THE LAW OF INTERNATIONAL CONTRACTING

The Law of International Contracting

by

Larry A. DiMatteo
Assistant Professor of Business Law and Legal Studies
University of Florida Graduate School of Business
Warrington College of Business
Gainesville, Florida

KLUWER LAW INTERNATIONAL
The Hague • London • Boston

Published by Kluwer Law International,
P.O. Box 85889, 2508 CN The Hague, The Netherlands.

Sold and distributed in the U.S.A. and Canada
by Kluwer Law International,
675 Massachusetts Avenue, Cambridge, MA 02139, U.S.A.
tel: (617) 354-0140; fax: (617) 354-8595

In all other countries, sold and distributed
by Kluwer Law International,
P.O. Box 85889, 2508 CN The Hague, The Netherlands
tel: 31 70 308 1562; fax: 31 70 308 1555

Library of Congress Cataloging-in-Publication Data

DiMatteo, Larry A.
The law of international contracting / by Larry A. DiMatteo.
p. cm.
Includes index.
ISBN 9041195920
1. Export sales contracts. I. Title.

K1030.D56 2000
341.7'53--dc21 00-042438

ISBN 9041195920

To my brother, Gary DiMatteo
Semper fidelis

PREFACE

The ability of a single volume or a series of volumes to deal with the many issues of international contracting is limited. The approach offered here is to review some of the key contract issues unique to various types of contracting such as sale of goods, licensing, intellectual property transfer, and the hiring of foreign agents and representatives. This work also attempts to analyze contract clauses and principles common to most international contracting scenarios. A number of contract clauses, such as the choice of law and the dispute resolution clauses, have become universally accepted. Along these same lines, the principles of good contract drafting are applicable to all types of international contracting. Thus, this is a book in fundamentals and not for one practicing in a narrow, highly specialized area of international business law; it is intended for the generalist, both legal and non-legal. It is for anyone interested in some of the more common legal aspects of international business contracting.

There are references throughout the text to a number of primary sources. All references to the Uniform Commercial Code or UCC are references to the law of the United States. The book also makes ample use of a variety of European Economic Community (EEC), European Community (EC), and European Union (EU) directives and regulations. I often refer to this body of law, apologetically, simply as EU Regulations. The reader may refer to the footnotes for the proper citation. Because of the overwhelming nature of national laws that impact upon international business transactions, the book can only provide a sampling of laws. For example, certain laws of the European Union, the People's Republic of China, and the Russian Federation have been singled out for purposes of illustration only. The use of national law serves to illuminate the typical issues found in international contracting.

I wish to thank the able research assistance of Hui Xue, along with the fine editorial assistance of Amy Reisinger. A special note of appreciation is to be given to those that provided materials including Steven Salbu, Ross Petty, Robert Emerson, Frances Zollers, Robert B. Bennett, Jr., and Virginia

Maurer. I also would like to thank John Berger of Kluwer Law International for his faith in the work and for ushering it through the editorial and publication process. Finally, I am especially grateful to the International Chamber of Commerce and ICC Publishing S.A. for allowing me to utilize their fine menu of publications.

SUMMARY OF CONTENTS

TABLE OF CONTENTS

CHAPTER 1

INTRODUCTION TO INTERNATIONAL CONTRACTING

"No written contract is ever complete; even the most carefully drafted document rests on volumes of assumptions that cannot be explicitly expressed."

Arthur Rosett, *Critical Reflections on the CISG,* 45 Ohio State Law Journal 265, 287 (1984)

****

"The transformation of international business law signifies more than just an incremental normative change; it signifies a quite radical revision in the very prism through which we view transnational deals and disputes."

Kenneth C. Randall & John E. Norris, *A New Paradigm for International Business Transactions,* 71 Washington University Law Quarterly 599, 624 (1993)

The above two quotes symbolize the limitations of this current undertaking. A book on international contracting, analogous to the driving of a new car out of its showroom, is immediately infected with a diminished value. The first quotation illustrates that a substantial core of international business transactions is non-legal in nature. Businesspersons prefer to talk in the language of business and are often unconcerned with the "memorialization" of their shared assumptions and tacit agreements into an enforceable form. Despite this informal attitude, such assumptions and agreements do have a tendency to be "codified" into legally recognizable custom and trade usage. This transformation is a well-worn tradition that harkens back to the medieval *lex mercatoria.* The general premise of this volume is that the astute international entrepreneur sees the written contract as a way of limiting the uncertainty of the transformation. A well-written contract serves to preempt misunderstandings along with managing the legal risks of an international transaction.

The second quote indicates that the latter half of the twentieth century has seen a broad expansion in international trade and business. This expansion has resulted in a transformation of international business law. The reality of trade liberalization and the rapid expansion of exporting in services and licensing have resulted in accelerating the number of international conventions and supranational responses to legal obstacles to further globalization. This volume will highlight some of these responses that international businesspersons should incorporate into their international business practices. Incorporating internationally recognized standards and practices in approaching international business transactions is important for a number of reasons. First, internationally based conventions and contracts often provide a vehicle for overcoming the cultural, language, and legal differences present in cross-border transactions. In a previous article I stated that:

> The acceptance of generally recognized contract principles, the trend towards economic trade unions, the adoption of international conventions, and the growth of international customary law has led to the convergence of national legal systems in the area of international contract law. In the long-term, this movement towards international unification and harmonization is likely to reduce transaction costs relating to contract formation.[1]

Second, the failure to take private international law developments into account will result in unexpected legal liability. For example, "an informal correspondence previously considered non-binding in nature may be transformed into an unexpected liability through an international recogni-

---

[1]Larry A. DiMatteo, *An International Contract Law Formula: The Informality of International Business Transactions Plus the Internationalization of Contract Law Equals Unexpected Contractual Liability*, 23 Syracuse Journal of Int'l Law & Commerce 67, 68 (1997).

tion of enforceability at odds with a given national legal system's holding of non-enforceability."[2]

The central purpose of this volume is to synthesize some of the major substantive terms and legal issues involved in the negotiations of international contracts. In order to best understand the legal ramifications for the international entrepreneur of negotiating certain terms or failing to negotiate such terms, the drafting attorney often looks to instances where negotiations have failed. A failure in negotiations means that the written contract fails to provide a clear answer to a disputed issue. Professor White, in discussing how to draft a contract, advises that it is best to "organize your thinking to visualize all of the potential plaintiffs and to speculate about all of the potential causes of action that they may assert against the seller."[3] Failures in the negotiation and drafting of contracts may be due to faulty language or inherent cultural or language differences. Given the universal nature of business transactions and the globalization of the marketplace, contractual failures attributable to inherent linguistic and cultural differences have significantly diminished. Most legal disputes stemming from written contracts are associated with poor writing or a lack of clarity, along with a failure to recognize and memorialize key substantive issues. Another cause of legal disputes is the existence of fundamental differences in the national default rules which pertain to the interpretation or implication of contractual terms. Thus, a primary source for understanding the pitfalls of international contracting is the researching of cases and arbitral decisions dealing with such failures in negotiations.

Secondary sources can be found in systemic attempts to prevent failures due to contractual misunderstandings. These secondary sources can be divided into two general groups. First, international conventions or regional initiatives aimed at harmonizing rules pertaining to specific issues commonly found in cross-border transactions. Examples include the Hague Rules[4] on the liability of international carriers of goods by sea and the Agreement on Trade Related Aspects of Intellectual Property (TRIPS)

[2] Ibid. at 67.

[3] James J. White, *How to Negotiate a Sales Contract,* in 19 ALI-ABA COURSE MATERIALS JOURNAL 47, 48 (1995).

[4] The Hague Rules were codified in the United States as the Carriage of Goods by Sea Act (COGSA) in 1936 which is applicable to an international export or import of goods involving a bill of lading for transport from or to a United States port.

within the General Agreement on Tariffs and Trade (GATT).[5] Regional harmonization efforts generally revolve around the major free trade areas such as NAFTA and the European Union, along with broader based institutions such as the Organization for Economic Coordination and Development (OECD). Second, the *lex mercatoria*[6] in all its manifestations, namely business customs or trade usage that have developed to bridge the language, cultural, and legal differences between businesspersons throughout the world. The materials produced by the International Chamber of Commerce (ICC)[7] in Paris provide good examples of the evolution of customary international law. The UCP 500 (Uniform Customs and Practices for Documentary Credits)[8] and the INCOTERMS manual (trade terms) are examples of international trade customs that have risen to near universal acceptance in the international banking and business communities.

Many legal disputes stemming from written contracts are associated with poor writing. A poorly written contract is one that stylistically lacks clarity or substantively fails to deal with an issue. This volume hopes to highlight some of the issues that are often left unattended by the interna-

---

[5]Agreement on Trade-Related Aspects of International Property Rights (TRIPS), General Agreement of Tariffs and Trade (GATT), April 15, 1994.

[6]The lex mercatoria or law merchant provides the mechanism in which day-to-day uses and practices are recognized by businesspersons, along with courts and arbitral tribunals, as international customary law. For, the importance of trade usage in American contract law see, Amy H. Kastely, Stock Equipment for the Bargain in Fact: Trade Usage, Express Terms, and Consistency under Section 1-205 of the Uniform Commercial Code, 64 No. Carolina L. Rev. 777 (1986). See also, M.T. Medwig, *The New Law Merchant: Legal Rhetoric and Commercial Reality,* 24 L & Pol. Int'l Bus. 589 (1993); E. Alan Farnsworth, *Unification and Harmonization of Private Law,* 27 Can. Bus. L. J. 48 (1996); A. Rosett, *Unification, Harmonization, Restatement, Codification and Reform in International Commercial Law,* 40 A. J. Comp. L. 683 (1982); R. Goode, *Usage and its Reception in Transnational Commercial Law,* 46 I.C.L.Q. 1 (1997); Lord Mustill, *The New Lex Mercatoria: The First Twenty Five Years,* 4 Arbitration Int'l 86 (1988).

[7]The International Chamber of Commerce is a non-governmental organization based in Paris. Its mission is to promote world trade, harmonize trade practices, and to provide practical services to businesspersons. These services include an International Court of Arbitration in Paris, Centre for Maritime Cooperation in London, Counterfeiting Intelligence Bureau in London, and the Institute of International Business Law and Practice in Paris.

[8]The UCP was first published in 1933 and subsequently revised in 1951, 1962, 1974, 1993, and 1993. UCP 500 came into effect on January 1, 1994.

tional entrepreneur. The importance of understanding the nuances of international transactional law cannot be overstated. Clarity of writing will not be able to overcome differences in the immutable rules of a given country. For example, a clearly written, principal-friendly termination clause in an agency agreement will not survive the *evergreen provisions*[9] found in a number of European countries. No level of drafting skills can substitute for a substantive understanding of the parameters of European agency laws. Good contract drafting, international or otherwise, requires a firm understanding of the substantive law of contracts.

Contract negotiators and drafters need to know the differences between national and international contracting. The issues selected for review in this volume are primarily private law issues and are transactional in nature. The impact of government intervention into trade matters is dealt with only tangentially. Instead, the focus is upon the private law issues that are controllable by the entrepreneur and her attorney through the *written* contract. The above emphasis upon the word "written" highlights the fact that legally, in some national legal regimes, a writing is not required for an enforceable contract. For example, under the United Nations Convention on Contracts for the International Sale of Goods (CISG),[10] a writing is not required and a contract may be proved by "any means including witness testimony."[11] In practice, many business transactions are characterized by a high degree of informality. An English court stated this premise simply as "[o]ne has to bear in mind that commercial men do not look at things from the lawyer's point of view." Surveys by Macaulay in the United States and Beale and Dugdale in the United Kingdom found that "many business executives are indifferent whether their agreements constitute binding contracts; business dealings are regulated more by mutual trust and shared conventions."[12] Beale and Dugdale found different types of contractual or quasi-contractual relations or exchanges ranging from highly negotiated customized contracts to highly "informalized" oral commitments. In re-

[9]An evergreen clause is a statutory preemption of the termination and commission clauses of an agency contract.

[10]United Nations Convention on Contract for the International Sale of Goods, April 11, 1980, U.N. Doc. A/CONF.97/18, Annex I, reprinted in, 19 I.L.M. 668.

[11]CISG at Article 11.

[12]Hugh Beale & Tony Dugdale, "Contracts Between Businessmen: Planning and The Use of Contractual Remedies," *British Journal of Law & Society* 2 (1975): 45, 49.

gards to the former, they concluded that "contracts formed as a result of detailed negotiation are comparatively rare."[13]

Despite the informal nature of business contracting and the common use of standard forms, it is likely that sophisticated businesspersons are fully aware of the default rules of contract and their supportive cadre of legal sanctions. This volume will proceed under the assumption that some formal or informal writing evidences most international business transactions. It is the recommendation of the author that even sale of goods transactions governed by the CISG should be based upon at least a semi-formal writing. This seems especially necessary given the difficulty of finding and procuring reputable business partners in foreign countries, along with the inherent obstacles of language and culture, including differences in negotiating styles. These factors, along with the potential difficulty of obtaining a legal remedy in a nationally diverse contractual relationship, justify the additional time and caution expended in writing and reviewing a written contract. A carefully written contract will often highlight the covert differences of language and law that can still be rectified prior to the execution of the contract. Such preventive contracting will diminish the likelihood of disputes resulting from culturally and nationally specific legal differences in the interpretation of contracts.

This book covers five general subject areas. Chapters 2 and 3 provide introductory materials on the drafting of an international contract. Drafting principles and the common clauses used in international contracts make-up the *shadow of the law* under which business transactions evolve. Behind every contract is the fear of non-performance and the threat of one party using the law to obtain a legal remedy. It is important to understand the issues of international dispute resolution in the area of contracts in order to negotiate and draft an effective contract. Just as prenuptial agreements are written in anticipation of a divorce, contracts should be written with the view towards contract breach and disputes. What can the negotiating or drafting parties write into the contract that would make dispute resolution less likely to be needed? What can be written into the contract that would make dispute resolution less painful or costly in the event it is necessary? What can be included in the contract to increase one's chances in a dispute resolution? Chapters 2 and 3 also look at issues common to all

[13]Ibid at 48.

contracts. Are their drafting techniques and principles that can be applied to all international contracts? What are some of the more common contract clauses found in most types of international contracts? Finally, what can be gleaned from actual cases and arbitral proceedings that provides guidance in drafting contracts in general or specific contract clauses?

The shadow or legal environment of international contracting continues in the coverage of international sale of goods found in Chapters 4 thorough 7. What are the generally recognized principles of international contract law? Also, what are some of the more fundamental contract law differences in the major national legal systems that the American entrepreneur should be aware? What are the typical characteristics of the export or import contract? Which clauses are the most important and thus should be carefully negotiated? What types of contracts are involved in documentary transactions? Chapter 8 focuses upon the often-neglected area of the sale of services. How do sale of services contracts differ from sale of goods contracts? Are their any international rules, conventions, or standards that pertain to the sale of services? Are there national law restrictions on the cross-border sale of services? More specifically, what are some of the important contract concerns in the sale of logistical, accounting, and marketing services? Chapter 9 reviews legal issues dealing with the growing area of intellectual property transfer and licensing. It reviews some of the substantive law issues that are a concern when crossing national borders. It then focuses upon the intellectual property transfer or licensing agreement. Chapter 10 investigates other mechanisms that have become popular in international business, such as franchising and joint ventures. Finally, the growing area of electronic contracting is investigated in Chapter 11.

A single volume on international contracting is necessarily limited in its scope and depth of coverage. This volume does not make the claim that it addresses all of the issues inherent in the drafting of an international contract. It does, however, provide a litany of issues that often arise in the drafting of an international contract. The clauses given are for purposes of illustration only and are not to be construed as model clauses. In cases of actual application, the clauses will need to be revised or customized for the particular context and to reflect the pertinent sections of substantive law. Although the clauses provided are not to be considered model, many of them should be viewed as *standard clauses.* I have attempted to write an accessible reference that can be used as an introductory or framework tool in the negotiating and drafting of international contracts. It is a framework that needs to be elaborated upon by the sophisticated international entrepreneur and his or her attorney.

A special note is necessary regarding the Appendices. The model laws and general principles of law are provided not so much for their potential roles as mandatory or customary international law, but as source material for the development of substantive contract clauses. The Convention on Limitation Period in the International Sale of Goods, Convention on Contracts for the International Sale of Goods (CISG), UNIDROIT Principles of International Commercial Contracts, and the Principles of European Contract Law should be reviewed before embarking on most international contract drafting projects. They provide general insight regarding the reasonableness of many contract clauses and the likelihood of their enforcement in a foreign jurisdiction. In the international sale of goods, the CISG and the associated Convention on Limitation Period provide a blueprint that negotiating parties can utilize in agreeing to compromise contract language. The material on INCOTERMS, Uniform Customs and Practices for Documentary Credits, UNCITRAL Model Law on Electronic Commerce, and the European Directives and Regulations provide guidance for specific types of contracts and issues. Finally, Appendix 1 (Internet Sources) provides some avenues for further research on international business transactions.

CHAPTER 2

Principles of Contract Drafting

This Chapter attempts to provide some general commentary on the difficulties of drafting international contracts. The drafter's knowledge base needs to be significantly broad in a number of areas. First, the difficulties due to differences in the cultures, languages, and legal systems of the contracting parties need to be overcome. The sections on the *Bernina* case and the limitations of language focus upon these difficulties. Second, general principles of international contract law, found in national laws and in supranational customary law, need to be understood by the drafting attorneys. This Chapter concludes with a review of the mechanics of drafting including the structure of an agreement, the use of model forms, and the phenomenon of standard form contracting. The importance of developing contract checklists in the drafting and reviewing of contracts is emphasized.

The *Bernina* Case

Because of differences in language, culture, and legal systems, the intentions of parties in an international transaction cannot be easily discerned from their contract. Therefore, it is imperative, more so than in a purely domestic undertaking, for the parties to carefully express intended rights and obligations in a written contract. At the time of execution, it is important that the parties, possibly with the assistance of their lawyers, review each contract clause to determine the parties' relative degrees of comprehension. When a certain level of comprehension is reached, then both parties should be required to initial each page. Some of the more important clauses, such as the *force majeure* and the liquidated damages clauses, may warrant initialing. Of course, such a model approach to contract review is not often practical. For example, in the typical export transactions there is no single form that both parties read and sign. The parties simply exchange their own forms in order to effectuate an offer and acceptance. Nonetheless, each party should take the time to carefully review the terms and conditions found in the other party's form before entering into the contract. This is especially important in the first transaction between the contracting parties. It is also important, especially in large transactions with an artificial entity, to verify the other party's authority to bind his company to such a contract.

Most contract law disputes can be prevented if the parties had anticipated future events and by carefully drafted contracts. Good legal drafting is a reflection of good legal thinking. The *Bernina Distributors v. Bernina Sewing Machines*[14] case illustrates how a party incurred more risks than were anticipated. A poorly written *open price term* resulted in significant monetary losses due to an unanticipated currency fluctuation. A distributor of sewing machines brought action against an importer for breach of contract. Defendant Bernina Sewing Machine Co. (Importer) imports and supplies Bernina sewing machines to plaintiff Bernina Distributors (Distributor). The problems that arose were related mostly to pricing and fluctuations of exchange rates. The case involved a long-term supply contract set-up to run for seven years. It contained an open price term which stated that "prices are automatically subject to change when factory costs are increased." Importer paid in Swiss francs to purchase the machines. The open price term allowed Importer to increase the price as follows: "(1) to the extent of any increase of factory invoice costs to Importer, (2) to the extent of any increase in duty charges, and (3) to the extent of increases in insurance, freight, handling, broker and port fees, or other similar charges. Increases to duty or factory invoice costs shall be adjusted as they occur. Increases to all other charges shall be adjusted at the commencement of each calendar year." A subsequent decline of the dollar (in relation to the Swiss franc) resulted in a dramatic increase in the Importer's costs.

The Importer maintained that the risk of currency fluctuations had not been considered or allocated in the contract and that under the Uni-

[14] 646 F.2d 434 (1981).

form Commercial Code the "open price term" should be adjusted according to what the court finds to be reasonable. The court rejected this argument holding that the contract provisions were quite comprehensive and hence the statutory provision was inapplicable. Therefore, the contract placed the risk of a diminishing profit margin due to currency fluctuations on the Importer. Importer also argued that due to the currency fluctuation the contract had become impracticable under § 2-615 of the Uniform Commercial Code. The U.C.C. excuses performance under a contract when performance "has been made impracticable by the occurrence of a contingency the nonoccurrence of which was a basic assumption on which the contract was made." However, the court rejected the applicability of the doctrine of impracticability. Comment 8 to § 2-615 states that the excuse does "not apply when the contingency in question is sufficiently foreshadowed at the time of contracting." Also, cost increases alone do not render a contract impracticable. The loss would have to be especially severe and unreasonable. The Importer was aware of the possibility of a reduction in profits due to exchange rate fluctuations and could have guarded against this contingency. For example, a cost-plus formula for determining the price could have been utilized. Furthermore, the Importer was represented by counsel throughout and should have known that the contract provided for price increases only to the extent of actual cost increases. In short, the court found an agreed-upon allocation of risk between commercial equals.

Often times the quality of a contract is evident not so much in what it says but in what it fails to say. Often times an international contract is the product of "studied ambiguity."[15] Vagueness or ambiguity in contractual language is employed in order to achieve the illusion of agreement. Johan Steyn describes the use of such techniques in drafting as "a kind of esperanto" in which "parties often leave a draft contract in ambiguous form in order to achieve agreement."[16] The roots of contract ambiguity come from two sources: (1) the parties negotiating the contract and (2) those charged with drafting the contract. A common scenario is that the principals negotiate the general framework for an agreement and then turn the task of writing the language of the agreement over to their attorneys. The brevity of such negotiations increases the risks of ambiguity inherent in in-

[15]Johan Steyn, *A Kind of Esperanto?*, in THE FRONTIERS OF LIABILITY 11 (Vol. 2, ed. P.B.H. Birks; New York: Oxford University Press 1994).
[16]Ibid. at 13.

terpersonal communication, especially within a cross-cultural context. A key issue for international businesspersons is determining at what stage they should enlist the services of a lawyer. Often businesspersons do not use lawyers in the negotiations stage of contracting. They view them generally as obstacles to agreement. The businessperson to businessperson, face to face exchange provides a strong symbol of how business is done. Lawyers are delegated the remedial task of acting as high priced scribes. In international contracting the businessperson, especially one new to international dealings, may be best served to use the services of an astute international transactional lawyer during the negotiations stage, along with seeking foreign counsel. The casual agreement, the foundation of many domestic transactions, may not be the proper model for international transactions. With the issue of trust aside, international dealings should be evidenced by clearly written and highly negotiated agreements due to the likelihood of misunderstanding stemming from differences in language, culture, and legal systems. The next section will briefly analyze the limitations of language. It is these limitations that a well-seasoned international lawyer will address in the negotiation and drafting of a contract.

The Limitations of Language

The shortcomings of human discourse and their roles in contractual drafting and interpretation were aptly noted by Justice Cardozo in *Wood v. Lucy, Lady Duff-Gordon.* "A promise may be lacking, and yet the whole writing may be instinct with an obligation, *imperfectly expressed.*"[17] The problem of converting the subjective to the objective is compounded by the difficulty of transforming promises into words, oral or written. Psychologists inform us that this problem is endemic to the fact that language is essentially nonnotational. To be notational linguistically, symbols need to have a single meaning or interpretation. Karl Llewellyn saw legal rules as a series of such nonnotational symbols. As such, these rules are infused with the flexibility inherent in word symbols. "What a word symbol signifies can extend beyond that which has already occurred or been conceived of only

[17] 118 N.E. 214 (N.Y. 1917) See also, McCall Co. v. Wright, 117 N.Y.S. 775 (1909); Moran v. Standard Oil Co., 105 N.E. 217 (N.Y. 1914).

in a normative sense, not in a descriptive sense."[18] The indeterminacy of words and their meanings provide both limitations and opportunities. The limitation of words precludes contracting parties from meeting absolute agreement. Words have no meaning by themselves but are infused with meaning based upon the particular experiences of the user of the words. However, words give law "an immanent expansive capacity" that allows for the fitting of new fact patterns into existing legal constructs.

The fragmentation of promises caused by human and linguistic shortcomings creates a divide between what is subjectively understood and what is *presentiated*[19] in the objective form. It results in "non-mutuality ranging from subtle to gross differences in understanding."[20] This non-mutuality is at the heart of the subjective-objective dialectic. "The promise made is never exactly the same as the promise received. Every promise is always *two* promises, the sender's and the receiver's."[21] This quality of contractual exchanges and of interpersonal communications is the source of the judicial search for interpretive guidance. Such guidance has been taken from a number of forms including community standards, custom, trade usage, and prior dealings. Courts have implied terms to fill the gaps in otherwise inchoate contracts. The mechanism for this contractual salvage effort is the default or *gap-filling* rules of contracts. The rationale behind these court-imposed rules is that the courts are merely extending the subjective intent of the two parties.

The judicial preference is decidedly in favor of using objective standards to determine the terms of a contract, the measurement of performance, and their remedial repercussions. The implication of terms and the measurement of performance are generally accomplished by the fabrication of the objective reasonable person. The reasonable person has been utilized to define ambiguous terms, to imply missing terms, and to determine if performance has been adequately rendered. The court does not have to look far to find the reasonable person. The gap filling provisions of the Uniform Commercial Code and the Convention on Contracts for the International

---

[18]KARL LLEWELLYN, *THE CASE LAW SYSTEM IN AMERICA* (ed. Paul Gewirtz 1989), 74, n. 1.

[19]For a fuller discussion of the notion of "presentiation" *see,* Ian R. Macneil, "Restatement (Second) of Contracts and Presentiation," *Virginia Law Review* 60 (1974): 589.

[20]IAN MACNEIL, *NEW SOCIAL CONTRACT* 9 (1980).

[21]Ibid.

Sale of Goods provide the courts a ready made guide for finding the terms that would satisfy the reasonable person standard.[22]

Interpreting Contracts: Fabricating the Reasonable Person

Drafting contracts is essentially an exercise in attempting to anticipate how a court or arbitration panel is likely to interpret certain contractual language. The courts traditionally view the contract from the perspective of the reasonable person. The courts' fabrication of the reasonable person is done through an examination of the customs of the times and of a business in order to determine the knowledge and skills the contracting parties brought to the negotiating table. "The law of contracts reflects, in an imperfect way, the needs and values of the communities it serves."[23] Savigny's historical school saw law as a mirrored reflection of community customs—"as an expression of the *folk spirit* and it was the task of law to capture what had been exhibited in the freely developed customs of the community."[24] Contract law serves not only a general *community*, that is society, but also a number of narrower communities, such as trades or professions.The Court in *Larwin-Southern Cal., Inc.* observed that "custom and usage within a trade may properly be used in clarifying what, on the face of a contract, ap-

---

[22]*See, e.g.,* Uniform Commercial Code § 1-102(3) (obligation of reasonableness); § 1-204 (reasonable time); § 1-205 (course of dealing and usage of trade); § 2-103(1)(b) (reasonable commercial standards), § 2-204(3) (manifested intent), § 2-305(1)(c) (reasonable price term); § 2-306 (output, requirements, and exclusive dealings); § 2-308 (place of delivery); § 2-503 (tender of delivery).

[23]Richard E. Speidel, "Some Reflections Upon Commercial Context and the Judicial Process," *Wisconsin Law Review* (1967): 822. See generally, James Q. Whitman, "Why Did the Revolutionary Lawyers Confuse Custom and Reason?," *University of Chicago Law Review* 58 (1991): 1321 (a review of the mingling and evolution of custom, reason, and the common law from their historical antecedents in the Middle Ages to the time of the American Revolution). The breeding ground for usage and custom are generally found in smaller communities within a societal or national umbrella. Examples include professional groups, trade unions and associations, and business associations. Custom and practice can also be found in a supranational community. The notion of the *lex mercatoria* or law merchant in international trade and business is such an example. See, e.g., Keith Highet, "The Enigma of the Lex Mercatoria," *Tulane Law Review* 63 (1989): 613.

[24]Martin P. Golding, "Jurisprudence and Legal Philosophy in Twentieth Century America—Major Themes and Developments," *Journal of Legal Education* 36 (1986): 441, 446.

pears to be an ambiguity."[25] Section 1-205 of the Uniform Commercial Code states that a "usage of trade is any practice or method of dealing having such regularity of observance in a place, vocation or trade as to justify the expectation that it will be observed with respect to the transaction in question."[26] Trade usage is a source used by courts in clarifying an ambiguity of intent. "The parties are considered, unless otherwise agreed, to have impliedly made applicable to their contract a usage of which the parties ought to have known and which in [international trade] is widely known to, and regularly observed by, parties to contracts of the type involved in the particular trade concerned."[27] Custom, usage, and practice can be seen as the background of contractual obligation. They are used to clarify any ambiguity of intent existing in the contractual instruments. If clarity is not forthcoming, then the courts must look to the existing rules of contract law for an answer. It is for the courts to decide whether contract law will provide recourse or whether the parties are to be left without recourse. Often courts will recognize customs and elevate them to a position equivalent to legal rules. The Court in *Lipschutz v. Gordon Jewelry Corp.* provides an example of this phenomenon. It acknowledged that "a *custom* is a practice which by its universality has acquired the force and effect of law."[28]

The imprimatur of the reasonable person approach can be seen throughout the *Restatement (Second) of Contracts* and the Uniform Commercial Code. It can be seen whenever reference is made to the fact that a party had reason to know or should have known. There is *reason to know* if a person "has information from which a person of similar intelligence would infer that the fact in question does or will exist." The line between *reason to know* and actual knowledge is often nonexistent. In contrast, *should know* is generally associated with a legal duty to know. "Should know imports a duty to ascertain the facts."[29] Thus, *should know* is relatively unconcerned with actual knowledge. The determination of whether a party had reason to know is accomplished through the "totality of the circum-

---

[25] 162 Cal. Rptr. 52 (1979). See also, Masterson v. Sine, 436 P.2d 561 (Cal. 1968).

[26] *Uniform Commercial Code* at § 1-205(2). See generally, Elizabeth Warren, "Trade Usage and Parties in the Trade: An Economic Rationale for an Inflexible Rule," *University of Pittsburg Law Review* 42 (1981): 515.

[27] Convention on Contracts for the International Sale of Goods, Article 9(2).

[28] 373 F.Supp. 375, 387 (S.D.Tex. 1974) (emphasis added).

[29] *Restatement (Second)* at § 19, Comment *b*.

stances" analysis. *Reason to know* is a factual determination based upon the circumstances and information available to the parties. *Should know* is more a judicial reflection regarding what is reasonable given the parties and the circumstances. The difference is that *reason to know* is a party-specific objectivity. In contrast, *should know* is community focused objectivity, that is, what is a reasonable interpretation or result as seen through the litmus test of community standards.[30] Modern contract law has witnessed an increasing preemption of this judicial reasonableness inquiry by way of statutory preemption. The *English Unfair Contract Terms Act of 1977* adopts a presumption of unreasonableness for indemnity clauses that "by reference to any contract term a party is made to indemnify another party in respect of liability for negligence or breach of contract."[31] For international sales contracts it voids any choice of law clause whose purpose is the avoidance of the Unfair Terms Act. These immutable rules preempt the objective contract theory's search for contractual intent.

A study in microcosm of the relationship between custom and the interpretation of contracts can be seen in Section 41 of the *Second Restatement.* Section 41 deals with the lapse of time as a common law way of automatically revoking an offer. The general rule is that an offeror is the master of her offer. Therefore, an offeror may revoke at her whim anytime prior to acceptance by the offeree. The law, however, limits the reach of the offer to a reasonable period of time. If the offer remains outstanding beyond a reasonable period of time, then a subsequent acceptance is converted into a new offer which the original offeror is then free to accept or reject. The issue is what is a reasonable period of time for an offer to remain viable? Reasonableness is an objective determination of fact based upon the totality of the circumstances of each case. Section 41 lists a litany of factors to be entered into the judicial analysis. These factors include the nature of the contract, the purpose of the parties, course of dealing, and trade usage and practice. This raises a supplemental issue of whether custom is part and parcel with the reasonable person. Does the fact that something has risen to the level of custom place an imprimatur of reasonableness upon it. The *Second Restatement* advocates the position that custom or trade usage do pos-

---

[30]For example, "what is reasonable depends on the circumstances; it may be reasonable to hold a nonmerchant to mercantile standards if he is represented by a mercantile agent." Ibid.at § 221, Comment *b.*
[31]Unfair Contract Terms Act § 4(1) (1977).

sess a strong presumption of reasonableness. Commentary to Section 222 states that "commercial acceptance by regular observance makes out a prima facie case that a usage of trade is reasonable."[32] Custom and trade usage are ready made arbiters of reasonableness. As such, their place within the judicial interpretation of contracts is secure.

Customary law, as imputed into the reasonable person, provides a stopgap that allows the judicial process to render decisions which reflect objective or commercial reality. This is likely to precede the reformulation of the formal rules to reflect that reality. Custom and usage has often been the vehicle by which the common law has mended itself and amended its rules to accommodate changing times. Justice Turley in the 1842 case of *Jacob v. State* convincingly states this grassroots metamorphosis. "Common law sources are to be found in the usage, habits, manners, and customs of a people. The common law of a country will be modified, and extended by analogy, *construction and custom,* so as to embrace new relations, springing up from time to time, from an amelioration or change of society."[33] The relationship between law and custom can be seen as reciprocal in nature. Custom is a source of law and law impacts upon custom. Aristotle saw law as a vehicle for inducing positive behavioral modifications within the populace. "The foundation of law is to lay down sound and balanced principles of character-formation to *accustom* various kinds of people, each in different ways, to refrain from greed."[34] The reasonable person acts as a receptacle for customary practice. The courts can also use the reasonable person standard more proactively to discourage unconscionable practices and encourage the development of judicially approved standards of reasonableness.

Karl Llewellyn asserted that trade practice provides the interpretative background of contract. "The background of trade practice gives a first indication; the line of authority rejecting unreasonable practice offers the needed corrective." He speaks of a *double-barreled objectivity* in which the words of a contract are to be read through two lenses. The interpretation of words through the lens of custom and practice provides a baseline. The courts must also look through a second lens in order to determine whether the parties attached a variant meaning. Words are to be interpreted "first in the light of trade usage, second in the light of the common meaning to the

[32] § 222, Comment *b.*

[33] 22 Tenn. 493, 514-515(1842) (emphasis added).

[34] W. von Leyden, *Aristotle on Equality and Justice* (1985), 82 (emphasis added).

hearer and the course of dealing of the parties." In supplying a missing term, the court can use trade practice or usage to imply what "a sane man might reasonably expect to find in the contract."

Trade usage often implies esoteric knowledge to which only those in a particular trade or profession are privy. The cases involving trade usage generally revolve around the expert testimony offered by the respective parties in support of their contentions regarding the meaning of the contract. In *Folk v. Central Nat. Bank & Trust Co.*, a series of experts were called to give testimony pertaining to the quality of pavement work at a raceway performed under a construction contract. The contractor was suing for contract damages arguing that he had substantially performed the contract. The owner's defense was that defective installation resulted in a material breach. The contractor called a consulting engineer who testified that the asphalt work was in accordance with standard procedures. A road contractor who specializes in asphalt installation testified that the new surface was "nice and tight" indicating a proper bonding. A number of race car drivers were called to testify that the surface was acceptable and "as good or better than other tracks."[35] The defense witnesses included a professional engineer who testified that deviations on the surface far exceeded acceptable standards. Another asphalt contractor testified for the defense stating that the workmanship was of substandard quality. Officials of a national racers association testified that it removed its certification of the raceway because of safety concerns pertaining to the track's surface. Two race drivers testified that the new surface was dangerous. Finally, a report from an engineer testing company provided measurements of variations in the track's surface. As illustrated by the wide variety of testimony from expert witnesses, the determination of usage or practice can be a harried one.

The jurisprudential issues in the above scenario revolve around the complexity of fabricating the reasonable person in the face of such conflicting testimony. The complexity of such a fabrication is increased due to the highly technical and specialized nature of the evidence. Is a judge equipped to handle the avalanche of evidentiary concerns pertaining to such testimony? Should we expect a jury of ordinary citizens to be able to decipher commercial and professional evidence and the assorted technicalities in applying the reasonable person standard? Karl Llewellyn was one who be-

[35]567 N.E. 2d 1, 5 (Ill. App. 1990).

lieved that the judge and jury are not equipped to handle this extension of the objective interpretation of contracts. He believed that the notion of reasonableness in a specific trade or profession would best be served through the use of expert arbitrators or the use of a merchant tribunal. The idea of a merchant tribunal to assist the courts in making an informed judgment of mercantile facts was never adopted. If our quest in contract interpretation is to find the understanding of the parties or to determine commercial reasonableness, then such expert judging would seem to make a good deal of sense. Can this be an explanation for the rise in use of *commercial arbitration*?

Standard Form Contracts

Karl Llewellyn recognized the courts' use of the reasonable person to "*construe* language into not meaning what the language is patently trying to say"[36] or what the parties intended. Llewellyn analyzed the use of creative misconstruction in the context of the categorization of terms as boilerplate or dickered. The advent of standard form contracts presented courts with a dilemma regarding the notion of mutual assent. How can the pretense of mutual assent be maintained when a standard form is supplied by one of the contracting parties, often given with a take it or leave it edict, and with fine print or boiler-plate passing unread by the assenting recipient? Llewellyn's solution to this dilemma was to bifurcate the contract into two contracts, the *dickered* deal and the *supplementary* boilerplate deal. This bifurcation of contract is accompanied by a similar bifurcation of the mutual assent requirement into specific assent to the dickered terms and a blanket assent to the remainder. The blanket assent is restricted to reasonable boiler-plate terms. Blanket assent is defined as assent "to any *not unreasonable* or indecent terms the seller may have on his form, which do not alter or eviscerate the *reasonable meaning* of the dickered terms."[37]

The *Second Restatement* pays homage to Llewellyn's creation in a comment to its Section 211 dealing with standardized agreements. It states that a party signing another's standard form agreement "assents to a few terms, typically asserted in blanks on the printed form, and gives *blanket assent* to

[36]Karl N. Llewellyn, *The Common Law Tradition* (1960), 364.
[37]Ibid. at 370 (emphasis added).

the *type of transaction* embodied in the standard form."[38] A contract, much like a constitution, allows the courts freedom to imply any term or meaning necessary and proper in carrying out its intent and spirit. The spirit of the contract stems from the fact that the voluntary engagement to the convention of contract commits the parties to a *common enterprise.* It is the consensual core and the notion of common enterprise that provide the justification for the courts' role in salvaging the contract. The specific solution provided by the court may be seen as a reflection of the parties' intent to share the risks and benefits of their common contractual enterprise. The parties remain free to preempt the court's intervention by better controlling "the meaning and extent of their relationship"[39] through the vehicle of specific, clear contract language.

The courts must determine if the term at issue is material and whether it is within the consensual core or *circle of assent.* If a term is not within the consensual core of an agreement it will be more susceptible to an attack upon the ground of unconscionability. The central factor within unconscionability is not unequal bargaining position but the lack of real assent. The Uniform Commercial Code states that the "principle is one of the prevention of oppression and unfair surprise and not of disturbance of allocation of risks because of superior bargaining power."[40] Two types of assent are needed in order to remove a term within a form contract by the doctrine of unconscionability. If the party raising unconscionability had a viable alternative to entering into the contract, then her assent was not coerced. Her assent can be determined to be real and not the product of duress, undue influence, or oppression. Secondly, she must have been conscious of the existence of the term in question at the time of the contract formation. If the term had been disclosed, then there was apparent consent. However, mere disclosure may not be sufficient to overcome a lack of apparent assent. The disclosure has to be of the type that would fully inform the reasonable person possessing the characteristics of this particular contracting party. The question is "whether a reasonable person, should have been aware of the material risk allocated to him." It is only when there is a choice (real assent) and disclosure (apparent assent) can there be a finding of meaningful

---

[38] *Restatement (Second)* at § 211, Comment *c.* (emphasis added).
[39] Ibid. at 73.
[40] *Uniform Commercial Code* § 2-302, Comment 1 (1990).

mutual assent. One may look to the ancient plea of *non est factum* for an ancestral analogy. This plea that "I did not make this contract" was generally used by the blind or illiterate who had been duped into signing a document. In other words, in the battle of the forms, the adverse party can be said to be blind to any unreasonable, boilerplate terms in the form contract. The operative question becomes whether the document was "in fact substantially, seriously or fundamentally different in its purport from what the signer believed to be the case?"[41]

This bifurcation of assent presents a problem of rationalization. A traditional adage of contract theory is that it is not for the court to make a contract for the parties. This notion is often framed within the rubric of certainty of contract. The lack of specific consent to the boilerplate of standardized contracts calls into question the courts' ability to preserve a contract as a reflection of intent while at the same time remaining faithful to the adage. Llewellyn makes an attempt at rephrasing the assent problem and venturing a solution in one brief statement. "A court's business is not the making of detailed contracts for parties; but a court's business is eminently the marking out of the limits of the permissible."[42] This solution sees the courts role as one of paring down the contract mainly through the elimination of unnecessary and unreasonable terms.[43]

How Do Lawyers Begin Drafting a Contract?

Lawyers often refer to preprinted forms or a previous written contract when drafting a new contract for a client. The problem with this approach is that the form or model agreement may have not been well written initially. Also, the law upon which the form or model was based may have become obsolete. At most, form or model agreements may be used as a checklist as to the types of clauses usually found in such agreements. The

---

[41]Phillip S. James, *English Law* (9th ed. 1976), 238-39.

[42]Llewellyn, *Common Law Tradition* at 367.

[43]Hugh Beale & Tony Dugdale, "Contracts Between Businessmen: Planning and The Use of Contractual Remedies," *British Journal of Law & Society* 2 (1975): 45, 50. This article represents the findings of interviews with engineering manufacturers in the City of Bristol, England. See also, Stuart Macaulay, "Non-contractual Relations in Business," *American Sociological Review* 28 (1963): 45.

most useful books provide summaries of the relevant law, along with the forms, and commentary on the use of such forms and how they can best be customized. The use of a form should be only the beginning of the drafting exercise. The language of the form should be reviewed in order to delete unnecessary legalese and outdated terminology. The form should be updated substantively by researching any changes in the law. Finally, the drafter should always ask what provisions are missing? An alternative approach to drafting is the use of provisions of the law in the writing of contract clauses. This approach can best be used in areas where the law is clear and settled or where there is a uniform codification of the law. In the drafting of an international sales contract, the drafter may utilize provisions of the Uniform Commercial Code or the Convention on Contracts for the International Sale of Goods as models for specific contract clauses.[44] For example, the CISG article on impediments and the UCC's doctrine of impracticability can be referenced in the drafting of a *force majeure* clause. The CISG provisions on *nachfrist notice* should be specifically opted out of in drafting a time of the essence clause. The UCC's Section 2-316 can be used in the drafting of a disclaimer of warranty clause. Furthermore, the surrounding case law to these codes can be used to determine what language has been most successful in contract litigation. The use of such statutory guidelines will help ensure against one-sided drafting and overreaching.[45]

Model Forms

In a perfect world in which sellers-buyers and exporters-importers are able to negotiate in person, a custom made, specific contract would be drawn together, with both parties reading, understanding, and signing the

---

[44]One commentator suggests that the provisions of the CISG can be used as a drafting technique in the writing of international sales contracts. The CISG can "be viewed as a drafting technique which [the drafter] uses the provisions of the CISG as a kind of model contract." Peter Schlechtriem, *Some Observations on the United Nations Convention on Contracts for the International Sale of Goods,* in THE FRONTIERS OF LIABILITY 29, 33 (Vol. 2, ed. Peter Birks; New York: Oxford University Press, 1994)

[45]One of the few texts available on contract drafting is Scott J. Burnham, *Drafting Contracts* (Charlottesville, Virginia: The Michie Company, 2d ed. 1993). See also, Peter N. Swisher, *Techniques of Legal Drafting: A Survival Manual,* 15 U. Richmond Law Review 873 (1981); Bloss, How to Review a Contract, 91 Case & Commentary 38 (1986); Ian Macneil, *A Primer of Contract Planning,* 48 Southern California Law Review 627 (1975).

contract. In the *battle of the forms* scenario, parties more often use separate forms that say different things and which neither party reads or understands. Contracting parties will continue to use standard forms because of their efficiency and trade use. More disputes would be prevented, however, if the parties at least read the entire form and negotiated specific language to overcome any differences in the forms. The International Chamber of Commerce has drafted a series of *model forms* that provide alternative solutions to different contract issues and that can be customized by the parties agreeing to one of the alternatives. For example, the ICC has developed a *Model Agency Agreement* and a *Model Distribution Agreement.* Unlike single-party generated standard forms, model forms can be seen as bilateral in nature because they can be prepared and signed by both parties in consultation with one another. The Introduction to the ICC *Model Contracts for International Trade* provides a number of suggestions and comments:

(1) The model contracts are not premised upon any specific national law. Therefore, any issues should be governed by the contract itself and generally recognized principles of international trade (*lex mercatoria*). This allows the parties to avoid the particularities of national laws. It is suggested that the parties agree to an arbitration clause because arbitrators are skilled in the enforcement of trade usage and general principles of law. International arbitration permits an international approach to contract interpretation and enforcement.
(2) The model contract's alternative terms should be carefully read and those terms that are not chosen should be deleted. The use of alternatives reflects the fact that versions of a term may not be enforceable in some legal systems. For example, a national law may supercede a termination at will provision in an agency agreement or employment contract. Some national laws mandate that the terminated agent is to be paid a *good will indemnity.* Thus, Alternative B in the ICC's *Model Contract* is to be used for EU countries that require such an indemnity payment.
(3) An exporter will often hire a foreign representative to act as its foreign sales agent or distributor. It is important to designate the party in the contract as an independent contractor. Designation as an independent contractor will enable the exporter to avoid host country laws such as labor, tax, and liability laws. However, some countries, by statute, will treat such parties as employees despite their designation as independent contractors in the contract. To avoid such laws, contracts

should be with companies and not individuals. It is generally held that an artificial legal entity (e.g., a corporation) cannot be considered as an employee.

(4) The parties, before signing the contract, should fill in and attach any riders or exhibits. Also, in order to avoid any confusion regarding which amendments or changes were agreed upon, both parties should initial each page of the contract.

Structure of Agreement

Before examining the structure of contracts, it is important to define the differences between representations, warranties, and declarations. *Representations* are statements of existing fact often made to *induce* someone to enter into a contract. *Warranties* are defined in Section 2-313(a) of the Uniform Commercial Code as "any affirmation of fact or promise which becomes part of the basis of the bargain." The terms "warranty" and "representation" are mere legal terms; meanings vary from context to context. Representations, whether promise, fact or warranty, should always lead the drafter to answer a further question. If a promise is given, what happens if the promise is not kept? If a fact is represented or assumed, what if the fact proves to be untrue? Upon failure of a fact, promise or warranty, what remedies are contemplated by the parties? *Declarations* are statements of the parties creating the private law that will govern their contract. The following are examples of clauses dealing with the parties' determination of the law of the contract: (1) *Force majeure:* What events will allow one of the parties to terminate the contract without liability for breach? (2) Choice of Law: In case of dispute, what law will apply? At times, the parties' choice of law may be abrogated by a court if the selection is held to be unconscionable or against public policy. (3) Merger: What makes up the agreement? Can evidence taken from the contract negotiations or writings dated prior to the execution of the contract be admitted in a contract dispute? (4) Modification: How can the agreement be modified? What is the procedure for modifying the parties' private law? (5) Severance: Does the invalidity of one provision render the entire contract unenforceable? What clauses are to be considered so central to the contract that they cannot be severed?

There is no universal model for structuring a contract. However, an "architecture analogy" has often be used to illustrate good contract drafting. The contract should be assembled according to a plan. This plan becomes must obvious when the drafter properly divides the contract into coherent parts with appropriate captions. For example, a traditional structure for an agreement includes: (1) a title and description of the agreement, (2) a preamble in which the parties are listed and the intended undertaking is described, (3) a transition or words of agreement, (4) recitals, (5) definitions and operative clauses, (6) *testimonium* or closing. The transition expresses the words of agreement. It may be traditional legalese such as "Now, Therefore, in consideration of the mutual promises herein contained, the parties agree as follows" or simply, "the parties agree as follows." The recitals are statements of fact and usually give the background to the agreement. The recitals are what lawyers know as the "Whereas" clauses. This section is often overlooked at the drafting stage. It should be carefully drafted. Any misstatements of fact by either party in the recitals may be grounds for a future cause of action for misrepresentation or breach of warranty. The definitional section may be found in the recitals or in the body of the agreement. Lawyers at best do not spend sufficient time in drafting clear definitions for the terms of art being used in the agreement. At worst, the terms are given different meanings in different portions of the contract. One cardinal rule is always change your words and language if you intend a change in meaning. The operative clauses provide the body of the agreement. They are generally a cadre of highly negotiated clauses and standard clauses taken from another form or model. The closing should clearly state the parties entering into the agreement. If the signatories are representatives of a company, then the type of company should be stated, along with the signatories capacity to sign on behalf of the company. One final note, the effective date of the agreement should be clearly stated for purposes of calculating necessary time frames such as the expiration of the agreement. Contracts sometimes display a number of dates. There may be one stated in the caption, another date stated in a performance clause, and a different date stated in the closing. It may be appropriate to have a separate clause that gives the legal, effective date. The following drafting points emphasize the correct use of the word *shall* and the use of the client as a key source for drafting the contract:

Exhibit 2.1: Practical Drafting Pointers

1. The word *shall* should be reserved for statements of duty or obligation. The use of the word *shall* should always indicate that one of the parties is agreeing to do or not to do something.

2. After drafting a *shall* clause, the drafter should ask and answer what if the party fails to perform as to that obligation? The remedial side of a contract should always be addressed within the four-corners of the document. For example, does a party have a right to rescind the contract for even a *de minimis* breach by the other party? Instead, the parties may want to agree to a graduated scheme of remedies that are triggered based upon the seriousness or frequency of the breaches.
3. The best source of information in the drafting of an agreement is the client-businessperson. The lawyer should always ask the client what he means by a term and use that meaning in defining the term in the contract. The lawyer should also ask what terms are most important to the client. These terms may dictate a more thorough review on the part of the lawyer and her client.

Principles of International Contract Law

It is impossible to adequately draft a contract without knowledge of the substantive law. This realization is compounded when drafting an international contract where there are at least three possible sources of law. The sources include the national laws of each of the parties and international contract law or the *lex mercatoria*. The ideal situation is to have a working knowledge of all three. Even if the drafter attempts to diminish his need to know a foreign law through the use of a choice of law clause, he still must be knowledgeable of the immutable rules and regulations found in the foreign law. Also, arbitrators often resort to a supranational law or *lex mercatoria* to trump the full application of a national law designated by a choice of law clause. Danish professor Ole Lando listed the following seven sources[46] of the *lex mercatoria* that can be used in the interpretation of contracts:

Public International Law: Lando notes that there are provisions in the Vienna Convention on Treaties that can be applied to private international contracts.

---

[46]Ole Lando, *The Lex Mercatoria in International Commercial Arbitration*, 34 Int'l & Comparative Law Quarterly 747 (1985).

Uniform Laws: The Hague Rules (codified as COGSA) and the Convention on Contracts for the International Sale of Goods (CISG) are examples of successful attempts at uniform international laws.

General Principles of Contract Law: The best example of a general principle of contract law found in most national legal systems is *pacta sunt servanda* or what is referred to in the common law as sanctity of contract.

Rules of International Organizations: Lando lists the following organizations: UN, UNCTAD, OECD, and UNIDROIT.

Custom and Usage: The clearest examples of custom and usage or customary international law that has reached a level of almost universal acceptance are the ICC's INCOTERMS and its Uniform Customs and Practices for Documentary Credits (UCP).

Standard Form Contracts: Once again, the ICC is a good source for standard form contracts and standard clauses. For example, the ICC publishes standard or model forms of Distribution and Agency Agreements. They also publish a manual to be used in the drafting of *force majeure* and hardship clauses.

Arbitral Decisions: Although not widely reported, arbitral decisions provide an outstanding resource for principles of private international law.

Generally recognized international contract principles have a direct bearing on how one approaches the drafting of an international contract. These principles are brought to bear by courts and arbitration panels in the interpretation of contracts. They are also used to determine the parties' rights and duties regarding performance and subsequent requests for adjustments in the contract. The general principle is that contracts should *prima facie* be enforced according to their terms under the doctrine of *pacta sunt servanda*. However, *pacta sunt servanda* is also qualified by the concept of *abus de droit* and the rule that unfair or unconscionable contracts and clauses should not be enforced. The general duty of good faith in international contracting is a more expanded version of the good faith requirement found in the Uniform Commercial Code. The civil law concept *culpa in con-*

trahendo requires that the parties negotiate in good faith.[47] The American concept of good faith is only applied to the area of performance and enforcement of contractual obligations. Thus, in international contracting there is a possibility of liability prior to the conclusion of contract negotiations. The principle of good faith is further extended to a duty to negotiate in good faith to adjust the contract in the event of unforeseen circumstances. This notion of good faith or civility should guide the American businesspersons' response to all communications from a foreign party. Failure to respond to a letter or request is often regarded as evidence of assent to its terms. This concept can be seen at work in the Convention on Contracts for the International Sale of Goods' (CISG) adoption of *nachfrist* notice in which a party makes a request for additional time to perform. In the event that the receiving party fails to respond or fails to give a commercially viable reason for a denial of the request, than the extension is automatically granted.[48] There is no counterpart to this notion in Anglo-American law. It is important for the international lawyer to understand these principles when drafting a contract. It is these principles of international contracting that foreign courts and arbitration panels use when interpreting an ambiguity in a contract.

Some contract codes, like the CISG, can be utilized in creating a checklist of issues or clauses that should be dealt with in an international contract. The CISG will be the topic of in-depth coverage in Chapter 7. Chapter 6 will discuss in more detail the non-binding UNIDROIT Principles of International Commercial Contracts (*Principles*). The following checklist of articles prepared by the International Chamber of Commerce (ICC) illustrates how a substantive body of law or principles may be utilized as a checklist in the drafting of a contract.[49] It is provides a list of issues that are covered in the *Principles.* These issues should be interfaced with custom drafted clauses in preparing a comprehensive contract. The material in the

---

[47]See seminal but outdated work, Friedrich Kessler & Edith Fine, Culpa in Contrahendo, *Bargaining in Good Faith, and Freedom of Contract: A Comparative Study*, 77 Harvard Law Rev. 401 (1964). For an analysis of the ethics of negotiation see, Gerald B. Wetlaufer, *The Ethics of Lying in Negotiations*, 75 Iowa Law Rev. 1219 (1990).

[48]See CISG Articles 47-48, 63. See, Chapter 7.

[49]INTERNATIONAL CHAMBER OF COMMERCE, THE UNIDROIT PRINCIPLES FOR INTERNATIONAL COMMERCIAL CONTRACTS: A NEW LEX MERCATORIA? (1995).

parenthesis refer to the relevant articles of the *Principles* which can be found in Appendix 6:

- Exclusion of trade usage (Articles 1.8, 4.3(f))
- Four corners clause (integration or merger clause) (Articles 2.17 & 2.18)
- Time of performance, early performance, late performance (Articles 6.1.1, 6.1.5, & 7.1.5)
- Order of performance (Article 6.1.4)
- Place of performance, place of payment (Article 6.1.6)
- Form of payment (Articles 6.1.7 & 6.1.8)
- Currency of payment (Article 6.1.9)
- Transportation costs, other expenses (Article 6.1.11)
- Government approvals (Articles 6.1.13-6.1.17)
- Hardship clause (Articles 6.2.1-6.2.3)
- *Force majeure* clause (Article 7.1.7)
- Termination clause, notice provisions (Articles 7.3.1 & 7.3.2)
- Forum Selection & Arbitration clauses (Article 7.3.5(3))
- Limitation of liability clause (Article 7.1.6)
- Interest on delinquent payments (Article 7.4.9)
- Damages, liquidated damages clause (Articles 7.4.1-7.4.4 & 7.4.13)

Contract Review Checklist

It is prudent to develop a contract review checklist for the different types of contracts that are commonly used in a particular business. This checklist can be developed using model forms, reviewing national and international contract principles, and by reviewing prior dealings. Examples of issues to be placed on the checklist include:

- Opening paragraphs or recitals should name contract, define the contract, give the effective date, and name the parties. Example: "The above parties desire to enter into an Agreement for the purpose of __________."
- Check individual state or foreign laws to determine if the given contract requires notarization or witnesses. If a corporate signatory is involved, is a corporate seal required?

- Has anything happened since the negotiations, such as the sending of letter of intent or an "agreement in principle?" Other examples include the subsequent filing of liens or the commencement of litigation by third parties.
- Has an alternative dispute resolution clause been considered? Are there clear choice of law and forum selection clauses?
- Does the contract settle the issue of assignment, transfer, or sub-licensing?
- Were there any third parties involved in the negotiations, e.g., brokers? Does the contract provide for obligations to pay for their services?
- Does the contract provide for modifications or adjustments, especially in long-term contracts?
- Is there a liquidated damages provision? Is it reasonable? Is there a late payment penalty clause? Is it reasonable? Check relevant usury laws. Does the contract provide for specific performance?
- Does the agreement state that it is intended to be the entire agreement between the parties (merger or integration clause)?
- Has the contract been legally executed?
- Is there proper referencing of exhibits to the contract? Have the parties seen and approved of the exhibits?
- If a corporate signatory: Require proof of incorporation and/or certificate of good standing. Also, require corporate resolution authorizing the representative to sign the contract on behalf of the corporation.
- Is there an expiration date requiring execution (signatures of all parties) by a certain date?
- Is the language gender-neutral?
- Are there adequate notice provisions?
- Are non-competition clauses reasonable as to scope, duration, and geography?
- Are there adequate confidentiality provisions?

The following items that deal with more substantive issues should also be incorporated into the checklist:

1. If there are two language versions of the contract, the contracts should specify the version that is the authoritative copy.

2. As a rule, a party should always add a choice of law and forum selection or arbitration clause to not only formal contracts, but also to letter agreements, telexes and other documents.
3. If the parties select a third or neutral country law to apply, they should develop a reasonable relationship between the choice of law and the contract in order to assure that a court will honor their selection. Reasonable contacts include place of payment, place of negotiations, and place of execution.
4. The choice of law or forum selection clause should provide for the means for service of process to commence a court action or for submission to arbitration.
5. Any arbitration clause should be custom drafted for the particular parties and type of transaction. At the minimum, the clause should include a specification of the arbitration tribunal, the place of arbitration, the language of the arbitration, the arbitration rules, any restrictions regarding the matters that are subject to arbitration, the allocation of costs for the proceeding and enforcement of any award, the currency of the award, and the calculation of interest.
6. If the contract is for a distribution of the seller's goods, the distributor should be labeled in the contract as an "independent contractor" in order to avoid the application of a foreign country's tax, employment, and liability laws.
7. A carefully worded and specific *force majeure* clause should be customized to take into account the characteristics of the transaction, the parties, and the types of risks that are of concern and that are not to be allocated to any one of the parties. The clause should also provide the consequences for the *force majeure* events including, termination of contract, suspension, and/or the allocation of additional costs.
8. To avoid misunderstanding and disputes, have both a lawyer and a technical expert review the contract documents before they are signed.
9. If some terms are considered so important to a party that the party would want to cancel the contract if they are not meet, then the party should specify in the contract that violation of those terms are to be considered a *fundamental breach* under the CISG or other relevant law and that the party shall have a right to avoid the contract.

10. As an American purchaser or importer, in order to protect your customers, specify that product warranties extend to any subsequent purchasers.

The contract review checklist needs to be customized for each particular transaction. A checklist for a sale of goods contract and a intellectual property transfer agreement will both incorporate some of the same items. However, a large number of different considerations will need to be added to reflect the fundamental differences between those types of contracts.

A Note on International Negotiations

A thorough knowledge of substantive law rules and principles is imperative to the drafting of a good contract. At the domestic level, for example, a working knowledge of the Uniform Commercial Code provides a solid foundation for the drafting of a sales contract. However, at the international level the general principles of contract law are less specific and applied sporadically by national courts. Thus, knowledge of the law of the country of your foreign contracting party may be necessary to avoid unnecessary misunderstandings. However, cultural and language differences may prevent a contract from ever being formed. A knowledge of the other party's culture and negotiating style is important if an initial inquiry is to develop into a long-term contractual relationship. Cross-cultural business behavior has been described along a number of parameters. Some cultures focus on the importance of developing a contractual and social relationship and not the deal-focused approach prevalent in the United States. Many cultures view a formal, detailed contract as unnecessary and a hindrance to a good faith, evolving contractual relationship where the parties mutually work through problems. "For many Asian cultures the contract may not represent finality but a starting point of a relationship. It is assumed that the contract will be reexamined, reinterpreted or renegotiated if conditions change. In these more traditional cultures, negotiators seek mainly broad-based agreements that are general, flexible and implicit."[50] Americans view

[50]Claude Cellich, Book Review, 10 Journal of Int'l Consumer Marketing 120 (1998) (Reviewing DONALD W. HENDON, REBECCA A. HENDON, & PAULA HERBIG, CROSS-CULTURAL BUSINESS NEGOTIATIONS (1996).

the contract as the operative tool for ensuring full and complete performance; something that should be honored at any costs to the other party. Many cultures view the negotiation phase of contracting as one in which a relaxed development of the relationship should be pursued. This is in opposition to the American "time is money" approach. Without a firm understanding of the cross-cultural differences in negotiating styles, the likelihood of successful completion of the negotiations is greatly diminished. This topic will be examined again in Chapter 6.

CHAPTER 3

Common International Contract Clauses

A survey by Beale and Dugdale found that a majority of firms surveyed "intended to make their contracts by the use of forms containing standard conditions."[51] This chapter will review some of the standard conditions or clauses found in international contracts. They are generally drafted and incorporated in standard forms on a one-sided basis. These clauses are not only found in standard forms, but are also highly negotiated terms in custom drafted contracts between parties of relatively equal bargaining positions. International conventions are useful sources for drafting "standard" clauses. Chapter 7 will review the United Nations Convention for the International Sale of Goods as a tool in the drafting of international sales contracts. More specialized international conventions can be utilized for specific types of contracts. A case in point is the 1988 Ottawa Convention on International Factoring. The Ottawa Convention defines a factoring contract as one in which a supplier assigns receivables arising from contracts for the sale of goods or services to another party (the factor). The factor must perform "at least two of the four functions listed in Article 1(2)(b) of the Convention: finance the supplier, keep the books relating to the receivables, collect the receivables, or protect the supplier against default in payment by the debtors."[52] Thus, if the transaction being contemplated falls

[51]Hugh Beale & Tony Dugdale, "Contracts Between Businessmen: Planning and The Use of Contractual Remedies," *British Journal of Law & Society* 2 (1975): 45, 49.
[52]Franco Ferrari, *The International Sphere of Application of the 1988 Ottawa Convention on International Factoring,* 31 The Int'l Lawyer 41, 47-48 (1997).

within this definition, then the Ottawa Convention should be reviewed as a guide in the drafting of the contract.

The bulk of this chapter examines three common international contract clauses: Choice of law, dispute resolution, and *force majeure*. In drafting a choice of law clause the drafter needs to understand the law that may abrogate his choice of law selection. In the area of dispute resolution, the prominence and nuances of drafting arbitration clauses will be examined. The general parameters of the *force majeure* clause are presented, along with their heightened importance in just-in time contracts. Other clauses to be reviewed include the handcuffs and termination clauses. The chapter concludes with a discussion of the operative clauses often found in sale of goods contracts. The Uniform Commercial Code is referenced as a guide to the drafting of sale of goods' contract clauses.

Choice of Law Clause

Internationally, courts and arbitration tribunals have generally enforced contractual choice of law clauses. However, courts will usually require that the choice of law have some connection to the parties or the contract. Conversely, arbitration tribunals are more likely to enforce a reasonable choice of law selection even if the choice is not connected to the contract or the transaction. Given the international nature of the transaction, an unconnected choice of law selection may be seen as a fair compromise. This is especially true if the parties choice is one of the more popular neutral country's laws. Popular neutral country choices of law include English, American, Swiss, and German law.

Judicial Abrogation of Choice of Law

Courts have used a number of factors in scrutinizing choice of law clauses. At times, statutory mandates may preempt this reasonableness inquiry. For example, the *English Unfair Contract Terms Act of 1977* adopts a presumption of unreasonableness for indemnity clauses that "by reference to any contract term a party is made to indemnify another party in respect of liability for negligence or breach of contract."[53] For international sales

[53]Unfair Contract Terms Act § 4(1) (1977).

contracts, it voids any choice of law clause whose purpose is the avoidance of the Unfair Contract Terms Act. The following excerpts from the *Second Restatement of the Law of Conflicts* provide a number of factors that courts review in deciding whether to honor a choice of law selection.

Section 1: Reason for the Rules of Conflict of Laws

The world is composed of territorial states having separate and differing systems of law. Events and transactions occur, and issues arise, that may have significant relationships to more than one state, making necessary a special body of rules and methods for their ordering and resolution.

Section 6: Choice of Law Principles

(1) A court will follow the statutory directive of its own state on choice of law.
(2) When there is no such directive, the factors relevant to the choice of law include:
   (a) the needs of the . . . international system,
   (b) the relevant policies of the forum,
   (c) the relevant policies of other interested states and the relative interests of those states in the determination of the particular issue,
   (d) the protection of justified expectations,
   (e) the basic policies underlying the particular field of law,
   (f) certainty, predictability and uniformity of result, and
   (g) ease in the determination and application of the law to be applied.

Section 187: Law of the State Chosen by the Parties

(1) The law of the state chosen by the parties to govern their contractual rights and duties will be applied if the particular issue is one which the parties could have resolved by an explicit provision in their agreement directed to that issue.

(2) The law of the state chosen by the parties to govern their contractual rights and duties will be applied, even if the particular issue is one which the parties could not have resolved by an explicit provision in their agreement directed to that issue, unless either
  (a) the chosen state has no substantial relationship to the parties or the transaction and there is no reasonable basis for the parties choice, or
  (b) application of the law of the chosen state would be contrary to a fundamental policy of a state which has a materially greater interest than the chosen state in the determination of the particular issue.

Section 188: Law governing in Absence of Effective Choice by the Parties

(1) The rights and duties of the parties with respect to an issue in contract are determined by the local law of the state which, with respect to that issue, has the most significant relationship to the transaction and the parties under the principles stated in Section 6.
(2) In the absence of an effective choice of law by the parties [under Section 187] the contacts to be taken into account in applying the principles of Section 6 to determine the law applicable to an issue include:
  (a) the place of contracting,
  (b) the place of negotiation of the contract,
  (c) the place of performance,
  (d) the location of the subject matter of the contract, and
  (e) the domicile, residence, nationality, place of incorporation and place of business of the parties.

  These factors are to be evaluated according to their relative importance with respect to the particular issue.
(3) If the place of negotiating the contract and the place of performance are in the same state, the local law of this state will usually be applied.

In weighing these factors, the modern judicial trend is to give great deference to the choice made by the parties in their contractual choice of law clause. "In the area of contracts, where choice-of-law rules are uncertain, some measure of predictability and certainty is achieved by allowing the parties, within broad limits, to select the law to govern the validity and effect of their contract."[54] This deference also advances the state policy goal of Section 6(d) of the Second Restatement, "the protection of the justified expectations" of the contracting parties.

In 1993 the European Union issued a *Directive on Unfair Terms in Consumer Contracts,* 93/13/EEC: L 95/29. Regulations pertaining to the Directive became effective on July 1, 1995. The Directive defines an unfair term as "any term which contrary to the requirement of good faith causes a significant imbalance in the parties' rights and obligations under the contract to the detriment of the consumer." *Exculpatory clauses* and clauses limiting the liability of the seller are considered to create such imbalances. However, unfair terms are not voidable if the term was "individually negotiated." What is the importance of the notion of individual negotiation? [Answer: The unfair term must appear in a standard form contract.] The regulations will void a term, despite the use by a seller, of a clause purporting to apply the law of another country. What factors will a court or arbitral tribunal look at in determining the validity of a choice of law clause? Courts are likely to void a choice of law clause where it appears that the clause was imposed in order to avoid the Directive. The court would than use conflict of law rules to decide the law of the case. These rules include factors such as the location of the parties' business or residence, the place where the contract was made, and the place where the contract is to be performed.

Dispute Resolution Clauses

Litigation is seen as the least-preferred method of dispute resolution in many countries. It is seen in some countries, most notably in Japan, as a failure of the businessperson *qua* businessperson. Alternatively, in "some cultures arbitration may prove a 'face-saving' approach to dispute resolution."[55] From a more practical perspective, it is seen as an expensive process likely to permanently damage the business relationship and is in-

---

[54] Willis Reese, *Conflict of Laws and the Restatement Second,* 28 Law & Contemporary Problems 679 (1963).

[55]Steven C. Nelson, *Alternatives to Litigation of International Disputes,* 23 Int'l Lawyer 187, 199 (1989). See also, Fox, *Dispute Resolution Techniques in International Contracts Involving the Sale of Goods,* 15 Int' Bus. Law 259 (1987).

herently unpredictable as to result. International litigation is often unduly delayed due to the lack of uniformity in procedural rules. The liberalized nature of United States discovery rules often meet with hostility in foreign courts. A number of international conventions can be utilized to overcome some of these foreign obstacles to full discovery. The ability to serve process and take evidence in foreign countries has been enhanced by the Hague Convention on the Service Abroad of Judicial and Extrajudicial Documents[56] and the Hague Convention on the Taking of Evidence Abroad.[57]

Another perceived problem of international litigation is the belief that judgments are more difficult to enforce than arbitral awards. The court in *Hunt v. BP Exploration Ltd.*[58] reviewed American law on the enforcement of foreign judgments. The case involved the enforcement of an English judgment against an American defendant. The court recognized that *Hilton v. Guyot*[59] was still good law. In *Hilton* the Supreme Court held that a foreign judgment is entitled to enforcement if the defendant had an opportunity for a fair trial. A fair trial is predicated on the foreign court possessing personal and subject matter jurisdiction, conducting trials using *regular* procedures, and acting "under a system of jurisprudence likely to secure an impartial administration of justice." However, despite this embrace of international comity, the Court failed to enforce the French judgment under a rule of *reciprocity.* Because of the convergence of national legal systems and the United States' recognition of other legal systems, the rule of reciprocity has rarely been used in recent years as a defense to the enforcement of a foreign judgment. Instead, the best grounds for attack are the procedural ones centered on due process and public policy concerns. The court held that given the historical deference received by English judgments, the *Hilton* due process standards were easily met given the similarities of the legal systems. Major substantive differences in the laws of the court rendering judgment will also be scrutinized during the enforcement stage.[60] However, American courts normally will not deny recognition "merely because the law or practice of the foreign country differs, even if markedly, from that of

[56]20 U.S.T. 361, T.I.A.S. No. 6638, 658 U.N.T.S. 163, Nov. 15, 1965.

[57]23 U.S.T. 2555, T.I.A.S. No. 7444, 847 U.N.T.S. 231, March 18, 1970.

[58]492 F. Supp. 885 (N.D. Tex. 1980).

[59]159 U.S. 113.

[60]For example, United States courts will generally not enforce foreign country penal and tax judgments.

the recognition forum."[61] Ultimately, the court in *Hunt v. BP Exploration* did not enforce the English judgment pending its appeal in the English court system. It cited the Uniform Foreign Money-Judgments Recognition Act which states that "if the defendant satisfies the court either that an appeal is pending or that he is entitled and intends to appeal from the foreign judgment, the court may stay the proceedings until the appeal has been determined or until the expiration of a period of time sufficient to enable the defendant to prosecute the appeal."[62]

The problems of international litigation become more pronounced when one of the parties is a government or a quasi-governmental entity. The doctrine of sovereign immunity protects governments from being sued on claims stemming from non-*commercial* activities. The problem with this type of categorization of activities is that government procurement has become increasingly commercialized making the distinction between sovereign and commercial activities difficult to define. The gravity of this problem becomes apparent in developing countries where almost by necessity a governmental entity is involved with international transactions. For example, a government partner is common in joint venture undertakings. It is important in such dealings to negotiate a contract clause in which the governmental entity *waives* its potential sovereign immunities[63] and *Act of State*[64] defenses.

It should be noted that an arbitration clause is not and should not completely separate the arbitration from the court system. At least in two instances the court system is crucial to the vitality of the arbitration process. The first is the most obvious—the arbitration award must be enforced through the court system. An unenforceable award renders the arbitration

[61]492 F. Supp. 885 at 900, *quoting*, von Mehren & Patterson, *Recognition and Enforcement of Foreign-Country Judgments in the United States*, 6 Law & Policy in Int'l Bus. 37, 61 (1974).

[62]The Uniform Foreign Money-Judgments Recognition Act, 13 Uniform Laws Annotated (U.L.A.) 263 (1962). The shortcoming of the act is that it has not received a significant degree of international adoption.

[63]The United States' doctrine of sovereign immunity has been codified as the *Foreign Sovereign Immunities Act of 1976*. Public Law 94-583, 90 Stat. 289, 28 U.S.C. §§ 1332 (a)(2), (3), (4), 1391(f), 1441(d), 1602-1611 (1982). For the English law counterpart (State Immunity Act of 1978) see, Chapter 33, 17 I.L.M. 1123 (1978).

[64]See, e.g., Banc Nacional de Cuba v. Sabbatino, 376 U.S. 398 (1964).

process an empty exercise. Fortunately, the New York Convention[65] has provided security of enforcement in most national jurisdictions. Nonetheless, the arbitration clause should expressly state that the parties consent to the jurisdiction of any competent court for purposes of the enforcement and satisfaction of any award. A device that makes enforcement of the award less problematic and court dependent is the establishment of an escrow account prior to the commencement of the arbitration. The parties can be required to deposit money, letters of credit, or insurance bonds. The arbitration clause should then provide that the arbitrator is empowered to release the funds held in escrow to satisfy any award.

A second role for the court system is the granting of injunctive relief pending the outcome of the arbitration. The arbitration clause may provide that application may be made to the arbitrators for such relief. However, the arbitrator's ability to restrain the parties may be legally ineffective. Thus, the clause should also allow the parties to resort to the court system. This provision is especially important in the area of intellectual property. The need to restrain the release of confidential information and trade secrets makes such injunctive relief a necessity. It is important for the aggrieved party to maintain the status quo pending the outcome of the arbitration process. The sensitivity of the information may also dictate a clause that places restraints on the release of information within the arbitration process. First, the clause should reiterate that all information provided in the arbitration is to remain private and confidential. Release of such information by one of the parties would be a ground for a separate claim. Second, the clause should provide that information is to be provided to the arbitrators during the resolution process and not during the arbitrator selection process.

Arbitration and Mediation Clauses

Arbitration is the most common vehicle for dispute resolution in international commercial transactions.[66] It can be institutionalized through

[65]Convention on the Recognition and Enforcement of Foreign Arbitral Awards (1958).

[66]"When businesses enter into transnational relationships such as contracts for the sale of goods, joint ventures, construction projects, or distributorships, the contract typically calls for arbitration in the event of any dispute." Yves Dezalay & Bryant Garth, *Merchants of Law as Moral Entrepreneurs: Constructing International Justice from the Competition for Transnational Business Disputes*, 29 Law & Society Rev. 27, 30 (1995). Compare,

the use of standard rules provided by such organizations as the American Arbitration Association (AAA) or the International Chamber of Commerce (ICC), or it can be done on an ad hoc basis.[67] Arbitration offers the potential for a shortened, cost effective, confidential, and hopefully more amicable means to resolve a dispute. It allows the parties to select arbitrators with the necessary expertise to understand the technicalities of the issues in dispute. Also, an unusual choice of law clause is more likely to be sustained by a panel of arbitrators then national courts of law. Unlike courts, arbitrators' primary mandate comes from the contractual arbitration clause and they do not have national public policy concerns. The importance of confidentiality, especially in areas involving sensitive information, makes alternative dispute resolution the preferred means for solving contractual disputes. Most businesspersons appreciate the finality of arbitration awards as compared to the multiple appeals process common in litigation. Most international contracts possess a standard arbitration clause such as the one discussed below. The arbitration clause should be viewed, along with the traditional material terms of price, quality, delivery, payment, trade term, and *force majeure,* as one of the most important terms in the contract. It should be custom designed to deal with the issues specific to the transaction and to the respective parties. The additional time spent negotiating and drafting the clause will be time well spent given the costs of international dispute resolution.

The Standard Clauses

A vague, simple arbitration clause often is not worth the paper it's printed on. Issues not dealt with will likely require a court proceeding to be resolved. The clause should state the specific rules to be applied, such as the rules of the International Chamber of Commerce[68] or the American Arbi-

---

Christina S. Romano, *1996 Brazilian Commercial Arbitration Law,* 5 Annual Survey of Int'l & Comparative Law 27 (1999) (Brazil was slow in accepting the desirability of international commercial arbitration).

[67]Dezalay & Garth note that the arbitration rules of the United Nations Commission on International Trade Law are often used for ad hoc arbitration. Ibid. at 31. To find the UNCITRAL arbitration rules see, 31 U.N. GAOR, Supp. No. 17, Doc. A/31/17 at 33 (1976, reprinted in, 15 I.L.M. 701 (1976).

[68]*International Chamber of Commerce,* Public Law No. 291, ICC 9-21, *Rules for the ICC Court of Arbitration* (1980).

tration Association. The American Arbitration Association's standard clause states that: "Any controversy or claim arising out of or relating to this contract . . . shall be settled by arbitration administered by the American Arbitration Association in accordance with its applicable rules and judgment may be entered in any court having jurisdiction thereof." This clause makes clear that *all* issues pertaining to the contract are to be arbitrated and it provides a complete set of rules and procedures by referring to the rules of the AAA. The *entry of judgment* language ("may be entered in any court") is essential to show intent that any arbitration award is to be final and binding. This is needed because arbitration awards are not automatically enforceable under 9 U.S.C. § 10. In order to avoid problems of enforcing an arbitration award, the arbitration clause can require the parties to post a bond before the submission of any dispute to arbitration. In short, in international contracting it is important "to make absolutely clear in the contract that both parties desire arbitration, are willing to accept judgment of an award, and are willing to accept entry of judgment in any jurisdiction."[69]

What the standard clause does not provide for is the vehicle of mediation or conciliation[70] as a way to efficiently resolve a dispute prior to a formal arbitration. It is highly recommended that a *Med-Arb* clause be utilized in most contracts. Conciliation or mediation as a required precursor to any arbitration is generally advantageous to both parties. First, mediation has been shown to be highly successful in promptly resolving a dispute and preserving the long-term solidarity of the contractual relationship. Second, if the mediation is unsuccessful, the parties will have a better understanding of the issues in dispute which will generally lead to a more efficient arbitration. One device to make mediation more appealing is to provide in the clause that the arbitrators may include the costs of the mediation in their arbitration award. The downside of mediation is minimal since either party retains the power to end the mediation at anytime in order to proceed to arbitration.

The standard arbitration clause can easily be transformed into a Med-Arb clause by inserting the following language after the ". . .": "The parties agree first to attempt to settle the dispute through mediation administered

---

[69]James H. Davis, Kenneth E. Payne, & John R. Thomas, *Drafting the Technology License Agreement,* in ALI-ABA COURSE MATERIALS JOURNAL 13, 27 (1996).

[70]Some commentators distinguish between mediation and conciliation. Since there is no generally accepted definition to base any such differences, the two words will be used interchangeably.

by the AAA and its Commercial Mediation Rules [or ICC Rules of Optional Conciliation] before resorting to arbitration." Conciliation especially makes sense in international business disputes because of the increased chances that misunderstandings are due to cultural and language differences. "It is precisely because misunderstandings brought about by cultural and other differences may lie at the heart of so many disputes between parties to international transactions that one might reasonably assume that in the international domain conciliation might have its greatest potential, at least where the parties concerned are acting in good faith."[71] Unfortunately, international mediation or conciliation is an underutilized dispute resolution device. Therefore, it is recommended that the arbitration clause expressly state that the parties have agreed to voluntarily submit to conciliation before proceeding with a formal arbitration. In order to stimulate interest in conciliation, the ICC updated its Conciliation Rules on January 1, 1988. The ICC Rules of Optional Conciliation are made up of eleven concise articles intended to encourage simplicity, flexibility, timeliness, cost-savings, and confidentiality in the conciliation process.

ICC Rules of Optional Conciliation

Articles 1 and 4 provide for simplicity in the commencement of conciliation. The parties simply submit an application for conciliation (along with a $500 application fee). A single conciliator is then appointed by the Secretary General of the ICC Court. The conciliator then sets a time-limit for the parties to present their arguments. Flexibility is enhanced by the fact that the Rules place few restraints upon the conciliator. For example, the conciliator may or may not make settlement recommendations and, unlike arbitration, may meet individually with either party. The ICC's position regarding costs is that they should be considerably less than the costs of arbitration. The Schedule of Conciliation and Arbitration Costs provides that ICC administrative expenses for conciliation are to be one-quarter of the amount of an arbitration.[72] Timeliness of the conciliation may become a concern because in a number of jurisdictions the commencement of a con-

---

[71]Eric A. Schwartz, *International Conciliation and the ICC*, 5 The ICC International Court of Arbitration Bulletin 5, 6 (Nov. 1994).

[72]Ibid at 9. The Schedule of Costs can be found in Appendix III to the ICC Rules.

ciliation conference does not toll the *statutes of limitations.*[73] The attorney should take the necessary steps to preserve her clients right to bring suit or to arbitrate.

Concerns for confidentially are emphasized in the rules.[74] Article 6 gives the general mandate that the "confidential nature of the conciliation process shall be respected by every person." Article 11 specifically prohibits the use of the following conciliation-generated information in a subsequent arbitration or court proceeding: (1) Any views expressed or suggested by any party with regards to a possible settlement, (2) Any proposals enunciated by the conciliator, and (3) The fact that one of the parties was agreeable to the conciliator's recommendations.

Custom Drafted Arbitration Clauses

The custom drafted clause may make use of an assortment of alternative dispute resolution devices such as mediation[75] and mini-trials.[76] Most arbitration clauses should also deal with the following fundamental concerns[77]:

> **Governing Law:** A clause that is as important as the forum selection clause (litigation) or the arbitration clause (alternative dispute resolution) is the choice of law clause. Given the diversity of national legal systems, all international contracts should have a clearly written choice of law clause. The arbitration clause and choice of law clause are intimately interconnected. For example:

---

[73]Ibid at 9, n. 22.

[74]See, e.g., Paulsson & Rawding, *The Trouble with Confidentiality,* 5 The ICC International Court of Arbitration Bulletin 48 (May 1994).

[75]The AAA has two sets of mediation rules: Commercial Mediation Rules and Construction Industry Mediation Rules.

[76]Mini-trial is a method in which officers from the contesting companies meet in the presence of a neutral advisor. The parties witness the presentation of cases supporting both sides and then attempt to agree to a voluntary settlement. The AAA has a separate set of rules for mini-trials—Mini-Trial Procedures. There are variations of the mini-trial. One example is the "mini-trial with penalties" where a stipulated penalty is paid by the party who rejects the settlement offer presented by the neutral advisor and who subsequently loses in the formal proceedings.

[77]Source: American Arbitration Association: http://www.adr.org.

i. The choice of law clause can direct the arbitrator away from any specific national law and require a decision based upon international law or the *lex mercatoria.*[78]

ii. The arbitration clause may remove the normal restrictions to strictly apply the substantive law stated in the choice of law clause. Instead, the arbitrator may be empowered to grant any remedy that fairness or equity dictates.

Provisional Remedies: The arbitration clause should clearly state whether or not provisional remedies, such as injunctions, may be obtained through application to the arbitrator. Failure to do so would require a party to incur the costs of obtaining a court order. The provision should also sanction the obtaining of interim relief pending the establishment of the arbitral tribunal. Alternatively, the clause may simply grant either party the option to seek provisional or interim relief from a court as a supplement to the arbitration proceeding.

Escrow Provision: Given the cost of enforcing judgments and arbitral awards in the international setting, the parties may want to ensure payment by requiring the establishment of an escrow fund. The fund may be established with the arbitration association (AAA, ICC), a law firm, or an independent escrow agent such as a commercial bank. The escrow may include a cash deposit, a letter of credit, or title documents (in a sale or lease of goods transaction, a bill of lading may be placed in escrow).

Venue of Arbitration: A specific city should be stated as the place of arbitration. The selection of the city of arbitration rests upon a number of factors:

i. Convenience of parties,

---

[78]See generally, M.T. Medwig, *The New Law Merchant: Legal Rhetoric and Commercial Reality,* 24 L & Pol. Int'l Bus. 589 (1993); E. Alan Farnsworth, *Unification and Harmonization of Private Law,* 27 Can. Bus. L. J. 48 (1996); A. Rosett, *Unification Harmonization, Restatement, Codification and Reform in International Commercial Law,* 40 A. J. Comp. L. 683 (1982); R. Goode, *Usage and its Reception in Transnational Commercial Law,* 46 I.C.L.Q. 1 (1997); Lord Mustill, *The New Lex Mercatoria: The First Twenty Five Years,* 4 Arbitration Int. 86 (1988).

ii. Availability of qualified arbitrators,

iii. Whether the state or country of the city is arbitration friendly. For example: Is the country a signatory to the New York Convention?

iv. Language of the proceeding.

Language of Proceeding: In transactions involving parties with multi-lingual skills, a language should be specified (generally, the language of the contract).

Selection of Arbitrators: The two types of selection are party-appointed and association appointed. The parties, especially when only one arbitrator is being used, may delegate her selection to the arbitration association. In the three-person arbitration panel, a common device is to have each party select one arbitrator from a list provided by the association. The third arbitrator is then selected jointly by the party-selected arbitrators. The clause should provide a time limit for party-selected appointments. This will prevent a party from using the arbitrator selection process as a means to delay the proceeding.

Failure of the parties to appoint an arbitrator or arbitrators and a failure of the arbitration clause to designate the association rules to be followed for appointment, will require that a court empanel the arbitrators. The Convention on the Recognition and Enforcement of Foreign Arbitral Awards, 9 U.S.C. Sections 1-14,[79] states that upon "the application of either party to a controversy the court shall appoint an arbitrator or arbitrators, as the case may require . . . and unless otherwise provided in the agreement the arbitration shall be by a single arbitrator."

Number of Arbitrators: Since the fees of the arbitrators are paid by the contesting parties, the monetary size of the dispute may dictate the preferred number of arbitrators. Because the parties are from different nationalities, each party may be more comfortable with se-

[79]Title 9 U.S.C. Sections 1-14 codify the United States Arbitration Act, the Convention on the Recognition and Enforcement of Foreign Arbitral Awards, and the Inter-American Convention on International Commercial Arbitration.

lecting an arbitrator of his own nationality with the third arbitrator having a neutral nationality. Also, the complexity of the transaction and the nature of the issues involved may suggest a number of arbitrators with various expertise.

Qualifications of Arbitrators: The parties may within their arbitration clause, list the requirements of the arbitrators to be appointed. In a complicated transaction, such as an intellectual property transfer, the parties may list different qualifications for each of the arbitrators who are to be subsequently appointed. For example, the parties could require that one arbitrator be a certified public accountant familiar with the determination of gross and net revenues and the calculation of royalties; that another be an intellectual property attorney who specializes is a specific area of intellectual property law; and that the third one be a former administrative law judge or governmental regulatory official with expertise in the regulatory side of intellectual property protection; or someone in the computer or technology transfer business.

Discovery: Most arbitration rules minimize the amount of discovery allowed to the parties. Depending on the complexity of the claims and sensitivity of the information, the parties may want to provide for discovery. It is suggested, however, that the contract language should be specific as to what type of discovery is to be permitted. Furthermore, the clause should limit the time frame available for discovery in order to avoid the dangers of creating a litigation-type of arbitration.[80] It may provide for discovery under the United States Federal Rules of Civil Procedure, but limit the discovery period to 120 days. Extended discovery can generally be rationalized in only large, complex cases. In those instances, the parties may elect to make use of the AAA's "Supplementary Procedures for Large, Complex Disputes" which is more party-controlled. The AAA also provides specialized rules for international arbitration, the Supplementary Procedures for International Commercial Arbitration. One device which would allow for discovery in a controlled

[80] "Arbitration has become increasingly formalized and more like U.S.-style litigation as it has become more successful and institutionalized." Dezalay & Garth at 29.

setting would be to provide for a pre-arbitration hearing in which the arbitrators may order a limited exchange of information including the production of requested documents, summaries of expected testimony of proposed witnesses, and depositions.

Remedies: The parties may want to restrict the type and amount of damages to be awarded through arbitration. For example, they may want to prohibit punitive damage awards or limit the amount of consequential damages. The clause may provide a "high-low" amount to which the arbitrator's award must conform. A high-low provision allows the parties to predict the greatest amount of damages that is likely to pay for breaching the contract.

Reasoned Awards: Most arbitration rules do not require the arbitrators to itemize their awards or to give reasons for their decision. At the very least, however, most contestants would like an itemization of the award amount. In a case involving multiple issues of law and fact, a reasoned award may provide guidance for the future activities of the parties. However, unless the arbitration clause requires an itemized or reasoned award such information is not likely to be provided. The propensity of arbitrators is not to give detailed, written opinions. Such opinions are time consuming and may open the award to criticism. In order to receive a reasoned award, the clause should state that the award shall be in writing and shall specify all findings of fact and conclusions of law.

Consolidation Clause: The arbitration clause may provide for the consolidation of multiple parties' claims and arbitration proceedings. For example, a dispute in a foreign construction project may entail claims of the general contractor, subcontractors, suppliers, and the owner, along with architects, engineers, lending institutions, and insurance companies. One of the advantages of litigation is its ability to handle disputes involving numerous parties. Arbitration clauses must be custom tailored to deal with multiple party, multiple issue disputes. For example, most arbitration rules base the selection of arbitrators scenario upon a two-party dispute. The United States Federal Rules of Civil Procedure 42(a) does authorize consolidation of multiple arbitration proceedings under the Federal Arbitration Act. However, it fails to adequately deal with the modification of procedural rules necessary to efficiently move from two-party to multiple party dispute resolution. Therefore, it is imperative for the arbitration clause to deal with the different procedural issues that multiple party disputes and consolidation generate.

The following is a single paragraph arbitration clause that in a succinct manner addresses a number of issues not dealt with in the common boilerplate clause.

> Any controversy, claim, or dispute arising out of, or relating to, this contract shall be resolved according to binding arbitration conducted in accordance with the Commercial Arbitration Rules of the American Arbitration Association then in effect. The decision of the arbitrator shall be final and binding on the parties and the award may be entered in any court of competent jurisdiction. The arbitrator shall not be authorized to award punitive damages. The costs of any arbitration, including the costs of the record or transcripts, administrative fees, attorney's fees, and any other fees shall be paid by the party determined by the arbitrator to not be the prevailing party or as otherwise allocated in an equitable manner as determined by the arbitrator.

The clause strongly emphasizes that the parties are giving up any rights to appeal the arbitration decision and both parties expressly consent to the entry of an arbitration award "in any court of competent jurisdiction." The preclusion of punitive damages is common and especially warranted in international contracts because of the fact that most legal systems do not recognize such damage awards. This clause also leaves all cost related to the arbitration proceeding to be allocated by the arbitrator.

Legality of Arbitration and Forum Selection Clauses

A well written arbitration clause will answer not only the question of "how" a contract dispute is to be resolved, but also "where" the dispute is to be resolved. In the latter sense, the clause is a form of a forum selection clause. Initially forum selection clauses were often voided by American courts as an usurpation of the court's jurisdiction or as "contrary to public policy." One of the public policy concerns was the preservation of the American plaintiff's right to bring a lawsuit in an American court. The United States Supreme Court in *The Bremen v. Zapata Off-Shore Co.*[81] case held that forum selection should only be voided in unusual cases. Forum selection clauses are to be fully enforced unless the attacking party meets "the heavy burden of showing that its enforcement would be unreasonable, unfair, or unjust." The grounds for voiding a forum selection clause were further limited by the court in *Bremen.* It explained that the challenging party needed to show that the "contractual forum will be so gravely difficult and inconvenient" that the plaintiff will, for all practical purposes, be deprived of her right to proceed with her claim. The court's stated rationale was that the expansion of American business would be retarded if "we insist on a parochial concept that all disputes must be resolved under our law and in our courts." It also asserted that the security and predictability of international contracts and contract dispute resolution needs to be ensured. "The elimination of uncertainties by agreeing in advance on a forum acceptable to both parties is an indispensable element in international trade and contracting."

However, in the area of consumer purchases, some courts continue to void arbitration clauses. In a 1999 case, a New York court voided an arbitration clause as unconscionable under Section 2-302 of the Uniform Commercial Code. *Bower v. Gateway*[82] involved the sale of a Gateway computer. After receiving an order either by mail, phone, or Internet, Gateway mails a copy of its "Standard Terms and Conditions of Agreement." The Standard terms provided that any dispute would be resolved under the arbitration rules of the International Chamber of Commerce. The court in *Bower* held that the high cost of arbitration would unconscionably deter the purchaser from invoking a claim. For an excellent recent case dealing with the enforcement of foreign arbitration awards see, *Europcar Italia, S.P.A. v. Maiellano Tours, Inc.*[83] The decision in *Europcar* states that any party to a foreign arbitration award may seek confirmation in a United States court within three years after the award was made.[84] The facts of the case involved the enforcement of an award made through an informal procedure in Italy. The

[81]407 U.S. 1 (1971).
[82]676 N.Y.S.2d 569 (App. Div. 1999).
[83]Docket No. 97-7224 (2d Cir. 1997).
[84]9 U.S.C. § 207.

United States Circuit Court held that "in light of the differences in arbitration among the signatory countries (New York Convention), the Convention should be read broadly to cover both formal and informal arbitration. A stay of confirmation should not be lightly granted lest it encourage abusive tactics by the party that lost in arbitration."[85]

Arbitration is an attractive vehicle for international dispute resolution due to the large number of signatories to the Convention on the Recognition and Enforcement of Foreign Arbitral Awards (New York Convention). The following is an edited version of the Convention that highlights its major principles.

CONVENTION ON THE RECOGNITION AND ENFORCEMENT OF FOREIGN ARBITRAL AWARDS (June 10, 1958)

Article I

When signing, ratifying or acceding to this Convention any State may on the basis of reciprocity declare that it will apply the Convention to the recognition and enforcement of awards made only in the territory of another Contracting State. It may also declare that it will apply the Convention only to differences arising out of legal relationships, whether contractual or not, which are considered as commercial under the national law of the State making such declaration.

Article II

Each Contracting State shall recognize an agreement in writing under which the parties undertake to submit to arbitration all or any differences which have arisen or which may arise between them in respect of a defined legal relationship, whether contractual or not, concerning a subject matter capable of settlement by arbitration.

The term "agreement in writing" shall include an arbitral clause in a contract or an arbitration agreement, signed by the parties or contained in exchange of letters or telegrams.

---

[85]See also, *Fertilizer Corp. of India v. IDI Management, Inc.*, 517 F.Supp. 948 (S.D. Ohio 1981).

Article III

Each Contracting State shall recognize arbitral awards as binding and enforce them in accordance with the rules of procedure of the territory where the award is relied upon, under conditions laid down in the following articles.

Article IV

To obtain the recognition and enforcement mentioned in the preceding article, the party applying for recognition and enforcement shall, at the time of the application, supply a duly authenticated original award or certified copy,

The United States is a signatory of the Convention and the People's Republic of China became the seventy-second country to ratify the Convention. The Convention provides for the full recognition of contract arbitration clauses. It does provide a narrow set of grounds for the non-enforcement or the vacating of an arbitration award. Section 10 and 11 provide for the vacating of an award on the following grounds:

(1) where an award was procured by corruption, fraud, or undue means,
(2) where there was evident partiality or corruption in the arbitrators,
(3) where the arbitrators were guilty of misconduct in refusing to postpone the hearing or in refusing to hear evidence pertinent and material to the controversy,
(4) where the arbitrators exceed their powers,
(5) where there was evident miscalculation of figures,
(6) where the arbitrators have awarded upon a matter not submitted to them.

Section 12 of the Convention requires that a motion to vacate must be served within three months after the award is filed or delivered.

Force Majeure Clause

The *force majeure* clause that excuses a breaching party from liability for non-performance is common under most national legal systems. Theo Rauh defines *force majeure* as "any occurrence outside the control of the parties preventing or delaying their performance of the contract. *Force majeure* means extraordinary events independent of the parties' will that cannot be foreseen or averted by them with due diligence, being beyond their control and preventing the contracting party from fulfilling the obligation undertaken in the contract. The expression *force majeure* includes circumstances which were beyond the control of the party concerned exercising the standard care of a reasonable and prudent operator"[86] Rauh states that most *force majeure* clauses require four criteria in order to satisfy the requirements of most national laws:

(1) the event must be external,
(2) it must render the performance radically different from that originally contemplated,
(3) it must have been unforeseeable (objectively) or at least unforeseen (subjectively),
(4) its occurrence must be beyond the control of the party concerned.[87]

He further states that it is imperative that the parties agree to the consequences of a *force majeure* event. The parties should clearly delineate the legal consequences including "detailed provisions dealing with the effect of a *force majeure* event on the contractual duties already and still to be performed."[88] The importance of a well drafted *force majeure* clause is illustrated by the case of *Bende & Sons, Inc. v. Crown Recreation, Inc.*[89] In that case an American seller of combat boots sought an excuse for nonperformance due to the derailment of the train transporting the boots. He sought the excuse of commercial impracticability under Section 2-615 of the Uniform Commercial Code. Section 2-615 provides for an excuse for non-performance when performance is "made impracticable by the occurrence of a contingency the non-occurrence of which was a basic assumption on which the contract was made." Surprisingly, the court rejected the defense holding that the derailment was an allocated risk because "common sense dictates that they could easily have foreseen such an occurrence [!]"[90] A well drafted *force majeure* clause could have preempted the courts finding of allocated risk.

---

[86]Theo Rauh, *Legal Consequences of Force Majeure Under German, Swiss, English and United States' Law*, 25 Denver J. Int'l Law & Policy 151 (1996).
[87]Ibid. at 152.
[88]Ibid.
[89]548 F. Supp. 1018 (E.D. Louisiana 1982).
[90]Ibid. at 1022.

In *Phillips Puerto Rico Core, Inc. v. Tradax Petroleum* liability rested upon the interpretation of a standard *force majeure* clause in relationship to the trade term. The clause in question read as follows:

> *FORCE MAJEURE:* In the event of any strike, fire or other event falling within the term *Force Majeure* preventing or delaying shipment or delivery of the goods by the seller . . . then the contract period of shipment or delivery shall be extended by 30 days on telex request made within seven days of its occurrence. Should shipment or delivery of the goods continue to be prevented beyond 30 days, the unaffected party may cancel the unfulfilled balance of the contract. Should the contract thus be cancelled and or performance be prevented during any extension to the shipment or delivery period neither party shall have any claim against the other.[91]

In the case the C & F contract was entered for the purchase of a product to be shipped from Algeria to Puerto Rico. The Coast Guard unexpectedly detained the ship while in transit. The purchaser brought suit against the seller for breach of contract. The seller claimed an excuse by invoking the *force majeure* clause. The court held that the defense was not necessary because under the C & F term the risk of loss had already passed to the purchaser at the port of shipment. The result may have been different if the purchaser proved that the ship was unseaworthy at the time of shipment and thus that was the reason it had been detained. The court held that the detainment was due to a general inspection of all ships of that type and was not due to the unseaworthiness of the particular ship in question. Thus, it is important for the parties to understand the interrelationship of contract provisions such as the trade term and the *force majeure* clause.

The *force majeure* clause should be a highly negotiated, customized provision dealing with the particulars of the specific parties and specific type of contract. Unfortunately, most contracts, domestic and international, utilize vaguely worded boilerplate excuse or exemption clauses. One example of a more elaborate type of *force majeure* clause has been developed

[91]Ibid,. at 318. As an aside, this clause does possess a number of features even though it does not adequately define the term *force majeure.* It does define the responsibilities of the party attempting to declare *force majeure.* It also provides an automatic 30-day performance extension before allowing the purchaser to cancel the contract. Such a graduated response to a *force majeure* event should be considered when drafting such a clause. The drafter should not only attempt to define the events to be considered as *force majeure,* but also the relative duties and rights of each party stemming from such an event.

by the International Chamber of Commerce.[92] The following is an edited version of the ICC clause:

> A party is not liable for a failure to perform if he can prove that: (1) the failure was due to an impediment beyond his control, (2) he could not have reasonably foreseen the impediment at the time of contract formation, and (3) he could not have reasonably avoided or overcome its effects. An impediment includes but is not limited to:
>
> (a) war, hostilities, and acts of piracy,
> (b) natural disasters
> (c) explosions, fires, and destruction of machinery,
> (d) boycotts, strikes, lock-outs, and work stoppages which occur in the enterprise of the party seeking relief.
> (e) acts of authority.
>
> A party seeking relief pursuant to this clause shall give notice as soon as practicable. Failure to give timely notice makes the party liable in damages for losses that could otherwise have been avoided. Notice shall also be given when the impediment ceases.
>
> The relief granted under this clause is a postponement of the time for performance for such period as may be reasonable. The non-breaching party may also suspend his own performance. Either party may terminate the contract in the event that the impediment persists for a period of ____ days. Upon the termination of the contract, each party may retain whatever he has received, but must account to the other party for any unjust enrichment.

Commentary: The notion of impediment can be found in Article 79 of the CISG. Therefore, research of Article 79 judicial and arbitral decisions can provide insight into the meaning of the word *impediment.* Impediment does not mean inconvenient, or more costly, or difficult to perform. The non-foreseeable requirement is generally interpreted as reasonably non-foreseeable since everything is technically foreseeable. "The clause refers to what a party could reasonably be expected to take into account and to make contingency plans for when entering into the contract." Regarding the above enumerated impediments, work stoppages or strikes at a supplier or subcontractor are generally not sufficient causes. This presumption may be overcome if, for example, the contract specifies the use of the particular

---

[92]ICC Publication No. 421, "Force Majeure and Hardship" (1985).

supplier or subcontractor. Acts of authority do not generally allow for an excuse of not being able to obtain a license, permit or governmental authorization that the contract allocates to one of the parties. The list of generally recognized impediments should be modified to reflect the particulars of the individual contractual subject matter and relationship. An excuse for a large currency fluctuation may be considered as an additional enumerated impediment, however, given the complexity of currency fluctuations and means to protect oneself, a separate clause dealing with currency fluctuations and inconvertibility problems is justified.

Since the *force majeure* clause generally does not recognize changes in circumstances that result in mere hardship, the parties may expand the clause from the recognition of excuse for events that render contract performance practically impossible to those events that make performance substantially more costly. For example, the ICC manual on "*Force Majeure* and Hardship" suggests potential options. Under all the options, an occurrence that "fundamentally alters the contractual equilibrium by placing an excessive burden on one of the parties" allows that party to request a revision of the contract. The requesting party must make the request within a reasonable time. The parties are to consult in good faith in the hope of amicably revising the contract. If no agreement is reached within a specified period of time then:

> Alternative A: The parties are to submit the case to the ICC Standing Committee for the Regulation of Contractual Relations for a non-binding [or binding] decision.
>
> Alternative B: Either party may submit the issue for binding arbitration pursuant to the contract's arbitration clause.

The hardship provision is especially warranted for long-term or multiple installment contracts. Another *force majeure*-type of clause that can be considered is the *government approval clause.* If some government permit, license or approval is required, then the parties may elect to have the approval be a *condition precedent* to the contract. This type of provision is especially appropriate in an intellectual property transfer in a country were government approval is required for such contracts. Such approvals may also be required in order to form a joint venture because some countries have registration requirements for certain contracts or import transactions. A simple government approval clause in an export contract would read:

"Seller shall obtain all necessary permits, licenses or approvals to export the goods. Buyer shall obtain all necessary permits, licenses or approvals to import the goods. This contract is not fully executed and enforceable until such approvals have been received."[93] This clause can be improved by including: (1) good faith or best efforts language regarding the parties' respective duties and (2) a time frame upon which the approvals must be obtained.

The *force majeure* clause is often overlooked in the international sales contract. The term *force majeure* means "superior force" and it allows a party to terminate its obligations under a contract due to the occurrence of something described in the *force majeure* clause. *Force majeure* events may include wars, blockades, strikes, governmental interference or approval, fire, transportation problems, and others. Any event described by the parties as such an event will be given *force majeure* effect. A *force majeure* clause should be custom drafted to take into account the type of industry, the countries, and type of carriage involved. The *Harriscom Svenska*[94] case, shows how a properly drafted *force majeure* clause enabled a seller to successfully avoid liability for not performing on a contract. A distributor filed a breach of contract claim against a manufacturer of radio communications products. The manufacturer claimed an excuse under the agreement's *force majeure* clause. It claimed that the United States government prohibition on all sales to Iran of goods it categorized as military equipment was a *force majeure* event. The U.S. State Department began a commodity jurisdiction proceeding, authorized by the Arms Export Control Act to decide whether the radio was a military product that should be on the government's "Munitions List." The placement on the list would require the manufacturer to obtain export licenses for all its sales of the radio, not just those to Iran. The manufacturer negotiated a compromise in which it agreed to "voluntarily withdraw from further sales to the Iranian market." In exchange, the government agreed that the radio was not subject to the stringent export controls of Munitions List products. One of the issues before the court was whether the manufacturer's failure to ship the spare radio parts was a voluntary act or a *force majeure*. A *force majeure* is an irresistible force, one that cannot be controlled. The issues include whether the defendant was re-

---

[93]WILLIAM F. FOX, JR., INTERNATIONAL COMMERCIAL AGREEMENTS: A PRIMER ON DRAFTING, NEGOTIATING AND RESOLVING DISPUTES 145 (2d ed. 1992).

[94]3 F.3d 576 (1993).

leased under the *force majeure* clause that excused performance under circumstances of governmental interference, whether the voluntary nature of defendant's compliance negated the excuse, and whether the defendant was required to give substituted performance through its Indian licensee. Despite the voluntary nature of the defendant's actions, the court held that the government had undoubted power to compel compliance. Like commercial impracticability, a *force majeure* clause in a contract excuses nonperformance when circumstances beyond the control of the parties prevent performance. The governmental interference in this case was such a circumstance. Furthermore, the court rejected the distributor's argument that the contracts' covenant of good faith required defendant to provide substituted performance from its Indian licensee. *Force majeure* clauses do not require substituted performance.

Just-In-Time Contracting

Force majeure, hardship, and limitation of liability clauses are of added importance in supply contracts premised on the concept of just-in-time. Just-in-time purchasing envisions the production and supplying of goods "in exactly the quantity needed and sending them to where they are needed, when they are needed."[95] Failure to provide the product when requested could lead to serious consequential damages. Where the product being supplied is a component part, failure to supply in time could lead to a production shut down and a resultant loss of profits. The supplier under a just-in-time arrangement should negotiate a broad *force majeure* clause for failures due to unexpected occurrences, along with a hardship clause to allow for adjustments in the contract. In order to limit his exposure to catastrophic consequential damage claims, the supplier should negotiate a limitation of liability or a liquidated damages clause.[96] The supplier may want, as a condition of a just-in-time contract, to require that purchaser (manufacturer) maintain a minimum "buffer inventory" of the product at all times in order to guard against serious consequential damages. In sum,

[95]Robert B. Bennett, Jr., *Just-In-Time Purchasing and the Problem of Consequential Damages,* Uniform Commercial Code Journal 332, 335 (1994).

[96]See, e.g., Hampton by Hampton v. Federal Express Corp., 917 F.2d 1119 (8th Cir. 1990).

the parties to a just-in-time contract should pay careful attention to the consequences of breach when negotiating their contract.

Handcuffs Clause

A contracting party that negotiates a choice of law clause designating the law of the other party's country is likely to be concerned that that law may hold some unexpected surprises. This is especially true when the other party is from a country with a strongly divergent culture and legal system. In order to limit its exposure, the other party may attempt to minimize the application of the law designated in the choice of law clause. The handcuffs clause attempts to provide a built-in menu of remedies available to a party in case of a breach. A simple handcuffs clause attempts to make the contract itself the source of any law to be applied to a future dispute. The following is a rather simple version of a handcuffs clause:

> The remedies agreed upon in this contract are exclusive and do not permit the parties to recur, for the enforcement of their contractual rights, to any remedies regulated outside of this contract in any statutory or non-statutory rule of the proper law of contract.[97]

The problem with handcuffs clauses is that a national court may see them as conflicting with the contract's own choice of law clause. In essence, the handcuffs clause's purpose is to prevent the operation of the choice of law clause. Thus, parties should not place heavy reliance on the handcuffs clause insulating them from the remedial nuances of a foreign law. One commentator concluded that "handcuff clauses are null and void if and insofar as they restrict the parties in the exercise of those of their contractual rights and remedies that have been granted to them by a public policy or mandatory law provision of the proper law of contract. However, they are binding and enforceable insofar as they exclude the exercise of substantive rights and remedies conferred upon them by any derogatory rule of the *lex contractus.*"[98]

---

[97]Otto Sandrock, *Handcuffs Clauses in International Commercial Contracts,* 31 The Int'l Lawyer 1105, 1106 (1997).
[98]Ibid. at 1116.

Termination Clause

All contracts of on-going duration should provide a termination provision. This may entail a period or date upon which the contract automatically terminates. It should also provide for an earlier, unilateral termination. For example, the following provisions were found in an exclusive distribution agreement between a German supplier and a Spanish distributor.[99] First, the contract provided for automatic termination:

> This contract is valid until December 31, 1990 and will be automatically renewed for another year provided that there has been no earlier written termination of the contract by either party.

The contract provides for a unilateral option for the seller to terminate in the event that the purchaser fails to meet certain sales quotas:

> Seller may terminate the contract at the end of the year provided that the following net purchase values have not been attained:
> 1988 DM 750,000
> 1989 DM 1,000,000
> 1990 DM 1,000,000
> In this case the contract will expire six months after the year in question.

The contract then provides for termination without cause after a certain period of time:

> In the case of termination after 3 years, no reasons will be required. The period of notice shall be three months.

It further provides for termination without notice upon the happening of certain events:

> The contract may be terminated by either party at any time, without notice, for the following reasons: Bankruptcy, insolvency or liquidation of one of the parties to the contract or breach of contract by one of the parties.

---

[99]See, ICC Arbitration Case No. 8611 of 1997.

Liquidated Damages Clause

This section will restrict its focus to comparing some of the substantive differences in liquidated damages law among different legal systems. The common law limits the courts to rescission of the liquidated damages clause judged to be a penalty. This is a minority approach under most national laws. A Council of Europe study noted that only the countries of England and Belgium (within Europe) prohibit their courts from rewriting penalty clauses.[100] In contrast, it cites Article 1152 of the French Civil Code that confers "a wider power on the courts to reduce penalties . . . and allows reduction to take place even if the penalty is not *manifestly excessive.*" In order to provide some uniformity between the common law's concept of penalty and the civil law, which tends not to scrutinize liquidated damages clauses, the Council of Europe adopted *Resolution (78) 3 on Penal Clauses in the Civil Law.*[101] The Resolution adopts language akin to the nomenclature of unconscionability. It provides for "judicial control over penal clauses . . . where the penalty is *manifestly excessive.*" The Resolution also provides for the reformation of such clauses. It states that the "sum stipulated may be reduced by the court when it is manifestly excessive." In its Explanatory Memorandum, the Committee on Legal Co-operation explained that some penal clauses are "*stricto sensu* whose main purpose [is] to act as a threat to induce the promisor to perform" while others are "a genuine pre-assessment of damages . . . or liquidated damages." However, unlike in the common law, the clauses that are *stricto sensu* are not invalid per se under a majority of the national laws. In short, it is acceptable for a liquidated damages clause to serve not only as a means for just compensation, but also as an incentive to induce performance.

Resolution (78) 3 provides a list of factors for determining if liquidated damages are "manifestly excessive." These factors include: the comparison of the pre-estimated damages with the actual damages suffered, "the legitimate interests of the parties including the promisee's *non-pecuniary* interests, the category of the contract and the circumstances under which it was

[100]Courts are required simply "to set aside a clause which is found to impose a true penalty." COUNCIL OF EUROPE, PENAL CLAUSES IN CIVIL LAW 15 (1978).

[101]Adopted by the Committee of Ministers on January 20, 1978 at the 281st Meeting of the Ministers' Deputies.

concluded, in particular the relative social and economic position of the parties . . . or the fact that the contract was a standard form contract," and whether the breach was in good or bad faith.[102] Three distinctions can be made regarding the inherent differences of Continental European and American law. First, the European threshold for voiding a liquidated damages clause is much higher than what is found in American law. The amount of damages must be more than merely disproportionate to actual damages, they must be "manifestly excessive." Second, the language of unconscionability is readily apparent in the law of Continental Europe. "Manifestly excessive" can be used as a synonym for substantive unconscionability. Also, the factors given for reviewing liquidated damages clauses include those often associated with procedural unconscionability including "the relative social and economic position of the parties" and the use of a standard form contract. Finally, the notion of *non-pecuniary interests* is especially noteworthy. This idea can be used to offset a less than accurate pre-estimate of damages, that is, one that is substantially disproportionate to actual damages.

A review of foreign national laws demonstrates that the common law approach to liquidated damages is not the only viable alternative. For example, the Foreign Contract Law of the People's Republic of China[103] does not deal directly with the issue of liquidated damages, but allows for the use of deposits as a way of fixing damages unrelated to actual damages. Article 14 of the law allows a party to retain the deposit if the other party fails to perform. Alternatively, if the party holding the deposit fails to perform, then it must return twice the amount of the deposit. This concept of deposit forfeiture mimics the doctrine of *arrhes* found in Article 1590 of the French Civil Code. Under the doctrine of *arrhes* a deposit is forfeited when the deposit giver cancels a contract. If the deposit holder cancels the contract, then that party must refund twice the amount of the deposit. The rules embodied in the doctrine of *arrhes* can be understood as the use of deposits as liquidated damages. Furthermore, the potentially penal nature of retaining the entire deposit or the doubling of the amount refunded is disregarded under this doctrine.

---

[102]Council of Europe, "Resolution (78) 3 on Penal Clauses in Civil Law (1978), Paragraph 26, Explanatory Memorandum (Commentary to Article 7).

[103]See generally, Zhang Yuqing & James S. McLean, *China's Foreign Economic Contract Law: Its Significance and Analysis,* 8 NW J INT'L L. & BUS. 120 (1987).

The French Civil Code deals directly with the issue of liquidated damages or penalty clauses. Article 1152 of the French Civil Code allows the courts to provide alternative relief if the stipulated amount is "manifestly excessive." It expressly grants courts the authority to reduce or increase the penalty if it is deemed to be manifestly excessive or low. In Japan, there is a strong presumption that penalty clauses are enforceable,[104] but Article 420(1) of the Japanese Civil Code precludes a court from reforming the contract amount. The laws of Denmark, Sweden, Finland, and Norway allow either the voiding or reformation of a penalty clause deemed to be unreasonable. Swedish law specifically provides for an evaluation of the relative bargaining power of the parties in making the reasonableness determination. Section 36(2) of the Swedish Commercial Code provides that "particular consideration" shall be given to protecting the party "in a subordinate position in the contractual relationship." The Swiss Code of Obligations deals directly with the "no actual damages defense." Article 61(1) provides that payment of the penalty is due "even if in the actual case the promisee has not suffered any damage." The Russian Civil Code also provides that "the debtor must pay the penalty established for the breach regardless of whether or not the creditor has suffered damages as a result of the breach." However, Article 190 of the Code allows a court to reduce the amount of the penalty or liquidated damages if it is "extraordinarily large in comparison with the creditor's actual losses." In contrast, Anglo-American common law simply allows for the voiding of a penalty clause and the assessment of actual damages when the stipulated amount is considered unreasonably large.

Operative Clauses in Sales Contracts

The following clauses are presented only for illustrative purposes. They represent only some of the more commonly used clauses. They are not offered as a form book, but as raw material from which intellectual inquiry and insight can be developed.

---

[104]Article 420(3) of the Japanese Civil Code states that "a penalty clause is presumed to be a determination in advance of the amount of compensation due for damages." INTERNATIONAL CHAMBER OF COMMERCE, GUIDE TO PENALTY AND LIQUIDATED DAMAGES CLAUSES 37 (1990).

<u>**Delivery Term:**</u> At times, delivery, performance, or transaction date will be seen as a target and may be controlled by a court's determination of reasonableness. To overcome such a presumption, a party may insert a time of the essence clause to convert the date of delivery from a minor to a material breach status: "TIME BEING OF THE ESSENCE AS PARTIES UNDERSTAND THAT THE EXACT TIME OF DELIVERY IS AN UNDERLYING PREMISE OF THE CONTRACT."

What is the remedy for late delivery? "In the event that there is a failure to deliver on the time and date provided in this contract, seller agrees to pay, as liquidated damages, a sum of $_____ per day of delay for a limit of 30 days. After 30 days of delay, the buyer has the right to terminate the contract." Should we define "time is of the essence"? Are there any other seller responsibilities? "Seller shall notify buyer of any expected delays and the reasons for the delays. Failure to seasonably notify shall be considered a breach of contract for which the buyer has the option to terminate."

<u>**Price Term:**</u> Section 2-305(1)(c) of the Uniform Commercial Code recognizes the notion of the open price term. Thus, the contracting parties are free to agree that the price is to be fixed in terms of some agreed market or other standard as set by a third party person or agency. How does the "open price term" and the excuse doctrine interrelate? Should cost factors be described in detail?

<u>**Bankruptcy Term:**</u> Bankruptcy does not automatically relieve the other party from its contractual obligations. Therefore, it is wise to expressly relieve the non-bankrupt party from his duty to perform:

"In the event of any bankruptcy or insolvency proceedings commenced by or against either party, or in the event of the assignment to a trustee or receiver, then the party not so affected is entitled to cancel any unfilled portion or promise under this contract."

<u>**Quality Disclaimer:**</u> The seller may want to disclaim certain warranty liabilities. A common example: SELLER DISCLAIMS ANY WARRANTY, INCLUDING A WARRANTY OF MERCHANTABILITY AND A WARRANTY OF FITNESS FOR ANY PARTICULAR PURPOSE, AS THE BUYER TAKES GOODS AS IS AND WITH ALL FAULTS. Does this language need to be capitalized? The CISG does not require that a disclaimer or limitation of liability clause be conspicuously displayed. In contrast, UCC Section 2-316(2) requires that the disclaimer mention the word "merchantability," and that it be conspicuously stated. For the implied warranty

of fitness the following language is sufficient: "There are no warranties which extend beyond the description on the face hereof." UCC Section 2-316(3): ". . . all implied warranties are excluded by expressions like *as is, with all faults,* or other language in common understanding." What happens if the disclaimer language conflicts with warranty language? UCC Section 2-316(1) states that if inconsistent, the warranty language prevails and the disclaimer becomes inoperative.

Force Majeure: A primary purpose for contracting is to assign risks. However, the contracting parties may want to provide an excuse for terminating the contract or avoiding damages for certain risks. A reasonable *force majeure* clause could be worded as follows: "The vendor's duty to deliver on time is suspended by reasons caused by an Act of God or strikes." A very broad, pro-seller clause would read as follows: "The vendor's duty to deliver on time is suspended by reasons of an Act of God, strikes, or when delay arises out of causes beyond the control and without the fault of the vendor." The problem with such a broadly worded clause is ambiguity. How would one define control or fault?

Confidentiality Clause: A common confidentiality clause reads as follows: "All information disclosed to the vendee/licensee shall be considered solely owned by the transferor and is communicated in confidence. The transferee shall take reasonable precautions to prevent any of the information being made available to any party who has no need to know. Transferee shall provide security measures that meet legal standards for the protection of trade secrets."

Modification: Parties may want to preclude any future attempt to change certain rights or obligations by post-formation modifications. They often do this by requiring any such modifications to be in writing: "This agreement, or any of its terms, may only be modified by a written agreement signed by both parties." How does waiver, estoppel, and course of performance impact upon this clause?

Anti-Assignment Clause: One method of attempting to structure an anti-assignment clause in a sale of services or "mixed sales" (goods-services) contracts is to phrase the contract as one for personal services that have traditionally been viewed in the common law as not subject to assignment without consent of the other party: "The parties agree that each relies on the other's skill, judgment and reputation in regard to the contractual undertakings promised. This contract cannot be assigned by either party without the express written consent of the other."

Indemnification Clause: "The second party agrees to hold the first party harmless from claims of any kind, including claims resulting from the activities of the party of the second part." An alternative version reads as follows: "First party shall defend, indemnify, and save harmless the second party from any and all liabilities, loss, damage, costs (including reasonable attorneys fees) for personal injury or property damage arising out of or in connection with the work or performance arising out of this agreement."

Choice of Law Clause: A typical choice of law clause reads as follows: "The validity, interpretation, and performance of this contract shall be governed by the laws of the State of New York." One may want to further designate a time frame for the applicable law such as the date of the contract execution, at time of performance, or time of trial. How does the CISG impact this clause?

Choice of Forum Clause: "In the event of dispute, the parties agree that any legal proceedings shall be instituted and prosecuted in State Supreme Court in Manhattan County, New York, and that each party accedes to the jurisdiction of that forum."

Arbitration Clause: "Any dispute or claim arising out of this agreement shall be settled by arbitration in accordance with the Commercial Arbitration Rules of the American Arbitration Association." How could one be more specific in fashioning the above clause? How does an arbitration interrelate with the forum selection clause? See material on arbitration clauses.

Limitation of Remedy Clause: "Vendor shall, at its option, repair or replace any defective products if notified of such defects within 60 days from time of delivery. This is the sole liability of the vendor. Vendor is not liable for any other damages of any kind, including, but not limited to consequential or incidental damages." How does this clause deal with the foreseeability rules of *Hadley v. Baxendale*? Compare to UCC Section 2-719: "(1)(a) the agreement may provide for remedies in addition or in substitution for those provided in this Article as by limiting the buyer's remedy to return of the goods and repayment of the price or to repair and replacement of non-conforming goods, (b) resort to a remedy as provided is optional unless the remedy is expressly agreed to be exclusive, in which case it is the sole remedy. (2) Where circumstances cause an exclusive or limited remedy to fail of its essential purpose, remedy may be had as provided in this Act. (3) Consequential damages may be limited or excluded unless the limitation or exclusion is unconscionable. Limitation of consequential damages for injuries in the case of consumer goods is prima facie unconscionable but limitation of damages where the loss is commercial is not." However, the law does not prevent a seller from narrowing the limitation period from which a cause of action must be commenced. UCC Section 2-725 provides that "an action for breach of any contract for sale must be commenced within four years after the cause of action has accrued. By the original agreement, the parties may reduce the period of limitation to not less than one year but may not extend it." For an international perspective see Appendix 3, *Limitation Period in the International Sale of Goods.*

Liquidated Damages Clause: What type of liquidated damages clause or penalty clause is likely to pass judicial scrutiny? UCC Section 2-718, "Liquidation or Limitation of Damages," provides that the clause should be "reasonable in light of anticipated *or* actual harm," used in instances were it is difficult to calculate or prove a loss, that it is inconvenient or non-feasible for the non-breaching party to obtain an adequate remedy, and any unreasonably large liquidated damages shall be void as a penalty. One drafting technique employed to overcome the above obstacles is to provide for "graduated" liquidated damages.

Time is of the Essence Clause: "Time is of the essence in regard to the performance dates required in Paragraphs _____. Failure to perform on such dates will be considered a material breach of the contract, permitting the other party to terminate the agreement." What is the importance of the second sentence? The second sentence attempts to transform what would generally be considered a minor breach of late delivery into a material breach. It does this by making the performance date a fundamental term in the contract. It should be noted that the "time of the essence" provision, which is popular in the United States, is not an internationally recognized concept. In fact, the civil law and the CISG recognize the concept of *nachfrist.* This device to extend the time for delivery or performance may be used by a foreign court to counteract the applicability of "time of the essence."

Evergreen Clause: "This agreement remains in effect for a term beginning on ______ and ending on ________ at which it remains in effect on a month to month basis until terminated by either party by the giving of sixty days written notice of termination." Which is the "evergreen" language? What is an evergreen statute?[105]

[105]See, Chapter 8, "Commercial Agency Contracts."

<u>**Covenant Not-To-Compete:**</u> The covenant not-to-compete is used in a number of different types of contracts including distribution, licensing, employment, and sale of business contracts. A typical one used in the employment contract states that "upon termination of employment for any reason, the employee agrees to neither directly or indirectly compete with the employer for a period of ____ year(s) in the geographical area of ____________." A prohibition regarding scope of duties and responsibilities that the employee must refrain from needs to be inserted.

CHAPTER 4

The Documentary Transaction

In order to alleviate the seller's risk of not being paid or the buyer's risk of not receiving the goods after paying, most export contracts require a documentary transaction. In short, a sale of goods contract is converted to a sale of documents contract. The buyer contracts to buy documents and the seller promises to provide conforming documents to the buyer while the goods are in transit. The seller is paid and the buyer receives title to the goods while the goods are in transit to the port of destination. In this way, the buyer's delivery and seller's payment risks are diminished. Upon receiving the documents, the buyer is in a position to re-sell the goods to downstream buyers or to use the documents as collateral to obtain financing. In the event that the buyer refuses to pay for the documents, the seller still retains title and control of the goods. He can mitigate his losses by selling the goods to someone else through negotiation of the documents.

The sales contract must carefully list and describe the types of documents that the seller will be required to present in order to receive payment. The mechanism for payment is the presentment of conforming documents as required in the export contract and as subsequently transcribed on the letter of credit through the listing of the documentary requirements on the letter of credit application by the buyer. The required documents are generally attached to a draft. The documentary draft is often drawn by the seller on the account of the buyer and made payable to the seller. Unlike a standard check or bank draft, the seller is both the drawer and payee of the documentary draft. In a non-documentary transaction, the draft would be clean and would be paid upon presentment. To better reduce the payment risk, the seller-exporter will want to negotiate a sight draft so that he will receive payment upon the presentation of the documents. However, some exporters will agree to wait for payment, especially when doing business with an established customer. In such cases, a time draft is utilized that provides for payment within so many days of presentment or from shipment. In that case, the buyer should be required to sign and note "accepted" on the time draft before obtaining possession of the documents. A time draft thus signed and stamped by a merchant is considered a trade acceptance and can be negotiated at a discount if the seller elects not to wait for the expiration of the time period. A more valuable form of acceptance is one signed by a commercial bank. Such an acceptance transforms the time draft into a more negotiable *banker's acceptance.*

To further diminish the seller's payment risk, the documentary contract can require that the buyer provide a letter of credit to the seller. Thus, in the above example of a buyer refusing to pay for conforming documents, the seller may demand payment through the letter of credit. In order to eliminate the payment risk, the exporter will need to negotiate a *confirmed* letter of credit. In the typical scenario, the letter of credit is issued by the importer's bank and then confirmed by the exporter's bank or another bank located near the exporter. The confirmed letter of credit also serves to eliminate the risk of foreign government restrictions on the repatriation of currency.

The Sales Contract and Documentary Transaction

The purchase order prepared by the buyer will include the payment terms of the transaction. The exporter may be paid in a number of ways. The purchase order may propose an open account transaction. Under open account, the exporter ships the goods and sends the documents directly to the purchaser. Payment is then made some time thereafter. Clearly, the open account transaction is risky from the seller's perspective. A "cash against documents" transaction or documentary transaction involves the sending of the documents to the buyer's agent who is authorized to pay the exporter. The documentary transaction utilizes the collection services of commercial banks. The exporter generally delivers the documents to a local bank that uses its banking correspondences to transmit the documents to a bank located near the buyer. That bank collects payment form the buyer prior to releasing the documents. To guarantee the payment to the exporter, the sales contract will often require that the buyer obtain a letter of credit naming the exporter as the beneficiary party. Under the letter of credit, the issuing or confirming bank is required to pay the exporter upon the presentation of conforming documents. The payment is not conditional upon receiving reimbursement from the buyer.

The typical exporting transaction proceeds along a chronological timeline beginning with the negotiation and execution of a sales contract. This is generally followed by: (1) procurement of a letter of credit by the purchaser, (2) delivery of the goods to the common carrier by the seller, (3) presentment and processing of the documents as required by the letter of credit through the international banking system, and (4) the taking of delivery of the goods by the purchaser.

At some point the negotiations either fail or result in the formation of a contract. The exact time of formation is often unclear. At times, the fact of formation becomes evident only when the parties begin to perform. If both parties fully perform, then the contract self-terminates at the time the second party completes her performance. If one of the parties breaches the contract by not performing or by delivering a faulty performance, then the other party may seek a legal remedy to compensate for any loss caused by the other party's breach. The preferred dispute resolution method in international contracting is arbitration rather than litigation.

The performance stage in the international sale of goods is more complicated than in the domestic sale of goods. The international sales contract normally provides for the utilization of a number of third parties to ensure the performance of the contract. Most contracts require the buyer to obtain a letter of credit on behalf of the seller in order to guarantee payment. The services of commercial banks are needed to obtain letters of credit and to process documentation. The international sales contract almost always provides shipment of the goods by ocean carriage. Under the standard CIF contract, the seller must transport the goods by obtaining the services of a freight forwarding company and a common carrier to transport the goods to the buyer. The contract will require that the seller obtain a bill of lading from the common carrier to prove that the goods have been sent as dictated by the contract. The seller will not be able to receive payment through the letter of credit unless he provides a conforming bill of lading, along with the other documents stated in the sales contract (and as transcribed in the letter of credit). Due to the length of transit in international sale of good transactions, a wise buyer will negotiate for inspection rights. The inspection of the goods will take place before the goods are loaded at the port of shipment. The inspection company provides an inspection certificate which the seller will send to the buyer, along with the other documents, through the banking system. The buyer will be able to review the inspection report before paying for the documents and taking possession of the goods at the port of destination. Some of the more common documents used in the documentary transaction are listed and briefly defined in the following "List of Export Documents."

LIST OF EXPORT DOCUMENTS

Bill of Lading: A title document issued by a shipping company. It also serves as a formal receipt of the goods and a carriage contract. The holder of the bill of lading has a right to claim delivery of the goods from the shipping company at the port of destination. The most common bill of lading in international transport is the ocean bill of lading. A multimodal transport bill of lading may be used when more than one form of transport is being used.

Letter of Credit: A document issued by the importer-purchaser's bank to guarantee the payment of the draft to the exporter for the purchase of the goods or upon the presentation of documents by the exporter. A transferable letter of credit allows the exporter (beneficiary) to make the credit payable to others (suppliers).

Letter of Indemnity: This document allows a carrier to release goods to the consignee not yet in possession of the bill of lading. It is a guarantee to indemnify the carrier from all liability related to the release. It is also, called a "steamer guarantee."

Export License: A government issued document granting permission to export the specific commodity to a specific country.

Dock Receipt: This document certifies the receipt of the goods by a carrier at the port of shipment. A "dock warrant" not only acknowledges receipt, but is also a document of a title.

Warehouse Receipt: Acknowledges receipt of the goods by a warehouse operator.

Commercial Invoice: This document is prepared by the exporter and lists and describes the goods. It generally also gives the prices, discounts, quantities, and the delivery and payment terms. It is used by governments to place an valuation of the goods for the assessment of customs duties.

Consular Invoice: An invoice certified by the consul of the country of import. It is used by customs officials to verify the value, quantity, and quality of the goods. Also, the consular may compare the export price with the market price in the exporting country to determine if dumping is evident.

Certificate of Inspection: An inspection certificate is issued by an independent inspection company to assure the purchaser of the quantity and quality of the goods being shipped.

Certificate of Origin: This document may be required by the country of import. It is provided by a third party such as an official of the local chamber of commerce or an official of the consular office.

Bill of Exchange or Draft: An order addressed to the importer or the importer's bank for the payment of a fixed sum at sight or in the future (time draft).

ATA Carnet: An international customs document for the temporary duty-free import of goods into a country for display, demonstration, or other purposes. A carnet is usually good for one year from the date of issuance. Generally, a bond or cash deposit of forty percent of the value of the goods is required. Carnets are sold in the United States by the U.S. Council for International Business, 1212 Avenue of the Americas, New York, New York 10036, (212) 354-4480.

ISO 9000 Certificate: International quality standards which certify that the exporter meets certain minimum requirements of quality.

Marine Insurance Certificate or Binder: Generic form of insurance available even in multimodal transport.

The international sales contract often triggers a host of contractual relationships. It does this by converting the typical domestic sale of goods into a documentary transaction. The documentary transaction, along with the logistics of international exporting, requires one or the other party to enlist the services of third parties. The purchaser is asked to guarantee payment by obtaining a letter of credit to the benefit of the seller.[106] The letter of credit appendage to the sale of goods produces a number of contractual relationships. The purchaser enlists the services of its commercial bank by way of a letter of credit application that provides the substance of their contractual undertaking. If successful, the bank will issue a letter of credit naming the seller as beneficiary. The issuing bank has a contractual obligation to pay the beneficiary upon the proper presentation of the required documents. Most often an intermediary bank located near the seller or the port of shipment is used to process the documents. If that bank confirms the letter of credit then two additional contractual relationships are formed: (1) between the confirming bank and the beneficiary, and (2) between the confirming and the issuing banks. Thus, the typical letter of credit transaction entails four contracts. Other third parties employed in the international sale of goods include marine insurers, common carriers, custom brokers, and freight forwarders.

It is the purpose of this chapter to explore these "other" contractual relationships associated with the international sale of goods and the documentary transaction. The first section will review the forms and rules pertaining to international letters of credit.

[106]See generally, DOLAN, THE LAW OF LETTERS OF CREDIT: COMMERCIAL AND STANDBY CREDITS (2d ed. 1991).

Letters of Credit

The typical scenario in an export transaction is that the seller and buyer negotiate a contract in which the buyer agrees to provide the seller with a letter of credit. Prior to signing a contract, the importer may seek the advice from a customs broker regarding import regulations and the documents that he should obtain from the seller for import purposes. After the execution of the contract, the buyer places an application for the letter of credit with the prospective issuing bank. Following credit approval, the bank issues the original letter of credit using the details supplied in the letter of credit application. The original letter of credit is forwarded (mail, telex, or SWIFT)[107] to the exporter's bank. The exporting bank then advises the exporter that the letter of credit has been issued. If required, the exporter's bank may also confirm the letter of credit. The beneficiary (exporter) reviews the letter of credit. In order to insure that the letter of credit is to be confirmed by exporter's bank, the exporter should negotiate clear language in the contract. The following clause would be sufficient for this purpose:

> The Letter of Credit is to be drawn in IRREVOCABLE form and be subject to the Uniform Customs and Practices for Documentary Credits as published and updated from time to time by the International Chamber of Commerce. The Letter of Credit must be advised through and CONFIRMED by a bank located at the port of shipment acceptable to the seller. It must be PAYABLE AT THE COUNTERS OF THE CONFIRMING BANK.

Upon approval by the beneficiary, the bank may be instructed to send the letter of credit to the freight forwarder with instructions to book shipment. The freight forwarder coordinates the movement of the goods, secures the bill of lading, and completes other documentation as required in the letter of credit. Generally, to initiate a relationship with a freight forwarder, the exporter completes a Power of Attorney form. The Power of Attorney allows the freight forwarder to complete documents in the name of

[107]The SWIFT network was set up to provide banks with a means of handling inter-bank transactions including bank transfers and foreign exchange confirmations. It is cooperatively owned by over 1000 banks in dozens of countries.

the exporter. The form must be signed by an authorized signatory of the company and witnessed by two people.

The original letter of credit and the shipping documents are presented to the advising or confirming bank. If the bank has confirmed the letter of credit, then it will review the documents and pay the exporter. The documents are sent to the issuing bank with a claim for reimbursement. Upon approval of the documents, the issuing bank will debit the importer's account for the amount of the letter of credit drawing and any charges due. Following payment, the importer may instruct the bank to forward the documents to a customs house broker. The customs house broker secures the release of the goods and customs clearance. The customs broker will need, among other items, a commercial invoice and a properly endorsed bill of lading. The importer will need to provide its customs broker with a Power of Attorney in order to act on his behalf.

The International Chamber of Commerce has developed a number of standard documentary credit forms, along with "Guidance Notes" for their proper use.[108] International purchasers and sellers should be familiar with the forms used to obtain and amend letters of credit. The ICC forms incorporate the requirements of the Uniform Customs and Practices for Documentary Credits (UCP 500). A review of the ICC forms and Guidance Notes will assist the purchaser in drafting instructions to the issuing bank and help the beneficiary (seller) in the preparation of the stipulated documents. For example, the drafter of letter of credit instructions should understand the repercussions of using broad terminology to describe items of value or amounts of something. The use of words like "approximate" in association with the amount of the credit or the quantity or unit price of the goods will be automatically translated under Article 39(b). The buyer will have to accept documents that vary the amount of goods in the range of 5%, more or less. In order to avoid such a variance, the applicant will want to state a specific number of packing units or words to the effect that "the quantity of the goods specified must not be exceeded or reduced."

The most important point in filling out letter of credit forms is to be simple, clear, and precise in drafting the instructions to the bank. A balance should be struck between filling out the letter of credit application com-

---

[108]See generally, ICC, *The New Standard Documentary Credit Forms for the UCP 500,* No. 516 (ed. Charles del Busto 1993). See also, James E. Byrne, *Fundamental Issues in the Unification and Harmonization of Letter of Credit Law,* 37 Loyola Law Rev. 1 (1991).

pletely and not using excessive detail. Excessive detail in the letter of credit application may led to unnecessary confusion given the different cultures represented in many international transactions. An overly detailed letter of credit is apt to result in an increased likelihood of documents being rejected by a bank which would have ultimately been acceptable to the account party (purchaser). The ICC manual makes these simple suggestions when filling out a letter of credit application:

- Do not call for documents which the Beneficiary cannot obtain. Article 13 (c) deals harshly with such instructions. "If a Credit contains conditions without stating the documents to be presented in compliance therewith, banks will deem such conditions not stated and will disregard them."
- Do not require a document to contain detail which is not within the issuer's knowledge.
- Do not state conditions whose observance cannot be ascertained from the face of a document.

It is imperative that the applicant (purchaser) does not place any conditions or instructions in the credit that cannot be satisfied by reasonable documentation. Also, Article 47 lists a series of rules for how dates and relevant phrases relating to dates are to be construed. This article should be reviewed in order to understand when documents or the presentation of documents become untimely.

A few comments gleamed from the ICC forms manual should be addressed when filling out the letter of credit application (Exhibit 4.1): (1) the name and address of the applicant should be complete including a street address or P.O. Box and zip code, and (2) the expiration date and place for the presentation of documents should be clearly stated.

The ICC manual suggests that in order to discourage forgery, all letter of credit forms should be printed on safety paper. The beneficiary of the letter of credit should inquire of the confirming bank what techniques are used to secure the authenticity of the forms. An alternative to traditional means of transmission is provided under Article 11 of the UCP (teletransmission). Standard Teletransmission Formats (MT 700 Message Formats) have been developed by and can be obtained through the Society for Worldwide Interbank Financial Telecommunication (SWIFT).

The sophisticated importer-purchaser should become familiar with the requirements and rules of the UCP 500. They have a direct bearing on how the applicant fills out a letter of credit application. If the applicant places a non-customary term or instruction in the application, the banks will often disregard them in favor of a default rule found in the UCP 500. The following is a list of some of the UCP 500 default rules:

- Care should be used in selecting an expiration date so that the bother of obtaining extensions is avoided. However, an unnecessarily prolonged expiration date should be avoided in order to avoid incurring additional bank charges.
- It is helpful to insert the beneficiary's telephone and fax or telex numbers. A full street address should also be included. A request by the beneficiary to use a P.O. Box should be carefully investigated by the applicant.
- For a letter of credit to be transferable, the applicant must request such designation. Article 48 of the UCP should be carefully reviewed before making such a request. If the first beneficiary of the transferable credit wants to retain the right to refuse to allow the transferring bank to make amendments to the original credit for the second beneficiaries, then he must irrevocably so instruct the transferring bank prior to the transfer of the credit.
- Under Article 9 of the UCP, the applicant must request that the letter be confirmed. The applicant may designate the confirming bank or leave it to the discretion of the issuing bank. Of course, the identity of the confirming bank should have been agreed to between the applicant and the beneficiary prior to the submitting of the credit application.
- The currency of the letter of credit should be designated using the ISO Currency Code: USD (United States Dollar), GBP (Pounds Sterling), DEM (Deutsche Marks).
- The applicant should designate the bank or banks (nominated banks) at which the credit will be available. If the space is left unfilled, then the issuing bank will choose the nominated bank. An alternative is to insert "freely negotiable by any bank" or "freely negotiable credit." This would allow the beneficiary to negotiate the documents at any bank willing to negotiate. However, it is desirable

for the applicant to limit the free negotiability to a specific country or city.

- The applicant should clearly instruct whether the credit will be made available for partial shipments ("partial shipments allowed" or "partial shipments not allowed"). Shipments by pre-agreed installments should also be clearly stipulated on the credit application.
- The applicant should provide transport details including where the shipment is to be "taken in charge, dispatched, or loaded on board" and to where the shipment must be made ("at the place of unloading, delivery or final destination"). The applicant should also state the latest date for shipment, dispatch or taking in charge under the space next to the phrase "not later than" on the credit application. Otherwise, the time limit will be the date of expiration as provided in Article 44 of the UCP. If the applicant uses the phrase "on or about," Article 46(c) of the UCP defines an acceptable period as five days before or after the specified date. Also, abbreviations for geographical designation should be avoided. Full names should be used for all cities, states, provinces, countries, etc.
- Under the rule of strict compliance, banks are authorized to reject documents even if they are technically in conformity. An example of this is the use of abbreviations or acronyms in the description of goods. People in the industry may use such devices in corresponding between themselves. However, banks are not required to know or to investigate trade custom or usage. This was the situation in the historically significant English case of *J.H. Rayner & Co. v. Hambros Bank, Ltd.*[109] in which the bank rejected a bill of lading that used the notation "C.R.S." in describing the goods. In the nut industry C.R.S. is the abbreviation for "Coromandel groundnuts." The letter of credit required that the bill of lading state "Coromandel groundnuts." The accompanying invoice did use the full name. Nonetheless, the court upheld the bank's right to reject the documents. Two rationales were given. First, "that even though the description of the goods in the bill of lading was correct in accordance with the custom of trade, the bank could not be held to be affected with a knowledge of the customs of the various trades in which its customers

[109] 112 K.B. 27 (1943).

Exhibit 4.1: Letter of Credit Application Form

Documentary Credit Application / Demande d'émission de crédit documentaire

Applicant / Donneur d'ordre

Issuing Bank / Banque émettrice

Date and place of expiry of the credit / Date et lieu d'expiration du crédit

Date of this application / Date de cette demande

Beneficiary / Bénéficiaire

☐ Issue by (air) mail
Emettre par courrier avion

☐ With brief advice by teletransmission
Avec bref avis par télétransmission

☐ Issue by teletransmission (which shall be the operative credit instrument)
Emettre par télétransmission (qui sera l'instrument permettant l'utilisation du crédit)

☐ Transferable credit / Crédit transférable

Amount / Montant

Confirmation of credit to the beneficiary / Confirmation du crédit au bénéficiaire

☐ not requested / non requise ☐ requested / requise

Partial shipments / Expéditions partielles

☐ allowed autorisées ☐ not allowed non autorisées

Transhipment / Transbordement

☐ allowed autorisé ☐ not allowed non autorisé

Credit available with / Crédit réalisable auprès de

☐ by sight payment par paiement à vue ☐ by acceptance par acceptation ☐ by negotiation par négociation

☐ deferred payment at / par paiement différé à

☐ Insurance will be covered by us / L'assurance sera prise en charge par nous

Loading on board/dispatch/taking in charge at/from
Mise à bord/expédition/prise en charge à/de

not later than / au plus tard le

for transportation to / à destination de

against the documents detailed herein / contre les documents précisés ci-après

☐ and beneficiary's draft at / et la traite du bénéficiaire à

on / sur

Goods (brief description without excessive detail) / Marchandise (brève description sans détail excessif)

☐ FOB ☐ C&F ☐ CIF CAF

Other terms / Autres termes

Documents to be presented within ☐ days after the date of issuance of the transport document(s) but within the validity of the credit
Documents à présenter dans les ☐ jours après la date d'émission du/des document(s) de transport mais dans la période de validité du crédit

Additional instructions / Instructions supplémentaires

We request you to issue your irrevocable documentary credit for our account in accordance with the above instructions (marked with an x where appropriate). The credit will be subject to the Uniform Customs and Practice for Documentary Credits (1983 Revision, Publication No. 400 of the International Chamber of Commerce, Paris, France), insofar as these are applicable.
We authorize you to debit our account.

Nous vous demandons d'émettre pour notre compte un crédit documentaire irrévocable conformément aux instructions ci-dessus (cochées d'une croix dans les cases choisies). Le crédit sera soumis aux Règles et Usances Uniformes relatives aux Crédits Documentaires (révision 1983, Publication nº 400 de la Chambre de Commerce Internationale, Paris France) dans la mesure où celles-ci sont applicables.
Nous vous autorisons à débiter notre compte.

Name stamp and authorized signature(s) of the applicant
Cachet et signature(s) autorisée(s) du donneur d'ordre

Consult the Issuing Bank for guidance if the completion of this form should raise to questions
Demandez conseil à la banque émettrice si vous vous posez des questions en remplissant la formule

might be concerned." Second, even if the bank possessed knowledge of the trade custom or usage, it must do exactly what its customers requires it to do. There may be some unknown reason why the account party (importer) wants the documents to be detailed in a certain way. It is not for the bank to impose common sense to abrogate a specific instruction in the letter of credit.

For the reasons described in the proceeding paragraph, the description of the goods should generally be as brief as possible. In the above case, the result would have been different under the UCP if the letter of credit had not specifically stated that the bill of lading should have that particular description. The UCP requires only that the commercial invoice reflect the description found on the letter of credit. Article 37 states that "the description of the goods in the commercial invoice must correspond with the description in the Credit. In all other documents, the goods may be described in general terms not inconsistent with the description of the goods in the Credit." Therefore, it is advisable to keep the description simple and clear. It should be noted that the use of terms like "about" or "approximately" in describing the quantity or unit price of the goods is defined under Article 39 of the UCP as a 10% tolerance .

- In the listing of documents other than transport documents, insurance documents and commercial invoices, the applicant should specifically state the issuing entity and what the content of the documents should entail. This is required under Article 21 of the UCP. The following designations in describing the issuer of a document should be avoided: qualified, independent, official, competent, etc. The use of these vague qualifiers will result in the bank accepting documents from any issuer as long as the documents are in facial compliance.
- Articles 23-30 of the UCP should be reviewed when determining the transport documents that will be required. The rules pertaining to two of the more common transport documents, the Marine/Ocean Bill of lading and those issued by a freight forwarder, are found in Article 23 and 30. If the shipment entails the use of more than one mode of transportation, then the applicant should require a Multimodal Transport Document as described in Article 26 of the UCP. For multimodal transport involving a sea leg and for carriage by sea under a bill of lading the applicant should specifically allow for

"shipment on deck" if that type of carriage is customary for the goods in question.

- The content of insurance documents is addressed under Articles 34-36 of the UCP. If the applicant fails to state the amount of the insurance to be procured, then Article 34 (f)(ii) of the UCP requires an amount equal to CIF value plus 10%. If the CIF value cannot be discerned from the documents, then the banks are likely to require 110% of the amount found in the commercial invoice.
- The applicant should specify the period of time when the documents need to be presented following shipment of the goods. If a period is not stipulated, then Article 43 (a) of the UCP sets the period as 21 days from the date of shipment. If the applicant wants to allow for presentation irrespective of the date of shipment, he must so state in the space provided for "Additional Instructions."
- In amending an irrevocable letter of credit it is advisable to use the standard form titled Irrevocable Documentary Credit Amendment Form (Exhibit 4.2).

Exhibit 4.3 further summarizes the rules pertaining to letters of credit by listing ten of the more important ones.

"Rule 6" notes that the banks have a reasonable time to review documents not to exceed three days under Section 5-112 of the Uniform Commercial Code (UCC) and seven days under UCP Article 13. An associated question is: After accepting non-conforming documents may the bank pursue an action against the beneficiary for reimbursement? An argument may be made that such an action is authorized by the warranty provision in Section 5-111 of the UCC. Section 5-111 states that "unless otherwise agreed the beneficiary, by transferring or presenting a documentary draft, warrants to all interested parties that the necessary conditions of the credit have been complied with." No such warranty requirement is found in the UCP 500. Nonetheless, the bank may sue the beneficiary party for presenting non-conforming documents if it proceeds in a timely fashion. This was the issue in *Habib Bank Ltd. v. Convermat Corp.*[110] In that case the bank paid on documents that included a bill of lading with a discrepancy in the shipping date. The account party subsequently rejected the documents. The bank waited a month before making a claim against the beneficiary party. The

[110] 554 N.Y.S.2d 757 (1990).

Exhibit 4.2: Letter of Credit Amendment Form

NAME OF ISSUING BANK - NOM DE LA BANQUE EMETTRICE	**Amendment to Documentary Credit** **Amendement au crédit documentaire**	Number - Numero
Date of amendment - Date d'amendement	Place and date of issue - Lieu et date d'émission	
Applicant - Donneur d'ordre	Beneficiary - Bénéficiaire	
Advising Bank - Banque notificatrice Ref. nr. - No. Réf.	This amendment is to be considered as part of the above mentioned credit and must be attached thereto. Cet amendement est à considérer comme faisant partie du crédit mentionné ci-dessus et doit y être joint.	

The above mentioned credit is amended as follows:
Le crédit mentionné ci-dessus est amendé comme suit:

All other terms and conditions remain unchanged
Tous les autres termes et conditions restent inchangés

The above mentioned documentary credit is subject to the Uniform Customs and Practice for Documentary Credits (1983 Revision, International Chamber of Commerce, Paris, France, Publication no 400)
Le susdit crédit documentaire est soumis aux Règles et Usances Uniformes relatives aux Crédits Documentaires (Révision 1983, Publication No. 400 de la Chambre de Commerce Internationale, Paris, France)

Please advise the Beneficiary Veuillez notifier le bénéficiaire	Advising Bank's notifications - Indications de la banque notificatrice.
Name and signature of Issuing Bank Nom et signature de la banque émettrice	Place, date, name and signature of the Advising Bank Lieu, date, nom et signature de la banque notificatrice

Exhibit 4.3: Ten Rules You Should (Must) Know Regarding Letters of Credit

Rule # 1

Rule of Facial Compliance: Banks are only required to review documents and compare them to the letter of credit's requirements for conformity (Not liable for "fraud in the transaction").

Rule # 2

Banks are not required to know or to investigate **trade or business usages,** custom, or practices.

Rule # 3

Rule of Strict Compliance: Banks may reject documents for **any** "discrepancies."

Rule # 4

A letter of credit must have an **expiration date** in order to be enforceable.

Rule # 5

UCP 500's "21 day rule": The beneficiary party must deliver documents within 21 days of receipt. Generally, 21 days from receipt of bill of lading.

Rule # 6

Bank's Period of Review: Banks have a **reasonable period** to review documents, not to exceed 3 days (UCC Art. 5) or 7 days (UCP 500).

Rule # 7

Presumption of Irrevocability: UCP 500 (not UCP 400) & UCC presume that a letter of credit is irrevocable unless it clearly states on its face that it is revocable.

Rule # 8

Insurance Binder/Certficate: Must not be dated later then date of loading and must be in the amount (generally) of CIF plus 10%.

Rule # 9

Commercial Invoice: Must include the exact description in the letter of credit. (other documents may use general descriptions not inconsistent with one found in letter of credit)

Rule # 10

A letter of credit is not transferable unless it specifically states that it is a **transferable credit.**

court held that the claim was not made in a timely fashion and dismissed the action. This duty of the bank to act quickly can be implied from Article 14 of the UCP. Article 14(d) requires the bank to give notice "by expeditious means" and such notice "must state all discrepancies in respect of which the bank refuses the documents."

Dispute Resolution Clause

The parties to a documentary credit should include a dispute resolution clause incorporating the new "ICC Rules for Documentary Credit Dispute Resolution Expertise" or the *DOCDEX Rules.*[111] These rules are intended to be applied in conjunction with the UCP 500 through the ICC's International Centre for Expertise. Upon a request, the Centre appoints a panel of three experts. The identities of the experts are kept secret from the contesting parties.

Any communications between the parties and the experts is to be transmitted in writing and processed through the Centre. In return, the experts are encumbered by strict rules of confidentiality. The decision of the experts is not binding on the parties. The ICC is authorized to publish any decisions, but only if it strikes the names of the contesting parties. The panel of experts must render a decision within thirty days of the submittal of all relevant information. Before the decision is disclosed to the contesting parties, it is reviewed by a Technical Adviser of the ICC Commission on Banking Technique & Practice for conformity to the UCP 500. The standard fee for the *DOCDEX* dispute resolution is $5,000 USD. That fee may be doubled if the amount in dispute exceeds $100,000 USD. For disputes involving a large letter of credit amount, the *DOCDEX Rules* offer a relatively quick dispute resolution process. More importantly, the double review by the panel of experts and Technical Adviser provides for an increased likelihood of a professional and technically correct decision.

New Standby Letters of Credit Rules

Standby letters of credit can be used to help secure a variety of contractual obligations associated with the export transaction. In addition to performance guarantees often associated with construction projects, standby letters have been used to guarantee "warranties, to support borrowers under international loans, to ensure availability of suppliers, to secure countertrade commitments, along with acting as deposits in the sale of goods and as prepayment of fees for services."[112] The UCP has traditionally been applied to both documentary credits and standby letters of credit. On

[111]ICC Publication No. 577. The *DOCDEX Rules* may be accessed at Docdex@iccwbo.org. See generally, ICC, *ICC DOCDEX Rules for Documentary Credit Dispute Resolution Expertise,* 10 Int'l Quarterly 507 (1998).

[112]Berman at 275-276.See also, Graham & Geva, *Standby Credits in Canada,* 9 Canadian Bus. Law Journal 180 (1982).

January 1, 1999 new international standby practices (ISP) governing standby letters of credit took effect. They are available as ICC publication "ISP98." They are much more detailed then the UCP 500 and therefore should be studied carefully. The Institute of International Banking Law and Practice recommends the following language in order to incorporate the ISP into standby letters of credit documents: "This letter of credit is issued subject to the International Standby Practices 1998 and shall, as to matters not governed by ISP98, be governed by and construed in accordance with the laws of the [State of or Country of ________]." The ISP98 recognizes the emergence of electronic delivery systems. It provides definitions of key terms like "electronic record," "electronic signature," and "authentication." The ISP98 does recognize the notion of automatic extensions known as "evergreen clauses," but it does not provide a definition. It is important that the documentation provide a clear explanation of such clauses. Other items of interest include: (1) the use of the word "exact" is interpreted to mean that the required language must be identical including any errors found in the original requirements, and (2) the beneficiary must negotiate for the acceptance of facsimiles as originals. The review period allotted to the bank is a reasonable period not to exceed seven days. Rule 5.01(a)(I) provides a safe harbor of three days to protect a bank from a charge of unreasonable delay in reviewing the documents. Therefore, it is left to the beneficiary to require a shorter period for review and payment. (3) In case of a discrepancy in the documents, the issuing bank is not required to approve a waiver given by the account party. (4) Unlike the UCP 500, ISP98 provides rules that govern the issuer-account party relationship through the letter of credit application. See, e.g., Rule 5.09 and Rule 8. The ISP98 can be obtained through the International Chamber of Commerce as Publication 590 or through the web site of the Institute of International Banking Law and Practice at http://www.isp98.com.

Demand Guarantees

An associated vehicle to guarantee performance is the demand guarantee. The documentary credit acts as the primary vehicle for fulfilling a payment obligation. It is triggered upon satisfactory performance (presentation of confirming documents). The standby credit can also be used to support a payment obligation. In contrast, the demand guarantee secures performance of a non-monetary obligation. It serves as a default device when performance is not satisfactory. "So whereas, a bank pays a documentary credit only if things go right, in the case of a demand guarantee it is intended that the bank will be called upon to pay only if things go wrong."[113] A special concern of demand guarantees is that the lack of rigid documentation requirements allows for the possibility of unfair calls.[114] Often all the beneficiary is required to do is make a written demand for payment. Both the ICC and UNCITRAL have developed rules to govern these types of instruments. The ICC has published *Uniform Rules for Demand Guarantees (Uniform Rules)*[115] and UNCITRAL has released its *Convention on Independent Letters of Guarantees and Standby Credits.*

In order to discourage unfair calls on demand guarantees, the *Uniform Rules* requires the beneficiary to provide a statement describing the way in which the principal is in breach.[116] However, the statement need only be a generalized description of the breach such as the principal is "guilty of delay, defective workmanship, or a shortfall in delivery of goods."[117] It has been suggested that in order to avoid confusion, the language of Article 20 should be incorporated into the language of the demand guarantee.[118] Another concern related to demand guarantees is the *extend or pay demand.* The beneficiary of a soon to expire demand will often make a demand that the guarantee's expiration be extended or if the extension is rejected that payment be made immediately. One immediate concern of the beneficiary is whether such a demand meets the dictates of Article 20. In order to be sure, the beneficiary should provide a statement of the underlying breach to fully conform to Article 20. The guarantor and principal should act quickly if such an extension is to be given. If they fail to respond prior to the expiration of the guarantee, then the guarantor will be forced to make payment.

---

[113]Roy Goode, *Abstract Payment Undertakings in International Transactions,* 22 Brooklyn Journal of Int'l Law 1, 15 (1996).

[114]"[T]he documentation required for a claim on a demand guarantee is skeletal in the extreme, entailing in most cases presentation of no more than the written demand itself." Ibid.

[115]ICC, Publication No. 458 (1992).

[116]Article 20.

[117]Goode at 17, note 47. See generally, ROY GOODE, GUIDE TO THE UCC UNIFORM RULES FOR DEMAND GUARANTEES 93-94 (1992).

[118]Ibid.

This occurs because the beneficiary has satisfied his documentary requirements by making a demand prior to the expiration.

Bills of Lading

There are a number of legal regimes that pertain to the responsibilities and liabilities of the common carrier under a bill of lading.[119] The three most common sets of rules are the Hague Rules, the Hague-Visby Rules, and the Hamburg Rules. All three of these provide a relatively fair allocation of liability between the carrier and the shipper. However, the rules become more pro-shipper as one moves from the Hague Rules to the Hamburg Rules. The Hague Rules cover the liability of the carrier from the time frame represented from "tackle to tackle" or from time of loading to time of discharge. This does not take into account the time when the goods are in the control of the carrier prior to the loading and after the unloading of the cargo. The Hamburg Rules extend the period of responsibility to include when the goods are in the control of the carrier but not on the ship. The Hague Rules limit carrier liability by providing sixteen specific exceptions to liability. The Hamburg Rules eliminate these exceptions and provide a presumption of carrier liability for loss except when occasioned by a fire. The Hague Rules technically only apply to carriage evidenced by a bill of lading. In contrast, the Hamburg Rules refer to "other documents evidencing the contract of carriage by sea." The Hague Rules require the consignee to make a notice of loss "before or after the time of the removal of the cargo, if apparent." It further provides a limitation period of one year for any claims of loss. The Hamburg Rules allow a claim of loss within one working day of delivery to the consignee. Also, the limitation period is extended to two years. The Hague Rules provide for liability when goods are lost or damaged but make no mention of liability for a delay in delivery. The Hamburg Rules designate "delay" as an equal ground for recovery.

Under the domestic enactment of the Hague Rules, the Carriage of Goods by Sea Act or COGSA,[120] the carrier is liable for damage or loss to the

[119]In the United States see Article 7 of the Uniform Commercial Code for domestic transactions. For international transactions involving bills of lading refer to the Federal Bills of Lading Act, 49 U.S.C.A. §§ 80101-16.
[120]46 U.S.C.A. § 1304.

goods in an amount not to exceed $500 per package. Section 1304(5) of COGSA provides the operative basis for common carrier liability.

> Neither the carrier nor the ship shall in any event be or become liable for any loss or damage to or in connection with the transportation of goods in an amount exceeding $500 per package lawful money of the United States, or in case of goods not shipped in packages, per customary freight unit, or the equivalent of that sum in other currency, unless the nature and value of such goods have been declared by the shipper before shipment and inserted in the bill of lading. This declaration, if embodied in the bill of lading, shall be prima facie evidence, but shall not be conclusive on the carrier. . . . In no event shall the carrier be liable for more than the amount of damage actually sustained.[121]

The package is the number of units specified in the bill of lading. Often a court will utilize the notion of a "customary freight unit" to quantify the package if the bill of lading does not expressly state a number. For example, in *Caterpillar Overseas v. Marine Transport, Inc.* the court determined that each tractor in a shipment of tractors was a customary freight unit (CFU).[122] However, this cap will be raised if the shipper declares a higher value on the bill of lading. The carrier will also be liable for an undeclared higher value if it failed to give the shipper "a *fair opportunity* to choose a higher liability by paying a corresponding greater charge."[123] Common carriers generally honor their duty to provide fair opportunity to declare a higher value by providing notice and a space to declare a higher value on the face of the bill of lading. Although good practice, some courts have held that such an approach (space on face of bill of lading) is not required. Language found in the boilerplate on the back of the bill of lading form may be sufficient.[124]

The bill of lading is the traditional transport document and acts as a document of title (See Exhibit 4.4 for an example of a typical Short Form Bill of Lading).[125] As such, it allows for the sale, transfer, and "collateraliza-

[121]46 U.S.C.App. § 1304(5).

[122]900 F.2d 714 (4th Cir. 1990).

[123]Cincinnati Milacron Ltd. V. M/V American Legend, 784 F.2d 1161 (4th Cir. 1986).

[124]See, e.g., Mori Seiki USA, Inc. v. M.V. Alligator Triumph, 990 F.2d 440 (9th Cir. 1993).

[125]See generally, Georgios Zekos, *The Contractual Role of Bills of Lading under United States Law*; *The Contractual Role of Bills of Lading under English Law;* and *The Contractual Role of Bills of Lading under Greek Law,* all in 39, Managerial Law (1997).

tion" of the goods while in transit. However, due to the containerization of the shipping industry, the newer multimodal transport documents have increasingly become popular. The legal and practical impact of this transformation is discussed in the materials on INCOTERMS. A future development that will transform documentary practice is the electronic bill of lading. Electronic bills of lading will enable a more efficient sale or transfer of goods while they are in transit. A highly negotiated bill of lading runs the risk of delaying the ability of the ultimate consignee of taking delivery. This will happen if the goods reach the port of destination while the bill of lading is still being negotiated. The first electronic bill of lading was developed in conjunction with rail transport (CMI Rules for Electronic Bills of Lading). Currently, a more expansive project to electronically transmit all standard documents is underway (BOLERO project).

Issues Pertaining to Bills of Lading

This section highlights some miscellaneous issues relating to the enforcement and interpretation of bills of lading, including the enforceability of arbitration clauses under COGSA, the impact of containerization, the continued importance of the distinction between on-board and received-for-shipment, and developments in the area of liability for the misdelivery of goods.

Arbitration Clauses. Is a placement of an arbitration clause in the bill of lading subject to challenge under COGSA, 46 U.S.C. App. § 1300 *et seq.*? The Supreme Court in *Vimar Seguros y Reaseguros v. M/V Sky Reefer*[126] found that an arbitration clause in the bill of lading was not subject to attack under COGSA. The Court referred to the Federal Arbitration Act[127] for the general premise that arbitration is a favored means of dispute resolution in the United States. Regarding COGSA, it held that an arbitration clause is not to be considered as a limitation of liability that is generally prohibited under COGSA. The arbitration clause was held not to lessen the liability of the common carrier by increasing the costs of obtaining relief. The added cost argument pertained not so much to the fact that arbitration was mandated but that the arbitration was to be held in Tokyo. The lessening of lia-

[126] 515 U.S. 526 (1995).
[127] 9 U.S.C.A. §§ 1, 2, 201 *et seq.*, 202.

Exhibit 4.4: Short Form Bill of Lading

SHORT FORM BILL OF LADING

SHIPPER/EXPORTER (1)	DOCUMENT NO. (9)
	EXPORT REFERENCES (10)
CONSIGNEE (2)	FORWARDING AGENT (NAME AND ADDRESS-REFERENCES) (11)
	PLACE OF ACCEPTANCE (12)
NOTIFY PARTY (3)	DOMESTIC ROUTING/EXPORT INSTRUCTIONS (13)
PIER/TERMINAL (4)	ORIGINAL
VESSEL (5) — PORT OF LOADING (6)	(*) PLACE OF FINAL DELIVERY (14)
PORT OF DISCHARGE (7) — FOR TRANSSHIPMENT TO (8)	

PARTICULARS FURNISHED BY SHIPPER (15)

MARKS AND NUMBERS	NO. OF PKGS.	DESCRIPTION OF PACKAGES AND GOODS	GROSS WEIGHT	MEASUREMENT

DECLARED VALUE (16) SEE CLAUSE 4

FREIGHT/CHARGES	PREPAID	COLLECT
TOTAL		

Received by for shipment by ocean vessel, between port of loading and port of discharge, and from place of acceptance to place of final delivery as indicated above; the goods to be delivered at the above mentioned port of discharge or place of final delivery, whichever applies, subject to terms contained on the reverse side hereof, to which the shipper agrees by accepting this Bill of Lading. In witness whereof three (3) original Bills of Lading have been signed, if not otherwise stated above, one of which being accomplished the other(s) to be void.

By ____________________

AS CARRIER

MO	DAY	YEAR	PLACE	B L NO.

bility argument was not strengthened by the fact that both Japanese and American laws were based upon the Brussels Convention for the Unification of Certain Rules Relating to Bills of Lading (Hague Rules).[128] The Court did outline one exception to the enforcement of arbitration clauses in bills of lading. This would be where a forum selection clause and a choice of law clause are used in tandem to prevent a shipper from be able to pursue his statutory remedies under COGSA.

Containerization. Containerization refers to the multimodal transport of goods. Goods placed within steel containers can be loaded and off-loaded on and by truck, rail, and ship.[129] The court in *DuPont de Nemours International v. Mormacvega,*[130] recognized an implied exception to the COGSA principle that carriage on the deck of the ship is a material deviation. It held, however, that it is not an unreasonable deviation from the carriage contract to carry the goods above deck if the ship is one designed for above deck containerized carriage. The common carrier generally prevents a material deviation claim for above deck carriage by inserting a *clause paramount* in the bill of lading. In essence, the shipper agrees to allow the common carrier to decide whether the goods are to be carried below or above deck. The clause asserts that the Hague Rules (Carriage of Goods by Sea Act) or other pertinent convention will apply to goods stowed above deck. The following is an example of a clause paramount:

> The bill of lading shall have effect subject to all the provisions of the Carriage of Goods by Sea Act of the United States, as approved on April 16, 1936. The defenses and limitations of said Act shall apply to goods whether carried on or under the deck, to carriage of goods between U.S. ports, or between non-U.S. ports, before the goods are loaded on and after they are discharged from the vessel, and throughout the entire time the goods are in the actual custody of Carrier, whether acting as carrier, bailee or stevedore. Carrier shall be entitled to the full benefit of all rights

---

[128]51 Stat. 233 (1924).

[129]See generally, Simon, *The Law of Shipping Containers,* Journal of Maritime Law & Commerce 507 (1974); Bissel, *The Operational Realities of Containerization and Their Effects on the 'Package' Limitation and the 'On-Deck' Prohibition: Review and Suggestions,* 45 Tulane Law Rev. 902 (1971); L. Alexander, *Containerization, the Per Package Limitation, and the Concept of 'Fair Opportunity',* 11 The Maritime Lawyer 123 (1986).

[130]493 F.2d 97 (2d Cir. 1974) See also, Electro-Tec Corp. v. S.S. Dart Atlantica, 598 F. Supp. 929 (D. Md. 1984).

> and immunity under and all limitations and exemptions from liability contained in any law of the United States or any other place whose law shall be compulsorily applicable. If any term of this bill of lading be repugnant to the Carriage of Goods by Sea Act or any other law compulsorily applicable, such term only shall be void. This bill of lading shall be construed and the rights of the parties determined according to the laws of the United States.[131]

Note that this clause does more than simply extend COGSA to above deck carriage. It also extends COGSA's coverage to beyond tackle to tackle (shore coverage) and for the entire period that the goods are in the possession of the carrier. Some courts have recognized this extension of COGSA even when the bill of lading fails to incorporate such a clause.[132] Second, it extends COGSA protection to all third parties involved with the transport of the goods by sea including stevedores (Himalaya clause). Third, it preempts the application of the Harter Act extending coverage to shipments between U.S. ports. Finally, it selects U.S. law as the law to be used to interpret the carriers' obligations and liabilities under the bill of lading (choice of law).

Containerization in the shipping industry also posed a challenge for the determination of the number of packages to be used in calculating COGSA's per package limitation of liability. The federal court in the Southern District of New York in *Marcraft Clothes, Inc. v. M.V. Kurobe Maru*[133] held that multimodal containers are generally not to be considered as a package for the calculation of COGSA liability of the common carrier. The enumeration on the bill of lading that the container was filled with 4,400 men's suits made each suit a COGSA package and eliminated the common carrier's argument that the container was the package. In the event that the package is valued above the $500 per package limit under COGSA, the common carrier's liability is limited to the $500 amount. The issue remains: Can the common carrier expressly designate the container as the package for purposes of COGSA's per package limitation? The following clause attempted to do just that: "The word *package* shall include a container used to ship goods under lump sum tariff." Generally courts have rejected the

---

[131]This clause was taken from St. Paul Fire & Marine Ins. V. Sea-Land Service, 745 F.Supp. 186, 188 (S.D.N.Y. 1990).

[132]See, e.g., Binladen BSB Landscaping v. M.V. Nedlloyd Totterdam, 759 F.2d 1006 (2d Cir. 1985).

[133]575 F. Supp. 239 (S.D.N.Y. 1983).

notion that a container can be designated as a package to limit the carrier's liability to five hundred dollars for the entire shipment. In *All Pacific Trading v. Vessel M/V Hanjin Yosu* the carrier inserted the following clause into the bill of lading: "Where the cargo has been packed into containers . . . it is expressly agreed that the number of such containers shown on the face hereof shall be considered the number of packages for the purpose of the application of the limitation of liability provided for herein." The carrier further argued that the container was the proper package because the rate agreement was determined based upon the number of containers and not by the number of packages within the containers. The court rejected the carrier's arguments that the containers were indeed the packages. It focused upon the fact that elsewhere on the bill of lading there was a listing of the number of packages in each container.[134] The law on this topic remains unsettled as indicated by the court in *St. Paul Ins. v. Sea Land Service:*

> The court notes with some trepidation that it is its view that the determination that the $500 per package or per customary freight unit limitation should not apply to a container said to contain packages should be re-examined. Cases seeking to apply the limitation to containers pursuant to bills of lading are all too common particularly because carriers have drafted bills of lading with all sorts of terms relating to its applicability to container shipments. Furthermore, because of reasons of reductions of cost and prevention of theft or damage, containers have become a *customary freight unit,* if not the customary freight unit [recognized by COGSA].[135]

The shipper should request a detailed description in the bill of lading expressly stating the number of packages within the container.

There are a limited number of exceptions to the per package limitation afforded to carriers, namely the common carrier materially deviated from the COGSA authorized terms of the bill of lading or the shipper was not given a fair opportunity to declare a higher per package value for the goods.

---

[134]See also, Universal Leaf Tobacco Co. v Companhia De Navegacao Maritima Netumar, 993 F.2d 414 (4th Cir. 1993) (courts will not consider a container as a package if the bill of lading discloses the number of packages within the container); Cia Panamena de Seguros, S.A. v. Prudential Lines, Inc., 416 F. Supp. 641 (D.C. 1976) (court rejected bill of lading definition of container as package).

[135]745 F. Supp. 186, 189.

Courts will generally look to the bill of lading itself in deciding whether the common carrier has fulfilled its *fair opportunity* responsibilities. The court in *Komatsu, Ltd. v. States S.S. Co.*[136] held that common carriers' fair opportunity obligations are satisfied when they incorporate the language of Section 1304(5) on the *face* of the bill of lading.

On-Board and Received-For-Shipment. The standard documentary sales contract requires an "on-board bill of lading." This type of bill ensures the buyer that the goods are in deed on the ship in transit to the port of destination. If the sale contract is silent regarding the type of bill of lading, must the buyer accept a "received-for-shipment" bill of lading when presented with the documents? The answer for the American exporter is different depending on whether the UCP 500 or Article 5 of the Uniform Commercial Code is applied. Section 1-201(15) of the UCC defines a document title simply as a "bill of lading." It does not differentiate between "on board" and "received-for-shipment." Section 1-201(6) further defines bill of lading as "a document evidencing the receipt of goods for shipment issued by a person engaged in the business of transporting or forwarding goods." Section 2-323 specifically authorizes the use of a "received-for-shipment" bill of lading in CIF or C & F contracts.[137] In contrast, Article 23 of the UCP states that "banks will, unless otherwise stipulated in the Credit, accept a document which: (ii) indicates that the goods have been loaded on board, or shipped on a named vessel."

Misdelivery of Goods. The common carrier is under a strict duty to deliver to a party holding a negotiable bill of lading. A cause of action accrues to the shipper in the event that delivery is made to someone not holding the bill of lading. This sometimes occurs when a country's import documentation allows for such a release or when the receiving party and the common carrier make alternative arrangements. An example of the former is presented in *Allied Chemical International Corp. v. Compania de Navegacao Lloyd Brasileiro.*[138] In that case, the goods were offloaded by the common carrier into a government warehouse pending payment of import duties.

---

[136] 674 F.2d 806 (9th Cir. 1982).

[137] "Where the contract contemplates overseas shipment and contains a term CIF or C & F or FOB vessel, the seller unless otherwise agreed must obtain a negotiable bill of lading stating that the goods have been loaded on board or, in the case of a term CIF or C & F, received for shipment." UCC § 2-323(1).

[138] 775 F.2d 476 (2d Cir. 1985).

The buyer paid the import fees and received a *carta declaratoria* from the carrier certifying their payment. The goods were released from the warehouse on the presentation of the *carta declaratoria,* but without the bill of lading. The common carrier was held liable for misdelivery because the carrier remains as bailee of the goods until they are delivered to the holder of the bill of lading. This case illustrates that even though the bill of lading is the universally accepted document of title national maritime customs and shipping practices need to be understood in order to protect against such occurrences.

An example of alternative arrangements is the practice where the common carrier agrees to release the goods to a consignee, not in possession of the bill of lading, upon the presentment of a bank guarantee. The bank guarantee indemnifies the carrier from any liability for misdelivery. In *C-Art, Ltd. v. Hong Kong Islands Line America, S.A.*[139] the parties' prior course of dealing allowed the importer to present a bank guarantee, rather than wait to receive the bill of lading. However, instead of presenting its normal bank guarantee, the buyer presented a corporate guarantee and received a release of the goods. The court held the carrier liable for misdelivery simply stating that "the carrier, the issuer of the bill of lading, is responsible for releasing the cargo only to the party who presents the original bill of lading."[140] It would seem that even if the importer had presented a bank guarantee, the carrier would remain liable to the shipper for misdelivery unless the shipper expressly agreed to such a delivery arrangement.

Air Waybill

Most transport of goods is performed through ocean carriage. However, in the event of transit by air, the operative transport document is the air waybill (Exhibit 4.5). Unlike the ocean bill of lading, the air waybill does not act as a document of title. Therefore, it is a non-negotiable instrument that serves as a contract of carriage and a receipt for goods. As a contract of carriage, it incorporates by reference the pertinent international carriage convention, namely the Warsaw Convention. Like the Hague Rules, the Warsaw Convention provides a limitation of liability for the common car-

[139] 940 F.2d 530 (9th Cir. 1991).

[140] Ibid. at 532. See also, The Caledonia, 157 U.S. 124 (1895).

Exhibit 4.5: Air Waybill Form

Shipper's Name and Address	Shipper's Account Number	Not negotiable **Air Waybill** Issued by
		Copies 1, 2 and 3 of this Air Waybill are originals and have the same validity.
Consignee's Name and Address	Consignee's Account Number	It is agreed that the goods described herein are accepted in apparent good order and condition (except as noted) for carriage SUBJECT TO THE CONDITIONS OF CONTRACT ON THE REVERSE HEREOF. ALL GOODS MAY BE CARRIED BY ANY OTHER MEANS INCLUDING ROAD OR ANY OTHER CARRIER UNLESS SPECIFIC CONTRARY INSTRUCTIONS ARE GIVEN HEREON BY THE SHIPPER, AND SHIPPER AGREES THAT THE SHIPMENT MAY BE CARRIED VIA INTERMEDIATE STOPPING PLACES WHICH THE CARRIER DEEMS APPROPRIATE. THE SHIPPER'S ATTENTION DRAWN TO THE NOTICE CONCERNING CARRIER'S LIMITATION OF LIABILITY. Shipper may increase such limitation of liability by declaring a higher value for carriage and paying a supplemental charge if required.
Issuing Carrier's Agent Name and City		Accounting Information
Agent's IATA Code	Account No.	
Airport of Departure (Addr. of first Carrier) and requested Routing		

to	By first Carrier (Routing and Destination)	to	by	to	by	Currency	Chgs Code	WT/VAL PPD	WT/VAL COLL	Other PPD	Other COLL	Declared Value for Carriage	Declared Value for Customs

Airport of Destination	Flight/Date	For Carrier Use only	Flight/Date	Amount of Insurance	INSURANCE – If carrier offers insurance, and such insurance is requested in accordance with the conditions thereof, indicate amount to be insured in figures in box marked "Amount of Insurance".

Handling Information

These commodities licensed by the U.S. for ultimate destination — Diversion contrary to U.S. law prohibited.

No. of Pieces RCP	Gross Weight	kg lb	Rate Class / Commodity Item No.	Chargeable Weight	Rate / Charge	Total	Nature and Quantity of Goods (incl. Dimensions or Volume)

Prepaid	Weight Charge	Collect	Other Charges
	Valuation Charge		
	Tax		
	Total other Charges Due Agent		Shipper certifies that the particulars on the face hereof are correct and that insofar as any part of the consignment contains dangerous goods, such part is properly described by name and is in proper condition for carriage by air according to the applicable Dangerous Goods Regulations.
	Total other Charges Due Carrier		
			Signature of Shipper or his Agent
Total prepaid		Total collect	
Currency Conversion Rates		cc charges in Dest. Currency	Executed on (Date) at (Place) Signature of Issuing Carrier or its Agent
For Carriers Use only at Destination		Charges at Destination	Total collect Charges

ORIGINAL 3 (FOR SHIPPER)

rier. The standard terms and conditions of the air waybill generally states that the liability limitation is "250 French Gold Francs per kilogram or approximately USD 20 per kilogram on the basis of USD 42.22 per ounce." Other common terms are an extension of coverage to other parties involved in the carriage. An example of such a Himalaya clause is that "any exclusion or limitation of liability applicable to the carrier shall apply to the benefit of the carrier's agents, servants and representatives and any person whose aircraft is used by carrier for carriage." The carrier is also protected from claims of material deviation as follows: "Carrier may substitute alternative carriers or may without notice and with due regard to the interests of the shipper substitute other means of transportation. Carrier is authorized to select the routing or to change or deviate from the routing shown on the face of the air waybill." In the area of notice of damage, the consignee or person entitled to take delivery must promptly inspect the goods. He then must make a written complaint "of visible damage to the goods, immediately after discovery of the damage and at the latest within 14 days from receipt of the goods." The Convention provides for a two year statute of limitation for the filing of claims.

The front of the air waybill makes a number of important representations. First, unless noted otherwise, the "goods are accepted in apparent good order and condition." Second, the shipper is directed to the reverse of the form for an explanation of the carrier's "limitation of liability." Third, the shipper is provided with notice of his right to increase carrier's liability. "Shipper may increase such limitation of liability by declaring a higher value for carriage and paying a supplemental charge." Also provided is a space for the "Amount of Insurance" requested by the shipper. Above the signature line, the shipper is notified that he is certifying that the goods are not dangerous unless described as such. If dangerous by nature, then the shipper certifies that the goods are in "proper condition for carriage by air according to the applicable Dangerous Goods Regulation."

Export License

The Export Administration Regulations (EAR) can be found in 15 C.F.R. Chapter VII. Part 730 of that Chapter provides a general overview of United States export restrictions as published by the Bureau of Export Administration (BXA). The BXA is organized into two branches: Export

Administration and Export Enforcement. The Export Administration implements and administers the export controls as detailed in the EAR. It consists of five offices: Office of Nuclear and Missile Technology Controls, Office of Chemical & Biological Controls and Treaty Compliance, Office of Strategic Trade & Foreign Policy Controls, Office of Strategic Industries & Economic Security, and Office of Export Services. The last office provides assistance to exporters and reexporters, conducts educational seminars, and maintains the EAR. The Export Enforcement branch has three offices: Office of Export Enforcement, Office of Environmental Support, and Office of Antiboycott Compliance. The last office enforces the Restrictive Trade Practices and Boycotts restrictions found in Part 760 of the EAR. The following index (Exhibit 4.6) of United States Export Regulations provides a good reference for the types of issues that pertain to United States export control.

Section 2403 of the export regulations explains the types of licenses that are available for exporting goods. The *general license* only requires the submission of the "Shipper's Export Declaration." *Validated licenses,* including those for specific exports along with those for multiple exports, require written approval from the Department of Commerce. The following excerpt from the Export Regulations lists the varieties of export licenses.

> Under such conditions as may be imposed by the Secretary which are consistent with the provisions of this Act [sections 2401 to 2420 of this Appendix], the Secretary may require any of the following types of export licenses:
>
> (1) A validated license, authorizing a specific export, issued pursuant to an application by the exporter.
>
> (2) Validated licenses authorizing multiple exports, issued pursuant to an application by the exporter, in lieu of an individual validated license for each such export, including, but not limited to, the following:
>
> (A) A distribution license, authorizing exports of goods to approved distributors or users of the goods in countries other than controlled countries, except that the Secretary may establish a type of distribution license appropriate for consignees in the People's Republic of China. The Secretary shall grant the distribution license primarily on the basis of the reliability of the applicant and foreign consignees with respect to the pre-

Exhibit 4.6: Export Regulations (Index)

EXPORT REGULATION
Public Law 96-72, 93 STAT. 503

Sec.

2401. Congressional findings.
2402. Congressional declaration of policy.
2403. General provisions.
 (a) Types of licenses.
 (b) Control list.
 (c) Foreign availability.
 (d) Right of export.
 (e) Delegation of authority.
 (f) Notification of public; consultation with business.
 (g) Fees.
2403-1 to 2403a. Repealed or Omitted.
2404 National security controls.
 (a) Authority.
 (b) Policy toward individual countries.
 (c) Control list.
 (d) Militarily critical technologies.
 (e) Export licenses.
 (f) Foreign availability.
 (g) Indexing.
 (h) Technical advisory committees.
 (i) Multilateral export controls.
 (j) Commercial agreements with certain countries.
 (k) Negotiations with other countries.
 (1) Diversion of controlled goods or technology.
 (m) Goods containing controlled parts and components.
 (n) Security measures.
 (o) Recordkeeping.
 (p) National Security Control Office
 (q) Exclusion for agricultural commodities.

TITLE 50, APPENDIX-WAR AND NATIONAL DEFENSE

2407. Foreign boycotts.
 (a) Prohibitions and exceptions.
 (b) Foreign policy controls.
 (c) Preemption.
2408. Procedures for hardship relief from export controls.
 (a) Filing of petitions.
 (b) Decision of Secretary.
 (c) Factors to be considered.
2409. Procedures for processing export license applications; other inquiries.
 (a) Primary responsibility of Secretary.
 (b) Initial screening.
 (c) Action on certain applications.
 (d) Referral to other departments and agencies.
 (e) Action by other departments.
 (f) Action by Secretary.
 (g) Special procedures for Secretary of Defense.
 (h) Multilateral controls.
 (i) Records.
 (j) Appeal and court action.
 (k) Changes in requirements for applications.
 (1) Other inquiries.
 (m) Small business assistance.
 (n) Reports on license applications.
 (o) Exports to members of coordinating committee.
 (q) Other authorities.
2410. Violations.
 (a) In general.
 (b) Willful violations.
 (c) Civil penalties; administrative sanctions.
 (d) Payment of penalties.
 (e) Refunds.
 (f) Actions for recovery of penalties.
 (g) Forfeiture of property interest and proceeds.
 (h) Prior convictions.
2410a. Multilateral export control violations.
 (a) Determination by the President.
 (b) Sanctions.
 (c) Exceptions.
 (d) Exclusion.
 (e) Definitions.
 (f) Subsequent modifications of sanctions.
 (g) Reports to Congress.
 (h) Discretionary imposition of sanctions.
 (i) Compensation for diversion of militarily critical technologies to controlled countries.
 (j) Other actions by the President.
 (k) Damages for certain violations.
 (1) Definition.
2410b. Missile proliferation control violations.
 (a) Violations by United States persons.
 (b) Transfers of missile equipment or technology by foreign persons.
 (c) Definitions.

vention of diversion of goods to controlled countries. The Secretary shall have the responsibility of determining, with the assistance of all appropriate agencies, the reliability of applicants and their immediate consignees. The Secretary's determination shall be based on appropriate investigations of each applicant and periodic reviews of licensees and their compliance with the terms of licenses issued under this Act [sections 2401 to 2420 of this Appendix]. Factors such as the applicant's products or volume of business, or the consignees' geographic location, sales distribution area, or degree of foreign ownership, which may be relevant with respect to individual cases, shall not be determinative in creating categories or general criteria for the denial of applications or withdrawal of a distribution license.

(B) A comprehensive operations license, authorizing exports and reexports of technology and related goods, including items from the list of militarily critical technologies developed pursuant to section 5(d) of this Act [section 2404(d) of this Appendix] which are included on the control list in accordance with that section, from a domestic concern to and among its foreign subsidiaries, affiliates, joint venturers, and licensees that have long-term, contractually defined relations with the exporter, are located in countries other than controlled countries (except the People's Republic of China), and are approved by the Secretary. The Secretary shall grant the license to manufacturing, laboratory, or related operations on the basis of approval of the exporter's systems of control, including internal proprietary controls, applicable to the technology and related goods to be exported rather than approval of individual export transactions. The Secretary and the Commissioner of Customs, consistent with their authorities under section 12(a) of this Act [section 2411(a) of this Appendix] and with the assistance of all appropriate agencies, shall periodically, but not less frequently than annually, perform audits of licensing procedures under this subparagraph in order to assure the integrity and effectiveness of those procedures.

(C) A project license, authorizing exports of goods or technology for a specified activity.

(D) A service supply license, authorizing exports of spare or replacement parts for goods previously exported.

(3) A general license, authorizing exports, without application by the exporter.

Subsections (1) and (2) describe the various types of *validated licenses* that are provided for under the regulations. The validated license described in subsection (1) covers only a single shipment of goods. Subsection (2) provides licenses for "multiple exports" including the distribution license, project license, service supply license, and the comprehensive operations license. Subsection (3) authorizes the generic *general license.* The term general license is a misnomer because it authorizes exports "without application by the exporter."

One important warning is that the EAR covers more than exports. It also covers re-exports, some foreign products (some products produced abroad under United States licenses), activities of United States citizens anywhere in the world involving technical assistance with respect to encryption commodities or software, and certain transactions within the United States. The last category includes the release of technology to a foreign national in the United States. It also includes the return of foreign equipment to its country of origin after repair in the United States, shipments from United States foreign trade zones, and the electronic transmission of non-public data.

Section 730.8 is titled "how to proceed and where to get help." It provides a simple schematic for the exporter. First, Part 732 of the EAR provides the steps to follow to determine the exporter's obligations under the EAR. Second, Part 734 defines the items and activities that are subject to the EAR. Third, Part 736 lists all the prohibitions that are contained in the EAR. Fourth, the EAR license requirements are best understood by reviewing, among others, the Commodity Control List, Parts 738, 740, 742, 744, and 746. The Commodities Control List is found in Supplement No. 1 to § 774.1 of the EAR. A license may be required for items on the Commodities Control List or if export is to a country found on the Country Chart in Part 738. If a license is required the exporter should consult Part 740 which describes the *License Exception.* Licenses required based on the end-use or end-user in the transaction are described in Part 744. The licensing requirements for exports to embargoed destinations are found in Part 746.

Once the exporter determines that a license will be required, the mechanics of filing an application for a license are found in Parts 748 and 750. The requirements for filing for a single license to cover a number of transactions is found in Part 752 (Special Comprehensive License). If the exporter is denied a license, Part 756 provides the rules for appealing the denial. Once a license is procured, Part 758 should be reviewed to determine the requirements for export clearance through the United States Customs Service. Finally, Part 762 sets out the exporter's record-keeping requirements. The BXA provides assistance on understanding the EAR, obtaining forms, training programs, and electronic services. This assistance can be obtained through the Office of Exporter Services (Exporter Counseling Division, Department of Commerce, 14th & Pennsylvania Avenue, Room H1099D, Washington, D.C. 20230, (202) 482-4811). United States export regulations (Export Administration Regulations) are available from the Superintendent of Documents, U.S. Government Printing Office, Washington, D.C. 20402.

A General License is not required for individual exporters. It is a grant of authority to all exporters for certain types of goods. In some instances, exporters must obtain a Validated License for certain products and for export to certain countries. The Validated License grants the authority to a specific exporter to export specific products. Whether a Validated License is required will be determined through a review of a number of regulations. First, whether the country of import is on the "Country Groups" list found in the "Export Administration Regulations" at 15 C.F.R. Part 370, Supplement No. 1. Second, whether the product being exported is on the "Commodity Control List" found at 15 C.F.R. Section 399.1, Supplement No. 1. Third, whether any "special restrictions" apply to the export as found in 15 C.F.R. Parts 376, 378, 385. If a Validated License is not required, then the goods may be exported under a General License without any specific application. However, the exporter will have to provide a "Shipper's Export Declaration" (SED) (Exhibit 4.7) and may have to provide a "Destination Control Statement." The Destination Control Statement requires that the following language be placed upon all export documents (bill of lading and commercial invoice): "These commodities, technology, or software were exported from the United States in accordance with the Export Administration Regulations. Diversion contrary to U.S. law is prohibited."[141] Title 15 of the Code of Federal Regulations (C.F.R.) provides information and guidance on the issuance of general and validated licenses.[142]

If a Validated License is required, the exporter must submit an "Application for a Validated Export License" (Form ITA-622P). In order to expedite the application process the exporter may have to obtain an "International Import Certificate" (Form ITA-645P/ATF-4522/DSP-53) and/or a "Statement of Ultimate Consignee and Purchaser" (Form ITA-629P) (Exhibit 4.8). The former is issued by the government of importation and certifies that the goods will be disposed of in the designated country. The Form ITA-629P is an assurance from the purchaser that the goods will not be resold or disposed of contrary to the requirements of the export license. A

---

[141]For a good overview on United States export documentation see, Braumiller & Rodriquez, *Export Process and Documentation: Focus on the New Export Administration Regulations,* 9 International Quarterly 697. They distill all of the Export Administration Regulations to five questions: What is the item (Commerce Control List)?, Where is it going?, Who will receive it?, What will be the item's end-use?, and What else does my end-user do (e.g., freight forwarder)?

[142]See, e.g., Information to Exporters, 15 C.F.R. § 770.11; The Commerce Control List, 15 C.F.R. § 799.1; and Export Administration Forms, 15 C.F.R. §770.12.

Exhibit 4.7: Shipper's Export Declaration

U.S. DEPARTMENT OF COMMERCE - BUREAU OF THE CENSUS - INTERNATIONAL TRADE ADMINISTRATION

FORM 7525-V (1-1-88) **SHIPPER'S EXPORT DECLARATION** OMB No. 0607-0018

1a. EXPORTER (*Name and address including ZIP code*)

ZIP CODE

2. DATE OF EXPORTATION

3. BILL OF LADING/AIR WAYBILL NO.

b. EXPORTER'S EIN (IRS) NUMBER

c. PARTIES TO TRANSACTION ☐ Related ☐ Non-related

4a. ULTIMATE CONSIGNEE

b. INTERMEDIATE CONSIGNEE

5. FORWARDING AGENT

6. POINT (STATE) OF ORIGIN OR FTZ NO.

7. COUNTRY OF ULTIMATE DESTINATION

8. LOADING PIER (*Vessel only*)

9. MODE OF TRANSPORT (*Specify*)

10. EXPORTING CARRIER

11. PORT OF EXPORT

12. PORT OF UNLOADING (*Vessel and air only*)

13. CONTAINERIZED (*Vessel only*) ☐ Yes ☐ No

14. SCHEDULE B DESCRIPTION OF COMMODITIES,
15. MARKS, NOS., AND KINDS OF PACKAGES } (*Use columns 17-19*)

D/F (16)	SCHEDULE B NUMBER (17)	CHECK DIGIT	QUANTITY - SCHEDULE B UNIT(S) (18)	SHIPPING WEIGHT (*Kilos*) (19)	VALUE (U.S. dollars, omit cents) (*Selling price or cost if not sold*) (20)

21. VALIDATED LICENSE NO./GENERAL LICENSE SYMBOL

22. ECCN (*When required*)

23. Duly authorized officer or employee

The exporter authorizes the forwarder named above to act as forwarding agent for export control and customs purposes.

24. I certify that all statements made and all information contained herein are true and correct and that I have read and understand the instructions for preparation of this document, set forth in the "Correct Way to Fill Out the Shipper's Export Declaration." I understand that civil and criminal penalties, including forfeiture and sale, may be imposed for making false or fraudulent statements herein, failing to provide the requested information or for violation of U.S. laws on exportation (13 U.S.C. Sec. 305; 22 U.S.C. Sec. 401; 18 U.S.C. Sec. 1001; 50 U.S.C. App. 2410).

Signature

Confidential - For use solely for official purposes authorized by the Secretary of Commerce (13 U.S.C. 301 (g).

Title

Export shipments are subject to inspection by U.S. Customs Service and/or Office of Export Enforcement.

Date

25. AUTHENTICATION (*When required*)

The "Correct Way to Fill Out the Shipper's Export Declaration" is available from the Bureau of the Census, Washington, D.C. 20233

Exhibit 4.8: Statement of Ultimate Consignee and Purchaser

OMB NO. 0625-0136

FORM ITA-629P (REV. 6-84)

U.S. DEPARTMENT OF COMMERCE
INTERNATIONAL TRADE ADMINISTRATION

STATEMENT BY ULTIMATE CONSIGNEE AND PURCHASER

GENERAL INSTRUCTIONS – This form must be submitted by the importer (ultimate consignee shown in Item 1) and by the overseas buyer or purchaser, to the U.S. exporter or seller with whom the order for the commodities described in Item 3 is placed. This completed statement will be submitted in support of one or more export license applications to the U.S. Department of Commerce. **All items on this form must be completed.** Where the information required is unknown or the item does not apply, write in the appropriate words "UNKNOWN" or "NOT APPLICABLE." If more space is needed, attach an additional copy of this form or sheet of paper signed as in Item 8. Submit form within 180 days from latest date in Item 8. Information furnished herewith is subject to the provisions of Section 12(c) of the Export Administration Act of 1979, 50 USC app. 2411(c), and its unauthorized disclosure is prohibited by law.

1. Ultimate consignee name and address

Name

Street and number

City and Country

Reference *(if desired)*

2. Request *(Check one)*

a. ☐ We request that this statement be considered a part of the application for export license filed by

____
U.S. exporter or U.S. person with whom we have placed our order (order party)

for export to us of the commodities described in item 3.

b. ☐ We request that this statement be considered a part of every application for export license filed by

____
U.S. exporter or U.S. person with whom we have placed or may place our order (order party)

for export to us of the type of commodities described in this statement, during the period ending June 30 of the second year after the signing of this form, or on ______________

3. Commodities

We have placed or may place orders with the person or firm named in Item 2 for the commodities indicated below:

COMMODITY DESCRIPTION	QUANTITY *(Fill in only if 2a is checked)*	VALUE *(Fill in only if 2a is checked)*

4. Disposition or use of commodities by ultimate consignee named in Item 1 *(Check and complete the appropriate box(es))*

We certify that the commodity(ies) listed in Item 3:

a. ☐ Will be used by us (as capital equipment) in the form in which received in a manufacturing process in the country named in Item 1 and will not be reexported or incorporated into an end product.

b. ☐ Will be processed or incorporated by us into the following product(s) ______________ *(Specify)*

to be manufactured in the country named in Item 1 for distribution in ______________ *(Name of country or countries)*

c. ☐ Will be resold by us in the form in which received in the country named in Item 1 for use or consumption therein.

The specific end-use by my customer will be ______________ *(Specify, if known)*

d. ☐ Will be reexported by us in the form in which received to ______________ *(Name of country(ies))*

e. ☐ Other *(Describe fully)* ______________

NOTE: If Item (d) is checked, acceptance of this form by the Office of Export Administration as a supporting document for license applications shall not be construed as an authorization to reexport the commodities to which the form applies unless specific approval has been obtained from the Office of Export Administration for such reexport.

(Reproduction of this form is permissible, providing that content, format, size and color of paper are the same)

Please continue form and sign certification on reverse side.

USCOMM-DC 84-21786

freight forwarder or customs broker may assist the exporter in the preparation of the documentation. However, it is important to know that the exporter is the one ultimately responsible for the accuracy of all the export documents. In order to protect oneself from violations of government re-export restrictions, a re-export prohibition clause should be written into the export contract. The clause should state the country of importation and prohibit the purchaser/importer from selling, delivering, or re-exporting the goods to another country or any country prohibited under United States law.

Most exporters will have to deal with one of two divisions within the Department of Commerce: the Bureau of Export Administration and the Office of Export Licenses. This is because the 1979 Export Administration Act delegated to the Department of Commerce the responsibility to promulgate regulations in conjunction with the enforcing of the Act. A number of other government agencies will also require approval for the exportation of certain specific goods (Exhibit 4.9).

Exhibit 4.9: Other Relevant Government Agencies

Types of Goods	*Agency*
Nuclear Technology	Department of Energy
Natural Gas	Department of Energy
Drugs	Department of Justice
Munitions	Department of State
Chemicals and Pesticides	Environmental Protection Agency
Nuclear Equipment & Materials	Nuclear Regulatory Commission
Technology in conjunction with foreign patent application	Patent & Trademark Office

Sources that may be used in order to ensure compliance include:

Exporter Assistance Division, U.S. Department of Commerce
Room 1099D
Washington, D.C. 20230
(202) 377-4811
(whether a Validated License is required)

Office of Antiboycott Compliance
Room 3886
International Trade Administration
U.S. Department of Commerce
Washington, D.C. 20230
(202) 377-2381
(special restrictions)

Public Health Service
Food & Drug Administration
5600 Fishers Lane
Rockville, MD 20857
(FDA restrictions)

Office of International Activities
U.S. Environmental Protection Agency
Washington, D.C. 20460
(EPA restrictions)

A good general source for information is the Overseas Private Investment Corporation (OPIC). OPIC is a U.S. Government owned corporation that offers specialized insurance and financing for United States exporters. OPIC offers political risk insurance that can protect exporters and contractors against the unfair drawing on a standby letter of credit by a foreign entity. It also offers insurance against the risks of currency inconvertibility. OPIC can be reached as follows: Overseas Private Investment Corporation, 1615 M Street, NW, Suite 400, Washington, D.C. 20527, (202) 457-7200 or (800) 424-6742.

The Office of Export Enforcement in the Department of Commerce has published the following "Helpful Hints" to help exporters in complying with the Export Administration Act and Regulations:

- Determine if a Validated Export License is required. When in doubt contact the Exporters Service Staff Office of Export Administration.
- Fully describe commodities or technical data on export shipping documents.
- Use the applicable destination control statement on commercial invoices, airway bills, and bills of *adirrgy* as required by Section 386.6 of the Export Administration Regulations.

- Avoid overshipments by maintaining an accurate account of the quantity and value of the goods being shipped against the validated export license.
- Avoid shipments after the expiration date on the validated export license.
- Enter the applicable validated export license number or general license symbol on the Shipper's Export Declaration.
- Make certain the export documents clearly identity the exporter, intermediate consignee, and ultimate consignee.
- Stay current with export control requirements by subscribing annually to the Export Administration Regulations.
- Avoid inadvertent sales to persons or firms denied U.S. export privileges by obtaining a copy of the Table of Denial Orders Currently in Effect available from the Office of Export Administration.
- Designate an appropriate person to monitor export transactions to ensure compliance with the Regulations.
- Enroll appropriate personnel in the Office of Export Administration's export licensing training program.

Foreign Import Restrictions and Requirements

A good source for general information on import restrictions and requirements of foreign countries is the Country Commercial Guides provided by Untied States government agencies. Country Commercial Guides can be obtained at http://www.state.gov. For example, the *Country Guide for Indonesia* provides information on trade regulations, standards, and import requirements. Beginning in 1996, the government began to drastically reduce tariffs, along with quantitative restrictions. "In May 1995, the Indonesian Government unveiled a comprehensive tariff reduction package covering roughly two thirds of all traded goods, designed to reduce most tariffs to under 5 percent by 2003." However, technical barriers remain in the area of services. "Foreign law firms, accounting firms, and consulting engineers must operate through technical assistance or joint venture with local firms." In the area of import control, the government has drastically reduced the types of good subject to import restrictions and special licensing requirements. However, goods such as alcoholic beverages, motor vehicles, hand tools, sweeteners, engines and pumps, tractors, rice, lube oil, and explosives continue to be regulated. Customs valuation has been transformed from an inspection system to one which relies on verification and auditing. Beginning in 1997, the Customs Directorate in the Ministry of Finance has operated an entry audit system. An electronic data interchange (EDI) system links importers, banks, and the Directorate. Import documentation generally includes the pro-forma invoice, commercial invoice, certificate of origin, bill of lading, and insurance certificate. The government requires an advance notification by which these documents are presented in diskette form. Like Indonesia's import tariff regime, export controls are in a state of rapid flux as the government works to implement reforms to reduce the restrictions and taxes placed on exports which affect agricultural products, including crops like rubber, palm oil, coffee, and copra.

The import regime of countries of the former Soviet-bloc is still evolving. New custom codes have been adopted, but enforcement may still be unpredictable.[143] For example, Russia has adopted customs valuation procedures as approved by GATT. Thus, valuation will generally be based upon CIF or DAF/Russian Border price of the goods. The tariff rate to be applied will be taken from a list of rates that became effective on May 15, 1996. If a preferential rate is being requested, for example for products originating from a less developed country, a certificate of origin will be required. Also, a number of exemptions can be obtained including for the importation for processing and sale, importation for processing and export, or importation of goods exported for processing. The former exemption is often difficult to obtain. The second type (processing and export) does not allow for an exemption for customs duties or value-added taxation (VAT), but does give a right to reclaim those taxes and duties if the processed goods are exported within two years. This exemption applies only to the processing value. Other than the certificate of origin, an importer must complete a customs declaration in the Russian language and may have to obtain bank approval pertinent to any hard currency transactions. Because of the evolving nature of the new customs laws, it is wise to contact the Russian Ministry of Foreign Economic Relations for updates and to enlist the services of a Russian customs agent to handle the import documentation.

---

[143]See, e.g., PRICE WATERHOUSE, DOING BUSINESS IN THE RUSSIAN FEDERATION 64-70 (1997).

Assessment of Import Duties

The viability of export contracts, especially long-term supply contracts, revolves around the parties' abilities to quantify and predict costs. The amount of customs duties to be paid is an important factor that needs to be analyzed prior to the signing of any long-term contract. A couple of items must be considered: (1) How will the goods be classified for purposes of obtaining the specific *ad valorem* rate?, and (2) How will the goods be valued? It would be prudent for the exporter to obtain an official ruling on the customs classification, rate, and other import fees before entering into a contract. The rest of this section will examine the customs valuation process in the United States.

The assessment of import tariffs or duties is a product of three variables: (1) classification of the goods being imported, (2) valuation of the goods, and (3) selection of the appropriate tariff rate (given a determination of classification) based upon a determination of the country of origin. The United States Customs Service administers tariff assessment and liquidation. The regulations governing this process are found in Title 19 of the Code of Federal Regulations (C.F.R.). The Customs Service web site can be assessed through http://www.customs.ustreas.gov. There are also a number of research services, such as *Customs Electronic Bulletin Board,* that will help in the development of a customs compliance procedure. A number of common sense techniques should be incorporated into a company's compliance procedure. First, a competent and responsible person within the company should review all customs documents, whether prepared by company personnel or outside experts, for completeness and accuracy. Second, the company must be sure the Customs Service is provided with a detailed product description and tariff classification for the imported goods. Third, the company needs to verify that the goods are properly marked with the correct country-of-origin. In 1997 the Customs Service published a *Reasonable Care Checklist*[144] as required by the Customs Modernization Act (Mod Act). Importers should refer to this Checklist in order to show that they have exercised reasonable care in complying with import regulations. The *Checklist* makes clear that responsibility remains with the importer even though

[144]62 Fed. Reg. 64,248 (1997).

the importation was handled by a licensed customs broker or other expert. Thus, the importer must exercise reasonable care in the selection of an import expert. Fourth, the company should become familiar with its record-keeping responsibilities as an importer.[145] "Administrative penalties between $10,000 and $100,000 per release of merchandise may be assessed for failure to produce records on reasonable demand by Customs within a reasonable time."[146] Even under the Customs Service new electronic entry system, the importer remains primarily responsible for maintaining proper records.

The documents required for entry into the United States include the "Entry/Immediate Delivery" (Form 3461), "Entry Summary" (Form 7501), bill of lading or transport document, pro forma or commercial invoice, packing slip, and other documents specific to the particular entry such as a certificate of origin. Penalties for material acts and omissions are provided in 19 U.S.C.A. §1592. In 1993 Congress passed the Customs Modernization and Informed Compliance Act. The law requires the Customs Service to develop an Automated Commercial System for the submission of entry documents electronically. The law also required the Customs Service to allow for a Remote Entry Filing system so that entry documents need not be processed solely at the port of entry. Therefore, importers could file documents through their custom brokers in order to obtain import clearance from distant ports.

The classification determination primarily entails the selection of the appropriate item within the Harmonized Tariff Schedule (HTS). The HTS can be accessed at http://www.customs.ustreas.gov/imp-exp/rulings/harmoniz or by writing the Superintendent of Documents, U.S. Government Printing Office, Washington, D.C., 20402. Despite the more than 5,000 tariff classifications in the HTS, often times there is no exact fit between the good being imported and a HTS tariff classification. The problem of classification was addressed in *Camel Manufacturing Co. v. United States.*[147] When the importer makes a selection of a tariff classification he should consult the "General Rules of Interpretation" found at the beginning

[145]"Recordkeeping Requirements," 62 Fed. Reg. 19,704 (1997) (proposed April 23, 1997).
[146]Matthew T. McGrath, Lawrence M. Friedman, & Robert A. Shapiro, *Customs Law,* 32 Int'l Lawyer 259, 260 (1998), citing, 62 Fed. Reg. 19,712, to be codified at 19 C.F.R. § 163.1.
[147]686 F.Supp. 912 (Ct. of Int'l Trade 1988).

of the HTS.[148] When there is more than one possible tariff selection, the Rules provide the means by which the importer and Customs Service make the final selection. The primary rule is the *rule of relative specificity* in which the more specific classification will apply over a broad or general classification.[149] The *rule of essential character* allows for a classification based upon the materials, attribute, or component that gives the product its essential character.[150] The *doctrine of entireties* allows the Customs Service to treat unassembled parts or components as an assembled product for purposes of classification. Thus, pieces of wood trim can be classified as picture frames.[151] The *last entry rule* holds that if two classifications seem equally applicable, the goods will be classified according to the most recent tariff heading (last in numerical order). Textile classifications are determined by the fibers with the chief weight.

The valuation of the goods is based upon the calculation of *transaction value.*[152] It is to the interest of the importer to keep the transaction value as low as possible. The issue becomes what items of costs need to be included in the transaction value. Those items most contested include commissions paid by the buyer,[153] royalties or fees paid by the buyer after importation,[154] the value of *assists*[155] (material, equipment, services provided to seller by the buyer), and proceeds of re-sales paid to the original seller.

The country of origin determination revolves upon two concepts. First, the general rule is that the country of origin is "that country where an article was grown, mined, produced, or manufactured." The second issue is whether there has been a subsequent *substantial transformation* of the original good or product in another country. The Supreme Court in *Anheuser-Busch Brewing v. United States* held that in order for there to be a substantial

---

[148]See also, United States Customs Service, Guidance for Interpretation of Harmonized System, 54 Federal Register 35127 (1989).

[149]See e.g., Humphrey's v. U.S., 272 F. Supp. 951 (1967).

[150]See, e.g., Better Home Plastics Corp. v. U.S., 119 F.3d 969 (Fed. Cir. 1997).

[151]See, e.g., Standard Brands Paint Co. v. United States, 511 F.2d 564 (1975) See also, Sears, Roebuck & Co. v. U.S., 723 F.Supp. 805 (1989).

[152]See, 19 U.S.C.A. § 1401a (a)(1)(A).

[153]See, 19 U.S.C.A. § 1401a (b) (1) (B). See also, Monarch Luggage Co. v. U.S., 715 F.Supp. 1115 (1989); Rosenthal-Netter, Inc. v. U.S., 861 F.2d 261 (Fed. Cir. 1988).

[154]See, 19 U.S.C.A. § 1401a (b)(1)(D).

[155]See, 19 U.S.C.A. §§ 1401a ((b)(1)(C) & 1401a (h)(1). See also, Texas Apparel Co. v. U.S., 698 F.Supp 932 (Ct. of Int'l Trade 1988).

transformation "a new and different article must emerge, having a distinctive name, character, or use."[156] Some of the factors used to justify a finding of a substantial transformation is that the process has added significant value to the item, that it has resulted in a change in tariff classification, and the item has been transformed from a producer to a consumer good.[157] The importer concerned with a classification issue may want to request an advanced ruling from the Commissioner of Customs as provided in 19 C.F.R. § 177.

A provision of United States customs law allows for a reduction in assessed duty for components manufactured in the United States and assembled abroad. Tariff Schedules, Item No. 807.00, 19 U.S.C.A. § 1202 provides that:

> Articles assembled abroad in whole or in part of fabricated components, the product of the United States, which (a) were exported in condition ready for assembly without further fabrication, (b) have not lost their physical identity in such articles by change in form, shape, or otherwise, and (c) have not been advanced in value or improved in condition abroad except by being assembled and except by operations incidental to the assembly process such as cleaning, lubricating, and painting . . .

The key issue of contention between the Customs Service and importers is the definition of "fabrication." In *Samsonite Corp. v. U.S.*[158] the Customs Service successfully challenged the importer's deduction for the value of assembling luggage in Mexico. Steel strips were produced in the United States and then sent to the company's assembly plant in Mexico. The case involved the deductibility of the costs of the steel strips upon importation into the United States. The Court agreed with the Customs Service that the shaping of the steel strips before placing them within the luggage constituted a further fabrication and not mere assembly as provided in 807.00.

The European approach to customs valuation follows the same approach as found in the United States. Council Regulation 2913/92 established the European Union's Customs Code. The valuation of imported goods is based on the notion of *transaction value* or the "price actually paid"

---

[156]207 U.S. 556, 562 (1908).

[157]To compare the customs law of another country see the web site for Japanese Customs at http://www.mof.go.ip/~customs/conte-e.htm

[158]889 F.2d 1074 (Fed. Cir. 1989).

(Article 28). Article 29 provides that transaction value must be adjusted for any proceeds of subsequent sales that are remitted by the buyer to the exporter, directly or indirectly. Article 32 provides a list of the types of charges that must be included in transaction value. Customs value includes the costs of packing, commission and brokerage fees, and royalty and license fees. Items that are not included in the customs valuation include freight charges, charges incurred subsequent to import, and finance charges (Article 33). One advantage of the EU tariff is that it is fully harmonized in the area of import licensing. The single tariff structure known as *Taric* provides rules for determining whether an import license is required for a particular good. It should be noted that most EU members maintain their own country lists of goods requiring an import license.[159]

Some countries require that an importer provide a surety bond as a condition of import For example, all United States importers are required to provide a bond to United States Customs. The Customs Service dictates the form and amount of the bond. The purpose of the bond is to provide the Customs Service with an agreement to pay duties, taxes, and charges. A Single Entry Bond secures the import involving a single transaction. Multiple import transactions can be secured by a Continuous Customs Bond. A knowledgeable customs broker can assist in determining the bonding requirements and in the placement of the bond.

Barter and Countertrade

Barter and countertrade or counterpurchase have become common methods to overcome currency convertibility and repatriation problems or capital shortcomings of a foreign party.[160] A barter transaction involves an exchange of goods or services. However, "barter agreements are not always simple, cashless, single document arrangements. They sometimes involve two separate documentary sales, often with letters of credit, and a linking

[159]Information on import forms for the EU is contained in Title VII of Council Regulation 2454/93 and Title III of Council Regulation 2913/92.

[160]See generally, Grabow, *Negotiating and Drafting Contracts in International Barter and Countertrade Transactions,* 9 No. Carolina Journal of Int'l Law & Commercial Regulation 255 (1984).

protocol agreement."[161] One definition of the countertrade transaction is it is an economic transaction in which one party sells goods to the second party and in return, the first party agrees to purchase goods from the second party, so as to achieve an agreed ratio between the reciprocal performances.[162] A variant is the *offset agreement*. "Offsets constitute an agreement by the foreign seller to include as part of the sale in the foreign nation the use of parts or services from local suppliers."[163] It acts as "a local content requirement."[164] The following excerpt describes the variations found in the area of countertrade.

MCVEY *Countertrade: Commercial Practices, Legal Issues and Policy Dilemmas,* 16 Law & Policy Int'l Bus. 1 (1984).

Countertrade frequently is confused with the concept of barter. Barter is an exchange of goods effectuated without the use of currency. Countertrade is most frequently used to refer to two reciprocal sales transactions in which each party is paid in currency. Despite this technical distinction most observers view barter transactions as a subcategory of countertrade. The two most common types of countertrade are known as "counterpurchase" and "compensation" or "buy-back."

COUNTERPURCHASE

In a counterpurchase arrangement, a private firm agrees to sell products to a sovereign nation and to purchase from the nation goods which are unrelated to the items which it is selling. For example, in a series of transactions between a major U.S. manufacturer of commercial aircraft and the government of Yugoslavia, the U.S. firm sold jet aircraft to Yugoslavia and agreed to purchase substantial quantities of Yugoslav crystal glassware, cutting tools, leather coats, and canned hams.

In a counterpurchase transaction, each party is paid in currency upon the delivery of its products to the other party. It is common in such transac-

---

[161]RALPH W. FOLSOM & MICHAEL W. GORDON, INTERNATIONAL BUSINESS TRANSACTIONS 32 (1995).
[162]See, UNCITRAL, "Preliminary Study of Legal Issues in International Countertrade" (1988).
[163]FOLSOM & GORDON at 35.
[164]Ibid.

tions for a private firm to be allowed a period of time following the delivery of the goods that it is selling in which to fulfill its purchase obligation. Periods of from three to five years, for example, are not uncommon in counterpurchase obligations imposed by Eastern European nations. Often, the parties agree upon a list of goods from which the private firm later will be able to select items to purchase.

Private firms resort to a variety of methods to dispose of goods which they are forced to purchase, but most frequently resell these goods to trading companies or directly to end users, often at a discount or "disagio." Sometimes the private firm will resell the countertraded goods at a price below that which it paid for them, seeking to offset this loss by larger profits generated by the sale of its own product to the nation.

COMPENSATION

The most common form of countertrade is referred to as "compensation" or "buy-back." In a compensation transaction, a private firm will sell equipment, technology, or even an entire plant to a sovereign nation and agree to purchase a portion of the output produced from the use of the equipment or technology. For example, in the celebrated $20 billion Occidental Petrolemn ammonia countertrade transaction with the Soviet Union, Occidental assisted the Soviets in constructing and financing ammonia plants and agreed to purchase quantities of ammonia produced in these plants over a twenty-year period.

Compensation transactions frequently involve significantly longer periods of time during which the private firm will be permitted to fulfill its purchase obligation than in counterpurchase. In addition, compensation transactions are generally of larger dollar value than counterpurchase transactions. Unlike counterpurchase transactions, the products which the private firm purchases in compensation are frequently of marketable quality and in demand in the international marketplace. Further, Western firms frequently are able to negotiate a purchase price for the output that is below the world market price so that the firm can earn a profit in reselling the product which it is forced to buy.

BARTER

Barter, swap, and other types of non-currency transactions are frequently viewed as forms of countertrade. In many cases, the sovereign nation will impose a barter requirement in a coercive fashion for purposes of disposing of surplus or low quality goods which it otherwise cannot sell.

Barter transactions are frequently utilized in crude oil transfers as a means of conveying crude below official OPEC prices. Similarly, barter is occasionally used as a means of "liberating" blocked currencies or otherwise circumventing foreign exchange controls.

IMPORT ENTITLEMENT PROGRAMS

An import entitlement is a government-imposed mechanism under which a party is afforded preferential treatment in obtaining an import license if it arranges an export transaction of equivalent value. In many partly-industrialized and Third World nations, hard currency shortages have forced national governments to impose import licensing programs under which only essential goods are allowed to be imported. Under such programs, exceptions will be made for non-essential items if the importer also arranges an export from that country of equivalent value.

An import entitlement program places the responsibility to arrange parallel purchases upon the importer and not upon the foreign private supplier; however, the importer often will shift the burden of arranging the export to the private supplier. Consequently, the private foreign supplier confronts what amounts to a countertrade requirement.

CLEARING AGREEMENTS

Although countertrade is conducted most frequently between a sovereign nation and a private firm, countertrade arrangements also occur between and among sovereign nations. Nations have historically entered into bilateral or multilateral "clearing agreements" under which they agree to purchase equal values of each other's products over a specified period of time. This is a form of reciprocal trading not unlike the private firm sovereign nation relationships discussed above. When an imbalance develops in an account that a nation cannot rectify, private firms known as "switch trading" firms offer to assist the recalcitrant nation in disposing of the goods which it is required to purchase, usually for a fee.

SWITCH TRADING

A switch trade is a device used to balance a bilateral clearing agreement. In a bilateral clearing arrangement between Romania and Brazil, for example, Romania may have taken more products from Brazil than Brazil has taken from Romania at the end of the clearing period. In this instance, Brazil will have a "credit" in its "clearing account," or as is frequently described, a surplus of Romanian "clearing dollars." The problem will arise when there are no available Romanian products which Brazil is interested in taking. In the switch trade, Brazil will locate a third party that is interested in purchasing Romanian goods and substitute the third party's purchase of Romanian goods in satisfaction of its own purchase obligation. Technically, Brazil sells its "clearing dollars" to the third party, and the third party uses these credits to pay for exports from Romania. Brazil sells the credits at a discount—discounts of up to 30 percent are not uncommon—and receives hard currency from the third party. It is common for a trading intermediary to assist Brazil in locating the third party purchaser. This intermediary, known as a "switch trader," would generally receive a portion of the discount for its services.

"PROGRESSIVE" OR "PROACTIVE" COUNTERTRADE

In "progressive" or "proactive" countertrade, a firm purchases goods from a nation prior to the point in time in which it is selling its product to the nation. This is done for the specific purpose of developing the right or opportunity to sell products to the nation in the future. This practice differs from traditional types of countertrade discussed above in that the private firm generates the hard currency for the purchasing nation prospectively, rather than simultaneously or over a period of time subsequent to the sale of its products to the nation.

Under variations of this type of arrangement, a firm may obtain the right to utilize its credits in serving as an agent for selling the products of other firms to the nation, or if the nation approves, the firm may transfer these credits to other private firms for a fee. Indonesia, for example, recently has announced that it will consider allowing the "crediting" of Indonesian exports generated by one firm against the countertrade commitments of another firm selling to Indonesia. In cases where a private firm is unable to locate desirable locally produced products for export from the nation to develop countertrade credit, firms have been known to transfer technology or establish plants in the nation in the effort to assist the nation to produce items for which the private firm has an established overseas market.

FRAMEWORK AGREEMENTS

In a countertrade "framework agreement" a private firm establishes a formal, long-term "crediting" mechanism with the host nation under which exports generated by the private firm are routinely credited to the countertrade commitments of numerous third party firms on an ongoing basis. The key to a framework agreement is that the "crediting" of the offsetting purchases or the escrowing and payment of funds is undertaken on a routine and ongoing basis under a prearranged agreement rather than on the more common case-by-case basis.

"POSITIVE" OR "REVERSE" COUNTERTRADE

In certain instances, private firms prefer countertrade arrangements over conventional transactions. In so-called "positive" or "reverse" countertrade, the private firm views the goods that it will be required to purchase as more valuable than hard currency. This is most often the case when a firm seeks to establish a guaranteed supply of a valuable commodity or production component when it anticipates future shortages of these items. For example, in one of the proposed East-West "gas-for-pipes" transactions, a group of private firms was negotiating with the Soviet Union to transfer equipment and technology for the transportation and production of natural gas to the Soviets in return for guarantees of quantities of natural gas produced through the use of this equipment and technology. In a similar transaction, a U.S. oil firm was reported to have assisted in the development of a $300 million export refinery and a separate $300 million petrochemical complex in Saudi Arabia in exchange for the right to purchase 1.4 billion barrels of Saudi Arabian crude oil over a fifteen-year period.

"DEVELOP-FOR-IMPORT" TRANSACTIONS

"Develop-For-Import" transactions are a specialized type of positive countertrade undertaken between an industrialized nation and a developing nation for the specific purpose of guaranteeing sufficient future supplies of strategic minerals or other scarce resources for the industrialized nation. Under these arrangements, a developed nation will provide the capital, equipment, and technology to develop mining and energy projects in nations that are rich in resources but lack the economic and technological capability to develop such resources. In exchange, the transferring nation will be guaranteed a long-term supply of the mineral or hydrocarbon produced from the mine or well which it assisted in developing.

These transactions differ from other "positive" compensation transactions discussed above in that the primary motive of the projects' proponents in undertaking these projects is to establish guaranteed future supplies of the strategic commodity rather than to conclude the sale of the equipment or technology.

PERFORMANCE REQUIREMENTS

A performance requirement is a condition imposed by a sovereign government that requires foreign parties who wish to undertake an investment in that nation to agree to take certain steps to increase exports from the nation. Such steps include the agreement by the foreign investors to export a certain percentage of the output from the investment project, to employ a certain level of local inhabitants in the project, to use a predetermined level of locally produced components in the manufactured product, and to transfer certain technology to the host nation. Performance requirements are distinguishable from other types of countertrade requirements in that the former involve a private firm's investment in the imposing nation rather than its sale of goods to the nation. Both practices involve intervention by the host nation in the free market process, however, and in view of their similarity are frequently treated as the same phenomenon.

One of the most frequently cited performance requirements is the "Mexican Automotive Decree" that requires foreign-owned automobile assembly enterprises operating in Mexico to generate sufficient exports to cover the value of all Mexican imports that occur as part of their respective assembly operations. Another example is the requirement imposed by the Canadian government that in order for a U.S. multinational corporation to be permitted to acquire a Quebec truck-body manufacturer, the U.S. firm had to commit to export 80 percent of the plant's output.

COLLECTION-THROUGH-EXPORT TRANSACTIONS

A major problem for U.S. firms doing business abroad is the collection of overseas funds which have been restricted from repatriation due to foreign exchange controls. In such instances, a private firm might be owed funds by a foreign party as a result of a trade debt or have profits denominated in local currency which are earned by a foreign subsidiary. The private firm will have possession of the local currency in the host country, but due to foreign exchange shortages will be unable to convert this currency into dollars. In a collection-through-export transaction, the firm will use the local currency to purchase locally produced goods, export the goods from the host nation, and sell the goods overseas for dollars or another convertible currency.

Another source for information and contract clauses dealing with countertrade is the United Nations Commission on International Trade Law (UNCITRAL). They publish a *Legal Guide on International Countertrade Transactions* that provides information on how best to structure a countertrade transaction. It also discusses the types of clauses generally found in countertrade contracts. The *Guide* discusses various types of countertrade including barter, counter-purchase, buy-back, direct offset, and indirect offset. It generally defines countertrade as an "undertaking to conclude a future contract or a series of supply contracts in one or both directions." The clauses discussed in the *Guide* include: type, quality, and quantity of goods; pricing of goods; participation of third parties; payment; restrictions on resale; liquidated damages; security for performance; failure to perform; choice of law; and settlement of disputes. One practitioner stresses the following concepts in drafting a countertrade agreement:

- Ensuring that products to be received are acceptable in quality and quantity, fit for a particular purpose specified in the contract,
- Ensuring that foreign currency risks are minimized,
- Establishing the time frame and time limits for supply/offset contracts,
- Avoiding particularly onerous penalties and one-sided breach provisions, including reasonable termination and *force majeure* provisions,
- Ensuring some flexibility in assignment/transferability of contract rights.[165]

---

[165]William G. Frenkel, *Legal Protection against Risks Involved in Doing Business in the Republics of the Former U.S.S.R.*, 10 International Quarterly 395, 431 (1998).

Because of the difficulty in finding marketable goods in a foreign country to fulfill a countertrade commitment, certain clauses take on added importance. First, an extended period of time should be allotted to the exporter to find the necessary goods. Second, a broad list of goods should be negotiated to enhance the exporter's chances of finding marketable goods. Third, because of the poor quality of some foreign goods, the exporter will want to negotiate broad inspection rights. Also, the costs and uncertainty of the countertrade arrangement may warrant the granting of a discount or *disagio* of the amount of goods needed to be purchased to fulfill the countertrade commitment.[166] Another provision included in countertrade contracts is a penalty clause for non-performance of the countertrade commitment. This clause can work to the benefit of the exporter in that payment of a penalty in substitute for purchasing unmarketable goods may make better economic sense. Of course, the penalty clause should make clear that payment of the penalty releases the exporter from any further liability.

Trade Liberalization

The 1980's and 1990's has witnessed a tremendous liberalization of international trade law. Tariff rates have been reduced to unprecedented levels and significant inroads have been made in the reduction of non-tariff barriers. The breadth of trade liberalization was evident in the successful conclusion of the Uruguay Round of the General Agreement on Tariffs and Trade (GATT).[167] The expansion beyond its traditional mandate of tariff reduction shows how pervasive the free trade movement has become. Its side agreements on investment, services, technology protection, and government procurement, along with the creation of the World Trade Organization (WTO), indicate that the internationalization of business transactions will continue to flourish. Tariffs in the range of five percent or less have become common. A number of provisions, mostly of a technical nature, of immediate importance to international exporters and importers include:

---

[166]FOLSOM & GORDON at 44.

[167]The United States Congress ratified and implemented the Uruguay Round agreements in December 1994 under the Uruguay Round Agreements Act. See, Public Law No. 103-465, 108 Stat. 4809.

Sanitary and Phytosanitary Measures, Agreement on Technical Barriers to Trade, Customs Valuation Code, Agreement on Pre-Shipment Inspection, Agreement on Rules of Origin, and Agreement on Import Licensing Procedures.

The Agreement on the Application of Sanitary and Phytosanitary Measures (SPS) is a parallel agreement to the Technical Barriers to Trade agreement. The SPS is aimed at promoting international standards to import restrictions aimed at protecting human, animal and plant life and health. SPS mandates that countries not use such measures or restrictions "as a disguised device" to restrict the importation of goods. "Countries are required to accept one another's measures as equivalent; but the exporting country may need to demonstrate that its measures achieve the importing country's SPS protection level and for this purpose to give the importing country access for inspection, testing and similar procedures."[168] The parallel Agreement on Technical Barriers to Trade requires that the importing country allow importers access to its testing and certification standards and procedures. Countries to this agreement are to "use international standards wherever possible; maintain transparency through publication and notification of all relevant information . . . through 'enquiry points' established in each country."[169]

The Customs Valuation Code attempts to standardize country challenges to the valuation placed on goods being imported. It places the burden of proof on the importer to provide additional evidence of valuation. However, a country must give adequate opportunity to the importer to respond to the country's challenge to its valuation. An associated agreement pertains to the importing country's right to pre-shipment inspection. This right to pre-inspect goods for quality, quantity, and value is afforded only to developing countries because of their limited resources. GATT recognizes their right to hire private companies to inspect the goods in the country of export. The Agreement on Import Licensing Procedures is based upon the principle that application procedures should be made as simple as possible. Finally, the work on developing uniform rules of origin is ongoing and should be monitored in the future.

[168]John Kraus, *The GATT Negotiations: A Business Guide to the Results of the Uruguay Round*, ICC Pub. No. 533 (E) 18 (1994).
[169]Ibid. at 22.

The "regionalization" of trade, as evidenced by the European Union and the North American Free Trade Agreement (NAFTA), have removed trade barriers and created larger markets for American goods. The impact of the broader macro concerns of international trade policy should be constantly monitored by exporters and importers. For example, the American exporter and importer should be fully aware of the pertinent provisions of NAFTA. NAFTA aims at reducing tariff and non-tariff barriers between the United States, Canada, and Mexico. On the tariff side, it has had an immediate impact on reducing barriers, especially on manufactured goods. Its long-term goal is the elimination of all tariffs over a fifteen-year period, however, the short-term effects on particular industries and companies are likely to be profound. With that in mind, NAFTA contains *snapback provisions* which allow for the reinstitution of previous tariff levels at times in order to alleviate short-term negative impacts on industry and business. NAFTA enacted a series of complicated rules of origin that the North American businessperson will need to master in order to earn the lower NAFTA tariff rates. Goods will need to be certified as *regional goods* in order to cross NAFTA borders freely. The traditional test of substantial transformation or a good going through a tariff classification change are not sufficient when certain goods are imported from outside of NAFTA and then moved within NAFTA. For example, textile products will need to go through a *triple transformation* in order to obtain regional goods status. Other products, like automobiles, electronics and machinery, have to pass stringent *cost tests.* Depending on the good, somewhere between fifty and sixty-two and one-half percent of the goods' costs must be regional.

NAFTA's ultimate long-term impact on trade is more likely to come in its non-tariff provisions. The non-tariff provisions include an agreement to reduce barriers to direct foreign investment, the elimination of performance standards, the free flow of capital, expropriation assurances, and a dispute resolution mechanism. The breadth of NAFTA and its potential impact on regional trade can be seen in the following chart's listing of some of the committees and groups authorized by NAFTA articles[170] (Reference to NAFTA Articles are in brackets).

[170]See, Leonard Waverman, *Post-Nafta: Can the United States, Canada, and Mexico Deepen Their Economic Relationships?,* in INTEGRATING THE AMERICAS: SHAPING FUTURE TRADE POLICY 89, 112 (ed. Sidney Weintraub 1994).

Working Groups:	Working Group on Rules of Origin [513] Working Group on Customs [513(6)] Working Group on Agricultural Subsidies [705(6)] Working Group on Trade & Competition [1504]
Committees:	Trade in Goods [316] Sanitary & Phytosanitary Measures [722] Financial Services [1412] Private Commercial Disputes [2022(4)] Land Transportation Standards [913(5)] Telecommunications Standards [913(5)] Automotive Standards [913(5)] Small Business [1021]

One of the areas where substantial work needs to be done is the removal of product and technical standards as a barrier to trade. The international businessperson has to prove to the country of import that its products meet its standards. The greatest obstacle to mastering standards is the non-transparency of national standards and the evaluating of different national standards. The European Union can be used as a benchmark. It has made significant strides under its *Common Community Customs Code* to lessen the paperwork problems of different national standards. "Technical regulations cannot now be used to keep imports out if the other country's technical requirements are *equivalent.* Where standards do not involve risks to health, safety, or the environment, the *rule of mutual recognition* holds. A country cannot prevent the importation of a product from another country simply because that product meets a different but qualified standard. Instead of harmonizing standards in these other areas, the Community relies on labeling and consumer choice."[171] The NAFTA provisions on standards are found in its Chapter 9. Other than a general mandate that the NAFTA countries are not to use standards as trade barriers, Chapter 9 re-asserts the individual countries' rights to set their own standards. Only time will tell whether the standing committees on standards will produce harmonization or mutual recognition of national standards. Such efforts should be closely monitored by the businessperson operating within the NAFTA countries.

[171]Ibid. at 102.

CHAPTER 5

National Laws Affecting International Sales

A fundamental difference between the common law and civil law is how they each approach the rights and duties of contracting parties during the negotiation stage of contracting. The common law approach is simply that there are no such duties or rights. A contracting party may terminate a long-term negotiation in bad faith without any legal repercussions. In contrast, the civil law recognizes a clear duty to negotiate in good faith. A bad faith termination could subject the withdrawing party to a lawsuit based upon *culpa in contrahendo* or fault in negotiating. Another area of potential pre-contractual liability is whether informal instruments and correspondences may become the basis for a breach of contract lawsuit. Once again, the common law approach to these writings, sometimes called comfort instruments, is that they do not rise to the level of contractual liability. The next section will examine how the potential for unexpected legal liability may exist for the issuer of such instruments in international business dealings.

Pre-Contractual Instruments

At the frontier of the contractual obligation are instruments that are imbued with an internal repugnancy. Such instruments are found in most areas of business and finance. Examples include the attorney opinion letter, letters of intent, accountant certifications, letters of support, letters of responsibility, and letters of assurance. They have no recognizable nomenclature, no universally accepted definition, and are generally considered to be *ex territorium* to the field of contractual liability. For want of a better term, they will be referred to as *comfort instruments.*[172] Comfort instruments are generally given to encourage another party to enter into a contractual obligation. The assurance is given with the intent of not incurring a legal obligation. If, however, the litmus test of reliance is used, then it is conceivable that these instruments may rise to the level of enforceable obligations.

The potential for contractual liability lies in the internal inconsistency of many of these instruments. The prototypical comfort instrument tries to provide a guaranty-type of assurance without the resultant guaranty-type of liability. The 1923 English case of *Rose & Frank Co. v. Crompton* is one of the earliest instances of a court coming to terms with a comfort instrument's internal repugnancy. The Court expressly recognized the doctrinal inconsistencies in the language of the letter. It weighed the assurance language with the disclaimer language, ultimately deciding that the disclaimer language was the more dominant. It determined that the operative phrase in the letter was that it was a *contract of honour.*[173] The word contract being a misnomer. Comfort instruments seem to exist in a doctrinal gray area between inchoate expectation and legally enforceable reliance. From a theoretical and doctrinal basis, this line between contract and noncontract remains ambiguous. The question of enforceability provides a framework for analyzing the twin pillars of contract, promissorial intent and promisee reliance.

Judge Vaisey in *Chemco Leasing Spa. v. Rediffusion plc.* sarcastically frames the issue of comfort instrument enforceability. It is a "*gentlemen's agreement* which is not an agreement, made between two persons neither of whom is a gentlemen, whereby each expects the other to be strictly bound without himself being bound at all."[174] If this was true, then there is little ground for enforcement under either express intent or reliance. On its face, the instrument's ambiguous nature would make it difficult to find the req-

[172]See generally, Larry A. DiMatteo & Rene Sacasas, "*Credit and Value Comfort Instruments,*" 47 *Baylor Law Review* 357 (1995).

[173]1924 All E.R. 245, 255 (Ct. App. 1923).

[174]Queen's Bench, affirmed, Court of Appeals (Commercial Court) (Transcript Assoc. 1985).

uisite intent either subjectively or objectively. The recipient of the comfort instrument would be hard pressed to prove justifiable reliance.

Internationally, courts have been more likely to enforce such instruments. The civil law system seems to place less weight on the semantic labeling of instruments when determining the existence of a legally enforceable obligation. The objective viewfinder of the civil law system is broader in scope than the one found in the common law system. The lack of dependency upon legal literalism, both in the labeling of instruments and in the words of art used within the instruments, allows for greater flexibility in the affixation of contractual liability in the civil law system. For example, in the Federal Republic of Germany "there are no specific provisions in the Civil or Commercial Codes concerning contractual guarantees."[175] The parties are at liberty to customize legal hybrids in the structuring of their business relationships. The expansiveness of the objective realm is evident in French jurisprudential thought. French law approaches the issue of contractual intent in a direct, commonsensical way. "The creation in the commercial world of a meaningless instrument is unthinkable."[176] Why would two commercial entities create unenforceable instruments? Anglo-American contract theory would hold that such instruments are unenforceable because they lack clear contractual intent. French jurisprudence renders a contrary presumption, finding that the objective person would presume that such commercial instruments possess an implied intent to be binding *obligations de faire.*

The objectiveness of the German law approach is more than a difference in the degree of formalism or in scope. The objective effect of the judicial interpretation plays a major role in the implication of intent. The goal of contractual interpretation, under this approach, is to give effect to the purpose of the instrument. The courts rather than restricting themselves to a "literal interpretation of the wording of a contractual term, they tend to consider the purpose of the contract and to interpret it in the way best suited to meet that purpose."[177] The focus of the objective inquiry has shifted away from the specific manifestations or intent of the promisor. In-

---

[175]Wolfgang Hering, "The Commercial Laws of the Federal Republic of Germany," in, Lester Nelson, ed., *Digest of Commercial Laws of the World* (1992), 62.

[176]L. Proscour, "France," Dennis Campbell, ed., *Legal Aspects* at 302.

[177]Hering, "Commercial Law of Federal Republic of Germany" at 206.

stead, the court looks to the purpose or essence of the contract to project a result in accord with that purpose. The Court in *Steller v. Thomas* stated that the intention of the parties is "not to be determined exclusively from the mere language of the contract, it must be construed in the light of the *nature,* subject, and purpose of the contract.

A *presumption of intentionality* can be deciphered from both the common law and the civil law systems. The presumption is grounded in the belief that parties generally do not intend to create meaningless contractual-type documentation.[178] Justice Hirst noted the constructional presumption in favor of enforceability. "It is for the party who claims there is no such intention to create legal relations to disprove it, and the onus is a heavy one."[179] Another rule of construction that favors a presumption of intentionality is the *contra proferentem rule.* This rule holds that "in case of ambiguity when all other rules of construction fail, the doubt is removed by construing the document adversely against the writer"[180] Thus, it encourages a finding of an intent that is favorable to the recipient of the writing.

The presumption of intentionality also plays a key role in the construction of instruments that are highly negotiated and ambiguously worded. In the field of comfort instruments the problem is compounded by internal repugnancy. The instrument possesses equally clear language and operative phraseology that support both findings of intentionality and non-intentionality. They often possess disclaimer-type language at the behest of the promisor and language that is contractual in nature in order to appease the promisee. It ultimately falls to the subjective determination of the court to decide who was the successful negotiator. In case of doubt, modern jurisprudential leanings regarding enforceability will win the day. The classically inclined jurist will look to the ambiguity of consent and hold that there is no contract. For those who believe it against reason for two reasonably sophisticated parties to pursue negotiations over the wording of a nonlegal instrument, a presumption of intentionality will be an attractive device. The key point of interest is the potential utilization of the presump-

---

[178]"There is a normal assumption that a business transaction is not meaningless and that the words have a purpose." Chelsea Industries, Inc. v. Accuray Leasing Corp., 699 F.2d 58, 60 (1st Cir. 1983). See also, Cincinnati Enquirer, Inc. v. American Security & Trust Co., 160 N.E.2d 392, 398 (Ohio 1958).

[179]Kleinwort Benson Ltd. v. Malaysia Mining Corp. Bhd., 1 W.L.R. 799 (1988).

[180]*See, e.g.,* U.S. v. Seckinger, 397 U.S. 203 (1970).

tion in the face of language not clearly reflective of mutual assent. The presumption of intentionality could simply be a factor to be weighed by a reasonable promisee. "Under the objective theory of contracts the test is whether a reasonable person in the position of the receiving party would conclude that the sending party had made a commitment."[181] The parameters used in the construction of this reasonable person are likely to be pivotal to the outcome of the judicial decision-making process.

Convergence and Divergence of National Laws

The interrelationship between national and international legal systems is critical to the entrepreneur and the legal practitioner in assessing the legal risks of a transaction. One commentator states that "with the world so interrelated, economic relations and their international aspect are influenced by the interests of and relations between subjects of civil (including commercial) law from various countries."[182] Even without the development of uniform international laws like the United Nations Convention on Contracts for the International Sale of Goods (CISG), there has been a significant convergence of contract law between different legal systems. The differences in contract law, for example, between the common law and the civil law systems is more one of style than substance. The first excerpt is a resolution from the Council of Europe pertaining to the enforceability of *penal clauses* or what American legal practitioners call *liquidated damage clauses.* First, take note that the Council of Europe's membership includes both common law and civil law countries. Therefore, the resolution is itself an example of contract law convergence in Europe. Second, the similarities between the resolution and American law, as described in the excerpts from the Uniform Commercial Code (UCC) and the Restatement (Second) of Contracts, are further evidence of convergence.

---

[181]Calamari & Perillo, *Contracts* at § 2-7 at 33.

[182]Tsvetana Kamenova, *Civil Law in Bulgaria: The Relationship Between International and Domestic Law and the Impact on Civil Law,* in, GEORGE GINSBURGS, DONALD D. BARRY & WILLIAM B. SIMONS, eds. THE REVIVAL OF PRIVATE LAW IN CENTRAL AND EASTERN EUROPE, 541(The Hague: Martinus Nijhoff Publishers (Kluwer) 1996).

Council of Europe Resolution (78) 3 On Penal Clauses in Civil Law

Preamble

Considering that the aim of the Council of Europe is to achieve greater unity between its members, in particular the adoption of common rules in the field of law and considering that it is necessary to provide judicial control over penal clauses in civil law in appropriate cases where the penalty is manifestly excessive.

Article 2

The promisee may not obtain concurrently performance of the principal obligation, as specified in the contract, and payment of the sum stipulated in the penal clause unless the sum was stipulated for delayed performance.

Article 7

The sum stipulated may be reduced by the court when it is manifestly excessive.

Explanatory Memorandum

The legal systems of member states have devised various means to enable courts to exercise a certain control over penal clauses, although the circumstances under which this control can be exercised differ considerably from one state to another. It is one of the essential aims of the present resolution to contribute towards a *harmonisation* of the laws of the member states. It is left to each legal system to determine under what precise circumstances the sum concerned is manifestly excessive. It is suggested that in a given case the courts may have regard to a number of factors such as:

i. comparing the damage pre-estimated by the parties at the time of contracting and the damage actually suffered by the promisee.
ii. the legitimate interests of the parties including the promisee's non-pecuniary interests.
iii. the category of contract and the circumstances under which it was concluded, in particular the relative social and economic position of the parties, or the fact that the contract was a standard form contract.

iv. the reason for the failure to perform, in particular the good or bad faith of the promisor.

Compare United States Law
Uniform Commercial Code,
Section 2-718: Liquidation or Limitation of Damages
Damages for breach may be liquidated in the agreement but only at an amount which is reasonable in the light of the anticipated or actual harm caused by the breach, the difficulties of proof of loss, and the inconvenience of obtaining an adequate remedy. A term fixing unreasonably large liquidated damages is void as a penalty.

Restatement (Second) of Contracts,
Section 356, Comment b.
Factor 1: The amount fixed is reasonable to the extent that it approximates the actual loss caused by the breach. Furthermore, the amount affixed is reasonable to the extent that it approximates the loss anticipated at the time of the making of the contract.
Factor 2: If the difficulty of proof is great, considerable latitude is allowed in the approximation of anticipated or actual harm.

Despite the growing similarities among the different legal systems, significant divergence remains. There are concepts within the civil law systems simply not found in common law. A review of the provisions taken from the French Civil Code demonstrates that there are foreign contract law principles still remaining that have no American law counterpart.

French Civil Code Section 1590

If the promise to sell was made with payment of a deposit (*arrhes*), each of the contracting parties is at liberty to withdraw: The one who paid the deposit, on forfeiting it, and the one who received it, on returning double the amount.

Section 1587
With regard to wine, oil and other things which it is customary to taste before buying, there is no sale so long as the buyer has not tasted and approved them.

> **Section 1674, 1681, & 1706**
> If the price of an immovable is inadequate by more than *seven-twelfths,* the seller has the right to demand rescission of the sale, even though he has expressly renounced in the contract the option to demand rescission. In case the action for rescission is upheld, the purchaser has the option either to return the thing upon recovering the price which he has paid, or to keep the property upon paying the balance of the *just price,* after deducting one-tenth of the total price. No rescission for inadequacy may take place in a barter contract.

Note the differences between the doctrine of *arrhes* and the normal deposit given in American business transactions. Does the doctrine of *arrhes* invite either party to breach the contract if they change their minds? Can the doctrine of *arrhes* be used as an implicit liquidated damages or penalty clause? Why are the inspection rights for wine and other similar products so different than what is found in most sale of goods transactions? Why do you think the just price provision allows the buyer to retain 10 percent of the value of the goods? Another example of idiosyncratic differences between the civil and common laws, is the civil law concept of *nachfrist* notice that has been adopted by the CISG in Articles 47-48 and 63. *Nachfrist* notice will be discussed in Chapter 7.

It is important also to realize that national differences in the requirements of and restrictions on contracting are often found throughout a country's regulatory network. These non-contract law regulations impact directly on contract issues. For example, Article 433 of the German Civil Code indicates that a producer or supplier of goods in an ongoing relationship (e.g., distribution agreement) has a "collateral obligation to have replacement parts ready for delivery even if there is no special agreement." In contrast, in the United States, issues of after-sales service and replacement parts supply are left to the private agreement of the contracting parties.

Another area of concern for the international entrepreneur is the difference between "law in fact" and "law in action." A number of countries have enacted modern, Westernized commercial codes, but uniformity in their interpretation and application is somewhat lacking. A classical example is the law of many Islamic countries where there is often a symbiotic relationship between religious and secular codes. The main body of law, the *Shari'a* is a body of religious, social, and legal mandates. The main body of this source of law was completed by the early tenth century, at least as practiced by the majority Sunni sect. However, beginning with the Ottoman Empire in the nineteenth century, "the *Shari'a* lost its exclusivity as the governing law of contracts to a combination of sacred and secular laws."[183] The secular laws have included a modern codification of contract and commercial law with which a Western businessperson would be quite comfortable. For example, Saudi Arabia has enacted a set of regulations including ones governing commercial law, negotiable instruments, and corporate law. The problem for an outside businessperson is that the principles of the *Shari'a* still take precedence over these secular statutes. Most of the judges in the secular court system have a religious training and their decisions are reviewed by a Commercial Board that ensures conformity with the dictates of the *Shari'a.*[184] The application and intrusion of religious principles into commercial law disputes is sporadic. However, it is also important to note that a party may seek to overcome a decision based upon the commercial codes by resorting to *Shari'a* principles. "Often it becomes a means of perverting the course of justice by allowing the strongest party in a dispute to select among the components of the law of contract those legal provisions which will settle that dispute on the most favorable terms."[185]

National Contract Codes and Restatements of Law

A person attempting to do business in a foreign country should make a good faith effort to acquaint herself with that country's contract and sales laws. Time constraints prevent a thorough examination, but the existence of restatements of law or statutory codes allow for a cursory review. Even a cursory review, however, will highlight some of the similarities and idiosyncrasies between home and host country laws. I have selected the Russian Civil Code, the Foreign Economic Contract Law of the People's Republic of China, and "The Principles of European Contract Law for review. The first two are examples of transitional economies enacting Western-style codes

[183]Nabil Saleh, *The Law Governing Contracts in Arabia,* 38 Int'l & Comparative Law Quarterly 761, 763 (1989).
[184]Ibid. at 765-766.
[185]Ibid. at 786-787.

compatible with an emerging market economy. The latter example is more of a "restatement" of general principles taken from the underlying national contract law systems.

Russian Civil Code

A special concern is the problem of assessing the laws in the countries of the former Soviet-bloc and those that remain under a centrally planned economy (China). The enormous change in the legal systems of the Soviet-bloc countries often means that the substantive and procedural laws are still in flux[186] and that their enforcement is uncertain. A brief look at selected provisions of the Russian Civil Code will illustrate some of the similarities and differences between this first generation commercial statute and American contract law. Chapter 9's coverage of intellectual property law will illustrate not only some of the substantive differences but also the problems with legal enforcement of these new substantive laws.

RUSSIAN CIVIL CODE

Article 158. Form of Transactions

1. Transactions shall be concluded orally or in written form (simple or notarial).
2. A transaction which may be concluded orally shall be considered to be concluded also when from the behavior of the person his will to conclude the transaction is manifest.
3. Silence shall be deemed to be an expression of will to conclude a transaction in the instances provided for by a law or by agreement of the parties.

---

[186]It was noted that in the first half-decade of transition "the Hungarian Parliament passed over 350 laws" aimed at effecting the transition to a market-oriented system. Ilonka Jankovich, *Recent Developments in Privatization Laws, Banking Laws, and Dispute Resolution in Hungary,* in, GINSBURGS, BARRY & SIMONS at 529.

Article 159. Oral Transactions

1. A transaction for which the written (simple or notarial) form has not been established by a law or by agreement of the parties may be concluded orally.
2. Unless otherwise established by agreement of the parties, all transactions to be performed by those who concluded them themselves may be oral, except for transactions for which the notarial form has been established and transactions the failure to comply with the simple written form of which entails their invalidity.
3. Transactions in performance of a contract concluded in written form may, by agreement of the parties, be concluded orally unless this is contrary to a law, other legal acts, or a contract.

Article 160. Written Form of Transaction

1. A transaction in written form must be concluded by means of drawing up a document reflecting the content thereof and signed by the person or persons concluding the transaction, or by persons duly empowered by them. Additional requirements to which the form of the transaction must conform may be established by a law, other legal acts, and by agreement of the parties (conclusion on a letterhead of a specified form; affixing of seal, and others), and consequences provided for the failure to comply with these requirements. If such consequences have not been provided, the consequences of the failure to comply with the simple written form of a transaction shall apply.
2. The use when concluding a transaction of a facsimile reproduction of a signature with the assistance of mechanical or other means of copying, electronic-cypher signature, or other analogue of a signature in one's own hand shall be permitted in the instances and procedure provided for by a law, other legal acts, or by agreement of the parties.
3. If a citizen as a consequence of physical defect, illness, or illiteracy can not sign in his own hand, then at his request another citizen may sign the transaction. The signature of the last must be certified

by a notary or by another official having the right to perform such a notarial action, specifying the reasons by virtue of which the person concluding the transaction could not sign it in his own hand. However, when concluding the transactions specified in Article 195(4) of the present Code and powers of attorney to conclude them, the signature of he who signs the transaction may be certified also by the organization in which the citizen who can not sign in his own hand works or by the administration of the inpatient treatment institution in which he is situated for care.

Article 161. Transactions Concluded in Simple Written Form

1. There must be concluded in simple written form, except for transactions requiring notarial certification:
   (1) transactions of juridical persons between themselves and with citizens;
   (2) transactions of citizens between themselves for an amount exceeding not less than ten times the minimum amount of payment of labour, and in the instances provided for by a law, irrespective of the amount of the transaction.
2. Compliance with the simple written form shall not be required for transactions which in accordance with Article 159 of the present Code may be concluded orally.

Article 162. Consequences of Failure to Comply with Simple Written Form of Transaction

1. The failure to comply with the simple written form of a transaction shall deprive the parties of the right in the event of a dispute to refer in confirmation of the transaction and its conditions to witness testimony, but shall not deprive them of the right also to cite written and other evidence.
2. In the instances expressly specified in a law or in the agreement of the parties the failure to comply with the simple written form of a transaction shall entail its invalidity.

3. The failure to comply with the simple written form of a foreign economic transaction shall entail the invalidity of the transaction.

Article 163. Notarially Certified Transactions

The notarial certification of a transaction shall be effectuated by means of the performing on the document of an endorsement of certification corresponding to the requirements of Article 160 of the present Code by a notary or other official having the right to perform such a notarial action.

Article 165. Consequences of Failure to Comply with Notarial Form of Transaction and Requirements for Registration Thereof

1. The failure to comply with the notarial form, and in the instances established by a law, the requirements concerning State registration of a transaction shall entail its invalidity. Such a transaction shall be considered to be void.
2. If one of the parties wholly or partially has performed a transaction requiring notarial certification, and the other party has evaded such certification of the transaction, the court shall have the right at the demand of the party who performed the transaction to deem the transaction to be valid. In this event subsequent notarial certification of the transaction shall not be required.
3. If a transaction requiring State registration has been concluded in the proper form but one of the parties evades the registration thereof, a court shall have the right at the demand of the other party to render a decision concerning registration of the transaction. In this event the transaction shall be registered in accordance with the decision of the court.

Article 427. Model Conditions of Contracts

1. It may be provided in a contract that its individual conditions shall be determined by model conditions worked out for contracts of the respective type and published in the press.

2. In instances when a reference to the model conditions is not contained in the contract, such model conditions shall apply to the relations of the parties as customs of business turnover if they correspond to the requirements established by Article 5 and by Article 421 (5) of the present Code.
3. Model conditions may be set out in the form of a model contract or other document containing these conditions.

Article 428. Contract of Adhesion

1. A contract of adhesion shall be deemed to be a contract whose conditions have been determined by one of the parties in records or other standard forms and which can be accepted by the other party not other than by means of adhering to the contract as a whole being offered.

...

4. A party which has adhered to the contract shall have the right to demand dissolution or change of the contract if the contract of adhesion, although not contrary to a law and other legal acts, deprives this party of the rights usually granted under contracts of that type, excludes or limits the responsibility of the other party for a violation of obligations, or contains conditions clearly burdensome for the adhering party which it, proceeding from its own reasonably understandable interests, would not accept if it had the opportunity to participate in determining the conditions of the contract.
5. When the circumstances provided for in point 2 of the present Article are present, the demand concerning dissolution or change of the contract presented by a party which has adhered to a contract in connection with the effectuation of its entrepreneurial activity shall not be subject to satisfaction, if the adhering party knew or should have known on what conditions the contract is concluded.

Article 429. Preliminary Contract

1. Under a preliminary contract the parties shall be obliged to conclude in future a contract concerning the transfer of property, ful-

fillment of work, or rendering of services (principal contract) on the conditions provided for by the preliminary contract.

2. The preliminary contract shall be concluded in the form established for the principal contract, and if the form of the principal contract has not been established, then in written form. The failure to comply with the rules concerning the form of the preliminary contract shall entail its being void.
3. A preliminary contract must contain conditions enabling the establishment of the subject, and also the other material conditions, of the principal contract.
4. A preliminary contract shall specify the period in which the parties are obliged to conclude the principal contract. If such period has not been determined in the preliminary contract, the principal contract shall be subject to conclusion within a year from the moment of concluding the preliminary contract.

Article 451. Change and Dissolution of Contract in Connection with Material Change of Circumstances

1. A material change of circumstances from which the parties proceeded when concluding a contract shall be a ground for the change or dissolution thereof unless provided otherwise by the contract or it arises from the essence thereof. A change of circumstances shall be deemed to be material when they have changed such that if the parties could reasonably foresee this, the contract would not have been concluded at all by them or it would have been concluded on significantly differing conditions.
2. If the parties have not reached agreement concerning bringing the contract into conformity with the materially changed circumstances or the dissolution thereof, the contract may be dissolved, and on the grounds provided for by point 4 of the present Article, changed by a court at the request of the interested party when the following conditions are present:
   (1) at the moment of concluding the contract the parties proceeded from the fact that such a change of circumstances would not occur;
   (2) the change of circumstances has been caused by reasons which the interested party could not overcome after they arose with that

degree of concern and care which are required of him by the character of the contract and the conditions of turnover;

(3) the performance of the contract without a change of its conditions would so violate the correlation of property interests of the parties which correspond to the contract and entail for the interested party such damage it would be deprived to a significant degree of that which it had the right to count on when concluding the contract;

(4) it does not arise from the customs of business turnover or the essence of the contract that the risk of the change of circumstances is borne by the interested party.

3. In the event of the dissolution of a contract as a consequence of a material change of circumstances the court at the demand of any of the parties shall determine the consequences of the dissolution of the contract by proceeding from the need for a just distribution between the parties of the expenses incurred by them in connection with the performance of this contract.
4. The change of a contract in connection with a material change of circumstances shall be permitted by decision of a court in exceptional instances when dissolution of the contract is contrary to social interests or entails damage for the parties which significantly exceeds the expenditures needed to perform the contract on the conditions changed by the court.

Article 469. Quality of Good

1. The seller shall be obliged to transfer a good to the purchaser when quality corresponds to the contract of purchase-sale.
2. In the absence in a contract of purchase-sale of conditions concerning the quality of a good the seller shall be obliged to transfer to the purchaser a good fit for the purposes for which a good of such nature is usually used. If the seller when concluding the contract was given notice by the purchaser of the specific purposes for the acquisition of the good, the seller shall be obliged to transfer to the purchaser a good fit for use in accordance with these purposes.
3. In the event of the sale of a good according to a sample and/or description, the seller shall be obliged to transfer to the purchaser of a good which corresponds to the sample and/or description.

4. If obligatory requirements for the quality of a good being sold have been provided in the procedure established by a law, then the seller effectuating entrepreneurial activity shall be obliged to transfer a good to the purchaser which corresponds to these obligatory requirements. By agreement between the seller and the purchaser a good may be transferred which corresponds to higher quality requirements in comparison with the obligatory requirements established in the procedure provided for by a law.

Article 475. Consequences of Transfer of Good of Improper Quality

1. If the defects of a good were not stipulated by the seller, the purchaser to whom the good of improper quality was transferred shall have the right at his choice to require from the seller: commensurate reduction of the purchase price; elimination without compensation of the defects of the good within a reasonable period; compensation of his expenses to eliminate the defects of the good.
2. In the event of a material violation of the requirements for the quality of a good (discovery of unremovable defects, defects which can not be eliminated without incommensurate expenses or expenditures of time or are elicited repeatedly, or manifest themselves anew after their elimination, and other similar defects), the purchaser shall have the right at his choice to: refuse to perform the contract of purchase-sale and to require the return of the monetary amount paid for the good; require the replacement of the good of improper quality by a good corresponding to the contract.

Taken from a broad perspective, the new Russian Civil Code displays many of the principles and concepts found in American contract law. Article 158 allows silence as a means of acceptance only if there was a prior agreement of the parties. Article 160 defines the requirements of the written form more broadly and is more modern than the definition currently found in Article 2 of the UCC. Paragraph 2 of Article 160 states that "the use when concluding a transaction of a facsimile reproduction of a signature with the assistance of mechanical or other means of copying, electronic-cypher signature, or other analogue of a signature in one's own hand shall be permitted in the instances and procedure provided by a law, other legal acts, or by agreement of the parties." Section 162, paragraph 3 expressly notes that foreign economic transactions are invalid unless in writing. Although oral contracts are recognized in some instances, the Civil Code places strong emphasis on formalities including the written form, notarial certifications, and in some cases, governmental registration. As a general rule, a foreign party should not contemplate moving forward on a business transaction without a formal written contract. It is also good practice, even if not technically required in a given transaction, for the parties' signatures to be notarized.

Section 428 recognizes the American notion of the contract of adhesion. It grants to the party that adhered to the contract a right to demand dissolution. Thus, terms that are not contrary to the law may be voided if they deprive the adhering party of the rights "usually granted under contracts of that type, or excludes or limits the responsibility of the other party." The importance of disclosure as a means to preclude the right to demand dissolution is also recognized. The adhering party cannot demand dissolution if he "knew or should have known on what conditions the contract is concluded." Section 451 recognizes an excuse for a "material change of circumstances." Paragraph 2 lists four conditions similar to those found in American excuse doctrines: (1) the contract was premised on the change of circumstances not occurring, (2) the party could not avoid the occurrence even when using reasonable care, (3) the occurrence materially alters the contract, and (4) it was not an allocated risk under the contract or through industry custom.

Article 429 recognizes the preliminary contract that is not recognized under American law. The parties have an affirmative obligation to conclude the contract under the Russian notion of preliminary contract. If the parties fail to provide a time for concluding the contract, then the law provides that it should be concluded within one year from the conclusion of the preliminary contract. Thus, the potential for pre-contractual liability seems to be much greater under the Russian Civil Code than under American law. Of course, the notion of a preliminary contract can be seen as a misnomer. It can be considered as a contract unto itself.

The final topic to be examined is the recognition of implied warranties. Paragraph 2 of Section 469 adopts the language, but not the nomenclature of the UCC's warranty of merchantability and warranty for a particular purpose. However, it provides a broader selection of remedial options to the receiving party. Like the CISG,[187] the buyer is granted a price reduction option. Under, the UCC the buyer must pay in full and then make a claim for damages under a breach of warranty claim. The price reduction remedy allows the buyer to reduce the price based on the diminishment of value caused by the defect. Also, Russian Civil Code allows the buyer the option to demand specific performance by requiring "the replacement of the good of improper quality by a good corresponding to the contract."

China's Foreign Economic Contracts Law

Another interesting codification of contract law, aimed at facilitating international trade, is the *Law of the People's Republic of China on Economic Contracts Involving Foreign Parties* (*Foreign Economic Contracts Law*). The law is divided into seven chapters: Chapter 1 deals with general provisions, Chapter 2 deals with contract formation, Chapter 3 deals with performance and remedies including the issues of breach, non-performance, *force majeure*, and liquidated damages, Chapter 4 deals with the transfer and assignments of rights, Chapter 5 deals with the modification and termination of contracts, Chapter 6 deals with dispute resolution, and Chapter 7 provides miscellaneous provisions including a statute of limitations. An important consideration is the authority of the Chinese party to the negotiations. The law applies to Chinese "enterprises or other economic organizations." It is important to determine that the other party is a member of such an entity and has authority to negotiate a foreign contract.[188]

A reading of the law reveals a great many similarities with the Anglo-American common law of contracts. Article 17 is a version of the American concepts of anticipatory repudiation and adequate assurance. Upon providing "definite evidence" of breach and the giving of "immediate notice," a party "may temporarily suspend performance." However, such suspension must cease if the other party "has provided a complete guarantee." Article 17, however, does note seem to allow for the anticipation of breach, only the suspension of performance on the occurrence of a breach. It also fails to de-

[187]See, Chapter 7.

[188]See generally, Zhang Yuqing & James S. McLean, *China's Foreign Economic Contract Law: Its Significance and Analysis,* 8 Northwestern Journal of Int'l Law & Business 120 (1987).

fine "complete guarantee" or "definite evidence." Article 19 adopts the *Hadley v. Baxendale* limitation on damages. Damages are not to exceed those that "should have been foreseen by the party breaching the contract." Article 20 is a general adoption of the American law of liquidated damages. Contracting parties "may agree on a certain amount of damages to be paid for breach." However, such stipulated damages may be reduced or increased by an arbitration panel or a court of law if they are "excessively higher or lower than the losses [actually] resulting." Such excessive damages would be considered as an unenforceable penalty under American law.[189] Article 22 adopts the common law's principle of mitigation. The non-breaching party "should take appropriate measures in a timely manner to prevent the increase of losses." Articles 24 and 25 recognize the excuse of *force majeure.* The requirements for a *force majeure* event are outlined in Article 24. Such events "shall mean events that are *unforeseeable*" at the time of contracting and whose "occurrence is *unavoidable* and cannot be overcome by the parties." The breaching party is required by Article 25 to notify the other party in a timely manner.

The foreign party should be aware of the high degree of formality required under the *Foreign Economic Contracts Law.* The law requires that all contracts be formalized in writing. It should be noted that the law does recognize the applicability of the CISG. The CISG does not require a writing in order to form a contract. However, China opted out of that provision. Therefore, an export or sale of goods contract must be in writing under Chinese law. In fact, Article 32 requires that any alteration or rescission of the contract must also be in written form. Article 7 does recognize that in international transactions there may be an exchange of instruments and not a single contractual document. It recognizes that an agreement may be reached through the exchange of letters, cables, or telexes, but it mandates that a contract is only formed when a "written confirmation is signed." The *Foreign Economic Contracts Law* also indicates that the written contract should display a high degree of certainty of terms. Article 12 states that contracts should contain the following provisions:

(1) title, name, nationality, and place of business of the parties,
(2) the date and place of its signing,

---

[189]See, U.C.C. § 2-718.

(3) the contract type, along with the category and scope of contractual objectives,
(4) objectives regarding technology terms, quality, standard, specifications and quantity,
(5) the time limit, place, and method of performance,
(6) conditions on price, amount, and method of payment,
(7) terms and conditions for assignment,
(8) compensation and liabilities for breach,
(9) methods of settlement,
(10) language of the contract.

Article 13 requires that the parties agree to the "limits of risk" and when necessary "the scope of insurance." Other articles provide a number of seemingly non-mandatory contract provisions. For long-term contracts Article 14 suggests that the parties should agree on "conditions for extension" and for early termination of the contract. Article 37, although not mandating alternative dispute resolution, encourages the meditation and then arbitration of any disputes. Finally, the law provides a four-year *statute of limitations* for bringing a lawsuit. The period begins from the "date the party knew or should have known that his rights were infringed."

Principles of European Contract Law

In 1998, the European Union's Commission on Contract published its revised *Principles of European Contract Law* (*Principles*).[190] The stated purpose of the *Principles* was to respond to a "need for a Community-wide infrastructure of contract law to consolidate the rapidly expanding volume of Community law regulating specific types of contracts."[191] Article 1.101 states that the Principles will apply to a contract dispute in two main scenarios; the parties selection of them as their choice of law and when the contract is to be governed by general principles of law or the *lex mercatoria.* The former scenario is likely to occur when the contracting parties are in disagreement over the application of a given national law. The *Principles,*

[190]See Appendix for complete copy.

[191]The *Principles of European Contract Law* may be accessed at http://www.jus.uio.no/lm/eu.contract. principles.1998/doc.html.

like the CISG, serve as a broad, fairly written compromise choice of law alternative. The CISG is a better choice in a sale of goods transaction, while the *Principles* apply to all types of contracts. The second scenario is likely to occur in the setting of international arbitration. Arbitrators, at times, want to avoid the application of an idiosyncratic rule of national law in favor of a "fairer" general principle found in international customary law. In time, arbitrators may recognize the Principles as evidence of customary law.[192]

A review of the *Principles* demonstrate a large amount of similarity with the United States' common law of contracts and the UCC. It also shows a number of significant differences that potentially could lead to unexpected liabilities to one who is only familiar with American law. The following review outlines some of the differences, along with noting comparative provisions in the CISG. One caveat should be noted: the American businessperson will find a great deal more of common ground than differences when comparing the *Principles* with American contract law. However, it is important to understand the differences in order to avoid certain liabilities. For example, the *Principles* adopt the CISG's approach to formalities. Article 2.101 is almost identical to Article 11 of the CISG: "A contract need not be concluded or evidenced in writing nor is it subject to any other requirement as to form. The contract may be proved by any means, including witnesses." Thus, the American businessperson must be aware that the statute of frauds or the parol evidence rule will not preclude breach of contract claims based upon oral representations. Ironically, despite rejecting statute of fraud requirements, the *Principles* give a definition of *written statements.* It defines written statements to include "communications made by telegram, telex, telefax and electronic mail and other means of communication capable of providing a readable record of the statement on both sides." The interesting feature of the definition is its breadth. Electronic means of communication are considered writings as long as they provide a "record."[193]

The *Principles* go farther than even the CISG[194] in rejecting provisions that reduce the admissibility of evidence in a contract dispute. The enforceability of common contract clauses, such as written modification and

[192]See coverage of the CISG as evidence of international customary law in Chapter 7.
[193]See, Chapter 11 on Electronic Contracting.
[194]See, CISG at Article 29(2).

merger clauses, is jeopardized under Articles 2.105 and 2.106. A *written modification clause* that requires a writing to make any changes to the contract only provides a presumption. The other party may still introduce parol evidence in order to rebut the presumption. It further states that "a party may by its statements or conduct be precluded from asserting such a clause." Also, a boilerplate *merger clause* found in a standard form or in the general conditions[195] section of a contract does not fair very well under the *Principles.* The standard merger clause states that the document into which it is incorporated is a final integration of the parties' agreement and supercedes all other statements, writings, or correspondences. A merger clause that is *individually negotiated* will be enforced otherwise, the clause only establishes a presumption. However, even when fully negotiated the clause can be avoided in the case of ambiguity in the contract or on grounds of waiver. Article 2.105 states that "the parties' prior statements may be used to interpret the contract." Regarding subsequent statements and conduct, it provides that such statements and conduct may preclude a party "from asserting a merger clause to the extent that the other party has reasonably relied."

In the area of notice, the *Principles* state that notice becomes effective "when it reaches the addressee." It qualifies this rule by stating that a properly dispatched notice of non-performance, which is subsequently lost or delayed in transmission, "shall have effect from the time at which it would have arrived under normal circumstances."[196] Notice plays a much larger role in the actual negotiation of contract terms than it does under the common law system. Article 2.104 states that "contract terms which have not been individually negotiated may be invoked against a party who did not know of them only if the party invoking them took reasonable steps to bring them to the other party's attention before or when the contract is concluded." Note that the individual negotiation rule is not confined to standard form contracting or merchant to consumer transactions. Article 4.110 allows a party to void an unfair term that was not individually negotiated.

---

[195]The following definition of *general conditions* is provided in Article 2.209(3) (Conflicting General Conditions): "General conditions of contract are terms which have been formulated in advance for an indefinite number of contracts of a certain nature, and which have not been individually negotiated between the parties."
[196]See, Article 1.303 (Notice).

It defines "unfair" as a term that "causes a significant imbalance in the parties' rights and obligations."[197]

A number of rules in the area of *offer* should be noted. First, the exporter should beware that a circular, advertisement, or proposal, considered by him as an invitation to offer, may be construed as a standing offer under the *Principles.* Article 2.201 states that "a proposal to supply goods or services at stated prices made by a professional supplier in a public advertisement or a catalogue, or by a display of goods, is *presumed* to be an offer to sell or supply at that price until the stock of goods, or the supplier's capacity to supply the service, is exhausted." Second, the firm offer principle is expanded to further restrict the maker of an offer's ability to revoke the offer. Unlike Section 2-205 of the Uniform Commercial Code, the offer need not be from a merchant, be in writing, signed, or not be for a period greater than three months. An offer may not be revoked if it indicates that it is irrevocable or fixes a time for acceptance. Thus, a statement that the offeree must accept within ninety days will be interpreted to be a firm offer for ninety days. Under American law, the offer would self-terminate after ninety days, but nothing prevents the offeror from prematurely revoking the offer; the offer must expressly assure the receiving party that the offer will remain open for a fixed period of time. More importantly, any offer may be recognized as a firm offer if it is "reasonable for the offeree to rely on the offer being irrevocable and the offeree has acted in reliance on the offer." Thus, the offer need not give any assurance that it is to remain open.[198]

In the area of acceptance, not surprisingly, the common law's dispatch or "mailbox rule is rejected for the civil law's receipt rule. A contract is concluded when the acceptance reaches the offeror.[199] It would seem that the latter time for acceptance would provide the offeror with an additional period to revoke the offer. But, like Article 18 of the CISG, the right to revoke an offer is frozen when the acceptance is dispatched[200] even though the acceptance is not effective until receipt. However, in the event that the accep-

[197]Article 4.110 makes an exception for terms that provide the "main subject matter of the contract" and are provided in "plain and intelligible language." Also, the adequacy of value exchanged between the parties is not a ground for voiding a term. See, Article 4.110(2)(b) (Unfair Terms Not Individually Negotiated).

[198]See also, CISG Article 16.

[199]Principles at Article 2.205 (Time of Conclusion of the Contract).

[200]Principles at Article 2.202 (Revocation of an Offer).

tance does not reach the offeror within a reasonable time, then it would seem that the revocation would be unfrozen and preclude the formation of a contract. In the case where a revocation has not already been sent, a late acceptance due to problems of transmission gives the offeror the option to reject the acceptance if he informs the offeree, "without delay," that the offer has lapsed.[201]

The *battle of forms* scenario[202] commonly found in international sale of goods transactions is dealt with in Article 2.208 titled "Modified Acceptance" and Article 2.209 titled "Conflicting General Conditions." The offeree's form that gives a definite assent to the offer creates a contract unless it possesses additional or different terms that materially alter the offer. Article 2.208 recognizes that the parties can include contract language to control the battle of the forms scenario. First, the offeror may incorporate a clause in its offer to the effect that it "expressly limits acceptance to the terms of the offer." Second, the offeree may condition its acceptance upon the offeror's assent to its additional terms. This Article requires that the offeror must expressly agree to the additional terms in order for the conditional acceptance to effectuate a contract. An agreement to the additional terms can be obtained by the offeree when he requires the offeror to sign and return the conditional acceptance. A conditional acceptance will be treated as a rejection if the offeror's assent to the additional or different terms "does not reach the offeree within a reasonable time. Article 2.209 provides that the fine print terms in offer and acceptance forms will generally be considered as "general conditions." As such, only the general conditions that are "common in substance" become a part of the contract. Thus, conflicting general conditions would not become a part of the contract.

The *Principles* also recognize a general area of pre-contractual liability and the duty of good faith negotiation not recognized under American contract law. The very real possibility of unexpected liability was discussed earlier in this chapter in the section on "Pre-Contractual Instruments." It is sufficient for our current purposes to note that parties have a general duty to negotiate in good faith. Failure to do so, such as never intending to enter into a contract, is grounds for contractual liability. Thus, the American perspective of terminating a negotiation without giving a viable reason is not

[201]Ibid. at Article 2.207(2) (Late Acceptance).

[202]Compare U.C.C. §2-207 and CISG Article 19.

an appropriate approach. A party can be held liable for losses caused to the other party.[203] Furthermore, either party to a negotiation may be held liable for a breach of confidentiality. Article 2.302 (Breach of Confidentiality) recognizes an affirmative duty not to disclose confidential information obtained in the course of negotiations. Also, statements made during the negotiations may provide separate grounds for an action. Article 6.101 (Statements Giving Rise to Contractual Obligation) states that a professional supplier gives information about the quality or uses of services or goods when marketing or advertising or otherwise before a contract is concluded then the "statement is to be treated as giving rise to a contractual obligation." This pre-contractual line of obligation is further extended to agents of the supplier. The supplier is contractually liable for statements made "by a person in *earlier links* of the business chain." It is imperative that the exporter-supplier review his advertisements, promotional brochures, and practices of foreign sales representatives in order to avoid such liability.

A unique feature of the *Principles* is its coverage of the agency relationship. Since the agency relationship is common in international transactions, such as in the hiring of a foreign sales representative or distributor, the section on agency law is apropos. Its coverage of the agency contract is limited to the relationship between third parties and the principle or agent. It does not govern the relationship between the principal and agent. The rules on agency are divided into those governing direct representation and those governing indirect representation. Direct representation is when the agent acts in the name of the principal. In contrast, indirect representation exists when a third party is unaware that the agent is acting as an agent. This section is consistent with most of the agency rules found in common law. However, a number of its specific rules are of note. First, in the case where the agent represents that it is acting as agent, it must identify the principal within a reasonable time of entering into the contract upon the request of the third party. If the agent unduly delays in disclosing the principal, then the agent becomes bound by the contract.[204] Second, if the third party is in doubt regarding the authority of the agent, "it may send a written confirmation to the principal or request ratification" from the principal.[205] If the

[203]Article 3.101 (Negotiations Contrary to Good Faith).

[204]Principles at Article 3.203 (Unidentified Principal).

[205]Ibid. at Article 3.208 (Third Party's Right with Respect to Confirmation of Authority).

principal does not respond in a timely fashion, then the agent's act is treated as being authorized.

In the area of genuineness of assent, *Principles* recognize many of the same contract avoiding events found in the common law. The terminology in parenthesis is the common law equivalent to the invalidating rule found in the *Principles.* Thus a party has the right to avoid a contract due to: Mistake as to Facts or Law (unilateral mistake),[206] Mutual Mistake,[207] Fraud,[208] Threats (duress),[209] Unfair Advantage (undue influence),[210] and Unfair Terms (unconscionability).[211] In the area of mutual mistake, the court is directly charged not with rescinding the contract but rather adapting (reforming) the contract. It states that "where both parties made the same mistake, the court may at the request of either party bring the contract into accordance with what might reasonably have been agreed had the mistake not occurred." The notion of economic duress is not placed under the threats (duress) umbrella but is placed within the notion of unfair advantage (undue influence). A party may avoid a contract if at the time of contracting "it was dependent on or had a relationship of trust with the other party, was in *economic distress* or had urgent needs, was improvident, ignorant, inexperienced or lacking bargaining skills." In contrast, the notion that the party had "no reasonable alternative" is found in the article on threats. The article on fraud recognizes a substantial duty to disclose information. The general duty of good faith and fair dealing is applied to require a duty to disclose under certain circumstances. The factors to be considered include whether one of the parties had "special expertise," the cost of obtaining the information, whether the other party could reasonably have acquired the information on his own, and whether the information would have been material to the decision-maker.[212]

In the area of interpretation, a number of traditional rules of interpretation are adopted. First, contractual ambiguity is strictly construed against the drafter under the *contra proferentem rule.* Second, terms of the contract

---

[206]Article 4.103 (Mistake as to Facts or Law).
[207]Article 4.105(3) (Adaptation of Contract).
[208]Article 4.107 (Fraud).
[209]Article 4.108 (Threats).
[210]Article 4.109 (Excessive Benefit or Unfair Advantage).
[211]Article 4.110 (Unfair Terms which have not been Individually Negotiated).
[212]Article 4.109(3) (Fraud).

are to be interpreted so that they are consistent with the contract as a whole. Alternatively, as under the civil law, other terms of the contract can be used by analogy to interpret ambiguous terms or imply missing terms. The *Principles* also recognize an excuse when an interpretation of contractual performance becomes a hardship due to a *change of circumstances.* Article 6.111 defines hardship as when a performance becomes "excessively onerous." In that case, the parties are obligated, unlike the common law, to enter into negotiations for purposes of adjusting the contract. In the event that the parties fail to reach an agreement within a reasonable time, a court may adjust or terminate the contract. Failure to negotiate in good faith gives the other party the right to sue for damages for bad faith.[213]

The *Principles* do adopt the notion of anticipatory repudiation and adequate assurance found in the Uniform Commercial Code.[214] Article 8.105 simply states that if one party reasonably believes that there will be a fundamental non-performance by the other party, then it may withhold performance and demand adequate assurance. In the area of the delivery of non-conforming goods, the seller has an expanded right to cure under the *Principles.* Section 2-508 of the Uniform Commercial Code allows the seller the right to cure only until the date specified for performance in the contract. The *Principles* allow the seller to cure even after the date of performance has passed if the "delay would not be such as to constitute a fundamental non-performance."[215] Furthermore, the *Principles,* as well as the CISG, adopt the civil law notion of *nachfrist* notice.[216] The non-performing party may obtain an extension of the time of performance by giving notice to the other party. Generally, the extension must be given unless the non-breaching party gives a commercially viable reason for not granting the extension. After the expiration of the extension, the non-breaching party may terminate the contract even for minor breaches. There is no such provision for requesting or granting additional time in American law.

In the area of contractual excuse and remedies for breach, the *Principles* adopt civil law rules not consistent with common law contracts. Article 8.108 recognizes the notion of impediment as a ground to excuse a breach-

[213]Article 6.111(3) (b) (Change of Circumstances).

[214]U.C.C. §§ 2-609 & 2-610. See also, CISG Articles 71-73.

[215]Article 8.104 (Cure by Non-Performing Party). Article 37 of the CISG provides a right to cure only up to the delivery date in the contract and only if it does not cause the buyer "unreasonable inconvenience or expense."

[216]See, CISG Article 47 & 63.

ing party for his non-performance. The test of impediment is similar to that found in the common law excuse doctrines. The impediment must not have been "reasonably expected," and must be beyond the control of the non-performing party.[217] The non-performing party must give prompt notice of the impediment or be liable for damages resulting from the non-receipt of the notice. In the event that the impediment is perceived to be temporary in nature, the non-performing party is not excused from the contract but is granted a temporary suspension of performance. In the area of remedies there are two fundamental differences when comparing the *Principles* with American law. First, the remedy of *price reduction* is given to the buyer of non-conforming goods. Under the UCC, the buyer may either reject non-conforming goods under the "perfect tender rule"[218] or accept the goods, pay in full, and make a breach of warranty claim. The price reduction remedy, also found in the CISG,[219] allows the buyer to unilaterally reduce the price paid for the goods based on the diminution of value due to the non-conformity. Second, the right to specific performance is not considered an extraordinary remedy. Article 9.102 simply states that "the aggrieved party is entitled to specific performance, including the remedying of a defective performance." In contrast, the UCC adopts the common law rule that specific performance is only warranted when the goods are *unique.*[220] Third, the liquidated damages clause is recognized in Article 9.509 (Agreed Payment for Non-Performance). It allows for the awarding of such stipulated damages fixed in the liquidated damages clause irrespective of the actual loss suffered but allows the court to reduce the amount where it is *grossly excessive.*

Conflict of Law Rules

How do courts determine which national laws apply in a given case? Generally, absent a choice of law clause, the law of the country most *closely connected* to the agreement will govern. Sometimes the courts may apply the principle of *depecage* to apply different governing laws to different parts of

---

[217]Article 8.108 (Excuse Due to an Impediment). Compare, U.C.C. § 2-615 (impracticability) and CISG Article 74.

[218]U.C.C. §2-601 (perfect tender rule).

[219]See, CISG Article 50.

[220]U.C.C. § 2-716 (Buyer's Right to Specific Performance or Replevin).

the contract. In short, different parts of the contract may have closer connections to different countries. The country of closest connection will often be the country of the residence of the performing party. If a specific contract clause or issue is invalid in a country with a close connection to the contract, that country's laws may be deferred to because of its strong interest in enforcing its laws and public policies. The doctrine of *renvoi* is when a court uses another country's conflict of law rules which direct the court to apply its own country's law. Other factors considered include the place the contract was negotiated, the place the contract was signed, the place of performance, and the place where the breach occurred.

Prior to drafting a contract and a choice of law clause, the conflict of law rules in the national law of the other party should be researched. This will help determine whether an express choice of law clause will be needed and if so, the factors used to determine if the national court will honor the choice of law selection. The following conflict of law rules are found in Hungarian law (Exhibit 5.1).[221]

Exhibit 5.1: Hungarian Conflict of Law Rules

Specific Rules

Sale/purchase contracts	law of the country of the seller
Lease contract	law of the country of the lessor
Banking/credit contract	law of the country of the financial institution
Employment contract	law of the country in which the services are performed when services are to be performed in more than one country, then law of the country of the employer

General Default Rule

specific rules are not applicable	law of the country of the party performing the principle obligation

[221]Jankovich at 538.

In the area of forum selection, Hungarian law illustrates the common phenomena that it is easier to enforce an arbitral award, as compared to a judicial award, in many countries. Also, the uncertainty of dispute resolution in a foreign country is generally more manageable through arbitration instead of resorting to the national court system. This is especially true of former Soviet-bloc countries and developing countries where the enforcement of new substantive laws is uncertain and uneven. Furthermore, even when enforced the remedies granted may be insufficient to fully protect the contract and property rights of the foreign party. "In general, arbitral awards rendered in other states that are contracting states (New York Convention) are readily enforceable in Hungarian courts."[222] Regarding arbitration in Hungary, it is best to select arbitration through the Hungarian Chamber of Commerce. The Chamber operates under the 1976 UNCITRAL Arbitration Rules and allows for the appointment of foreign arbitrators.

Issue Specific Regulations: Marking and Standards

"Marking" requirements are found in most national customs laws. Section 304(a) of the United States Tariff Act of 1930 states that "every article of foreign origin imported into the United States shall be marked in a conspicuous place as legibly, indelibly, and permanently as the nature of the article will permit in such a manner as to indicate to an ultimate purchaser in the United States the English name of the country of origin of the article."[223] The Customs Regulations dealing with this marking requirement are found at 19 C.F.R. § 134. Civil actions pertaining to the marking requirements are placed with the Court of International Trade.

Another area of concern is the imposition of national-specific requirements of product standards and certifications. For example, a European Union requirement mandates metric-only labeling of United States exports.[224] At the international level, standards, certifications, and testing pro-

---

[222]Ibid. at 538.

[223]19 U.S.C. § 1304(a) (1982). See generally, David Silverstein, *Country-Of-Origin Marking Requirements: Under Section 304 of the Tariff Act: An Importer's Map Through the Maze,* 25 American Bus. Law Journal 285 (1987). See also, Joseph A. LaNasa III, *Rules of Origin and the Uruguay Round's Effectiveness in Harmonizing and Regulating Them,* 90 American Journal of Int'l Law 625 (1996).

[224]It should be noted that the date of implementation of metric-only labelling may be postponed until the year 2005 or perhaps the year 2010.

cedures vary widely from country to country. The trend, however, is in the direction of harmonization. The success of ISO (International Standards Organization) standards,[225] and the inclusion of standards provisions in NAFTA and GATT, evidences the weakening of national standards as obstacles to international trade. The activities of the European Union (EU) deserve special attention. EU requirements include the placement of a CE mark by the manufacturer on all regulated products. Importers who obtain the CE mark will be guaranteed access to the markets of all members of the European Union. The CE mark relates to the mandatory health, safety, and environmental requirements of the EU. The CE mark cannot be affixed unless the product complies to all relevant directives pertaining to that type of product. Therefore, in the area of products' standards, the exporter is still confronted with the need to conform to both EU and individual national standards. A newer development is the establishment of a voluntary mark known as the "EU Ecolabel." Products without the Ecolabel may still enter the EU, but the label, if used, replaces the existing national equivalents. In order to obtain an Ecolabel, the manufacturer must show that its products are less harmful to the environment than similar products.

The latest EU technical standards may be accessed through the Standards Information Service of the National Institute of Standards and Technology (NIST) at (301) 975-4040. This service obtains the most recent information published by the two European standards organizations, the European Committee for Standards (CEN) and the European Committee for Electrotechnical Standardization (CENLEC). Other sources include the American National Standards Institute (ANSI), 1430 Broadway, New York, New York 10018, (212) 354-3300 and the Department of Commerce's National Technical Information Service at (703) 557-4733.

In the area of service standards, the General Agreement on Trade in Services (GATS) requires that all countries review their laws so that "qualification requirements and procedures, technical standards and licensing re-

---

[225]See, e.g. Paulette L. Stenzel, *Can the ISO 14000 Series Environmental Management Standards Provide a Viable Alternative to Government Regulation?*, 37 American Business Law Journal 237 (2000). See also, MIKE MIRAMS & PAUL MCELHERON, GAINING AND MAINTAINING THE NEW QUALITY STANDARDS: THE BS EN 9000 TOOL KIT (1995). ISO 9000 SERIES QUALITY MANAGEMENT STANDARDS are available from the American National Standards Institute (ANSI), 11 West 42nd Street, New York, NY, 10036; Phone 212-624-4900; <http//www.ansi.org>.

quirements do not constitute unnecessary barriers to trade in services." Any such requirements should be "based on objective and transparent criteria." In the area of professional services, each country "shall provide for adequate procedures to verify the competence of professionals" of any other country.

Anti-Bribery Laws

The international entrepreneur should always be cautioned against partaking in activities that involve the corruption of a foreign official. Most national laws outlaw the payment of bribes in order to obtain a service, contract, license, approval, or other regulatory consideration from a government official. Unfortunately, anti-corruption laws in some countries are not enforced and the soliciting of bribes is openly practiced.[226] There is a temptation that in order to level the competitive playing field, the foreign businessperson will need to make bribes. For the American businessperson this is especially troublesome because of the severe civil and criminal penalties available through the Foreign Corrupt Practices Act.[227] The act applies extraterritorially to foreign activities of United States citizens, companies, and foreign entities controlled by them. Furthermore, a U.S. firm is liable for bribes made by its foreign agents. Actual knowledge of the bribery is not required; only that the firm should have been aware of a high probability of bribing need be shown. Incorporated within the Act is stringent accounting provisions that require companies doing business abroad to maintain records and auditing controls that provide reasonable assurances that unauthorized bribing is not occurring. A company will be liable for violating the accounting provisions even if no illegal bribing has occurred. Violations of the statute can result in fines as large as two million dollars for a company and imprisonment for up to five years for an individual.

The magnitude of foreign bribery has resulted in some recent movement at the international and regional levels. For example, on February 15, 1999 the OECD Convention on Combating Bribery of Foreign Public Offi-

[226]See generally, Transparency International, *Corruption Perception Index* at http://www.transparency.de/documents/cpi/index.html

[227] Amended in 1988 in 15 U.S.C. § 78. Further amended in 1998 by the International Anti-bribery and Fair Competition Act, 15 U.S.C. § 78 dd-1(a)(2)(iii) (1998).

cials in International Business Transactions went into effect.[228] The Convention provides a framework and guidance to signatories regarding the steps to be taken to combat bribery of their public officials. It defines public officials broadly to include public agencies, public enterprises, and public international organizations.[229] It mandates that countries prosecute their nationals for offenses committed abroad.[230] In the accounting area, it requires that each signatory enact "dissuasive civil, administrative or criminal penalties for such omissions and falsifications in respect of the books, records, accounts and financial statements."[231] Companies will be required to disclose, on their financial statements, any potential liabilities under the act that rise to the level of a material contingent liability.

---

[228] See, OECD Convention on Combating Bribery of Foreign Public Officials, http://www.oecd.org/daf/cmis/bribery/ 20nov1e.htm.

[229] Article 1.

[230] Article 4.

[231] Article 8.

CHAPTER 6

International Sales Contract

The sales contract is the center of the export-import transaction.[232] The other contracts often found in international exporting, the carriage contract, the insurance contract, and letter of credit contracts, are tangential to the underlying sales contract. As such, the contracting parties should periodically review the sales contract before they engage other parties in transaction-related contracts. For example, one of the sales contract's operative terms is the trade term. This term controls the parties' respective obligations regarding contracting for shipping and insurance services. The trade term is also important in determining the conformity of documents in the documentary transaction. Use of the FOB trade term generally dictates that the bill of lading need not show that the freight has been paid since freight costs and shipping arrangements are delegated to the buyer in an FOB contract. However, the buyer can negotiate an *additional services clause* into the contract. This clause often requires the seller to secure liner space and an insurance certificate as agent for the buyer. This type of clause acts as a compromise for the seller who wants to avoid the risk of paying for any escalation in insurance or freight costs. Additionally, such a clause benefits the buyer who is willing to incur such costs but does not possess the sophistication or wants to avoid the inconvenience of booking a ship or in-

[232]Professor Berman has written a clear explanation of the documentary transaction that is a must read for novices to the export transaction. Harold J. Berman, *The Law of International Commercial Transactions (Lex Mercatoria)*, 2 Journal of Int'l Dispute Resolution 245 (1988).

surance at the port of shipment. Other risk shifting clauses that are negotiated in exporting contracts include choice of law, forum selection or arbitration, hardship, open price, and escalation clauses. The last three clauses are more common in long-term sales contracts involving numerous installments or for commodities prone to price fluctuations.

In selecting trade terms, the parties should also be concerned with any conflicts between the chosen trade term and other terms in the contract. For example, a CIF contract shifts the risk of loss to the buyer at the port of shipment. If the contract provides that the seller guarantees a certain weight or quality at arrival, then the risks of loss below that weight would seem to shift back to the seller. What term will dictate liability for loss during transit? "The tendency of courts (in the United States) has been to subordinate conflicting terms to the CIF term."[233] Under the Uniform Commercial Code (UCC) a guarantee of quality clause is likely to be construed only as a guarantee of "ordinary deterioration, shrinkage, and the like in transportation."[234] All other causes of loss or damage remain with the buyer. Furthermore, an occurrence within the "quality clause" does not provide the buyer with a right of rejection but only a right of adjustment. Professor Berman notes that comments to UCC Section 2-321(3) make such a presumption.

> [T]he express language used in an agreement is frequently a precautionary, fuller statement of the normal CIF terms and hence not intended as a departure or variation from them. Moreover, the dominant outlines of the CIF term are so well understood commercially that any variation should, whenever reasonably possible, be read as falling within those dominant outlines rather than as destroying the whole meaning of a term which essentially indicates a contract for proper shipment rather than one for delivery at destination.[235]

Nonetheless, it important for contracting parties not to vary recognized trade terms. In international contracting, the terms as defined in IN-

---

[233]Berman at 250. Professor Berman notes a more drastic example of inconsistency when a CIF term is coupled with a "no arrival, no sale clause." "With full risk of loss on the seller, it makes no sense for the buyer to have the right to the insurance proceeds." Ibid. at 251.

[234]Ibid. at 253, citing, U.C.C. § 2-321(2).

[235]U.C.C. § 2-320, Comment 14.

COTERMS 1990 or INCOTERMS 2000 should be utilized.[236] A classic example of the dangers of varying the trade term and the problems caused by other terms in the contract is *Kumar Corp. v. Nopal Lines, Ltd.*[237] Kumar entered into a contract to sell goods to Nava in Venezuela on a consignment basis. The contract trade term was CIF. Unfortunately, the goods were stolen while in possession of the common carrier at the port of shipment. Since payment was not due until a resale of the goods in Venezuela, Nava was under no obligation to pay against documents. In bringing suit against the common carrier, Kumar would have to overcome the defense that under the CIF term, risk of loss had passed to the buyer and therefore, Kumar had no standing to sue. Failure to overcome that defense would result in Kumar not having any recourse except for a claim under an applicable insurance policy.[238]

Negotiating an International Contract

International contract negotiation is a very difficult and complicated affair. The nuances of language and culture make international negotiations a risky enterprise for the unsophisticated importer or exporter. The negotiation of the export or sales contract is generally more time-consuming than in a domestic transaction. Foreign contractors need to develop a trust in their American counterpart before entering into a contract. It is important for the American businessperson to understand these cultural differences. The added time invested in the negotiation of an international contract will provide significant dividends in the long-term. First, additional time is needed to overcome any language, cultural, and legal differences. If successful in overcoming these differences, the agreement will better reflect basic

[236]Reference to Incoterms will generally be to INCOTERMS 1990. However, the International Chamber of Commerce recently published the ICC GUIDE TO INCOTERMS 2000, ICC Pub. No. 620 (1999). See also, Appendix 8 for coverage of INCOTERMS 1990 and some of the changes made in INCOTERMS 2000.

[237]462 So.2d 1178 (Fl. Ct. Appeals 1985).

[238]Ironically, Kumar's negligence in not procuring insurance coverage enabled it to sue the common carrier. The court held that since Kumar had failed to obtain insurance as required by the CIF term the risk of loss remained with Kumar. Thus, Kumar had the requisite standing to sue the common carrier.

understandings and minimize misunderstandings. Second, the trust developed early in a contractual relationship will help ensure a long-term international business contact. The following excerpt discusses some of the nuances associated with Japanese negotiators and business practices.

> The story about Japanese contracting that emerges is that law is largely irrelevant. Instead, the business relationship is paramount, and the Japanese favor unwritten, or very brief agreements; do not regard themselves bound by the letter of such agreements but rely on the notion of *changed circumstances* to seek renegotiation; and, in the case of a dispute, will seldom, if ever, allow the matter to proceed to court. *** The relationship, rather than the formalities or potential legal sanctions, traditionally gave the contract its binding force in Japan. *** Commercial custom in contemporary Japan often revolves around transaction types identified as *traditional contracting practices*. My personal favorite is the *cry-yourself-to-sleep* transaction, in which the seller is faced with a sudden cancellation of an order and simply absorbs the consequent loss, in the hope that it will be made up in the future. Not all of these practices are supported by classical contract law, but all represent commercial expectations, and to that extent, they can be viewed as a kind of [*unwritten*] law. *** In Japan, a continuing contract will invite some relational analysis. Specifically, it is not improbable that a court would seriously consider the effect of removing a retailer's *ikigai* (reason for living) as well as the legal merits and economic rationality of a termination.[239]

Such cultural differences have crucial practical importance in the negotiation and formation of a contract. The Confucian influence of harmony permeates contracting in Japan. Thus, the American style of hard bargaining and pressure tactics are likely to meet with failure. It is important to state a position firmly and at the same time not disturb the *wa* or harmony of the negotiation. This notion of harmony permeates all aspects of contracting including dispute resolution. The Japanese aversion to litigation stems from the belief that it is their societal "duty to avoid discord."[240] Interestingly, the Japanese also dislike arbitration. They believe that parties

---

[239] Veronica L. Taylor, "Continuing Transactions and Persistent Myths: Contracts in Contemporary Japan," 19 *Melbourne University Law Review* 352, 353, 356, 364, 393, & 395 (1993).

[240] Note, *'Working it Out': A Japanese Alternative to Fighting it Out,* 37 Cleveland St. Law Rev. 149, 157 (1989).

should negotiate directly in resolving disputes. In case of failure in negotiating a solution, the Japanese prefer the use of conciliation or *chotei.*[241] The *wa* concept is reflected in the Japanese approach to negotiation as the process of developing a trusting business relationship and not the simple formation of a contract. From a practical perspective, this results in Japanese contracts being simple, short, and vague. All problems are to be dealt with through acts of conciliation. All questions are to be answered through a process of *reconcilement.* "Reconcilement is the process by which parties in the dispute confer with each other and reach a point at which they come to terms and restore *harmonious* relationships."[242] The contract provides a basic framework that allows for modification and flexibility. Performance standards are not restrictively defined. Thus, the American businessperson may have to modify his proclivity for long, detailed agreements.

Cultural differences in the negotiation and the entering into a contract can have a profound impact on new business relationships. The American exporter should be careful in how he approaches a prospective contact in Japan. Once again, the Japanese place a high premium on personal exchange. The Japanese importer may not respond to written inquiries. Therefore, any initial inquiry is best followed by a personal contact. The more successful approach is to be introduced by an intermediary known to the other party.[243] Another example is the American businessperson's propensity to send a written agreement when negotiations have entered into their final stages. An American businessperson may want his attorney to confirm the terms discussed and agreed upon before the completion of the negotiations.[244] The lawyer may respond by sending a letter or a proposed agreement. "But the letter may get no response because the unexpected arrival of a contract probably appears abrupt and possibly coercive to a foreign recipient." In order to avoid cultural *faux pas* one attorney gives this common sense advice:

---

[241]Ibid. at 164. See generally, Kawashima, *Dispute Resolution in Contemporary Japan,* in, LAW IN JAPAN 42 (1963); D. HENDERSON, CONCILIATION AND JAPANESE LAW (1965).

[242]Ibid. at 163.

[243]See, Elliot Hahn, *Negotiating Contracts with the Japanese,* 14 Case Western Reserve Journal Int'l Law 377 (1982).

[244]See, e.g., Henderson, *The Role of Lawyers in U.S.-Japanese Business Transactions,* 38 Washington Law Rev. 1 (1963).

> Do some reading on the country—at least you'll know where it is. Know something of the history. Talk to someone who's done business there, an American businessman or someone from the Department of Commerce—find out who the trade specialist is in that country and talk to that person. And once you get there, don't hop off the plane and set up meetings . . . Don't do the trilogy of hotels, restaurants and office buildings. Instead of staying in your hotel room answering e-mail, get up in the morning and walk around.[245]

Finally, it is important to understand the authority of the other negotiating party and her place in the chain of command. A longer negotiation period may not be due to the other party's reluctance or gamesmanship but her lack of authority to complete a deal on her own. For example, the Japanese often make business decisions based upon a consensus or *ring-sho* which takes time to formulate.

Pre-Contractual Liability

Under American and English common law, a negotiating party owes no duty of good faith to the other party.[246] One may terminate negotiations in bad faith and not be liable for the other parties' expenses. Two major exceptions to this freedom of negotiation should be mentioned. If the parties have entered into a "preliminary agreement," the courts will be more willing to hold a party liable for bad faith termination of the negotiations. *Reliance theory* may be used to extend contractual liability to protect someone who reasonably relied upon the belief that the parties would conclude a final agreement. In the old common law writ of assumpsit, informal contracts could be enforced based upon justifiable reliance. Section 90 of the *Restatement (Second) of Contracts,* often referred to as *promissory estoppel,* allows a court to give a remedy if a person's promise (a promise to conclude

[245]Laurel-Ann Dooley, "Culture Clashes Hinder Deals," in *National Law Journal* at B1, B4 (September 13, 1999).

[246]For an analysis of precontractual liability in conjunction with the Convention on Contracts for the International Sale of Goods see, Michael Joachim Bonnell, *Formation of Contracts and Precontractual Liability Under the Vienna Convention on International Sale of Goods,* in FORMATION OF CONTRACTS AND PRECONTRACTUAL LIABILITY 157 (Paris: ICC Publishing, S.A. 1990).

negotiations) is reasonably relied upon and injustice can only be prevented by the enforcement of the promise. For example, the court in *Nimrod Marketing v. Texas Energy Corp.*,[247] held that a subcontractor who expended money in reliance on obtaining a contract from one of its clients could sue for damages when the customer hired another subcontractor. The client had sent a letter to the subcontractor that stated: "Acting pursuant to your responsibilities as our purchasing agent, it is our hope to begin construction of the housing shortly upon obtaining a contract with the foreign government." The court ruled that based upon the doctrine of promissory estoppel, the subcontractor had reasonably relied upon the assurance in the letter (See Exhibit 6.1 for List of "Reliance Factors"). The second major exception to non-liability for pre-contractual conduct is *misrepresentation*. If the parties conclude a contract based at least partially on the untrue statements of one of the parties, then the innocent party may sue for a rescission of the contract and damages.

Exhibit 6.1: Reliance Factors[248] (Liability for Oral Statements and Informal Business Letters)

1. Does the language in the statement or letter border upon a promise or a guaranty?
2. Is there a disclaimer of liability in the statement or letter?
3. Does the statement or letter invite one of the parties to take steps to insure performance of an underlying obligation?
4. What was the intent of the party giving the statement or letter?
5. Did either party receive legal advice as to the legality of the statement or letter?
6. What was the relative sophistication of the parties regarding the purpose or legality of the statement or letter?
7. What were the prior dealings between the parties regarding such letters or statements?
8. What is the custom or practice in that particular business regarding the purpose and legality of such statements or letters?

---

[247] 769 F.2d 1076 (5th Cir. 1985).

[248] See, Larry A. DiMatteo & Rene Sacasas, *Credit and Value Comfort Instruments: Crossing the Line from Assurance to Legally Significant Reliance and Toward a Theory of Enforceability*, 47 Baylor Law Rev. 357 (1995).

9. What was the length of negotiations pertaining to the statement or letter?
10. Was there actual reliance upon the statement or letter?

The Federal Republic of Germany provides a comparative example of how other legal systems deal with the potential liability of pre-contractual correspondences and instruments. German law is less dependent upon the literal designation of writings or instruments as legal or non-legal as is found in American law. An example of this informalism is reflected in the fact that a merchant's guaranty is valid even if given orally. This informalism provides parties greater flexibility in structuring their transactions. The German courts look to the purpose of a letter or a writing to determine if it creates an enforceable contractual obligation. One may argue that even informal business letters, seemingly not binding on the surface, are more likely to have legal consequences under this purpose-oriented or teleological approach to enforceability. The presumption is that most businesspersons would not spend time negotiating and drafting letters and documents unless they believed them to be legally binding. A German court often asks the following question when reviewing an instrument for enforceability purposes. Would two sophisticated commercial entities spend time to create a meaningless, unenforceable instrument?

Model International Sales Contract

The core document in the international documentary transaction is the export sales contract. The intricacies and importance of the sales contract are explained in the following excerpt.

> In international trade, the sales contract is the core of the export-import transaction. It is, however, always supported by several other related contracts, reflecting the complexity of the transaction and the number of parties involved. First, the contract of carriage by sea. Second, there is the contract for marine insurance. Third, the sale is usually financed by means of a banking transaction, often in the form of a letter of credit.
>
> **The Export-Import Contract**
>
> Many of the risks inherent in an international transaction can be allocated by the importer and exporter through their contract of sale, under

familiar principles of contract law. *** Out of the price-delivery term, and especially out of the term "c.i.f." which is probably the most widely used term in international trade contracts, has come a great deal of law. The price-delivery term defines the title to the goods, time and place of delivery, time and place of payment, importer's right of inspection, the risk of loss or damage to the goods in transit, and the cost of transportation.

***

An international sales contract typically contains other risk-shifting clauses. *Force majeure* and other contingency clauses are added to escape liability where unforeseen circumstances prevent performance of an assumed obligation. Choice of law, choice of forum, and arbitration clauses seek to avoid the vagaries, uncertainties, and delays of foreign litigation. The tendency to spell out in detail such matters as inspection rights and remedies for breach may also be an attempt to substitute the law of the contract for that of any national legal system.

***

Destination and Shipment Contracts

An importer may ask his foreign supplier to place the goods on board a vessel bound for the country of destination and to bear the risks of the voyage. Such a contract is called a "destination contract." *** "Shipment contracts" cast the risk of loss upon the purchaser from the moment of loading or shipment. The seller typically agrees to place the goods on board or alongside the vessel, but the risks of transit are shifted to the buyer. Typical shipment contracts include f.a.s., f.o.b., c.i.f., and c & f.

***

Customs as a Source of Law in International Commercial Transactions

In interpreting terms generally used in international commercial transactions, courts and arbitration tribunals are inevitably concerned with the common understandings of such terms by merchants, ship-owners, insurance underwriters, bankers, and others engaged in international trade.[249]

---

[249]Harold J. Berman, *The Law of International Commercial Transactions (Lex Mercatoria)*, 2 Journal on International Dispute Resolution 245-248, 276 (1988).

The International Chamber of Commerce has produced a *model contract* for the international sale of goods.[250] It provides a sound source or checklist for standard types of terms that are incorporated in most sales contracts. The "Specific Conditions" allow the parties to customize their contract by offering alternatives or spaces to be filled. The ICC commentary[251] states that the model form is intended for independent transactions between merchants and not for use in long-term supply contracts. For example, the *model contract* does not possess a price adjustment clause often found in long-term supply contracts. An example of a price adjustment clause is provided in *Bernina Distibutors, Inc. v. Bernina* Sewing.[252]

> The foregoing prices of the above described sewing machines shall be subject to increase or decrease as follows:
>
> (a) To the extent of any increase or decrease of factory invoice costs charged to the Importer.
>
> (b) To the extent of any increase or decrease in duty charges.
>
> (c) In the event charges or insurance, freight, handling, broker, port fees or other similar charges are increased 20% over present charges, the prices of sewing machines sold to Distributor shall increase likewise to the extent of the entire increase over present charges. Increase or decreases in duty charges and in factory sewing machine costs to Importer shall be adjusted as they occur. Increases in all other charges mentioned above shall be adjusted at the commencement of each calendar year.

The contract in this case was between an American importer of Swiss made sewing machines and an American distributor of the sewing machines. The importer's purchase agreement with the manufacturer called for payment in Swiss francs. Unfortunately, the American dollar was devalued in relationship to the Swiss franc, seriously eroding the importer's profit margin. The importer attempted to pass the costs of the currency fluctuations through the price adjustment clause to the distributor. As an alternative, it

---

[250] ICC, "The ICC Model International Sale Contract, Pub. No. 556 (E) (1997).

[251] The following material has been taken from ibid. at 5-11.

[252] 646 F.2d 434 (1981).

asked the court pursuant to the open price provision of the UCC to fix a reasonable price.[253] The court rejected both of the arguments. First, the currency fluctuations could not be charged to the distributor because the price adjustment clause did not authorize such a pass through. Second, the court could not imply a "reasonable price" because it held that currency fluctuations were an allocated risk. Since currency fluctuation is a common risk in international trade, the risk falls to the party whose currency is devalued unless expressly allocated in the contract otherwise. Finally, the court held that the diminishment in the importer's profit margin was not so great to excuse him from the contract under the doctrine of impracticability.[254] A price adjustment or escalation clause is an important part of a long-term supply contract. It is also one of the most difficult to draft and is a common source of litigation. For example, the clause may fail to recognize a cost component as in the *Bernina* case.

In the ICC *model contract*, the parties can use both the Specific Conditions and General Conditions (Exhibit 6.2) or use the General Conditions in conjunction with the parties' contract. Also, the contract is best used for the sale of manufactured goods and not the sale of raw material, agricultural, or perishable goods. Furthermore, the contract is not appropriate for specially-manufactured goods but rather is intended for the sale of goods used in general commerce.

The Commentary to the Model Contract also notes the following points. First, the intended substantive law to be applied is the Convention for the International Sale of Goods (CISG). For issues not dealt with by the CISG, the Model Contract states that the "law of the country where the seller has his place of business" is to be the law applied. Second, despite CISG Article 29's authorization of oral modification, the Model Contract states that modifications must be made in writing. Third, it suggests that contracting parties avoid the use of the CFR and CIF Incoterms because "manufactured goods are rarely sold or pledged in transit and rarely require the use of a transferable transport document (e.g., Bill of lading)." Accordingly, the contract should expressly state the type of transport document

---

[253]"The parties if they so intend can conclude a contract for sale even though the price is not settled. In such a case the price is a *reasonable price at the time of delivery.*" U.C.C. § 2-305(1).

[254]See, U.C.C. § 2-615.

that is to be provided by the seller. The most common documents and mode of shipment are as follows: bill of lading (ocean carriage or multimodal), multimodal document (bill of lading or combined transport document), seaway bill (also known as line waybill or non-negotiable bill of lading), mate's receipt (ocean carriage), air waybill, consignment note (CIM for rail or CMR for road), warehouse warrant (ocean or land), and freight forwarder documents (all modes of transport). It also suggests the avoidance of the FAS, FOB, DES, and DEQ Incoterms because they focus upon the discharge of the goods from a ship. In contrast, "manufactured goods are normally handed over for carriage at terminals." Therefore, the more appropriate Incoterms are the EXW, FCA, CPT, CIP, DAF, DDU, and DDP terms. In conjunction with the selected Incoterm, when agreeing on the time of delivery the "parties should check carefully the stage at which delivery occurs under the Incoterm."

Fourth, the seller should check national laws if he wants to retain title of the goods until full payment is received. See ICC Pub. No. 501, "Guide on Retention of Title." The retention or reservation of title clause provides some security to the seller who is delivering goods on open account. It provides that title remains in his name until full payment by the purchaser. This clause is generally intended to protect the seller in the event that his trading partner becomes insolvent. Such clauses have been expanded to include a claim to the proceeds from the sale of the unpaid goods. The problem with proceeds of sale clauses is that if the purchaser becomes insolvent, then the chances of recovering the proceeds is highly unlikely. One technique would be to contractually require that all such proceeds are to be placed in an escrow account until the seller is paid in full. The legal complexity grows when the goods supplied become component parts of a finished product. Such a clause may still be effective if the goods are not lost in the process of making the finished product. If the identity of the supplied goods is lost due to the production process, then a clause specifically giving the supplier title to the new product would be necessary. If the goods remain identifiable in their original state and can be extricated without undue harm or costs, then the clause may still be effective. An even broader clause is the "all accounts clause" which retains title to all goods supplied as long as some of them remain unpaid. The problem with this type of clause is that unspecified amounts of the goods are eventually sold to third parties. The enforcer of the clause has the difficult task of linking goods to unpaid invoices. The enforceability of the above permutations of the retention of title clause requires investigation of national law. For example, national bankruptcy laws are less likely to recognize the reservation in its broadest forms.[255]

Fifth, the Model Contract limits the liability of the seller for late or non-delivery of the goods. The buyer may collect a late delivery charge of .5 percent of the contract price per week of delay. The amount is capped at a total of 5 percent, which is reached after ten weeks of delay. After ten weeks of delay the buyer may terminate the contract and claim the five percent as liquidated damages. Upon termination, the buyer may make an additional claim for damages not to exceed ten percent of the contract price.

Sixth, the delivery of non-conforming goods does not give the buyer an automatic right to terminate the contract. The seller is entitled to cure the non-conformity. If successful, the buyer is limited to the liquidated damages provided specifically for late delivery. Upon the giving of notice for non-conformity, the seller has three options: to repair the goods, replace the goods, or to reimburse the price. If the buyer decides to accept the non-conforming goods he is "entitled to recover from the seller the difference in value compared with conforming goods, subject to a limit of 15 percent of the contract price."

Seventh, the Model contract provides for three instances when the buyer may terminate the contract: (1) where the seller fails to deliver by the "cancellation date" stated in the contract, (2) where the seller fails to deliver within the ten weeks provided in the liquidated damage provision for late delivery, or (3) where the seller fails to repair or replace non-conforming goods within the ten week period provided in the late delivery provision. Of course, the late delivery provision should be read in conjunction with the contract's *force majeure* clause.

Exhibit 6.2: ICC Model International Sales Contract

A. SPECIFIC CONDITIONS

These specific conditions have been prepared to permit the parties to agree to particular terms by completing the spaces or by choosing between alternatives.

---

[255]For in-depth coverage of the retention of tile clause see, SALLY WHEELER, RESERVATION OF TITLE CLAUSES (1991).

SELLER:	CONTACT PERSON	BUYER:	CONTACT PERSON

A-1 **GOODS SOLD: Description of the Goods**

A-2 **CONTRACT PRICE** (ART. 4)
Currency:______________________
Amount in Numbers:____________ Amount in Letters:______________

A-3 **DELIVERY TERMS**

Recommended Terms (according to INCOTERMS 1990/2000)

EXW Ex Works	named place:
FCA Free Carrier	named place:
CPT Carriage Paid To	named place of destination:
CIP	named place of destination:
DAF Delivered At Frontier	named place:
DDU Delivered Duty Unpaid	named place of destination:
DDP Delivered Duty Paid	named place of destination:

Other Terms (according to INCOTERMS 1990/2000)

FAS Free Alongside Ship	named port of shipment:
FOB Free On Board	named port of shipment:
CFR Cost and Freight	named port of destination:
CIF Cost Insurance and Freight	named port of destination:
DES Delivered Ex Ship	named port of destination:
DEQ Delivered Ex Quay (duty paid)	named port of destination:

Other delivery terms
CARRIER (where applicable)
Name and Address: Contact Person:

The present contract of sale will be governed by these Specific Conditions (to the extent that the relevant boxes have been completed) and by the ICC General Conditions of Sale (Manufactured Goods Intended for Resale) which constitute part B of this document.

Seller:	**Buyer:**
signature	signature
Date:	Date:
Place of Signature:	Place of Signature:

A-4 **TIME OF DELIVERY**
Indicate here the date or period (e.g. week or month) at which or within which the Seller must perform his delivery obligations according to clause A.4 of the respective Incoterm

A-5 **INSPECTION OF THE GOODS BY BUYER** (ART. 3)
Before shipment:_______place of inspection:________
Other:_________________________________

A-6 **RETENTION OF TITLE** (ART. 7)

A-7 **PAYMENT CONDITIONS**
Payment on open account (art. 5.1)
Time for payment: _____ days from date of invoice. Other: _____
Open account backed by demand guarantee or standby letter of credit
Payment in advance (art. 5.2)
Date: ________ Total price ____ ____% of the price
Documentary Collection (art. 5.5)
___D/P Documents against payment ___D/A Documents against acceptance
Irrevocable documentary credit (art. 5.3) ___Confirmed ___Unconfirmed
Place of issue (if applicable): _____Place of confirmation:_____
Credit available: Partial shipments:Transhipment:
__ By payment at sight __ Allowed __ Allowed
__ By deferred payment at: ___ days __ Not allowed__ Not allowed
__ By acceptance of drafts at: ___ days
__ By negotiation

Date on which the documentary credit must be notified to seller (if different from art. 5.3)
____days before date of delivery other: ____________________

Other: ____
(e.g. cheque, bank draft, electronic funds transfer to designated bank account of seller)

A-8 **DOCUMENTS**

Indicate here documents to be provided by Seller. Parties are advised to check the Incoterm they have selected under A-3 of these Specific Conditions. (As concerns transport documents, see also Introduction)
__ Transport documents: indicate type of transport document required:
____

__ Commercial Invoice	__Certificate of origin
__ Packing list	__Certificate of inspection
__ Insurance document	__Other: ____________

A-9 **CANCELLATION DATE**

To be completed only if the parties wish to modify article 10.3
If the goods are not delivered for any reason whatsoever (including *force majeure*) by: (date) _______ the Buyer will be entitled to CANCEL THE CONTRACT IMMEDIATELY BY NOTIFICATION TO THE SELLER

A-10 **LIABILITY FOR DELAY**

To be completed only if the parties wish to modify art.10.1,10.4 or 11.3
Liquidated damages for delay in delivery shall be:
______% (of price of delayed goods) per week, with a maximum of ____% (of price of delayed goods)
or:
____________(specify amount)
In case of termination for delay, Seller's liability for damages for delay is limited to ____ % of the price of the non-delivered goods

A-11 **LIMITATION OF LIABILITY FOR LACK OF CONFORMITY** (ART. 11.5)

To be completed only if the parties wish to modify art.11.5.

Seller's liability for damages arising from lack of conformity of the goods shall be:

________ limited to proven loss (including consequential loss, loss of profit, etc.) not exceeding ___ % of the contract price;

or:

________ as follows (specify):

A-12 **LIMITATION OF LIABILITY WHERE NON-CONFORMING GOODS ARE RETAINED BY THE BUYER** (ART. 11.6)
To be completed only if the parties wish to modify art. 11.6

The price abatement for retained non-conforming goods shall not exceed:
___ ___% of the price of such goods

or:

___ ________ (specify amount)

A-13 **TIME-BAR** (Art.11.8)
To be completed only if the parties wish to modify art.11.8.

Any action for non-conformity of the goods (as defined in article 11.8) must be taken by the Buyer not later than _________ from the date of arrival of the goods at destination

A-14 **APPLICABLE LAW** (Art. 1.2)
To be completed only if the parties wish to submit the sale contract to a national law instead of CISG. The solution hereunder is not recommended. (a) This sales contract is governed by the domestic law of _________

To be completed if the parties wish to choose a law other than that of the seller for questions not covered by CISG

(b) Any questions not covered by CISG will be governed by the law of

____

A-15 **RESOLUTION OF DISPUTES** (Art. 14)
The two solutions hereunder (arbitration or litigation before ordinary courts) are alternatives: parties cannot choose both of them. If no choice is made, ICC arbitration will apply, according to art. 14

ARBITRATION	**LITIGATION**
ICC	In case of dispute the courts of ________
Place of arbitration ________	______________________(place)
Other ______________(specify)	shall have jurisdiction

A-16 OTHER

B. GENERAL CONDITIONS

Art. 1 GENERAL

1.1 These General Conditions are intended to be applied together with the Specific Conditions (part A) of the International Sale Contract (Manufactured Goods Intended for Resale), but they may also be incorporated on their own into any sale contract. Where these General Conditions (Part B) are used independently of the said Specific Conditions (Part A), any reference in Part B to Part A will be interpreted as a reference to any relevant specific conditions agreed by the parties. In case of contradiction between these General Conditions and any specific conditions agreed upon between the parties, the specific conditions shall prevail.

1.2 Any questions relating to this Contract which are not expressly or implicitly settled by the provisions contained in the Contract itself (i.e. these General Conditions and any specific conditions agreed upon by the parties) shall be governed:

A. by the United Nations Convention on Contracts for the International Sale of Goods (Vienna Convention of 1980, hereafter referred to as CISG), and

B. to the extent that such questions are not covered by CISG, by reference to the law of the country where the Seller has his place of business.

1.3 Any reference made to trade terms (such as EXW, FCA, etc.) is deemed to be made to the relevant term of Incoterms published by the International Chamber of Commerce.

1.4 Any reference made to a publication of the International Chamber of Commerce is deemed to be made to the version current at the date of conclusion of the Contract.

1.5 No modification of the Contract is valid unless agreed or evidenced in writing. However, a party may be precluded by his conduct from asserting this provision to the extent that the other party has relied on that conduct.

ART. 2 CHARACTERISTICS OF THE GOODS

2.1 It is agreed that any information relating to the goods and their use, such as weights, dimensions, capacities, prices, colours and other data contained in catalogues, prospectuses, circulars, advertisements, illustrations, price-lists of the Seller, shall not take effect as terms of the Contract unless expressly referred to in the Contract.

2.2 Unless otherwise agreed, the Buyer does not acquire any property rights in software, drawings, etc. which may have been made available to him. The Seller also remains the exclusive owner of any intellectual or industrial property rights relating to the goods.

ART. 3 INSPECTION OF THE GOODS BEFORE SHIPMENT

If the parties have agreed that the Buyer is entitled to inspect the goods before shipment, the Seller must notify the Buyer within a reasonable time before the shipment that the goods are ready for inspection at the agreed place.

ART. 4 PRICE

4.1 If no price has been agreed, the Seller's current list price at the time of the conclusion of the Contract shall apply. In the absence of such a current list price, the price generally charged for such goods at the time of the conclusion of the Contract shall apply.

4.2 Unless otherwise agreed in writing, the price does not include VAT, and is not subject to price adjustment.

4.3 The price indicated under A-2 (contract price) includes any costs which are at the Seller's charge according to this Contract. However, should the Seller bear any costs which, according to this Contract, are for the Buyer's account (e.g. for transportation or insurance under EXW or FCA), such sums shall not be considered as having been included in the price under A-2 and shall be reimbursed by the Buyer.

ART. 5 PAYMENT CONDITIONS

5.1 Unless otherwise agreed in writing, or implied from a prior course of dealing between the parties, payment of the price and of any other sums due by the Buyer to the Seller shall be on open account and time of payment shall be 30 days from the date of invoice. The amounts due shall be transferred, unless otherwise agreed, by teletransmission to the Seller's bank in the Seller's country for the account of the Seller and the Buyer shall be deemed to have performed his payment obligations when the respective sums due have been received by the Seller's bank in immediately available funds.

5.2 If the parties have agreed on payment in advance, without further indication, it will be assumed that such advance payment, unless otherwise agreed, refers to the full price, and that the advance payment must be received by the Seller's bank in immediately available funds at least 30 days before the agreed date of delivery or the earliest date within the agreed delivery period. If advance payment has been agreed only for a part of the contract price, the payment conditions of the remaining amount will be determined according to the rules set forth in this article.

5.3 If the parties have agreed on payment by documentary credit, then, unless otherwise agreed, the Buyer must arrange for a documentary credit in favour of the Seller to be issued by a reputable bank, subject to the Uniform Customs and Practice for Documentary Credits published by the International Chamber of Commerce, and to be notified at least 30 days before the agreed date of delivery or at least 30 days before the earliest date within the agreed delivery period. Unless otherwise agreed, the documentary credit shall be payable at sight and allow partial shipments and transhipments.

5.4 If the parties have agreed on payment by documentary collection, then, unless otherwise agreed, documents will be tendered against payment (D/P) and the tender will in any case be subject to the Uniform Rules for Collections published by the International Chamber of Commerce.

5.5 To the extent that the parties have agreed that payment is to be backed by a bank guarantee, the Buyer is to provide, at least 30 days before the agreed date of delivery or at least 30 days before the earliest date within the agreed delivery period, a first demand bank guarantee subject to the Uniform Rules for Demand Guarantees published by the International Chamber of Commerce, or a standby letter of credit subject either to such Rules or to the Uniform Customs and Practice for Documentary Credits published by the International Chamber of Commerce, in either case issued by a reputable bank.

ART. 6 INTEREST IN CASE OF DELAYED PAYMENT

6.1 If a party does not pay a sum of money when it falls due the other party is entitled to interest upon that sum from the time when payment is due to the time of payment.

6.2 Unless otherwise agreed, the rate of interest shall be 2% above the average bank short-term lending rate to prime borrowers prevailing for the currency of payment at the place of payment, or where no such rate exists at that place, then the same rate in the State of the currency of payment. In the absence of such a rate at either place the rate of interest shall be the appropriate rate fixed by the law of the State of the currency of payment.

ART. 7 RETENTION OF TITLE

If the parties have validly agreed on retention of title, the goods shall remain the property of the Seller until the complete payment of the price, or as otherwise agreed.

ART. 8 CONTRACTUAL TERM OF DELIVERY

Unless otherwise agreed, delivery shall be "Ex Works" (EXW).

ART. 9 DOCUMENTS

Unless otherwise agreed, the Seller must provide the documents (if any) indicated in the applicable Incoterm or, if no Incoterm is applicable, according to any previous course of dealing.

ART. 10 LATE-DELIVERY, NON-DELIVERY AND REMEDIES THEREFOR

10.1 When there is delay in delivery of any goods, the Buyer is entitled to claim liquidated damages equal to 0.5% or such other percentage as may be agreed of the price of those goods for each complete week of delay, provided the Buyer notifies the Seller of the delay. Where the Buyer so notifies the Seller within 15 days from the agreed date of delivery, damages will run from the agreed date of delivery or from the last day within the agreed period of delivery. Where the Buyer so notifies the Seller after 15 days of the agreed date of delivery, damages will run from the agreed date of delivery or from the last day within the agreed period of delivery. Where the Buyer so notifies the Seller after 15 days of the agreed date of delivery, damages will run from the date of the notice. Liquidated damages for delay shall not exceed 5% of the price of the delayed goods or such other maximum amount as may be agreed.

10.2 If the parties have agreed upon a cancellation date in Box A-9, the Buyer may terminate the Contract by notification to the Seller as regards goods which have not been delivered by such cancellation date for any reason whatsoever (including a *force majeure* event).

10.3 When article 10.2 does not apply and the Seller has not delivered the goods by the date on which the Buyer has become entitled to the maximum amount of liquidated damages under article 10.1, the Buyer may give notice in writing to terminate the Contract as regards such goods, if they have not been delivered to the Buyer within 5 days of receipt of such notice by the Seller.

10.4 In case of termination of the Contract under article 10.2 or 10.3 then in addition to any amount paid or payable under article 10.1, the Buyer is entitled to claim damages for any additional loss not exceeding 10% of the price of the non-delivered goods.

10.5 The remedies under this article are exclusive of any other remedy for delay in delivery or non-delivery.

ART. 11 NON-CONFORMITY OF THE GOODS

11.1 The Buyer shall examine the goods as soon as possible after their arrival at destination and shall notify the Seller in writing of any lack of conformity of the goods within 15 days from the date when the Buyer discovers or ought to have discovered the lack of conformity. In any case the Buyer shall have no remedy for lack of conformity if he fails to notify the Seller thereof within 12 months from the date of arrival of the goods at the agreed destination.

11.2 Goods will be deemed to conform to the Contract despite minor discrepancies which are usual in the particular trade or through course of dealing between the parties but the Buyer will be entitled to any abatement of the price usual in the trade or through course of dealing for such discrepancies.

11.3 Where goods are non-conforming (and provided the Buyer, having given notice of the lack of conformity in compliance with article 11.1, does not elect in the notice to retain them), the Seller shall at his option:

(a) replace the goods with conforming goods, without any additional expense to the Buyer, or
(b) repair the goods, without any additional expense to the Buyer, or
(c) reimburse to the Buyer the price paid for the non-conforming goods and thereby terminate the Contract as regards those goods.

The Buyer will be entitled to liquidated damages as quantified under article 10.1 for each complete week of delay between the date of notification of the non-conformity according to article 11.1 and the supply of substitute goods under article 11.3(a) or repair under article 11.3(b) above. Such damages may be accumulated with damages (if any) payable under article 10.1, but can in no case exceed in the aggregate 5% of the price of those goods.

11.4. If the Seller has failed to perform his duties under article 11.3 By the date on which the Buyer becomes entitled to the maximum amount of liquidated damages according to that article, the Buyer may give notice in writing to terminate the Contract as regards the nonconforming goods unless the supply of replacement goods or the repair is effected within 5 days of receipt of such notice by the Seller.

11.5. Where the Contract is terminated under article 11.3(c) or article 11.4, then in addition to any amount paid or payable under article 11.3 as reimbursement of the price and damages for any delay, the Buyer is entitled to damages for any additional loss not exceeding 10% of the price of the non-conforming goods.

11.6 Where the Buyer elects to retain non-conforming goods, he shall be entitled to a sum equal to the difference between the value of the goods at the agreed place of destination if they had conformed with the Contract and their value at the same place as delivered, such sum not to exceed 15% of the price of those goods.

11.7 Unless otherwise agreed in writing, the remedies under this article 11 are exclusive of any other remedy for non-conformity.

11.8 Unless otherwise agreed in writing, no action for lack of conformity can be taken by the Buyer, whether before judicial or arbitral tribunals, after 2 years from the date of arrival of the goods. It is expressly agreed that after the expiry of such term, the Buyer will not plead non-conformity of the goods, or make a counterclaim thereon, in defence to any action taken by the Seller against the Buyer for non-performance of this Contract.

ART. 12 COOPERATION BETWEEN THE PARTIES

12.1 The Buyer shall promptly inform the Seller of any claim made against the Buyer by his customers or third parties concerning the goods delivered or intellectual property rights related thereto.

12.2 The Seller will promptly inform the Buyer of any claim which may involve the product liability of the Buyer.

ART. 13 FORCE MAJEURE

13.1 A party is not liable for a failure to perform any of his obligations in so far as he proves:

(a) that the failure was due to an impediment beyond his control, and

(b) that he could not reasonably be expected to have taken into account the impediment and its effects upon his ability to perform at the time of the conclusion of the Contract, and

(c) that he could not reasonably have avoided or overcome it or its effects.

13.2 A party seeking relief shall, as soon as practicable after the impediment and its effects upon his ability to perform become known to him, give notice to the other party of such impediment and its effects on his ability to perform. Notice shall also be given when the ground of relief ceases. Failure to give either notice makes the party thus failing liable in damages for loss which otherwise could have been avoided.

13.3 Without prejudice to article 10.2, a ground of relief under this clause relieves the party failing to perform from liability in damages, from penalties and other contractual sanctions, except from the duty to pay interest on money owing as long as and to the extent that the ground subsists.

13.4 If the grounds of relief subsist for more than six months, either party shall be entitled to terminate the Contract with notice.

ART. 14 RESOLUTION OF DISPUTES

14.1 Unless otherwise agreed in writing, all disputes arising in connection with the present Contract shall be finally settled under the Rules of Arbitration of the International Chamber of Commerce by one or more arbitrators appointed in accordance with the said Rules.

14.2 An arbitration clause does not prevent any party from requesting interim or conservatory measures from the courts.

General conditions and terms are considered by most businesspersons as supplemental to the specific terms. This view is incorrect and may lead to unfortunate legal consequences. Specific and general terms together form the contract and are equally enforceable. The parties, therefore, should carefully review the general conditions and terms before executing their contract. The use of a model form, like the one above, guards against unnecessary surprises through the insertion of dramatically one-sided terms by one of the parties. Also, a model form can be used as a checklist of clauses that should be incorporated into a custom drafted contract. A few general rules of thumb should be kept in mind when negotiating an international sales contract. The contracting parties should attempt to carefully define any technical or general terminology in their contract. They should also select an appropriate Incoterm (without modification). Along with selecting an Incoterm, the parties should detail any rights and obligations associated with the shipment of the goods, including any special marking, packaging, inspection, and testing requirements. Other contract clauses that should be negotiated and closely reviewed include those dealing with warranty, default, *force majeure*, and dispute settlement.

Choice of Law

As mentioned previously, the Model Form assumes that the substantive law to be applied will be the CISG. In order to prevent the application of the CISG, the contract should expressly stipulate to that fact. The following clause serves as an illustration:

> The rights and obligations of the parties to this Agreement shall not be governed by the 1980 United Nations Convention on Contracts for the International Sale of Goods; rather, these rights and obligations shall be governed by the law of the State of New York including the provisions of the Uniform Commercial Code enacted in the state of New York and as construed by the courts of New York State.[256]

This type of clause overcomes the problem represented by a more generic choice of law clause, such as the "Law of New York." Simply stating the applicable law to be the "Law of New York" may lead a court to apply the CISG and not the UCC.

[256]Michael L. Sher in UNITED NATIONS, UNIFORM COMMERCIAL LAW IN THE TWENTY-FIRST CENTURY 97-98 (1992).

INCOTERMS

The trade term is one of the most important terms to be negotiated in an export or import contract. The rules for interpreting trade terms are of primary importance in international sale of goods transactions. Trade terms are used to allocate the costs of freight and insurance, along with stating the time that the risk of loss passes to the purchaser. The rules of interpretation for trade terms also determine who is responsible for dealing with customs agents and the payment of tariffs and other important import and export fees, and who pays for the cost of loading and off loading. Traditionally, national laws provide the rules of interpretation.[257] In international trade, trade terms as defined in the INCOTERMS 1990 and 2000 manuals, published by the International Chamber of Commerce, has obtained almost universal acceptance. The 1990 version of INCOTERMS provides 13 terms categorized into 4 groups: E Group (EXW), F Group (FCA, FAS, FOB), C Group (CFR, CIF, CPT, CIP), and D Group (DAF, DES, DEQ, DDU, DDP). The superiority of the INCOTERMS is that they have been consistently updated to reflect contemporary commercial practice. As a result, the CISG elected not to provide any competing terms and the current Revision of Article 2 of the Uniform Commercial Code eliminates its provisions dealing with trade terms. The main theme enunciated by the ICC, pertaining to its manuals, is the belief that international business should be self-regulated. The universal acceptance of its rules dealing with international letters of credit (UCP 500), for example, demonstrates the ability of people in countries with differing legal systems to apply their own private mechanisms for the conduct of trade.

The ICC has stated a number of *Golden Rules*[258] when using Incoterms. First, always cite to "Incoterms 1990 (now "Incoterms 2000"). Thus, in selecting an Incoterm state it as follows: "CIF as defined in Incoterms _____." Second, obtain the full set of Incoterms and familiarize yourself with the responsibilities of each party under the term selected for your contract. Incoterms can be obtained through the ICC as Publication 460 and a "Guide to Incoterms 2000" as Publication No. 620. Third, use one of the thirteen In-

[257]See, e.g., Uniform Commercial Code Sections 2-319 to 2-322.

[258]The material in this paragraph was taken from ICC, "The ICC Model International Sale Contract," Pub. No. 556(E) (1997) at 30-31.

coterms by simply stating the three letter abbreviation. Do not attempt any variation of the terms. Fourth, understand that some of the terms are to be used for only certain modes of transportation, while others can be used for all modes of transportation. The FAS, FOB, CFR, CIF, DES, and DEQ terms are used for the carriage of goods by sea. The EXW, FCA, CIP, CPT, DAF, DDU, and DDP terms can be used generally, including for multimodal means of shipment. Fifth, Incoterms are used to set the relative responsibilities of the seller and the buyer. They do not directly affect the relationship between the shipper and the common carrier. The carriage contract should be carefully reviewed in order to make sure that it conforms to the Incoterm used in the contract of sale. Sixth, Incoterms generally allocate the risk of loss, insurance and freight costs, and some customs responsibilities. The Incoterms manual lists ten obligations that the terms may allocate. These obligations include obtaining necessary export licenses, and authorizations; satisfying import requirements and formalities; giving notice regarding a vessel hired for transport (buyer); giving notice of delivery to common carrier (seller); the checking, packaging, and marking of goods; obtaining transport and other documents. By way of example, under FOB, the seller must deliver conforming goods on board the vessel named by the buyer at the stipulated time and must give notice to the buyer of the delivery. The seller bears all costs up to the passing of the ship's rail at the port of shipment including exportation fees, the packing and checking of the goods, and the costs of obtaining a document evidencing the loading of the goods. He is also obligated to obtain a certificate of origin at the buyer's request and expense. In turn, the buyer must book the carriage and give notice to seller of the name, loading berth, and dates for delivery to vessel. The buyer, along with bearing the costs of freight and insurance, pays the costs of obtaining most documents including the certificate or origin, consular invoice, and in some incidences the bill of lading.[259] Under the CIF term the seller's responsibilities include the obtaining of a marine insurance policy and a carriage contract. He must also at his expense obtain any export license and arrange for the loading of the goods. The marine insurance policy shall be in the amount of CIF value plus ten percent. The seller must also obtain war risk coverage at the request and expense of the buyer. He must obtain a

[259]The need for the buyer to obtain a bill of lading may occur when he charters a vessel and the seller is issued a mate's receipt instead of a bill of lading.

"clean, on-board bill of lading." However, it should be noted that some clauses commonly inserted into the bill of lading that go to the condition of the packaging do not render the bill of lading "unclean." For example, clauses that note that the packages are "used" or "second-hand" are considered descriptive and not a notation of perceived damage or non-conformity. Such statements as "condition unknown" in the above clauses does not remove the presumption that the carrier guarantees that the goods were "in apparent good order and condition." The costs of packing and checking the goods are that of the seller. In turn, the buyer is required to pay the cost of unloading, along with lighterage and wharfage charges. The buyer can transfer the costs of unloading by negotiating a "CIF landed" term. The buyer also pays for the costs of obtaining the certificate of origin and any necessary import licenses or permits, along with all customs duties.

Other related responsibilities should be expressly allocated in the contract. For example, the CIF term only requires the seller to obtain a basic ("free of particular average") marine insurance policy in the currency of the contract. The parties should agree to any special risk endorsements that may be appropriate including theft, pilferage, leakage, breakage, and other risks of concern for the particular goods and the particular point of destination. The contract should specify how delivery is to take place, who is responsible for loading and unloading, how much insurance coverage is required, as well as the contract's duration and geographical scope, and details regarding the type of carriage (e.g., above deck or below, refrigerated container, etc.). Also, the party responsible for customs clearance or delivery should negotiate a *force majeure* or time-extension clause in case of delay in clearing customs or making delivery. Understand that the "C terms" are "shipment contracts and not "arrival or destination contracts." The risk of loss is transferred, like in the "F terms," at the port of shipment.

Professor Ramberg has noted that under Incoterms 1990 (and 2000) the traditional prevalence of the FOB, CFR and CIF terms is likely to give way to increased use of the CPT, CIP, and FCA terms.

> It is important to note that the traditional supremacy of FOB, CFR and CIF contracts will, in modern carriage, have to yield to FCA, CPT and CIP respectively, simply because the traditional function of the ship's rail as the dividing point between the functions of sellers and buyers has been replaced by other points, such as cargo terminals or other reception facilities. This has also influenced documentation and significantly reduced the use of on-board bills of lading. Thus, even in the carriage of

goods by sea, bills of lading have been replaced by non-negotiable sea waybills.[260]

He notes that the FCA term is the one most likely to become more important because it applies to all modes of transport.

Ramberg also notes that under the FOB and FCA, practice often overtakes the legal obligation that the seller need only turn over the goods to the carrier hired by the buyer. In practice, it is the seller who generally books the shipment for carriage. This practice is noted in the Incoterms' FCA trade term: "If requested by the buyer or if it is commercial practice and the buyer does not give an instruction to the contrary in due time, the seller may contract for carriage on usual terms at the buyer's risk and expense. The seller may decline to make the contract and, if he does, shall promptly notify the buyer accordingly."[261] In practice, there are a variety of FOB contracts. Under the strict definition of the term, the buyer nominates the ship, the seller delivers the goods to that ship in exchange for the bill of lading. Another version is FOB with "additional services" in which the shipping and insurance are actually arranged by the seller on behalf of the buyer. The only distinction with the CIF contract is that in FOB additional services, the arrangements are made at the expense of the buyer. Finally, the FOB (buyer contracting with carrier) version requires that the bill of lading be sent directly from the carrier to the buyer.[262] It is also important to note that the allocation of costs for loading and unloading under FOB, CIF, and C & F may be impacted by the customs of a given port.

It is important, as discussed in *Phillips Puerto Rico v. Tradax Petroleum*,[263] to examine the interrelationship between the trade term and other terms in the contract. This is especially necessary if other language in the contract can be construed as modifying the trade term. This was the issue in *Warner Bros. & Co. v. Israel.*[264] That case involved the purchase of Philippine sugar for shipment to New York City. The trade term in the contract stated "Philippines–C.I.F. Terms." Another provision in the contract pro-

[260]Jan Ramberg, "Novel Features of the ICC Incoterms 1990 in UNITED NATIONS UNIFORM COMMERCIAL LAW IN THE TWENTY-FIRST CENTURY 80 (1992).
[261]Ibid.
[262]RALPH H. FOLSOM, MICHAEL W. GORDON, & JOHN A. SPANOGLE, JR., INTERNATIONAL BUSINESS TRANSACTIONS 90 (3d ed. 1995).
[263]Chapter 3, "Force Majuere."
[264]101 F.2d 59 (2d Cir. 1939).

vided that the seller was to deliver sugar of a "net delivered weight." The sugar was delayed entry into the United States due to the imposition of a government sugar quota. The buyer attempted to avoid payment by arguing that the "net delivered weight" language converted the contract to a delivery contract. It argued that the net delivered weight could only be determined at the port of destination. The court rejected the argument holding that there was a CIF contract where the purchaser must pay upon the presentation of documents. It held that the "net delivered weight" language referred to the adjustment of the price based upon the weight of the sugar actually delivered, but was not enough to convert the express trade term into a destination contract. It further noted the general proposition that a delivery term (to be delivered to New York City) does not change an express trade term. "Under the ordinary CIF contract . . . delivery of the goods would not be a condition precedent to be performed at the risk of the seller. Nor is it made so merely because the obligation to contract for the carriage is expressed in the form of the delivery of the goods at a designated place."[265] The result may be different, however, if the destination term is included in the same provision as the trade term. Thus, it is important to use the trade term without further explanation and to make sure that other terms in the contract do not expressly conflict with the term chosen.

Unfair Contract Terms

Some countries will void, generally in consumer contracts, terms that are deemed unfair or unconscionable. Section 2-302 of the Uniform Commercial Code (UCC) provides that "if a court, as a matter of law, finds any clause of a contract to have been unconscionable . . . it may refuse to enforce the clause . . . or it may so limit the application of any unconscionable clause as to avoid an unconscionable result." This applies to commercial as well as consumer contracts. Some countries have enacted separate acts to deal with the issue of unfair terms. One example is the United Kingdom's Unfair Contract Terms Act of 1977. However, unlike the UCC, it targets only consumer contracts. The statute invalidates unreasonably broad exculpatory and indemnity clauses. In the area of exculpatory clauses, Section 2 states that a party cannot "exclude or restrict his liability for death or personal injury resulting from negligence." Indemnification clauses are void if

[265]Ibid. at 61.

a consumer is made to indemnify another person "in respect of liability that may be incurred by the other for negligence or breach of contract." Section 27 also voids any choice of law clause that enables the party imposing it "to evade operation of this Act." Finally, some international supply contracts are expressly exempted from the statute.[266] A similar law, the Standard Contract Terms Act, is found in Germany.[267]

Council Directive 93/13/EEC[268] provides similar protection for consumer contracts within the European Union. Its stated aim is to protect consumers "against the abuse of power by the seller or supplier of goods and services, in particular against one-sided standard contracts and the unfair exclusion of essential rights in contracts." Article 3 of the Directive provides a presumption of unfairness where a term has not been "individually negotiated" and "it causes a significant imbalance in the parties' rights and obligations." Article 5 provides a plain language requirement. "Terms must always be drafted in plain, intelligible language." Any terms not so written will be construed in a manner most favorable to the consumer. Article 6 voids any choice of law clause if it results in the consumer losing the protection provided by the Directive. Article 7 allows third parties to sue on behalf of consumer protection. Thus, trade forms and standard clauses can be attacked by a third party seeking "a decision as to whether contractual terms drawn up for general use are unfair." An Annex to the Directive provides an illustrative list of clauses that are considered susceptible to charges of fairness. These include limitation of liability, liquidated damages, unilateral termination, automatic renewal, price escalation without a right to cancel, unilateral right to alter terms, and surprisingly, arbitration clauses.

Securing Payment

As discussed in Chapter 4, a crucial concern of the exporter is securing payment for the goods shipped. This security is often provided through a third-party guarantee, the letter of credit. However, between trusted parties or when a letter of credit is not cost-effective, alternatives may be sought to

[266] See, Section 26.

[267] Gesetz zur Regelung des Rechts der Allgemeinen Geschäftsbedingungen, AGB-Gesetz.

[268] Council Directive 93/13/EEC of 5 April 1993 on Unfair Terms in Consumer Contracts. For an example of the Directive's enactment into national law see United Kingdom's Unfair Terms in Consumer Contracts Regulations of 1994.

secure payment. The documentary transaction without a letter of credit is still utilized. The payment is through a sight or time draft. The draft may be sued upon independent of the underlying export contract. The following is a sample of an acceptance and payment clause relating to a time draft:

> Buyer shall pay for the goods ordered by means of a documentary collection whereby Seller shall draw a time draft which shall be accepted by buyer against buyer's receipt of documents (specify documents) not less than sixty days after shipment, and payable sixty days after such acceptance. Payment of the draft shall be made by buyer's bank upon presentation at bank located near seller as shall be designated by buyer's bank and acceptable to seller.[269]

Other devices that should be considered to minimize the exporter's payment risk include retention of title, acquiring a chattel mortgage or security interest, and requiring the buyer to obtain a banker's acceptance.

Product Liability

It is important to note that a disclaimer of liability clause that is enforceable in one country may not be enforceable in another. This is especially true when the end user is a consumer. Many countries place restrictions on the ability of the manufacturer or even suppliers of component parts from disclaiming liability due to injury or loss caused from the use of their products. A review of European Union Directive 85/374 of July 25, 1985[270] provides an example of a law controlling products liability. Its

---

[269]Dennis J. Murphy, *How to Document International Commercial Transactions,* Int'l Quarterly 70, 85 (1985).

[270]Council Directive of 25 July 1985 on the Approximation of the Laws, Regulations and Administrative Provisions of the Member States Concerning Liability for Defective Products (85/374/EEC). See generally, Sandra N. Hurd & Frances E. Zollers, *Desperately Seeking Harmony: The European Community's Search for Uniformity in Product Liability Law,* 30 American Business Law Journal 35 (1992) (reviews the substantive provisions of this Directive and summarizes the laws of the "Member States"). See also, Council Directive 92/59/EEC on General Product Safety issued on 29 June 1992, Council Directive 93/13/EEC concerning Unfair Contract Terms, and Directive on Consumer Guarantees and After Sales Service as issued on 18 June 1996 (Draft). For a review of recent developments in this area see, Frances E. Zollers, Sandra N. Hurd & Peter Shears, *Consumer Protection in the European Union: An Analysis of the Directive on the Sale of Consumer Goods and Associated Guarantees,* 20 University of Pennsylvania Journal of International

general premise is that "all producers involved in the production process should be made liable" and that "liability should extend to *importers* of products."[271] Article 3 states that any one who imports into the European Union is also liable for product liability. It also provides that "where the producer cannot be identified each supplier of the product should be treated as its producer." The Directive also requires that the product or its packaging must identify the supplier, producer, or importer, but it leaves to national law the determination of the nature of the marking requirements. It further makes a commitment to strict products liability when it states that "liability without fault on the part of the producer is the sole means of adequately solving the problem of a fair apportionment of the risks inherent in modern technological production." It provides that the measurement of *defectiveness* is not the fitness of the product for a particular purpose, but the lack of the safety that the public is entitled to expect.

Article 7 provides a number of potential defenses to a claim of strict products liability. First, the defect was due to compliance with mandatory regulations. Second, a "state of the art" defense is provided in Article 7(e). It states that "the state of scientific and technical knowledge at the time when the product was placed into circulation was not such as to enable the existence of the defect to be discovered." Third, a manufacturer of a component part is absolved from liability if the defect is due to product design. Fourth, Article 10 provides for a statute of limitations defense. The injured party must bring suit within a three-year limitations period. The limitation period begins to run "from the day the plaintiff became aware, or should reasonably have become aware, of the damage, the defect and the identity of the producer." Any tolling of the limitations period is to remain based upon national laws.

Economic Law 97 (1999) (discusses the April 1998 "Amended Proposal for a Directive of the European Parliament and of the Council on the Sale of Consumer Goods and Associated Guarantees" and compares it to relevant provisions of the Uniform Commercial Code). It should be noted that the European equivalent to "warranty" is "guarantee." For an update of developments in this area see: European Commission, *Consumer Protection in the EU: Progress and Priorities for the Future* at <http://www.cec.org.uk/pubs/br/br96/br9612.htm>

[271] "However, on its true construction, the rule may enable an importer to avoid liability provided the products brought into the European Economic Area are imported for use, as opposed to distribution." PATRICK KEELY & REBECCA ATTREE, eds., EUROPEAN PRODUCT LIABILITIES 12-13 (1997).

Limitation Period

Another important issue is the statute of limitations or warranty period that will be applied to any future claims of the parties. It is always advisable for the parties to agree upon a reasonable limitation period. But, what is considered to be a reasonable limitation period? When does the limitation period commence? Should there be any instances when the limitation period should cease or be tolled? The United Nation's sponsored Convention on the Limitation Period in the International Sale of Goods[272] provides uniform rules governing the period of time within which a party may bring a claim in conjunction with a contract for the international sale of goods. The Convention prescribes a four-year limitation period for most claims. Article Two of the Convention defines an international sale as one in which "the buyer and seller have their places of business in different states." Article Twenty-two provides that the limitation period cannot be modified through contract, however it does make an exception for arbitral proceedings. "The provisions of this Article shall not affect the validity of a clause in the contract of sale which stipulates that arbitral proceedings shall be commenced within a shorter period of limitation." However, the four-year limitation period, even if applicable, can become truncated through the adoption of restrictive notice provisions. Article One states that "this Convention shall not affect a particular time-limit within which one party is required, as a condition for the acquisition or exercise of his claim, to give notice to the other party or perform any act other than the institution of legal proceedings." Also, the Convention does not apply to certain types of claims. For example, claims for personal injury caused by defective products and claims on bills of exchange or drafts are not governed by the Convention (Article Five).

The Convention provides rules for the determination of the commencement of the limitation period and when the period is to be tolled. Article Nine provides the general rule that the limitation period commences on the date that the "claim accrues." This date is further defined in Article

[272] The Convention on the Limitation Period in the International Sale of Goods was concluded in New York on June 14, 1974. An amendment to the Convention, known as the 1980 Protocol, was concluded in Vienna on April 11, 1980. Both instruments entered into force on August 1, 1988. See, Appendix 3.

Ten as the date when a breach of contract occurs. Other commencement dates are provided for acts of fraud and claims of defects. "A claim arising from a defect or other lack of conformity" accrues on the date on which the "goods are handed over to or their tender is refused by the buyer." The period for a claim of fraud commences on the date which the fraud was discovered or "reasonably could have been discovered." A tolling of the limitation period is granted when there is a submission to arbitrate the claim. Article Fourteen states that when the parties submit a claim to arbitration, "the limitation period shall cease to run when either party commences arbitral proceedings" in accordance with an arbitration clause. In the absence of an arbitration agreement, "arbitral proceedings shall be deemed to commence on the date on which a request that the claim in dispute be referred to arbitration is delivered at the habitual residence or place of business of the other party." Other tolling provisions for specific types of claims and events are provided elsewhere in the Convention. For example, Article Fifteen provides for a tolling of the limitation period when a creditor asserts a claim in conjunction with a dissolution or bankruptcy proceeding. Article Eighteen provides for a further tolling when there are multiple debtors. It states that "where legal proceedings have been commenced against one debtor, the limitation period prescribed in this Convention shall cease to run against any other party jointly and severally liable with the debtor, *provided that the creditor informs such party in writing within that period that the proceedings have been commenced.*" Note the importance of notifying any potential debtors. Article Seventeen provides for an additional one year limitation period when a legal proceeding is concluded "without a decision binding on the merits of the claim." The Convention does place an outer limit for the tolling of the limitation period through the above provisions. Article Twenty-three states that "notwithstanding the provisions of this Convention, a limitation period shall in any event expire no later than ten years from the date on which it commenced."

Associated limitation periods vary greatly from country to country and from cause of action to cause of action. Two common statutes of limitation periods are generally provided for breach of warranty and products liability claims. For example, European Union law provides for an extended ten year statute of limitation for product liability claims. The producer remains liable for damage caused by a defect in his product. In comparison, a proposed limitation period for warranty claims is two years starting from the date of delivery.

UNIDROIT Principles of International Commercial Contracts

UNIDROIT is a specialized agency of the United Nations that promotes the unification of law. In May 1994 it published the Principles of International Commercial Contracts (*Principles*) (See Appendix 6). Its primary differences in comparison to the CISG are threefold. First, it is not for adoption as a domestic law of international contracts. It is intended merely to provide neutral principles acceptable for guidance for lawyers and businesspersons from different legal systems. Second, it provides a set of general principles applicable to all types of contracts. In contrast, the CISG applies only to the commercial sale of goods and supplies a number of specific rules for that transaction type. Third, the *Principles* cover contract negotiations, while the CISG merely deals with the mechanics of offer and acceptance. The following excerpt explores the *Principles*' coverage of pre-contractual liability for conduct during the negotiation phase. Hans van Houtte describes the fine line between negotiation and contract, along with the potential of liability for bad faith negotiation under the *Principles.*

> First, a contract does not require an agreement of all details of the transaction. The fact that no agreement needs to be reached on all details of a transaction implies that parties may not know exactly when they enter a transaction. Article 2.13 suggests that if a party wants to avoid being "dragged" into a contract by surprise, it must specify in advance, that agreement on an issue it considers important has also to be reached; if no agreement on that specific item is reached, there will be no contract. Second, sometimes negotiations are not actually finished when one of the parties starts to perform. For instance, the legal departments of the two companies may still be discussing the contract terms when the sales department of the seller already delivers. In such a situation, the shipment of the goods can be considered as acceptance of the offer. Thus negotiations can be overtaken by contract performance. Third, sometimes parties to a contract intentionally leave terms open; terms on which they have to agree in future negotiations. Article 2.14 states that "if the parties intend to conclude a contract, the fact that they leave a term to be agreed upon in further negotiations or to be determined by a third party, does not prevent a contract from coming into existence.
>
> Anglo-American law appears not to require that negotiations are conducted in good faith. German, French, Italian, and Belgian law, on the other hand, have elaborate rules on "pre-contractual liability" for

> conducting or terminating negotiations. One of the great innovations of the Principles is that they provide standards for conducting negotiations. Article 2.15 states that "a party who negotiates or breaks off negotiations in bad faith is liable for the losses caused to the other party." Also, Article 2.16 makes a party liable when it discloses or improperly uses confidential information obtained in the course of negotiations. Breach of confidentiality entitles the other party to compensation for either the loss suffered by the breach of good faith or for the benefit the party in breach received by disclosing the information.[273]

The UNIDROIT Principles are indicative of how most civil law legal systems are more likely to affix liability in the negotiation stage. Parties are generally required to act in good faith during the negotiation phase. For example, a termination of lengthy negotiations without a justified reason will be considered bad faith and subject the party to a suit for damages or expenses. Such *pre-contractual liability* may include claims for expenses directly related to the negotiations including travel, research, and consulting expenses. It may also support a claim for indirect damages such as lost profits from other potential deals that the innocent party gave up to pursue negotiations with the terminating party. The Civil Code countries make a distinction between mere negotiations and preliminary agreement. The line between the two is a very subtle one. The key difference is that recognition of a preliminary agreement entitles the non-breaching party to the remedy of *specific performance.* In contrast, specific performance is almost always denied under the Uniform Commercial Code even for breaches of formal contracts. Section 2-716 of the U.C.C, allows for specific performance only if the suing party can prove that the goods were unique. The CISG writers could not engineer a compromise for this fundamental difference between common law and civil law remedies. Thus, a court applying the CISG is directed to reference a national law to determine if specific performance is to be granted. In contrast, a violation of the duty of good faith negotiations or *culpa in contrahendo* limits a party to a suit for damages. A court is likely to reject a claim for breach of a preliminary agreement if it is missing any essential elements of the final contract. Also, the Civil Code countries provide for extended periods of time for the bringing of lawsuits. The statute of limitations to bring a breach of the duty of good faith negotiations is five years

[273]Hans van Houtte, "The UNIDROIT Principles of International Commercial Contracts," 11 *Arbitration International* 373, 374-378 (1995).

under the Italian Civil Code and is extended to ten years for a breach of contract. In contrast, there is no cause of action in the United States for bad faith negotiation, while the statute of limitations under Section 2-725 of the Uniform Commercial Code is four years and the contracting parties are authorized to reduce the period to as little as one year.

Those drafting an international contract of any type may want to review the UNIDROIT Principles for International Commercial Contracts. Although they are non-binding general principles, some courts may utilize them in the interpretation of an international contract. Professor Bonell has stated that "with the assistance of the Principles, judges or arbitrators called upon to decide questions of interpretation or to supplement international legislative texts will find it easier to . . . adopt an autonomous and internationally uniform solution."[274] A number of features of the *Principles* should be noted.

The first group of features involves the formation of contracts. First, like the CISG, there is no writing requirement. This translates into a rejection of the parol evidence rule. It simply states that a contract "may be proved by any means, including witnesses."[275] Thus representations made during the negotiation stage may be entered into evidence even if they conflict with the written contract. However, Article 2.17 recognizes the ability of the parties to exclude such evidence through a merger clause. Nonetheless, prior statements or agreements may be used to "intepret the writing." Second, international trade usage is recognized. The parties are "bound by a usage that is widely known to and regularly observed in international trade."[276] Second, an offer may not be revoked if it is reasonable for the offeree to rely on it.[277] This is an expanded version of the Uniform Commercial Codes' firm offer rule. Fourth, an acceptance binds the contract not upon dispatch but "when the indication of assent reaches the offeror."[278] Fifth, an oral (telephone) offer "must be accepted immediately" or it self-terminates.[279] Sixth, in the "battle of the forms" scenario, an attempted acceptance with materially different terms is in reality a rejection (coun-

[274]Michael J. Bonell, "Non-Legislative Means of Harmonization" in UNITED NATIONS, UNIFORM COMMERCIAL LAW IN THE TWENTY-FIRST CENTURY 38 (1992).
[275]Article 1.2. Compare, U.C.C. §§ 2-201 & 2-202.
[276]Article 1.8. Compare, U.C.C. § 1-205.
[277]Article 2.4. Compare, U.C.C. § 2-205.
[278]Article 2.6.
[279]Article 2.7.

teroffer). If the additional terms are not material, then the contract includes the additional or modifying terms.[280] Article 2.22 acknowledges the use of pre-printed standard terms and provides for a presumption that a contract is formed despite conflicting standard terms. "A contract is concluded on the basis of the agreed terms and of any standard terms which are common in substance." Seventh, Article 2.16 recognizes a duty of confidentiality for information obtained during the course of negotiations. Eighth, Article 2.18 recognizes the efficacy of a written modification clause.[281] However, the party wanting to enforce such a clause must be careful that his conduct (prior acts) are not taken as a waiver of the clause. Article 2.18 states that "a party may be precluded by its conduct from asserting such a clause." Ninth, Article 2.20, titled "Surprising Terms," provides a means for a party to void boilerplate terms in a standard form contract. It provides that terms that a party "could not reasonably have expected" will not be enforced. However, "surprising terms" are enforceable if the other party should have been aware of their existence. This determination is to be based upon the terms' "content, language and representation." Thus, a conspicuously and clearly written term should be enforced.

In the area of validity, the *Principles* recognize a number of common contract voiding defenses including mistake, misrepresentation, fraud, and threat (duress). It does not deal with invalidity due to incapacity, lack of authority, or public policy. Courts would make those determinations through the application of a national law. Article 3.10 on "Gross Disparity" is a counterpart to the doctrine of unconscionability found in Section 2-302. It states that a party "may avoid the contract or an individual term if, at the time of the conclusion of the contract, it unjustifiably gave the other party an *excessive* advantage." In its place, "a court may adapt the contract or term in order to make it accord with reasonable commercial standards of fair dealing."

In the area of interpretation, Article 4.1 and 4.2 recognize the use of the reasonable person standard.[282] In fabricating the reasonable person a

[280]Article 2.11. Compare, U.C.C. § 2-207.

[281]Compare, U.C.C. § 2-209.

[282]For a more complete explanation of the reasonable person standard in Anglo-American law see, LARRY A. DIMATTEO, CONTRACT THEORY: THE EVOLUTION OF CONTRACTUAL INTENT (1998). See also, Larry A. DiMatteo, *The Counterpoise of Contracts: The Reasonable Person Standard and the Subjectivity of Contract,* 48 So. Carolina Law Rev. 293 (1997).

court or arbitration panel is authorized to take into account the preliminary negotiations, practices established between the parties (prior dealings), subsequent conduct (course of performance), nature and purpose of the contract, common meanings in the trade, and usages.[283] The *contra proferentem rule* is adopted in Article 4.6 so that ambiguous contract language is construed against the drafter. Article 4.4 recognizes the civil law notion that all terms should be interpreted "in the light of the whole contract." Article 5.4 recognizes the implied duty of best efforts in the performance of contractual obligations.

In the area of performance, the *Principles* provide a section on *hardship.* Hardship is defined as "where the occurrence of events fundamentally alters the equilibrium of the contract."[284] In order for a party to claim a hardship he must show that the event causing the hardship could not have reasonably been taken into account at the time of contracting, the event was beyond his control, and the risks were not assumed by the party in the contract. Hardship allows the party to "request negotiations." In the event that the parties do not agree to an adjustment or settlement, the court is instructed to either terminate the contract or adjust the contract to restore its equilibrium.[285] The related excuse of *force majeure* is recognized in Article 7.1.7. Article 7.1.4 gives a party the right to cure a non-performance unless the aggrieved party has a "legitimate interest in refusing cure."[286] Exemption or "limitation of liability clauses" are generally enforceable, unless they are "grossly unfair."[287] The demand of specific performance, unlike under the common law, is recognized as an ordinary remedy available to the non-breaching party.[288] The UCC notions of anticipatory repudiation and adequate assurance are recognized in Articles 7.3.3 and 7.3.4. Finally, the ability of the parties to agree on liquidated damages in their contract is authorized. The counterpart to the UCC notion of unenforceable penalties is that stipulated amounts may be reduced if they are "grossly excessive in relation to the harm resulting from non-performance."[289]

[283]Article 4.3. Compare, U.C.C. §§ 1-205 (course of dealing and usage of trade) & 2-208 (course of performance).
[284]Article 6.2.2. Compare, U.C.C. § 2-615.
[285]Article 6.2.3.
[286]Compare, U.C.C. § 2-508.
[287]Article 7.1.6. Compare, U.C.C. § 2-719.
[288]Article 7.2.2. Compare, U.C.C. § 2-716.
[289]Article 7.4.13. Compare, U.C.C. § 2-718.

CHAPTER 7

The CISG

This chapter incorporates a number of recent cases, and ICC Arbitration Tribunal decisions, including the recent American case of *MCC-Marble Center v. D'Agostino.*[290] The chapter attempts to blend an assortment of domestic and comparative law materials. However, this chapter serves primarily as an introduction to the United Nations Convention on Contract for the International Sale of Goods (CISG). It also attempts to highlight the major differences between the CISG and the Uniform Commercial Code (UCC). The contract law issues to be discussed include offer-acceptance rules, battle of the forms, firm offer rule, parol evidence rule, inspection and notice duties and rights, right to cure, anticipatory repudiation, disclaimer of warranty, damages, and contractual excuses. Special emphasis will be placed on the civil law concept of *nachfrist* notice. A case study is developed using some recent German court decisions.

International Sales Law

Most legal issues in international trade are settled by application of domestic national laws. At the end of the twentieth century, however, we can begin to discuss the evolution of a truly international law of sales or a new *lex mercatoria*. *Lex mercatoria* or law merchant refers to a system of rules of law created by international merchants, independent of any national legal

---

[290] 144 F.3d 1384 (1998).

system, for the purpose of governing international business transactions. The adoption in 1980 of the United Nations Convention for the International Sale of Goods (CISG)[291] marked a milestone in the development of the new *lex mercatoria.* Professor Farnsworth, the Reporter of the Second Restatement of Contracts, has predicted that the CISG will become the governing law of most export and import of goods transactions.[292] The CISG went into effect in the United States on January 1, 1998. Thus, the United States has two laws of contracts for the sale of goods: the Uniform Commercial Code and the CISG. In a case where two contracting parties are residents of the United States and another CISG country, an American court will apply the CISG rather than the Uniform Commercial Code. The CISG, however, is an optional law and the parties may *opt out* of it through a choice of law clause in their contract. As of April 25, 1999, the United Nations Treaty Section reported that fifty-five countries have adopted the CISG (Exhibit 7.1). The list of the contracting states includes most of the United States major trading partners such as Canada, Mexico, Germany, France, Russia, China, Italy, and Australia. The major exceptions include Japan, South Korea, Britain and Brazil. For an update on recent signatories and international case and arbitral law on the CISG refer to the following web cite: http://www.cisg.law.pace.edu.

Choice of Law and Conflict of Laws

There are three grounds for the jurisdiction and application of the CISG. Article 1 of the CISG states that unless there is an express choice of law clause in the contract, the CISG will be the law of a dispute in two situations. First, if the two parties have their places of business in countries that have ratified the CISG. Article 10 provides guidance regarding how one determines *place of business* for multinational enterprises. "If a party has more than one place of business, the place of business is that which has the clos-

[291]See generally, ALBERT H KRITZER, GUIDE TO PRACTICAL APPLICATIONS OF THE UNITED NATIONS CONVENTION ON CONTRACTS FOR THE INTERNATIONAL SALE OF GOODS (Deventer & Boston: Kluwer 1989); Symposium, *Convention on the International Sale of Goods,* 21 Cornell Int'l Law Journal 419-589 (1988).
[292]21 Cornell Int'l Law Journal 439-440 (1988).

Exhibit 7.1: Contracting Parties to the CISG

Argentina	Australia	Austria	Belarus
Belgium	Bosnia-Herzegovina	Bulgaria	Burundi
Canada	Chile	China	Croatia
Cuba	Czech Republic	Denmark	Ecuador
Egypt	Estonia	Finland	France
Georgia	Germany	Greece	Guinea
Hungary	Iraq	Italy	Latvia
Lesotho	Lithuania	Luxembourg	Mexico
Moldova	Mongolia	Netherlands	New Zealand
Norway	Peru	Poland	Romania
Russian Federation	Singapore	Slovakia	Slovenia
Spain	Sweden	Switzerland	Syria
Uganda	Ukraine	United States	Uruguay
Uzbekistan	Yugoslavia	Zambia	

est relationship to the contract and its performance." Therefore, if a foreign subsidiary of a corporation enters into a contract, the place of business for determining the jurisdiction of the CISG is the location of the subsidiary not the parent company. The second ground for jurisdiction is when only one of the parties is from a CISG country. In that event, the court or arbitral tribunal, is instructed to use their *conflict of law rules* to determine the law of the dispute. If the conflict of law rules direct the court or tribunal to the party whose country has ratified the CISG, then the CISG becomes the law of the dispute. It should be noted, however, that the United States opted out of the second ground for jurisdiction. A United States court or arbitral tribunal will only apply the CISG when the parties are from different CISG countries. A third ground for the use of the CISG in a dispute is not as direct law, but as customary international law. An arbitral panel or a court may use the CISG as evidence of trade usage instead of applying the law of an individual country. The following excerpts from International Chamber of Commerce Arbitration Case No. 5713 of 1989 and an article from the Dispute Resolution Journal explains this use of the CISG.

Seller v. Buyer, ICC Case No. 5713 of 1989

The contract contains no provisions regarding the substantive law (no choice of law clause). Therefore, the arbitrators will apply the law designated as the proper law by the rule of conflicts which they deem appropriate. The law of the country of the Seller appears to be the proper law governing the contract. However, the Tribunal finds that there is no better source to determine the prevailing trade usage than the terms of the United Nations Convention on the International Sale of Goods (CISG) of 11 April 1980, usually called the "Vienna Convention." This is so even though neither the country of the Buyer nor the country of the Seller are parties to that Convention.

The following excerpt discusses this potential application of the CISG as customary international law.

Larry A. DiMatteo, *Resolving International Contract Disputes*, American Arbitration Association, Dispute Resolution Journal 75, 76-77 (Nov. 1998)

The CISG may be voluntarily applied as evidence of customary international law. Arbitration tribunals are more likely than courts to recognize it as a source of customary international contract law. It is the product of compromise between the world's major legal systems—common law, civil law, and socialist law. Thus, it possesses a universal appeal that many arbitrators will find appealing in their search for a *lex mercatoria*-type of justification for their awards. The movement towards the unification and internationalization of contract law stems from numerous sources. These sources include the increase in economic and legal unions, most noticeably in Europe, the use of "neutral" country laws, and the increased recognition of general principles of contract law. The most profound evidence of the move towards the unification of contract law is the adoption of the CISG. Merchants have long developed usage and practices that have given them the ability to communicate with one another without the distractions presented by the nuances of culture, language, and national legal systems. The terse, clear, and non-legal language of the CISG provides arbitrators a source of supranational rules of commerce. Arbitration tribunals can imply the CISG into a contract as trade usage. For example, an ICC Tribunal in *Case No. 5713 of 1989* dealt with the issue of the amount of time a purchaser had to give notice of defect. The arbitration tribunal disregarded the domestic law's shorter statute of limitations period in favor of the two-year period provided in the CISG. In short, the arbitral tribunal used the CISG as evidence of international trade usage to avoid what it deemed to be an unfair domestic law. "As the applicable provisions of the law of the country where the seller had his place of business appeared to deviate from the generally accepted trade usage as reflected in the CISG in that it imposed extremely short and specific requirements in respect of the buyer giving notice to the seller in case of defects, the tribunal elects to apply the CISG." In sum, the CISG, along with the UNIDROIT Principles for Commercial Contracts, provide arbitrators a suitable framework for deciding international contract disputes by the application of general principles.

Choice of Law Under the CISG

The use of a choice of law clause to avoid application of the CISG must be carefully drafted. For example, the parties may intend that the Uniform Commercial Code is to be the law of the transaction. To that end the parties negotate the following choice of law clause: "the law of the State of New York shall apply to any disputes." Under Article 1(1)(a) of the CISG, the law of New York is the CISG if the two parties are from different CISG countries. An interesting side issue is what type of evidence will a court admit to interpret the choice of law clause. If it uses cases involving the Uniform Commercial Code, then its parol evidence rule would prevent testimony that the parties intended the Uniform Commercial Code to be the law of the dispute. Thus, the court would likely be forced to apply the CISG as the law of New York. If the court uses the CISG to interpret the clause, it could allow testimony as to the parties intent because the CISG lacks a parol evidence rule. It would than decide that the law of New York was meant to refer to the Uniform Commercial Code! In order to avoid such a quagmire, clear choice of law clauses should be drafted.

Sale of Goods Defined

The CISG's coverage is limited to transactions for the sale of goods. Article 2 excludes certain types of goods from coverage, including goods purchased at auction, electricity, securities, ships, vessels, and aircraft. Thus, sales of services and transfers of intellectual property rights would not come under the jurisdiction of the CISG. There are many transactions, however, that include more than one type of subject matter. For example, the sale of computer software is often a *mixed sale* involving the sale of a tangible item,[293] like a disk or a CD-ROM, along with a service or technical assistance agreement, and a license pertaining to intellectual property rights. Is this type of transaction covered by the CISG? Article 3 provides a two-part test to distinguish a service contract from a sale of goods. First, a contract is not for the sale of goods if the buyer provides a substantial part of the materials used in the production of the goods. This would be considered a contract for labor or assembly services. Second, a preponderant part of the contract is not for the supply of labor or services. A computer software sale normally mixes the characteristics of a sale of goods, a sale of services, and a lease or license of technology. Thus, software possesses both tangible and intangible elements. According to Article 3's second test it will only be considered within the scope of the CISG if a preponderant part of the transaction is for tangible goods. If, for example, a company contracts for software to computerize its inventory the court may look to the allocation of the price within the contract among the different components. Thus, if the contract provided for $20,000 worth of database software and $15,000 worth of support service and labor for data-entry, the contract would be considered predominately one for the sale of goods and covered by the CISG. However, if it is possible to separate the goods portion of the contract from the services portion, then the CISG would apply to the goods portion of the contract. One suggested approach to the intangibility problem of technology and software is to treat such items as "virtual goods."[294] This is the approach taken in applying the UCC to software. *Virtual goods* are treated just like conventional goods for purposes of the UCC. Time will tell whether such an approach will be applied to the CISG.

---

[293]See generally, Thomas L. Lockhart & Richard J. McKenna, *Software License Agreements in Light of the UCC and the Convention on the International Sale of Goods,* 70 Michigan Business Journal 646 (1991); L. Scott Primak, *Computer Software: Should the U.N. Convention on Contracts for the Sale of Goods Apply? A Contextual Approach to the Problem,* 11 Computer Law Journal 197 (1991).

[294]See, Marcus Larson, *Applying Uniform Sales Law to International Software Transactions,* 5 Tulane Journal of International & Comparative Law 445 (1997).

The Parol Evidence Rule and the CISG

The UCC requires that any sale of goods for a price of $500 or more must be evidenced by "some writing sufficient to indicate that a contract of sale has been made." Also, the writing must be signed by the party against whom enforcement is sought. Under the CISG, the use of parol evidence is liberalized and there are no writing or signature requirements. The CISG applies the view of many of the civil law countries where a writing is not required in order to enforce an agreement. Instead, the CISG generally admits all parol evidence under its "all relevant circumstances" approach. The Uniform Commercial Code writing requirement or *statute of frauds* prevents the admission of evidence that contradicts the writing by its adoption of the common law's parol evidence rule. Along with stating the requirements for a legally sufficient writing, UCC Section 2-201 lists a number of exceptions including the *written confirmation rule*, an order for *specially manufactured goods*, and where the parties' conduct has overtaken the lack of a sufficient writing such as the payment or receipt of goods. The written confirmation rule is only available in commercial transactions since it requires that both parties be merchants. It states that a writing sent by one of the parties confirming the conclusion of a contract is sufficient to satisfy the writing requirement. The other party need not sign or acknowledge receipt of the confirmation in order to be bound by it. Section 2-201 does allow the receiving party to object to the confirmation and thus, prevent the formation of a contract. The notice of objection must be given within ten days of the receipt of the written confirmation. The court in *GPL Treatment Ltd. v. Louisiana-Pacific,*[295] analyzed the intricacies of the written confirmation rule. The plaintiff (GPL) sued defendant (Louisiana-Pacific) for breach of an oral contract to buy 88 truckloads of cedar shakes. Louisiana-Pacific denied the alleged contract and asserted the UCC statute of frauds as an affirmative defense. The relevant text of GPL's form was entitled and read:

---

[295] 914 P.2d 682 (Or. Sup. Ct. 1996).

"ORDER CONFIRMATION"

"Conditions of Sale:"

All orders accepted subject to strikes, labor troubles, car shortages, or other contingencies beyond our power.	GPL LTD.
Any freight rate increases, sales, or use taxes is for buyers account.	BY:____________________

"SIGN CONFIRMATION COPY & RETURN"

BY:______________________________

Thereafter, the price of cedar shakes dropped and defendant's needs changed. The defendant refused to place orders for more than 13 truckloads. Plaintiff brought a breach of contract action for lost profits. The court held that a written confirmation sent pursuant to the merchant's exception need not contain all material terms of the contract; it must simply confirm a contract and include a quantity term. A merchant who receives a confirmatory writing may escape being bound only by giving a written objection within 10 days. Silence by the receiver does not affect a valid confirmation. A determination that the writing satisfies the merchant's exception does not prove the existence of a contract, however. It merely prevents the party against whom enforcement is sought from raising the UCC statute of frauds as an affirmative defense. The defendant raised the issue that the "Sign Confirmation Copy and Return" language on the confirmation required the defendant to sign before a binding contract would be formed. The court held that there is no single correct answer to the question of the effect of a "sign and return" clause. Each writing must be examined independently and in light of its own contents and context. Considering GPL's writing in its entirety, it concluded that notwithstanding the "sign and return" clause, GPL's order confirmation form was sufficient to satisfy the merchant's exception.

The parol evidence rule seeks to preserve the integrity of written contracts by refusing to allow the admission of oral statements or previous correspondence to contradict the written agreement. Under this rule, when parties place their agreement in writing, all previous oral and written documents merge into the final written agreement. However, final written agreements may be explained or supplemented by prior dealings, trade usage, or course of performance information. *Prior dealings* include prior conduct and performances under prior contracts between the parties, which are regarded as establishing a common basis of understanding. *Trade usage* refers to the customs and practices regularly observed in a given trade or business. "Usages of trade furnish the background and gives meaning to the language used by merchants in that trade."[296] The concept of *course of performance* is premised on the fact that the parties conduct in performing under the contract is a good indication of what they believe to be its meaning. Section 2-208 of the UCC states that "any course of performance accepted or acquiesced in without objection shall be relevant to determine the meaning of the agreement."

Unlike the UCC, the CISG in its Article 11 states that a "contract need not be evidenced by writing." Also, a contract and its terms may be proven "by *any* means," including witness testimony. Therefore, the potential for liability for representations made during the negotiation stage is greater under the CISG. The Uniform Commercial Code's parol evidence rule allows a party to avoid liability for statements made during the negotiations if those statements are not placed within the final written contract. Under the CISG, prior oral statements regarding anything, including quality and performance, would potentially be enforceable. The unknowledgeable businessperson could be charged with unexpected liability for oral statements or representations made in an informal correspondence. The CISG's elimination of the writing requirement and the parol evidence rule allows the receiver of a letter or document a strategic advantage in proving enforceability. Also, oral assurances given to persuade another party to enter into a contract may be used to prove contractual intent.

The lack of a writing requirement is further complicated by Articles 12 and 96 which allow contracting states to *opt out* of Article 11's no writing requirement. Some countries, mostly former countries of the Soviet Union and socialist law countries, have opted out in favor of domestic laws that require a writing. These countries include Russia, Ukraine, Belarus, Estonia, Hungary, Argentina, Chile, and China. The 1998 case of *MCC-Marble v. D'Agostino*,[297] is the most recent American case involving the interaction of the CISG with other American laws. The court was asked to determine if the

[296]U.C.C. Section 1-205, Comment 4.

[297]144 F. 3d 1384 (1998).

American parol evidence rule is to be applied to cases involving the CISG. "MCC" was a Florida corporation engaged in the retail sales of imported tiles. "D'Agostino" was an Italian manufacturer of tiles. At a trade show they orally agreed on a sale of tiles. The agreed terms were placed on one of D'Agostino's standard pre-printed order forms. The executed forms were printed in Italian. MCC brought suit claiming a breach of the requirements contract when D'Agostino failed to satisfy a number of orders. D'Agostino responded that it was under no legal obligation to fill the orders because MCC had defaulted on payment for previous shipments. MCC responded that the earlier tiles they received were of a lower quality than contracted for and that it was entitled to reduce payment in proportion to the defects. D'Agostino replied that a clause on the reverse side of the purchase order form required that all complaints for defects must be made in writing not later than 10 days after receipt of merchandise and this had not been done by MCC. MCC argued that the parties never intended the terms and conditions printed on the reverse of the order form to apply to their agreement. Article 8 of the CISG provides: "For purposes of this Convention statements made by and other conduct of a party are to be interpreted according to his intent where the other party knew or should have been aware what that intent was. Due consideration is to be given to *all* relevant circumstances of the case including negotiations." The plain language of the Convention, therefore, requires an inquiry into a party's subjective intent as long as the other party to the contract was aware of that intent. MCC argued that it did not intend to be bound by the terms on the manufacturer's form since it was entirely in Italian. The court found it "nothing short of astounding that an individual, purportedly experienced in commercial matters, would sign a contract in a foreign language and expect not to be bound simply because he could not comprehend its terms." The general proposition is that parties that sign contracts will be bound, regardless of whether they have read them or understand them.[298] Nonetheless, Article 8(1) of the CISG requires a court to consider evidence of the parties' subjective intent. Affidavits of agents of MCC acknowledged that D'Agostino's representatives were aware of MCC's subjective intent not to be bound by the fine print terms.

---

[298]See, Samson Plastic Corp. v. Battenfeld Extrusionstechnik GMBH., 718 F.Supp. 886 (1989).

The key issue of the case was whether the parol evidence rule of the American court applies to the CISG. It was crucial in determining whether the testimony of MCC's subjective intent and D'Agostino's awareness of it would be admitted to contradict or vary the terms of the written contract. The court asserted that the parol evidence rule, contrary to its title, was a substantive rule of law, not a rule of evidence. As such, courts cannot simply apply the parol evidence rule as a procedural matter — as it might if excluding a particular type of evidence under the Federal Rules of Evidence. The Uniform Commercial Code includes a version of the parol evidence rule that states that "a writing intended by the parties as a final expression of their agreement may not be contradicted by evidence of any prior agreement or contemporaneous oral agreement." The CISG contains no express statement on the role of parol evidence. Moreover, Article 8(3) expressly directs the courts to give "due consideration to all relevant circumstances of the case including the negotiations." It is a clear instruction to admit and consider parol evidence regarding the negotiations to the extent they reveal the parties' subjective intents.

Another court, however, appears to have arrived at a contrary conclusion. In *Beijing Metals & Minerals Import/Export Corp. v. American Bus. Ctr., Inc.*,[299] a defendant sought to avoid a dismissal of its contract claim by relying on evidence of negotiated oral terms that the parties did not include in their written agreement. The court held that the parol evidence rule would apply regardless of whether Texas law or the CISG governed the dispute. The court in *MCC-Marble* rejected the *Beijing* court's analysis of the applicability of the parol evidence rule to the CISG. It argued that Article 8(3) of the CISG is a rejection of the parol evidence rule. Furthermore, one of the primary factors motivating the negotiation and adoption of the CISG was to provide parties to international contracts for the sale of goods with some degree of certainty as to the principles of law that would govern potential disputes. Courts applying the CISG should not upset the parties reliance on the Convention by substituting familiar principles of domestic law, such as the parol evidence rule, when the Convention requires a different result. Moreover, to the extent parties wish to avoid parol evidence problems they may attempt to do so by including a *merger clause* in their agreement that

[299] 993 F.2d 1178 (5th Cir. 1993).

extinguishes any and all prior agreements and understandings not expressed in the writing.

Issues of Contract Law: CISG and Uniform Commercial Code

This section will focus on the substantive provisions of the CISG to provide instruction as to the potential for unintended legal liability in international contracting. These substantive provisions will be compared to relevant provisions in the UCC (Exhibit 7.2).[300] Although the UCC acted as a blueprint in the drafting of the CISG, the American exporter must be cognizant of the fundamental differences between the two laws. Ten years after its adoption by Congress, the CISG remains a complete unknown to many businesspersons and lawyers. It is important that the CISG be understood and effectively applied by United States exporters and importers. It not only places some unique responsibilities on sellers and buyers of goods, it also provides a number of rights and remedies not found in American law.

Whether applying the CISG, the UCC, or the law of another legal system, the issues of contract law remain the same. The broad topical areas to be examined include formation, performance, warranty, interpretation, remedies, and excuses. All of these issues of contract law are dealt with in the CISG. There are, however, a number of areas where an issue of law would not be covered under the CISG. These include product liability, the legality of a contract, the capacity of the parties to contract, and whether the non-breaching party is entitled to specific performance. These substantive areas would be decided under a national law of contract. The national law to be applied would be determined by applying the courts' conflict of law rules. By way of background and preview, the following is a list of 65 rules derived from the CISG. This list of rules can be used as a quick reference guide to the substantive provisions of the CISG. The numbers placed within the brackets refer to the relevant articles of the CISG.

---

[300]See generally, HENRY GABRIEL, PRACTITIONER'S GUIDE TO THE CISG AND UCC (1994); WILLIAM HANCOCK, ed., GUIDE TO THE INTERNATIONAL SALE OF GOODS (1986). See also, B. Blair Crawford, *Drafting Considerations Under the 1980 United Nations Convention on Contracts for the International Sale of Goods*, 8 Journal of Law & Commerce 187 (1988).

Exhibit 7.2: Selective Comparison of CISG & UCC

CISG Description	*CISG Articles*	*UCC Description*	*UCC Sections*
Writing Requirement	11, 13, 14	Statute of Frauds	2-201
Parol Evidence Rule	8, 9	Parol Evidence Rule	2-202
Fomation	14, 19, 20-21, 23	Formation	2-204
Obligation of Good Faith	None	Obligation of Good Faith	1-202
Revocability of Offer	16	Firm Offer Rule	2-205
Acceptance Upon Receipt	18	Mailbox Rule	2-206
Battle of the Forms	14, 19	Additional Terms	2-207
Fixing Price Term	14, 55, 56	Open Price Term	2-305
Fixing Place of Delivery	57	Place for Delivery	2-308
Time for Delivery; *Nachfrist*	33, 63	Time for delivery, performance	2-309
Place of Payment	57	Time for Payment	2-310
Avoidance; Rejection	81, 86	Manner of Rejection	2-602
Limited Right to Reject Goods	49	Perfect Tender Rule	2-601
Warranty Against Third-Party Claims of Infringement	41, 42	Warranty of Title	2-312
Warranties	35	Warranties	2-313, 314, 315, 316
Inspection; Documents	518	Right to Inspection	2-513
Nonconformity; Non-delivery Partial Delivery	36, 49, 51	Rights on Improper Delivery	2-601
Notice of Avoidance	49	Waiver of Failure to Particularize	2-605
Failure to Notify	49	Acceptance of Goods	2-606
Notice of Nonconformity (particularized notice)	39	Notice of Defect (generalized notice)	2-607(3)(a)
Fundamental Breach; Notice; Installments; Avoidance	25, 49, 73, 81-82	Revocation of Acceptance	2-608
Anticipatory Breach	71, 72, 73	Anticipatory Repudiation	2-609, 610
Price Reduction Remedy	50	Not Available	
Nachfrist Notice	47, 48, 63	Not Available	
Impediment Exemption	79	Commercial Impracticability	2-615
General Notice	27	Notice of Excuse	2-616
Specific Performance (S.P.)	45	Limited Right to S. P.	2-716

Exhibit 7.3: List of 65 CISG Rules

1. **The CISG is structured along the typical timeline of an international contract of sale: formation, obligations of the parties, passing of risk.**

2. **The CISG favors an *original interpretation* of its content and terms, and not as defined in a given national legal system.**

3. **The CISG applies to sales of goods between parties from different countries, when the counties are both signatories to the CISG, and the rules of international law lead to the law of one of those signatories. [1] Place of business is the one closest to the contract and its performance. [10]**

4. **The CISG does not apply to (1) personal goods, (2) goods sold at auction or by a governmental proceeding, (3) securities and negotiable instruments, (4) ships and aircraft, and (5) electricity. [2]**

5. Mixed sales of goods and services may or may not come under the CISG depending on whether the party ordering the goods supplied a *substantial part of the materials* or if the *preponderant part* of the contract is for labor or services. [3]

6. The CISG only governs the formation of contracts and the rights and obligations of the seller and the buyer. [4]

7. National laws continue to govern issues dealing with the validity of contracts, such as capacity and legality. [4]

8. Liability for injuries caused by goods are governed by national product liability laws. Damages to property caused by defective goods are subject to the CISG. [5]

9. Parties may contract out the application of the CISG. If there is a doubt there is a presumption that the CISG applies. [6]

10. Parties are implied to have agreed to a usage they knew or should have known which is widely known and observed in international trade (for that particular trade and type of good), such as INCOTERMS. [9]

11. A contract need not be in writing and can be proved by *any* means, including witnesses. [11] A writing is required if an adopting state opted out of Article 11 and the applicable national law requires a writing. [96] Writing includes telegram and telex. [13]

12. An offer must show intent, be sufficiently definite including a description of the goods and provisions for determining quantity and price. [14]

13. A proposal not addressed to specific persons (newspaper advertisements or price circulars) is presumed to be an invitation, unless it states otherwise. [14]

14. An offer, even if irrevocable, can be revoked if withdrawal reaches offeree before the offer. [15]

15. An offer may be revoked if revocation reaches offeree prior to dispatch of acceptance. [16]

16. An offer may not be revoked if offeree reasonably relied upon it. [16]

17. A statement or conduct may act as an acceptance. [18]

18. Offeree may indicate acceptance by performing an act (based on usage or prior dealings) if performed within the required time. [18]

19. An acceptance becomes effective upon receipt by the offeror if received within a *reasonable time* ("reasonable" based upon circumstances of transaction, including means of transmission used by offeror). [18] The period of time for acceptance of an offer sent by letter begins to run from the date shown on the letter. [20]

20. Oral offers must be accepted immediately. [18]

21. Assent to an offer with additions or modifications is a counteroffer. [19]

22. Additions or modifications that do not materially alter an offer is an acceptance unless offeror objects. [19]

23. Non-materially altering terms of offeree become part of the contract. [19]

24. Material terms include price, quantity, place and time of delivery, warranties, liability limitations, choice of law, and choice of forum. [19]

25. An acceptance dispatched belatedly is effective if offeror notifies offeree of his "acceptance" of the acceptance. [21]

26. A properly transmitted acceptance belatedly received is effective unless the offeror notifies otherwise. [21]

27. A fundamental breach is a condition for the immediate avoidance of a contract. [25]

28. The parties may agree to the fundamental nature of an obligation, such as "time is of the essence." [25]

29. A violation of the time for performance is fundamental if the party cannot use the late delivery or time is made of the essence. [25]

30. A violation of quality requirements (non-conformity) is fundamental if it impedes the use of the goods and is irreparable. [25]

31. The rejecting party must notify the breaching party of her intent to avoid the contract. [26]

32. A court is to issue a judgment for specific performance based upon its own national law. [28]

33. A contract may be modified by agreement. [29]

34. If a contract is silent as to place of delivery, then delivery is the handing the goods over to a common carrier. At that time the risk of loss passes. [31]

35. If a contract for specially manufactured goods is silent as to delivery, the place of delivery is seller's factory or warehouse. [31]

36. The seller must properly mark goods or give notice to buyer upon delivery to common carrier. [32]

37. If insurance is to be obtained by the buyer, then seller must at buyer's request provide all necessary information. [32]

38. If the seller hands over non-conforming documents before the required time, she has the right to cure the lack of conformity up to the time provided. [34]

39. For goods to be in conformity they must be fit for the purposes ordinarily used, are of the quality as indicated by a sample or model, and are packaged properly. [35]

40. The CISG treats differing quantities as a lack of conformity and not as a partial delivery. [35]

41. The seller has a right to cure a non-conformity if the goods had been delivered early. [37]

42. The buyer must examine the goods promptly after taking delivery. [38]

43. The buyer must give notice of non-conformity within a reasonable time after a defect is discovered or should have been discovered but no later than two years from delivery. [39] This period does not apply if seller knew or should have known about the non-conformity. [40]

44. The buyer may demand delivery of substituted goods or repair to the non-conforming goods. [46]

45. The buyer may grant an additional time for performance (*nachfrist* extension). [47]

46. If seller request additional time and buyer does not reply, then seller may perform within time indicated in her request. [48]

47. Buyer may declare a contract avoided if there is a fundamental breach or in case of non-delivery during the *nachfrist* extension. [49]

48. The buyer may reduce the price, in the same proportion as the reduced value of the non-conforming goods, as compared to the value of conforming goods. [50]

49. A buyer may avoid a contract of there is a partial delivery only if it constitutes a fundamental breach. If not fundamental, then may only avoid the non-conforming portion. [51]

50. A (reasonable) price may be implied by a court. It is the price generally charged in the trade at the time of the conclusion of the contract. [55]

51. Under the normal documentary transaction the buyer will not have the right to examine the goods before delivery. [58]

52. Buyer is obligated to do what is reasonably required to take delivery. [60]

53. If buyer fails to take delivery, seller must take reasonable steps to preserve the goods. He is entitled to retain them until he has been reimbursed for expenses related to the preservation. [85]

54. Buyer has an obligation to preserve the goods if she has received them even though she plans to reject them. [86]

55. The seller may fix an additional time for performance by the buyer (*nachfrist* extension). [63]

56. If buyer fails to provide specifications as required (specially made goods), then seller may make the specifications and provide them to the buyer. If the buyer fails to provide different specifications within a reasonable time, then the seller's specifications are binding. [65]

57. Unless stated otherwise, risk of loss passes to buyer upon delivery to the *first carrier.* If a particular place is specified, then it is upon delivery to the carrier at that place. [67]

58. A party may suspend performance if it becomes apparent the other party will not perform due to creditworthiness or failing to prepare to perform (anticipatory repudiation). [71]

59. A party suspending performance must give immediate notice to the other party. [71]

60. A party must continue performance if the other party provides adequate assurance. [71]

61. The non-breaching party has a duty to mitigate damages. [77]

62. A party is excused from performance if she cannot perform due to (1) an impediment beyond her control and (2) it was nor reasonably expected at the time of the contract formation. [79]

63. The excuse is only good for the duration of the impediment. [79]

64. Examples of impediments include: natural phenomena, decisions of countries, war, accidents, blockades, sabotage, robbery. [79]

65. The party claiming the excuse must give notice of the impediment to the other party within a reasonable time. [79]

Mechanics of Formation

The CISG can be divided into four groupings: General Provisions (Articles 1-13), Contract Formation (Articles 14-24), Rights and Obligations (Articles 25-88), and Ratification (Articles 89-101). This section will examine the grouping dealing with Contract Formation, along with articles in the Ratification grouping that bear on formation. All legal systems recognize the formation of a contract when an offer and acceptance is exchanged.[301] The key issue is determining the exact time of formation. This determination is important in order to decide the effectiveness of attempted revocations by the offeror and attempted rejections (subsequent to the sending of an acceptance) by the offeree. An exception is when the offer invites the offeree to accept by the commencing of performance. However, commencement of performance may not be sufficient. Most legal systems require the offeree to notify the offeror within a reasonable time that performance has commenced. Section 2-206(2) of the Uniform Commercial Code states that "where the beginning of a requested performance is a reasonable mode of acceptance an offeror who is not notified of acceptance within a reasonable time may treat the offer as having lapsed before acceptance." The common law rule known as the dispatch or *mailbox rule* holds that a contract is formed upon the sending of the acceptance by placing it into a reasonable means of transmission. All other legal systems of the world find a contract only when and if the acceptance or notice of the acceptance is received by the original offeror. Article 1326 of the Italian Civil Code states that an acceptance needs to be communicated to the offeror within the term which is deemed reasonable according to the nature of the business or trade customs.

Most international commercial transactions involve long-term negotiations, along with numerous exchanges of correspondences and documents. It is often the difficult task of a court or arbitral tribunal to analyze

---

[301]See generally, Ronald A. Brand & Harry M. Fletcher, *Arbitration and Contract Formation in International Trade: First Interpretations of the U.N. Sales Convention,* 12 Journal of Law & Commerce 239 (1993); Burt A. Leete, *Contract Formation Under the United Nations Convention on Contracts for the International Sale of Goods and the Uniform Commercial Code: Pitfalls for the Unwary,* Temple Int'l & Comparative Law Journal 193 (1992).

the numerous exchanges to determine if and when a contract was formed. Articles 14-24 of the CISG, similar to those found in American law, provide a number of offer-acceptance rules to be used to answer formation issues. A Hungarian court in *Pratt & Whitney v. MALEV Hungarian Airlines*[302] was the first to apply these rules. MALEV Airlines (defendant) entered into negotiations with Pratt & Whitney (plaintiff) to supply it with jet engines to be installed on jumbo jets that defendant was purchasing from Boeing Aircraft and Airbus of France. After carrying on thorough negotiations, Pratt & Whitney sent a meticulously written proposal of 15 pages to defendant on December 14, 1990 with a deadline for the proposal of December 21, 1990. Defendant "accepted the proposal on December 21, 1990. After numerous other discussions and correspondences, defendant informed plaintiff in a March 25, 1991 letter that it no longer planned on buying plaintiff's engines. The issues for the court included whether the proposal without a fixed price was an offer, whether the defendant's response was an acceptance, and whether aircraft parts were covered under the CISG? On the last issue, Article 2 of the CISG excludes from coverage the sale of "ships, vessels, hovercraft or aircraft." Does this exclusion include aircraft engines and parts? The court held that such component parts are covered as contracts relating to the production of goods as defined in Article 3 of the Convention.

Regarding the issues of formation, according to Article 14 of the CISG, a proposal to be an offer need only be addressed to one or more definite persons, be adequately specified, and indicate the offeror's intention to bind itself. A proposal is adequately defined if it indicates the goods and fixes the quantity and price expressly or contains provisions for the their definition. The court held that the proposal left no doubt about its subject because it indicated unambiguously the goods subject of the sale. It simply left to the buyer the right to designate the exact engine to be purchased. The quantity of engines was to be decided based upon the number of airplanes the defendant decided to buy. Also, the proper indication of the goods was not affected by the condition that according to the proposal the buyer could choose from among the enumerated engines. Therefore, plaintiff's proposal of December 14, 1990 was a legal offer under the CISG.

[302] 13 Bp. P.O.B. 16 (Metropolitan Court of Budapest) (1991).

The next issue was whether defendant's response of December 21, 1990 was an acceptance under Article 18 of the CISG. It is noted that the offer contained the language that the defendant's "acceptance of this proposal is conditional upon the approvals of the governments of Hungary and the United States." The court held that this condition did not prevent the formation of a contract. Article 23 of the CISG states that a contract becomes valid when the offeror receives a notification of acceptance. The defendant's response of December 21, 1990 established a valid agreement.

A New York case dealt with similar issues under the UCC.[303] The case applied Section 2-206 of the Uniform Commercial Code to a unilateral or "contract by conduct" situation. A New York company sent a purchase order to a buying agent in Hong Kong. The buying agent failed to sign and return the order, but proceeded to represent the New York company in procuring the goods. The court, citing Section 2-206, stated that "an order or offer to buy goods for prompt or current shipment shall be construed as inviting acceptance either by a prompt promise or by the prompt or current shipment of conforming or non-conforming goods" It held that the Hong Kong agent had entered into a contract when it filled in the terms of the purchase order and by subcontracting for the production of the goods.

Firm Offer Rule

Section 2-205 of the Uniform Commercial Code provides an exception to the rule that an offeror is the *master of the offer.* The "master of the offer" rule gives the offeror the right to revoke his offer at any time. The firm offer exception provides that "an offer given by a *merchant* in a *signed writing* which gives *assurance* that it will be held open is not revocable, but in no event may such period of irrevocability exceed three months." The *firm offer rule* found in Article 16 of the CISG is broader then the one provided in the UCC. It provides that an offer cannot be revoked "if it indicates that it is irrevocable or if it was reasonable for the offeree to rely on the offer being irrevocable and the offeree has acted in reliance on the offer." In short, the offeror need not give a fixed period of time for which the offer is to remain

[303]Kahn Lucas Lancaster, Inc. v. Lark International Ltd., 1997 WL 458785 (S.D.N.Y. 1997).

open or give any assurance that the offer is being left open. The CISG allows for the designation of an offer as firm if it is determined that such offers are generally relied upon in a given trade or industry.

Battle of Forms

Most international export transactions make use of standard forms to expedite the negotiation and conclusion of contracts. Exhibits 7.4 and 7.5 are examples of a standard purchase order and some of the fine print or *boilerplate* terms found on the reverse side of a pro forma invoice. The purchase order and pro forma invoice are examples of forms, along with others such as price quotations or written confirmations, that act as the offers and acceptances in the contract formation process. The chronological order of communication will determine if a purchase order acts as an offer or acceptance. Most exporters and importers will review the front page of the other party's form (Exhibit 7.4). Few exporters or importers take the time to read and understand the "Terms and Conditions" on the reverse side of the other party's form. The problem is that the terms on the reverse side of the respective forms are often in conflict or contain terms that the other party would not have consciously agreed to at the time of formation. For example, the "Terms and Conditions" found in Exhibit 7.5 absolves the seller of any responsibility for the goods when they are delivered to any third party such as a freight forwarder or common carrier (Paragraphs 1,2,3). This term may conflict with the trade term located on the face of the other party's form. Paragraph 4 makes the sellers' quotations as to freight and insurance *nonbinding*. Paragraph 5 limits the seller's liability for his negligent acts to $50 per shipment. Paragraph 6 requires the buyer to notify the seller of any defects in the goods within 60 days of the date of exportation or the buyer will lose his right to sue for breach of warranty. Paragraph 7 allows the seller to retain a lien on the goods for "all charges or expenses incurred by the Seller in connection with the shipment to the Purchaser." Paragraph 8 absolves the seller from any governmental requirements pertaining to the shipment of goods including marking and health regulations. Paragraph 9 mandates that any dispute needs to be settled in a court near the seller (City of Miami) and using the law of the seller's place of business (State of Florida). Paragraph 10 passes the costs of any litigation brought by the

Exhibit 7.4: Purchase Order

Purchase Order

(orden de compra)

January 15, 1999

To: Latin America Exporting Co.
P.O. Box 54321
Miami, Florida 33152
USA

No. 7777895
Date Required: March 15, 1999
Deliver to: Compania Mundial
Mexico City, Mexico
Payment: Irrevocable LOC

______ Terms of Payment

CASH AGAINST DOCUMENTS

Shipped By: Final Destination

Payment Against the Following Documents:

Commercial Invoice	( )	Packing List	( )
Insurance Certificate	( )	Bill of Lading	( )
Quality Certificate	( )	Airway Bill	( )
Forwarders Receipt	( )		

Forwarders Insurance Taken By

Trade terms governed by INCOTERMS 1990

Identifying Marks	Quantity	Description	Unit Price	Amount
			CIF Mexico City	
C & M "Made in USA"	350	Model #345 HTS # 8059101345	US $45.99	$
C & M "Made in USA"	150	Model #198 HTS #8059101152	US $74.50	$
			Total	$

Packing: Each in Cardboard Box, 144 per double export carton, weighing 14 & 16 kilograms and measuring 25 X 25 X 10 cm.

Shipment: via M/V Hathaway from Port of Miami

Payment: Irrevocable Letter of Credit for 110% of CIF value at sight, through Banco de Mexico to Nations Bank, Miami, Florida

Notify Party: Towers of Mexico Customs Broker

Confirmed By:________________

seller, including attorneys fees, to the purchaser. The one-sided nature of these terms becomes important only if the parties are involved in a contract dispute. By the time of a dispute, it is too late for one party to object to the

Exhibit 7.5: Pro Forma Invoice — Terms and Conditions

Pro Forma Invoice
Terms and Conditions

(Please Read Carefully)

1. Services by Third Parties: Unless the Company carries, stores or otherwise physically handles the shipment, and the loss, damage, or delay occurs during such activity, the Company assumes no liability as a carrier, but undertakes only to use reasonable care in the selection of carriers, truckmen, lightermen, forwarders, customhouse brokers, warehousemen, and others to whom it may entrust the goods for delivery unless a separate bill of lading or other contract of carriage is issued by the Company, in which event the terms thereof shall govern.

2. Liability Limitations of Third Parties: The Company is authorized to select all necessary third parties as required to transport the goods, all of whom shall be considered as the agents of the Purchaser and subject to all conditions as to limitation of liability and to all rules and regulations and conditions appearing in bills of lading or receipts issued by such third parties. The Company shall not be liable for any loss, damage, expense or delay to the goods for any reason whatsoever when the goods are in the possession of third parties.

3. Choosing Routes or Agents: Unless specified by the Customer in writing, the Company has complete freedom in choosing the means, route and procedure to be followed in the handling, transportation, and delivery of the goods.

4. Quotations Not Binding: Quotations as to fees, rates of duty, freight charges, insurance premiums or other charges are for informational purposes only and are subject to change without notice unless the Company in writing specifically undertakes the transportation of the shipment at the specified rate.

5. Limitation of $50 per shipment: The Customer agrees that the Company shall in no event be liable for any loss, expense, or delay to the goods resulting from the negligence or fault of the Company for any amount in excess of $50 per shipment.

6. Presenting Claims: In no event shall the Company be liable for any act or omission or default unless the claim is presented to it at its office within 60 days from the date of exportation of the goods in a written statement to which sworn proof of claim shall be attached.

7. General Lien on Any Property: The Company shall have a general lien on any and all property and documents relating thereto of the Purchaser in its possession or en route, for all claims for charges, expenses or advance incurred by the Company in connection with any shipments to the Purchaser, and if such claims remain unsatisfied for a period of thirty days, the Company may sell at public auction or private sale, and apply the net proceeds of the sale to the payment of the amount due Company. The Purchaser remains liable for any deficiency in the sale.

8. No Responsibility for Governmental Requirements: It is the responsibility of the Purchaser to know and inform the Company of the marking requirements of the country of importation, and all other safety and health regulations, and all other requirements of law or official regulations. The Company shall not be responsible for action taken or fines or penalties assessed by any governmental agency against the shipment.

9. Construction of Terms and Venue: The foregoing terms and conditions shall be construed according to the laws of the State of Florida. Unless otherwise consented to in writing by the Company, no legal proceeding against the Company may be instituted by the Purchaser, its assigns or subrogee except in the City of Miami, Florida.

10. Costs of Collection: Purchaser shall pay all costs, charges, and expenses including attorney's fees, reasonably incurred or paid by the Company (including attorney's fees for any appeals taken) because of the failure of the Purchaser to perform and comply with the terms and conditions of this agreement including payment of monies due and every such payment shall bear interest from the date at the highest rate permitted by law.

onerous terms found in the other party's forms. This exchange of forms containing conflicting or varying terms is referred to as the battle of the forms.

An American businessperson who is familiar with the terms of the UCC will encounter unexpected results under the CISG in the "battle of the forms" scenario.[304] Article 19 of the CISG resolves a conflict in the exchange of forms differently than does Article 2-207 of the Code. For example, a seller responds to a purchase order ("the offer") with a confirming invoice ("the acceptance"), but the confirming invoice includes an *additional term* that limits the purchaser's ability to make a claim for breach of warranty by providing a short notice period. What is the legal effect of the additional notice requirement? If the addition is construed as a non-material modification, both the CISG and the Code would acknowledge the formation of a contract which incorporates the additional term. However, Article 19(3) of the CISG broadly defines material to include "among other things, to price, payment, quality and quantity of the goods, place and time of delivery, *extent of one party's liability to the other* or relating to the settlement of disputes." In essence, the CISG adopts the old common law mirror image rule in which the acceptance must be a mirror image of the offer. Thus, under the CISG the additional term converts the attempted acceptance into a counteroffer and thus no contract is formed. The strict rules of the CISG may be a reason for opting out of the CISG in favor of the UCC or another domestic contract law.

The pro forma invoice or price quotation should include: the buyer's name and address, any buyer reference number, date of inquiry, unit price per item (stated in the exporter's currency), gross and net shipping weights (if applicable), total cubic volume and dimensions when packed for export, terms of payment, estimated date of shipment, costs of insurance and freight (CIF contract), place of delivery, charges to be paid by customer (e.g., customs fees and duties), the country of origin, any applicable trade discount, and the expiration date of the quote. The seller may elect to stipulate that the quoted price is subject to change without notice. The document should be clearly labeled as a "Pro Forma Invoice" so as not to be

---

304 See generally, Paul C. Blodgett, *The U.N. Convention on the Sale of Goods and the 'Battle of Forms',* 18 Colorado Law Review 421 (1989).

confused with the commercial invoice prepared as part of the collection process.

The impact of the CISG's adoption of the mirror image rule should make international contract formation more difficult. In reality, the use of standard forms in the formation of a modern contract is a universal practice. Invariably, any time seller's and buyer's forms are exchanged there will be conflicting terms in the fine print which neither party are likely to read unless a dispute arises. Under the CISG's broad materiality standard, these transactions are technically based upon unenforceable contracts. The German Court of Baden-Baden seemed to recognize the reality of standard form contracting and ignored the broad materiality definition of Article 19(3). It held that a restrictive notice provision pertaining to claims of defects was not a material term. The notification requirements for nonconfomities would seem to come within the purview of Article 19(3)'s "any term relating to the extent of one party's liability to the other party." The German court's decision demonstrates that until there are enough cases interpreting the CISG, contracting parties are likely to be surprised by some of the decisions produced by national courts applying the CISG. The battle of the forms situation was illustrated in *Filanto, S.p.A. v. Chilewich International Corp.*[305] in which an offer attempted to incorporate another document by reference. A belated acceptance attempted to delete the reference in order to avoid the inclusion of the arbitration clause in the contract.

In *Filanto* an Italian footwear manufacturer brought action against a New York export-import firm, alleging breach of contract. This case is a striking example of how a lawsuit involving a relatively straightforward international commercial transaction can raise an array of complex questions. Defendant Chilewich signed a contract with a Russian importer for a long-term supply of footwear. This "Russian Contract" contained an arbitration clause which stated that "[a]ll disputes are to be settled by the arbitration tribunal of the Chamber of Commerce in Moscow, Russia." Chilewich then entered into negotiations with Filanto, an Italian manufacturer, to supply the shoes needed for the Russian contract. After a negotiation meeting Chilewich sent Filanto a letter, dated July 27, 1989, that stated: "Attached please find our contract to cover the purchases from you. Same is

[305] 789 F. Supp. 1229 (S.D.N.Y. 1992).

governed by the conditions which are enumerated in the standard contract in effect with the Russian buyers, copy of which is also enclosed." Subsequently, Chilewich procured a letter of credit to the benefit of Filanto as required under the contract. Soon thereafter, Filanto began to perform on the contract. On September 2, 1989 Chilewich received a letter from Filanto that included the following statement: "Returning back the enclosed contracts signed for acceptance, if we do not misunderstand, regarding the Russian contract, we have to respect only the following points: Packing and marking, way of shipment, delivery." After the Russian buyer rejected a shipment of shoes, Chilewich never purchased a subsequent order of 90,000 pairs of boots from Filanto. Chilewich commenced an arbitration action in Moscow against Filanto. Filanto moved to enjoin the arbitration, or alternatively, for an order directing that arbitration be held in New York rather than Moscow because of unsettled political conditions in Russia.

The court noted that Chapter 2 of the *Federal Arbitration Act* incorporated the *Convention on the Recognition and Enforcement of Foreign Arbitral Awards*. The Arbitration Convention requires courts to recognize "any agreement in writing under which the parties undertake to submit to arbitration." The term "agreement in writing" is defined as "an arbitral clause in a contract or an arbitration agreement, signed by the parties or contained in an exchange of letters or telegrams." The threshold question is whether these parties actually agreed to arbitrate their disputes in a certain forum. State law is applicable to govern the validity, revocability, and enforceability of arbitration agreements. However, this court concluded that federal law (Arbitration Convention) is to be applied in determining whether the parties agreed to arbitrate their disputes. Also, the court held that under the CISG an offeree who, knowing that the offeror has commenced performance, fails to notify the offeror of its objection to the terms of the contract within a reasonable time will be deemed to have assented to those terms. The August 7, 1990 acceptance, noting its objection to the arbitration clause, to Chilewich's March 13, 1990 Memorandum Agreement was untimely because Filanto knew that Chilewich had commenced performance. Furthermore, Filanto's June 21, 1991 letter makes reference to the "Master Purchase Contract" (the Russian contract). This letter comes within the purview of CISG Article 8(3) directive that "in determining the intent of a party due consideration is to be given to any *subsequent conduct* of the parties." Heeding the presumption in favor of arbitration, which is even stronger in the context of international commercial transactions, the court held that Filanto was bound by the terms of the March 13th Memorandum Agreement and so must arbitrate its dispute in Moscow

Contract Interpretation

A famous case of contract interpretation involved the judicial attempt to define the word "chicken." The *Frigaliment Importing v. BNS International*[306] case illustrates how a court attempted to define terms in a contract through its reading of the contract itself and its use of evidence of prior dealings, course of performance, and trade usage. It involved an action by a buyer of fresh, frozen chicken against a seller for breach of warranty of two sales contracts. In the first contract, a New York sales corporation confirmed the sale to the plaintiff, a Swiss corporation, of "US fresh Frozen Chicken, Grade A, Government Inspected, 2½ to 3 lbs. each, all chickens individually wrapped, packed in secured fiber cartons suitable for export." The second contract was identical except for the quantity term. When the initial shipment arrived in Switzerland, plaintiff found that the birds were not young chickens suitable for broiling and frying but stewing chickens or "fowl." A protest ensued, nevertheless, a shipment of stewing chickens was made under the second contract. The issue before the court was what is a chicken? The plaintiff argued that "chicken" meant a young chicken, suitable for broiling and frying. Defendant argued that "chicken" meant any bird of the genus that met contract specifications on weight and quality, including what it called "stewing chicken" and plaintiff pejoratively termed "fowl." Assuming that both parties were acting in good faith, the case nicely illustrates Oliver Wendel Holmes remark "that the making of a contract depends not on the agreement of two minds in one intention, but on the agreement of two sets of external signs—not on the parties' having *meant* the same thing but on having *said* the same thing."

Since the word "chicken" standing alone is ambiguous, the court turned to the contract first to see whether it offered any aid to the interpretation of the word "chicken." The contract failed to provide any definition or clarification for the word "chicken." Plaintiff's agent testified that when asked by defendant's agent what kinds of chickens were wanted, he received

---

[306] 789 F. Supp. 1229 (S.D.N.Y. 1992).

the answer "any kind of chickens." Defendant argued that if plaintiff were sincere in thinking it was entitled to young chickens, plaintiff would not have allowed the shipment under the second contract to go forward. Plaintiff's next contention was that there was a definite trade usage that "chicken" meant "young chicken." Plaintiff endeavored to establish such a trade usage by the testimony of witnesses. However, one witness stated that a careful businessperson protected herself by using "broiler" when that was what he wanted and "fowl" when he wished older birds. Defendant provided a witness that said that in the trade "chicken" would encompass all the various classifications of chicken. Defendant also provided a regulation of the Department of Agriculture that defined "chickens" as various classes including "*Broiler or fryer,* Roaster, Capon, Stag, Hen or *stewing* chicken or *fowl.*" The court ultimately held in favor of the defendant because plaintiff failed to meet its burden of showing that "chicken" was used in the narrower rather than in the broader sense.

The Importance of the *Frigaliment* Case

This *Frigaliment* case illustrates the hierarchy of tools that courts use in interpreting contracts.[307] The first level of analysis is to study the language of the contract in order to determine its meaning. This is sometimes referred to as a *four-corners analysis* or the plain meaning rule. If the language is unclear, the court proceeds to the next level of analysis. It will analyze the relationship between and actions of the contracting parties by looking at evidence of "course of performance." For example, the post-formation conduct of the parties will be analyzed to determine what the parties believed that the contract meant. If the meaning is still unclear, the court will study any prior contracts or dealings between the parties to find a previously established meaning. The final level of analysis is to imply a meaning from an outside source such as a trade usage or custom. In *Frigaliment* none of these levels of analysis provided a clear meaning for the word "*chicken.*" The result was that the plaintiff lost due to the failure to meet its burden of proof regarding the meaning of the word.

[307]For an analysis of the CISG's gap-filling role see, Mark N. Rosenberg, *The Vienna Convention: Uniformity in Interpretation for Gap-Filling—An Analysis and Application,* 20 Australia Business Law Rev. 442 (1992).

The second and third levels of analysis are referred to as a *totality of the circumstances* analysis. The courts often look to circumstances surrounding the execution of a written contract to find the parties' intent. Lord Wilberforce in *Reardon Smith Line Ltd.*[308] defined the totality of the circumstances analysis as the need in "commercial contracts for the court to know the commercial purpose of the contract which pre-supposes knowledge of the genesis of the transaction, background, context, and the market in which the parties were operating." The background and context includes oral negotiations, prior dealings, trade usage, and customs.

The common law has long used the *reasonable person standard* as an aid in interpreting and enforcing contracts. The reasonable person standard is a reflection of the totality of the circumstances analysis because it is often constructed using the trade usage, customs, and practices of businesspersons in a particular trade or business. The role of the reasonable person standard has become more important in recent years because of the modern innovation of standard forms. Most of the terms of standard forms are not the product of negotiations and conscious agreement. The reasonable person is used to interpret the so-called fine print or boiler plate terms—to see if the terms meet the measure of commercial reasonableness.

Larry A. DiMatteo, *The Counterpoise of Contracts: The Reasonable Person Standard and the Subjectivity of Judgment*, 48 South Carolina Law Review 293, 338-41 (1997)

The role of the reasonable person has expanded with the advent of form contracts. The standardization of contracts has removed the narrow focus of the reasonable person from the four corners of the contract. The traditional focus held that the act of signing a standard form was evidence that the signer intended to accept all of its terms. This approach became increasingly untenable when it became apparent that in reality there was no such actual consent. The fact of the matter was that at least one of the parties did not read or understand the fine print of the preprinted form. The role of the reasonable person was thus expanded to determine what reasonable terms would be included and what unreasonable terms would be excluded. Professor Karl Llewellyn devised two roles for the reasonable person standard in the area of standard form contracts: (1) to interpret the meaning of the terms expressly negotiated by the parties, and

[308] [1976] 1 W.L.R. 989.

(2) to determine what non-dickered terms are to be reconstructed or expelled due to unreasonableness or alternatively, what reasonable terms are to be implied to fill in gaps in the contract. For purposes of determining reasonableness, the reasonable person looks to the terms generally found in such contracts. The reasonable person is used to conform the boilerplate terms to the spirit of the contract as represented by the dickered terms and the type of transaction being undertaken.

Warranty Law

The CISG's warranty provision mimics the warranty provisions found in the Uniform Commercial Code.[309] The warranties that are of concern to most seller-exporters are any implied warranties that a court may use to hold the seller liable for non-conforming goods. Section 2-614 of the Uniform Commercial Code recognizes the two common law implied warranties of merchantability and particular purpose. A sale of fungible commodities is normally governed by the *implied warranty of merchantability.* Section 2-614 states it is implied that for the goods to be merchantable they must be "fit for the ordinary purposes for which such goods are used." A toaster should brown toast within a reasonable amount of time. A 20,000 BTU air-conditioning unit should produce 20,000 BTU of air-conditioning. The *implied warranty for a particular purpose* entails the conveying of specific requirements from the buyer to the seller. The buyer communication of particular needs is generally done to take advantage of the seller's superior knowledge or expertise in selecting or producing the product. Article 35 of the CISG states that the goods are to conform to "any purpose expressly or impliedly made known to the seller" at the time of the formation of the contract. Thus, if a buyer visits a licensed air-conditioning company and discusses his needs for air-conditioning, the seller is implied to warrant that the unit being provided is sufficient for the buyer's needs. If the air-conditioning company sells the buyer a 20,000 BTU unit that performs as advertised by producing 20,000 BTU, it will be considered defective when in fact the buyer's needs dictated a unit with a 50,000 BTU capacity. The CISG

[309]For an analysis of warranty of title and against infringement in intellectual property see, Allen M. Shinn, Jr., *Liabilities Under Article 42 of the U.N. Convention on the International Sale of Goods,* 2 Minnesota Journal of Global Trade 115 (1993).

also specifically makes it a breach of warranty if the seller fails to adequately package the goods for shipment.

The court in *T.J. Stevenson & Co.*[310] discussed the warranty of merchantability and the importance of the buyer giving notice when receiving defective or non-conforming goods. The action was brought by an ocean carrier which claimed it had a lien on the cargo for costs incurred by freight, detention, and expenses, and also sought recovery of damages from the milling company (seller) and shipper consignee (buyer), the Republic of Bolivia. The miller filed counterclaims against Bolivia and the carrier, and Bolivia counterclaimed for breach of warranty due to insect infestation in the flour. The Republic of Bolivia had entered into a contract for the purchase of 26,618 metric tons of flour from ADM Milling Co. The contract contained the following delivery term: "Delivery of goods by SELLER to the carrier at point of shipment shall constitute delivery to BUYER." Upon satisfactory delivery, the cost was payable by irrevocable letter of credit. The contract also contained an express warranty of merchantability: "Seller warrants that the product sold shall be of merchantable quality." The warranty clause contained the following notice requirements: "BUYER hereby waives any claim based on the quality of the goods unless, within twenty days of the arrival of goods at destination, BUYER sends SELLER a letter by registered mail specifying the nature of the complaint".

The court held that the flour failed to meet the express warranty provision of the contract. The issue being the infestation and whether the flour was of merchantable quality. The Uniform Commercial Code Section 2-314(2) defines merchantable as goods that "are fit for the ordinary purposes for which such goods are used." Official Comments 2 and 8 provide helpful clues to divining the parties' intent. Comment 2: "Goods delivered under an agreement made by a merchant in a given trade must be of a quality comparable to that generally acceptable in that line of trade." Comment 8: "Merchantable goods must be honestly re-salable in the normal course of business because they are what they purport to be." Under these standards, the infested flour failed to conform to the warranty of merchantability. However, in order for Bolivia to win on its warranty claim it must satisfy the relevant notice requirements. Section 2-607(3)(a) of the UCC states that "the buyer must within a reasonable time after he discovers or should have discovered any breach notify the seller of breach or be barred from any rem-

[310] 629 F.2d 338 (1980).

edy." Furthermore, the contract added the requirement that notice must be in writing "within twenty days after arrival of the goods." ADM contends that under the requirements of Section 2-607(3)(a) and the contract provision, it never received adequate notice of the defects. The facts showed that there were informal communications throughout the time that indicated problems with the flour. The parties were in "continuous communication" with one another at the time the infestation problems were found. Also, Bolivia telexed ADM that no further payments would be permitted under the "irrevocable" letter of credit. From this view of the parties' course of conduct, the court inferred that ADM was aware of Bolivia's dissatisfaction with the flour, as such the parties' conduct operated to waive the contract notice requirements. ADM's reply to the telex, as well as its informal communications, dealt with the substance of Bolivia's complaint and did not fault Bolivia for failing to comply with the contract's notice requirements. ADM's responses to Bolivia's initial complaints established a course of performance in which the registered mail requirement of the contractual notice provision could be disregarded. The defendant was held liable for a breach of warranty and its argument that it did not receive adequate notice was rejected.

Disclaimer of Warranty

Oftentimes a seller will attempt to disclaim all warranties, express or implied, or will want to limit its liability through a *limited express warranty.* Section 2-316 of the UCC allows for such a disclaimer only through the use of clear and conspicuous language. Any disclaimers of tort liability should expressly state what torts are being disclaimed. The most common disclaimers pertain to the torts of fraud, misrepresentation, negligence, and strict product liability. In contrast, the CISG provides no formal requirements for disclaimers. Any form of disclaimer is enforceable under the CISG. The following capsule was taken from the American Bar Association's *Collection of Software Contract Forms*[311] and provides an example of the type of disclaimer language often used by merchants.

[311] American Bar Association, "Software Contract Forms" at 1-3 (1992).

Exhibit 7.6: Limited Liability & Disclaimer in a Software Sales Contract

LICENSE

The User shall have a nontransferable license to modify and use the product for functions performed in User's business. This product is sold to the purchaser under this Agreement to be an end user, to be modified for certain functions as specified in the documentation for the product. The product includes both hardware and firmware that is proprietary to the seller who retains said rights. RESALE OR OTHER TRANSFER OF THE PRODUCT BY THE FIRST PURCHASER IS A VIOLATION OF THE TERMS OF THIS AGREEMENT. ANY AND ALL WARRANTIES ARE TERMINATED UPON SUCH A TRANSFER.

The User may NOT duplicate, disassemble, modify, translate, or use the Firmware other than as expressly authorized in this Agreement. Upon termination of the license, the User shall destroy all copies of and modifications to the Firmware.

LIMITED WARRANTY & DISCLAIMER

EXCEPT AS EXPRESSLY SET FORTH, THE PRODUCT IS PROVIDED TO THE ORIGINAL USER "AS IS," WITHOUT WARRANTY OF ANY KIND, EITHER EXPRESSED OR IMPLIED, INCLUDING, BUT NOT LIMITED TO, ANY IMPLIED WARRANTIES OF MERCHANTABILITY OR FITNESS FOR A PARTICULAR PURPOSE

LIMITATION OF REMEDIES

Seller's entire liability and User's exclusive remedy shall be: (1) Repair and replacement including materials and labor for a period of one year unless the product has been abused, misused, or modified. IN NO EVENT WILL SELLER BE LIABLE TO THE USER FOR ANY DAMAGES, INCLUDING ANY LOST PROFITS, INCIDENTAL OR CONSEQUENTIAL DAMAGES ARISING OUT OF THE USE OR INABILITY TO USE THE PRODUCT.

THE USER FURTHER AGREES THAT THIS DOCUMENT IS THE COMPLETE AND EXCLUSIVE STATEMENT OF THE AGREEMENT BETWEEN THE USER AND THE SELLER WHICH SUPERSEDES ANY PROPOSAL OR PRIOR AGREEMENT, ORAL OR WRITTEN.

The above disclaimer responds to the requirements set out in Section 2-316 of the UCC. Language such as the "Original User Takes As Is" is recognized as clear disclaimer language by Section 2-316. Also, the disclaimer satisfies the UCC's conspicuousness requirement; it is likely to be easily noticed when the contract is subject to a reasonable review. The technique of capitalizing the letters takes the clause outside a claim that it is non-conspicuous fine print.

Buyer's Duty to Inspect, Give Timely and Proper Notice

A purchaser of goods may reject delivered goods if it gives timely and effective notice of a non-conformity.[312] The issue becomes what is considered proper notice under the CISG. The buyer has three duties that relate to the notice requirement. First, Article 38 (1) requires the buyer to inspect the goods "within as short a period as is practicable." Second, the buyer must inform the seller of the non-conformity "within a reasonable time after he has discovered it or ought to have discovered it." Any claim for non-conformity is time barred if not reported within two years of delivery to the buyer. Third, the notice to the seller must specify the nature of the non-conformity.

The inspection requirement is actually a two-fold requirement. The inspection will be reviewed not only for its promptness, but also for the quality of the inspection. A German court dealt with the issue of the quality of an inspection. In short, it held that due diligence should be exhibited in the inspection of goods. In that case,[313] following customer complaints about measurements, sewing quality, and colors fading, a German retailer of shoes attempted to cancel a second order with an Italian manufacturer. The goods were shipped nonetheless. The retailer inspected only a selected sample of the shoes and failed to detect any non-conformities. Following additional customer complaints, the retailer attempted to reject the second order due to non-conformity. This time the court found in favor of the seller holding that the expiration of sixteen days rendered the buyer's notice as untimely. The court's rationale is analogous to the American concept of due diligence. Because the buyer was aware of non-conformities stemming from the first order, it should have performed a more detailed inspection of the shoes in the second order. The court presumed that such an inspection would have uncovered the non-conformity at an earlier date.

Another German case dealt with the content requirements for a satisfactory notice of non-conformity.[314] Pursuant to an installment contract, a

---

[312]For a general discussion of conformity see, Eyal Zamir, *Toward a General Concept of Conformity in the Performance of Contracts,* 52 Louisiana Law Rev. 1 (1991).

[313]General Court of Stuttgart, 3 KFh 97/89, The CLOUT Case No. 4 (Case Law on UNCITRAL Text).

[314]General Court of München, 17 HKO 3726/89, The CLOUT Case No. 3, UNCITRAL Abstract, A/CN.9/SER.C/Abstracts/1(May 19, 1993).

German clothing retailer gave notice to an Italian seller of fashion goods eight and twelve days respectively, after the delivery of two separate shipments. The German court bypassed the issue of timeliness and held the notice ineffective due to its lack of specificity. The notice stated that the goods failed to conform because of "poor workmanship and improper fit." The court held that this description was not specific enough and therefore was ineffective notice.

The notice specificity of the UCC, however, is less demanding than the requirements of the CISG. Initially, the rejecting party only needs to state in general terms the reason for the rejection. Comment One states that it is the policy of this Section to permit the "buyer to give a quick and informal notice of defects in a tender without penalizing him for omissions in his statement."[315] There appears to be one exception to the general character of the UCC notice requirement: "Where the defect in a tender is one which could have been cured by the seller, a buyer who merely rejects without stating his objections is probably acting in commercial bad faith." Thus, except for the situation where the seller has the ability and right to cure, this clarification indicates that general notice rather than a particularized one is sufficient to meet the dictates of the UCC. The UCC does provide that the seller may make a formal request in writing for a more particularized listing of the defects. The German court's determination that "poor workmanship and improper fit" was not specific enough indicates that the degree of specificity required under the Convention is much greater than under the UCC. Vagueness in a notification of non-conformity can result in the preclusion of the buyer from exercising her right of rejection and associated warranty claims.

Nachfrist Notice

Another concept foreign to Anglo-American contract law is the civil law notion of *nachfrist* notice. The notion allows a buyer or seller to fix an additional time for performance beyond that which is specified in the contract. The ability to affix additional time onto the time fixed in the contract was adopted in Articles 47-48 and 63 of the CISG. The buyer may give no-

---

[315]U.C.C. § 2-605, Comment 1 (1990).

tice to the seller that she will accept delivery beyond the time prescribed. The buyer is then enjoined from taking legal action during the *nachfrist* period and must accept any proper tender of performance during that period. If the seller makes a request for a *nachfrist* extension, then the buyer is obligated to respond to the request. Failure to do so results in the automatic granting of additional time.

An American businessperson unaware of this practice may subject herself to unintended liabilities. She may mistake a *nachfrist* notice as a meaningless, nonlegal request for more time. Failure to respond in a proper way could result in an unintended granting of additional time and a freezing of her legal options. Furthermore, the subsequent rejection of the "delayed" delivery of goods during the *nachfrist* period would subject her to liability for the purchase price, along with possible additional freight and storage costs. The existence of an express "time of the essence" clause in a contract is unlikely to provide a party any protection from the use of *nachfrist* notice. It is important for a businessperson to realize that the receipt of seemingly meaningless communications should be fully investigated for legal consequences.

Nachfrist Case Study

A contract between an Italian clothing manufacturer and a German retailer provided for a schedule of delivery dates stating that the clothes were "autumn goods, to be delivered July, August, September, plus or minus."[316] The first delivery of the goods was made on September 26th. The buyer rejected the delivery of the goods as untimely. The court rejected the buyer's argument that the term "autumn goods" translated into the delivery of three equal shipments for the months of July, August, and September. Such misunderstandings are common given the problems attributable to linguistic and cultural differences, along with the tendency of businesspersons towards brevity in their business communiqués. *What could the German buyer have done differently to avoid such a misunderstanding?* First, he should have defined the term "autumn goods" more carefully in order to ensure timely and qualitatively effective delivery of the goods. Second, as suggested by the German court, he could have made use of the *nachfrist* notice provisions in the CISG. Article 47 states that the "buyer may fix an additional period of time of reasonable length for performance by the seller." Article 48 allows a seller to "request" additional time for per-

---

[316]Municipal Court of Holstein, 5 C 73/89, The CLOUT Case No. 7.

formance. The granting of additional time to perform is normally given in conjunction with a fixed and known delivery date. The German court held that "the buyer did not effectively avoid the contract by refusing acceptance of the goods *without fixing an additional period* in the previous cases of non-delivery." The implications of this decision support a number of interpretations regarding *nachfrist* notice. First, the use of *nachfrist* notice in this situation would have indicated that the parties had indeed intended multiple delivery dates throughout the autumn months. Second, the decision holds the possibility that *nachfrist* notice may be used to fix an unspecified delivery date. At the minimum, notice would have placed a burden upon the exporter to respond to the buyer's request for delivery. The failure of the exporter to respond would have allowed the German buyer to declare the contract as avoided and to seek substituted goods elsewhere. Article 49 provides that the "buyer may declare the contract avoided in the case of non-delivery, if the seller does not deliver goods within the additional period of time fixed by the buyer."

Seller's Right to Cure

The seller's right to cure under the CISG is similar to the right offered in the UCC. Section 2-508 of the UCC allows a seller to cure the delivery of defective goods if the time for performance has not expired. The Revised UCC, discussed towards the end of this chapter, allows for an extended time to cure beyond the period for the performance provided for in the contract. Article 48 of the CISG allows the seller to cure after the contract date for delivery unless such late delivery would cause the buyer "unreasonable inconvenience or uncertainty."[317] However, an ICC Tribunal held that if the seller is guilty of a fundamental breach, then he has no right to cure beyond the contract due date without the buyer's consent.[318] The problem for the American trader is that the CISG defines fundamental breach narrowly. Under the UCC's perfect tender rule almost any defect can be grounds for rejection. If the buyer would like to obtain such a perfect tender right where the CISG is applicable, then it should negotiate a clause providing that failure to comply with certain specified terms shall be considered a fundamental breach for purposes of rejection, contract avoidance, and the right to

[317]The buyer retains the right to sue for damages and expenses caused by the delay or by the initial delivery of non-conforming goods.

[318]ICC Case No. 7531 of 1994.

cure. An example of such a clause is as follows: "any non-conformity to the product specifications expressly stated in the contract will be considered a fundamental breach."

Anticipatory Breach and Adequate Assurance

Article 71 of the CISG allows a party to suspend its performance if it becomes clear that the other party will not perform. The CISG gives two broad grounds for *anticipatory breach.* First, the other party has become seriously deficient in its ability to perform or in its creditworthiness. Second, the other party's preparation, lack of preparation, or insufficient performance to date has called into question its ability or willingness to perform under the contract. When one party anticipates a breach of the other party and suspends performance, it must give immediate notice of the suspension. However, the suspending party must lift its suspension in the event that the other party provides *adequate assurance* that it will perform as contracted. Section 2-609 of the Uniform Commercial Code provides a similar device for suspending performance. It states that when reasonable grounds for insecurity arise with respect to performance, the concerned party "may in writing demand adequate assurance of due performance" and may suspend performance until such time as such assurance is given. Failure to give such adequate assurance within a reasonable time, not exceeding thirty days, results in a repudiation of the contract. Although nearly identical, do you see any differences between the CISG and the UCC on this issue?

Damages

The damage provisions in the CISG are found in Articles 74 to 77.[319] The granting of the remedy of specific performance is delegated to the applicable national law.[320] Article 74 provides the general measure of damages.

---

[319]See generally, Graham Corney, *Obligations and Remedies Under the 1980 Vienna Sales Convention,* 23 Queensland Law Society Journal 37 (1993).; Franco Ferrari, *Comparative Ruminations on the Foreseeability of Damages in Contract Law,* 53 Louisiana Law Rev. 1257 (1993).

[320]See generally, Steven Walt, *For Specific Performance Under the United Nations Sale Convention,* 26 Texas Int'l Law Journal 211 (1991).

It adopts the common law rule that damages should be limited to losses that were foreseeable at the time of contract formation—what are popularly known as the rules of *Hadley v. Baxendale.*[321] The non-breaching party is owed damages resulting from the breach, including lost profits. There are three restrictions on the damages that can be collected. First, only foreseeable *consequential damages* related to the breach may be sued upon. Article 74 states that "damages may not exceed the loss which the party in breach foresaw or ought to have foreseen at the time of the conclusion of the contract." Second, damages will be limited to those that are provable with some degree of certainty. Therefore, purely speculative damages may not be collected. Third, Article 77 provides that even if the loss was foreseeable and its amount is certain, the non-breaching party will be limited in his recovery in the event he failed to *mitigate* his damages. Article 77 provides that if he "fails to take such measures to mitigate the loss, the party in breach may claim a reduction in damages in the amount by which the loss should have been mitigated." For example, if a buyer has a source for substituted goods, he must make efforts to obtain those substituted goods. If he does not, he will be precluded from collecting full loss profit damages. Article 77 is similar to the rule adopted in Section 2-715 of the UCC which holds the breaching party liable for all damages that *could not reasonably be prevented.* In the case of a fundamental breach, Article 75 allows the non-breaching party to avoid the contract. It also authorizes the non-breaching party to obtain substituted goods. He may than sue the breaching party for the difference between the contract price (of the avoided contract) and the price, if higher, of the substituted goods. If the non-breaching party elects not to procure substituted goods, he may in the alternative sue for lost opportunity damages. Article 76 of the CISG allows him to recover for the difference between the contract price and the market price at the time of avoidance.

The 1995 case of *Delchi Carrier SpA v. Rotorex Corp.*[322] illustrates the types of damages allowable under the CISG. The case involved a warranty dispute between a U.S. seller of compressors ("Rotorex") and an Italian purchaser ("Delchi"). The trial court determined that the compressors failed to conform to either the specifications provided in the contract or the sample provided by Rotorex to Delchi. After Rotorex failed to cure the defects, Delchi brought suit for breach of contract and recovery of damages, in-

[321] 156 Eng. Rep. 145 (1854).

[322] 71 F.3d 1024 (2d Cir. 1995).

cluding consequential damages for lost profits. The lost profits were allegedly due to lost volume caused by a closing of the assembly line for four days until the compressors were repaired and for lost profits from a loss in the volume of goods for the upcoming selling season. They also sued for incidental damages such as the cost to repair the compressors, the cost of storage, and the costs of expediting substitute goods.

Article 74 of the CISG allowed for Delchi to collect monetary damages that equaled its losses, including lost profits. Those damages were limited, however, to damages foreseeable at the time of the formation of the contract. Its first claim of damages was the cost of repairing the non-conforming compressors. These damages were recoverable because they were a foreseeable result of Rotorex's breach. Hence, Delchi was entitled to expenses for repairing the units, including labor costs, costs of extraordinary inspections, and testing of the units. Pursuant to Article 77 of the CISG, Delchi attempted to mitigate its losses by expediting a shipment of previously ordered Sanyo compressors. The expedited shipment was not considered as a "cover" under Article 75, because they were previously ordered. Nonetheless, the court held that Delchi's actions in expediting the shipment were both commercially reasonable and reasonably foreseeable. Therefore, Delchi was granted the additional costs of air shipment over the cost of ocean shipment. Delchi was also granted the incidental costs of handling and storage of the rejected compressors.

The CISG permits the recovery of lost profits resulting from a diminished volume of sales. In conformity with the common law, to recover for lost profit under the CISG, a party must provide sufficient evidence to estimate the amount of damages with reasonable certainty. Delchi proved, with reasonable certainty, actual lost profits. The court held, however, that Delchi did not prove with reasonable certainty lost sales from "anticipated profits". Delchi's claim of 4,000 additional lost sales in Italy was supported only by the speculative testimony of Italian sales agents who stated that they would have ordered more if additional items were available. Delchi provided no documentation of additional lost sales in Italy or evidence that Delchi's inability to fill those orders was directly attributable to Rotorex's breach. Thus, as illustrated in the *Delchi* case, a plaintiff, under the CISG, is entitled to compensatory damages for expenses incurred in repairing nonconforming goods, obtaining substitute goods, storage of rejected goods, and reasonably certain lost profits. Lost profits do not include profits which may arise from anticipated sales that cannot be determined by reasonable certainty.

Unlike the Uniform Commercial Code, the CISG does not allow recovery for breach of warranty that results in injury to persons or property. Article 5 of the CISG states that it does not cover claims resulting from the "liability of the seller for death or personal injury caused by the goods to any person." Therefore, under the CISG, product liability is still determined under national tort laws. In contrast, Section 2-715 of the UCC allows for the recovery of consequential damages, stemming from the seller's breach, due to "injury to person or property proximately resulting from any breach of warranty." Also, punitive damages or penalty clauses are not specifically precluded under the CISG. The ability to collect punitive damages would have to be determined under national laws. Penalty clauses are held to be unenforceable under the U.C.C.'s liquidated damage provision in Section 2-718.

Contractual Excuses

All legal systems provide relief for someone who, despite good faith intentions, is unable to perform. Although in technical breach of the contract, the court will excuse the breaching party from claims of damages. The common law fabricated the *doctrine of impossibility* and the *doctrine of frustration.* The former required the contracting party be objectively prevented from performing. This generally entailed the destruction of the subject matter of the contract. Under the doctrine of frustration the performance may still be objectively possible, but the reason for the performance has ceased. The availability of contractual excuses in the civil law countries varies. In Belgium and France, *pacta sunt servanda* or sanctity of contract generally prevails over any request for an excuse. If the contract does not provide an excuse through a *force majeure* clause, then the contract will be enforced without any modification to its terms. In the United Kingdom, the doctrine of frustration remains the premier excuse doctrine. The parties are relieved of their contractual obligations as of the date of frustration. The courts do not have the authority to modify or reform the contract. In Germany, if the "basis of the transaction" has evaporated, then the court is free to excuse a party or to reform the contract in accordance with the changed circumstances.

The UCC and the CISG possess their own excuse provisions. The UCC provision found in Section 2-615 is popularly referred to as the *doctrine of impracticability.* It excuses a party from performing if the performance has been "made impracticable by the occurrence of a contingency, the nonoccurrence of which was a *basic assumption*" of the contract. Article 79 of the CISG allows for an excuse if nonperformance is due to an *impediment* that is beyond the control of the breaching party and was not foreseeable at the time of contract formation. However, if the excuse is not permanent, performance is suspended only for the duration of the impediment. The person attempting to exercise an Article 79 impediment must give prompt notice of the impediment to the other party. Failure to do so exposes the party to damages resulting from not giving notice. All of the excuse doctrines revolve around some of the following parameters: unforeseeability, undue hardship, and "beyond the control." Most of the excuse doctrines require that the changed circumstances were *objectively unforeseeable* at the time of contract formation. If they were foreseeable, then the losses resulting from the breach will be considered an allocated risk. The breaching party will be susceptible to full contract damages. The requirement of *undue hardship* generally means more than a mere loss. The fact that the contract becomes unprofitable for one of the parties is an insufficient reason to avoid the contract. Instead, the loss must be near catastrophic. The *beyond control* requirement means the event is a type of *force majeure* or superior force and that there are no feasible alternatives for the party to perform on the contract. The UNIDROIT Principles summarize these factors. It defines hardship (Article 6.2.2) as an occurrence that *fundamentally alters* the contractual equilibrium due to a change in costs or values (hardship). It further states that the occurrence must not have been known and the events could not *reasonably* have been taken into account at the time of the conclusion of the contract, and the events are *beyond the control* of the breaching party. Before requesting a rescission or reformation of the contract, a party must request a re-negotiation with the other party. Upon failure of the re-negotiation, a party may petition the court for relief.

The Excuse of Frustration

In some countries, such as the United Kingdom, the excuse of commercial frustration remains the primary excuse doctrine. Commercial frustration does not require that the contract become objectively impossible to perform, but rather due to changed circumstances, that the purpose or the value of the subject matter of the contract has been severely diminished. International Chamber of Commerce arbitration *Case No. 6281 of 26 August 1989* involved a seller's attempt to claim frustration for an increase in the market price of steel. On August 20, 1987, the parties entered into a contract for the sale of 80,000 metric tons of steel bars at a price of US$ 190 per ton and for delivery to a port in Yugoslavia. The contract provided the buyer with an option to purchase an additional 80,000 metric tons. On November 27, 1987, the buyer informed the seller that it would exercise the option. The seller requested US$ 215 per ton for the additional delivery. On January 26, 1988, the buyer purchased 80,000 tons from another supplier at a price of $216 and brought suit against seller for the difference between the original contract price and the price spent for the substituted goods. The arbitrator noted that Article 133 of the Yugoslav Law on Obligations allowed for a rescission of a contract due to "changed circumstances." The seller argued that it should be released from the contract due to changed circumstances, namely the increase in the market price of steel. Article 133 does list "economic events, such as extremely sudden and high increases or decreases of prices" as one of the reasons resulting in a frustration of a contract. The arbitrator held, however, that a party cannot make such a claim if he should have taken such circumstances into account at the time of contracting. The world market prices of products, such as steel, fluctuate and this fact should be known from experience. Also, the amount of damage must exceed a reasonable entrepreneurial risk. An increase in market prices from $190 to $215, amounts to slightly less than 13.16%. The arbitrator held that such an increase was well within the customary margin. The arbitrator additionally stated that the outcome would have been the same under the CISG.

Summary

In summary, the American practitioner attempting to draft an international contract based upon the CISG should be mindful of the above issues (Exhibit 7.7 summarizes the CISG by way of a "Topical Review"). For example, by placing the contract in writing, she will be avoiding the "no writing" requirement of the CISG and will not have to be concerned with whether the other party is from a country that elected to opt out of the no writing requirement. The attorney and entrepreneur should be aware that the CISG does not have a parol evidence rule; evidence from the negotiation stage may be entered into evidence to contradict the written agreement. Therefore, a merger or integration clause should be incorporated into the contract to prevent the admission of parol evidence. However, there is no indication that a court applying the CISG would honor the merger clause in precluding the admission of such evidence. A better approach would be specific language agreeing that the UCC's parol evidence rule would be applied. Other clauses that should be highly negotiated and customized for the particular transaction are the choice of law, arbitration, *force majeure,* and clauses requiring letters of credit or performance bonds. The *force majeure* clause should list specific foreseeable hardships including cost escalations and currency fluctuations

Exhibit 7.7: A Topical Review of the CISG (Articles of CISG in brackets)

1. CISG's Application

   The CISG applies to sales of goods (1) between parties from different countries, that are signatories to the CISG, and (2) where the rules of international law (conflict of law rules) lead to the law of one of those signatories [Note: U.S. opted out of jurisdiction (2)]. [1] Place of business is the one closest to the contract and its performance. [10]

2. CISG Coverage: Types of Goods

   The CISG does not apply to (1) personal goods, (2) goods sold at auction or by a governmental proceeding, (3) securities and negotiable instruments, (4) ships and aircraft, and (5) electricity. Mixed sales of goods and services may or may not come under the CISG depending on whether the party ordering the goods supplied a *substantial part of the materials* or if the *preponderant part* of the contract is for labor or services. [3]

3. CISG Coverage: Substantive Law

   The CISG only governs the formation of contracts and the rights and obligations of the seller and the buyer. National laws continue to govern issues dealing with the validity of contracts, e.g., capacity and legality. [4] Liability for injuries caused by goods are governed by national product liability laws. Damages to property caused by defective goods are subject to the CISG. [5] Parties may contract out the application of the CISG. If there is a doubt then the presumption is that the CISG applies. [6] A court is to issue a judgment for specific performance based upon its own national law. [28]

4. Articles 11, 13, & 96: Writing Requirement

   A contract need not be in writing and can be proved by *any* means, including witnesses. [11] A writing is required if an adopting state opted out of Article 11 and its national law requires a writing. [96]

   A writing includes telegrams and telexes. [13]

5. Article 16: Firm Offer Rule

   An offer may be revoked if revocation reaches the offeree prior to dispatch of acceptance. An offer may not be revoked if the offeree reasonably relied upon it.

6. Articles 18, 20, 21: Contract Formation

   An acceptance dispatched belatedly is effective if the offeror notifies the offeree of his "acceptance" of the acceptance. [21] A properly transmitted acceptance belatedly received is effective

unless the offeror notifies otherwise. Thus, the risk of transmission is borne by the offeree. [21 An acceptance becomes effective upon receipt by the offeror if received within a *reasonable time* ("reasonable" based upon circumstances of transaction, including means of transmission used by the offeror). Oral offers must be accepted immediately. [18]

7. Article 19: Battle of Forms:

(1) Is there a contract? If so, do the additional terms become a part of the contract? Assent to an offer with an addition or modification is a counteroffer. An addition or modification that does not materially alter an offer is an acceptance unless the offeror objects. Non-materially altering terms of the offeree become part of the contract. Material terms include price, quantity, place and time of delivery, warranties, liability limitations, choice of law, and choice of forum.

8. Place of Delivery

If a contract is silent as to place of delivery, then delivery is the handing the goods over to a common carrier. At that time the risk of loss passes. [31] If a contract for specially manufactured goods is silent as to delivery, the place of delivery is the seller's factory or warehouse. [31]

9. Warranty

The seller must properly mark goods or give notice to buyer upon delivery to common carrier. [32] In order for goods to be in conformity they must be fit for the purposes ordinarily used, be of the quality as indicated by a sample or model, and be packaged properly. [35]

10. Delivery of Goods; Inspection; Notice of Nonconfomity

The seller has a right to cure a non-conformity if the goods were delivered early. [37] If the seller hands over non-conforming documents before the required time, she has the right to cure the lack of conformity up to the time provided. [34] The buyer must examine the goods within a short period from delivery. [38] The buyer must give notice of non-conformity within a reasonable time after a defect is discovered or should have been discovered but no later than two years from delivery. [39] This period does not apply if the seller knew or should have known about the non-conformity. [40] The buyer may demand delivery of substituted goods or repair of the non-conforming goods. [46]

11. Article 50: Price Reduction (Remedy)

The buyer may reduce the price in the same proportion as the reduced value of the non-conforming goods as compared to the value of conforming goods.

12. Article 63: *Nachfrist* Notice (Extension of time for Performance)

The seller may fix an additional time for performance by the buyer (*Nachfrist*). [63] The buyer may grant an additional time for performance (*Nachfrist*). [47] If the seller requests additional time and the buyer does not reply, then the seller may perform within the time indicated in her request. [48]

13. Article 67: Risk of Loss

Unless stated otherwise, risk of loss passes to the buyer upon delivery to the *first carrier*. If a particular place is specified, then it passes upon delivery to the carrier at that place.

14. Article 71: Anticipatory Repudiation and Adequate Assurance

A party may suspend performance if it becomes apparent that the other party will not perform due to creditworthiness or failing to prepare to perform (anticipatory repudiation). A party suspending performance must give immediate notice to the other party. A party must continue performance if the other party provides adequate assurance.

15. Article 79: Excuse for Impediment (force majeure)

A party is excused from a contract if she cannot perform due to (1) an impediment beyond her control and (2) the impediment was not reasonably expected at the time of the contract formation. The excuse is only good for the duration of the impediment. Examples of impediments include: natural phenomena, decisions of countries, war, accidents, blockades, sabotage, and robbery. The party claiming the excuse must give notice of the impediment to the other party within a reasonable time.

16. Buyer's Obligations

The buyer is obligated to do what is reasonably required to take delivery. [60] The buyer has an obligation to preserve the goods if she has received them even though she plans to reject them. [86] If the buyer fails to provide specifications as required (specially made goods), then the seller may make the specifications and provide them to the buyer. If the buyer fails to provide different specifications within a reasonable time, then the seller's specifications are binding. [65] The non-breaching party has a duty to mitigate damages. [77]

Uniform Commercial Code: Revision of Article 2

The Permanent Editorial Board to the Uniform Commercial Code instructed the revisers to give "due consideration to the harmonization of domestic and international law." The revisers have made numerous references to the CISG being more in step with modern commercial practices than the UCC. There are no fewer than thirty-five substantive references to the CISG. However, the reconciliation is not complete as some significant differences remain. We will first look at some of the major changes that have reconciled the Revised UCC with the CISG. We will finish with a recognition of some of the remaining differences.

The Seller's *right to cure* found in Section 2-508 has been broadened to allow for an extended time for performance beyond the time fixed in the contract. The Revised UCC (Section 2-709) allows the seller to "provide a cure that is appropriate and timely under the circumstances and the buyer has no reasonable grounds to refuse the cure." This may be seen as at least a partial recognition of the *nachfrist notice* concept in the CISG. The CISG allows either party to request a time extension in order to perform. The broadened cure remedy in the Revised UCC recognizes the civility of granting the seller additional time to perform. Unless the receiving party can provide a good faith reason for denying the extension of time, a rejection is likely to be construed as a bad faith act. This revision is also in line with the UNIDROIT Principles of International Commercial Contracts. "The UNIDROIT principle on cure allows the party in breach to cure its failure to perform if it gives notice of the intent to cure, cure is appropriate in the circumstances, the aggrieved party has no legitimate interest in refusing cure, and cure is affected promptly."[323]

The Revised UCC retains the "perfect tender rule." A buyer may reject goods that fail in any respect to conform to the goods described in the contract. In contrast, the CISG only allows for a rejection of goods that are fundamentally non-conforming. Also, Article 50 of the CISG, unlike the UCC, allows for a *price reduction remedy* for non-conforming goods that are delivered. Although the buyer does not have a right to reject, as provided under the UCC's *perfect tender rule,* the CISG price reduction remedy allows for an immediate reduction in the price before remitting payment. Another area of difference is the extent that a warranty under the CISG or UCC is extended to *remote purchasers.* The Revised UCC clearly extends warranty protection to all purchasers of the goods and not just the immediate or first purchaser. The CISG, however, limits a seller's warranty liability for non-conforming goods to the immediate purchaser. The difference may be due to the fact that the UCC covers sale of goods to merchants and consumers, while the CISG applies only to commercial sale of goods.

Fundamental differences still remain in the area of the *battle of the forms.* The Revised UCC significantly changes its handling of this problem. The notion of *additional terms* is eliminated and replaced with *varying terms.* The varying terms enter the contract only if one of the parties sign the other party's form or the term is a matching term that is in fundamental agreement with a term in the other party's form. The major difference in the Revised UCC is that when there is an exchange of forms, without a signature of the other party's form, the varying terms do not become part of the contract. In the current UCC, the additional (varying) terms in the second document do enter the contract unless they materially alter the offer. However, the way the CISG and UCC define *material terms* remains dis-

---

[323]Linda J. Rusch, *The Relevance of Evolving Domestic and International Law of Contracts in the Classroom: Assumptions about Assent,* 72 Tulane Law Rev. 2043, 2065 (1998).

tinctly different. The UCC will generally enforce the contract by simply deleting the varying terms. Any gaps in the contract will be filled using the UCC's gap-filler provisions. In contrast, varying terms are more likely to be considered material under the CISG. Under its mirror image approach, the second form will be considered a counteroffer and thus no contract will have been formed.

After some thought of eliminating the writing requirements of the statute of frauds, the Revised Section 2-201 retains it with a number of important changes. First, electronic contracting is recognized in that the requirement of a "writing" has been replaced in favor of a requirement of a "record." Also, the requirement of a signature is replaced with the notion of "authentication." Second, the threshold amount for a requirement of a "record" (writing) has been raised from $500 to $10,000. Thus, relatively small international commercial transactions will escape the mandates of the statute of frauds. This may become important in the area of after-purchase contracts where the cost of replacement parts may fall below the $10,000 amount. Thus, the parties will need to be aware that the fact that the initial contract was in a written form does not mean that an oral contract will not be sufficient in related contracts.

CHAPTER 8

General Principles of Service Contracting

Exporters contemplating an initial penetration into a foreign market have at least three legal alternatives in structuring relationships for such an entry. First, the utilization of employees, whether those already in place or new foreign hires. Second, the hiring of an independent contractor, usually foreign based, to act as their foreign sales representative. Third, the entering into a distribution relationship with a foreign distributor. It is estimated that over half of world trade is handled through sales representatives and distributors.[324] This chapter will focus upon the differences and importance of the employment-independent contractor relationships and on the law pertaining to the use of foreign sales representatives and distributors. It will finish with a brief review of some issues dealing with risk insurance, international accounting, and advertising.

Sale of Services

A major development in cross-border commercial transactions is the expansion in the size and types of services being sold. Historically, the most common types of services that were sold internationally were construction and engineering services. Two sources for standard service contracts and clauses in this area are the International Federation of Consulting Engineers

---

[324]Barry M. Fisher, *Product Distribution in Canada*, 20 The Int'l Lawyer 45, 46 (1986), *citing*, King, *Legal Aspects of Appointment and Termination of Foreign Distributors and Representatives*, 17 Case Western Int'l Law Journal 91 (1985).

and the UNCITRAL "Legal Guide on Drawing up International Contracts for the Construction of Industrial Works (1988). This chapter will focus on the use of the services of foreign representatives, sales agents and distributors, in the marketing, sale, and distribution of goods. The crucial determination is on how best to structure the relationship. The two fundamental options are the implementation of either an employment or an independent contractor relationship. This determination is not purely a matter of private contracting. Foreign laws heavily impact the classification of a given relationship as one of employment or independent contracting. Also, once designated as an employment or independent contractor relationship, a number of host country laws regulate areas such as notice, termination, and remuneration. It is important to note that the terminology of agency, employment, and independent contractor as used in the United States often differs in other countries. For example, "the general meaning of *agent* may differ from country-to-country, which emphasizes the need for contractual clarity in defining the relationship."[325] It is important to understand the local terminology and factors used in a host country's law before drafting relevant clauses, such as an independent contractor clause. The following excerpt from the U.S. State Department's Country Commercial Guide for Indonesia illustrates some of the nuances in hiring foreign sales representatives and agents:

> The main difference between a representative office and an agent is that the former cannot sell or sign contracts but only market and do research, while the latter can perform all trade activities. Only Indonesians can function as agents.
>
> Foreign principals often work out a management agreement that allows the foreign company in Indonesia to play a more active role in the marketing efforts of its Indonesian agent or distributor. In many cases, a separate agreement is signed between the expatriate personnel and the foreign employer to regulate this relationship. The tax liability of the foreign firm is limited to the income of the expatriates assigned to the representative office, while any other taxes are assessed to and borne by the agent. Types of management agreements include: (1) technical assis-

---

[325]RALPH H. FOLSOM & MICHAEL W. GORDON, INTERNATIONAL BUSINESS TRANSACTIONS 4, n. 1 (1995).

tance agreements; (2) management agreements; and (3) management agreements coupled with financial agreements.

The technical assistance agreement limits the foreign firm's function to providing technical assistance to the Indonesian company. The management agreement allows the foreign firm to manage the company or a division within the company. In the management agreement coupled with a financial agreement, the foreign firm also finances the Indonesian operation, either under the name of the Indonesian company or a division thereof. Remuneration to the foreign company can be in one of the following forms: (1) fixed fee; (2) commission; or (3) profit-sharing. Whatever basis is used for remuneration, it must be formulated clearly in the agreement, and it must be applicable under the present Indonesian laws. To protect the foreign company's interests properly, a bona fide and comprehensive agreement should be drawn between the parties concerned.

A subsequent determination or conversion of an independent sales agent to employment status subjects the exporter to a wide array of foreign laws including tax and labor laws. An employment designation may also "establish" the company for purposes of personal jurisdiction in the courts of that country. Thus, the structuring and wording of the services contract as one of independent agency, and not dependent agency, is crucial for avoiding such host country laws. The profound differences between civil law and common law countries in the area of agency law require the advice of foreign legal counsel when entering such a relationship. The next three sections on employment, independent contractor, and commercial agency relationships will further flesh out the types of issues and contract clauses that relate to these determinations.

The Employment Relationship

The philosophical foundation of the American employment relationship is the *employment at will doctrine.* It provides that except for expressed employment contracts the employment relationship may be terminated at the will of either party. In order to prevent employee-generated lawsuits of unfair dismissal based upon the breach of an implied contract of employment, companies should avoid the use of employment contracts and make clear at the time of hiring that the employment is "at will." A United States based international company's employment manual should make this clear. First, the manual should state that the general employment policy applies to all subsidiaries. Of course, one should bear in mind that the *at will* concept may be defined differently in other legal systems. Second it should clearly state that "all employees are hired as *at will* employees. The employer's *code of conduct* should delineate prohibited conduct that generally are the basis of employee-generated lawsuits (e.g., sexual harassment) or direct losses to the company. Prohibited conduct should include the following items: (a) rude or discourteous behavior, (b) theft or personal dishonesty, (c) use or possession of alcohol or controlled substances on company premises, (d) maintenance of inappropriate files on the company's internal network, (e) transmission of confidential information over the E-mail system, (f) disclosing non-public information, including trade secrets, (g) duplicating software products, and (h) engaging in any act of harassment or discrimination.

The employment manual should also provide a separate sexual harassment policy. It should give guidance to the types of acts that constitute harassment and a procedure for reporting such acts. Three typical sections of a sexual harassment policy include:

> General Policy: Management personnel are responsible for maintaining a harassment-free environment and are strictly prohibited from stating or in any way implying that submitting or refusing to submit to sexual advances will have any affect upon an individual's hiring, placement, compensation, training, promotion, or any other term or condition of employment.
>
> Definition: All employees are prohibited from making offensive remarks or engaging in unwelcome overtures, either verbal or physical. Such prohibited conduct includes, but is not limited to, offensive and unwelcome flirtations, advances or propositions; verbal abuse of a racial, ethnic, religious, or sexual nature; graphic or degrading comments about an individual or his/her appearance; the display of sexually suggestive objects or pictures; or any offensive or abusive physical contact. Acts of harassment by any employee are strictly prohibited and will result in disciplinary action which may include termination of employment.
>
> Complaint Procedure: When a complaint is received an immediate investigation will be conducted impartially and confidentially by the company's ethics officer or Human Resources Department. At the con-

clusion of the investigation, the officer or representative of Human Resources will advise the employee of the results.

The employment relationship is viewed differently both culturally and legally throughout the world. The differences in the legal status of the employment relationship varies from the employment at will doctrine in the United States to the view of employment as a property right in Germany and the notion of "lifetime employment" in Japan. Understanding these differences is vital to the American exporter contemplating the hiring of foreign nationals. In Germany, for example, the hiring of a single employee can result in the company being designated as having "permanent status" which can lead to the taxation of the exporter's German-generated revenues. Thus, a clearly written contract designating the German national as an independent contractor would be prudent. The decision to hire foreign employees, especially in most European Union countries, should be made with full knowledge of the obstacles the employer has to overcome under European law in order to terminate the employment relationship. In Germany, the required notice required to discharge an employee may vary from four weeks to seven months depending on the longevity of the employment. All intended dismissals can only occur following consultation with statutorily mandated Workers Councils. Also, workers can sue for reinstatement and damages if the dismissal is determined to be "unjustified."[326] There are also a number of protected classes, such as pregnant women and members of the Worker's Council, not subject to dismissal. Furthermore, severance payments can range as high as a full year salary or more for long-term employees. Thus, the employment decision should be cautiously entered into.

Under the French Labor Code, immediate termination is impossible due to the notice requirements and a required meeting with the employee being discharged. A suit for unfair dismissal, like in Germany, is recognized. "In order to avoid civil sanctions for breach of contract, the employer must be able to prove that there were real and serious grounds for the dismissal."[327] The employee also has a right to a severance payment based upon seniority. He may waive this right in favor of a statutorily mandated *conversion contract.* Under the conversion contract, the employee receives, at the cost of the employer, enhanced government unemployment benefits and

[326]PRICE WATERHOUSE, DOING BUSINESS IN GERMANY 84 (1996).
[327]PRICE WATERHOUSE, DOING BUSINESS IN FRANCE 102 (1995).

retraining or educational opportunities. If the ground for dismissal is economic, then the discharged employee has: (1) a right to a transfer if another position is available within the company and (2) a right to re-employment for a period of one year in the event that the economic factors change. The employment relationship in the former Soviet countries is also heavily regulated. For example, the Russian Labor Code "makes it very difficult for the employer to terminate employment. Another policy grants maternity leave of up to *three years* per child."[328] Furthermore, the written contract is the basic form for commencing an employment relationship and there are detailed requirements for dismissing employees. "Before dismissing an employee, it is most advantageous to seek legal consultation."[329]

The Independent Contractor Contract

If the contract for services is intended to be on an independent contractor basis, then the contract should clearly designate it as such. The independent contractor agreement should also include a "non-partnership clause" to prevent the principal from being vicariously liable under agency principles.

> Non-Partnership Clause: The party being hired is to perform as an independent contractor and nothing contained herein should be construed as creating a partnership between the parties to this agreement.

Also, a "work for hire clause" should be inserted into any employment or independent contractor agreement in which the employee or independent contractor is being paid to develop new technology or to perform research and development. This clause makes it clear that all rights to the research and intellectual property rights are to revert to the employer.

> Work for Hire Clause: All inventions, creations, and research of the employee during the term of his employment shall be work for hire and shall be the property of the employer. All rights to to such intellectual property shall be assigned by the employee to the employer.

It is important that the independent contractor status be preserved in both the written contract and in the actual carrying out of the contractual

---

[328]PRICE WATERHOUSE, DOING BUSINESS IN THE RUSSIAN FEDERATION 86-87 (1997).
[329]Ibid at 89.

relationship. In some countries in order to avoid host country laws, especially income tax laws, the exporter-principal should retain control over each sales transaction. The agency contract should specifically require principal approval for each sales contract. Furthermore, transactional approval at the principal's home office should be documented.

Commercial Agency Contracts: The Foreign Sales Representative

The most common use of the agency (independent contractor) vehicle for transacting business is the hiring of a foreign sales representative. This relationship has been defined has the hiring of an agent "to prospect for and visit customers with a view to negotiating and when appropriate concluding sales agreements in the name and for account of the principal (exporter of goods, services, technology)."[330] Under European Union regulations the mere supplying of marketing services does not fall within the definition of commercial agency.[331] The ICC's *Commercial Agency—Guide for the Drawing up of Contracts* notes some domestic laws grant special status to the commercial agent. For example, many European countries grant the agent a right upon the termination of the agency relationship to either an *indemnity* payment (based upon the length of the relationship, along with the level of past or anticipated performance) or a claim for damages (anticipated costs due to termination). Therefore, laws of the foreign country of the commercial agent need to be researched "to ensure that nothing contained in a commercial agency contract is repugnant to imperative [mandatory] provisions"[332] of any law applicable to the contract. Even if the contract is enforceable as written, foreign laws will need to be studied in order to avoid their application to the principal. The clearest example of this is the application of foreign tax liability to the principal:

> In many countries a non-resident principal will be liable for tax if the agent has, and habitually exercises, a general authority to negotiate and

[330]ICC, *Guide for the Drawing up of Contracts — Commercial Agency* 5 (1993).

[331]See, EC Directive 86/653/EEC of December 18, 1986.

[332]Ibid. at 6. For example, in Belgium if the contract subordinates the agent to the authority of the principal, then there is a legal presumption that an employment relationship has been formed. However, this presumption can be overcome if the agent is a corporate entity. Ibid. at 6, note 1.

> conclude contracts on behalf of the principal. For instance, when a principal appoints an agent in a foreign country, with a fixed office therein and with power to make contracts on his behalf, the principal may be deemed to be carrying on business in that foreign country and be taxed accordingly.[333]

Clearly the use of foreign counsel is required in order to avoid such liability traps. The ICC *Guide* can be used as a checklist in order to draft an agency contract. The following summary of the Guide illustrates the types of issues that an international agency contract should address:

> **Independent Contractor Status:** The heading of the agreement should clearly state that it is a commercial agency contract. In order to be absolutely clear as to the intended contractual relationship, the heading and preamble, or a provision in the body, should state that it is an independent contractor arrangement.
> **Identity, Capacity, and Status of Parties:** The nationality and legal form of each party should be stated, along with the foreign entity's capacity to act as a commercial agent. For example, in some countries only nationals may act as agents and in others commercial agents must be registered with the government.
> **Assignments:** Generally, the parties intend that their contract is not subject to assignment and thus, the contract should state that it is not to be assigned. If the parties intend to allow assignment, the contract should state the conditions and procedure for assignments.
> **Language of the Contract:** If the contract is written in two languages, it should state which language is to control in the enforcement of the contract. If both languages are to control, then the translation should be carefully reviewed by an expert.
> **Dates of Commencement and Expiration:** Since there may be a lag between the first and second signature to the contract or between execution and when the relationship is to be commenced, the contract should expressly state the commencement and expiration dates of the contract.
> **Products:** The contract should be clear regarding the products that are to be sold on behalf of the principal. If the principal produces different classes of products, then the contract should state which classes are the

[333] Ibid. at 7.

subject of the agency contract. If the products have different uses, the contract should state for which uses the products are to be marketed and sold. The contract should also address the issue of the development of new products or subsequent improvements of the products listed in the contract. It should state whether the agent will have rights to sell those products. The parties may also consider minimum or maximum amounts of the products to be supplied by the principal.

Agency Territory: The contract should precisely delineate the sales territory that is being given to the agent. A further restriction may be placed upon the sales to third parties who are likely to export the goods to another territory. Host country laws should be reviewed to see if territorial restrictions will violate anti-competition laws.

Exclusivity: The parties should agree as to whether the contractual territory is being given exclusively to the agent. It should also state any rights reserved to the principal to operate within the territory as some foreign buyers may contact the principal directly or may want to only deal with the principal. The agreement should provide what are the relative rights of the principal and the agent in such situations.

Solicitation of Customers: The parties should agree to the groups to be targeted by the agent as potential customers. Also, the parties should append a list of customers, if any, in which the principal has previously done business within the contract territory.

Acceptance of Orders: The agreement should clearly state whether the agent has the authority to bind the principal. However, if the agent is authorized merely to pass on orders, then the principal is generally free to accept or reject them. A notice provision setting a reasonable time for the principal to advise the agent of its decision should be incorporated into this provision.

Promotional and Sales information: The contract should stipulate the manner in which the agent shall be kept informed of the principal's sales policy, particularly with regard to any visits the principal may make to customers within the contractual territory and to what extent the principal is obligated to send copies of correspondence, documentation, and invoices exchanged between the principal and customers or potential customers. The clause should provide the manner in which the principal is to notify the agent of any changes in its price structure, terms of delivery, terms of payment or standard conditions of sale. It should also stipulate when such changes will become effective in the contractual territory.

Manufacturing Licenses: The agreement should define the rights and obligations of the parties in the event that the principal licenses with a third party to manufacture the goods within the territory of the agency contract.

Intellectual Property Rights Infringement: The relative responsibilities of the parties as to infringement of intellectual property rights should be defined. For example: (1) the obligations of the principal to prevent unfair competition or the appearance on the market of infringements of its property rights, (2) the agent's responsibility to notify the principal of any such infringements.

Advertising and Marketing Materials: The contract should stipulate whether the principal is to provide any samples or advertising materials, and which party is to pay the costs of such materials including any duties and clearance charges for samples or materials. The contract should make clear whether the principal has the right of prior consent for any materials or advertising produced by the agent. Also, the agent's rights to take part in fairs and exhibitions or whether prior approval is required should be detailed.

Expenses: If the principal is to share any of the agent's expenses in the marketing and selling of the products, then the agreement should state what expenses are to be allocated to the principal. Note, however, that in some countries the sharing of expenses may be enough to convert an independent contractor relationship into an employment relationship.

Best Efforts Provision: The principal will want to negotiate a clause that requires the agent to use "best efforts" in marketing and selling the principal's products. The agent should be required to make every effort to safeguard the principal's property and property rights. The agreement should attempt to define the meaning of "best efforts" or "every effort," possibly tying them to generally accepted business practices.

Disclosure of Authority: It is advisable to stipulate that it is the agent's duty when dealing with third parties to act in such a manner as to avoid any ambiguity and dispute as to the source, nature, and extent of its authority to bind the principal. If the agent is given the authority to bind the principal, that authority should be made conditional upon the agent's complying with instructions of the principal regarding any changes in the prices or terms of sale.

Non-competition Clause: This provision prohibits the agent from selling the products of a competitor. The contract should list the agency relationships already in place at the time of the signing of the contract. This clause should be narrowly constructed so not to violate national laws that view such restrictions harshly.

Agent as Distributor: If an agent enters into separate agency and distributor relationships with the principal, the contracts should reference one another. It is important that the agreements describe what obligations the agent is accepting as an agent and as a distributor.

Consignment: The parties should agree in detail on the terms to govern all matters relating to consignment stocks. They should specify if the principal can take back the whole inventory or part of it and if the agent is allowed to send back unsold goods. It is essential that the consignment stocks be properly insured. The contract should also provide that the agent is to take all necessary safeguards to protect the principal's right of ownership. Note, in some countries the creation of consignment lays the principal open to being taxed as a resident.

Parts and Service: The obligations of the agent should be detailed with regards to providing after-sales service and spare parts.

Customer and Legal Information: A clause may be inserted that obligates the agent to keep the principal informed as to changes in the market and the financial status of customers. It may also require the agent to inform the principal of any changes in national laws or regulations relating to technical requirements, labeling, and customs regulations. This should include information regarding any national requirement to register the agency contract. It should also require the agent to cooperate in the termination of the registration when the contract expires.

Confidentiality: The agreement should require the agent to maintain the secrecy of the principal's trade secrets even after the termination of the relationship.

Sub-agents: It may be stipulated that the agent is responsible for hiring sub-agents and covering any related expenses. It should make clear that there is no intended relationship between the sub-agents and the principal.

Due Diligence: The agent is required to satisfy itself by means of proper inquiries as to the solvency of prospective customers.

Escrow: The principal may require the agent to place any sales revenues into a separate bank account. This will protect the principal from aggregation with assets of the agent in the event of bankruptcy or sequestration.

Del Credere Status: In some countries the agency may be subject to certain mandatory statutory rules. A *del credere* relationship is generally recognized when the agent guarantees to its customer's payments to the principal. The contract should explain the extent of the agent's liability.

Intellectual Property Rights Registration: The contract should provide in whose name any such registration is to be made and who will bear the cost. In order to protect its rights, the principal should perform the registration prior to entering any agency relationship or intellectual property licensing agreement.

Minimum Sales: The principal may want to negotiate that the agent is required to meet certain minimum sales levels. It should specify the consequences for the failure to meet sales quotas such as termination, reduction of territory, or loss of exclusivity. Alternative or supplementary sales commissions may be provided in the event that the agent meets or fails to meet its sales quotas. Also, the contract should provide excuses for failing to meet sales quotas such as changes in economic climate, non-acceptance of orders by the principal, and the imposition of import restrictions.

General Conditions of Sale: The parties should incorporate, by reference, the general terms or conditions of sale that will apply to the principal-customer relationship. Note, domestic laws should be checked regarding the legality or enforceability of the different terms.

Commissions: The basis of calculation and the rate of commissions should be clearly stated. If the net amount is used as a basis, then the deductions (e.g., freight, insurance, discounts, taxes, packing) should be delineated. The contract should explain what commissions will be owed for transactions executed outside the territory, those made directly between the principal and a customer within the territory, or on repeat orders. The time when the commission is due should be stipulated (when the order is accepted, upon delivery of goods, or upon payment of purchase price). It should also stipulate the place and currency of payment.

Termination: The contract may be for a fixed period or an indefinite time period subject to reasonable notice. Some national laws require that the notice be of a certain length of time. It may be stipulated that certain events (bankruptcy, merger, assignment, resignation of a key employee) give a party the right to terminate. Some national laws (e.g., Germany, France, Brazil, Switzerland) require the principal to pay compensation for termination.

Choice of Law & Forum Selection Clauses: The parties should agree on the law that will apply to any disputes. It should also select the court or arbitration panel in which such disputes are to be brought.

Merger Clause: This clause states that all the terms of the contract are found in the agency contract and that all previous dealings and agreements are being replaced by this contract.

The most difficult laws to avoid are national agency termination laws. These laws often impose minimum notice requirements for terminating an agent or require the payment of an indemnity upon termination unless the termination is based upon a just cause. In countries like France, a decision not to renew an agency contract is construed as a termination requiring remuneration. European Union directive 86/653 provides that agency contracts should be in writing and expressly state any grants of exclusivity and the agent's marketing area. The termination clauses should provide for a minimum notice of termination. A reasonable notice period is one month per year of service through the sixth year and six months thereafter. A commercial agent will be owed an indemnity upon termination to the extent that he has brought new customers to the principal or significantly increased the principal's volume of business.[334] The EC Directive also allows national laws to provide for a damage claim to the agent, especially if at the time of termination the agent had not completely amortized his costs and expenses relative to the representation.[335] The best approach is to enter into a fixed term contract with no renewal options. The contract should also provide a detailed list of performance standards upon which termination for just cause may be based. The ICC Guide recommends the selection of the alternative (Alternative A) in its model contract whenever the right to an indemnity is recognized under the national law of the agent's country. Alternative B (Article 21) would conflict with many of the national laws of the countries within the European Union. Also, some country laws, as in Belgium and France, presume that the agent is an employee even if the contract designates the agent as an independent contractor. Therefore, the easiest way to avoid this presumption is to only deal with agents who are artificial entities (corporations). National labor and employment laws will need to be checked for obligations of the principal pertaining to social security and other "employment-related" statutory requirements. Under Italian law, the principal and the agent must pay five percent each on all commissions paid to the national agency (ENASARCO) as social security contributions. The principal is legally obligated to withhold the agent's contribution and remit it to the agency, along with an amount to be used towards the severance indemnity. A certain percentage is paid on a sliding scale based on the amounts of the commissions paid, ranging from 4% to

[334]EC Directive 86/653, Article 17(2).

[335]Ibid. at Article 17(3). The agent must notify its principal of a claim for indemnity or damages within one year from the date of termination. Ibid. at Article 17(5).

1% for exclusive and nonexclusive agents. The 1% rate is not reached until thirty-six million lire is paid for exclusive agents, while the rate of 1% is lowered for amounts over eighteen million lire for nonexclusive agents.

A variation of the foreign sales representative is the foreign consultant. The same issues of host country labor laws and agency termination laws apply to the consulting relationship. The *consulting contract* should be specific as to the scope of the engagement (surveying, advertising, etc.). The independent status of the consultant should be emphasized. The agreement should state that the services are being provided on a nonexclusive basis and that the principal takes no responsibility for the manner in which the consultant performs on the contract. Compensation should be structured to highlight the independent basis of the relationship. Overhead expenses should not be passed on to the principal. A separate "independent contractor status clause" should be incorporated into the agreement. The factors often utilized in making the employee-independent contractor distinction should be incorporated into this clause: (1) the consultant is not an employee and is not entitled to any employee-type of benefits, (2) the consultant is to perform his tasks based on his own discretion and skills and will be responsible for any acts or omissions, (3) the consultant is responsible for hiring any sub-agents or assistants, (4) the consultant provides its tools, equipment, and materials, and pays its own overhead expenses.

Logistical Services

An exporter must become knowledgeable of packing, labeling, and documentation requirements. Because of the importance and complexity of these requirements, most exporters will enlist the services of freight forwarders and customs brokers. Freight forwarders and customs brokers act as agents of the exporter and/or importer in transporting cargo worldwide and for the importation of the goods into a given country. Freight forwarders are familiar with foreign import regulations, methods of shipping, documentation, and United States export regulations. They are a good source for freight and insurance cost information for the exporter preparing a pro forma invoice or price quotation. In the documentary transaction, the freight forwarder can be enlisted to review the letter of credit, bill of lading, and other documents. The freight forwarder can also help in the packaging and the marking of the goods for transport. The marking of the export shipping cartons is especially important. Proper markings are needed to meet shipping regulations, to assure proper handling, and to help the purchaser identify the goods. The most common markings are the shipper's mark, country of origin, weight markings, number of packages, handling marks, cautionary markings, port of entry, and hazardous materials labels. The freight forwarder will be aware of the internationally recognized symbols for handling and shipping.

The next section analyzes the most crucial relationship in the exportation and distribution of goods internationally. The success of foreign exporting often rises or falls based upon the strength of the exporter-distributor relationship. Because of the differences in language, culture, and the legal treatment of such relationships, it is important to negotiate a foreign distribution agreement that is detailed regarding the respective duties and responsibilities of the parties.

The Distribution Agreement

A common form of service contract for the movement and sale of goods once they are imported into a foreign country is the distribution agreement.[336] Unlike an agency relationship where the sales contract is between the principal and the purchaser, the distributor generally sells the goods on its own account. The sales contract is between the distributor and the purchaser. Because of this, the foreign distributor is by necessity an independent contractor in relationship to the exporter or manufacturer. The selection of a competent and trustworthy foreign distributor or agent is crucial. The U.S. Department of Commerce can be used as a resource in the selection process. They provide information on foreign distributors and agents through Agent-Distributor Searches (ADS). Also, it provides Customized Market Analysis (CMA) reports that identify potential representatives.

---

[336]See generally, Herold & Knoll, *Negotiating and Drafting International Distribution Agency and Representative Agreements: The United States Exporter's Perspective,* 21 Int'l Lawyer 939 (1987); King, *Legal Aspects of Appointment and Termination of Foreign Distributors and Representatives,* 17 Case Western Reserve J. Int'l Law 91 (1985); Saltoun & Spudis, *International Distribution and Sales Agency Agreements: Practical Guidelines for U.S. Exporters,* 38 Business Lawyer 883 (1983).

The International Chamber of Commerce *Guide to Drafting International Distribution Agreements*[337] outlines the underlying risks of the distribution relationship and the ways to deal with such risks in the distribution contract. A brief review of this guide is a good starting point for analyzing this pivotal contractual relationship for the international manufacturer-exporter. Distributor is defined in the *Guide* as "not a middleman, but a dealer who buys goods in order to resell them in his own name, even if he is often called an agent." Thus the referencing of a distributor as an agent is a misnomer. The agent is generally an independent contractor owing certain fiduciary obligations to the principal. The foreign sales representative, as an independent agent, acts as a middleman between its principal (manufacturer-exporter) and third party customers. It should be noted that a party may act as both an agent and as a distributor. It is important to analyze these different roles independently of each other. The distributor's relationship with the manufacturer-exporter is purely contractual and is very much akin to a sale of goods transaction. However, it is a special kind of sales relationship in that the distributor often (1) "deals with the promotion and organization of distribution within its contractual territory, (2) generally the contractual territory is exclusive to the distributor," (3) it is not a one-shot transaction but lasts for a certain duration, (4) there exists a certain heightened level of loyalty, namely "an obligation to refrain from competition," and (5) almost always relates to the distribution of "branded products."

Before drafting an international distribution agreement it is imperative to research the law of the distributor's country in order to comply with mandatory legal provisions. Unlike in the United States, the distributor (along with commercial agency) relationship is regulated under some foreign statutes. Some countries like Saudi Arabia require distributors to be nationals and register as distributors with the government. Some countries, by statute or case law, require that the distribution agreement provide some minimal level of protection. In France, the case law is rich with instances where judges have ordered additional compensation to be paid by the principal when severing a distribution relationship. Germany recognizes a "goodwill indemnity" that is owed to the distributor upon the termination

[337]ICC, *Guide to Drafting International Distribution Agreements,* ICC Pub. No. 441 (E) (1988).

of the distribution agreement. Finally, foreign competition laws need to be researched to see if exclusivity in a distribution agreement will be enforceable. European Union (EU) law has been used at times to challenge territorial restrictions as restrictive trade practices. However, certain "block exemptions" can be utilized to defend against such challenges. EU Regulation 1983/83 deals with the legality of exclusive distribution agreements. For example, it generally disfavors clauses that prohibit a distributor from selling within the territory of another distributor. Because of the complexity of EU competition law, it is advisable to have a specialist review your distribution agreement. Another source for nation-specific regulation of the distribution agreement is a series of articles found in the *International Lawyer*.[338]

The *Guide* discusses the following issues that should be handled in a distribution agreement[339]: the uniqueness of a principal, its goods, and the country of the distributor require that all distribution agreements be custom tailored. This list of issues is best used as the beginning checklist for drafting of international distribution contracts. One note of caution, because most distribution agreements entail some transfer of intellectual property, it is imperative that the exporter protect his rights under the foreign law of the distributor prior to entering into an agreement.

> **The Parties:** The agreement should deal with the ability of the parties to assign their rights and duties. It should also deal with the issue of changes in key personnel. If certain employees are considered essential, they should be recognized in the contract. The contract could then provide for a termination in the event that essential persons cease to be associated with the distributor. The parties should be required to give notice of key personnel changes and changes in the ownership or management of the

[338]*See, e.g.*, H.T. King, Jr., *Legal Aspects of Appointment and Termination of Foreign Distributors and Representatives,* Int'l Lawyer at 91 (1985); T.W. Simon, *Termination of Sales Agents and Distributors in Belgium,* Int'l Lawyer at 752 (1983); G. Vorbrugg & D.H. Mahler, *Agency and Distribution Agreements Under German Law* at 607 (1985); David M. Dobson & Rita Gaudenzi, *Agency and Distribution Laws in Italy: Guidelines for the Foreign Principal* Int'l Lawyer at 997 (1986).

[339]*See also,* Barry Michael Fisher, *Product Distribution in Canada,* 20 The International Lawyer 45, 48-54 (1986).

company. A special clause should deal with the issue of the parties' rights to assign the contract. Generally, an exporter will want the contract to preclude assignments or at least to require prior consent.

Commencement and Expiration: The contract should specify a specific commencement date and not leave it to be extrapolated from the date of execution. The same is true for the date of expiration. In order to minimize the changes of large indemnity payments under certain national laws, indefinite contract terms should be avoided. Also, renewals should be kept to a minimum. It is better for indemnity purposes to enter into an entirely new contract at the expiration of the first contract.

Contractual Products: Products subject to the agreement should be listed. The range of products to be distributed should be clearly defined. The contract should specify if the distributor will have the right to distribute future products. If the products are being sold under specific trademarks, then the agreement should state that similar products sold under a different trademark are not covered by the agreement. Furthermore, the contract should state whether the distributor has the right to appoint sub-distributors and sub-dealers. The exporter should retain the right not to have to continue to supply a product that has been discontinued.

Host Country Regulations: The exporter will want the distributor to take responsibility for product compliance with local health, safety, and packaging regulations. Also, in order to avoid foreign tax, employment (including *evergreen statutes*), and labor laws, the agreement should specify that the relationship is one of independent contracting in which neither party has the right to bind the other. Also, foreign income tax and currency control laws should be reviewed by the exporter; a request for payment by the distributor into an account located outside the host country should be viewed as possible violations of those laws.

Contractual Territory: The agreement should deal with issues of competition and the exclusivity of the contractual territory. It may provide a restriction prohibiting the distributor from selling a rival's products. The exporter may want to restrict the distribution rights to certain classes of customers (e.g., only manufacturers that the use product as a component part or only retailers). Also, the exporter may be prohibited from selling products to customers who are likely to import them into the distributor's territory. However, terms preventing the distributor from selling outside its contractual territory may be illegal under some legal regimes (e.g., EU Competition Law). It is important for the licensor to receive host country legal advice on the legality of exclusivity provisions. In some countries such provisions are illegal as potential restraints of trade.[340]

General Conditions of Sales: The parties will attach the exporter's general condition of sales to the distribution agreement. The distribution agreement should provide that in case of conflict the distribution agreement shall prevail over the general conditions of sale. The exporter should reserve the right to change its prices at its sole discretion. The right of the distributor to set retail pricing should also be specified. Foreign antitrust or anti-competition laws should be checked to determine the legality of any price ceilings. The contract should specify the time, method, and currency of payment. The exporter may want to set a minimum amount of the product that can be ordered at any one time. Also, the contract should detail the method of placing orders and the method of accepting or rejecting such orders, including any time limits. The distribution agreement should specify that its terms control over any conflicting terms found in subsequent purchase orders. The exporter is generally obligated to pay excess transportation and storage charges for failure to comply with shipping instructions it has accepted. However, the exporter will want to limit any consequential damages. The agreed trade term should reference the International Chamber of Commerce's INCOTERMS manual.

Best Efforts (Licensee): The exporter should include a clause requiring the distributor to use best efforts to achieve a maximum of sales. The distributor should agree to refrain from selling or promoting competitive products. The best efforts provision may also provide minimum sales quotas in order to meet the best efforts obligation. The "minimum sales quota" may be used to trigger an exporter option to terminate the contract or to preclude a renewal of the contract. The clause should provide for an annual review of the minimum sales quota. The best efforts requirements should also be interrelated with the *force majeure* clause. For example, the

[340] *See, e.g.,* Jesse A. Finkelstein, *Legislative and Judicial Regulation of Exclusive Distribution Agreements in France,* Int'l Lawyer 539 (1981); S. Sharma & W. Morrison, *The Use of Local Representatives in Saudi Arabia,* Int'l Lawyer at 453 (1977). It should be noted that these articles are somewhat dated and should be used only as general background reading.

distributor should be excused from meeting his minimum sales obligation in the event that import restrictions prohibit the importation of material to the licensee.

Products Liability: The exporter may want to place a clause in the agreement assigning the risk of product liability claims to the distributor. However, the foreign national law may impose such liability on both the manufacturer-exporter and the distributor (e.g., EU Directive of 25 July 1985). Instead, the parties may agree to obtain a proscribed level of products liability insurance to protect both their product liability risks.

Warranties: The product warranty provisions provided by the distributor should be consistent with those of the exporter. Both parties may require the other to procure a specific minimum amount of product liability insurance. Responsibility for transportation charges on warranty claims should be specified. Also, a specific limitation on special or consequential damages should be set.

Directives: If the exporter wants to maintain some control over the distribution of its products, then it should negotiate a clause requiring the distributor to comply with its directives.

Sales Promotion: The obligations of the distributor to promote sales of the product should be detailed in the agreement. Instead of a minimum quantity clause (see below) the agreement may require the distributor to commit a minimum sum of money for advertising and sales promotion.

After-Sales Service: The distributor's duties regarding after-sales service and the providing of spare parts should be detailed, along with any corresponding rights to additional compensation.

Sub-Distributors: The contract should provide the extent of the distributor's rights to use agents or sub-distributors. It should answer the following question: How much control will the exporter exercise over the identity of any such agents or sub-distributors?

Minimum Quantity Clause: This clause requires the distributor to buy a minimum quantity of goods. It is important that it specify the consequences of not meeting the required quota such as a right to terminate, a reduction in contractual territory, or a discontinuance of exclusivity.

Advertising: The distribution agreement should specify the extent of any advertising that the distributor is required to undertake. If brand image is a concern of the exporter, then it should negotiate a right to control the content of advertisements. If the costs are to be shared, then the contract should specify the criteria for sharing costs.

Conditions of Sales: Often the manufacturer will want to ensure that each of its distributors offer the same conditions of sales to their customers especially regarding guarantees and after-sales service. However, the validity of such clauses as restrictions regarding the types of customers to be solicited, resale pricing, and territorial restrictions is questionable under some national laws. For example, the laws of France, Germany, United Kingdom, and the Scandinavian countries should be closely checked especially with regards to the area of retail price maintenance.

Export Prohibition: The manufacturer will often insert a clause that obligates the distributor to transmit orders from customers outside its territory to the manufacturer or a distributor within that territory. Such a provision is likely to be held invalid under EU law. Before drafting such a clause in a European distribution agreement, Regulation 1983/83 should be reviewed. Under that regulation, a properly drafted clause prohibiting a distributor from openly soliciting outside its territory is likely to be upheld.

Disclosure of Information: This clause obligates the distributor to provide a variety of types of information to the exporter. It may include information regarding changes in host country regulations (rules of origin, packaging or marking requirements, custom law changes, safety and health standards). It may also require the distributor to provide information on customers (e.g., customer list). However, the providing of customer information is enough in some countries to convert the distributor into an agent and thus entitle it to a goodwill indemnity at the expiration of the agreement.

Notice of Infringement: The distributor should be required to promptly notify the exporter of any infringements on the exporter's intellectual property rights that come to its attention.

Manufacturer's Duty to Cooperate and Provide Information: This clause requires the manufacturer to keep the distributor informed of product changes and supply problems. It may entail the duty to supply advertising materials or to provide technical assistance. The manufacturer may also be required to provide training courses or to provide specialized staff. The agreement should state the additional costs of such assistance. The exporter's obligations to provide technical information on products and subsequent improvements, and to provide promotional assistance, should be specifically described. The exporter may also want to provide a right of prior approval for any promotional materials developed by the distributor. Also, some national laws (Germany) require that the exporter-manufacturer maintain a minimum level of parts inventory. Any obligations of the exporter to maintain a minimum level of parts to service the distribution agreement should be specified.

Limitation of Remedies: Typically, exporters reserve the right to replace products found to be defective or in short supply. The exporter should reserve the right to require the distributor to return any rejected goods (at exporter's expense) or to otherwise dispose of the defective products.

Assignment: The agreement should expressly prohibit the distributor from assigning the agreement, in whole or in part.

Notice of Termination: The contract should provide reasonable notice in order to terminate the agreement or to prevent a renewal of the agreement. The rights of the exporter to terminate the agreement should be specified, including the types of breaches that may result in immediate termination. The parties should agree to reasonable termination notice for either party to terminate the agreement without cause. Upon termination, the distributor should be required to refer any future inquires, orders, and correspondence concerning the products to the licensor.

Force Majeure: The standard *force majeure* clause should be customized to provide an excuse for governmental regulations. "The United States party ought to include a provision which allows suspension, or possibly termination, of any obligations to provide products to fulfill orders, when the United States government imposes restrictions on exports."[341] It may be prudent to expand the excuse by negating any responsibilities to supply substitute goods from sources outside of the United States.

Trial Period: Some manufacturers prefer an initial trial period before committing to a long-term relationship. The agreement should provide that the parties may terminate without notice at a certain specified date or during a certain trial period or on very short notice.

Post-Termination Provisions: The contract should provide for the disposition of distributor's inventory of products or spare parts. It should provide for the price to be paid by the manufacturer if it is required to buy back stock as is required under French law. Another clause should deal with the termination of the distributor's use of the manufacturer's intellectual property rights. The distributor should be required, on termina-

---

[341]FOLSOM & GORDON at 18.

tion of the agreement, to cease using the name and trademarks of the exporter and to cooperate in the cancellation of any user registration. This clause should provide for a return of any sensitive materials, discontinuance of trademark usage, and post-termination confidentiality. Another provision may require the terminated distributor to cooperate in the transfer of after-sales service (supplying parts, technical assistance, and guarantee servicing) to the new distributor.

Choice of Law and Forum Selection: A clear choice of law clause and forum selection clause should be negotiated. However, it should be noted that choice of law will not be honored if it results in the avoidance of mandatory national laws pertaining to distribution agreements. Also, in some countries (e.g., Belgium) the distributor will be allowed to bring suit in its home country notwithstanding a forum selection clause that states otherwise. The preferred means of dispute resolution in international contracting is arbitration.

Host Country Restrictions

Contractual restrictions on the rights of the distributor or licensee are dealt with in a number of different ways under national laws. The developing countries look with skepticism on any such restrictions and generally will not enforce restrictive contract provisions in their courts. Other countries prohibit only certain types of clauses such as non-reciprocal grant-back clauses. Most developed countries allow the contracting parties full freedom to contract and will enforce most restrictive clauses. The one main exception is that certain restrictions will be scrutinized under antitrust or competition laws. Thus, some forms of exclusivity may be deemed to be anti-competitive. EU and national agency laws are highly protective of their citizens that are acting as foreign agents. These laws should be consulted before drafting agency contracts.[342] Generally, the following clauses need to be carefully drafted to be legally enforceable in certain countries: Grant-back, Price-fixing, Non-competition, No-Challenge, Quantity Limitations, Field-of-Use, Quality Controls and Tying clauses.

Price-fixing and *tying clauses* are those most likely to be held as illegal. For example, most legal regimes prohibit the principal or licensor from set-

[342]See, EU Council Directive Regarding Commercial Agents, Council Directive 86/653.

ting downstream pricing, especially at the retail level. Tying clauses that require the distributor or licensee to purchase other items along with the licensed product are generally unenforceable. One exception is when such a tying of products or services is needed to ensure the quality of the licensed or distributed product. In such cases, a requirement that the licensee purchase materials from certified suppliers is likely to be enforced. However, in some countries the courts may review the tie-in arrangement to prevent excessive pricing.

Non-competition and *validity or no-challenge clauses* and are also susceptible to non-enforcement. Generally, a distribution or sales contract cannot prohibit the agent or representative from also selling the products of another company. The one major exception is that U.S. courts will allow such clauses in cases involving patented property rights where the licensee is given an exclusive license. Another strategy to increase the chances of enforceability is to tie exclusivity to non-competition. The distributor or licensee has the right to sell the goods of a competitor but in doing so converts the license from an exclusive to a non-exclusive one. Validity or no-challenge clauses prohibit the licensee from challenging the exclusiveness or validity of the licensor's intellectual property rights. No-challenge clauses are unenforceable under antitrust or competition law because of the notion that a party should have a right to challenge a patent that it believes to be fraudulent or inappropriate. One exception is that the United States does allow no-challenge clauses in trademark licenses.

Exporters and licensors often attempt to prevent *gray market* problems by negotiating *field-of use* and *quantity restrictions* into their transfer agreements. An example is Japan's *Antimonopoly Act Guidelines for International Licensing Agreements.* It expressly permits such restrictions as proper exercise of statutory patent, copyright, and trademark rights. The *Guidelines* permit limitations on "field of technology" and "limited field of sales." It also allows the licensor to "restrict the amount of output or the amount of sales of patented goods."[343] Chapter 9 of this volume reviews European Union Regulations pertaining to such restrictions. Generally, the EU provides a *block exemption* that allows for such limitations. The licensor can be prohibited from "actively" selling outside of its contractual territory, however, it cannot be prohibited from filling orders "passively" acquired.

---

[343]See, RAY AUGUST, INTERNATIONAL BUSINESS LAW 484 (2d ed. 1997).

The *grant back clauses* are highly valued by most licensors. One-sided grant back clauses give all rights to title and to use of any improvements made by the licensee to the licensor. The non-reciprocal version of this clause is not enforceable in some countries.[344] Thus, it may be necessary, depending upon the country, to provide for reciprocity or sharing within the grant back clause. Thus, any subsequent improvements made by the licensor may also have to be made available to the licensee. Another technique for increasing the likelihood of enforceability is to provide for reasonable compensation for the grant back of licensee's improvements. Also, the grant back can be made to be non-exclusive. Thus, the licensee is allowed to continue to use its improvement within the geographical scope of the license.

Carriage of Goods Contracts

In order to transport goods throughout the world, a number of different types of common carriers are utilized. Each type of carriage contract is governed by its own unimodal transport convention. The most popular conventions are listed in Exhibit 8.1:

Exhibit 8.1: International Transport Conventions

Type of Carriage	Convention
Carriage by Air	Convention for the Unification of Certain Rules Relating to International Carriage by Air (Warsaw Convention)
	Additional Protocols Nos. 1-4 to Amend the Warsaw Convention (Montreal Accord)
Carriage by Rail	International Convention Concerning the Carriage of Goods by Rail (CIM Convention)
	Protocol to Amend the Convention Concerning International Carriage by Rail (COTIF) (1990)

[344]In contrast, such non-reciprocal grant back clauses are generally enforceable in United States courts unless hey are held to violate the antitrust laws. See, e.g., Santa Fe Pomeroy. Inc. v. P. & Z. Co., 569 F.2d 1084 (9th Cir. 1978)

Carriage by Road	Convention on the Contract for the International Carriage of Goods by Road (CMR)
Carriage by Sea	Brussels Convention on Bills of Lading or International Convention for the Unification of Certain Rules of Law Relating to Bills of Lading (Hague Rules)
	Protocol to Amend the Hague Rules (Hague-Visby Rules)
	Hamburg Rules 1978
Multimodal Transport	UNCTAD/ICC Rules for Multimodal Transport Documents 1991

The application of different carriage liability regimes in an international transport of goods is potentially overwhelming. The leg of the transport in which the loss-inducing event occurs (land, rail, ocean) determines the type of convention to be applied. The scene is further complicated by the existence of different legal regimes for a given mode of transport. For example, if the loss is sustained during an ocean voyage, then it must be determined which ocean carriage convention (Hague, Hague-Visby, or Hamburg) is applicable.

The Hague-Visby rules updated the Hague rules, but some countries, including the United States, have failed to ratify the update. The liability of the carrier and ancillary companies is directly impacted depending upon which version is applied. Under the Hague-Visby rules, the limit of liability is significantly increased. The liability limitations under the Hague-Visby Rules are 2 SDR[345] per kilogram. The Hamburg Rules are even more pro-shipper than the Hague-Visby Rules. The Hamburg Rules cap carrier liability at 2.5 SDR per kilogram or 835 SDR per unit or package. Carrier liability protections are automatically extended to the servants of the carriers in the Hamburg Rules, where as under the Hague Rules, a properly worded *Himalaya Clause* is of paramount importance to extend the coverage to third parties.[346] However, the third party need not be specifically named in the Himalaya clause in order for the protection of a carriage convention to be extended. General language is sufficient to extend defenses under the bill of lading to stevedores.[347] Even marine terminal operators have been extended

[345]SDR stands for "Special Drawing Rights" which is the unit of calculation of the International Monetary Fund. Its value is determined by a basket of national currencies.
[346]See, e.g., Brown & Root, Inc. v. M.V. Peisander, 648 F.2d 415 (5th Cir. 1981).
[347]See, *Secrest Machine Corp. v. S.S. Tiber,* 450 F.2d 285 (5th Cir. 1971).

protection under a general Himalaya Clause.[348] For example, the following general clause was held to be sufficient to extend coverage to a stevedore company and a consultant hired to supervise the stowage of the cargo.

> No servant or agent of the Carrier (including every independent contractor from time to time employed by the Carrier) shall in any circumstances whatsoever be under any liability whatsoever to the Merchant. Every right, exemption, defense and immunity of whatsoever nature applicable to the Carrier shall also be available and shall extend to protect every such servant or agent of the Carrier.[349]

A still unresolved issue is how best to deal with multimodal or combined transport contracts. The current approach is the recognition that the different unimodal conventions form a network of liability. Each segment of the transport is governed by the convention applicable to that type of transportion. Under the ICC Rules," the carrier must prove during which stage of the multimodal transport the damage occurred." It also places a presumption in favor of the shipper in the event that the carrier does not meet its burden. "If the stage cannot be established, the system of liability most favorable to the claimant of the relevant modes of transport is deemed to apply."[350]

Law of Freight Forwarding

The freight forwarder plays a crucial role in the transportation of products under an international sales contract. The services provided by the freight forwarder, and to some extent the customs broker, have expanded in modern times.

> Traditionally they are mainly engaged in assisting merchants in connection with preparing and booking the cargo for subsequent carriage. In doing so, they would perform a number of services ancillary to the carriage and also contract for carriage as agent for the merchant. In some

[348]See, *Wemhoener Pressen v. Ceres Marine Terminals,* 5 F.3d 734 (4th Cir. 1993).

[349]General Elec. Co. v. Inter-Ocean Shipping, 862 F.Supp. 166, 169 (S.D. Tex. 1994).

[350]Frank G.M. Smeele, "The Contract of Carriage" in Marieele Koppenol-Laforce, ed., *International Contracts: Aspects of Jurisdiction, Arbitration and Private International Law* 257 (1996).

> cases, freight forwarders would act as agents for carriers, particularly liner shipping companies for the carriage of goods by sea. The freight forwarding services would normally include the clearance of goods for export and for import. Also, freight forwarders would have cooperating partners in other countries to whom instructions could be given for the receipt of the cargo and for customs clearance.[351]

A key issue is whether a freight forwarder can be sued as a principal to the carriage contract. The answer revolves on whether in a given freight forwarding contract the freight forwarder is determined to be a mere agent or a principal. In its role as a cargo consolidator, especially where it quotes a fixed price, the freight forwarder can be sued under certain national laws as a carrier.[352] The demands of international, multimodal transport have transformed the freight forwarder from a mere agent of the shipper to that of an operator with carrier liability. This realization was noted in the UCP 500 (documentary credit rules). Article 30 of the UCP allows the operative bill of lading to be issued by a freight forwarder if the freight forwarder is acting as a carrier or multimodal transport operator. The multiple roles played by the freight forwarder leads to some ethical concerns. As the agent of the shipper, the freight forwarder is supposed to work on the shipper's behalf as an unbiased advisor.[353] However, his multiple roles may generate temptations to give preferential treatment to certain customers or to work more in favor of the carrier than the shipper. Thus, the shipper is best advised to perform independent checks on the services being provided.

Associated issues involving freight forwarder liability include: (1) whether the freight forwarder can further limit its liability through contract provisions and (2) what international carrier convention applies in determining the scope of the freight forwarder's liability. In some countries, like the Nordic countries, the answer to the first issue is the adoption of industry or country-specific standards of agreed conditions of the contract. The second answer is partially determined by the first. If the freight forwarder is

---

[351]Jan Ramberg, *Unification of the Law of Freight Forwarding,* http://www.unidroit.org/english/publications/art-98-1.htm.

[352]Ibid. citing German HGB § 413 or French Civil Code Article 94.

[353]P.R. Murphy, J.M. Daley, & P.K. Hall, *Transportation Ethics: A Comparison of Shipper and Carrier Perspectives,* 63 Journal of Transportation Law, Logistics & Policy 370 (1996); Paul R. Murphy & James M. Daley, *Ethics and the International Freight Forwarder: User Perspectives,* 65 Journal of Transportation Law, Logistics & Policy 95 (1998).

held to be a carrier, then its ability to contractually limit its liability will be determined by the relevant carriage convention. The issue becomes what convention will be applied to determine the freight forwarder's liability, especially in the context of multimodal transport. A number of attempts have been made to provide a uniform answer to this question, the FIATA Model Rules for Freight Forwarding Services and the UNCTAD/ICC Rules for Multimodal Transport Documents. However, the existence of uniform rules for carrier liability is still only wishful thinking. Currently, liability is likely to be determined by the application of a unimodal carriage convention based on what segment of the transport that the goods sustained a loss.[354]

Risk Insurance

One avenue for minimizing the risks of international business transactions is to obtain commercial and political risk insurance. These policies are mostly utilized in conjunction with large investment or construction projects. One of the more popular providers is Overseas Private Investment Corporation (OPIC) which is a wholly owned corporation of the United States government. It insures against losses due to inconvertibility of currency, expropriation by foreign governments, and business interruption.[355] Other sources for insurance include the Multilateral Investment Guarantee Agency (MIGA) (investment in developing countries), Export-Import Bank of the United States (EXIMBANK) (supports U.S. exports) and its Eximbank Export Credit Insurance Program (ECIP) (provides political and commercial risk insurance), along with private carriers like Lloyds.

The determination of whether political or commercial risk insurance will be required should be made when negotiating the underlying contract. The cost and type of insurance to be procured should be stated in the contract but may be limited by government regulation. In China, for example, insurance in conjunction with a joint venture must be obtained through a Chinese insurance company. The decision to obtain commercial insurance

[354]One response to the mass of different carriage conventions and their applicability to multimodal transport, is the use of contract logistics agreements. Under such contracts, the shipper no longer deals directly with a carriage or service provider. Instead, the shipper contracts with a third party to provide the necessary logistical services.
[355]22 U.S.C. § 2194 (1988).

may be dictated by the commercial lender. Provisions in the underlying contract need to be reviewed for their potential impact on subsequent insurance claims. For example, *force majeure* and choice of law clauses should be reviewed to determine if there are events or laws that preclude the insured from making a claim under its insurance policy.

The application for insurance, like the application for a letter of credit, is contractual in nature. The applicant should read the form carefully and answer it as honestly and comprehensively as possible. The general rule is that the applicant must disclose any information that would "materially" influence the insurance company's decision.[356] In the related area of marine insurance, a court stated that "an applicant for a marine insurance policy is bound to reveal every fact within his knowledge that is material to the risk."[357] In that case, an owner of a company failed to disclose that he had previously filed claims for over two dozen losses at sea. The court found that there was sufficient evidence to find fraud in intentionally concealing material facts to allow for rescission of the insurance policy. Typical provisions in the application and insurance contract include accounting method, description of insured property, definition of "expropriatory act," waiting period, notice, warranties, recoveries, duty to minimize loss,[358] and definition and computation of loss.[359] The definition of what expropriatory acts can trigger an insurance claim should be closely scrutinized. Does the policy cover both partial and total losses or acts of expropriation? A "waiting period" is often required between the expropriatory act or loss and collecting on the insurance policy. In large projects the waiting period can be as long a year. The duties of the insured regarding the preservation of the investment and any claims pertaining to the loss should be clearly defined. A warranty provision requires the insured to take proactive steps in order to preserve its coverage. For example, the insured may have to certify its compliance with relevant host country laws and that the uninsured portion of the investment will remain uninsured. Also, rights to recoveries made after

[356]See, e.g., NEW YORK INS. LAW § 3105 (McKinney's).

[357]Cigna Property & Casualty Insurance Co. v. Polaris Pictures Co., 1998 WL 734391 (9th Cir. 1998).

[358]See, related "sue and labor doctrine." See, e.g., Slay Warehousing Company Inc. v. Reliance Insurance Co., 471 F.2d 1364 (8th Cir. 1973).

[359]S. Linn Williams, *Political and Other Risk Insurance: OPIC, MIGA, EXIMBANK, and Other Providers*, 5 Pace Int'l Law Rev. 59, 106-112 (1993).

payment on the claim should be defined. A typical provision states that any recovery is to be "shared between the insurer and the insured in the proportion to which they shared the loss."[360]

Transit Insurance

Due to the advent of containerization, an insurance policy or policies will need to cover multiple modes of transportation. Insurance claims often involve multiple insurance providers and polices. This is dictated by the highly specialized nature of the transit insurance business. The shipping of goods across national boundaries, from one inland destination to a port of shipment and then to a port of destination and on to the inland point of destination, involves different types of insurance (marine, war risk, comprehensive general liability, protection and indemnity, excess, umbrella insurance). This is further complicated by the fact that insurance providers will often dispute the risk through reinsurance.[361] In order to deal with these different issues of coverage, the transit insurance industry has produced a host of standard forms and clauses. The existence of such standardization, however, should not cloud the fact that the transit insurance policy is often a highly specialized, custom contract. "Even with the extensive use of form policies there are inevitable variations negotiated by the parties. There is simply no substitute for a thorough review of the particular insurance contract in the manner of its negotiation and placement."[362]

There are numerous types of policies that shippers procure to protect themselves from an assortment of exposures including damage to goods, damage to the ship, damage to other's property, and liability for injury and death. The most common property coverage is provided by hull insurance. Within the standard hull policy contains a "running down clause" that pro-

[360]Ibid. at 112.

[361]Marine insurance is a contractual relationship between an underwriter and the insured (shipper), while reinsurance is a contract between different underwriters. As a general rule the insurer may not reinsure on broader terms than are found in the underlying policy.

[362]Raymond P. Hayden & Sanford E, Balick, *Marine Insurance: Varieties, Combinations, and Coverages*, 66 Tulane Law Rev. 311, 313 (1991). See generally, ARTHUR E. BRUNCK, ET AL., OCEAN MARINE INSURANCE (1988).

vides coverage for liability due to collision. Liability coverage is provided through protection and indemnity insurance. These are offered through associations of shipping companies, popularly known as P & I clubs. Indemnity policies only become operative upon payment by the insured. They can provide protection against claims stemming from personal injury, cargo loss, collision, pollution, towage, and general *average* loss. Of importance to the shipper, P & I insurance can provide "through-transport" coverage, thus providing coverage to container transport during the inland phase of shipment.[363] Another, shipper policy relevant to the shipper of goods is the comprehensive general liability coverage (CGL). The Insurance Services Office, Inc. (ISO) drafts this policy.[364] Two points will be made regarding this type of policy. First, its most salient feature is its comprehensiveness. For this reason, some marine insurance policies include a CGL clause. Second, it provides a rather broad duty to defend. Thus, ship owners are provided with the luxury of having legal services paid for by the insurance company even on claims where insurance coverage is suspect.

Another type of insurance commonly obtained by shippers is excess or umbrella insurance. Insurance is often multi-layered due to the fact that the underlying insurance provider may be unwilling to provide the amount of coverage requested by the insured. The insured may further limit its exposure by obtaining excess coverage for claims that exceed the amount of the underlying policies. The excess insurance policy incorporates one of a number of popular clauses that control when that coverage becomes operational. These clauses relate the excess coverage to the coverage provided by underlying policies. For example, an escape clause precludes any recovery if the type of claim is covered under an existing policy even if that claim exceeds the amount of coverage provided by the underlying policy. An excess clause covers all claims outside the coverage of the underlying policy. The pro rata clause proportions the amount paid under the policy based upon the limits provided by all relevant policies.[365]

Direct coverage to the shipper is provided by the standard marine or cargo insurance policy. This is the policy obtained by the seller on behalf of the buyer-importer under a CIF contract. Three general limitations are gen-

---

[363]Ibid. at 327.

[364]Ibid. at 339.

[365]Ibid. at 357.

erally found in such polices. First, the policy is *free of particular average* (F.P.A.), which means the shipper is only protected against total loss. The only remedy for partial losses will be a claim against the carrier. In order to cover such losses, one will want to negotiate for *with average* (W.A) protection. Second, the standard policy will not cover risks associated with war, revolution, riot, or strikes. These areas of loss are exempted by the F.C. & S. Clause (capture and seizure) and the S.R. & C.C. clause (strikes and riots). Once again, coverage may be requested through an endorsement on the underlying policy or through a separate war risk policy. This decision is likely to be based upon the particular places of shipment and destination, along with the expected route of transport and the types of goods being transported. Third, the standard policy is a *perils policy* which only protects against stated perils. If this is the provided policy, the shipper should make sure that it includes an *Inchmaree clause.* The Inchmaree clause adds losses due to the negligence of the ship's personnel, errors in navigation, or latent defect as covered perils. The more shipper-friendly policy is the all-risk policy, which protects against all losses except for those specifically exempted. The pro-shipper aspect of an all-risk policy is that the shipper need not prove the exact cause of the loss. Given the nature of the transport of goods, whether one obtains a perils or an all-risk policy, the policy should incorporate a *marine extension* or *warehouse to warehouse* clause. This clause extends the standard marine coverage to the period before the loading of the goods and the period between offloading and delivery to the consignee. It is important to make sure that the clause does not limit the extended coverage through a time limit provision. The best way to ensure this is to provide that the policy remains in operation until the goods are delivered to the consignee.[366] Finally, the sophisticated international exporter or importer should familiarize herself with the standard forms and clauses published by the Institute of London Underwriters (I.L.U.), the American Institute of Marine Underwriters (A.I.M.U.), and Lloyd's of London. An example of such publications is the manual on Cargo Clauses published by the A.I.M.U. Familiarization with the standard forms is important because underwriters will often create their own policies by using the clauses found in the standard forms. "Frequently, the standard clauses will be removed from the standard form and used as building blocks in custom policies. In addi-

[366]Ibid. at 323.

tion the I.L.U. and A.I.M.U. have drafted standard terms for particular trades."[367]

Liberalization of Trade in Services

The General Agreement on Trade in Services (GATS) established a framework for the removal of obstacles to the international trade in services. The pillars of the General Agreement on Tariffs and Trade (GATT) are reiterated with requirements for most-favored nation treatment and transparency in technical standards and certifications. In the area of professional services, "each Member shall provide for adequate procedures to verify the competence of professionals of any other Member." A number of follow-up agreements and protocols offer real hope of easier market entry in certain service sectors. On February 15, 1997, a WTO working group successfully passed the Agreement on Basic Telecommunications Services or GBT.[368] The GBT will provide market entry and national treatment in local and long-distance telephone, mobile radio (cellular), international telecommunications, and satellite services. At the end of 1997, the WTO Financial Services Agreement was completed. It requires the elimination of barriers to market access and investment in the areas of banking, insurance, securities, and financial data services.

At the bilateral level, the United States and the European Union reached a number of Mutual Recognition Agreements (MRA). These agreements are aimed at reducing trade barriers in a number of industries. "The MRA package covers trade in telecommunications equipment, electronic products, medical devices, pharmaceuticals, and recreational craft."[369] This is to be achieved through the mutual recognition of each other's product testing and certification procedures. At the non-governmental level, the Trans-Atlantic Business Dialogue (TABD) "endorsed bilateral and multilateral cooperation in the area of electronic commerce and identified five priority issues: protection of personal data and privacy; digital signatures and

[367]Ibid. at 325.

[368]Fourth Protocol to the Agreement on Trade in Services.

[369]Charles O. Verrill, Jr., Peter S. Jordan, & Timothy C. Brightbill, *International Trade,* 32 Int'l Lawyer 319, 326 (1998).

harmonized legal framework; encryption; tax, tariff, and customs; and intellectual property, protection, and associated liabilities."[370]

Internationalization of Accounting and Taxation

The GATT's expansion to include the liberalization of trade in services has lead to the creation of two bodies: the Council for Trade in Services and the Working Party on Professional Services (WPPS). The later group has focused upon internationalization in accounting services. The internationalization of business has placed pressure upon the accounting profession to provide necessary support services. Accounting services, as with most professional services, can be internationalized on a number of fronts. First, domestic regulations can be modified to take into account the special issues of cross-border transactions. Second, international standards can be enumerated for professional services. Third, countries can mutually recognize each other's professional qualifications and national standards.[371] The adoption of harmonized international standards provides the greatest possibility for increased trade in international accounting services. The areas where international accounting services are needed include: transfer pricing, currency translation,[372] and joint venture accounting. International Accounting Standards (IAS) have been drafted by the International Accounting Stan-

[370]Ibid.

[371]The problem of recognition is especially acute in former non-market countries. It was not until 1996 that Russian accountants first received national qualifications for professional accountants. On the substantive side, Russia has adopted international accounting practices, but some idiosyncrasies remain. For example, the fundamental accounting assumption that financial statements are reviewed so that they are a "true and fair view of financial position, performance, and changes in the financial position of a company" is replaced with a lower threshold that the financial statements are "satisfactory trustworthy" or *dostovernost.* Trustworthiness is defined as compliance with law and regulations. PRICE WATERHOUSE, DOING BUSINESS IN RUSSIA 104 (1997).

[372]Currency translation is the process of expressing amounts denominated in one currency in terms of another currency by use of an exchange rate. Translation adjustments result from the process of translating financial statements from the entity's functional currency (primary currency or currency in which its books are maintained) into the reporting currency. See, Statement of Financial Accounting Standards, No. 52 (1981). The translation risk of currency devaluation needs to be addressed on both the management and accounting sides. Translation exposure may result in lower reported earnings. See,

dards Committee (IASC). Copies can be obtained from the International Accounting Standards Committee, 166 Fleet Street, London, England, EC4A2DY or by e-mail: publications@iasc.org.uk.[373]

In the area of transfer pricing, multinational corporations need to develop a transfer pricing policy that will be generally accepted in the countries that they do business. This is needed in order to avoid complicated tax disputes and the potential for double taxation. Tax planning should be done on a country by country basis. For example, the social security rates in European Union countries range from twenty to as high as forty percent. Some guidance can be obtained through the use of recently developed guidelines for transfer pricing and documentary requirements produced by the Organization on Economic Coordination and Development (OECD). One approach for taxing multinational corporations or cross-border business transactions is through *unitary taxation.* It is an approach in which corporate profits are apportioned to the different taxing authorities using a formula based on sales, payroll and property within each jurisdiction. Transfer pricing issues become more confusing in the growing area of international Internet or electronic commerce. The United States' policy on Internet commerce, as stated in a 1997 release titled "A Framework for Electronic Commerce," adopts the following principles regarding the issue of taxation of Internet commerce:

- No tax system should discriminate among types of commerce.
- The system should be transparent.
- The system should accommodate tax systems of other countries.

Currently, the two most influential bodies in the movement to harmonize accounting standards and financial statements are the International Accounting Standards Committee (IASC) and the International Organization of Securities Commissions (IOSCO). The diversity of accounting practices throughout the world is seen as an encumbrance to the development of truly global capital markets. For example, the ability to provide comparable financial statements to be used in cross-border security offerings would significantly decrease the number and types of required filings. Such

---

e.g., C. O. Houston, *Translation Exposure Hedging Post SFAS No. 52,* 2 Journal of Int'l Management & Accounting 145 (1990).

[373]See also, International Federation of Accountants (IFAC): http://ifac.org

statements would need to be based upon internationally recognized accounting standards. Companies currently wishing to raise capital in foreign markets have to contend with costly and complicated national disclosure and reporting requirements. The European Commission has sought to harmonize such reporting requirements at the regional level. At the international level, IASC has developed a number of International Accounting Standards (IAS). IOSOC has deferred to IASC by accepting IAS and has focused its attention on the development of a common international prospectus that could be used for listing and filing in all exchanges. These efforts will continue and are essential to further enhance the free flow of capital and related services.

Advertising Law

National laws dealing with deceptive advertising vary in scope and enforcement. Due to cultural differences, an advertising campaign that is legal in one country may be illegal in another. Almost all developed countries possess laws that make illegal the use of misleading advertising.[374] Advertising laws are policed by administrative agencies, through private litigation, and via industry self-regulation. These three means of enforcement vary dramatically throughout the world. All three are utilized in the United States. The Federal Trade Commission (FTC) regulates virtually all forms of advertising in the United States. They are empowered to prevent "unfair and deceptive practices."[375] Section 43(a) of the Lanham Act[376] created a private cause of action for anyone injured by false advertising.[377] There are also many examples of industry and media self-regulation. One example is the National Advertising Division of the Council of Better Business Bureaus. In contrast, there is no national self-regulation in Saudi Arabia. Instead, a

---

[374]See, e.g., Barbara S. Baudot, *International Advertising Handbook* (1989); Peter L. Tracey, *International Advertising: Regulatory Pitfalls for the Unwary Marketer,* 7 Dickinson Journal of Int'l Law 229 (1989); Norbert Reich & Hans W. Micklitz, *Consumer Legislation in the EC Countries: A Comparative Analysis,* (1980).

[375]15 U.S.C. § 45(a)(1)(1982).

[376]15 U.S.C. 1125(a) (1988).

[377]See generally, Ross D. Petty, *Supplanting Government Regulation with Competitor Lawsuits: The Case of Controlling False Advertising,* 25 Indiana Law Rev. 351 (1991).

number of agencies, including the Organization for the Prevention of Sins and Order of Good Deeds, seek the enforcement of Islamic laws.[378] In Italy, "industry self regulation deals with most of the country's advertising disputes."[379] Many other civil law countries, including Germany, "rely on advertising law that authorizes private litigation to control misleading advertising."[380] The Scandinavian countries make use of the consumer ombudsman to enact advertising guidelines and to resolve disputes.[381] Because of the vast differences in advertising law enforcement, it is important for the international entrepreneur to seek local counsel before embarking on a marketing campaign. The local counsel can provide information on the substantive law of advertising. However, most exporters will use private advertisement agencies to handle their marketing campaigns. At a minimum, the prospective agency should be a member of that country's professional advertisement association. For example, in Chile most advertising agencies are members of the Asociacion Chilena de Agencias de Publicidad (Chilean Association of Advertising Agencies, ACHAP).

Comparative Advertising

Internationally, the development of supranational rules has been sporadic. The best example of a multi-national effort is the Marketing Supervision Network. The United States and about twenty other countries have agreed to cooperate in resolving advertising disputes that cross national boundaries.[382] At the regional level, the European Union has enacted two directives aimed at harmonizing European law on misleading and compar-

---

[378]Mushtaq Luqmani, *Advertising in Saudi Arabia: Content and Regulation,* 6 Int'l Marketing Rev. 59 (1989).

[379]Ross D. Petty, *Advertising Law and Social Issues: The Global Perspective,* 17 Suffolk Transnational Law Rev. 309, 319 (1994).

[380]Ibid. at 318. See also, Warren S. Grimes, *Control of Advertising in the United States and Germany: Volkswagen has a Better Idea,* 84 Harvard Law. Rev. 1769 (1971).

[381]J.J. Boddewyn, *The Swedish Consumer Ombudsman System of Advertising Self-Regulation,* 19 Journal of Consumer Affairs 140 (1985).

[382]Allyson L. Stewart, *International Marketing Police Resolve Trading Disputes,* Marketing News 15 (June 7, 1993).

ative advertising.[383] Prior to the enactment of the 1997 Directive 97/55/EC on comparative advertising, such advertising was banned in Italy, Belgium, and Luxembourg, and highly restricted in such countries as Germany and France. In contrast, in the United States more than twenty-five percent of all advertising is comparative.[384] The 1997 Directive legalizes the use of comparative advertising which is defined as "any advertising which explicitly or by implication identifies a competitor or goods or services offered by a competitor." However, such advertising is strictly constrained. Comparative advertising is permitted only if:

(1) it does not mislead,
(2) it compares goods or services meeting the same needs or serving the same purpose,
(3) it objectively compares one or more material, relevant, verifiable and representative features of the goods and services,
(4) it does not create confusion in the market place between the advertiser and a competitor or with the competitor's trademarks or trade names,
(5) it does not discredit or denigrate the trademarks, trade names, goods, or services of a competitor,
(6) for products with designation of origin, it relates in each case to products with the same designation, and
(7) it does not present goods or services as imitations or replicas of trademarked goods or services.

The EU Directive also requires that the advertiser demonstrate promptly the accuracy of its comparative claim. In contrast, the U.S. Federal Trade Commission only requires the proof of a "reasonable basis."[385]

---

[383]DIRECTIVE 84/450/EEC (1984) ("Misleading Advertising Directive") and DIRECTIVE 97/55/EC (1997) ("Comparative Advertising Directive").

[384]Paul Spink & Ross Petty, *Comparative Advertising in the European Union,* 47 Int'l & Comparative Law Quarterly 855 (1998). See also, Ross D. Petty, *Advertising Law in the United States and European Union,* 16 Public Policy & Marketing 2 (1997); Keith B. Murray & Edward T. Popper, *Competing Under Regulatory Uncertainty: A U.S. Perspective on Advertising in the Emerging European Market,* 12 Journal of Macromarketing 38 (1992).

[385]Spink & Petty at 859.

The use of subjective features such as taste or feel is permitted in the United States. Under the EU Directive's requirement of objective proof, such comparative advertising is prohibited. "Comparison on the basis of subjective factors, and opinion-based puffery are therefore prohibited under the Directive. Furthermore, it seems that the adopted formula bans the use of objectively administered consumer preference tests."[386] Thus, the American exporter should not assume that its comparative advertisements are automatically legal under the new Directive. This is especially true in countries that traditionally prohibited such advertisements. The Directive's form and method of implementation is left to the member countries.

Professional Standards of International Advertising

The International Chamber of Commerce has sponsored a number of ethical codes relating to international advertising and marketing. The following is a list of ICC Codes: International Code of Advertising Practice, International Code of Sales Promotion, International Code of Practice on Direct Marketing, Code on Environmental Advertising, Code on Sponsorship, and the ICC/ESOMAR International Code of Marketing and Social Research Practice. The ICC International Code of Advertising Practice was first issued in 1937 and was recently revised in 1997. The main principles contained in the ICC code on advertising summarized in Exhibit 8.2. It applies to advertising in any medium for the sale of goods *or* services. The importance of the concept of *any* medium is that an advertisement may be appropriate for use in one medium, such as the Internet, and be inappropriate for use in another, such as broadcast or outdoor advertising. The introduction to the Code describes it as a voluntary, self-regulating ethical code, but noted its use in a legal proceeding: "The Code is designed primarily as an instrument of self-discipline but it is also intended for the use of the courts as a reference document within the framework of applicable law."[387] The underlying principle of the Code is that "all advertising should be legal, decent, and truthful." Articles 3 through 17 provide some details regarding the meaning of "decent and truthful."

---

[386]Ibid. at 866.

[387]ICC International Code of Advertising Practice, Introduction (1997 edition).

Exhibit 8.2: ICC International Code of Advertising Practice

Art. 2: Decency	Should not offend prevailing standards of decency.
Art. 3: Honesty	Should not exploit consumers' lack of experience or knowledge.
Art. 4: Social Responsibility	Should not condone any form of discrimination, play on fear or play on superstition
Art. 5: Truthful Presentation	Should not mislead with regards to characteristics, value, terms of guarantee, intellectual property rights, or official recognition or approval and should not misuse research results.
Art. 6: Comparisons	Comparison to other products should be based on facts which can be substantiated and should not be unfairly selected.
Art. 7: Denigration	Should not denigrate any firm, organization, profession or product.
Art. 8: Testimonials	No use of personal testimonials or endorsements unless genuine, verifiable, relevant, and based upon personal experience or knowledge. Testimonials that have become obsolete should not be used.
Art. 11: Imitation	Should not imitate other advertisements or unduly imitate others advertising campaigns in other countries.
Art. 12: Identification	Should not be made to appear as an editorial or news item. Should be presented so that it is readily recognized as an advertisement.
Art. 14: Children Advertisements	Applies to children as defined as minors under applicable national laws. Should not exploit their inexperience or give unreal perception of the true value of the product. For example, the use of the word "only" should be avoided. Should not directly appeal to children to persuade their parents to buy the advertised products.
Art. 15: Guarantees	Should not contain any reference to a guarantee which does not provide the consumer with additional rights to those provided by law.
Art. 10: Exploitation of Goodwill	Should not infringe upon the intellectual property or goodwill.

CHAPTER 9

Law of Intellectual Property Transfer

The law as applied to international intellectual property transfer is multi-layered and complex. Three avenues of applicable law need to be studied: (1) whether home country law (law of licensor) applies extraterritorially, (2) whether an international convention can be used in protecting the property being transferred, and (3) whether the nuances of the foreign host country's laws provide sufficient protection. A key concern for many licensors is the creation of a *gray market* problem in which goods produced under a foreign license agreement are imported into the sales territory of the licensor or other licensees. The intellectual property transfer agreement must deal with the gray market issue, along with other areas of intellectual property rights protection. The restrictions placed in the agreement or license are especially important when the licensee's place of business is in a country with a propensity for not protecting foreign intellectual property rights. In such countries, the restrictions placed in the transfer agreement may be the only means by which a licensor can protect his intellectual property rights. Thus, the importance of *due diligence* is crucial before the contemplation of entering a transfer agreement. Due Diligence should provide answers to the following questions: (1) What formalities are needed to register or protect the rights in the host country?, (2) Will the transfer agreement need to be registered and approved by foreign government authorities?, (3) What types of clauses are likely to be disapproved or chance violating foreign competition laws?, and (4) Are there other mandatory legal rules that are specific to that particular country?

In the area of the extraterritorial application of United States law, the discussion begins with a brief review of the *Scotch Whiskey Assoc.* and

Bulova Watches cases. These cases essentially held that the Lanham Act applies extraterritorially against United States companies in order to prevent trademark infringement. The material on international conventions provides an in-depth review of the provisions of the Agreement on Trade Related Aspects of Intellectual Property (TRIP). This extended coverage is warranted because it was only recently enacted and it has the potential to provide near universal protection for intellectual property rights. The material on national laws, such as the laws of Russia and China, along with European Union Regulations, will be used to highlight major areas of concern. The impact of national law is further expanded upon in the material on foreign transfer restrictions. The foreign transfer restrictions found in the law of the People's Republic of China and European Union Regulations are examined to illustrate the legal restrictions placed upon negotiators and drafters of licensing agreements. The nuances of national laws are also detailed in the last section on "Mandatory Legal Rules." That section addresses the issue of the standing of licensees to sue third-party infringers under United States law. The remaining portions of the chapter examines the types of clauses that are used to overcome the shortcomings found in foreign intellectual property law regimes.

Extraterritorial Application of United States Law

The Lanham Act, 15 U.S.C.A. §§ 1125 (a) and 1127, allows for a claim for the false designations of origin.[388] The Court of Appeals in *Scotch Whiskey Assoc. v. Barton Distilling*[389] held that the Lanham Act could be applied extraterritorially where an American producer supplies false labels to

[388] 5 U.S.C. § 1125(a) states:

> Any person who shall affix, apply, or annex or use in connection with any goods or services, or any container for goods, a false designation of origin, or any false description or representation, including words or other symbols tending falsely to describe or represent the same, and shall cause such goods or services to enter into commerce, and any person who shall with knowledge of the falsity of such designation or origin or description or representation cause or procure the same to be transported or used in commerce or deliver the same to any carrier to be transported or used, shall be liable to a civil action by any person or business in the locality falsely indicated as that of origin or . . .

[389] 489 F.2d 809 (7th Cir. 1972).

a foreign licensee. In that case, the American company supplied labels designating the product as "Scotch Whiskey" to a Panamanian licensee. There was no evidence that the adulterated whiskey filtered into the United States. Nonetheless, the court held that the Lanham Act applied to the American defendant stating that "no principal of international law bars the United States from governing the conduct of its own citizens." The court relied on the Supreme Court decision in *Steele v. Bulova Watches.*[390] In that case, an American citizen registered the Bulova name in Mexico. He then manufactured watches, using the Bulova name, for sale in Mexico. However, there was evidence that some of the watches had been imported into the United States. The Supreme Court broadly defined "commerce" in the Lanham Act to include activities of United States citizens outside of the country. The court in *Scotch Whiskey* held that "the purpose underlying the Lanham Act, to make actionable the deceptive use of false designations of origin, should not be evaded by the simple device of selecting a foreign license."

International Conventions

The most recent development in international intellectual property rights protection is the Agreement on Trade Related Aspects of Intellectual Property (TRIPS). This framework agreement is to be enforced under the auspices of the World Trade Organization (WTO). The constitutionality of TRIPS was the issue in *U.S. v. Moghadam.*[391] The U.S. circuit court held that the statute enacting TRIPS into the law of the United States was constitutional under the Commerce Clause. The statute was held to be based upon a legally ratified treaty "called for by the World Trade Organization whose purpose was to ensure uniform recognition and treatment of intellectual property in international commerce." The American defendant was found guilty of bootlegging compact discs of illegal recordings of a live performance.

With the full force of GATT implementation, TRIPS promises to be the best hope for the recognition of minimum standards for national intellectual property law regimes. The need for more specific standards and understandings has already resulted in the adoption of a number of protocols

[390] 344 U.S. 280 (1952).

[391] 175 F.3d 1269 (11th Cir. 1999).

to TRIPS in the areas of telecommunications services (Agreement on Basic Telecommunications Services), information technology (Information Technology Agreement), and financial services (WTO Financial Services Agreement). The "General Provisions" of TRIPS restates the foundational principles of the GATT system including national treatment and most-favored nation treatment, along with the current role of the World Intellectual Property Organization (WIPO). Article Three also recognizes the continuing roles of existing international conventions, namely the Paris Convention, Berne Convention, Rome Convention, and the Treaty on Intellectual Property in Respect of Integrated Circuits. Article Eight "Principles" recognizes countries' rights to limit the grant of intellectual property rights when they violate antitrust laws, that is, when there are unreasonable restraints of trade.

AGREEMEENT ON TRADE-RELATED ASPECTS OF INTELLECTUAL PROPERTY RIGHTS, INCLUDING TRADE IN COUNTERFEIT GOODS

Desiring to establish a mutually supportive relationship between the MTO and the World Intellectual Property Organization (WIPO) as well as other relevant international organizations.

PART I: GENERAL PROVISIONS AND BASIC PRINCIPLES

Article 3

National Treatment

1. Each Member shall accord to the nationals of other Members treatment no less favorable than that it accords to its own nationals with regard to the protection of intellectual property, subject to the exceptions already provided respectively in the Paris Convention (1967), the Berne Convention (1971), the Rome Convention and the Treaty on Intellectual Property in Respect of Integrated Circuits.

[In this Agreement the] "Paris Convention" refers to the Paris Convention for the Protection of Industrial Property; "Paris Convention (1967)" refers to the Stockholm Act of this Convention of 14 July 1967. "Berne Convention" refers to the Berne Convention for the Protection of Literary and Artistic Works: "Berne Convention (1971)" refers to the Paris Act of this Convention of 24 July 1971. "Rome Convention" refers to the International Convention for the Protection of Performers, Producers of Phonograms and Broadcasting Organizations adopted at Rome on 26 October 1961. "Treaty on Intellectual Property in Respect of Integrated Circuits" (IPIC Treaty) refers to the Treaty on Intellectual Property in Respect of Integrated Circuits adopted at Washington on 26 May 1989.

Article 4
Most-Favoured-Nation Treatment

With regard to the protection of intellectual property, any advantage, favour, privilege or immunity granted by a Member to the nationals of any other country shall be accorded immediately and unconditionally to the nationals of all other Members.

Article 8
Principles

2. Appropriate measures, provided that they are consistent with the provisions of this Agreement, may be needed to prevent the abuse of intellectual property rights by right holders or the resort to practices which unreasonably restrain trade or adversely affect the international transfer of technology.

TRIPS established the Council for Trade-Related Aspects of Intellectual Property. The Council, along with the WIPO, should be used as a resource for those interested in intellectual property protection. Article 69, at least implicitly, recognizes the problem of illegal gray market imports. It requires each country to establish "contract points" in their governments in order to coordinate with other countries in preventing the importation of goods produced in violation of rights recognized under TRIPS. It specifically instructs customs authorities to cooperate in preventing trade in counterfeit trademark goods and pirated copyright goods.

Article 68
Council for Trade-Related Aspects of Intellectual Property Rights

The Council for Trade-Related Aspects of Intellectual Property Rights shall monitor the operation of this Agreement and, in particular, Members' compliance with their obligations hereunder, and shall afford Members the opportunity of consulting on matters relating to the trade-related aspects of intellectual property rights. It shall carry out such other responsibilities as assigned to it by the Members, and it shall, in particular, provide any assistance requested by them in the context of dispute settlement procedures. In carrying out its functions, the Council may consult with and seek information from any source it deems appropriate. In consultation with the World Intellectual Property Organization, the Council shall seek to establish, within one year of its first meeting, appropriate arrangements for cooperation with bodies of that Organization.

Article 69
International Cooperation

Members agree to cooperate with each other with a view to eliminating international trade in goods infringing intellectual property rights. For this purpose, they shall establish and notify contact points in their national administrations and be ready to exchange information on trade in infringing goods. They shall, in particular, promote the exchange of information and cooperation between customs authorities with regard to trade in counterfeit trademark goods and pirated copyright goods.

Transitional provisions were incorporated into TRIPS in recognition of the demands it places on developing countries and former communist countries. These countries are given five years to implement the requirements of TRIPS. The least developed countries are given ten years before needing to fully implement TRIPS. It is imperative for the international licensor of intellectual property to check the status of a given country's implementation of TRIPS.

Article 65
Transitional Arrangements

1. Subject to the provisions of paragraphs 2, 3 and 4 below, no Member shall be obliged to apply the provisions of this Agreement before the expiry of a general period of one year following the date of entry into force of the Agreement Establishing the MTO.
2. Any developing country Member is entitled to delay for a further period of four years the date of application, as defined in paragraph 1. above.
3. Any other Member which is in the process of transformation from a centrally-planned into a market, free-enterprise economy and which is undertaking structural reform of its intellectual property system and facing special

problems in the preparation and implementation of intellectual property laws, may also benefit from a period of delay as foreseen in paragraph 2 above.

Article 66
Least-Developed Country Members

1. In view of their special needs and requirements, their economic, financial and administrative constraints, and their need for flexibility to create a viable technological base, least-developed country Members shall not be required to apply the provisions of this Agreement, other than Articles 3, 4 and 5, for a period of 10 years from the date of application as defined under paragraph 1. of Article 65 above. The Council shall, upon duly motivated request by a least-developed country Member, accord extensions of this period.

Part II provides the core protections that national laws should recognize and enforce. The intellectual property rights that are recognized are copyrights (§ 1), trademarks (§ 2), industrial designs (§ 4), patents (§5), integrated circuits (§ 6), and confidential information or trade circuits (§ 7). Article 9 expressly delegates the recognition of moral rights under copyright law to the Berne Convention. It does recognize computer programs, both object and source codes, and data bases as literary works protected under copyright law (Articles 10 & 11). The minimum period of protection shall be fifty years from the end of the author's life, otherwise fifty years from the year of publication or the year of its making (Article 12).

PART II: STANDARDS CONCERNING THE AVAILABILITY, SCOPE AND USE OF INTELLECTUAL PROPERTY RIGHTS

SECTION 1: COPYRIGHT AND RELATED RIGHTS

Article 9
Relation to Berne Convention

1. Members shall comply with Articles 1-21 and the Appendix of the Berne Convention (1971). However, Members shall not have rights or obligations under this Agreement in respect of the rights conferred under Article 6bis of that Convention or of the rights derived therefrom.
2. Copyright protection shall extend to expressions and not to ideas, procedures, methods of operation or mathematical concepts as such.

Article 10
Computer Programs and Compilations of Data

1. Computer programs, whether in source or object code, shall be protected as literary works under the Berne Convention (1971).
2. Compilations of data or other material, whether in machine readable or other form which by reason of the selection or arrangement of their contents constitute intellectual creations shall be protected as such. Such protection, which shall not extend to the data or material itself, shall be without prejudice to any copyright subsisting in the data or material itself.

Article 11
Rental Rights

In respect of at least computer programs and cinematographic works, a Member shall provide authors and their successors in title the right to authorize or to prohibit the commercial rental to the public of originals or copies of their copyright works.

Article 12
Term of Protection

Whenever the term of protection of a work, other than a photographic work or a work of applied art, is calculated on a basis other than the life of a natural person, such term shall be no less than fifty years from the end of the calendar year of authorized publication, or, failing such authorized publication within fifty years from the making of the work, fifty years from the end of the calendar year of making.

Article 14
Protection of Performers, Producers of Phonograms

1. In respect of a fixation of their performance on a phonogram, performers shall have the possibility of preventing the following acts when undertaken without their authorization: the fixation of their unfixed performance and the reproduction of such fixation. Performers shall also have the possibility of preventing the following acts when undertaken without their authorization: the broadcasting by wireless means and the communication to the public of their live performance.

Article 9, Paragraph 1. Recognizes the superiority of Article 6bis of the Paris Convention. Article *6bis* of the Paris Convention gives the owner of a *well known* trademark the right to block or cancel an unauthorized registration of its marks in a foreign country. This illustrates the importance in reviewing established intellectual property conventions and comparing them to TRIPS. It is also important to realize that conflict of law rules still play an important role in the application of national intellectual property laws. A United States Circuit Court held that under international conventions, Russian copyright protects all works created in Russia.[392] The issue then becomes whether the owner could sue the infringer in an American court. In the case, a Russian language newspaper in New York had copied articles that were originally published in Russia by a Russian newspaper. The court held that under the Berne Convention and the Universal Copyright Convention, the ownership of the materials is to be determined under the law of the country of origin. However, since the articles were copied in the United States, the Russian owner has standing to sue in an American court. The court noted that under Russian copyright law, the Russian owner had rights only to the arrangement and display of the articles, but not to the actual text.

Section Two provides the parameters for trademark protection. Article 15 provides a broad definition of trademark akin to the more recent judicial recognition in the United States. Thus, under Article 15 combinations of colors can be registered as trademarks. Article 17 recognizes the copyright fair use concept and applies it as an exception to trademark protection. The period of protection for trademarks, and any renewals, is set at a minimum of seven years (Article 18). TRIPS recognizes the principle that trademark rights may be lost through abandonment or nonuse, but rejects the notion of compulsory licensing (Article 21) found in some national laws. Article 19 allows a country to cancel a trademark registration if it is unused for a period of three years. It prohibits such cancellation if the reason for nonuse was due to events outside the control of the registrant, such as import restrictions or government regulation. The importance of geographical indications or country of origin to the sale of certain products is recognized in Article 22. It recognizes the rights of others to prevent the false use of geographical indications "where a given quality, reputation or

---

[392]Itar-Tass Russian News Agency v. Russian Kurier, Inc., 153 F.3d 82 (2d Cir. 1998).

other characteristic of the good is essentially attributable of its geographical origin."

SECTION 2: TRADEMARKS

Article 15
Protectable Subject Matter

1. Any sign, or any combination of signs, capable of distinguishing the goods or services of one undertaking from those of other undertakings, shall be capable of constituting a trademark. Such signs, in particular words including personal names, letters, numerals, figurative elements and combinations of colours as well as any combination of such signs, shall be eligible for registration as trademarks. Where signs are not inherently capable of distinguishing the relevant goods or services, Members may make registrability depend on distinctiveness acquired through use. Members may require as a condition of registration, that signs be visually perceptible.
3. Members may make registrability depend on use. However, actual use of a trademark shall not be a condition for filing an application for registration. An application shall not be refused solely on the ground that intended use has not taken place before the expiry of a period of three years from the date of application.

Article 16
Rights Conferred

1. The owner of a registered trademark shall have the exclusive right to prevent all third parties not having his consent from using in the course of trade identical or similar signs for goods or services which are identical or similar to those in respect of which the trademark is registered where such use would result in a likelihood of confusion.

Article 17
Exceptions

Members may provide limited exceptions to the rights conferred by a trademark, such as fair use of descriptive terms, provided that such exceptions take account of the legitimate interests of the owner of the trademark and of third parties.

Article 18
Term of Protection

Initial registration, and each renewal of registration, of a trademark shall be for a term of no less than seven years. The registration of a trademark shall be renewable indefinitely.

Article 19
Requirement of Use

1. If use is required to maintain a registration, the registration may be cancelled only after an uninterrupted period of at least three years of non-use, unless valid reasons based on the existence of obstacles to such use are shown by the trademark owner . . . such as import restrictions on or other government requirements for goods or services protected by the trademark.

Article 21
Licensing and Assignment

Members may determine conditions on the licensing and assignment of trademarks, it being understood that the compulsory licensing of trademarks shall not be permitted and that the owner of a registered trademark shall have the right to assign his trademark with or without the transfer of the business to which the trademark belongs.

Article 22
Protection of Geographical Indications

1. Geographical indications are, for the purposes of this Agreement, indications which identify a good as originating in the territory of a Member, or a region or locality in that territory, where a given quality, reputation or other characteristic of the good is essentially attributable to its geographical origin.

In respect of geographical indications, Members shall provide the legal means for interested parties to prevent:

(a) the use of any means in the designation or presentation of a good that indicates or suggests that the good in question originates in a geographical area other than the true place of origin in a manner which misleads the public as to the geographical origin of the good;

An entire section of TRIPS is devoted to the protection of "industrial designs." Section Four recognizes "independently created industrial designs" as a separate category of protection. It recognizes a protection period of ten years for qualifying designs.

SECTION 4: INDUSTRIAL DESIGNS

Article 25
Requirements for Protection

1. Members shall provide for the protection of independently created industrial designs that are new or original. Members may provide that designs are not new or original if they do not significantly differ from known designs or combinations of known design features. Members may provide that such protection shall not extend to designs dictated essentially by technical or functional considerations.
3.The duration of protection available shall amount to at least ten years.

Article 27 defines *patentable* as something that is "new, involves an inventive step and is capable of industrial application." For the purposes of this Article, the terms "inventive step" and "capable of industrial application" may be deemed by a Member to be synonymous with the terms "non-obvious" and "useful," respectively. The immediate impact of the TRIPS patent protections for the United States was the extension of the period of protection from seventeen to twenty years.

SECTION 5: PATENTS

Article 27
Patentable Subject Matter

1. Patents shall be available for any inventions, whether products or processes, in all fields of technology, provided that they are new, involve an inventive step and are capable of industrial application.

Article 28
Rights Conferred

1. A patent shall confer on its owner the following exclusive rights:

(a) where the subject matter of a patent is a product, to prevent third parties not having his consent from the acts of: making, using, offering for sale, selling, or importing for these purposes that product;

(b) where the subject matter of a patent is a process, to prevent third parties not having his consent from the act of using the process, and from the acts of: using, offering for sale, selling, or importing . . .

2. Patent owners shall also have the right to assign, or transfer by succession, the patent and conclude licensing contracts.

Article 33
Term of Protection

The term of protection available shall not end before the expiration of a period of twenty years counted from the filing date.

Additionally, instead of recognizing integrated circuit designs as patentable, TRIPS recognizes such designs separately (Section Six) and provides for a ten year period of protection from the date of application or from the date of the "first commercial exploitation."

SECTION 6: LAYOUT-DESIGNS (TOPOGRAPHIES) OF INTEGRATED CIRCUITS

Article 35
Relation to IPIC Treaty

Members agree to provide protection to the layout-designs (topographies) of integrated circuits (hereinafter referred to as "layout-designs") in accordance with Articles 2-7 (other than paragraph 3 of Article 6), Article 12 and paragraph 3 of Article 16 of the Treaty on Intellectual Property in Respect of Integrated Circuits and, in addition. to comply with the following provisions.

Term of Protection

1. In Members requiring registration as a condition of protection, the term of protection of layout designs shall not end before the expiration of a period of ten years counted from the date of filing an application for registration or from the first commercial exploitation wherever in the world it occurs.

2. In Members not requiring registration as a condition for protection, layout-designs shall be protected for a term of no less than ten years from the date of the first commercial exploitation wherever in the world it occurs.

3. Notwithstanding paragraphs 1 and 2 above, a Member may provide that protection shall lapse fifteen years after the creation of the layout-design.

Trade secrets are recognized under Section Seven's "protection of undisclosed information." Trade secret is defined as information having commercial value that is not commonly known and to which reasonable steps have been taken to maintain its secrecy. The importance of confidentiality agreements and clauses in employment contracts is clearly recognized under the notion of reasonable steps. Furthermore, the owner of the information may prevent the disclosure of such information if disclosure would be contrary to "commercial practices." The term *commercial practice* is further defined in a footnote as, among other things, "breach of contract." Thus, reasonable confidentiality and non-disclosure agreements would be enforceable commercial practices.

SECTION 7: PROTECTION OF UNDISCLOSED INFORMATION

Article 39

1. In the course of ensuring effective protection against unfair competition as provided in Article 10bis of the Paris Convention (1967), Members shall protect undisclosed information in accordance with paragraph 2 below and data submitted to governments or governmental agencies in accordance with paragraph 3 below.
2. Natural and legal persons shall have the possibility of preventing information lawfully within their control from being disclosed to, acquired by, or used by others without their consent in a manner contrary to honest "commercial practices" so long as such information: (1) is secret in the sense that it is not, as a body or in the precise configuration and assembly of its components, (2) generally known among or readily accessible to persons within the circles that normally deal with the kind of information in question; (3) has commercial value because it is secret; and (4) has been subject to reasonable steps under the circumstances, by the person lawfully in control of the information, to keep it secret.

Article 40 and subsequent interpretations are of special importance to licensors of intellectual property rights. Countries are allowed to prohibit certain contractual restrictions that have "adverse effects on trade and *may* impede the transfer of technology." Article 40 allows Member States to single out for scrutiny contractual restrictions found in exclusive grantback clauses and clauses that prohibit challenges to the validity of the licensor's rights.

SECTION 8: CONTROL OF ANTI-COMPETITIVE PRACTICES IN CONTRACTUAL LICENCES

Article 40

1. Members agree that some licensing practices or conditions pertaining to intellectual property rights which restrain competition may have adverse effects on trade and may impede the transfer and dissemination of technology.
2. A Member may adopt, consistently with the other provisions of this Agreement, appropriate measures to prevent or control such practices, which may include for example exclusive grantback conditions, conditions preventing challenges to validity and coercive package licensing, in the light of the relevant laws and regulations of that Member.

Part III provides a menu of penalties and remedies to parties seeking the enforcement and protection of their intellectual property rights. Countries are required to provide civil and criminal remedies, along with procedures for the seizing and destruction of illegal goods. Civil remedies include damages for lost profits and attorney's fees (Article 45), along with the granting of injunctions to prevent imported goods from entering "the channels of commerce" (Article 44). Other provisions allow for the removal or destruction of infringing goods and the providing of the identity of the infringing party to the owner of the intellectual property (Articles 46, 47, 57 and 59). Regarding counterfeited goods, Article 59 instructs the customs authorities not to permit "the re-exportation of the infringing goods in an unaltered state." Special provisions are included to prevent entry of infringing goods through the customs authorities. An owner of intellectual property rights may petition the government to suspend the importation or exportation of infringing goods (Article 51). The administrative or judicial authority may require that the petitioner supply security before granting the suspension (Article 53). The security can be used to indemnify a party who's goods were wrongfully enjoined or suspended (Article 48 and Article 56). Article 55 provides for an initial period of suspension of ten days. During that period the petitioner must move forward with a proceeding on the merits or request an additional ten-day suspension. Article 57 gives the rights owner the right to inspect the suspended goods in order to substantiate his claim. Criminal remedies, imprisonment and/or penalties, are to be enacted into law for "cases of willful trademark counterfeiting or copyright piracy on a commercial scale (Article 61)."

Article 44
Injunctions

1. The judicial authorities shall have the authority to order a party to desist from an infringement, *inter alia* to prevent the entry into the channels of commerce in their jurisdiction of imported goods that involve the infringement of an intellectual property right, immediately after customs clearance of such goods. Members are not obliged to accord such authority in respect of protected subject matter acquired or ordered by a person prior to knowing or having reasonable grounds to know that dealing in such subject matter would entail the infringement of an intellectual property right.

Article 45
Damages

2. The judicial authorities shall also have the authority to order the infringer to pay the right holder's expenses, which may include appropriate attorney's fees. In appropriate cases, Members may authorize the judicial authorities to order recovery of profits and/or payment of pre-established damages even where the infringer did not know or had no reasonable grounds to know that he was engaged in infringing activity.

Article 46
Other Remedies

In order to create an effective deterrent to infringement, the judicial authorities shall have the authority to order that goods that they have found to be infringing be, without compensation of any sort, disposed of outside the channels of commerce in such a manner as to avoid any harm caused to the right holder, or, unless this would be contrary to existing constitutional requirements, destroyed.

Article 47
Right of Information

Members may provide that the judicial authorities shall have the authority, unless this would be out of proportion to the seriousness of the infringement, to order the infringer to inform the right holder of the identity of third persons involved in the production and distribution of the infringing goods or services and of their channels of distribution.

Article 48
Indemnification of the Defendant

1. The judicial authorities shall have the authority to order a party at whose request measures were taken and who has abused enforcement procedures to provide to a party wrongfully enjoined or restrained adequate compensation for the injury suffered because of such abuse. The judicial authorities shall also have the authority to order the applicant to pay the defendant's expenses, which may include appropriate attorney's fees.

Article 51
Suspension of Release by Customs Authorities

Members shall, in conformity with the provisions set out below, adopt Procedures to enable a right holder, who has valid grounds for suspecting that the importation of counterfeit trademark or pirated copyright goods may take place, to lodge an application in writing with competent authorities, administrative or judicial, for the suspension by the customs authorities of the release into free circulation of such goods. Members may enable such an application to be made in respect of goods which involve other infringements of intellectual property rights, provided that the requirements of this Section are met. Members may also provide for corresponding procedures concerning the suspension by the customs authorities of the release of infringing goods destined for exportation from their territories.

Article 53
Security or Equivalent Assurance

1. The competent authorities shall have the authority to require an applicant to provide a security or equivalent assurance sufficient to protect the defendant

and the competent authorities and to prevent abuse. Such security or equivalent assurance shall not unreasonably deter recourse to these procedures.

Article 55
Duration of Suspension

If, within a period not exceeding ten working days after the applicant has been served notice of the suspension, the customs authorities have not been informed that proceedings leading to a decision on the merits of the case have been initiated by a party other than the defendant, or that the duly empowered authority has taken provisional measures prolonging the suspension of the release of the goods, the goods shall be released, provided that all other conditions for importation or exportation have been complied with, in appropriate cases, this time-limit may be extended by another ten working days.

Article 56
Indemnification of the Importer
and of the Owner of the Goods

Relevant authorities shall have the authority to order the applicant to pay the importer, the consignee and the owner of the goods appropriate compensation for any injury caused to them through the wrongful detention of goods or through the detention of goods released pursuant to Article 55 above.

Article 57
Right of Inspection and Information

Without prejudice to the protection of confidential information, Members shall provide the competent authorities the authority to give the right holder sufficient opportunity to have any product detained by the customs authorities inspected in order to substantiate his claims. The competent authorities shall also have authority to give the importer an equivalent opportunity to have any such product inspected. Where a positive determination has been made on the merits of a case, Members may provide the competent authorities the authority to inform the right holder of the names and addresses of the consignor, the importer and the consignee and of the quantity of the goods in question.

Article 59
Remedies

Without prejudice to other rights of action open to the right holder and subject to the right of the defendant to seek review by a judicial authority, competent authorities shall have the authority to order the destruction or disposal of infringing goods in accordance with the principles set out in Article 46 above. In regard to counterfeit trademark goods, the authorities shall not allow the re-exportation of the infringing goods in an unaltered state or subject them to a different customs procedure, other than in exceptional circumstances.

Article 61
Criminal Penalties

Members shall provide for criminal procedures and penalties to be applied at least in cases of willful trademark counterfeiting or copyright piracy on a commercial scale. Remedies available shall include imprisonment and/or monetary fines sufficient to provide a deterrent, consistently with the level of penalties applied for crimes of a corresponding gravity. In appropriate cases, remedies available shall also include the seizure, forfeiture and destruction of the infringing goods and of any materials and implements the predominant use of which has been in the commission of the offence. Members may provide for criminal procedures and penalties to be applied in other cases of infringement of intellectual property rights, in particular where they are committed willfully and on a commercial scale.

It is important to note that even with the full implementation of the TRIPS protection, the acquisition and maintenance of intellectual property rights remains the domain of national laws. TRIPS does require that those laws be transparent (Article 63) and that the acquisition process permits the granting or registration of rights within "a reasonable period of time (Article 62)."

Article 62
Formalities/Registration

1. Members may require, as a condition of the acquisition or maintenance of the intellectual property rights provided for under Sections 2-6 of Part II of this Agreement, compliance with reasonable procedures and formalities. Such pro-

cedures and formalities shall be consistent with the provisions of this Agreement.
2. Where the acquisition of an intellectual property right is subject to the right being granted or registered, Members shall ensure that the procedures for grant or registration, subject to compliance with the substantive conditions for acquisition of the right, permit the granting or registration of the right within a reasonable period of time so as to avoid unwarranted curtailment of the period of protection.

Article 63
Transparency

1. Laws and regulations, and final judicial decisions and administrative rulings of general application, made effective by any Member pertaining to the subject matter of this Agreement (the availability, scope, acquisition, enforcement and prevention of the abuse of intellectual property rights) shall be published, or where such publication is not practicable made publicly available, in a national language, in such a manner as to enable governments and right holders to become acquainted with them.
2. Members shall notify the laws and regulations referred to in paragraph 1 above to the Council for Trade-Related Aspects of Intellectual Property Rights in order to assist that Council in its review of the operation of this Agreement.

Under Article 63's transparency standards, countries are required to transmit copies of their laws and regulations to the Council for Trade-Related Aspects of Intellectual Property. Thus, the licensor must continue to research foreign laws to ascertain the formalities and procedures for acquiring intellectual property rights in a given country.

At the regional level, primarily Europe, the intellectual property owner may want to make use of any devices that provide multi-nation protections. One example is the availability of a Single European Patent. The problem is that the EU Patent Convention has not been ratified and thus does not provide for the intended uniformity and efficiency of application. However, the single patent is recognized in a number of EU countries, along with Switzerland, Sweden, Austria, and Liechtenstein. In order to acquire the Single European Patent, an application needs to be submitted to the European Patent Office in Munich. In the area of trademarks, the EU Trademark Office in Alicante, Spain issues a single EU trademark that is valid in all fifteen EU countries. It should be noted that national trademarks continue to co-exist with the EU trademark. On January 1, 1998, the EU Directive on the protection of databases went into effect. The Directive extends copyright protection to electronic and manual databases.

National Intellectual Property Laws

National intellectual property laws vary substantially in substance and even more on issues of enforcement and remedies. As a matter of terminology, some countries still use the older nomenclature of "industrial property. One explanation of the differences in meanings of the terms industrial property and intellectual property follows:

> *Industrial property* is a term disappearing from Anglo-American legal terminology. It used to include the protection of inventions, industrial designs, and trademarks. *Copyright* in contrast designated the system for protection of literary and artistic works. This dichotomy has now broken down. Many countries have entered the postindustrial era, where the line between goods production and information production is increasingly blurred. Copyright protects purely utilitarian items, such as computer operating systems; patent protects quite abstract ideas for ways of doing business. Trademarks have taken on functions quite different from their traditional role of identifying producers of goods. For instance, trademark owners sell their marks as decorations for T-shirts. English-language terminology has also changed. The broader and more attractive term *intellectual property* has become the designation for the combination of what used to be industrial property, copyright law, and other related fields.[393]

The author of the above definition cautions that the "unification of terminology has not yet led to a unification of legal institutions." Therefore, it is important to research all the different laws relating to intellectual property. It is important to see how patent and copyright laws interrelate in the foreign country of interest. The following excerpt taken from the State Departments Country Commercial Guide for Indonesia illustrates some of the

[393]Peter B. Maggs, *Industrial Property in the Russian Federation,* in, GEORGE GINSBURGS, DONALD D. BARRY & WILLIAM B. SIMONS, eds., THE REVIVAL OF PRIVATE LAW IN CENTRAL AND EASTERN EUROPER 377, note 1 (1996).

common sense strategies that the licensor may have to undertake in order to protect his intellectual property. One technique used, due to the failure of governmental enforcement actions, is to track down the counterfeiters and sign them as legal licensees.

Protecting Your Product from IPR Infringement

Protection of intellectual property rights (IPR) in Indonesia is hampered by inadequate enforcement of the relevant laws and regulations. Foreign companies therefore must be vigilant in protecting their products from IPR infringement. Some choose to go through the Indonesian legal system, but cases may take several years before they are finally resolved.

Occasionally, foreign companies work with local law firms and law enforcement officials to conduct police raids on counterfeiters. Others conduct periodic seminars on the adverse effects of IPR infringement on the Indonesian economy, one of which is reduced investment by foreign companies.

Ultimately, the course taken by companies to protect their intellectual property rights will depend on their product. As an example, one United States company first identifies the counterfeiters of its products and then proceeds to work with them and sign them as legal licensees of its products. Some computer software companies provide free training and/or sell their software at competitive prices, while warning that copies of their product may contain damaging viruses. Also, companies with well-known trademarks must be vigilant in defending their marks by registering them early or seeking a cancellation of an unauthorized registration through the Ministry of Justice. In general, acquiring a strong local partner or agent can help in defending trademarks and intellectual property, as long as the arrangement remains amicable.

The new intellectual property law regimes in former Soviet-bloc countries need to be highly scrutinized. The former inventor's certificate system that gave recognition to an inventor, but did not grant a monopoly on profits from the invention, has been mostly abandoned. The response of the newly democratic governments has been to adopt Western-style intellectual property laws in a somewhat bifurcated manner. Often their laws begin with a full recognition of international conventions like the Paris Convention, Berne Convention, Patent Cooperation Treaty, and Universal Copyright Convention. Since these conventions provide minimum standards, an upgrading of domestic legislation is needed to provide the higher standards found in most legal regimes of the developed countries. The problem then becomes that the lack of developed remedies under the old inventor's certificate system has carried over to the new system. The court systems are not well equipped to handle claims of intellectual property infringement. Upon recognizing an infringement, the lack of appropriate remedies or the disposition not to impose harsh remedies results in an under-enforcement decision. The under-enforcement of substantive intellectual property protection laws is not a phenomena unique to developing countries or former Soviet-bloc countries. For example, the U.S. Trade Representative placed Italy on its intellectual property rights "watch list" under Section 301 of the United States Trade Act of 1988. It accused the Italian government of lax enforcement of the pirating of protected computer software, sound recordings, and film videos.

The experience in Russia highlights some of the pitfalls of licensing intellectual property rights in such countries. First, as in almost all other countries, the United States' "first to invent" principle is not recognized. Russian patent law[394] adheres to the "first to register" principle in which legal rights are given "solely to those who file applications with a national patent office."[395] Thus, an American patent holder may find it difficult to prevent infringement unless he takes the necessary steps to obtain a Russian patent. The best approach is to secure the services of a *patent agent*[396] in order to obtain the necessary patents (and trademarks) within in foreign country. A second issue is the ownership and protection of inventions created by an employee. "The Russian Patent Law provides that employee inventions belong to the employer, but that the employer must remunerate the employee for the invention."[397] The law requires the employee to give

---

[394]Patent Law of the Russian Federation, adopted September 23, 1992, available in LEXIS, Intleg Library, Rusleg File.. See generally, Mark Douma & Rudolph Chistyakov, *The First Patent Law of the Russian Federation,* 1 U. Baltimore Intellectual Property Law J. 162 (1993). See also, Andrew A. Baev, *Recent Changes in Russian Intellectual Property Law and Their Effect upon the Protection of Intellectual Property Rights in Russia,* 19 Suffolk Transnational Law Rev. 361 (1996).

[395]Maggs at 383. It should be noted that Russia is a signatory of the Paris Convention. Therefore, the true inventor should have twelve months from the filing date in another country to file for a patent in Russia.

[396]Russian patent agents are certified under the Statute of Patent Agents enacted in 1993, available in LEXIS, Intleg Library, Rusleg File.

[397]Maggs at 384.

timely notice to her employer of the invention. The employer then must take a proactive step within four months to preserve its title to the invention. If it fails to respond by filing a patent application or notifying the employee of its plans to retain the invention as a trade secret, then the employee will gain the right to file for a patent. From a contractual perspective, a written employment contract should provide for a formal notification procedure, establish the obligation of the employee to cooperate in the filing of a patent application, and detail the amount of remuneration that will be paid to the employee.

A third issue under Russian patent law is the notion of *compulsory licensing.*[398] If a licensee or a third party makes an improvement on a patent that has not been used for four years, then the law provides that the patent holder must grant the improvement owner a license to use the underlying patent or technology. The "junior" patent holder must argue that it cannot use its patent without infringing on the rights of the other "senior" patent holder. The danger of this provision in the Patent Law is that "a minor improvement by a second inventor theoretically gives him the right to a license without a reciprocal requirement to license the first."[399] Under United States law, "if the first inventor refuses to grant a license, the second inventor has no remedy. Russian law provides for compulsory licensing in this situation, thus lessening the value of patent protection."[400] For this reason it is important to periodically use or "work" the patent in order to preclude the creation of second inventor rights. One alternative is to retain the property as a trade secret. In such a situation, all employment contracts should prohibit the post-employment use of trade secrets. However, foreign labor law should always be researched before drafting such clauses in an employment contract. Labor law provisions may protect employees by voiding such clauses.[401]

---

[398]Compulsory licenses are government grants of statutory rights to use someone else's intellectual property rights. Such licenses are found in some countries where an owner of intellectual property rights is required to use the rights or suffer a loss of exclusivity. See generally, Michael Scott, *Compulsory Licensing of Intellectual Property in International Transactions,* 10 European Intellectual Property Rev. 319 (1988).

[399]Marina Portnova, *Ownership and Enforcement of Patent Rights in Russia: Protecting an Invention in the Existing Environment,* 8 Indiana Int'l & Comparative Law Rev. 505, 516 (1998).

[400]Maggs at 385.

[401]Ibid. at 387.

The contract, whether a license, employment, franchise, or joint venture agreement, is, at this time, the only mechanism available to protect intellectual property. Breach of contract claims may be the best avenue for preventing "direct-party" infringement or abuse of the granted rights. Regarding the protection of intellectual property rights through the enforcement of patent, copyright, and trademark law, enforcement has not been consistent. "Russia has now adopted industrial property legislation generally complying with international standards. However, until it has a strong and functioning commercial court system with serious enforcement powers, there is a great risk that the new legislation will remain on paper."[402] A recent positive development was the creation of the Supreme Patent Chamber by Presidential Edict issued on September 11, 1997. We can only hope that the new judicial body will provide a level of expertise currently lacking in the civil courts. However, its jurisdiction is limited to a number of matters such as the granting of compulsory licenses. The bulk of litigation involving disputes over patent ownership, patent infringement, and licensing contracts remains the jurisdiction of the lower courts.

A number of tangential issues should be explored by the licensor before proceeding with a Russian license agreement. First, all protections provided by international conventions should be explored. International treaties subscribed to by Russia will supercede its new Patent Law. Russia is currently a party to the Patent Cooperation Treaty, Madrid Protocol, Berne Convention, and Universal Copyright Convention, along with the Paris Convention. Second, after obtaining a Russian patent it is important to pay periodic maintenance fees. Failure to pay such fees can result in a termination of the patent.[403] Third, a licensor is required to record any transfer or assignment of property rights. For example, patent transfers or licenses must be registered with the Patent Office. Fourth, the licensee should be required to enter into employment contracts with their employees which clearly delineate ownership of rights to any improvements made to the licensed technology. Fifth, because of the poor track record of enforcement by the Russian civil court system, negotiating license agreements with infringing parties may be the best alternative. Sixth, a strong "best efforts" clause should be incorporated into any transfer agreement to prevent claims of abandonment and the issuing of compulsory licenses. Seventh,

[402]Ibid. at 390. This statement is equally applicable to a host of other countries.
[403]See, Article 30 of Patent Law.

the recently enacted Eurasian Patent Convention should be utilized when appropriate. This convention allows a Russian patent to be expanded to include a number of other former Soviet republics. The foreign licensor may file an application in the Eurasian Patent Office in Moscow.[404] Finally, the licensor may want to enlist the services of International Searching Authorities (ISA) when filing foreign patent applications. A number of national patent offices, including Russia, United States, Japan, and the European Patent Office, recognize patent search certificates produced by this company. ISA will forward the search report and the international patent application authorized under the Patent Cooperation Treaty to signatory countries.

The Gray Market

The importation of counterfeited goods is prohibited under 19 U.S.C. Section 1526(e) (Section 526 of the Tariff Act). Under 19 C.F.R. Section 133.23a, the Customs Service is authorized to seize such goods at the point of entry into the country. In order to assist the Customs Service, trademarks and copyrights should be *recorded* with the Service. Section 133 set forth the procedures governing recordation of trademarks with the Customs Service. For additional information, contact the Customs Service's Intellectual Property Rights Branch. The more difficult legal issue is the *gray market* problem.[405] This problem involves goods which are legally produced under a license and that are imported or re-imported into the United States. Also referred to as parallel imports, they include goods produced outside the United States pursuant to an international transfer agreement and those licensed in the United States for export only that are subsequently re-imported into the United States.[406] Thus, an American licensor attempting

---

[404]The Eurasian Patent Convention went into effect on January 1, 1996 and provides protection in the countries of Russia, Azerbaijan, Belarus, Kazakhstan, Tajikistan, Turkmenistan, Kyrgystan, Moldova, and Armenia. See, Portnova at 524.

[405]See, Lawrence M. Friedman, *Business and Legal Strategies for Combating Grey-Market Imports,* 32 Int'l Lawyer 27 (1998).

[406]The Supreme Court attempted to deal with the different gray market scenarios in *K Mart v. Cartier, Inc.,* 486 U.S. 281 (1988).

to increase foreign royalty revenues may find its own market territory undercut by identical goods produced under a foreign licensing agreement. The Customs Service generally does not act to prevent the importation of gray market goods. Its authority does not include the policing of goods produced under a legal license.[407] The Customs Service makes an exception to section 526 in cases where the American trademark owner and the foreign producer are under *common control.* In order to monitor the gray market problem, all goods sold through a foreign distributor should be marked with identification numbers. "Knowing which distributors are responsible for supplying gray market retailers is of assistance in choosing future distributors and in pursuing [breach of contract] claims against the distributor."[408] This, however, does not impact the more prevalent problem of foreign production of the licensed goods unless the licensor provides marked packaging for the products being produced. Of course, the licensee could discard such packaging to avoid identification.

The Lanham Act may be used to prevent the importation of foreign goods that infringe on an American trademark. However, a large portion of the gray market is considered legal. Trademark law generally does not reach the sale of genuine goods produced outside the United States and subsequently imported to compete against the same goods produced domestically. This was the situation in the 1987 case of *NEC Electronics v. Cal Circuit ABCO.*[409] The defendant had purchased gray market chips from a foreign source and imported them to compete against the trademark owner's California subsidiary. The court held that if the trademark owner "chooses to sell abroad at lower prices than those it could obtain for the identical product in the United States, it cannot look to United States trademark law to insulate the American market or to vitiate the effects of international trade."[410]

A number of causes of actions are available against unauthorized resellers of a manufacturer's goods, such as phonorecords. One such cause of action is found in Section 602(a) of the Copyright Act. Section 602 provides:

---

[407]See generally, 19 C.F.R. § 133.42 (a) & (b).

[408]Lawrence M. Friedman, *Business and Legal Strategies for Combating Grey-Market Imports,* 32 The Int'l Lawyer 27, 50 (1998).

[409] F.2d 1506 (9th Cir. 1987).

[410]810 Ibid. at 1511, See also, A. Bourjois & Co. v. Katzel, 260 U.S. 689 (1923); Olympus Corp. v. United States, 792 F.2d 315 (2d Cir. 1986).

(a) Importation into the United States, without the authority of the owner of the copyright, of copies of phonorecords of a work that have been acquired outside of the United States is an infringement of the exclusive right to distribute copies or phonorecords under section 106, actionable under section 501.

This section gives a copyright owner the right to prohibit the importation of copies if the product was manufactured overseas. However, the cause of action is more limited where a product has been manufactured in the United States and then exported to another country. The unauthorized resellers would be protected from such a suit under the *first sale doctrine* found in Section 109(a) of the Copyright Act. Section 109(a) states that the "owner of a particular copy or phonorecord lawfully made under this title or any person authorized by such owner [e.g., through a license], is entitled, without the authority of the copyright owner, to sell or otherwise dispose of the possession of that copy or phonorecord."[411]

Foreign Transfer Restrictions

Some foreign countries attempt to regulate or restrict the transfer of technology and intellectual property to its nationals.[412] These transfer regulations may include the requirement of government approval. The People's Republic of China's regulations on the importation of technology will be briefly examined as an example of a restrictive type of transfer regulations. First, the European Union transfer regulations will be explored. These regulations offer the importer of technology or the licensor of intellectual property the hope for a more harmonized system throughout the European Union.

---

[411]A recent case dealing with this issue is Quality King Distributors, Inc. v. L'Anza Research International, Inc., 140 L.Ed.2d 254 (1998). See also, Columbia Broadcasting System v. Scorpio Music, 569 F. Supp. 47 (1983); Independent News Co. v Williams, 293 F.2d 5410 (3d Cir. 1961); Bobbs-Merrill Co. v. Straus, 210 U.S. 339 (1908); Burke & Van Heusen, Inc. v. Arrow Drug., Inc., 233 F. Supp. 881 (E.D.Pa.1964).

[412]See e.g., Ohara, *New Japanese Guidelines for the Commission Regulations of Restrictive Clauses in Patent and Know-How Licensing Agreements,* Int'l Rev. Industrial Property & Copyright Law 656 (1991).

European Union Regulations

On January 31, 1996, new Technology Transfer Regulation 240/96 went into effect.[413] The new Regulation is actually two regulations, one pertaining to "patents" (2349/84)[414] and the other dealing with the transfer of "know-how" (556/89).[415] The purpose of Regulation 240/96 was to simplify patent and know-how licensing. The simplification included clarifying the legality of certain restrictions within transfer agreements in relation to European Union Competition Law. Exclusive licenses of patents or know-how where the licensor also agrees not to work the licensed territory are now expressly exempted from EU Competition Law. However, the duration of such licenses is limited. An exclusive patent license may extend for a period equivalent to the parallel license of the licensee. A *parallel license* is defined under the Regulation as the period that such patents would be granted under the national laws of the licensee. Know-how licensing agreements are limited to a period of ten years from the time that a licensee markets the product.

Regulation 240/96 also sanctions certain restrictions placed upon the licensee. Provisions dealing with gray market issues are expressly allowed. Thus, a license grant prohibiting a licensee from using the license outside the licensed territory, or more specifically, in the territory of the licensor, is valid. Furthermore, the licensee can be required to designate itself as the manufacturer of a product when licensed to affix the licensor's trademark. The Regulation also expands the so-called number of *white-listed clauses* that can be used in know-how and patent transfer agreements. It allows for the following contractual restrictions:

(a) confidentiality provisions prohibiting the licensee from disclosing licensor's know-how,

(b) a prohibition on the continued use of the licensor's technology after the expiration or termination of the license

---

[413]See generally, Pierre V. F. Bos & Marco M. Slotboom, *The EC Technology Transfer Regulation—A Practitioner's Perspective,* 32 The Int'l Lawyer 1 (1998).

[414]See, Appendix 9.

[415]See, Appendix 10.

(c) nonexclusive grant back clauses are authorized, however the licensor may be required to grant an exclusive license to the licensee for subsequent improvements made by the licensor,
(d) best efforts clauses requiring the licensee to fully work the technology in the licensed territory,
(e) the right of the licensor to terminate the license in the event that the licensee challenges the validity of the licensor's patents,
(f) field of use restrictions are permitted,
(g) production limitations when the licensed product is a component in the licensee's own products.

Also, the obligation to pay royalties on sales of non-licensed products, a practice which was formerly black-listed, is now permitted. Thus, momentum clauses are generally permitted. See Commission Regulations 556/89, Art. 3(3) & 2349/84, Art. 3(4).

The Regulation also lists a number of clauses that are prohibited. These *black-listed clauses* include:
(a) clauses that prohibit *gray market* imports,
(b) grant back clauses that require the licensee to assign the rights to its improvements to the licensor,
(c) general limits on production amounts,
(d) allocation of customers between former competitors.

It is important to note that other types of contracts may be impacted by the new regulations. Joint ventures between competitors involving technology transfers may not benefit from the new Regulation. However, some licensing agreements between competitors are covered by the Regulation "if certain market share thresholds are respected." The parents of the joint venture may not have a combined market share of more than twenty percent (production joint venture) or ten percent (distribution joint venture).[416] Another extension of the Regulation is in the area of software licensing. "Software licensing agreements based on copyright may now be covered by the Regulation as soon as they are accompanied by patents or know-how within the meaning of the Regulation."[417] Thus, the black and white lists of exempted and prohibited contract clauses are applicable to most types of

---

[416]Pierre V. F. Bops & Marco M. Slotboom, *The EC Technology Transfer Regulation—A Practitioner's Perspective,* 32 Int'l Lawyer 1, 22 (1998).
[417]Ibid. at 24.

technology transfer agreements. "Skillful draftsmanship is called for to match the contractual restrictions with the appropriate territories and industrial property. The block exemption (Regulation) provides a map with which to steer a safe but effective course through the common market."[418]

Therefore, an American exporter contemplating an intellectual property transfer to the European Union should give consideration as to whether Directorate IV will need to be notified. The American exporter must also conform to the requirements found in United States export regulations. For example, will a validated export license for sensitive technologies be required? In order to answer such a question, United States export law should be reviewed including 15 C.F.R. §370 *et. seq.*, (export regulations), 50 U.S.C. App. 2401 *et. seq.* (Export Administration Act), and 22 U.S.C. § 2778 (Arms Control Export Act).

Regulations of the People's Republic of China

China's regulations regarding the importation of technology represent a serious obstacle to a foreign licensor. The *Regulations Governing Contracts for the Importation of Technology* defines imported technology as including the transfer of patents, technical know-how, and technical services. The licensor and licensee must enter into a formal written contract that is to be subsequently submitted to the Ministry of Foreign Economic Relations & Trade. The Ministry has sixty days to approve or reject the contract. It should be noted that other agencies of the government also need to be consulted. For example, approvals often need to be obtained from both the local municipality and the provincial government. The disturbing feature of the *Regulations* is that it imposes numerous prohibitions on the substantive content of the transfer contract. Article 6 requires the licensor to guarantee his title to the technology. Article 8 limits the duration of the agreement to ten years or "the time period for the Recipient to master the imported technology."

The most troublesome provisions are found in Article 9 of the Regulations. Article 9 prohibits a number of contractual provisions commonly

[418]Walter Kinn, *New European Union Technology Transfer Block Exemption Regulation,* 9 Int'l Quarterly 320, 329 (1996).

used by licensors to protect their rights and the rights of other licensees. Some of the prohibited provisions include: (1) restrictions on the selection of sources for materials, spare parts, or equipment, (2) restrictions on acquiring similar technology from a competitor, (3) unequal conditions for exchanging improvements, (4) restrictions on the sales channels or exportation of licensed products, and (5) restrictions on post-termination use of the technology. The first two provisions are generally found in exclusive licenses or distribution contracts. The third provision prevents the licensor from negotiating a favorable grant-back clause for improvements to the technology. The fourth provision prohibits clauses aimed at preventing a *gray market* problem for the licensor or other licensees. The last provision heightens concern for the confidentiality of trade secrets and other sensitive information. These are only a few of the prohibitions found in the *Regulations.* The *Measures for the Examination of Contracts for the Importation of Technology* provide added insight into the restrictive nature of the regulations. Article 6 of the *Measures* mandates that the government review the contract for, among other things, fairness in price, reasonableness of provisions pertaining to property rights, and to ensure that the rights and obligations of the parties are "definite, reciprocal and reasonable." Thus, the ability of the exporter of technology or licensor of intellectual property rights to protect themselves through a contract is heavily circumscribed. The foreign licensor attempting to negotiate contractual protections may want to take advantage of the provision for preliminary approval in order to prevent an unexpected disapproval of the final agreement. Article 7 provides that the "recipient may prior to or during negotiation seek the opinion of the Approval Authority or submit the contract for preliminary examination with respect to the major contents or certain articles of the contract."

Intellectual Property Transfer Agreement

There are numerous reasons for using licensing agreements to tap into foreign markets. The licensor can avoid the costs and time of exporting and importing goods across national borders. He also avoids the panoply of host country laws, such as tax, labor, and environmental laws, that would need to be addressed when directly investing and developing a foreign market. Licensing, from the licensor perspective, provides an inviting means of generating revenues without committing large amounts of capital. The major pitfall of international licensing is the necessity to disclose confidential information such as trade secrets to parties outside the reach of United States' intellectual property laws. Therefore, the drafting of the international licensing agreement takes on an added importance.[419] What follows is a list of steps that a potential licensor should undertake when contemplating licensing its rights and technology to a foreign entity. This list is followed by a review of some of the more common clauses found in intellectual property transfer agreements.

Preventive Due Diligence

In contemplating the exportation of intellectual property rights (patents, copyrights, trademarks, trade secrets) a preventive (legal) due diligence should be undertaken. For example, foreign national and international property rights protection laws need to be reviewed in order to take the necessary steps to best protect the licensor's rights. Also, the licensor should review past transfers and infringements of his rights in order to understand the types of warranties that he is able to make in future transfers. A preventative law checklist should be developed to address these and other concerns.

Checklist for Intellectual Property Transfers

Intellectual Property Review Team

Assemble an intellectual property review team. This team should include representatives from: management; local and foreign legal counsel; technical personnel, such as representatives from research and development, engineering, and production; management; sales and marketing; human resources; and possibly financial.

[419]See generally, Byington, *Planning and Drafting of International Licensing Agreements*, 6 No. Carolina Journal of Int'l Law & Commercial Regulation 193 (1984).

Due Diligence[420]

Patents:

- What are the terms remaining on the patents?
- Have patents been used in countries that require *working*?
- Identify all U.S. and foreign patents associated with the transfer.
- Search U.S. and foreign patent office records for title and payment of all necessary fees.
- Identify other research & development projects which may be exposed to competition in the event of a transfer.
- Identify procedures for protecting inventions, including procedures for determining whether an invention should remain a trade secret, making foreign filing decisions, and ensuring the timeliness of patent filings.
- Determine which patents cover which products.
- Identify all markings to be used in conjunction with the production of the licensed product.
- Identify all existing and pending agreements dealing with the patents.
- Whether a licensor or licensee, always ask: Are the patents or licenses transferable? Are improvements included in the transfer? Are there any non-compete provisions? What are the termination dates on the patents and licenses? Are there any security interests on file with the U.S. Patent Office and have applicable state records been reviewed?
- Review all correspondence relating to patent disputes, claims of infringement, and letters threatening lawsuits or other notices received by licensor or licensee.
- What steps have been taken to insure patent rights in the foreign country of the licensee or the geographic area of the license grant? Has the patent been registered under the appropriate foreign national law?

---

[420]See generally, Mary Ann Tucker, *Checklist for Due Diligence in Intellectual Property Transactions,* 14-1 Corporate Counsel's Quarterly 68 (1997).

Trademarks

- Identify all federal, state and foreign trademarks registrations and pending applications.
- Check title and payment of renewal fees.
- Identify all procedures for protecting trademarks, including procedures for deciding whether to seek registrations.
- Determine the products on which each trademark is used. Provide licensee with samples of the proper use of the trademarks.
- Review copies of all product advertising and promotional materials.
- Check use of the trademark on the Internet.
- Has there been any period of nonuse of the trademarks?
- Have there been any previous assignments of the trademarks? Have these assignments been recorded?
- Are the trademarks and any licenses pertaining to them transferable or assignable? Are there any restrictions or limitations in the licenses?
- Check for security interests with the U.S. Trademark Office and applicable state records, and conduct comparable foreign searches.
- How has the licensor and licensee protected their trademarks in the past?
- Review renewal dates on trademarks.

Copyrights

- Identify all copyrighted materials associated with the transfer or license.
- Check title to copyrights and payment of renewal fees for copyrights by searching the U.S. Copyright Office.
- Review procedures for identifying "copyrightable" material, and the protecting of those materials, including procedures for deciding whether to mark materials or to register them.
- Review all agreements dealing with the copyrights. Are they assignable or transferable? Are there any restrictions or limitations on their use or transfer?
- Check for security interests by searching the U.S. Copyright Office and state records.

- Have the licensor and licensee enforced their copyrights in the past?
- Does any action need to be taken in the country of the licensee to protect the copyrights?

Miscellaneous

- What procedures should the licensee be required to undertake in order to protect the rights being licensed? Review site security, employee access, and monitoring of third parties.
- Review employment agreements relating to intellectual property and confidentiality. Does the licensee conduct employee exit interviews?
- What procedures and responsibilities should the licensee be required to undertake in relationship to third party infringements?

A licensor's due diligence checklist should include the determination of whether the transfer agreement or license needs to be approved by an agency of the licensee's government. Some countries, unlike the United States, require the registration of the license with a government agency. For example, in Russia all licensing agreements need to be registered. Failure to register results in the inability to deduct royalty payments from a tax and accounting perspective.[421]

The intellectual property agreement or license takes on added significance in international transactions as compared to purely domestic transfers in the United States. The wide variety of intellectual property protection offered by foreign laws requires the American exporter of technology to take added precaution in drafting a contract that is protective of its intellectual property rights. It is important that the contract provide avenues for lawsuits for breach of contract where an infringement claim is unlikely to be sustained under a foreign intellectual property law regime. Following the *identification* of the parties, the generic licensing agreement will have a number of recitals and a definitional section. These parts of the preamble take on added significance in an international transfer agreement. The *recitals* will often list the rights being licensed. Any untruthful recitals can become the basis for lawsuits asserting breach of warranty or misrepre-

[421]PRICE WATERHOUSE, DOING BUSINESS IN THE RUSSIAN FEDERATION 53 (1997).

sentation. The licensor should verify the status of all its trademarks, copyrights, and patents, along with any patents pending. Extra care should be taken in defining terms in the *definitional section.* Given the differences in language, culture, and national intellectual property regimes, the agreement should possess a carefully negotiated and drafted list of definitions. For example, the meaning of terms such as "net sales" or "gross sales" for the purposes of calculating royalties will often be at the center of disputes if they are not carefully defined.

The root of the intellectual property transfer agreement is the *grant clause* which describes the rights and know-how being transferred, along with any restrictions or limitations on their use. The grant clause should itemize all the intellectual property rights and know-how being transferred. Referencing exhibits that are attached to the agreement can best do this. The grant should make clear whether the license is exclusive or non-exclusive. The difference is fundamental to issues regarding the degree of competition that may be expected by the licensee and in the setting of the royalty rate. Also, exclusivity is interconnected to issues dealing with infringement. In an exclusive license,[422] the licensee should negotiate the right to demand that the licensor sue any third-party infringer or in the alternative, the right to sue in the name of the licensor for any infringements in the license territory. A non-exclusive license grant may include a *most-favored license* provision in which the licensor is required to amend the license to include the more favorable terms negotiated in a subsequent license to another licensee. This would insure that earlier licensees are not placed in an unfair competitive disadvantage.[423] The problem with such clauses is the difficulty in determining the relative values of different terms. All things being equal, the negotiation of a more favorable royalty rate would be considered to be subject to a most favorable license clause. A well written most-favored license clause would require the licensor to notify the licensee of any new licenses affecting its territory and to provide a copy of any such licenses so that the licensee can determine if the terms of the other license are more favorable. Finally, the most-favorable license clause should provide that if the licensee demands an amendment to its license in order to incorporate any more fa-

[422]A hybrid to the exclusive license is the sole license in which the licensor retains the right to produce, sell, or use its rights within the licensed territory.

[423]Most favored license clauses were held to be enforceable in Carpenter Tech. Corp. v. Armco, Inc., 800 F. Supp. 215 (E.D. Pa. 1992).

vorable terms, it must also accept the incorporation of other less favorable terms included in the subsequent license.

The grant clause should also define the grant in terms of its geographic scope, as well as its duration. If the license is for the right to produce, sell, and use the rights in the United States, then the Patent Act implies that the grant is for the entire United States, along with its possessions and territories.[424] If the license is silent as to duration, then a court may imply that it was intended to grant rights for the entire statutory term of the patent, copyright, or trademark.[425] The grant clause may also restrict the nature of the rights being transferred. For example, for technology with different fields of use, the grant clause may restrict the type of use for which the transferred rights are to be utilized.

A major issue that should be addressed in the license is the right of the licensee to export goods from the licensed territory. Of great concern is the licensee's ability to import goods into the country of the licensor. This *gray market* issue has become hotly contested throughout the world. If the mobility of the goods being produced under the license is a concern for the licensor, then it should place restrictions in the license in order to prevent gray market imports. The TRIPS agreement as codified in 35 U.S.C. § 271 (a) grants the licensor or intellectual property owner the rights to prevent "imports into the United States." These additional rights should be clearly delineated in the agreement. The licensor may also want to negotiate caps on the maximum amount of units of the licensed product that can be produced by the licensee in a given year. It could also limit the amount of units that the licensee may sell to individual purchasers in a given year. Also, it should clearly state that the licensee is precluded from selling to anyone who is known to import goods into other markets.

Important Contractual Provisions

Most licensors have developed a standard licensing agreement for use in domestic transactions. The previous material exposed the reader to some of the foreign laws that will impact the operation of some of the clauses found in standard licensing agreements. Foreign competition, technology

[424] 35 U.S.C. §§ 100, 271 (a) (1994).

[425] See, e.g., United States v. Radio Corp. of America, 117 F. Supp. 449 (D. Del. 1954).

transfer, and consumer protection laws cannot be avoided through contractual agreement. For example, some foreign contract or consumer laws limit the scope of disclaimers or limitation of liability clauses. Thus, it is imperative that the international licensor determine how such laws, along with differences in customs and trade usage, will impact the operation of their standard clauses. The following sections focus upon some of the standard clauses found in intellectual property.[426]

Grant Clause and Liability Limitation Clauses

The single most important clause in any intellectual property, technology, or software licensing agreement is the "grant clause." The licensor will want to emphasize that he is only granting to the licensee the right to use the items being transferred. Therefore, the grant clause should: (1) limit or prohibit the licensee's right to copy the licensed material, (2) prohibit the licensee from reverse engineering, (3) clearly state that the licensor retains all title, copyrights, patents, and other proprietary rights, and (4) provide that upon termination the licensee must cease using the information and shall return or destroy all copies. Other protective provisions that should be considered are discussed below, along with examples of such clauses.

(1) Compliance with Export Laws: The licensee agrees to comply with the export regulations of the licensor's country.

"The licensed products shall not be exported, directly or indirectly, in violation of the export regulations of the United States or be used for any purposes prohibited by the export regulations."

(2) Merger or Integration Clause: This is especially important where the individual products being transferred come with their own licenses.

"This contract supercedes the terms of any purchase order or ordering document, along with the terms of any unsigned or "shrinkwrap" license included in any product package."

[426]See generally, James H. Davis, Kenneth E. Payne, & John R. Thomas, *Drafting the Technology License Agreement,* ALI-ABA COURSE MATERIALS JOURNAL 13 (Dec. 1996)

The licensor would only want to supercede such "individual licenses" if it has provided adequate terms of the license in the master license or transfer agreement.

(3) Limitation of Liability: The parties will generally want to exclude liability for indirect, incidental, special or consequential damages. The licensor may want to limit the extent of its liability to an amount no greater then the total fees paid by the licensee. Furthermore, the parties may want to exclude the possibility that an unexpected event may trigger a claim for an adjustment of the contract.

"The provisions of this Agreement allocate the risks between the licensor and licensee. The licensor's pricing reflects this allocation of risk and the limitation of liability hereto specified."

(4) Exclusive Remedy Clause: An ancillary clause to the limitation of liability clause is one that limits the types of remedies available to the parties. The following one limits the remedies of the licensee.

"The licensee's exclusive remedy and the licensor's total liability shall be the correction of defects in the licensed product or the re-performance of services rendered. Upon failure by the licensor to correct the defects within a reasonable period of time, the licensee may terminate the license and recover any fees paid for the product or for the unsatisfactory services."

(5) Infringement Indemnity Clause: The licensee will want assurance that the licensor will defend it against any infringement claims. In turn, the licensor will want to limit its exposure to defending such claims.

"Licensor will defend and indemnify licensee against claims of infringement of patent, copyright or other intellectual property rights provided that (a) the licensee notifies licensor in writing within 45 days of receiving the claim, (b) the licensor shall have full control over the defense of the claim, (c) the licensee shall assist the licensor in defending the claim. The licensor shall reimburse the licensee for reasonable expenses incurred in providing such assistance. The licensor shall have the option to (a) modify the licensed products to make them non-infringing or (b) to obtain a valid license for the licensee. If the licensor determines that it is not commercially reasonable to perform either (a) or (b), then the licensor may terminate this license and refund the license fees. This shall be licensor's entire liability and the licensee's exclusive remedy for third-party claims of infringement.

(6) Most Favored Licensee Clause: Such a clause requires the licensor to provide the same royalty rate and terms to the licensee that he subsequently gives to another competitive licensee. Such a clause is likely to place the burden in future litigation on the licensor to prove that the most favored licensee's competitor was not given a license at a more favorable or lower royalty rate. The purpose of such a clause is to "ensure that the favored licensee remains on an equal competitive footing with other licensees."[427]

The licensee, at the very least, should contractually require that the licensor join him in any infringement claim made by the licensee against a third party. This is important because under United States law a patent holder is a necessary party to any infringement claim.[428]

Generic Transfer Clauses

A number of contract provisions are found in most generic intellectual property licensing agreements.[429] The sample clauses are brief in nature and would need to be customized and detailed for a particular transfer. The

427 Carpenter Technology Corp. v. Armco, Inc., 800 F. Supp. 215 (E.D.Pa. 1992).

428 See, e.g., Yarway Corp. v. Eur-Control USA, Inc., 775 F.2d 258 (Fed. Cir. 1985) (licensee brought claim of infringement against a holder of another patent under the "doctrine of equivalence" where a patent is filed for something that is the design equivalent of another patented device but in which minor changes have been made in order to avoid an infringement claim).

429 Mary Ann Tucker, *Checklist for Due Diligence in Intellectual Property Transactions,* 14-1 Corporate Counsel's Quarterly 68 (1997). Tucker lists the following clauses as those that should be clearly written: Exclusivity or non-exclusivity of license; assignability or non-assignability of license by licensee; rights or cross-licenses for improvements made by licensee or licensor; rights of licensor to terminate license; licensor's warranty of title; confidentiality provision; post-transaction requirements, e.g., due diligence in returning

sample clauses are generally written from the perspective of the licensor. The term "Licensed Property" refers to the intellectual property rights being transferred under the agreement. "Licensed Products" refers to the products to be produced or sold under the authority granted by the agreement.

- **Definitions:** Given the cross-cultural problems of language and the differences in national intellectual property laws, added attention should be given to defining technical and non-technical terms. For example, terms like *gross sales* or *net sales* should be defined in detail. Such detail should include a definition of each of the items that the licensee can deduct in determining the net sales amount for purposes of the royalty calculation.
- **Channels of Distribution (exclusivity):** The licensor may want to define the appropriate avenues for sales or channels of distribution for the licensed product. This is especially important when the license is non-exclusive or the licensor is retaining substantial rights in the licensee's intended market. For example, an American licensor may want to retain the right to sell the licensed product to other American companies doing business in the license territory.

Example: "The licensee may not distribute or sell licensed product to grocery stores or supermarkets [define grocery store and supermarkets]. The licensee may sell the licensed product through the following channels of distribution: Gift stores, souvenir stores, and theme parks."

The licensor will generally want to restrict the licensee's ability to sell products outside of the licensed territory. However, such restrictions may be invalidated under foreign competition laws. For example, European Union law requires that a licensee be able to sell outside its territory in order to fill unsolicited orders. In order to accommodate such a law, the agreement may prohibit the active solicitation of customers outside the licensee's territory.

- **Reservation of Rights:** The licensor should always include a reservation of rights clause in the license, even if it is intended to be an exclusive license.

---

know-how; details for consulting and support necessary to transfer the technology; and a dispute resolution clause.

Example: Licensor reserves all rights not expressly conveyed to the licensee. [Licensor reserves the right to grant any such reserved rights to other licensees.]

- **Modifications Clause:** The licensor will want to stipulate that any modifications or improvements made by the licensee shall revert to the ownership of the licensor. The clause should require the licensee to assign all its rights to any modification to the licensor. In order to protect the integrity of its intellectual property rights, the licensor will want to require prior approval over any modifications.
- **Royalties:** There are three general parameters involving the payment of monies from the licensee to the licensor: the Royalty Rate, Guaranteed Consideration, and Momentum Royalties. Guaranteed Consideration may be a schedule of payments, including a good faith deposit, not connected with sales by the licensee. This is used to ensure that the licensee will make reasonable efforts to produce, market, and sell the licensed product. The licensee should negotiate that any advance payments ("Guaranteed Consideration") are to be credited against future royalties. In turn, the licensor should place a time limit upon which the Guaranteed Consideration can be applied against royalties. Momentum Royalties are paid when the licensee sells other product lines. These royalties are based upon increases in the licensee's overall sales. This notion is similar to the rental provisions in commercial leases that make the rental amount based upon the tenant's sales. Momentum Royalties are negotiated in licenses of marquee products that are likely to draw customers to the licensee. The generic Royalty Clause is based upon a percentage of sales. The key issue is the determination of the amount of sales. A percentage of gross sales is generally favorable to the licensor, while net sales favors the licensee. However, this distinction between the use of gross sales and net sales terms is not always true. A "net sales" definition which allows for very few offsets or deductions will be very close to a gross sales amounts. Conversely, a "gross sales" definition that allows for a liberal amount of setoffs can mimic a net sales figure.

Example: "Guaranteed Consideration": The sum of $________ is payable upon the following dates: ______________.

These sums as set forth above shall be applied against such royalties as become due to the licensor. No part of such Guaranteed Consideration shall be repayable to the licensee.

"Royalty Payments": The Royalty Rate shall be five percent (5%). The licensee shall pay a sum equal to the Royalty Rate of all "net sales" by the licensee of the Licensed Product. The term "net sales" shall mean gross invoice price billed customers, less actual quantity discounts and actual returns (actual returns not to exceed 5%). No deductions are to be made for non-collectible accounts or costs incurred in the manufacture, marketing, advertisement or sale of the Licensed Product.

- **Accounting:** The accounting provision should provide for periodic statements of sales and the payment of royalties. It should also provide for some form of certification and audit of the sales amount and royalties owing. The licensor should provide for the payment of interest on delinquent payments and for assurances in the case of default.

Example: Within thirty (30) days of the end of every month, the licensee shall furnish to licensor complete and accurate statements certified by an officer of the licensee with respect to the number of units sold, their gross sale prices, and itemized deductions from the gross sale prices. Upon demand, the licensee shall at its own expense furnish to licensor a detailed statement by an independent certified public accountant pertaining to the above items. Any payments made after the required due date shall bear interest at the then current prime rate. The licensee agrees to provide, in the event of default, a letter of credit issued in favor of the licensor from a financial institution to be approved by the licensor. In the alternative, the licensor may request the granting and perfecting of a security interest or lien on any contract rights, accounts receivable, or proceeds associated with the sale of the Licensed Products.

- **Record-keeping:** The licensee should be required to retain records pertaining to the license and the sales of the Licensed Products.

Example: The licensee shall maintain and preserve records pertaining to the license at its principal place of business for at least two years following termination or expiration of the license term or any renewals. These records shall include, without limitation, purchase orders, inventory records, invoices, correspondence, banking and financial records, and any other records pertaining to the Licensed Products. Such records and accounts shall be available for inspection and audit at any time during or after the license term during reasonable business hours and upon at least three (business) days written notice by the licensor.

- **Best Efforts Clause:** A best efforts clause is vital in an exclusive license agreement. The licensor is dependent upon the licensee to generate sales and royalty payments. Courts have implied such clauses in exclusive licenses.[430] However, the licensor would be better served by negotiating a specific best efforts clause with appropriate timetables, benchmarks for production and sales, the amount of monies to be expended and minimum royalty levels. It may provide "penalties" for failure to reach stated goals and for the termination of the license. A well-written best efforts clause will adequately define the words "best" and "efforts." Another unrelated purpose of the best efforts clause is to prevent a foreign country from issuing a compulsory license on the licensor's technology to a third party. Some countries require a patent owner to use the patent in order to avoid losing the exclusive rights to exploit that patent in the country. The granting of a license to a national of that country usually satisfies these so-called "working requirements". The threat remains, however, if the licensee fails to work the license. Therefore, a best efforts clause should be inserted to require that the licensee use the license enough to prevent any compulsory licensing.
- **Indemnification Clause:** Indemnification clauses work both ways between the licensor and the licensee. The licensee generally wants to be indemnified for any liability stemming from the licensor's title or product warranties. Alternatively, the licensor wants to be indemnified for any misuse of the license by the licensee.

Example: The licensor shall indemnify the licensee and hold it harmless from any loss or liability arising out of any claims brought against the licensee by reason of the breach by the licensor of the warranties and representations stated within this License Agreement.

---

[430]The court in Shearing v. Iolab Corp., 712 F. Supp. 1446 (D. Nev. 1989) extended the implication of best efforts to "improvements.": "It is normal and customary in an exclusive licensing arrangement to imply an obligation of the licensee to use its reasonable best efforts with respect to improvements on the invention for which the licensee purchased rights." Ibid. at 1455.

> The licensee shall indemnify the licensor and hold it harmless from any loss or liability arising out of any claims brought against the licensor by reason of the licensee's breach of any provision of this License Agreement including any unauthorized use by the licensee, any improper use of trademarks, copyright, patent, design or process not specifically granted or approved by the licensor, any non-compliance by the licensee of federal or state laws or regulations, and for any defects attributable to the licensee's production of the Licensed Products.

In order for a disclaimer of warranty to be effective against end users, the licensor may have to obtain the signature of the end user. If that is the case, the licensor will want to insert language requiring the licensee to obtain customer signatures. It should be noted that where this is not possible (e.g., shrinkwrap license) the disclaimers or limitations of product liability may not be enforceable outside of the United States. A good technique, which should be coupled with the indemnification clause, is to require the licensee to obtain a product liability insurance policy.

> **Example:** The licensee agrees, at its own expense, to obtain a products liability insurance policy in the minimal amount of $_______________ per occurrence to the benefit of the licensee and the licensor with the licensor being named as an additional insured. The procurement and delivery of the insurance policy to the licensor shall be a material obligation of the license.

- **Quality Control:** Quality control is a key concern to most licensors when the license relates to the production of goods. The following is an abbreviated example of quality control language that the licensor may use.

> **Example:** The licensee agrees to strictly comply and maintain compliance with the quality standards, specifications, and rights of approval of the licensor in respect to any and all usage of the Licensed Property. Any modification of the Licensed Product must be submitted in advance for the licensor's written approval as if it were a new product. Approval or disapproval shall be in the licensor's sole discretion. Licensee shall permit the licensor, upon three days notice, to inspect the licensee's manufacturing operations, testing records, and inspection reports.

• **Warranties and Representations:**[431] Often licensing agreements will informally place warranties and representations in the preamble ("whereas clauses"). It is better to place such statements within the body ("operative clauses") of the agreement due to their importance to subsequent liability claims for negligence, misrepresentation, or breach of warranty. The licensor should insert language specifying that only express warranties are expressly enforceable. To further prevent the implication of warranties, the licensor should insert pertinent *negations.* An example of negation includes the statement that the license does not grant the licensee the rights to any subsequent know-how or to additional technical support or information. Another negation may preclude the licensee from using the licensor's trade name. The license should also detail the rights and duties of the respective parties in the event that a third party sues the licensee for infringement. The most licensee-friendly provision would be an express covenant requiring the licensor to defend and indemnify the licensee against such claims. The licensor, on the other hand, would prefer to exclude or limit its obligations regarding such infringement claims. One compromise solution would be to grant the licensee the right to indemnification but limiting the maximum amount of such indemnification. In *Hewlett-Packard Co. V. Bausch & Lomb Inc.,*[432] the court upheld such a cap on indemnification. Another compromise clause would be an agreement to share the costs of defending any third-party infringement claims.[433] If the license contains an arbitration clause, then either it or the warranty or infringement clause should state that the parties should submit to arbitration any disagreement on whether there is a third party infringement.

Example:
Licensor Warranties. The licensor warrants that it possesses the right to license the Licensed Products, including any patents, copyrights, or

[431]See, Brunsvold, *Negotiating Techniques for Warranty and Enforcement Clauses in International Licensing Agreements,* Vanderbilt Journal of Transnational Law 281 (1981).
[432]909 F.2d 1464 (Fed. Cir. 1990).
[433]See, e.g., Ortho Pharm. Corp. v. Genetics Institute, Inc., 52 F.3d 1026, *cert. Denied,* 116 S. Ct. 274 (1995).

trademarks, in accordance with the provisions of this License Agreement. The making of this License Agreement does not violate any agreements or rights of any other person, firm, or corporation.

This clause is sometimes referred to as an intellectual property indemnity. The problem with such clauses is that a licensor with a United States patent cannot be assured that this is enough to preclude an infringement claim under a foreign law. Therefore, the licensor should avoid any expansion of this warranty beyond the scope of United States patent rights. Also, the licensor may want to further limit its exposure by providing that it will have the option to pay a specified amount to the licensee and to terminate the license instead of defending the licensee against an infringement claim.

Licensee Warranties. The licensee warrants that it will not harm, misuse or bring in disrepute the Licensed Property. The licensee will manufacture, sell, and distribute the Licensed Products in accordance with the terms of this License Agreement, and in compliance with applicable government regulations and industry standards. It will not cause or allow any liens or encumbrances to be placed against the Licensed Property. It will provide the licensor with the dates and locations of the first and last use of the Licensed Property. It will not produce, sell, or deliver the Licensed Products outside the Territory provided in this License Agreement. Upon reasonable notice, the licensee shall permit the licensor to inspect testing records and procedures with respect to the production and sales of the Licensed Products for compliance with applicable quality standards provided in this License Agreement and for compliance with applicable, governmental, regulatory, industry, and certification standards.

- **Confidentiality:** A type of warranty given by the licensee, but included in a separate clause, is the promise to secure the confidentiality of all proprietary information given by the licensor.

Example: The licensee warrants that it will use its best efforts to maintain the confidential nature of all proprietary information and to prevent unauthorized access, reproduction, use, or disclosure of that information. It will restrict access to employees on a need to know basis. In furtherance of this obligation it shall: (a) maintain all copyright notice, trademark notice, and other proprietary markings, (b) not copy or reproduce the proprietary information except as authorized under this agreement, and (c) not disassemble, de-compile, or reverse engineer any of the information or products provided.

- **Copyright and Trademark Protection:** The licensee should be required to take all reasonable measures to protect the licensor's copyrights and trademarks. These measures include the affixation of appropriate marks and patent numbers[434] to the products being licensed and the notification of the Licensor of trademark or copyright infringements by third parties. The court in *Yarway Corp. v. Eur-Control USA, Inc.*[435] held that a licensor has a cause of action for damages resulting from the licensee's failure to mark goods as required under the License.

Example: The licensee shall cause to be imprinted on each Licensed Product sold under the License Agreement, and on all advertising, promotional, and packaging material, the proper copyright notices and trademarks as instructed by the licensor. The licensee shall promptly notify the licensor in writing of any infringements by others of the Licensed Property.

An ancillary issue is whether the licensor should be required to bring suit in order to prevent third-party infringement impacting the licensee's ability to fully work its license. Generally, there is no implied duty on the part of the licensor to protect the licensee in this manner.[436] Thus, the licensee will want to negotiate a clause requiring the licensor to sue third-party infringers. This is especially important because United States patent law authorizes infringement actions only by the patentee-licensor[437] or the assignee of an exclusive license.[438] The clause should also state the repercussions for the licensor failing to fulfill its obligations under the clause. For example, it may authorize the licensee: (1) to sue on behalf of the licensor and for the licensor to reimburse the licensee for the costs of the litigation, (2) it may require the licensor to waive any claims to damages recovered un-

[434]Failure to affix the patent numbers may prevent the licensor from collecting damages for past infringements. See, 35 U.S.C. § 287.

[435]775 F.2d 268 (Fed. Cir. 1985).

[436]See, e.g., Water Technologies Corp. v. Calco, Ltd., 576 F. Supp. 767 (N.D. Ill. 1983). U.S.C. § 261 authorizes such actions by "assignees, grantees, and successors."

[437]35 U.S.C. § 281.

[438]See, e.g., Rite-Hite Corp. v. Kelly, 56 F.3d 1538 (Fed. Cir. 1995).

der the licensee's suit or, (3) it may provide for the cessation of royalty payments. Finally, the clause should detail who is responsible for the cost of bringing such suits and who is entitled to any damages recovered. In international intellectual property transfers, where it is often unclear whether the licensor's intellectual property rights have or can be perfected in the foreign country, a provision requiring the licensee to assist the licensor in the perfection and protection of its property rights is recommended.

> **Example:** The licensee shall assist the licensor [at the licensor's expense] in the procurement, protection, and maintenance of the licensor's rights in the Licensed Property. The licensee agrees to cooperate with the licensor in connection with any claims or suits relating to infringements on the licensor's property rights.

- **Validity or No-Challenge Clause**: The licensor may want to insert a provision prohibiting the licensee from challenging the validity of its intellectual property rights. Such clauses are generally valid in the United States. However, these types of clauses may be invalid under some national laws[439] where they are considered illegal restrictive trade practices and are also often prohibited in the transfer of technology codes found in developing countries. It should be noted that a claim of invalidity of a patent or other intellectual property right must be proven by "clear and convincing evidence" under United States law.[440]
- **Assignability and Sublicensing:** The License Agreement should make clear the licensee's rights to assign or sublicense the rights being transferred by the licensor. The licensor will generally require that the license is non-assignable and cannot be sublicensed.

> **Example:** This License Agreement is personal to the licensee. The licensee shall not sublicense, franchise, assign or delegate to third parties any of the rights acquired hereunder. Neither this License Agreement nor any of the rights hereunder shall be sold, transferred or assigned by the licensee.

- **Non-Partnership Clause:** The purpose of inserting this type of clause is to make clear that the licensee is not acting as an agent or

[439]See, section titled "Host Country Restrictions" in Chapter 8.
[440]See, e.g., Shearing v. Iolab Corp., 712 F.Supp. 1446 (D. Nev. 1989); Bausch & Lomb, Inc. v. Barnes-Hind/Hydrocurve, 796 F.2d 443 (Fed. Cir. 1986).

partner of the licensor. This will hopefully prevent the licensor from being held vicariously liable for the actions of the licensee under agency law principles.

Example: The licensee is an independent company. Nothing in this agreement is intended to represent that the licensee is to act as an agent or partner of the licensor. The licensee is not granted any rights or authority, express or implied, to bind the licensor in any manner.

- **Termination:** The termination clause should provide the specific grounds upon which the licensor may unilaterally terminate the License Agreement. An ancillary issue is the effect of termination on existing sublicenses. The licensor should make clear that the termination of the license requires the termination by the licensee of any sublicenses.

Example: The licensor shall have the right to terminate this Agreement without prejudice to any rights which it may have upon the occurrence of any of the following events:

The licensee fails to deliver or maintain the required product liability insurance policy.

The licensee becomes delinquent on any payments due under this License Agreement.

The licensee fails to provide assess to the premises or access to the records required to be maintained under this License Agreement.

The licensee fails to comply with applicable laws, regulations, or industry standards.

The licensee makes any assignment for the benefit of creditors or files a petition under the bankruptcy or insolvency laws of any jurisdiction or where a receiver or trustee is appointed for its business.

The licensee does not commence in good faith to manufacture, distribute or sell the Licensed Products throughout the Licensed Territory.

The licensee undergoes a substantial change of management or control.

The licensee delivers or sells Licensed Products outside the Licensed Territory or knowingly sells Licensed Products to a third party who the licensee knows intends to or reasonably should suspect intends to sell or deliver[441] such Licensed Products outside the Licensed Territory.[442]

The licensee has made a material misrepresentation or failed to disclose a material fact.

The licensee breaches any other agreement in effect between the licensee and the licensor.

The licensee defaults on any of its other obligations required in this License Agreement.

Under some foreign laws the unilateral termination of a licensing agreement by the licensor may require the payment of an indemnity. It is advisable that the licensor attempt to objectify in the agreement the events that can trigger a termination. For example, the failure of the licensee to meet certain prescribed minimum sales quotas could result in an automatic termination of the licensee. It is important to have foreign legal counsel advise you of the validity of the termination clause under foreign termination law.

- **Liquidated Damages Clause:** One means of attempting to discourage the development of a gray market problem is an agreement on a pre-set amount of damages for gray market violations. This provision can provide a strict liability standard for determining such violations of the licensing agreement. The damages are to be paid if the licensor can prove that the goods produced under the license are found in the United States market. "Such a clause shifts the burden of enforcement to the distributor or licensee, who must then ensure that its customers do not sell in the gray market."[443] Of course, such

[441]The "reason to know" concept would place a requirement of "due diligence" upon the licensee to investigate the third party purchaser, especially in large volume sales.

[442]This provision is clearly aimed at preventing a *gray market* problem for the licensor. In larger cost products, it would also be prudent to place production caps on the number of units to be produced under the license and the maximum number of units that can be sold to any one purchaser. The overall cap could be determined by calculating an estimate of the amount of sales expected for the Licensed Territory based upon its demographics or based upon sales figures of similar territories.

[443]Lawrence M. Friedman, *Business and Legal Strategies for Combating Grey-Market Imports,* 32 The Int'l Lawyer 27, 50 (1998).

a liquidated damage clause would need to meet the standards of enforceability required under American law.[444]

- **Choice of Law Clause:** Given the unevenness of national intellectual property law protections, a United States licensor should require that United States intellectual property law is the law of any future dispute. However, if patents, copyrights, or trademarks have only been registered in another country, then it would be appropriate to authorize that any interpretation of those rights be determined under the law of the country in which they are registered. Also, a court in the licensee's country is unlikely to honor a choice of law that avoids the competition, intellectual property transfer, consumer protection, and termination laws of the host country. In many transactions involving technology transfer, the contract provides for the sale of both goods and services. Does the CISG apply to such contracts? Such transactions are called *mixed sales.* Article 3 provides that the CISG does not apply if the "preponderant part" of the contract consists of labor or other services. Also, if a "substantial part" of the materials used in the production of the goods are supplied by the buyer, then the transaction is not a sale of goods transaction that is covered by the CISG, but is a contract for labor or assembly.
- **Forum Selection Clause:** The most popular forum selection clause in international licensing agreements is the arbitration clause. For the specifics of drafting an adequate arbitration clause refer to Chapter 3. However, to enhance one's ability to obtain and enforce a foreign arbitral award, the place of arbitration should be in a country that has ratified the Convention on the Recognition and Enforcement of Foreign Arbitral Awards ("New York Convention") and where the courts do not have a reputation for interfering with arbitration proceedings.
- **Notice Provisions:** Foreign laws should be researched to determine the minimal period required to notify a party of a default or termi-

---

[444]See, e.g., Uniform Commercial Code § 2-718. The amount of damages set must: (1) be reasonable in light of the anticipated loss or be reasonable in light of the actual loss, and (2) the amount of loss is difficult to estimate at the time of contracting or is difficult to prove, and (3) a term fixing unreasonably large liquidated damages is void as a penalty." Ibid. at § 2-718 (1).

nation. Also, it is advisable to provide that notice may be given by fax or by private courier delivery.

If protection of intellectual property rights and trade secrets remains a concern after drafting a pro-licensor licensing agreement, the next option may be the negotiation of an ancillary *management contract.* A management contract coupled with a long-term licensing agreement "insures that the process subject to the license will be properly performed"[445] and properly protected. Other ancillary agreements to be considered would require the licensee to have its employees sign individual confidentiality agreements and any other third parties to sign non-disclosure agreements. The licensor may want to require that the licensee's employees' sign a form provided by the licensor which would include a promise to maintain all proprietary information in the strictest confidence, a description of what constitutes proprietary information, and a promise to return all such information upon termination of employment.

Foreign Registration and Approval

A considerable number of countries, mainly less developed and emerging countries, require some form of government input into the culmination of a transfer or licensing contract. This government regulation can generally be categorized into two types. First, the types of regulation that require a formal government approval before such agreements become valid. For example, it was noted earlier that Chinese regulations require submissions to numerous governmental agencies. Second, there are regulations that require the registration of the agreement with a government agency after its execution. The less onerous type of regulations relating to registration should not be discounted in importance. In some countries, such as Russia, failure to register the agreement may result in severe penalties, including the cancellation of the contract.

In those countries that require approval, the type of approval varies in scope and application. In some countries such approval is only required for

[445]WILLIAM F. FOX, JR., INTERNATIONAL COMMERCIAL AGREEMENTS: A PRIMER ON DRAFTING, NEGOTIATING AND RESOLVING DISPUTES 71 (2d ed. 1992).

certain types of technology transfers. When approval is required, the parties have to submit documentation that usually includes the draft agreement, financial statements, and proof of ownership of the technology. The provisions of the contract are generally reviewed with the view of protecting the national licensee. "Governmental bodies charged with reviewing technology transfer agreements often refer to statutory lists of objectionable business practices which must be excised from any agreement as a condition of approval."[446] The most troublesome clauses under approval schemes are those that provide a long duration for the license term, overly restrictive control by the licensor, one-sided grant back clauses, dispute resolution and choice of law clauses that remove any disputes from the law and jurisdiction of the host country's courts. It may be necessary to locate a foreign agent or a licensee with experience in obtaining such approvals.

Mandatory Legal Rules

It is important, in drafting a transfer agreement, to recognize the limits placed upon the parties under national legal regimes. For example, the granting of a right to sue third parties for patent infringement on a patent licensee is not sufficient under United States patent law. The licensor-patentee must be joined to any such infringement suit. The rationale for this rule was explained in *Western Electric Co. v. Pacent Reproducer Corp.*[447]

> In its simplest form, a license means only leave to do a thing which the licensor would otherwise have a right to prevent. Such a license grants to the licensee merely a privilege that protects him from a claim of infringement by the owner of the patent. . . . He has no property interest in the patent, nor any contract with the patent owner that others shall not practice the invention. Hence the patent owner may tolerate infringers, and in [such a] case no right of the patent licensee is violated. Practice of the invention by others may indeed cause him pecuniary loss, but it does him no legal injury.

[446] Alan S. Gutterman, *Regulation of Foreign Inbound Technology Transfers and Direct Investments,* 7 Int'l Quarterly 599, 600 (1995).

[447] 42 F.2d 116, 118 (2d Cir. 1930). See also, Ortho Pharmaceutical Corp. v. Genetics Institute, Inc., 52 F.3d 1026 (Fed. Cir. 1995).

The Supreme Court has long recognized that the patent owner is an indispensable party to an infringement suit.[448] The courts have also held that granting the licensee the right to sue for third party infringement does not imply any obligations on the part of the licensor to assist in such actions. "There is no implied agreement by a licensor to protect the licensee by suing . . . In the absence of a covenant to protect the licensee against infringers there is no obligation on the part of the licensor to do so."[449] However, courts have recognized the right of an exclusive licensee to join the licensor as an involuntary plaintiff to an infringement action.[450] In order to best protect its interests, the licensee will want to negotiate a clause either requiring the licensor to sue third-party infringers or to join the licensee in any such actions.

---

[448]Waterman v. Mackenzie, 138 U.S. 252 (1891).
[449]Water Technologies Corp. v. Calco Ltd., 576 F.Supp. 767, 772 (N.D.Ill. 1983). See also, Heidelberg Brewing Co. v North American Service Co., 26 F.Supp. 342 (E.D.Ky. 1939); Martin v. New Trinidad Lake Asphalt Co., 255 F. 93 (1919).
[450]Independent Wireless Telegraph Co. v. Radio Corporation of America, 269 U.S. 459 (1926).

CHAPTER 10

Joint Venture and Franchise Contracts

An international joint venture or franchising arrangement is attractive for a number of reasons.[451] First, it allows a party to utilize a partner's or franchisee's local expertise, marketing skills, and established lines of distribution. Second, it may provide a means to avoid the host country's protective trade requirements. Joint ventures are used to provide technology to a foreign partner who has production facilities and access to the local market. The joint venture and franchise mode of business are well suited for entry into a foreign market through the involvement of a national familiar with the local language, law, and culture. The theory behind franchising is that each franchise owner acts as an independent operation with the benefit of a central organization.

Due Diligence

Before entering into a joint venture or franchising contract with a foreign entity, it is important to thoroughly research the investment climate in the host country. One source of information is the Department of State's Country Commercial Guides. Individual Country Commercial Guides can be obtained at http://www.state.gov. The Guides provide a good introduc-

---

[451]See generally, KAREN J. HLADIK, INTERNATIONAL JOINT VENTURES (1985); Robert Radway, *Overview of Foreign Joint Ventures,* 38 Business Lawyer 1040 (1983); SUSAN GOLDENBERG, HANDS ACROSS THE OCEAN: MANAGING JOINT VENTURES WITH A SPOTLIGHT ON CHINA & JAPAN (1988)

tion to the nuances of doing business in a given country. General topics of coverage include: foreign representatives and agents, market research and trade events, franchising, joint ventures, licensing, opening a representative office, intellectual property rights infringement, conversion and transfer policies, expropriation and compensation, dispute settlement, political environment, countertrade policy, trade regulations and standards, labeling and marking requirements, customs, import and export controls, investment climate, transparency issues, trade financing options, business infrastructure, economic and trade statistics, and country contacts.

The Country Guide for Indonesia, for example, notes that franchising was becoming a popular vehicle for foreign entry until the devaluation of the rupiah. "The depreciation of the rupiah has made virtually impossible the payment of franchise royalties in foreign exchange." Aside from the convertibility issue, Indonesia places no major restrictions on the repatriation of profits. Indonesia maintains no capital controls and foreign exchange may flow freely in and out of the country. No prior permits are necessary to transfer foreign exchange. Foreign investors have the right to repatriate capital and profits at the prevailing rate of exchange. The Commercial Guide summarizes the law pertaining to franchising as follows:

> Although there is no specific law regulating franchising, the legal underpinnings for franchising are specified in article 1338 of the Indonesian Civil law (KUH Perdata - Kitab Undang Undang Hukum Perdata) which states that business persons are free to conclude contracts. Further legal grounding for franchising can be found in the 1992 law on trademarks No. 19, article 44-50.
>
> There are no widely accepted models for business contracts covering franchise agreements. However, the foreign principal usually provides the franchisee with his own standard contract format which is used as a basis for developing franchise agreements with the local business enterprise. The franchise agreement should be reviewed and notarized by a public notary in Indonesia in order to make it legally binding.
>
> Franchise agreements should be accompanied by other contractually binding arrangements such as loan agreements, site leases, building agreements, graphics, employee selection, standard description and promotion. Franchise agreements should also include a provision regarding the settlement of disputes through arbitration which may arise out of breach of contract or disagreements between the contracting parties.

Indonesian law, thus, does not prescribe any specific form or registration requirements for franchise agreements. Therefore, the foreign franchisor is free to use its standard forms. The agreement must be reviewed and notarized in Indonesia to become legally binding. The Guide notes that *joint venturing* with an established Indonesian company is the preferred way of market entry. This means of market entry has been enhanced by recent developments. First, in 1994 the Indonesian government removed most local participation requirements. Second, there are a number of firms that will provide background and credit checks on Indonesian firms. Third, the Indonesian' company can provide the necessary knowledge and contacts with the local market. One drawback to establishing an Indonesian franchise relationship is the difficulty of dissolving a joint venture or franchise partnership under Indonesian law. Therefore, careful background research, prior dealings, and a clear, comprehensive agreement is necessary.

Other sections of interest for those contemplating franchising, licensing, or joint venturing in Indonesia include the protection of intellectual property rights, the use of a local attorney, conversion, transfer, and expropriation and dispute settlement polices.[452] Generally, intellectual property protection is wanting in Indonesia. "One United States' company first identifies counterfeiters and then proceeds to sign them as legal licensees of its products." Nonetheless, its is important to register your intellectual property as soon as possible and to challenge any unauthorized registrations. Once again, the Guide suggests the acquiring of a local partner as the best way to defend against the infringement of intellectual property rights. In the area of dispute resolution, Indonesia is a party to the New York Convention on the enforcement of arbitration. However, the record for the enforcement of foreign arbitration awards is dismal. Therefore, the Guide

[452]"Because Indonesia's legal system is currently being overhauled and modernized, firms are strongly advised to locate and retain a local attorney early in the investment process. In the event of a commercial dispute, one should first attempt to reach consensus through negotiation, using a mediator acceptable to both parties if necessary. If deliberation fails to achieve consensus, then companies may enter into arbitration. To prepare for this eventuality, an arbitration clause should be included in any commercial contract with Indonesia chosen as the site of arbitration. This is recommended because foreign arbitral awards have proven difficult to enforce locally. Badan Arbitrase Nasional Indonesia (BANI) is the local arbitration board and companies may employ BANI or select their own arbitration vehicle and procedures (i.e. ICC or UNCITRAL)." Department of State, Country Commercial Guide for Indonesia (1999).

suggests an arbitration clause that designates Indonesia as the place of arbitration. The conversion, transfer, and expropriation polices of the government are conducive to foreign entry. Indonesia maintains no capital controls and no permits are required to transfer foreign exchange. Foreign investors have the right to repatriate capital and profits. The 1967 Foreign Capital Investment Law stipulates that nationalization will only occur when necessary in the interest of the state.

The Commercial Guide also provides general information for a foreign company seeking to enter the Indonesian market whether by exporting, establishing an office, or entering a joint venture, franchising, or licensing relationship. Although it does not provide in-depth answers to questions, it raises key issues that the foreign entity will need to fully research. For example, only Indonesians or Indonesian companies may act as *agents* for a foreign exporter. However, foreign principals are allowed to exert substantial control over their agents through *management agreements.* These management agreements do not establish the foreign entity for purposes of tax liability. The tax liability of the foreign company is restricted to the income of any expatriates assigned to the representative office. The Guide advises that the management agreement be as comprehensive as possible and clearly formulate the remuneration to be paid to the agent. The foreign entity may elect to establish its own *representative office.* This still entails appointment of an Indonesian' company or citizen to act as a representative. A business permit is required which usually entails considerable filings with a number of government agencies. For example, the foreign company must register as a legal entity with the Indonesian government. Also, the activities of a representative office are limited to signing sales contracts, collecting payments, and other general business activities.

Defining Joint Venture[453]

A simple definition of joint venture is "a contract that creates a partnership for the purpose of performing some kind of business opera-

---

[453]The term joint venture is not legally defined in numerous foreign legal systems. One important exception is the European Union which has adopted rules for joint ventures. Therefore, there is often no foreign joint venture law. It is important to research foreign

tion."[454] However, a joint venture is an elastic vehicle for doing business and can take numerous forms. For example, the parties can enter into an agreement to work together in order to achieve certain business goals as joint venturers or they can agree to create an entirely separate entity, such as a corporation, in order to transact business. The following definitions[455] describe two of the common uses of the joint venture vehicle for conducting international business: (1) Single "Project" Joint Venture: A number of parties or companies agree to enter into a partnership in order to develop specific business opportunities with a single, identifiable goal. These single "project" joint ventures generally have a relatively short life span. (2) Business Alliance Joint Venture: This type of joint venture envisions a more fluid, long-term business relationship. A major limitation on selecting the joint venture form of doing business is that it is not recognized in many foreign countries. Under American law, they are generally viewed as a general partnership. The core issues in the partnership agreement include the scope of the business enterprise, the capitalization of the venture, the organization and management of the venture, and the termination of the business.

A major concern in most joint venture agreements is providing the mechanisms for decision-making. The most obvious risk in joint venturing is the uncertainty and unpredictability of developing a new business or project. The joint venturers may disagree on how best to deal with post-formation events, especially those that were not foreseeable. It is important, especially in the long-term joint venture agreement, to provide a mechanism to prevent decisional deadlock.

Key Joint Venture Negotiation Issues

In negotiating and structuring joint ventures, proper attention should be given to the issues of share allocation, financing the enterprise, protect-

---

law to familiarize oneself with the forms of doing business recognized under the national law that can be utilized to approximate the joint vehicle concept.

[454]WILLIAM F. FOX, JR., INTERNATIONAL COMMERCIAL AGREEMENTS: A PRIMER ON DRAFTING , NEGOTIATING AND RESOLVING DISPUTES 79 (1992).

[455]See, Mark Pery-Knox-Gore, *Joint Ventures* in STRUCTURING INTERNATIONAL CONTRACTS 87 (ed. Dennis Campbell 1997).

ing minority interests, confidentiality, and the transfer and continuation of the business.[456]

Allocation of Shares: Shares may be allocated based upon each party's contribution. A problem arises in the valuation of non-monetary contributions. A joint venture may authorize different classes or types of shares in order to attract other investors such as venture capitalists. "In Ireland, a common capital structure would include two classes with each class of shares carrying the right to appoint a certain number of directors."[457]

Funding the Joint Venture: Funding decisions have a direct impact on the location of profits for tax purposes.[458] The equity or loan funding determination should give full consideration to all accounting and tax ramifications. For example, one would like to avoid the European Union's 1 percent duty on company capital. A key issue for a successful joint venture agreement is to provide the means to make future funding decisions. The most likely cause of joint venture failures is the parties' disagreement regarding future capital infusions. If external funding is sought, an agreement is needed as to whether the joint venture partners will provide guarantees in order to procure the external financing. The parties should agree whether to provide formal guarantees or more informal comfort letters.[459] Also, the joint venture agreement should have a "counter-indemnity clause" in which the joint venture partners agree to be responsible on multiple party guarantees only to the proportion of their shareholdings.

The joint venturers need to establish the initial level of capitalization. This should include the amount and form of currency to be invested by each partner and a method for adjusting foreign currency differences. If non-currency contributions are contemplated, then a valuation method should be specified. Also, the parties should expressly agree to the adoption

---

[456]See generally, Hooton, *Structuring and Negotiating Joint Ventures,* 27 Creighton Law Rev. 1013 (1994).

[457]Ibid at 88.

[458]See, Dolan, *Special Issues in Structuring International Joint Ventures,* 22 Tax Management Int'l Journal 51 (1993).

[459]For a fuller analysis of the use of comfort instruments or letters in international business transactions see, Larry A. DiMatteo, *The CISG and the Presumption of Enforceability: Unintended Contractual Liability in International Business Dealings,* 22 Yale Journal of International Law 111 (1997). See also, Larry A. DiMatteo, and René Sacasas, *Credit and Value Comfort Instruments: Crossing the Line from Assurance to Legally Significant Reliance and Toward a Theory of Enforceability,* 47 Baylor Law Rev. 357 (1995).

of accounting standards such as United States or European Union accounting standards and practices. The agreement should also specify the level and type of indebtedness the venture is authorized to undertake. Establishing an acceptable debt to equity ratio for the venture would be prudent.

Super-Majority Vote Provision: If the joint venture is between numerous parties, then provisions in the joint venture agreement to protect minority interests may be necessary. One way to protect minority interests is to categorize decisions as "ordinary" or "extraordinary." *Extraordinary decisions* would then require a super-majority vote to pass. For example, a two-thirds or 75 percent vote would be required to approve extraordinary decisions. Extraordinary decisions could include: capital expenditures in excess of a certain amount, borrowings in excess of a certain amount, increasing of share capital, issuing of new stock or admitting a new joint venture partner, the giving of guarantees, appointment or removal of directors, the setting of employee remuneration above a certain level, any material change in the business operation or nature of the business, sale or transfer of assets, making contracts with principals of the joint venture, and approval of budgets.[460]

Confidentiality and Non-Competition Provisions: Joint venture agreements should have strict *confidentiality* and *non-competition* provisions. The joint venture partners may be prohibited from competing with the joint venture including, not hiring employees of the joint venture for a period of time, maintaining the secrecy of all confidential information, and not soliciting customers of the joint venture. Of course, these restrictions have to be reasonable or may be subject to challenge as illegal restraints of trade under United States common law or the European Union's Competition Law pertaining to ancillary restrictions.

Continuation and Transfer of Ownership Provision: In case of a deadlock regarding an important decision, a party may be afforded the right to leave the joint venture. A provision should provide for a transfer or sale of ownership to the other joint venture partners interested in continuing the joint venture. The sale of shares should be at a fair price, to be determined possibly by an independent accounting firm, to all remaining joint venture partners in proportion to their existing ownership shares. The agreement should also provide whether, in the event of termination, the joint venture

[460]This list of extrordinary events was gleaned from Pery-Knox-Gore at 94.

partners have the right to continue in the same business after the termination.

Salbu and Brahm[461] have made a number of valuable suggestions for those considering a joint venture contract. They assert that the "purposes clause" is a crucial clause for maintaining the long-term viability of the joint venture arrangement. The *purposes clause* should map out the scope and goals of the business enterprise. This scope should be defined along three parameters: geographic scope, products and services, and duration. A careful balance needs to be struck between a clause that is precise, but restricts future expansion, and one that allows "the venture to develop in unforeseeable directions."[462] The drafter should use contractual language that establishes a "venture purpose that is sufficiently fluid and non-specific to avoid any undesirable, inadvertent termination." This can be accomplished by a *specific purposes clause* coupled with an *exceptions clause* that allows for adjustments by the parties to the purposes clause along prescribed parameters. An alternative provision would allow for a periodic review of the purposes clauses with a re-negotiation requirement.

The next crucial set of provisions needed for the ongoing viability of the venture is the management provisions. Salbu and Brahm note the pervasive problem of *double parenting* in which both joint venturers attempt to assert independent control over the joint venture. The degree of managerial control to be placed with the different joint venturers needs to be carefully delineated in the agreement. "Will the venture be a 50/50 collaboration, or will one parent own a greater share? Will the owner of the greater share have greater managerial control? Or, will a desirable minority partner be allowed a degree of contractual control greatly exceeding its proportional ownership?"[463] Other issues that will need to be dealt with by the management clauses[464] include: (1) Should a veto power be given to the partners, including minority partners, for particular classes of important decisions?, (2) How will the selection of the top manager and management team be decided?, (3) What reporting and information systems will be used to communicate between the joint venture and its owners? Salbu and Brahm suggest the best solution will be for "the parents to work up front with the

---

[461]Steven R. Salbu & Richard A. Brahm, *Strategic Considerations in Designing Joint Venture Contracts,* 1992 Columbia Business Law Review 253 (1992).
[462]Ibid. at 259.
[463]Ibid. at 291.
[464]The following material was taken from Salbu & Brahm at 292-294.

venture management team to design a simplified reporting and information system compatible with the common requirements of both parents." Ultimately, these provisions will reflect the essential nature of the joint venture as either one being controlled by a dominate parent or as one in which a shared management structure is envisioned.

The joint venture should have a detailed termination provision stating the events that allow the parties to terminate their involvement. The following list provides the types of considerations that should be discussed in drafting a termination clause.[465]

- Failure of a participant to make required capital contributions,
- Failure of a participant to obtain necessary government approvals,
- Failure of the venture to reach a pre-agreed level of profitability,
- Defined management deadlock,
- Failure of one participant to purchase the shares of another under a buy-sell agreement,
- Occurrence of a *force majeure* event,
- An adverse and debilitating change in the law,
- Bankruptcy or insolvency of one of the participants,
- Mutual consent of a majority of participants.

Ancillary Agreements and Documentation

The joint venture agreement is likely to be one of only a number of documents that need to be drafted or prepared for any well-planned joint venture undertaking. Other documentation commonly used include a formal business plan, distribution agreement, intellectual property transfer or licensing agreement, management agreement, service contracts, and secondment agreements. A carefully written *business plan* is vital to maintaining cordial relationships among the joint venture partners. It should be sufficiently long-term in nature, set realistic revenue and profit goals, and provide for a "cushion" in capital and time in meeting the plan's objectives. The business plan should include other necessary studies such as a long-term strategic plan and a marketing plan. *Secondment agreements* are used to require the "lending" of employees of the joint venture partners to the

[465]Taken from William G. Frenkel, *Legal Protection against Risks Involved in Doing Business in the Republics of the Former U.S.S.R.*, 10 International Quarterly 395, 467 (1998).

joint venture. It is important to determine whether these employees are to be treated as independent contractors or employees of the joint venture. From the point of view of the joint venture, treatment as independent contractors is preferred. The joint venture partner would then remain primarily obligated to the employees being lent. *Service contracts* between the partners and their joint venture could also be utilized in the management of the joint venture enterprise. At times, one of the joint venture partners is given the responsibility to manage the joint venture. In this case, the managing partner should enter into a formal *management agreement* with the joint venture. The management agreement, among other things, should provide for an allocation of costs between the partner's core business and the management of the joint venture business. Often one of the contributions of a joint venture partner is its expertise in its home country regarding the distribution of goods or services. A formal *distribution agreement* should be entered into between that partner and the joint venture. The distribution agreement's termination provisions should be tied to those in the joint venture agreement. This may be important in the event that the distributor is removed as a joint venture partner. International joint ventures may include the use of one of the joint venture partner's know-how or intellectual property rights. In such a situation, an independently negotiated *intellectual property transfer* or licensing agreement will be necessary. It should deal with the issue of the withdrawal of the licensor-partner. In that case it may require a name change of the joint venture if the existing name is associated with the intellectual property of the withdrawing partner. Pery-Knox-Gore recommends a provision that makes the licensing of intellectual property rights "coterminous with the licensor's involvement in the joint venture."[466]

Foreign Government Regulation

Foreign governments commonly regulate joint venture transactions. The most common restrictions are foreign participation requirements in which control of the enterprise must vest in a local company. More unique types of government regulations can be found on a country by country basis. For example, The People's Republic of China enacted *Regulations on Labor Management in Joint Ventures Using Chinese and Foreign Investment.* It

[466]Pery-Knox-Gore at 99.

requires that a labor contract be entered into between the joint venture and a trade union. The labor contract must be approved by the government. It further provides that all workers of the joint venture "shall be selected for employment through examinations conducted by the joint venture." The joint venture's ability to discharge employees is also restricted. "Punishment by discharge must be reported to the department in charge of enterprises and the labor management department for approval."

China's more generic law on joint ventures, the *Law of the People's Republic of China on Chinese-Foreign Cooperative Joint Ventures*, was promulgated on April 13, 1988. It should be carefully reviewed before beginning any negotiations. It provides that the parties should agree in a *cooperative venture contract* on the terms and conditions of cooperation, the distributions of earnings or products, the sharing of risks and losses, the form of operation and management, and the ownership of property (Article 2). All such contracts need to be approved by the relevant "Examination and Approval Authority." The process for the approval and establishment of a joint venture are outlined in Exhibit 10.1.

The above discussion demonstrates that governmental regulation is pervasive in the establishment and operation of a joint venture in China. The cooperative joint venture law however, is merely a framework or enabling statute. Detailed regulations will need to be consulted before establishing a joint venture. Also, ancillary laws must be reviewed in conjunction with the operation of the joint venture. Article 13 states that "matters such as the employment, discharge, remuneration, welfare, labor protection and labor insurance of staff and workers should be stipulated through the making of contracts in accordance with the law." This was previously noted in the discussion of the *Regulations on Labor Management.* In contemplating a joint venture in China it is good practice to obtain copies of form contracts (available in English) used by Chinese enterprises and to consult with Chinese Ministry of Foreign and Economic Relations and Trade (MOFERT) which was created in 1982 to expedite foreign trade contracts.

The State Department's Country Commercial Guide for Indonesia summarizes the practice and law of joint venturing in that country.

Exhibit 10.1
Approval and Establishment of Joint Venture

Step 1

Signing of Cooperative Joint Venture Contract

Step 2

Submission of Joint Venture Contract and Articles of Association to the "Examination and Approval Authority" (as designated by the State Council)
[Approval Authority must render a decision within forty-five days]
[Article 5]

Step 3

Application for Registration (to appropriate industry & commerce agency)
[Within thirty days of receipt of approval certificate from Approval Authority]
[Article 6]

Step 4

Receipt of Business License
(date of establishment)

Step 5

Register Venture with appropriate tax authority
[Article 6]

Post-Establishment Concerns

Any changes in the joint venture contract must be submitted to the Approval Authority.
[Article 7]

Any transfers or rights and obligations under the cooperative joint venture contract must be approved by the Approval Authority.
[Article 10]

Any changes in the management and operation of the joint venture (to a party not an original partner) must be by unanimous vote of the board of directors and with the approval of the Approval Authority.
[Article 12]

Record-keeping and certifications must be verified by an accountant registered in China.
[Article 9]

The joint venture must establish and support a labor union to represent its employees.
[Article 14]

Open a foreign exchange account.
[Article 16]

Joint Ventures/Licensing

Since 1994 the government has removed most requirements for domestic equity and joint ventures. Foreign investors who opt for 100 percent initial ownership are obligated to divest to Indonesians some share — as little as one percent — after 15 years. This can be accomplished through the stock market. This requirement is too new to have been tested yet.

As a practical matter a local joint venture partner is often essential for success in this market, for the same reason that an Indonesian agent or distributor has advantages over a foreign trade representative office. The choice of an Indonesian joint venture partner is critical for many reasons, especially for knowledge of the local scene and contacts, which are important for successful operations in Indonesia. A few experienced firms provide background, credit-type reports on Indonesian entrepreneurs and firms.

A partnership in Indonesia is difficult to dissolve. Consequently, the first choice has to be the correct choice. Business sense is as crucial to any commercial endeavor and contacts in Indonesia as anywhere else; "contacts" alone, while important in Indonesia, can not substitute for business skills in an Indonesian partner.

Because Indonesians place great importance on personal relationships and mutual understanding, partnerships tend to be based primarily on genuine accord, with the written contract playing a less significant role. It is therefore important that any agreement be well understood by both sides. A contract over which there are conflicting interpretations is certain to cause future problems.

Franchising

The advantage of franchising is aptly stated as its method for facilitating "the transfer of know-how and managerial expertise to the franchisee companies while simultaneously allowing the franchisor to quickly establish a presence in the country. Under a typical franchising agreement, the franchisor receives royalties and fees as stipulated in the contract. In exchange, the franchisee has the right to use (and manufacture) copyrighted, patented or service-marked materials identifying the enterprise. The franchisor typically provides training and organizational guidance in return for a guarantee that the franchisee will follow these operational directions."[467] The fact that the franchise usually consists of a bundle of intellectual property rights relating to trademarks, copyrights, know-how, designs, and patents requires careful attention in the franchise agreement. The same considerations involved in the licensing of each of those rights are present in the franchise arrangement. The franchisor will want to protect its intellectual property by placing restrictions on the franchisee on its use of those rights.

United States Franchise Law and the Franchise Agreement

Even more so than the joint venture, the franchise relationship is not a legally recognized way of doing business in some countries. It is a uniquely American creation. "Over half a million franchises operate in the United States, and they account for more than a third of the nation's total retail sales."[468] The United States has developed an extensive body of law regulating the franchise relationship.[469] A large number of states regulate the offer and sale of franchises. A number of state laws require franchisors to register a detailed offering before being able to solicit franchisees.[470] Other statutes provide the franchisee a right to cure and a minimum notice period prior to termination.

The popularity of franchising in the United States, along with increased governmental regulation, has produced a number of franchise clauses that are commonly used and recognized in the franchise industry. Professor Emerson surveyed retail and fast food franchise agreements and found the following seven commonly used clauses that place a fiduciary obligation upon the franchisor in their application. A *site selection clause*

---

[467]Department of State, Country Commercial Guide for Indonesia (1999).

[468]Robert W. Emerson, *Franchise Contract Clauses and the Franchisor's Duty of Care Toward its Franchisees*, 72 No. Carolina Law Rev. 905, 909 (1994) (hereinafter *Franchise Contract Clauses*).

[469]See, e.g., Robert W. Emerson, *Franchise Contract Clauses*; Robert W. Emerson, *Franchising Covenants Against Competition*, 80 Iowa Law Rev. 1049 (1995); Robert W. Emerson, *Franchisors' Liability When Franchisees are Apparent Agents: An Empirical and Policy Analysis of 'Common Knowledge' About Franchising*, 20 Hofstra Law Rev. 609 (1992).

[470]Emerson, *Franchise Contract Clauses* at 911.

should clearly delineate the franchisor's responsibilities in the site selection process. Such clauses range from placing an affirmative duty on the franchisor to find an appropriate site to simply requiring the franchisor's approval. An approval clause should state the criteria for the franchisor's disapproval of a site. In *Brennan v. Carvel Corp.*[471] the court went outside the boundaries of the franchise site selection clause in finding that the franchisor had failed to meet its obligations in the site selection process. It looked to the language of the franchisor's promotional materials, Application and Deposit Agreement, and the state required Uniform Franchise Offering Circular (UFOC). The Deposit Agreement stated that the franchisor would expend a "substantial amount of time and effort in seeking, surveying, and showing locations available for a store." The UFOC stated that the franchisor would "assume responsibility for selecting, obtaining and negotiating a suitable location for the store." This case illustrates the importance in reviewing all franchise documentation for consistency. A merger clause in the final franchise agreement is unlikely to prevent courts from reviewing preliminary agreements, ancillary agreements, promotional materials, and governmental filings for purposes of clarification or to substantiate a claim of misrepresentation. This is even more likely to be the case internationally where the parol evidence rule is not uniformly recognized.

Physical layout and signage, along with operational standards, are important areas of control for the franchisor. "Package" and "Layout" clauses, and their enforcement, are essential to maintain system-wide integrity and uniformity of standards. Most retail franchises provide for a "package" of "systematized layouts."[472] Such layouts are generally utilized to maintain the uniformity of appearance of all franchise locations. "This design or display *package* may be in conjunction with the trademarks and service marks provided by the franchisor or as part of the advertising controls."[473] Failure of the franchisee to adhere to these and other operational standards generally provides the franchisor with good cause for termination of the franchise operation. Most layout clauses give the franchisor the absolute right of approval. An operational standards clause should provide a detailed description of quality standards and operational goals. The clause generally refers to an operating manual provided by the franchisor. It normally gives the

[471]929 F.2d 801 (S.D.Fla. 1992), as discussed, Emerson at 937.

[472]Ibid. at 938.

[473]Ibid. at 938, n. 143.

franchisor the unilateral right to revise the manual in order to maintain system wide quality controls. In order to defend its decision to terminate, the franchise agreement should have a clear notice provision and provide for a reasonable period of time to cure the deficiencies. An associated concern is the training of the franchisee and its employees. The heart of many franchise arrangements is the training and consultation provided by the franchisor. The training programs should be described in detail. The nature of the consulting often requires a more flexible consultation clause. "Training typically involves a well-defined program for new franchisees and their key employees, with almost all of the activity in the early stages of a franchise. Consultation, on the other hand, may occur at any point during the franchise, and it is more likely to involve problems peculiar to a particular franchise than the more generalized training programs." Clearly, a franchisor's failure to provide adequate training and consultation under these clauses would be grounds for a lawsuit by the franchisee.

Other areas where the expertise of the franchisor is reflected in the franchise contract include the opening and financing of the franchise, along with the means and content of advertisement. Contractual clauses pertaining to the franchisor's assistance in the obtaining of financing and opening the franchise should state specific obligations. In the area of advertisement, the clause should state the franchisor's control over the content and placement of advertisements. Also, it may mandate a minimum level of franchisee expenditures on advertisements. It should also state any advertisement obligations of the franchisor. Some franchise agreements provide for a pooling of funds contributed by franchisees that the franchisor then uses to place the advertisements. The franchisee would want language in the agreement detailing how advertisement monies are to be spent by the franchisor. For example, the franchisee may want a clause allocating advertisement monies between a national or international campaign and local advertisement.

Most franchise systems are premised upon a uniformity of treatment between the franchisor and all its franchisees. However, franchisors sometimes incorporate a clause in their franchise agreements that allow them to vary contractual terms among their different franchisees. Company attorneys should carefully review these clauses. Such clauses have been grounds for claims of discriminatory treatment.[474] Other common clauses include

---

[474]Ibid. at 941.

those on territorial exclusivity and protection, non-competition, transfers and assignments, terminations and non-renewals, and those pertaining to pricing, purchase of supplies, hours of operation, franchisor's rights of inspection and audits. Many territorial clauses grant the franchise an exclusive territory for which the franchisor is barred from competing with the franchisee. The problem with such clauses is that the franchisor and franchisee may disagree regarding the scope of expansion of franchise operations within the territory. An alternative would be to give the franchisee a period of time to fully develop the franchise territory. After the expiration of that time, the franchisor would then be allowed to further develop the territorial market. The franchisee would be somewhat protected by being granted a right of first refusal for any new locations within its territory.

A number of clauses should be incorporated into the franchise agreement to deal with any fundamental changes in the franchise relationships. These clauses should deal with the transfer, assignment, and termination of franchise rights. The rights of both the franchisor and the franchisee to transfer or assign their rights should be clearly stated. Sometimes these provisions provide for a right of first refusal. Also, the transfer provisions should delineate among the different types and purposes of transfer. A transfer by inheritance or change of the corporate entity by merger, acquisition or otherwise, and an outright sale of the franchise may be treated differently.

The termination of the franchise by the franchisor, either for cause or non-renewal, is the most likely action to lead to litigation. Thus, drafters of franchise agreements should be especially diligent in the writing of termination clauses. Most franchise agreements contain a clause that allows the franchisor to terminate for any violation. The problem with such a clause is that termination for a minor breach will not be viewed favorably by most courts. Likewise, the renewal clause often provides an absolute right of the franchisor not to renew. Instead of such absolute rights to terminate or not to renew, such clauses should specify the violations that are to be considered material for termination and the grounds for non-renewal. Emerson lists the loss of a lease, failure to operate the business, franchisee insolvency, denial of franchisor access to inspect, and requested violations of quality standards[475] as appropriate grounds for termination or non-renewal. Internationally, termination without good cause or without a reasonable period

[475]See, e.g., Dayan V. McDonald's Corp., 466 N.E.2d 958 (Ill. 1984).

to correct will be vulnerable to legal challenge. In the United States, a number of state statutes require good cause for the termination of franchises.[476]

It is important for the franchisor to provide for post-termination protection of its trade secrets and intellectual property rights. This is generally done through the incorporation of a non-competition clause. Such a clause is especially vulnerable to non-enforcement as an unfair restraint of trade. It is also important for the drafter to delineate a legitimate business interest for which the restriction is needed. It should also state specific duration and geographic parameters in order to provide for a defense of unreasonableness.

Other provisions deal with the mechanics of the franchise relationship. Foremost is the remuneration of the franchisor. The franchise agreement commonly provides that an initial fee be paid for the right to obtain a franchise and then for payment of royalties based upon a percentage of gross or net sales. The agreement is generally for a fixed, as compared to an indefinite time period. It should provide for a commencement and expiration date. One common means of fixing the commencement and expiration dates is to provide for expiration following a certain number of years from commencement, that being the date the franchise opens for business.[477] Since most franchise arrangements include the transfer of intellectual property rights, the agreement should expressly retain the title to those rights to the franchisor. The following is an example of a franchise clause dealing with the transfer of trade secrets and intellectual property:

> FRANCHISEE acknowledges that ownership of all right, title and interest to the ABC franchise system and its marks are and shall remain vested solely in the franchisor, and the FRANCHISEE disclaims any right or interest therein or the goodwill derived therefrom. FRANCHISEE agrees that all materials loaned or otherwise made available to him by the franchisor at any time before or during the term of this Agreement relating to the franchise system, including, without limitation, the Manual in its entirety, financial information, marketing strategy and programs are to be considered trade secrets of the franchisor and shall be kept confidential and used by FRANCHISEE only in connection with the franchise operation. FRANCHISEE agrees not to divulge any of the trade secrets

---

[476]See, Robert W. Emerson, *Franchising and the Collective Rights of Franchisees,* 43 Vanderbilt Law Rev. 1503, 1511, n. 27 (1990).

[477]Emerson, *Franchise Contract Clauses* at 956, n. 262.

> to any person other than its employees and then only to the extent necessary for the operation of the franchise and, specifically, that FRANCHISEE will not, nor permit anyone to, reproduce, copy or exhibit any portion of the Manual or any other trade secrets of the franchisor. FRANCHISEE shall immediately notify franchisor of all infringements or limitations of franchisor's marks which come to its attention.[478]

"In essence, these clauses remind the franchisee that the franchisor owns the intellectual property being licensed, that this property's use is restricted to purposes related to the maintenance of the franchised business, and that — on the franchise's termination — all of the property rights remain with the franchsior."[479]

The final two clauses to be discussed are the insurance and the franchisee review clauses. It is prudent for the franchisor, especially in the international setting, to require the franchisee to maintain certain types and amounts of insurance. The contract should provide that the franchisor should be an "additional endorsee" on all such policies. Emerson provides the following example:

> FRANCHISEE agrees to carry at its expense throughout the term of this Agreement comprehensive general liability insurance, including products liability and broad form contractual liability, in an amount of not less than ____________ USD per occurrence for property damage, or in such increased amounts as the franchisor may reasonably request from time to time. Each policy shall name the franchisor as additional insureds and will provide that the policy cannot be canceled without thirty days prior written notice to the franchisor. Prior to the Commencement Date, FRANCHISEE shall furnish to the franchisor a Certificate of Insurance reflecting that the above insurance coverage is in effect.

The insurance clause should be coupled with a hold harmless clause that requires the franchisee to defend the franchisor against any liability claims arising from or related to its operation of the franchise.

The final clause to be discussed is the franchisee review clause. These clauses are used to combat future claims of misrepresentation or overbearing by the franchisor. They generally incorporate a number of provisos including "a statement that the franchisee has received no guarantees,

---

[478]Ibid. at 958, n. 268.
[479]Ibid. at 957-958.

representations, warranties or the like as to the profitability of the franchise being purchased and that the franchise has conducted its own independent investigation of the merits of the investment."[480] Other clauses vital to the franchisor's defense are the merger and independent contractor clauses discussed previously. The merger clause attempts to prevent the entry of any parol evidence in a subsequent adversarial proceeding.[481] The independent contractor clause attempts to preclude a finding of an employment or agency relationship between the franchisor and franchise.[482]

International Franchising

The principles recognized under American franchise law do not always translate well into other legal systems.[483] For example, the State Department's Country Commercial Guide for Russia downplays the use of franchising as a viable option in entering the Russian market. "Franchising is little understood in Russia. Several early attempts to establish franchise distribution have floundered, due to confusion regarding ownership and the responsibilities of the parties to a franchise agreement." However, the Guide qualifies the previous statement by noting that "some have been quite successful, and the potential remains quite high." Two crucial issues in the franchise relationship are termination and the use of trade secrets. The court in *McAlpine v. AAMCO Automatic Transmission, Inc.* described the synergy of franchising and the inherent seeds for its own destruction:

> The franchise arrangement starts as a mutually advantageous business relationship. Both the franchiser and the franchisee contribute to this arrangement in order to obtain benefits they could not obtain independently. The franchiser's contribution is a combination of factors: trademark, recognized product or service, experience, advertising, and management support. The franchisee's contribution is capital, day-to-day management and the payment of franchise fees. The franchiser benefits from the use of franchisee capital, fees, and lower-level manage-

---

[480]Ibid. at 959.

[481]See, Chapters 6 & 7.

[482]See, Chapter 8.

[483]See generally, Avner, *Franchising in Eastern Europe and the Soviet Union,* 3 DePaul Business Law J. 307 (1991).

> ment, for it allows the franchise organization to expand more rapidly. As the franchise becomes successful, the partnership arrangement which seemed reasonable at its inception begins to appear burdensome to the franchisee who comes to regard the payment of franchise fees as restricting its profitability.[484]

Thus, it is important for the franchise agreement to provide the appropriate means of termination and the protection of the franchisor's trade secrets. Trade secrets is a much broader concept than merely statutorily protected intellectual property rights (patent, copyright, trademark). The problem is that there is no generally accepted definition of trade secrets. The Uniform Trade Secrets Act offers this definition:

> "Trade Secret" means information, including a formula, pattern, compilation, program, device, method, technique, or process, that: (i) derives independent economic value, actual or potential, from not being generally known to, and not being readily ascertainable by proper means by other persons who can obtain economic value from its disclosure or use, and (ii) is the subject of efforts that are reasonable under the circumstances to maintain its secrecy.[485]

The franchisor should determine if the information being given is a trade secret. If so, it should expressly list the information that it intends to be treated as trade secrets. An express recital is important to overcome the lack of a presumption that a particular piece of information is a trade secret.[486] Also, the agreement may list information not generally considered as trade secrets and expressly state that the information is to be deemed "secret and confidential." For example, customer lists provided by the franchisor have been held to be legally protected trade secrets. This determination is enhanced if: (1) the information is not readily obtainable through alternative sources and (2) the franchisor treats the lists as "secret and confidential." The agreement can further protect the franchisor with a separate confidentiality clause and a non-competition clause. The drafting of an appropriate non-competition clause is an art form. The drafter needs to balance the goal of protecting the franchisor with the need to devise reasonable restrictions

[484]461 F. Supp. 1232, 1238-39 (E.D. Mich. 1978).
[485]UNIFORM TRADE SECRETS ACT § 1(4), 14 U.L.A. 541 (1980).
[486]Scott P. Sandrock, *Trade Secret Protection and the Terminated Franchise,* Franchise Law Journal 3 (1988).

regarding scope, duration, and territory. Non-competition clauses are highly scrutinized by courts in meeting a standard of reasonableness.

Another concern is that a franchise agreement that provides for a large amount of franchisor control may create problems of host country regulation. "Excessive control or the public appearance of such control may give rise to an agency relationship between the franchisor and the franchise"[487] under foreign law. If viewed as a dependent agency relationship, as discussed in Chapter 8, the franchisor may become susceptible to the tax and labor laws of the host country, along with making it amenable to lawsuits such as products liability. This increases the importance of negotiating strong indemnification and insurance clauses into the franchise agreement.

UNIDROIT Guide to International Master Franchising

The International Institute for the Unification of Private Law (UNIDROIT) has published an elaborate document titled *UNIDROIT Guide to International Master Franchise Arrangements.*[488] It provides an array of information, along with standard clauses to be used in the drafting of a master franchise contract. The approach of the publication is to provide clauses that are fair to all parties concerned and are based on "best practices." Some of the issues addressed include the types of franchising arrangements available (Annex 1), the relationship between the franchising arrangement and other types of agreements (commercial agency, license, technology transfer, distribution), and the differences in the Franchisor-Franchisee and Sub-Franchisor-Sub-Franchisee relationships. The contract issues discussed include the nature and extent of the rights granted (e.g., exclusivity of rights granted to sub-franchisor); duration of agreement and provisions for renewal; alternative fee structures; calculation of payments (timing, accounting, currency, tax issues); costs and control of advertising; supply of equipment, products, and services; the transfer and protection of intellectual property (confidentiality clauses, non-competition clauses,

---

[487]RALPH H. FOLSOM & MICHAEL W. GORDON, INTERNATIONAL BUSINESS TRANSACTIONS 428 (1995).

[488]This Guide may be obtained from UNIDROIT Publications, Via Panisperna 28, 00184 Rome, Italy.

grant-back clauses, post-termination clauses); assignment and transfer; indemnification and insurance (franchisor liability to third-parties); remedies for breach; and termination. Other important clauses presented include severability, integration, waivers, *force majeure,* hardship, cumulative rights, notice, damages, field of use restrictions, and right of first refusal.

Regulation of Franchising

Franchising is a uniquely American form of doing business. Other countries may possess similar devices, but no other country has witnessed the growth of franchising on the level of the United States. A number of restrictions are found in both domestic and foreign laws. For example, a number of state franchise statutes limit the unfettered ability of the franchisor to terminate the franchise at will. Internationally, some countries offer a less friendly environment for franchising then is found in the United States. The European Union (EU) places restrictions on franchises which require them to conform to its competition (antitrust) law.[489] *See,* Regulation No. 4087/88, "Application of the Treaty to Categories of Franchise Agreements" (Nov. 30, 1988). However, EU regulations do provide for a number of protections for the franchise network. For example, the franchisee can be required to sell products specifically manufactured by the franchisor or by designated suppliers. Also, the franchisee is obligated to meet minimum quality standards established by the franchisor for all of its franchisees. The franchisee is precluded from directly competing in the territories of other franchisees. Finally, the franchisee can be precluded from assigning any rights or obligations without the consent of the franchisor. The next subsection will review EU Franchise Regulations for purposes of drafting a legally enforceable agreement.

The importance of reviewing host country law before entering into a master franchise contract is noted in the UNIDROIT *Guide to International Master Franchise Arrangements.* The variety of host country laws vary from laws that do not even recognize the franchise form of business to laws that limit the types of contract provisions that will be enforced. The use of

[489]See, Schmitz & Van Hamme, *Franchising in Europe—The First Practical EEC Guidelines,* 22 The Int'l Lawyer 717 (1988).

model forms is limited by the fact that vast differences in contractual issues occur from industry to industry and in what is permitted under various host country laws. Annex 3 provides an overview of host country laws regulating the franchise relationship. The specific countries reviewed are the United States, Canada, France, Spain, Brazil, Mexico, Japan, Russia, and Australia. The law of the European Union is also reviewed, along with a number of ethical codes (Code of Ethics of the European Franchise Federation and Code of Ethics of National Franchise Associations).[490]

EU Franchise Regulations

The EU Regulations on Franchise Agreements[491] is a good example of a foreign regulation that provides insight to the contract drafter regarding what types of clauses should be incorporated into a franchise agreement. As mentioned in the previous section, this Regulation provides an exemption from the application of EU competition law found in Article 85 of the Treaty of Rome.[492] However, it is also an indispensable source to be used in the drafting of a franchise agreement. Commission Regulation 4087/88 (Appendix 11) pertains only to certain types of franchise agreements, namely those involving the distribution of goods or services, along with master franchise agreements.[493] The Regulation expressly exempts from its coverage industrial franchises that generally include the manufacture of products. It notes that those types of franchises may make use of the block exemptions pertaining to patent and know-how licensing previously discussed in Chapter 9.

From an overarching philosophical perspective, contract restrictions

---

[490]A good source for information on international franchising is the International Franchising Association at http://www.franchise.org.

[491]Commission Regulation (EEC) No 4087/88 of 30 November 1988 on the Application of Article 85(3) of the Treaty to Categories of Franchise Agreements.

[492]For a fuller explanation on how European Union competition law relates to franchising, see Paul Ridgeway, *Franchising in the Common Market: A Survey of the Application of Competition Law of the European Community to Retail Franchising,* 13 No. Carolina J. Int'l Law & Commercial Regulation 74 (1988).

[493]Master franchise agreements are defined in the Regulations as those in which "the relationship between franchisor and franchisees is made through a third undertaking, the master franchisee."

will be more likely to sustain judicial scrutiny if they can be tied to the "preservation of the common identity and reputation of the (franchise) network." Also, contract restrictions are more likely to be enforced if they are "needed to prevent the know-how made available and the assistance given by the franchisor from benefiting competitors." Alternatively, the Regulation recognizes that some restrictions on the rights of the franchisee are needed in order to maintain the "homogeneity of the network and the constant cooperation between franchisor and franchisees [in order to] ensure a constant quality of the products and services" being provided. Thus, Article 2 provides a list of clauses that, although restrictive of competition, have a strong nexus to the above philosophical goals. They allow for the development of exclusive franchise territories and prohibit franchisees from actively seeking customers outside their franchise territories. Along those lines, a master franchisee can be prohibited from entering a sub-franchise agreement with an entity outside the territory of the master franchise. The agreement may also prohibit the franchisee from selling the goods or services of a competitor of the franchisor. The franchisor may insert clauses mandating that the franchisee only sells goods or services "matching minimum objective quality specifications." Generally, the franchisee cannot be restricted in determining its sources of supply. However, an exemption from this prohibition is given if requirements to purchase supplies from the franchisor or other designated third party suppliers are necessitated in order to meet "objective quality specifications." Other clauses that are expressly permitted include best efforts,[494] minimum sales quotas,[495] customer service and warranty requirements,[496] advertising requirements,[497] confidentiality (including post-termination confidentiality),[498] training requirements,[499] rights to improvements,[500] location restrictions,[501] non-assignment without prior consent,[502] sales restricted to end users, other franchisees and re-

[494]Article 3(1)(f).
[495]Ibid.
[496]Ibid.
[497]Article 3(1)(g).
[498]Article 3(2)(a).
[499]Article 3(2)(e).
[500]Article 3(2)(b).
[501]Article 2(c).
[502]Article 3(2)(j).

sellers,[503] and notice of infringement.[504] Prohibited clauses include those that restrict a franchisee from purchasing from another franchisee, from filling orders from parties outside its territory that were not actively sought, "unduly limiting the franchisee's choice of suppliers or customers, and restrictions on pricing. These prohibited restrictions relate to a stated purpose of the Regulation that ensures that "parallel imports and cross deliveries between franchisees remain possible."[505] Article 5 expressly renders no-challenge or validity clauses non-enforceable. In the event that a contract clause restriction does not come within one of the "approved restrictions enumerated in the Regulation, then the parties will have to *notify* the European Commission for an approval or "negative clearance." This should not be necessary for the United States franchisor because the Regulation approves many of the standard types of clauses found in American franchise agreements. However, attempts at creating closed territorial restrictions should be carefully drafted or abandoned.

503Article 3(1)(e).
504Article 3(2)(c).
505Whereas clause (12).

CHAPTER 11

Electronic Contracting

The potential of Internet marketing and sales makes it the most important concept to impact the international marketplace.[506] However, because it is within the public domain, the Internet and electronic commerce (e-commerce) markets pose a number of risks that have yet to be fully resolved. The foremost is the security of information. Trade secrets or payment transmissions may be stolen by the other party or by third parties. Also, the same issues that are found in more traditional international business transactions apply to Internet transactions.[507] For example, does an Internet transaction bring the seller within the scope of the laws of the buyer? Will he be liable for foreign income, sales and value-added taxes?[508] Is the

---

[506]See generally, Jeffrey B. Ritter, *Defining International Electronic Commerce,* 13 NW Journal of Int'l Law & Business 3 (1992).

[507]For problems of applying traditional contract and commercial law constructs to electronic commerce and cyberspace see, Joel R. Reidenberg, *Governing Networks and Rule-Making in Cyberspace,* 45 Emory Law Journal 911 (1996); David R. Johnson & David Post, *Law and Borders — The Rise of Law in Cyberspace,* 48 Stanford Law Rev. 1367 (1996); John T. Delacourt, *The International Impact of Internet Regulation,* 38 Harvard Int'l Law Journal 207 (1997).

[508]The evolving law and issues relating to internet taxation is beyond the scope of this Chapter. See generally, David L. Forst, *Old and New Issues in the Taxation of Electronic Commerce,* 14 Berkeley Technology Law Journal 711 (1999); Patrick Thibodeau, *Europe Wants U.S. Firms to Pay E-Commerce Taxes,* 33 Computerworld 41 (Aug. 30, 1999); John K. Sweet, *Formulating International Tax Law in the Age of Electronic Commerce: The Possible Ascendancy of Residence-Based Taxation in an Era of Eroding Traditional Income Tax Principles,* 146 University of Pennsylvania Law Review 1949 (1998); Anne Murrath, Stan

transaction subject to foreign consumer protection laws? Does a transaction bring you within the jurisdiction of a foreign court? The chapter begins with a brief look at how national contract laws are being applied to electronic transactions. It then focuses directly on issues specific to e-commerce, after a brief introduction to electronic data interchange (EDI). The source materials reviewed include the International Chamber of Commerce's *General Usage for Internationally Digitally Ensured Commerce* (GUIDEC) and UNCITRAL'S *Model Law on Electronic Commerce.* The chapter concludes with analysis of an assortment of mostly unresolved issues including domain name registration and trademark infringement, personal jurisdiction determination, "shrinkwrap" contracting, electronic documentation, and e-commerce ethics.

National Contract Laws and E-Commerce

The White House has released a paper titled *A Framework for Global Electronic Commerce* in which it sets out United States' policy regarding electronic commerce.[509] Its general premise is that regulation of the Internet and e-commerce should be primarily by private and not public means. "Governments must adopt a non-regulatory, market-oriented approach to electronic commerce, one that facilitates the emergence of a transparent and predictable legal environment to support global business." The market approach is one in which the parties through private contract police their rights and obligations. Nonetheless, there will be a need for international agreement and governmental regulation in a number of areas. It states, however, that even when regulation is needed "private entities should take the lead in organizing them." The paper then notes that there are three areas of issues that require international agreement: financial, legal, and market access. Under the legal issue area, the paper calls for a "Uniform Commercial Code for Electronic Commerce," enhanced intellectual property protection, privacy protection, and security initiatives. In the area of developing domestic and international rules and norms, the paper ac-

---

Beelen, & Martin Fish, *European Union: The Internet and VAT in the EU,* 8 International Tax Review 49 (1997).

[509]William J. Clinton & Albert Gore, Jr., *A Framework for Global Electronic Commerce,* http://www.iitf.nist.gov/ eleccomm/ecomm.htm.

knowledges the work of the United Nations Commission on International Trade Law (UNCITRAL) in developing its *Model Law on Electronic Commerce.* Two fundamental principles are given to guide the development of such rules. First, contract and other rules should be technology-neutral. Second, existing rules should be applied or modified before the adoption of new rules for electronic contracting. It advises that these principles are best meet internationally through the efforts of organizations like UNCITRAL, UNIDROIT, and the International Chamber of Commerce in developing model provisions and uniform principles. In the area of intellectual property, the Administration specifically recognizes the problem of trademark infringement and domain names. The preferred solution is the "development of a global market-based system to register Internet domain names." In the area of security, the paper highlights the need to develop "trusted certification services" that permit the secured use of digital signatures.

Amelia Boss aptly stated the sporadic nature of national laws pertaining to electronic commerce.

> As of yet, none of the developing and developed countries, common law and civil law countries, and countries of different cultural and legal heritages, have developed a comprehensive legal structure governing electronic commerce. Thus, the challenge is to take countries of divergent economic capabilities, legal heritage, telecommunications infrastructures, and needs, and bring them together to develop common analysis of, and approaches to, problems never encountered previously.[510]

The enactment, however, of a set of comprehensive and generally accepted international rules for governing electronic commerce is unlikely in the foreseeable future. Instead, the law of contracts is likely to remain the governing institution for electronic commerce. The establishment of a contractual relationship in e-commerce generally begins with customer registration. By requiring customers to register, the international vendor is able to better alleviate the concerns for authentication, security, and payment. In order to place an order, the customer must provide her digital signature. Encryption is used to secure the transmission of the digital signature and credit card information. The customer by clicking at appropriate places accepts the terms of the contract. It should be noted that sales over the Inter-

---

[510]Amelia H. Boss, *The Emerging Law of International Electronic Commerce,* 6 Temple Int'l & Comparative Law Journal 293, 301-304 (1992).

net that resemble "catalog sales" are likely to come under the purview of consumer protection laws. As such, the e-commerce contract will need to comply with legal disclosure requirements. Within the United States, compliance can be achieved through the use of icons and linkages. The purchaser would only need to click the appropriate icon or link to obtain the required disclosures. Foreign consumer protection laws will need to be reviewed to determine their applicability to e-commerce.

National contract law raises numerous issues when applied to electronic contracting. Which communication is to be considered an offer and which one is the acceptance? When and where does an electronic acceptance reach the offeror? This will depend on the type of communications and information being provided. A non-interactive web page is more like an advertisement or an invitation to make an offer. Conversely, an interactive web page designed to accept payment information such as credit card numbers could be construed as a standing offer. The use of e-mail to negotiate contracts opens up the offeror to an acceptance by e-mail. However, does the acceptance reach the offeror upon receipt by the service provider's storage of it in the offeror's mailbox or is acceptance when the offeror opens his mailbox? The better answer would seem to be the former because the offeror is inviting acceptance by e-mail and is thus under an implied duty to retrieve his mail in a timely fashion.[511]

Other issues that need to be considered include:

- Under the ***acceptance rules*** of § 2-206 of the uniform commercial code can the downloading of information constitute an acceptance? Can the *clicking* of approval to terms be considered an acceptance? The answer to both of these questions seems to be yes. Both fulfill the fundamental requirement that an acceptance merely must be a definite expression of acceptance. A related issue is whether an e-mail confirmation between merchants satisfies the requirements of the written confirmation rule found in § 2-201(2)? In shrinkwrap licensing how is the ***additional terms*** scenario of § 2-207 likely to be handled? This is answered under the proposed revised Article 2 in which the notion of additional terms is replaced with *varying terms.*

[511]This information was gleaned from Christoph Glatt, *Comparative Issues in the Formation of Electronic Contracts,* 6 Journal of Law & Information Technology 34, 50-53 (1996).

Thus, terms inside the package will be considered as varying and do not become a part of the contract. See, section on The "Shrinkwrap" Contract latter in this chapter.[512]

- Do ***statutory warranty laws*** apply to Internet transactions? In the United States the *Magnuson-Moss Act* (15 U.S.C. § 2301, *et seq.*) does pertain to Internet commerce since most Internet transactions are consumer transactions. Therefore, all product warranties for products sold through the Internet must expressly state: (1) the protected parties, (2) any limitations on the implied warranties, (3) any limitation of damages, (4) availability of alternative dispute resolution, (5) the coverage of the warranty (parts, characteristics of product), (6) the responsibility of the seller in case of defect, (7) the procedure for making a warranty claim, and (8) the commencement and expiration of the warranty period. Of course, foreign statutory warranty laws would need to be researched for sales in other countries.
- Use of ***Electronic Agents***. What if one of the entities making an offer or acceptance is a computer? What if a human makes a conditional acceptance to a computer or digital voice system? Is a contract formed? Do the conditional or additional terms become a part of the contract? The Uniform Computer Information Transactions Act (UCITA) (previously the Uniform Commercial Code's proposed Article 2B),[513] provides rules for such a situation. Section 206 provides the general rule that "a contract may be formed by the interaction of electronic agents" and "a contract may be formed by the interaction of an electronic agent and an individual."[514] The contract is formed if the individual takes actions or makes statements that he knows will cause the electronic agent to perform. Additional terms incorporated into the acceptance do not become a part of the

---

[512]See, Step-Saver Data Systems v. Wyse Technology, 939 F.2d 91 (3d Cir. 1991); Arizona Retail Systems v. Software Link, 831 F. Supp. 759 (Ariz. 1993).

[513]Approved by the National Conference of Commissioners on Uniform State Laws in July 1999. For a copy of this law see the following website: http://www.upenn.edu/bll/ulc/ucita/cita10st.htm.

[514]An "electronic agent" is defined as a "computer program, or electronic or other automated means, used by a person to initiate an action, or to respond to electronic messages or performances, on the person's behalf without review or action by an individual at the time of action, or response to a message or performance. UCITA, Section 102 (27).

contract if the individual "had reason to know that the electronic agent could not react to the terms as provided."

Developments in e-commerce and Internet law are on-going at both the national and international levels. On June 13, 1997, Germany enacted a broad Internet-Multimedia Law. It is titled the Federal Act Establishing the General Conditions for Information and Communications Services or "Information and Services Act." One of the substantive provisions of the Act provides for at least a limited amount of liability for independent service providers for the content of materials accessed through their services. However, this liability extends only if the independent service provider knew of the content and has the technical means of preventing its use. The law provides for a "reasonableness standard in determining if the independent service provider is jointly liable with the creator or provider of the material.[515]

The major obstacle to electronic letters of credit is the need to have a signed writing as is required by the Uniform Commercial Code's Section 5-104 for letters of credit. The Uniform Customs and Practices for Documentary Credits (UCP 500) recognized this problem by replacing *signed* with the notion of *authentication.* UNCITRAL has also issued standards to deal with the issues posed by electronic commerce.

Exhibit 11.1: UNCITRAL Model Law for EDI Contracting[516]

The model law validates electronic contracting practices and eliminates common law legal assumptions concerning transactions on paper. Its features include:

A. Validation of intent to contract — the model law makes it clear that trade data messages may be used to conclude contracts.

B. Guidelines for establishing offer and acceptance.

C. Modification of definitions — "writing," "signature," "original."

   1. "Writing" is expanded to include any information record.

   2. "Signature" includes any method of identification.

---

[515]For more information on the German Internet-Multimedia Law see, http://www.iid.de, http://www.iukdg.de, or http://www.bmbf.de.
[516]U.N. Doc. A/CN.9/406 (1994).

3. "Original" includes any reproduction of an electronic record so long as the data integrity is reasonably certain.

D. Standards for Use as Evidence—the model law provides a liberal rule for admission of trade data messages leaving questions of integrity and reliability to the judge or jury.[517]

Electronic Data Interchange

Electronic Data Interchange (EDI) is the computer-to-computer communication of information.[518] The use of EDI for purposes of forming contracts will continue to grow.[519] Instead of the use of paper documents in the documentary transaction, the documents will be transferred electronically. Contracts will be electronically formed, electronic bills of lading will be sent to a third party record-keeping service, letters of credit will be issued based upon a pre-existing template,[520] and other necessary documents like insurance certificates will be requested and transmitted by computers. The closed nature of the EDI system allows private parties to create their own law to fill the void created by a lack of legislation.[521] "In the absence of appropriate statutory revisions to accommodate electronic commercial practices, parties doing business electronically began to execute 'trading partner agreements' or 'interchange agreements' in an attempt to resolve contractually the legal certainties they faced."[522] However, the open nature of the next

---

[517]R. David Whitaker, *Letters of Credit and Electronic Commerce,* 31 Idaho Law Review 699 (1995).

[518]See generally, H. PERITT, LAW AND THE INFORMATION SUPERHIGHWAY: PRIVACY, ACCESS, INTELLECTUAL PROPERTY, COMMERCE AND LIABILITY (1996); P SOKOL, FROM EDI TO ELECTRONIC COMMERCE: A BUSINESS INITIATIVE (1995); B. WRIGHT, THE LAW OF ELECTRONIC COMMERCE: EDI, E-MAIL, AND INTERNET TECHNOLOGY, PROOF AND LIABILITY (2d ed. 1995).

[519]See generally, BERNARD D. REAMS, JR., ET AL., ELECTRONIC CONRACTING LAW: EDI AND BUSINESS TRANSACTIONS (1993-94 ed.).

[520]See, e.g., Whitaker, *Letters of Credit and Electronic Commerce,* 31 Idaho Law Rev. 699 (1995).

[521]See ABA Model Agreement as reported in *Model Electronic Data Interchange Trading Partner Agreement and Commentary,* 45 Business Lawyer 1717 (1990).

[522]Amelia H. Boss & Jane Kaufman Winn, *The Emerging Law of Electronic Commerce,* 52 The Business Lawyer 1469, 1477 (1997). See generally, Amelia H. Boss, *Electronic Data Interchange Agreements: Private Contracting Toward a Global Environment,* 13 NW Journal Int'l Law & Business 31 (1992); AMELIA H. BOSS & JEFFREY B. RITTER, ELECTRONIC DATA INTERCHANGE AGREEMENTS (ICC 1993).

generation of electronic commerce requires a more proactive role for government regulation. A legal framework needs to be provided to ensure the security and integrity of open network transactions (Internet, etc.).

The European Union has made recent strides to deal with the issues impeding the development of EDI and electronic commerce. In 1997 the European Commission published the "European Initiative in Electronic Commerce" or COM (97) 157.[523] Prior to that initiative, the first foray into e-commerce was the publication of a *Model EDI Agreement*. This may be accessed through Commission Recommendation 94/820/EC (OJ L 338/98 1994) and Council Decision 87/499/EEC (OJ 1987 L 285/35). "The Commission states that the objective of the *Model Agreement* is to provide a contractual basis for EDI users. The users need a mandatory legal basis regulating their obligations and duties deriving from an EDI agreement."[524] It should be noted that national law preempts the *Model Agreement*. The *Model Agreement* is intended to act only as a guide. As a guide, it provides contracting parties with a number of important provisions including the regulation of the processing and acknowledging of EDI messages, security precautions, operational requirements, and confidentiality protections.

Electronic Commerce

Amelia Boss and Jane Winn lists three major commercial effects of the increased use of electronic technologies: "(1) commercial parties have begun to restructure their business practices using such technologies to communicate internally as well as externally, (2) new industries have emerged to provide needed services to companies engaging in electronic commerce, and (3) new types of property with commercial value have become the subject of trade domestically and internationally." They then note two current trends, one revolving around the way businesspersons conduct business and the other revolving around the changing nature or subject matter of business transactions. The first trend is the increasing use of electronic contracting instead of relying on paper transactions. The development of elec-

[523]The European Initiative on Electronic Commerce can be accessed at http://www2.echo.lu/bonn/final.html.

[524]Zekos, *The Legal Framework Governing the Use of Electronic Technology in the European Union*, [1998] 3 Web JCLI, http://webjcli.ncl.ac.uk.

tronic bills of lading and letters of credit are examples of this trend, along with the use of electronic purchase orders and confirmations. The second trend is evidenced by the growing business of selling and transferring information.

The first generation of electronic contracting was Electronic Data Interchange (EDI).[525] The future will likely see the Internet as the vehicle for electronic commerce. Unlike the Internet, EDI generally involves dealings between sizable commercial entities. Also, unlike the Internet, EDI provides a closed, secured environment in which known contracting parties transact business. The legal framework for the interchange is based upon standardized trading agreements, rules, and standards. Currently, the risk in Internet commerce, especially unsecured payment systems, makes the need for a standardized legal framework imperative for future growth. The legal framework needed for secured Internet contracting will likely involve the modification of current legal regimes,[526] such as Article 2 of the Uniform Commercial Code, in addressing the nuances of electronic contracting. The following excerpt lists a number of issues and the current proposals to modify the Uniform Commercial Code in order to deal with them.

> Several types of issues need to be considered in electronic transactions. First, is the issue of attribution. How should the law allocate the risk of communications that are not authentic? For example, who should bear the risk of having his electronic communication system violated by a *hacker*? Second, is the issue of errors in communication. How should the law allocate the risk of garbled communication? This is complicated by the fact that electronic messages may be relayed through unknown and unknowable intermediaries. Third, when should electronic messages be considered to have legal effect [for purposes of offer and acceptance and the formation of contracts]? [Fourth,] how should the evidentiary issues be resolved in an electronic environment? For example, should there be a statute of frauds type of requirement and if so how should its require-

525See, e.g., Randy V. Sabett, *International Harmonization in Electronic Commerce and Electronic Data Interchange: A Proposed First Step Toward Signing on the Digital Dotted Line,* 46 American U. Law Rev. 511 (1996).

526See generally, Raymond T. Nimmer, *Electronic Contracting: Legal Issues,* 14 J. Marshall Journal of Computer & Information Law, 211 (1996). *See also,* Raymond T. Nimmer, *Breaking Barriers: The Relation Between Contract and Intellectual Property Law,* 13 Berkeley Technology Law Journal 827 (1998) and *Information Age in Law: New Frontiers in Property and Contract,* 68 New York State Bar Journal 28 (1996).

> ments be defined? How can we ensure the integrity of electronic records? [R]egarding the fourth series of questions, [UCITA] and the Revised Article 2 of the Uniform Commercial Code, indicate that electronic commerce will not be prevented due to evidentiary issues. The word "writing" in the statute of frauds is replaced with "records" and the requirement of a "signature is replaced with the term "authentication."[527]

The three major concerns for international electronic contracting are authenticity, enforceability, and confidentiality. Authenticity involves the verification of the person that one is dealing with electronically. Enforceability includes the legal scope of the license granted or the warranty given under a national law. It also includes the provability and verification of the contractual terms of an on-line transaction. Confidentiality revolves around the protection of sensitive information such as payment information and trade secrets. The fear is that the public domain nature of e-commerce makes such information susceptible to fraud and misappropriation by third parties. The minimum level of due diligence pertaining to these three concerns entails a workable knowledge of the legal requirements of forming and proving a contract formed through the Internet.

The most secure means of Internet contracting is the entering into a trading partner agreement with a known party.[528] This form of contracting makes sense only when one contemplates a long-term contractual relationship with a relatively modest number of contracting parties. The American Bar Association has developed a *Model Electronic Data Interchange Trading Partner Agreement*[529] that can be tailored to particular types of transactions. However, entering into such a detailed agreement prior to commencement of the commercial transaction is impractical, if not impossible, when contemplating transactions with a large number of other parties. Other techniques that can be used to authenticate the existence of the other party and to confirm the terms of the contractual undertaking include acknowledgment, use of independent agents or value-added networks, and encryption.

---

[527]Linda J. Rusch, *The Relevance of Evolving Domestic and International Law of Contracts in the Classroom: Assumptions About Consent,* 72 Tulane Law Review 2043, 2056-2058 (1998).

[528]See, Gary S. Weinstein, *Forming Contracts on the Internet,* 14 Corporate Counsel's Quarterly 1 (1998).

[529]See, *ABA's Model Electronic Data Interchange Trading Partner Agreement,* 45 Business Lawyer 1645 (1990).

Acknowledgement can be as simple as an e-mail or a facsimile to confirm the on-line transaction. Private computer networks have become a popular means to broker e-commerce. They provide the vital independent record-keeping function needed to respond to the evidentiary concerns of proving the contract in case of a future breach. Finally, encryption provides the strongest vehicle for alleviating concerns over confidentiality. The use of "private" and "public" keys enables contracting parties to secure their confidential information against theft. Ultimately the use of public key encryption to create *digital signatures* provides the means for increased e-commerce security. The American Bar Association has published guidelines for the creation of digital signatures.[530]

The International Chamber of Commerce published in 1997 a guide titled *General Usage for International Digitally Ensured Commerce* (GUIDEC) which addresses some of the definitional and legal aspects relating to methods aimed at overcoming e-commerce authentication and confidentiality problems. It provides a general framework for the ensuring (authenticating) and certifying of digital messages. GUIDEC is national law neutral as its goal is to harmonize legal and trade practices across national legal systems.[531] In order to do this it developed some original nomenclature and provides "clear descriptions of the rights and responsibilities of subscribers, certifiers, and relying parties." GUIDEC's operative concept of affixing a signature or verifying the author of the data message is referred to as the process of *ensuring*. The stated goals of GUIDEC are "to enhance the ability of the international; business community to execute secure digital transactions, to establish legal principles that promote reliable digital ensuring and certification practices, and to define and clarify the duties of participants in the emerging ensuring and certification system."

Open system or Internet commerce is a natural evolution of the emerging global electronic trading system. As discussed above, closed network systems, such as EDI, provided a secure means for known trading or business entities to engage in large numbers of inter-party transactions. Because of the standardized nature of EDI, a genre of standard electronic

---

[530]ABA's Section of Science and Technology, *Digital Signature Guidelines: Legal Infrastructure for Certification Authorities and Secure Electronic Commerce,* www.abanet.org/scitech.

[531]The following has been gleaned from a review of GUIDEC, A Living Document accessed at http://www.iccwbo.org/guidec2.htm.

forms developed which further streamlined the process. Most elements of uncertainty and risks were addressed through trading or interchange agreements. These agreements attempted to fill in the legal gap that had not yet been adequately dealt with in the substantive law. "The development of model trading agreements established the foundation for a contractually based legal structure for electronic commerce." The movement toward open networks rekindled the same security concerns that were addressed in the EDI trading agreements. However, because of the open nature of Internet access, it is unlikely that security concerns can be adequately dealt with through contracts. Some level of governmental regulation, hopefully international in scope, will be needed to ensure the integrity of e-commerce over open networks. GUIDEC provides a starting point because it provides the language and framework for dealing with the issues of security and authentication.

GUIDEC focuses upon existing legal formalities found in national legal systems. It addresses the issues of how to interrelate paper-based requirements with the technology of e-commerce. How can electronic commerce conform to the Statute of Frauds requirement found in Section 2-201 of the Uniform Commercial Code?[532] How can the notion of a written signature be applied to digital communication. How can the civil law's notarial requirements be accommodated electronically? The answers to these questions most likely revolve around a common sense approach to satisfying the intent or purpose of these formality requirements. For example, instead of focusing upon the physical rendering of a human signature, the focus should be upon the notion in Section 2-201 of the "intent to authenticate." The ensuring of a document with a digital signature through public key encryption is seen as the solution to ensuring and security issues. However, the key to the digital signature system for broad-based e-commerce is the development of a system of third-party certification.

The third-party certifier issues a certificate guaranteeing the identity of the sender of an electronic message.[533] The liability of the certifying company is likely to be contractual in nature. GUIDEC provides that the certifi-

---

[532]See generally, Richard A. Horning, *Has Hal Signed a Contract: The Statute of Frauds in Cyberspace,* 12 Santa Clara Comp. & High Tech. Law Journal 253 (1996).

[533]For a discussion of the emerging role of certificate authorities in electronic commerce see, Michael Froomkin, *The Essential Role of Trusted Third Parties in Electronic Commerce,* 75 Oregon Law Rev. 49 (1996).

cate should indicate its scope both in duration and transactional longevity. It should state a time period of coverage and whether it certifies a single transaction or a number of transactions. The certificate should also possess a *certification practice statement* that describes the practices utilized by the certifier in issuing the certificate. The certifying company will be tempted to place a disclaimer on its certification. "A certifier may seek to restrict liability for the contents of a certificate either through the contractual relationship with the subscriber, or by means of a general disclaimer in the practice statement, or even in the certificate itself." The prudent trader should examine those instruments for such disclaimers. It should be noted that these disclaimers may not be enforceable under a given national law. National laws should also be reviewed to determine any required formalities. For example, whether notarial practice will be required under a civil law system.

Other contractual issues addressed in GUIDEC include indemnity insurance, connecting the message being ensured with the ensuring party, and notice requirements. First, the integrity of the certifier is a key concern for purposes of transactional security. As stated above, a certifier who places an overly broad disclaimer on its product or process should be viewed with concern. Another integrity enhancing device is to find a certifier willing to provide professional indemnity insurance. Second, GUIDEC places a responsibility on the ensurer to indicate the scope of the ensured message. Defining the limit of the message is important to secure against fraud and alteration of the original message. The linkage between the digital signature and the message should be dealt with by agreement between the parties. The parties should agree as to the form of their messages and the degree of acceptable variation. Third, GUIDEC provides a duty of notice standard that does not require actual notice of the recipient. "A duty to notify may be satisfied, even though the intended recipient of the notice fails to become aware of its contents. In an electronic setting, dispatching a reliable ensured message addressed to the intended recipient through a technologically reliable system should suffice as a means of notification." That said, it is best if the parties specifically agree to notice requirements.

The domestic response in the United States has been initially to revise the existing commercial law.[534] The earliest recognition of the need to de-

[534]See generally, Jeffrey B. Ritter, *Scope of the Uniform Commercial Code: Computer Contracting Cases and Commercial Practices*, 45 Business Lawyer 2533 (1990).

velop rules pertaining to electronic communications was Article 4A (wire transfers). Like EDI, liability is based upon the following of a pre-agreed security procedure. A party to a wire transfer agreement can avoid liability if it can prove that a message was fraudulently sent by a third-party. This limitation on liability can be challenged if the contracting party failed to follow the security procedures provided for in the wire transfer agreement. Article 2 (sales of goods) is being revised to more openly recognize electronic contracting. The statute of fraud formalities will be satisfied not by a "writing," but by the production of a "record." The notion of "record" was first recognized in Article 5 (letters of credit). The "signature" requirement will be replaced by the need to provide an "authentication." UCITA will provide rules for sales of software and the licensing of information. Although more along the lines of an intellectual property law development, its close relationship to electronic commerce is obvious. The formation of a contract under UCITA is dependent on the receipt of the acceptance by the offeror. This is opposite of the common law's acceptance upon dispatch or mailbox rule. However, receipt is not defined as "actual receipt." Receipt of an electronic notice is defined as "coming into existence in an information processing system or at an address in that system in a form capable of being processed by or perceived from a system of that type by a recipient, if the recipient uses, or otherwise has designated or holds out, that place or system for receipt of notices.[535] Thus, a contract is formed even if the receiving party fails to open or read the message of acceptance.

In 1996, the American Bar Association issued its *Digital Signature Guidelines* with the stated purposes of minimizing electronic forgeries, enabling the reliable authentication of documents in computer form, and giving legal effect to technical standards for the authentication of computer messages. Similar to GUIDEC, the ABA guidelines recommend the use of public and private key cryptography conducted through a third-party certificate authority. At the state level, more than a dozen states have passed legislation recognizing digital signatures. The 1995 Utah Digital Signature Act[536] has served as a sort of model law. It provides that a digital signature is as valid as a written signature. Digital signature legislation can also be found in other countries. Germany recently enacted the Digital Signature Act,[537]

[535]UCITA, Section 102 (52).

[536]UTAH CODE ANN. § 46-3-101.

[537]Act on Digital Signatures (Gesetz zur digitalen Signatur), enacted as Article 3 of the Information and Communication Services Act (1997).

which calls for the establishment of a governmental authority to license certification authorities. The Act further provides the minimal content for signature key certificates. The signature key certificate must contain: the name of the owner of the signature key, the public signature key assigned, names of the algorithms, serial number of the certificate, the beginning and termination of the validity period of the certificate, name of the certification authority, and any restrictions to the scope and type of use of the signature key.

The long-term viability of e-commerce is partially dependent on the development of secure payment systems. Two of the more promising methods are the use of *trusted third parties* and the use of *digital cash.* In the former, confidential payment information (such as credit card information) is sent to a trusted third party. An example would be the use of the electronic interbank system used by banks to transfer funds. Digital cash requires a type of EDI framework with a financial institution being one of the parties. "A digital cash system employs software held by the participating financial institutions, their customers, and merchants. A merchant that receives the digital cash can send it onto its bank and have its account credited or it can spend the digital cash."[538] The downside of digital cash is that it is based upon the debit method. Therefore, a paying party does not receive the float that one obtains when using a credit card. Although, this may be true for consumer purchases, digital cash remains a strong possibility for merchant to merchant transactions, especially when the merchants carry out a long-term relationship.

UNCITRAL Model Law on Electronic Commerce

The United Nations Commission on International Trade Law (UNCITRAL) adopted a Model Law on Electronic Commerce on June 12, 1996.[539] The law potentially serves three purposes. Individual governments can use it as a model or guide in drafting national legislation. More important to this text, it can be used as source of language for contract drafting purposes

[538]James J. McAndrews, *Making Payments on the Internet.* Business Rev. (Federal Reserve of Philadelphia) 3, 7 (January/February 1997).
[539]UNCITRAL MODEL LAW ON ELECTRONIC COMMERCE: http://www.un.or.at/uncitral>; U.N. Doc. A/51/17 Annex I (1996), reprinted in, 36 I.L.M. 200 (1997). See, Appendix 6 for the complete text.

or as a set of default rules incorporated into a contract by reference. In 1997 the United Nations published a guide to be used in conjunction with the formal text.[540] The *Guide* states that the "principles expressed in the *Model Law* are also intended to be of use to individual users of electronic commerce in the drafting of some of the contractual solutions that might be needed to overcome legal obstacles to the increased use of electronic commerce." Finally, courts and arbitration panels "in interpreting existing international conventions and other instruments as far as they impede electronic commerce" may also use it.[541]

The *Guide* states that "it is a *framework* law that does not itself set forth all the rules and regulations that may be necessary to implement those techniques in an enacting country."[542] The *Model Law* is not intended to displace national rules of contracting. It takes no position on whether a contract is formed upon dispatch of the acceptance (common law) or upon receipt (civil law). However, it does provide uniform rules for determining when something is dispatched or received (*time of dispatch* or *receipt*). Article 15 provides that an offer or acceptance is dispatched when the sender presses the "enter button". They are received when the message enters the information system of the addressee. It further notes that an e-mailbox can be the information system of the addressee. Also of importance is the *place of dispatch or receipt* for determining the law of the contract and the appropriate court in which to bring a lawsuit. Under Article 15 (4) of the *Model Law*, the place of dispatch is the place of business of the sender. Therefore, the contract is concluded at the place of the sender. This will be important when there is no express choice of law. In Europe, the Brussels and Lugano Conventions provide further guidance regarding the appropriate jurisdiction for disputes. Under the Brussels Convention, the fundamental ground for jurisdiction is the domicile of the defendant. However, Article 5 provides that the place of performance can be an alternative ground for jurisdiction. For delivery of goods, this would generally be the customer's address. For the payment of goods and services, the place of performance will be the creditor's place of business. Interestingly, for the on-line sale and transmission of software, the place of performance will be the place of the service

540 United Nations Commission on International Trade, UNCITRAL Model Law on Electronic Commerce with Guide to Enactment (Guide No. 3) (1997).

541 Glatt at 57.

542 UNCITRAL Guide at ¶ 13 (1996).

provider where the data is received which may not be the same country as where the defendant is located.[543] Regarding choice of law, the Rome Convention on law applicable to contractual obligations provides, absent a choice of law clause, the contract is to be governed "by the law of the country with which it is most closely connected." Article 4(2) provides a presumption in favor of the performing party's principal place of business.

The *Model Law's* definition of electronic commerce is intended to be broadly construed. Electronic commerce includes "communication by means of EDI defined narrowly as the computer-to-computer transmission of data in a standardized format; transmission of electronic messages involving the use of either publicly available standards or proprietary standards; and transmission of free-formatted text by electronic means [such as the INTERNET]." The *Guide* notes that the definition of "data message" is all encompassing. It is intended to cover "all types of messages that are generated, stored, or communicated in essentially paperless form." The *Model Law* has three conceptual parts. Chapter I of Part One contains general provisions such as the sphere of application (Article 1) and definitions (Article 2). Chapters II and III provide rules for the formation of electronic contracts. They expressly define "writing," "signature", and "originality" which are central features in most laws of contracts. Chapter II reviews existing legal requirements and their application to electronic contracting such as writing requirements (Article 6) and the signature requirement (Article 7). Article 7 adopts the *Model Law*'s functional equivalent approach to formal requirements. An electronic signature should be recognized as long as it identifies the author of the document and confirms that the author approved of its content. The *Guide* states that these provisions provide mandatory-type of rules or "minimum acceptable form requirements." Chapter III provides specific rules including the formation and validity of electronic contracts (Article 11), along with the determination of the time of dispatch and receipt of data messages (Article 15). "Chapter III of Part One contains a set of rules of the kind that would typically be found in agreements between parties such as *interchange agreements* and *system* [default] *rules*." The second part of the Model Law is titled "Electronic Commerce in Specific Areas." It presently contains provisions for the adoption of electronic contracting for the carriage of goods. This part should be

[543]The above information was taken from Glatt at 61-63.

checked from time to time because it may be expanded into other specific areas of electronic contracting.

The *Model Law* recognizes the existing legal obstacles to the formation of electronic commerce in national contract laws. These obstacles generally revolve around the formality requirements found in some national laws, namely "writing," "signature" and "original copy" requirements. Article 1 provides two important concepts in determining the sphere of application of the *Model Law.* First, it is to be used in the "context of commercial activities," although it does not negate its application to consumer transactions. Second, it is intended to provide "media-neutral rules." Its goal is to eliminate any differences between the legality of electronic contracts and paper-based contracts. Article 5 of the *Model Law* establishes the fundamental principle that under law "there should be no disparity of treatment between data messages and paper documents." Also, it is meant to be open-ended in order to be adaptable to future developments in technology. The *Guide* states that the use of "similar means" is intended "to reflect the fact that the *Model Law* was not intended only for application in the context of existing communication techniques but also to accommodate foreseeable technical developments." One area that the Model Law fails to directly address is the role of intermediaries.[544] "The *Model Law,* which is focused on the relationships between originators and addressees, does not, in general, deal with the rights and obligations of intermediaries."

The notion of *incorporation by reference* is highlighted in Section 46 of the *Guide.* It states that "incorporation by reference is regarded as essential to the widespread use of electronic data interchange (EDI), electronic mail, digital certificates, [public key certificates], and other forms of electronic commerce. For example, electronic communications are typically structured in such a way that large numbers of messages are exchanged, with each message conveying bits of information, and relying much more frequently than paper documents on reference to information accessible elsewhere." Major obstacles to such contracting by reference are national laws such as consumer protection laws. Thus, incorporation by reference in electronic contracting should be done with the rules of mandatory laws in

[544]The *Guide's* definition of "intermediaries" includes those entities that receive, store, or transmit data messages on behalf of other parties. It should be noted that a single person can be both an originator or addressee of one data message and act as an intermediary with respect to another.

mind. The *Guide* suggests the following conditions: (1) the reference clause should be inserted into the data message, (2) the document being referenced should actually be known to the other party, and (3) the reference document should be accepted by the other party. Therefore, in an on-line contracting environment where reference is made to the "general terms and conditions" of the seller, the application or form contract should clearly reference the document and make it available for review. For first time users, the on-line site may automatically bring up the referenced document before allowing the user to effectuate a transaction.[545]

Domain Names and Trademark Infringement

A recurring problem in Internet commerce has been the misappropriation of names by so-called "cybersquatters."[546] Cybersquatters are parties that register a famous brand name or trademark as their domain name. The owner of trademark in developing a presence on the world wide web is likely to want to obtain a domain name that is readily associated with its brand name or trademark. The cybersquatter will then attempt to extort a payment for its registered domain name. Network Solutions, Inc administers the United States' domain registration system. The Department of Commerce has recommended the development of new registries, along with the creation of five additional generic top-level domain names. The problem with the Network Solutions dispute resolution process is that it often results in the freezing of the domain name and makes it unavailable to anyone. The two statutory recourses available to the trademark owner are the Lanham Act[547] and the Federal Trademark Dilution Act of 1995.[548] The problem with the Lanham Act is that it requires a likelihood of confusion between the junior user (infringing party) and the senior user. Courts have

---

[545]One may obtain additional information on the *Model Law* directly from UNCITRAL at the following address: International Trade Law Branch, Office of Legal Affairs, United Nations Vienna International Centre, P.O. Box 500, A-1400, Vienna, Austria, Telephone: (43-1) 26060-4060 or 4061 or by E-mail: uncitral@unov.un.or.at.

[546]This term and coverage was taken from L. Keith Whitney, *Defeating the Cybersquatter: Protecting Trademarks and the Internet* (unpublished manuscript) (1999).

[547]15 U.S.C. 1114.

[548]15 U.S.C. 1125 (c).

held that when the goods or services are unrelated to the trademark owner's products, such as when the domain name is registered on behalf of no particular product or service, there is no likelihood of confusion. However, the Federal Trademark Dilution Act does not require proof of a likelihood of confusion. Courts have held that the registering of a domain name for the purpose of selling it to a trademark owner is actionable under the Act.[549] This was confirmed in *Avery Dennison Corp. v. Sumpton*[550] where the court labeled the defendant as a "cybersquatter." The court concluded that the defendant's use diluted the well-known trademark of the plaintiff. In holding against the defendant, the court noted that it had registered over 12,000 domain names.

Personal Jurisdiction

A key issue for the person making an initial foray into Internet commerce is whether he will become amenable to the jurisdiction of a foreign court. Does advertising or processing an order over the Internet provide enough contact with the jurisdiction of the other party to give a foreign court personal jurisdiction? A number of recent American court decisions offer some guidance. A federal Circuit Court in *Bensusan Restaurant Corp. v. King*[551] held that the creation of a web site did not constitute transacting business in a foreign jurisdiction. A restaurant operated under the same name as a trademarked nightclub in New York City. The trademark owner brought suit for tortious infringement of trademark in federal court in New York. The court held that the mere creation of a web site accessible in New York was not sufficient to prove sufficient intent to do business in New York. The case was dismissed for lack of personal jurisdiction. A similar decision was reached in *Cybersell, Inc. v. Cybersell, Inc.*[552] A Florida company created

[549]See, Intermatic, Inc. v. Toeppen, 947 F. Supp. 1227 (N.D. Ill. 1996); Panavision Int'l L.P. v. Toeppen, 945 F. Supp.1296 (C.D. Cal. 1997).

[550]1998 U.S. Dist. LEXIS 4373 (C.D. Cal. 1998).

[551]126 F3d 25 (2d Cir. 1997). Compare, Inset Systems, Inc. v. Instruction Set, Inc., 937 F. Supp. 161 (D. Conn. 1996).

[552]130 F3d 414 (9th Cir. 1997). For a case finding personal jurisdiction see, CompuServe, Inc. v. Patterson, 89 F.3d 1257 (6th Cir. 1996) (a subscriber to a service held to have purposefully availed himself of doing business in the state of the shareware distributor).

a web page to advertise its web page construction services. An Arizona company had a trademark for the same name. In dismissing the case, the court stated that "no court has ever held that an Internet advertisement alone is sufficient to subject the advertiser to jurisdiction in another state." The court further emphasized that the Florida company had not contracted or sold to anyone in Arizona. Despite the tortious nature of the claim, the court elected not to invoke Arizona's long-arm statute. A federal District Court held that actual sales may not even be sufficient to trigger the application of a long-arm statute. In *E-Data Corp v. Micropatent Corp.*[553] the court held that the purchasing of services by downloading material from the Internet was insufficient for purposes of obtaining personal jurisdiction. A key factor in the case was that the accused infringer did not actively advertise its web site. A user had to obtain its web address, access it, browse the information and then download. The result was different in *Zippo Manufacturing Co. v. Zippo Dot Com, Inc.*[554] where the web advertisement was followed by the sale of services to over three thousand subscribers in the state. The number of contacts and sales within a given state is likely to be considered the major factor in the personal jurisdiction decision. In order to avoid being amenable to suit in a given jurisdiction, it is advisable to place clear disclaimers within a web site that your intent is not to engage in transactions with residents in that jurisdiction.

The "Shrinkwrap" Contract

United States law has increasingly recognized the shrinkwrap license or contract. This form of contract has primarily been used in the sale of computer software. The seller places a statement on the exterior of the package to the effect that if the purchaser opens the package she has agreed to the contractual terms found within the package. The agreement found in the package, or subsequently sent by the vendor, typically states something to this effect: "Purchaser's receipt of services (or software) constitutes acceptance of all terms and conditions of this Agreement." Some contracts go further and state boldly that the vendor "reserves the right to change the

[553]— F.Supp. — (D. Conn. 1997), 1997 WL805282.
[554]952 F. Supp. 1119 (W.D.Pa. 1997). See also, Maritz, Inc. v. Cybergold, 947 F.Supp. 1328 (E.D.Mo. 1996).

terms and conditions." The purchaser's only option is to cancel the service or return the product. One particular contract states that upon cancellation, the purchaser-customer is "not entitled to a refund of any prepaid fees." A number of states have passed laws recognizing the shrinkwrap contract. For example, Illinois passed the following law in 1986: "A person who acquires a copy of computer software will be conclusively deemed to have accepted and agreed to those provisions of the license agreement accompanying the copy." However, it places a number of requirements on the seller-licensor before granting the presumption of enforceability. First, there must be a "written legend or notice affixed to [the package] that states clearly that the opening of the sealed package will constitute acceptance of the terms of the accompanying license agreement." Second, the notice must be "clearly and conspicuously visible so as to be readily noticeable to a person viewing the package." Third, conspicuously means "in all capital letters and in language which is readily understandable."

If software is considered a good, then the issue becomes whether the shrinkwrap license is considered a contract under the Uniform Commercial Code (UCC). The court in *Arizona Retail Systems v. Software Link*[555] applied Section 2-207 (additional terms) and 2-209 (modification) to a shrinkwrap license. The issue in the case was whether a disclaimer of implied warranties found in the license had become a part of the contract. The case provides a common scenario in which two merchants discuss the terms of an order over the telephone. The items discussed in the process of placing the order are the specification of the goods, quantity, and the price. The court determined that it was this discussion, along with the placing of the order and the shipment of the software, which formed the contract. The court rejected the argument that the terms of the shrinkwrap license included in each package of software were not additional terms under Section 2-207's battle of the forms scenario or a modification of the contract under Section 2-209. The court also rejected the claim that the license agreement constituted a written confirmation of the telephone discussions. "The license agreement cannot reasonably be described as an attempt to embody, in one form, the agreement between the parties." At best, the license agreement was "a proposal to modify the contract between the parties." Thus, un-

[555]831 F.Supp. 759 (D.Ariz 1993). See also, Step-Saver Data Systems v. Wyse Technology, 939 F.2d 91 (3d Cir. 1991).

less expressly agreed to by the purchaser, the warranty disclaimer did not become a part of the contract since the license was delivered after the contract had already been formed. The court suggested that sellers can protect themselves by not shipping until they obtain assent to those terms they consider essential to the formation of a contract.

The problem with shrinkwrap contracts is that they are generally an American phenomenon. It is important to determine if such a contract will be recognized in the country of importation. In order to protect your software, it may be necessary to require your foreign sales representative or agent to procure a signature on the license agreement from the foreign purchaser. Once enacted, UCITA will provide some parameters for the drafting of shrinkwrap contracts in the United States. For example, UCITA presumes that a license is freely transferable unless the license contract specifically prohibits transfers.[556] Also, warranty law under UCITA possesses similarities and differences when compared to Article 2. Since licensing entails a right to use and not title or ownership of the underlying property, it provides an implied warranty of title and protection against third-party infringement from the licensor to the licensee.[557] Section 401 provides, however, two means by which the licensor may limit its liability under this implied warranty. The licensor may disclaim "by specific language . . . that the licensor does not warrant that competing claims do not exist."[558] The following language is suggested for this purpose: "There is no warranty against interference with your enjoyment of the information or against infringement." In an automated transaction, this language must be stated conspicuously. A second means of disclaiming the implied warranty is provided in Section 401(e). It states that (between merchants) a "grant of a *quitclaim* grants the information or informational rights without an implied warranty as to infringement or misappropriation or as to the rights actually possessed or transferred by the licensee."

---

[556]"A party's contractual interest may be transferred unless the transfer (A) is prohibited under other law; or (B) would materially change the duty of the other party, materially increase the burden or risk imposed on the other party, or materially impair the other party" property or its likelihood or expectation of obtaining return performance." UCITA, Section 503(1).

[557]UCITA, Section 401 (Warranty and Obligations Concerning Interference and Noninfringement).

[558]UCITA, Section 401(d).

UCITA also recognizes implied warranties of *merchantability* and *for a particular purpose.* Section 403 provides an implied warranty of merchantability of computer programs. Section 405 provides an implied warranty that the information provided in the licensed material will achieve an intended purpose. Section 404 recognizes an implied warranty of informational content. It states that a merchant "collects, compiles, processes, provides, or transmits informational content warrants that there is no inaccuracy in the informational content caused by the merchant's failure to perform with reasonable care." An issue left unresolved is whether a warranty may be implied that the software or information does not contain any computer viruses.

In the area of remedies, the ability to use electronic self-help remedies is limited by Section 816.[559] It requires that "the licensee separately manifest assent to a term authorizing the use of electronic self-help."[560] Before using an electronic self-help remedy, the licensor must give a 15-day notice to the licensee. The notice must state the nature of the claimed breach and provide contact information to which the licensee may communicate concerning the alleged breach.

Given the technological nature of shrinkwrap products, the traditional notice provision is often expanded to provide different avenues for notice. One example of such a notice provision follows:

> **Notice:** Notices are deemed given when deposited in the mail and addressed to the recipient's last known address. A right is reserved to give notice electronically or by telephone, and such notice is deemed given when left with the recipient. Purchaser's notice is deemed given when received by us.

Note that this pro-vendor notice provision adopts a dispatch or mailbox rule for the vendor's notice, but a receipt rule for the purchaser's notice. The provision does not adequately define what is meant when an electronic notice is "left" with the purchaser. Other clauses commonly found in shrinkwrap contracts include: (1) a clause stating that the customer has not

[559]Boss and Kaufman note the development of electronic devices like "software locks," "logic bombs," and "drop-dead" to provide the licensor with self-help remedies to terminate and police their licenses.

[560]UCITA, Section 816(c). See generally, Esther C. Roditti, *Is Self-Help a Lawful Contractual Remedy?*, 21 Rutgers Computer & Technology Law Journal 431 (1995).

purchased the software itself, but merely has obtained a personal, non-transferable license to use the program, (2) a disclaimer of all warranties, except for a warranty covering physical defects in the diskettes, (3) a clause purporting to limit the purchaser's remedies to repair and replace of defective disks, and to exclude all consequential or incidental damages caused by the software, (4) an integration clause providing that the license is the final and complete expression of the agreement, (5) a provision prohibiting assignment of the program or license without the express prior consent of the seller, and (6) a provision triggering the purchaser's acceptance of the shrinkwrap license upon opening the package.

Electronic Documentation

The "paper" in the documentary transaction that is central to the exportation of goods is becoming less vital. Cost savings generated by electronic transmission are likely to foster increased use of the electronic communication of documents. "In the transport industry, the cost of raising conventional documents and the attendant delays involved in their issuance and verification constitute 10% to 15% of total transportation costs."[561] In response, the *Comité Maritime International* (CMI) produced the 1990 Rules for Electronic Bills of Lading. The CMI Rules are voluntary in nature. As important as the drafting of the Rules, was the establishment of a central registry for registering the electronic keys needed to effectuate the transfer of the electronic bill of lading.[562] Professor Ramberg discusses the use of a "private key" to effectuate the transfer.

> The electronic transfer itself is achieved by connecting the so-called right of control and transfer to a "private key," which is unique to each successive holder and transferable by him. This private key must be separate and distinct from any means used to identify the contract of carriage and any security password or identification used to access the

[561]Commission of the European Communities, The Legal Position of the Member States with Respect to Electronic Data Interchange: Final Report (Sept. 1989), as cited in, Amelia H. Boss, *The International Commercial Use of Electronic Data Interchange and Electronic Communication Technologies,* 46 Business Lawyer 1787 (1991).

[562]See, Comment, *The CMI Charts a Course on the Sea of Electronic Data Interchange: Rules for Electronic Bills of Lading,* 16 Tulane Maritime Law Journal 349 (1992).

> computer network. The carrier is only entitled to take instructions from or deliver the goods to a person able to verify his possession of the right of control and transfer by reference to the private key which could be passed on to a new holder by the carrier's cancellation of the previous key and issuance of a new one to the next holder following a notification and confirmation procedure according to Rule 7.[563]

The obstacle to electronic conveyance presented by the document of title function of bills of lading is not present in other transport documents. Therefore, sea waybills, air waybills, and rail consignment notes are easily transmitted through EDI software. Also, most of the documents involved in the contract formation process (pro forma invoice, purchase order, confirmations) can be transmitted through EDI. Professor Ramberg also notes that Incoterms 1990 (and Incoterms 2000) recognizes the trend toward electronic transmissions. Section A8 of Incoterms states that "where the seller and buyer have agreed to communicate electronically, the document referred to in the proceeding paragraph may be replaced by an equivalent electronic date interchange (EDI) message."

The New Electronic Services Industry

As electronic commerce grows, so does the need for companies to service the industry in the form of third party providers and value added networks. These service companies will perform a number of vital functions including "protocol conversion; storage, transmission and retrieval services; format translation; message tracing, delivery notification and integration reports; record retention services; implementation training and consultation; security enhancement; and database development."[564] A first generation example of this phenomenon is the SWIFT system (Society for Worldwide Interbank Financial Telecommunications) which provides a set of rules that govern banks in their telecommunications transactions. The

563Jan Ramberg, "Novel Features of the ICC Incoterms 1990 in UNITED NATIONS, UNIFORM COMMERCIAL LAW IN THE TWENTY-FIRST CENTURY 81 (1992).

564Amelia Boss, "Electronic Commerce and the Law" in UNITED NATIONS, UNIFORM COMMERCIAL LAW IN THE TWENTY-FIRST CENTURY 163 (1992).

SWIFT system has accelerated the transmission of payments in documentary collections through a private, high-speed communications network between member banks.[565]

E-Commerce Ethics

Along with the development of an adequate legal support structure, electronic commerce poses numerous ethical concerns. The e-commerce industry needs to develop its own self-regulatory code of ethics in order to provide aspirational guidance to those using the World Wide Web, Internet, and other electronic networks to transact business. The International Chamber of Commerce recognized this need by developing *Guidelines on Advertising and Marketing on the Internet.* The *Guidelines*' main philosophical mandate is to encourage advertisers and marketers "to create an electronic environment which all the world's consumers can fully trust." Article 1 states that "all advertising and marketing should be legal, decent, honest, and truthful." Because of the potential for fraud, someone purchasing on the Internet should not base his decision to purchase solely on information obtained online. Depending upon the size of the transaction, there is no substitute for obtaining the financial statements of the other party, along with obtaining references of suppliers and other customers. Although aspirational in character, the *Guidelines* do provide some concrete rules. Advertisers and marketers should identify themselves and the nature of their connection to any commercial messages placed on the Internet (Article 2). The addressees of commercial messages should be clearly informed of the cost of accessing the message or of a service (Article 3). Also, "advertisers and marketers should take reasonable precautions to safeguard the security of their files (Article 5)." Finally, advertisers and marketers should post a *privacy policy statement* on their online site.

---

[565]It has been estimated that electronic funds transfers have reduced the costs of some transaction in half. G. Mitshell, *Introduction to Electronic Funds Transfer Systems,* 2 Computer Law Journal 2 (1980). See also, Fred M. Greguras & Lynn Kerr, *Transborder Payments: The Legal Issues,* 19 Computer L. Rep. 628 (1994); Symposium, *The Electronic Future of Cash,* 46 American U. Law Rev. 967 (1997).

Exhibit 11.2: Internet Sources and Terms

A number of terms related to the Internet are defined below:

Bulletin Board System (BBS) — A computerized meeting and announcement system where people can have discussions, and download files, without all the persons being connected to the computer at the same time.

BITNET — A network of educational sites independent of the Internet.

Browser — Software program that is used to look at various Internet resources.

Domain Name — The name that identifies an Internet site. It consists of both a general and more specific part. A given domain name points to only one computer.

Homepage — Main web page for a person, business, or organization.

Host — Any computer on a network that is a repository for services available to other computers on the network.

Hypertext — A text that contains links to other documents. Words when chosen cause another document or file to be retrieved.

HyperText Markup Language (HTML) — The coding language that creates hypertext documents.

HyperText Transport Protocol (HTTP) — the most important protocol for moving hypertext files across the Internet.

Intranet — Unlike the Internet, which connects tens of thousands of independent networks, this is a private network inside a company or organization.

Integrated Services Digital Network (ISDN) — A newer way to move large amounts of data over existing telephone lines.

Internet Service Provider (ISP) — An entity that provides access to the Internet.

Maillist — A system that allows one to send a message to a single address whereupon the message is copied and sent to the other subscribers to the maillist or mailing list.

Portal — The initial site when entering the World Wide Web. It provides a menu of web sites or a search engine.

Secure Sockets Layer (SSL) — A Netscape Communications designed protocol that allows for the encryption and authentication of messages across the Internet.

Uniform Resource Locator (URL) — The standard method of giving an address for any source on the Internet.

Wide Area Information Servers (WAIS) — Commercial software that allows the indexing of large amounts of information. One can then search the Internet and the software will rank sources according to closeness to the search request.

The Internet provides an almost unlimited amount of access to information relevant to international trade and international business transactions. The following is a selective sampling of some web sites: (1) CyberSpace Law Center: www.cyberlaw.com. This site focuses on legal issues concerning computer technology including information on international piracy and patent infringement. (2) Internet Legal Services: www.legalethics.com. This site covers legal issues dealing with advertising on the Internet and the confidentiality of E-mail. (3) Trade Compass: http://www.tradecompass.com. This site provides a number of valuable services including the electronic filing of customs forms with the United States Customs Service. (4) GINS/World Business Network (@WBN) provides access to the credit reporting services of Dunn & Bradstreet. Other Internet sources are presented in Appendix 1.

APPENDIX 1

Internet Sources

INTELLECTUAL PROPERTY LAW

American Bar Association's Intellectual Property Law Section: www.abanet.org/intelprop
Business Software Alliance (BSA): www.bas.org. BSA is an association that represents U.S. software companies in preventing international software piracy.
United States Copyright Office: http://lcweb.loc.gov/copyright
United States Patent and Trademark Office: www.uspto.gov
World Intellectual Property Organization (WIPO): www.wipo.org

ELECTRONIC COMMERCE

Committee on the Law of Commerce in Cyberspace, ABA Section of Business Law: http://www.abanet.org/buslaw/cyber/
Department of Commerce (Business, economic, and trade information data base) (subscription service): http://www.statgov/BEN/subject/trade.html
Digital Signature Guidelines, ABA Information Security Committee, Section of Science and Technology: http://www.abanet.org/scitech/ec/isc/dsg-toc.html
Digital Signature Resource Center (worldwide laws on digital signatures), Internet Law and Policy Forum: http://www.ilpf.org/digsig/digsig2.htm
Electronic Agent (example): Cisco Systems, *Networked Commerce:* http://www.cisco.com/public/ordsum.html

Electronic Communications in Contractual Transactions (National Conference of Commissioners on Uniform State Laws), *Drafts of Uniform and Model Acts:* http://www.law.upenn.edu/library/ulc.htm
Framework for Global Electronic Commerce, White House Paper: http://www.iitf.nist.gov/eleccomm/ecomm.htm
GUIDEC: General Usage for International Digitally Ensured Commerce: http://www.uscib.org/frame6a.htm
UNCITRAL, *Model Law on Electronic Commerce* (with Guide to Enactment): http://www.un.or.at/uncitral/texts/electcom/ml-ec.htm
Uniform Electronic Transactions Act (UETA) (National Conference of Commissioners on Uniform State Laws): http://www.law.upenn.edu/bll/ulc/ulc.htm

INTERNATIONAL TRADE

Convention on Contracts for the International Sale of Goods (CISG) cases and materials: http://www.cisg.law.pace.edu
Exchange Rates: http://cnn.com/travel/currency
INCOTERMS **Information:** http://itl.irv.uit.no/trade law/documents/sales/incoterms/nav/inc.html
International Chamber of Commerce: http://www.iccwbo.org
Comprehensive site on **international shipping:** http://www.tradeport.org
International Trade Administration: http://www.ita.doc.gov/
International Trade Law Monitor: http://ra.irv.uit.no/tradelaw
"Maritime Global Net" (Links to **ocean carriers** and shipping schedules): http://www.mglobal.com
"Tradeport" (comprehensive site on international trade): http://www.tradeport.org
UNCITRAL: http://www.un.or.at/uncitral
UNIDROIT (International Institute for the Unification of Private Law: http://ra.irv.vit.no/trade-law/organizations/unidroit.html
UNIDROIT Principles of International Commercial Contracts: http://www.unidroit.org/english/principles/pr-main.htm
UNIDROIT Conventions: http://www.unidroit.org/english/conventions/c-main.htm
United States Federal Maritime Commission: http://www.fmc.gov
World Bank: http://www.worldbank.org/

APPENDIX 2

United Nations Convention on Contracts for the International Sale of Goods (1980)*

THE STATES PARTIES TO THIS CONVENTION,

BEARING IN MIND the broad objectives in the resolutions adopted by the sixth special session of the General Assembly of the United Nations on the establishment of a new International Economic Order,

CONSIDERING that the development of international trade on the basis of equality and mutual benefit is an important element in promoting friendly relations among States,

BEING OF THE OPINION that the adoption of uniform rules which govern contracts for the international sale of goods and take into account the different social, economic and legal systems would contribute to the removal of legal barriers in international trade and promote the development of international trade,

HAVE AGREED as follows:

PART I Sphere of Application and General Provisions

Chapter I: Sphere of Application

---

*(Part IV Final Provisions, Article 89-101, have been deleted)

Article 1

(1) This Convention applies to contracts of sale of goods between parties whose places of business are in different States:

- (a) when the States are Contracting States; or
- (b) when the rules of private international law lead to the application of the law of a Contracting State.

(2) The fact that the parties have their places of business in different States is to be disregarded whenever this fact does not appear either from the contract or from any dealings between, or from information disclosed by, the parties at any time before or at the conclusion of the contract.
(3) Neither the nationality of the parties nor the civil or commercial character of the parties or of the contract is to be taken into consideration in determining the application of this Convention.

Article 2

This Convention does not apply to sales:

- (a) of goods bought for personal, family or household use, unless the seller, at any time before or at the conclusion of the contract, neither knew nor ought to have known that the goods were bought for any such use;
- (b) by auction;
- (c) on execution or otherwise by authority of law,
- (d) of stocks, shares, investment securities, negotiable instruments or money,
- (e) of ships, vessels, hovercraft or aircraft;
- (f) of electricity.

Article 3

(1) Contracts for the supply of goods to be manufactured or produced are to be considered sales unless the party who orders the goods undertakes to supply a substantial part of the materials necessary for such manufacture or production.
(2) This Convention does not apply to contracts in which the preponderant part of the obligations of the party who furnishes the goods consists in the supply of labour or other services.

Article 4

This Convention governs only the formation of the contract of sale and the rights and obligations of the seller and the buyer arising from such a contract. In particular, except as otherwise expressly provided in this Convention, it is not concerned with:

(a) the validity of the contract or of any of its provisions or of any usage;

(b) the effect which the contract may have on the property in the goods sold.

Article 5

This Convention does not apply to the liability of the seller for death or personal injury caused by the goods to any person.

Article 6

The parties may exclude the application of this Convention or, subject to article 12, derogate from or vary the effect of any of its provisions.

Chapter II: General Provisions

Article 7

(1) In the interpretation of this Convention, regard is to be had to its international character and to the need to promote uniformity in its application and the observance of good faith in international trade.

(2) Questions concerning matters governed by this Convention which are not expressly settled in it are to be settled in conformity with the general principles on which it is based or, in the absence of such principles, in conformity with the law applicable by virtue of the rules of private international law.

Article 8

(1) For the purposes of this Convention statements made by and other conduct of party are to be interpreted according to his intent where the other party knew or could not have been unaware what that intent was.

(2) If the preceding paragraph is not applicable, statements made by and other conduct of a party are to be interpreted according to the understanding that a reasonable person of the same kind as the other party would have had in the same circumstances.
(3) In determining the intent of a party or the understanding a reasonable person would have had, due consideration is to be given to all relevant circumstances of the case including the negotiations, any practices which the parties have established between themselves, usage and any subsequent conduct of the parties.

Article 9

(1) The parties are bound by any usage to which they have agreed and by any practices which they have established between themselves.
(2) The parties are considered, unless otherwise agreed, to have impliedly made applicable to their contract or its formation a usage of which the parties knew or ought to have known and which in international trade is widely known to, and regularly observed by, parties to contracts of the type involved in the particular trade concerned.

Article 10

For the purposes of this Convention:

(a) if a party has more than one place of business, the place of the business is that which has the closest relationship to the contract and its performance, having regard to the circumstances known to or contemplated by the parties at any time before or at the conclusion of the contract;

(b) if a party does not have a place of business, reference is to be made to his habitual residence.

Article11

A contract of sale need not be concluded in or evidenced by writing and is not subject to any other requirement as to form. It may be proved by any means, including witnesses.

Article 12

Any provision of article 11, article 29 or Part 11 of this Convention that allows a contract of sale or its modification or termination by agreement or any offer, acceptance or other indication of intention to be made in any form other than in writing does not apply where any party has his place of business in a Contracting State which has made a declaration under article 96 of this Convention. The parties may not derogate from or vary the effect of this article.

Article 13

For the purposes of this Convention "writing" includes telegram and telex.

PART II: Formation of the Contract

Article 14

(1) A proposal for concluding a contract addressed to one or more specific persons constitutes an offer if it is sufficiently definite and indicates the intention of the offeror to be bound in case of acceptance. A proposal is sufficiently definite if it indicates the goods and expressly or implicitly fixes or makes provision for determining the quantity and the price.
(2) A proposal other than one addressed to one or more specific persons is to be considered merely as an invitation to make offers, unless the contrary is clearly indicated by the person making the proposal.

Article 15

(1) An offer becomes effective when it reaches the offeree.
(2) An offer, even if it is irrevocable, may be withdrawn if the withdrawal reaches the offeree before or at the same time as the offer.

Article 16

(1) Until a contract is concluded an offer may be revoked if the revocation reaches the offeree before he has dispatched an acceptance.
(2) However, an offer cannot be revoked:

(a) if it indicates, whether by stating a fixed time for acceptance or otherwise, that it is irrevocable; or
(b) if it was reasonable for the offeree to rely on the offer as being irrevocable and the offeree has acted in reliance on the offer.

Article 17

An offer, even if it is irrevocable, is terminated when a rejection reaches the offeror.

Article 18

(1) A statement made by or other conduct of the offeree indicating assent to an offer is an acceptance. Silence or inactivity does not in itself amount to acceptance.
(2) An acceptance of an offer becomes effective at the moment the indication of assent reaches the offeror. An acceptance is not effective if the indication of assent does not reach the offeror within the time he has fixed or, if no time is fixed, within a reasonable time, due account being taken of the circumstances of the transaction, including the rapidity of the means of communication employed by the offeror, An oral offer must be accepted immediately unless the circumstances indicate otherwise.
(3) However, if, by virtue of the offer or as a result of practices which the parties have established between themselves or of usage, the offeree may indicate assent by performing an act, such as one relating to the dispatch of the goods or payment of the price, without notice to the offeror, the acceptance is effective at the moment the act is performed, provided that the act is performed within the period of time laid down in the preceding paragraph.

Article 19

(1) A reply to an offer which purports to be an acceptance but contains additions, limitations or other modifications is a rejection of the offer and constitutes a counter-offer.
(2) However, a reply to an offer which purports to be an acceptance but contains additional or different terms which do not materially alter the terms of the offer constitutes an acceptance, unless the offeror, without undue delay, objects

orally to the discrepancy or dispatches a notice to that effect. If he does not so object, the terms of the contract are the terms of the offer with the modifications contained in the acceptance.
(3) Additional or different terms relating, among other things, to the price, payment, quality and quantity of the goods, place and time of delivery, extent of one party's liability to the other or the settlement of disputes are considered to alter the terms of the offer materially.

Article 20

(1) A period of time for acceptance fixed by the offeror in a telegram or a letter begins to run from the moment the telegram is handed in for dispatch or from the date shown on the letter or, if no such date is shown, from the date shown on the envelope. A period of time for acceptance fixed by the offeror by telephone, telex or other means of instantaneous communication, begins to run from the moment that the offer reaches the offeree.
(2) Official holidays or non-business days occurring during the period for acceptance are included in calculating the period. However, if a notice of acceptance cannot be delivered at the address of the offeror on the last day of the period because that day falls on an official holiday or a non-business day at the place of business of the offeror, the period is extended until the first business day which follows.

Article 21

(1) A late acceptance is nevertheless effective as an acceptance if without delay the offeror orally so informs the offeree or dispatches a notice to that effect.
(2) If a letter or other writing containing a late acceptance shows that it has been sent in such circumstances that if its transmission had been normal it would have reached the offeror in due time, the late acceptance is effective as an acceptance unless, without delay, the offeror orally informs the offeree that he considers his offer as having lapsed or dispatches a notice to that effect.

Article 22

An acceptance may be withdrawn if the withdrawal reaches the offeror before or at the same time as the acceptance would have become effective.

Article 23

A contract is concluded at the moment when an acceptance of an offer becomes effective in accordance with the provisions of this Convention.

Article 24

For the purposes of this part of the Convention, an offer, declaration of acceptance o any other indication of intention "reaches" the addressee when it is made orally to him or delivered by any other means to him personally, to his place of business or mailing address or, if he does not have a place of business or mailing address, to his habitual residence.

PART III: Sale of Goods

Chapter I: General Provisions

Article 25

A breach of contract committed by one of the parties is fundamental if it results in such detriment to the other party as substantially to deprive him of what he is entitled to expect under the contract, unless the party in breach did not foresee and a reasonable person of the same kind in the same circumstances would not have foreseen such a result.

Article 26

A declaration of avoidance of the contract is effective only if made by notice to the other party.

Article 27

Unless otherwise expressly provided in this Part of the Convention, if any notice, request or other communication is given or made by a party in accordance with this Part and by means appropriate in the circumstances, a delay or error in the transmission of the communication or its failure to arrive does not deprive that party of the right to rely on the communication.

Article 28

If, in accordance with the provisions of this Convention, one party is entitled to require performance of any obligation by the other party, a court is not bound to enter a judgement for specific performance unless the court would do so under its own law in respect of similar contracts of sale not governed by this Convention.

Article 29

(1) A contract may be modified or terminated by the mere agreement of the parties.
(2) A contract in writing which contains a provision requiring any modification or termination by agreement to be in writing may not be otherwise modified or terminated by agreement. However, a party may be precluded by his conduct from asserting such a provision to the extent that the other party has relied on that conduct.

Chapter H: Obligations of the Seller

Article 30

The seller must deliver the goods, hand over any documents relating to them and transfer the property in the goods, as required by the contract and this Convention.
Section 1. Delivery of the goods and handing over of documents

Article 31

If the seller is not bound to deliver the goods at any other particular place, his obligation to deliver consists:

(a) if the contract of sale involves carriage of the goods — in handing the goods over to the first carrier for transmission to the buyer;
(b) if, in cases not within the preceding subparagraph, the contract relates to specific goods, or unidentified goods to be drawn from a specific stock or to be manufactured or produced, and at the time of the

conclusion of the contract the parties knew that the goods were at, or were to be manufactured or produced at a particular place — in placing the goods at the buyer's disposal at that place;

(c) in other cases — in placing the goods at the buyer's disposal at the place where the seller had his place of business at the time of the conclusion of the contract.

Article 32

(1) If the seller, in accordance with the contract or this Convention, hands the goods over to a carrier and if the goods are not clearly identified to the contract by markings on the goods, by shipping documents or otherwise, the seller must give the buyer notice of the consignment specifying the goods.
(2) If the seller is bound to arrange for carriage of the goods, he must make such contracts as are necessary for carriage to the place fixed by means of transportation appropriate in the circumstances and according to the usual terms for such transportation.
(3) If the seller is not bound to effect insurance -in respect of the carriage of goods, he must, at the buyer's request, provide him with all available information necessary to enable him to effect such insurance.

Article 33

The seller must deliver the goods:

(a) if a date is fixed by or determinable from the contract, on that date;
(b) if a period of time is fixed by or determinable from the contract, at any time within that period unless circumstances indicate that the buyer is to choose a date; or
(c) in any other case, within a reasonable time after the conclusion of the contract.

Article 34

If the seller is bound to hand over documents relating to the goods, he must hand them over at the time and place and in the form required by the contract. If the seller has handed over documents before that time, he may, up to that time, cure any lack of conformity in the documents, if the exercise of this right does not cause the buyer unreasonable inconvenience or unreasonable expense. However, the buyer retains any right to claim damages as provided for in this Convention.

Section 11. Conformity of the goods and third party claims

Article 35

(1) The seller must deliver goods which are of the quantity, quality and description required by the contract and which are contained or packaged in the manner required by the contract.

(2) Except where the parties have agreed otherwise, the goods do not conform with the contract unless there:

- (a) are fit for the purposes for which goods of the same description would ordinarily be used;
- (b) are fit for any particular purpose expressly or impliedly made known to the seller at the time of the conclusion of the contract, except where the circumstances show that the buyer did not rely, or that it was unreasonable for him to rely, on the seller's skill and judgement;
- (c) possess the qualities of goods which the seller has held out to the buyer as a sample or model,
- (d) are contained or packaged in the manner usual for such goods or, where there is no such manner, in a manner adequate to preserve and protect the goods.

(3) The seller is not liable under subparagraphs (a) to (d) of the preceding paragraph for any lack of conformity of the goods if at the time of the conclusion of the contract the buyer knew or could not have been unaware of such lack of conformity.

Article 36

(1) The seller is liable in accordance with the contract and this Convention for any lack of conformity which exists at the time when the risk passes to the buyer, even though the lack of conformity becomes apparent only after that time.

(2) The seller is also liable for any lack of conformity which occurs after the time indicated in the preceding paragraph and which is due to a breach of any of his

obligations, including a breach of any guarantee that for a period of time the goods will remain fit for their ordinary purpose or for some particular purpose or will retain specified qualities or characteristics.

Article 37

If the seller has delivered goods before the date for delivery, he may, up to that date, deliver any missing part or make up any deficiency in the quantity of the goods delivered, or deliver goods in replacement of any non-conforming goods delivered or remedy any lack of conformity in the goods delivered, provided that the exercise of this right does not cause the buyer unreasonable inconvenience or unreasonable expense. However, the buyer retains any right to claim damages as provided for in this Convention.

Article 38

(1) The buyer must examine the goods, or cause them to be examined, within as short a period as is practicable in the circumstances.
(2) If the contract involves carriage of the goods, examination may be deferred until after the goods have arrived at their destination.
(3) If the goods are redirected in transit or redispatched by the buyer without a reasonable opportunity for examination by him and at the time of the conclusion of the contract the seller knew or ought to have known of the possibility of such redirection or redispatch, examination may be deferred until after the goods have arrived at the new destination.

Article 39

(1) The buyer loses the right to rely on a lack of conformity of the goods if he does not give notice to the seller specifying the nature of the lack of conformity within a reasonable time after he has discovered it or ought to have discovered it.
(2) In any event, the buyer loses the right to rely on a lack of conformity of the goods if he does not give the seller notice thereof at the latest within a period of two years from the date on which the goods were actually handed over to the buyer, unless this time limit is inconsistent with a contractual period of guarantee.

Article 40

The seller is not entitled to rely on the provisions of articles 38 and 39 if the lack of conformity relates to facts of which he knew or could not have been unaware and which he did not disclose to the buyer.

Article 41

The seller must deliver goods which are free from any right or claim of a third party, unless the buyer agreed to take the goods subject to that right or claim. However, if such right or claim is based on industrial property or other intellectual property, the seller's obligation is governed by article 42.

Article 42

(1) The seller must deliver goods which are free from any right or claim of a third party based on industrial property or other intellectual property, of which at the time of the conclusion of the contract the seller knew or could not have been unaware, provided that the right or claim is based on industrial property or other intellectual property:

- (a) under the law of the State where the goods will be resold or otherwise used, if it was contemplated by the parties at the time of the conclusion of the contract that the goods would be resold or otherwise used in that State; or
- (b) in any other case, under the law of the State where the buyer has his place of business.

(2) The obligation of the seller under the preceding paragraph does not extend to cases where:

- (a) at the time of the conclusion of the contract the buyer knew or could not have been unaware of the right or claim; or
- (b) the right or claim results from the seller's compliance with technical drawings, designs, formulae or other such specifications furnished by the buyer.

Article 43

(1) The buyer loses the right to rely on the provisions of article 41 or article 42 if he does not give notice to the seller specifying the nature of the right or claim

of the third party within a reasonable time after he has become aware or ought to have become aware of the right or claim.
(2) The seller is not entitled to rely on the provisions of the preceding paragraph if he knew of the right or claim of the third party and the nature of it.

Article 44

Notwithstanding the provisions of paragraph (1) of article 39 and paragraph (1) of article 43, the buyer may reduce the price in accordance with article 50 or claim damages, except for loss of profit, if he has a reasonable excuse for his failure to give the required notice.

Section III: Remedies for Breach of Contract by the Seller

Article 45

(1) If the seller fails to perform any of his obligations under the contract or this Convention, the buyer may:

(a) exercise the rights provided in articles 46 to 52; (b) claim damages as provided in articles 74 to 77.

(2) The buyer is not deprived of any right he may have to claim damages by exercising his right to other remedies.
(3) No period of grace may be granted to the seller by a court or arbitral tribunal when the buyer resorts to a remedy for breach of contract.

Article 46

(1) The buyer may require performance by the seller of his obligations unless the buyer has resorted to a remedy which is inconsistent with this requirement.
(2) If the goods do not conform with the contract, the buyer may require delivery of substitute goods only if the lack of conformity constitutes a fundamental breach of contract and a request for substitute goods is made either in conjunction with notice given under article 39 or within a reasonable time thereafter.
(3) If the goods do not conform with the contract, the buyer may require the seller to remedy the lack of conformity by repair, unless this is unreasonable having regard to all the circumstances. A request for repair must be made either in conjunction with notice given under article 39 or within a reasonable time thereafter.

Article 47

(1) The buyer may fix an additional period of time of reasonable length for performance by the seller of his obligations.
(2) Unless the buyer has received notice from the seller that he will not perform within the period so fixed, the buyer may not, during that period, resort to any remedy for breach of contract. However, the buyer is not deprived thereby of any right he may have to claim damages for delay in performance.

Article 48

(1) Subject to article 49, the seller may, even after the date for delivery, remedy at his own expense any failure to perform his obligations, if he can do so without unreasonable delay and without causing the buyer unreasonable inconvenience or uncertainty of reimbursement by the seller of expenses advanced by the buyer. However, the buyer retains any right to claim damages as provided for in this Convention.
(2) If the seller requests the buyer to make known whether he will accept performance and the buyer does not comply with the request within a reasonable time, the Seller may perform within the time indicated in his request. The buyer may not, during that period of time, resort to any remedy which is inconsistent with performance by the seller.
(3) A notice by the seller that he will perform within a specified period of time is assumed to include a request, under the preceding paragraph, that the buyer make known his decision.
(4) A request or notice by the seller under paragraph (2) or (3) of this article is not effective unless received by the buyer.

Article 49

(1) The buyer may declare the contract avoided:
- (a) if the failure by the seller to perform any of his obligations under the contract or this Convention amounts to a fundamental breach of contract; or
- (b) in case of non-delivery, if the seller does not deliver the goods within the additional period of time fixed by the buyer in accordance with paragraph (1) of article 47 or declares that he will not deliver within the period so fixed.

(2) However, in cases where the seller has delivered the goods, the buyer loses the right to declare the contract avoided unless he does so:

(a) in respect of late delivery, within a reasonable time after he has become aware that delivery has been made;

(b) in respect of any breach other than late delivery, within a reasonable time:

(i) after he knew or ought to have known of the breach;

(ii) after the expiration of any additional period of time fixed by the buyer in accordance with paragraph (1) of article 47, or after the seller has declared that he will not perform his obligations within such an additional period; or

(iii) after the expiration of any additional period of time indicated by the seller in accordance with paragraph (2) of article 48, or after the buyer has declared that he will not accept performance.

Article 50

If the goods do not conform with the contract and whether or not the price has already been paid, the buyer may reduce the price in the same proportion as the value that the goods actually delivered had at the time of the delivery bears to the value that conforming goods would have had at that time. However, if the seller remedies any failure to perform his obligations in accordance with article 37 or article 48 or if the buyer refuses to accept performance by the seller in accordance with those articles, the buyer may not reduce the price.

Article 51

(1) If the seller delivers only a part of the goods or if only a part of the goods delivered is in conformity with. the contract, articles 46 to 50 apply in respect of the part which is missing or which does not conform.
(2) The buyer may declare the contract avoided in its entirety only if the failure to make delivery completely or in conformity with the contract amounts to a fundamental breach of the contract.

Article 52

(1) If the seller delivers the goods before the date fixed, the buyer may take delivery or refuse to take delivery.

(2) If the seller delivers a quantity of goods greater than that provided for in the contract, the buyer may take delivery or refuse to take delivery of the excess quantity. If the buyer takes delivery of all or part of the excess quantity, he must pay for it at the contract rate.

Chapter III: Obligations of the Buyer

Article 53

The buyer must pay the price for the goods and take delivery of them as required by the contract and this Convention.

Section 1. Payment of the price

Article 54

The buyer's obligation to pay the price includes taking such steps and complying with such formalities as may be required under the contract or any laws and regulations to enable payment to be made.

Article 55

Where a contract has been validly concluded but does not expressly or implicitly fix or make provision for determining the price, the parties are considered, in the absence of any indication to the contrary, to have impliedly made reference to the price generally charged at the time of the conclusion of the contract for such goods sold under comparable circumstances in the trade concerned.

Article 56

If the price is fixed according to the weight of the goods, in case of doubt it is to be determined by the net weight.

Article 57

(1) If the buyer is not bound to pay the price at any other particular place, he must pay it to the seller:

(a) at the seller's place of business; or

(b) if the payment is to be made against the handing over of the goods or of documents, at the place where the handing over takes place.

(2) The seller must bear any increase in the expenses incidental to payment which is caused by a change in his place of business subsequent to the conclusion of the contract.

Article 58

(1) If the buyer is not bound to pay the price at any other specific time, he must pay it when the seller places either the goods or documents controlling their disposition at the buyer's disposal in accordance with the contract and this Convention. The seller may make such payment a condition for handing over the goods or documents.

(2) If the contract involves carriage of the goods, the seller may dispatch the goods on terms whereby the goods, or documents controlling their disposition, will not be handed over to the buyer except against payment of the price.

(3) The buyer is not bound to pay the price until he has had an opportunity to examine the goods, unless the procedures for delivery or payment agreed upon by the parties are inconsistent with his having such an opportunity.

Article 59

The buyer must pay the price on the date fixed by or determinable from the contract and this Convention without the need for any request or compliance with any formality on the part of the seller.

Section H: Taking delivery

Article 60

The buyer's obligation to take delivery consists:

(a) in doing all the acts which could reasonably be expected of him in order to enable the seller to make delivery; and

(b) in taking over the goods.

Section 111. Remedies for breach of contract by the buyer

Article 61

(1) If the buyer fails to perform any of his obligations under the contract or this Convention, the seller may:

(a) exercise the rights provided in articles 62 to 65;

(b) claim damages as provided in articles 74 to 77

(2) The seller is not deprived of any right he may have to claim damages by exercising his right to other remedies.

(3) No period of grace may be granted to the buyer by a court or arbitral tribunal when the seller resorts to a remedy for breach of contract.

Article 62

The seller may require the buyer to pay the price, take delivery or perform his other obligations, unless the seller has resorted to a remedy which is inconsistent with this requirement.

Article 63

(1) The seller may fix an additional period of time of reasonable length for performance by the buyer of his obligations.

(2) Unless the seller has received notice from the buyer that he will not perform within the period so fixed, the seller may not, during that period, resort to any remedy for breach of contract. However, the seller is not deprived thereby of any right he may have to claim damages for delay in performance.

Article 64

(1) The seller may declare the contract avoided:

(a) if the failure by the buyer to perform any of his obligations under the contract or this Convention amounts to a fundamental breach of contract; or

(b) if the buyer does not, within the additional period of time fixed by the seller in accordance with paragraph (1) of article 63, perform his obligation to pay the price or take delivery of the goods, or if he declares that he will not do to with in the period so fixed.

(2) However, in cases where the buyer has paid the price, the seller loses the right to declare the contract avoided unless he does so:

(a) in respect of late performance by the buyer, before the seller has become aware that performance as been rendered; or

(b) in respect of any breach other than late performance by the buyer, within a reasonable time:

(i) after the seller knew or ought to have known of the breach; or

(ii) after the expiration of any additional period of time fixed by the seller in accordance with paragraph (1) of article 63, or after the buyer has declared that he will not perform his obligations within such an additional period.

Article 65

(1) If under the contract the buyer is to specify the form, measurement or other features of the goods and he *fails* to make such specification either on the date agreed upon or within a reasonable time after receipt of a request from the seller, the seller may, without prejudice to any other rights he may have, make the specification himself in accordance with the requirements of the buyer that may be known to him.
(2) If the seller makes the specification himself, he must inform the buyer of the details thereof and must fix a reasonable time within which the buyer may make a different specification. If, after receipt of such a communication, the buyer fails to do so within the time so fixed, the specification made by the seller is binding.

Chapter IV: Passing of Risk

Article 66

Loss of or damage to the goods after the risk has passed to the buyer does not discharge him from his obligation to pay the price, unless the loss or damage is due to an act or omission of the seller.

Article 67

(1) If the contract of sale involves carriage of the goods and the seller is not bound to hand them over at a particular place, the risk passes to the buyer when

the goods are handed over to the first carrier for transmission to the buyer in accordance with the contract of sale. If the seller is bound to hand the goods over to a carrier at a particular place, the risk does not pass to the buyer until the goods are handed over to the carrier at that place. The fact that the seller is authorized to retain documents controlling the disposition of the goods does not affect the passage of the risk.
(2) Nevertheless, the risk does not pass to the buyer until the goods are clearly identified to the contract, whether by markings on the goods, by shipping documents, by notice given to the buver or otherwise.

Article 68

The risk in respect of goods sold in transit passes to the buyer from the time of the conclusion of the contract. However, if the circumstances so indicate, the risk is assumed by the buyer from the time the goods were handed over to the carrier who issued the documents embodying the contract of carriage. Nevertheless, if at the time of the conclusion of the contract of sale the seller knew or ought to have known that the goods had been lost or damaged and did not disclose this to the buyer, the loss or damage is at the risk of the seller.

Article 69

(1) In cases not within articles 67 and 68, the risk passes to the buyer when he takes over the goods or, if he does not do so in due time, from the time when the goods are placed at his disposal and he commits a breach of contract by failing to take delivery.
(2) However, if the buyer is bound to take over the goods at a place other than a place of business of the seller, the risk passes when delivery is due and the buyer is aware of the fact that the goods are placed at his disposal at that place.
(3) If the contract relates to goods not then identified, the goods are considered not to be placed at the disposal of the buyer until they are clearly identified to the contract.

Article 70

If the seller had committed a fundamental breach of contract, articles 67, 68 and 69 do not impair the remedies available to the buyer on account of the breach.

Chapter V: Provisions Common to the Obligations of the Seller and of the Buyer
Section 1. Anticipatory breach and installment contracts

Article 71

(1) A party may suspend the performance of his obligations if, after the conclusion of the contract, it becomes apparent that the other party will not perform a substantial part of his obligations as a result of:

(a) a serious deficiency in his ability to perform or in his creditworthiness; or

(b) his conduct in preparing to perform or in performing the contract.

(2) If the seller has already dispatched the goods before the grounds described in the preceding paragraph become evident, he may prevent the handing over of the goods to the buyer even though the buyer holds a document which entitles him to obtain them. The present paragraph relates only to the rights in the goods as between the buyer and the seller.

(3) A party suspending performance, whether before or after dispatch of the goods must immediately give notice of the suspension to the other party and must continue with performance if the other party provides adequate assurance of his performance.

Article 72

(1) If prior to the date for performance of the contract it is clear that one of the parties will commit a fundamental breach of contract, the other party may declare the contract avoided.

(2) If time allows, the party intending to declare the contract avoided must give reasonable notice to the other party in order to permit him to provide adequate assurance of his performance.

(3) The requirements of the preceding paragraph do not apply if the other party has declared that he will not perform his obligations.

Article 73

(1) In the case of a contract for delivery of goods by installments, if the failure of one party to perform any of his obligations in respect of any installment con-

stitutes a fundamental breach of contract with respect to that installment, the other party may declare the contract avoided with respect to that installment.
(2) If one party's failure to perform any of his obligations in respect of any installment gives the other party good grounds to conclude that a fundamental breach of contract will occur with respect to future installments, he may declare the contract avoided for the future, provided that he does so within a reasonable time.
(3) A buyer who declares the contract avoided in respect of any delivery may, at the same time, declare it avoided in respect *of* deliveries already made or of future deliveries if, by reason of their interdependence, those deliveries could not be used for the purpose contemplated by the parties at the time *of* the conclusion of the contract.

Section VI: Damages

Article 74

Damages for breach of contract by one party consist of a sum equal to the loss, including loss of profit, suffered by the other party as a consequence of the breach. Such damages may not exceed the loss which the party in breach foresaw or ought to have foreseen at the time of the conclusion of the contract, in the light of the facts and matters of which he then knew or ought to have known, as a possible consequence of the breach of contract.

Article 75

If the contract is avoided and if, in a reasonable manner and within a reasonable time after avoidance, the buyer has bought goods in replacement or the seller has resold the goods, the party claiming damages may recover the difference between the contract price and the price in the substitute transaction as well as any further damages recoverable under article 74.

Article 76

(1) If the contract is avoided and there is a current price for the goods, the party claiming damages may, if he has not made a purchase or resale under article 75, recover the difference between the price fixed by the contract and the current price at the time of avoidance as well as any further damages recoverable under article 74. If, however, the party claiming damages has avoided the contract af-

ter taking over the goods, the current price at the time of such taking over shall be applied instead of the current price at the time of avoidance.
(2) For the purposes of the preceding paragraph, the current price is the price prevailing at the place where delivery of the goods should have been made or, if there is no current price at that place, the price at such other place as serves as a reasonable substitute, making due allowance for differences in the cost of transporting the goods.

Article 77

A party who relies on a breach of contract must take such measures as are reasonable in the circumstances to mitigate the loss, including loss of profit, resulting from the breach. If he fails to take such measures, the party in breach may claim a reduction in the damages in the amount by which the loss should have been mitigated.

Article 78

If a party fails to pay the price or any other sum that is in arrears, the other party is entitled to interest on it, without prejudice to any claim for damages recoverable under article 74.

Section IV: Exemptions

Article 79

(1) A party is not liable for a failure to perform any of his obligations if he proves that the failure was due to an impediment beyond his control and that he could not reasonably be expected to have taken the impediment into account at the time of the conclusion of the contract or to have avoided or overcome it or its consequences.
(2) if the party's failure is due to the failure by a third person whom he has engaged to perform the whole or a part of the contract, that party is exempt from liability only if-

- (a) he is exempt under the preceding paragraph; and
- (b) the person whom he has so engaged would be so exempt if the provisions of that paragraph were applied to him.

(3) The exemption provided by this article has effect for the period during which the impediment exists.

(4) The party who fails to perform must give notice to the other party of the impediment and its effects on his ability to perform. If the notice is not received by the other party within a reasonable time after the party who fails to perform knew or ought to have known of the impediment, he is liable for damages resulting from such nonreceipt.
(5) Nothing in this article prevents either party from exercising any right other than to claim damages under this Convention.

Article 80

A party may not rely on a failure of the other party to perform, to the extent that such failure was caused by the first party's act or omission.

Section V: Effects of avoidance

Article 81

(1) Avoidance of the contract releases both parties from their obligations under it, subject to any damages which may be due. Avoidance does not affect any provision of the contract for the settlement of disputes or any other provision of the contract governing the rights and obligatons of the parties consequent upon the avoidance of the contract.
(2) A party who has performed the contract either wholly or in ~art may claim restitution from the other party of whatever the first party has supplied or paid under the contract. If both parties are bound to make restitution, they must do so concurrently.

Article 82

(1) The buyer loses the right to declare the contract avoided or to require the seller to deliver substitute goods if it is impossible for him to make restitution of the goods substantially in the condition in which he received them.
(2) The preceding paragraph does not apply:

(a) if the impossibility of making restitution of the goods or of making restitution of the goods substantially in the condition in which the buyer received them is not due to his act or omission;

(b) if the goods or part of the goods have perished or deteriorated as a result of the examination provided for in article 38; or if the goods or part of the goods have been sold in the normal course of business or have been consumed or transformed by the buyer in the course of normal use before he discovered or ought to have discovered the lack of conformity.

Article 83

A buyer who has lost the right to declare the contract avoided or to require the seller to deliver substitute goods in accordance with article 82 retains all other remedies under the contract and this Convention.

Article 84

(1) If the seller is bound to refund the price, he must also pay interest on it, from the date on which the price was paid.
(2) The buyer must account to the seller for all benefits which he has derived from the goods or part of them:
- (a) if he must make restitution of the goods or part of them; or
- (b) if it is impossible for him to make restitution of all or part of the goods or to make restitution of all or part of the goods substantially in the condition in which he received them, but he has nevertheless declared the contract avoided or required the seller to deliver substitute goods.

Section VI: Preservation of the goods

Article 85

If the buyer is in delay in taking delivery of the goods or, where payment of the price and delivery of the goods are to be made concurrently, if he *fails* to pay the price, and the seller is either in possession of the goods or otherwise able to control their disposition, the seller must take such steps as are reasonable in the circumstances to preserve them. He is entitled to retain them until he has been reimbursed his reasonable expenses by the buyer.

Article 86

(1) If the buyer has received the goods and intends to exercise any right under the contract or this Convention to reject them, he must take such steps to pre-

serve them as are reaso nable in the circumstances. He is entitled to retain them until he has been reimbursed his reasonable expenses by the seller.
(2) If goods dispatched to the buyer have been placed at his disposal at their destination and he exercises the right to reject them, he must take possession of them on behalf of the seller, provided that this can be done without payment of the price and without unreasonable inconvenience or unreasonable expense. This provision does not apply if the seller or a person authorized to take charge of the goods on his behalf is present at the destination. If the buyer takes possession of the goods under this paragraph, his rights and obligations, are governed by the preceding paragraph.

Article 87

A party who is bound to take steps to preserve the goods may deposit them in a warehouse of a third person at the expense of the other party provided that the expense incurred is not unreasonable.

Article 88

(1) A party who is bound to preserve the goods in accordance with article 85 or 86 may sell them by any appropriate means if there has been an unreasonable delay by the other party in taking possession of the goods or in taking them back or in paying the price or the cost of preservation, provided that reasonable notice of the intention to sell has been given to the other party.
(2) If the goods are subject to rapid deterioration or their preservation would involve unreasonable expense, a party who is bound to preserve the goods in accordance with article 85 or 86 must take reasonable measures to sell them. To the extent possible he must give notice to the other party of his intention to sell.
(3) A party selling the goods has the right to retain out of the proceeds of sale an amount equal to the reasonable expenses of preserving the goods and of selling them. He must account to the other party for the balance.

APPENDIX 3

United Nations Convention on the Limitation Period in the International Sale of Goods

Article 1

(1) This Convention shall determine when claims of a buyer and a seller against each other arising from a contract of international sale of goods or relating to its breach, termination or when it can no longer be exercised by reason of the expiration of a period of time. Such a period of time is hereinafter referred to as "the limitation period".
(2) This Convention shall not affect a particular time-limit within which one party is required, as a condition for the acquisition or exercise of his claim, to give notice to the other party or bring any act other than the institution of legal proceedings.
(3) In this Convention:

(a) buyer , seller" and "party" mean persons who buy or sell, or agree to buy or sell, goods, and the successors to and assigns of their rights or obligations under the contract of sale;
(b) "creditor" means a party who asserts a claim, whether or not such a claim is for a sum of money;
(c) "debtor" means a party against whom a creditor asserts a claim;
(d) "breach of contract" means the failure of a party to perform the contract or auy-performance not in conformity with the contract;

(e) "legal proceedings" includes judicial, arbitral and administrative proceedings;
(f) "person" includes corporation, company, partnership, association or entity, either private or public, which can sue or be sued;
(g) "writing" includes telegram and telex;
(h) "year" means a year according to the Gregorian calendar.

Article 2

For the purposes of this Convention:

(a) a contract of sale of goods shall be considered international, if at the time of I M conclusion of the contract, the buyer and the seller have their places of business in different States;

(b) the fact that the parties have their place of business in different States shall be disregarded whenever this fact does not appear either from the contract or from any dealings between, or from information disclosed by, the parties at any time before or at the conclusion of the contract;

(c) where a party to a contract of sale of goods has places of business in more than one State, the place of business shall be that which has the closest relationship to the contract and its performance, having regard to the circumstances known to or contemplated by the parties at the time of the conclusion of the contract;

(d) where a party does not have a place of business, reference shall be made to his habitual residence;

(e) neither the nationality of the parties nor the civil or commercial character of A M parties or of the contract shall be taken into consideration.

Article 3

(1) This Convention shall apply only

(a) if, at the time of the conclusion of the contract, the places of business of the parties to a contract of international sale of goods are in Contracting States; or

(b) if the rules of private international law make the law of a Contracting State applicable to the contract of sale.

(2) This Convention shall not apply when the parties have expressly excluded its application.

Article 4

This Convention shall not apply to sales:

(a) of goods bought for personal, family or household use, unless the seller, at any time before or at the conclusion of the contract, neither knew nor ought to have known that the goods were bought for any such use;

(b) by auction;

(c) on execution or otherwise by authority of law;

(d) of stocks, shares, investment securities, negotiable instruments or money;

(e) of ships, vessels, hovercraft or aircraft;

(f) of electricity.

Article 5

This Convention shall not apply to claims based upon:

(a) death of, or personal injury to, any person;

(b) nuclear damage caused by the goods sold;

(c) a lien, mortgage or other security interest in property;

(d) a judgement or award made in legal proceedings;

(e) a document on which direct enforcement or execution can be obtained in accordance with the law of the place where such enforcement or execution is sought;

(f) a bill of exchange, cheque or promissory note.

Article 6

(1) This Convention shall not apply to contracts in which the preponderant part of the obligations of the seller consists in the supply of labor or other services.

(2) Contracts for the supply of goods to be manufactured or produced shall be considered to be sales, unless the party who orders the goods undertakes to sup-

ply a substantial part of the materials necessary for such manufacture or production.

Article 7

In the interpretation and application of the provisions of this Convention, regard shall be had to its international character and to the need to promote uniformity.

THE DURATION AND COMMENCEMENT OF THE LIMITATION PERIOD

Article 8

The limitation period shall be four years.

Article 9

(1) Subject to the provisions of articles 10, 11 and 12 the limitation period shall commence on the date of which the claim accrues.
(2) The commencement of the limitation period shall not be postponed by:
- (a) a requirement that the party be given a notice as described in paragraph 2 of article 1, or
- (b) a provision in an arbitration agreement that no right shall arise until an arbitration award has been made.

Article 10

(1) A claim arising from a breach of contract shall accrue on the date on which such breach occurs.
(2) A claim arising from a defect or other lack of conformity shall accrue on the date on which the goods are actually handed over to, or their tender is refused by, the buyer.
(3) A claim based on fraud committed before or at the time of the conclusion of the contract or during its performance shall accrue on the date on which the fraud was or reasonably could have been discovered.

Article 11

If the seller has given an express undertaking relating to the goods which is stated to have effect for a certain period of time, whether expressed in terms of a specific period of time or otherwise, the limitation period in respect of any claim arising from the undertaking shall commence on the date on which the buyer notifies the seller of the fact on which the claim is based, but not later than on the date of the expiration of the period of the undertaking.

Article 12

For the purposes of articles 13, 14 and 15, any act performed by way of counterclaim shall be deemed to have been performed on the same date as the act performed in relation to the claim against which the counterclaim is raised, provided that both the claim and the counterclaim relate to the same contract or to several contracts concluded in the course of the same transaction.

Article 17

(1) Where a claim has been asserted in legal proceedings within the limitation period in accordance with article 13, 14, 15 or 16, but such legal proceedings have ended without a decision binding on the merits of the claim, the limitation period shall be deemed to have continued to run.
(2) If, at the time such legal proceedings ended, the limitation period has expired or has less than one year to run, the creditor shall be entitled to a period of one year from the date on which the legal proceedings ended.

Article 18

(1) Where legal proceedings have been commenced against one debtor, the limitation period prescribed in this Convention shall cease to run against any other party jointly and severally liable with the debtor, provided that the creditor informs such party in writing within that period that the proceedings have been commenced.
(2) Where legal proceedings have been commenced by a subpurchaser against the buyer, the limitation period prescribed in this Convention shall cease to run

in relation to the buyer's claim over against the seller, if the buyer informs the seller in writing within that period that the proceedings have been commenced.
(3) Where the legal proceedings referred to in paragraphs I and 2 this article have ended, the limitation period in respect of the claim of the creditor or the buyer against the party jointly and severally liable or against the seller shall be deemed not to have ceased running by virtue of paragraphs 1 and 2 of this article, but the creditor or the buyer shall be entitled to an additional year from the date on which the legal proceedings ended, if at that time the limitation period had expired or had less than one year to run.

Article 19

Where the creditor performs, in the State in which the debtor has his place of business and before the expiration of the limitation period, any act, other than the acts described in
Articles 13, 14, 15 and 16, which under the law of that State has the effect of recommencing a limitation period, a new limitation period of four years shall commence on the date prescribed by that law.

Article 20

(1) Where the debtor, before the expiration of the limitation period, acknowledges in writing his obligation to the creditor, a new limitation period of four years shall commence to run from the date of such acknowledgement.
(2) Payment of interest or partial performance of an obligation by the debtor shall have the same effect as an acknowledgement under paragraph (1) of this article if it can reasonably be inferred from such payment or performance that the debtor acknowledges that obligation.

Article 21

Where, as a result of a circumstance which is beyond the control of the creditor and which he could neither avoid nor overcome, the creditor has been prevented from causing the limitation period to cease to run, the limitation period shall be extended so as not to expire before the expiration of one year from the date on which the relevant circumstance ceased to exist.

MODIFICATION OF THE LIMITATION PERIOD BY THE PARTIES

Article 22

(1) The limitation period cannot be modified or affected by any declaration or agreement between the parties, except in the cases provided for in paragraph (2) of this article.
(2) The debtor may at any time during the running of the limitation period extend the period by a declaration in writing to the creditor. This declaration may be renewed.
(3) The provisions of this article shall not affect the validity of a clause in the contract of sale which stipulates that arbitral proceeding shall be commenced within a shorter period of limitation than that prescribed by this Convention, provided that such clause is valid under the law applicable to the contract of sale.

GENERAL LIMIT OF THE LIMITATION PERIOD

Article 23

Notwithstanding the provisions of this Convention, a limitation period shall in any event expire not later than ten years from the date on which it commenced to run under Articles 9, 10, 11 and 12 of this Convention.

CONSEQUENCES OF THE EXPIRATION OF THE LIMITATION PERIOD

Article 24

Expiration of the limitation period shall be taken into consideration in any legal proceedings only if invoked by a party to such proceedings.

Article 25

(1) Subject to the provisions of paragraph (2) of this article and of article 24, no claim shall be recognized or enforced in any legal proceedings commenced after the expiration of the limitation period.

(2) Notwithstanding the expiration of the limitation period, one party may rely on his claim as a defence or for the purpose of set-off against a claim asserted by the other party, provided that in the latter case this may only be done:

(a) if both claims relate to the same contract or to several contracts concluded in the course of the same transaction; or
(b) if the claims could have been set-off at any time before the expiration of the limitation period.

Article 26

Where the debtor performs his obligation after the expiration of the limitation period, he shall not on that ground be entitled in any way to claim restitution even if he did not know at the time when he performed his obligation that the limitation period had expired.

Article 27

The expiration of the limitation period with respect to a principal debt shall have the same effect with respect to an obligation to pay interest on that debt.

CALCULATION OF THE PERIOD

Article 28

(1) The limitation period shall be calculated in such a way that it shall expire at the end of the day which corresponds to the date on which the period commenced to run. If there is no such corresponding date, the period shall expire at the end of the last day of the last month of the limitation period.
(2) The limitation period shall be calculated by reference to the date of the place where the legal proceedings are instituted.

Article 29

Where the last day of the limitation period falls on an official holiday or other dies non Juridicus precluding the appropriate legal action in the jurisdiction where the creditor institutes legal proceedings or asserts a claim as envisaged in articles 13, 14 or 15, the limitation period shall be extended so as not to expire until the end of the first day following that official holiday or *dies non juridicus* on which such proceedings could be instituted or on which such a claim could be asserted in that jurisdiction.

INTERNATIONAL EFFECT

Article 30

The acts and circumstances referred to in articles 13 through 19 which have taken place in one Contracting State shall have effect for the purposes of this Convention in another Contracting State, provided that the creditor has taken all reasonable steps to ensure that the debtor is informed of the relevant act or circumstances as soon as possible.

APPENDIX 4

UNIDROIT Principles of International Commercial Contracts

PREAMBLE (Purpose of the Principles)

These Principles set forth general rules for international commercial contracts.
They shall be applied when the parties have agreed that their contract be governed by them.
They may be applied when the parties have agreed that their contract be governed by general principles of law, the *lex mercatoria* or the like.
They may provide a solution to an issue raised when it proves impossible to establish the relevant rule of the applicable law.
They may be used to interpret or supplement international uniform law instruments.
They may serve as a model for national and international legislators.

CHAPTER I — GENERAL PROVISIONS

Article 1.1 (Freedom of contract)

The parties are free to enter into a. contract and to determine its content.

Article 1.2 (No form required)

Nothing in these Principles requires a contract to be concluded in or evidenced by writing. It may be proved by any means, including witnesses.

Article 1.3 (Binding character of contract)

A contract validly entered into is binding upon the parties. It can only be modified or terminated in accordance with its terms or by agreement or as otherwise provided in these Principles.

Article 1.4 (Mandatory rules)

Nothing in these Principles shall restrict the application of mandatory rules, whether of national, international or supranational origin, which are applicable in accordance with the relevant rules of private international law.

Article 1.5 (Exclusion or modification by the parties)

The parties may exclude the application of these Principles or derogate from or vary the effect of any of their provisions, except as otherwise provided in the Principles.

Article 1.6 (Interpretation and supplementation of the Principles)

(1) In the interpretation of these Principles, regard is to be had to their international character and to their purpose including the need to promote uniformity in their application.
(2) Issues within the scope of these Principles but not expressly settled by them are as far as possible to be settled in accordance with their underlying general principles.

Article 1.7 (Good faith and fair dealing)

(1) Each party must act in accordance with good faith and fair dealing in international trade.
(2) The parties may not exclude or limit this duty.

Article 1.8 (Usages and practices)

(1) The parties are bound by any usage to which they have agreed and by any practices which they have established between themselves.

(2) The parties are bound by a usage that is widely known to and regularly observed in international trade by parties in the particular trade concerned except where the application of such a usage would be unreasonable.

Article 1.9 (Notice)

(1) Where notice is required it may be given by any means appropriate to the circumstances.
(2) A notice is effective when it reaches the person to whom it is given.
(3) For the purpose of paragraph (2) a notice reaches a person when given to that person orally or delivered at that person's place of business or mailing address.
(4) For the purpose of this article notice includes a declaration, demand, request or any other communication of intention.

Article 1.10 (Definitions)

In these Principles
— court" includes an arbitral tribunal;
— where a party has more than one place of business the relevant "place of business" is that which has the closest relationship to the contract and its performance, having regard to the circumstances known to or contemplated by the parties at any time before or at the conclusion of the contract;
— "obligor" refers to the party who is to perform an obligation and "obligee" refers to the party who is entitled to performance of that obligation;
— writing" means any mode of communication that preserves a record of the information contained therein and is capable of being reproduced in tangible form.

CHAPTER 2 — FORMATION

Article 2.1 (Manner of formation)

A contract may be concluded either by the acceptance of an offer or by conduct of the parties that is sufficient to show agreement.

Article 2.2 (Definition of offer)

A proposal for concluding a contract constitutes an offer if it is sufficiently definite and indicates the intention of the offeror to be bound in case of acceptance.

Article 2.3 (Withdrawal of offer)

(1) An offer becomes effective when it reaches the offeree.
(2) An offer, even if it is irrevocable, may be withdrawn if the withdrawal reaches the offeree before or at the same time as the offer.

Article 2.4 (Revocation of offer)

(1) Until a contract is concluded an offer may be revoked if the revocation reaches the offeree before it has dispatched an acceptance.
(2) However, an offer cannot be revoked
- (a) if it indicates, whether by stating a fixed time for acceptance or otherwise, that it is irrevocable; or
- (b) if it was reasonable for the offeree to rely on the offer as being irrevocable and the offeree has acted in reliance on the offer.

Article 2.5 (Rejection of offer)

An offer is terminated when a rejection reaches the offeror.

Article 2.6 (mode of acceptance)

(1) A statement made by or other conduct of the offeree indicating assent to an offer is an acceptance. Silence or inactivity does not in itself amount to acceptance.
(2) An acceptance of an offer becomes effective when the indication of assent reaches the offeror.
(3) However, if, by virtue of the offer or as a result of practices which the parties have established between themselves or of usage, the offeree may indicate assent by performing an act without notice to the offeror, the acceptance is effective when the act is performed.

Article 2.7 (Time of acceptance)

An offer must be accepted within the time the offeror has fixed or, if no time is fixed, within a reasonable time having regard to the circumstances, including the rapidity of he means of communication employed by the offeror. An oral offer must be accepted immediately unless the circumstances indicate otherwise.

Article 2.8 (Acceptance within a fixed period of time)

(1) A period of time for acceptance fixed by the offeror in a telegram or a letter begins to run from the moment the telegram is handed in for dispatch or from the date shown on the letter or, if no such date is shown, from the date shown on the envelope. A period of time for acceptance fixed by the offeror by means of instantaneous communication begins to run from the moment that the offer reaches the offeree.
(2) Official holidays or non-business days occurring during the period for acceptance are included in calculating the period. However, if a notice of acceptance cannot be delivered at the address of the offeror on the last day of the period because that day falls on an official holiday or a non-business day at the place of business of the offeror, the period is extended until the first business day which follows.

Article 2.9 (Late acceptance. Delay in transmission)

(1) A late acceptance is nevertheless effective as an acceptance if without undue delay the offeror so informs the offeree or gives notice to that effect.
(2) If a letter or other writing containing a late acceptance shows that it has been sent in such circumstances that if its transmission had been normal it would have reached the offeror in due time, the late acceptance is effective as an acceptance unless, without undue delay, the offeror informs the offeree that it considers the offer as having lapsed.

Article 2.10 (Withdrawal of acceptance)

An acceptance may be withdrawn if the withdrawal reaches the offeror before or at the same time as the acceptance would have become effective.

Article 2.11 (Modified acceptance)

(1) A reply to an offer which purports to be an acceptance but contains additions, limitations or other modifications is a rejection of the offer and constitutes a counter-offer.

(2) However, a reply to an offer which purports to be an acceptance but contains additional or different terms which do not materially alter the terms of the offer constitutes an acceptance, unless the offeror, without undue delay, objects to the discrepancy. If the offeror does not object, the terms of the contract are the terms of the offer with the modifications contained in the acceptance.

Article 2.12 (Writings in confirmation)

If a writing which is sent within a reasonable time after the conclusion of the contract and which purports to be a confirmation of the contract contains additional or different terms, such terms become part of the contract, unless they materially alter the contract or the recipient, without undue delay, objects to the discrepancy.

Article 2.13 (Conclusion of contract dependent on agreement on specific matters or in a specific form)

Where in the course of negotiations one of the parties insists that the contract is not concluded until there is agreement on specific matters or in a specific form, no contract is concluded before agreement is reached on those matters or in that form.

Article 2.14 (Contract with terms deliberately left open)

(1) If the parties intend to conclude a contract, the fact that they intentionally leave a term to be agreed upon in further negotiations or to be determined by a third person does not prevent a contract from coming into existence.
(2) The existence of the contract is not affected by the fact that subsequently
- (a) the parties reach no agreement on the term; or
- (b) the third person does not determine the term, provided that there is an alternative means of rendering the term definite that is reasonable in the circumstances, having regard to the intention of the parties.

Article 2.15 (Negotiations in bad faith)

(1) A party is free to negotiate and is not liable for failure to reach an agreement.
(2) However, a party who negotiates or breaks off negotiations in bad faith is liable for the losses caused to the other party.

(3) It is bad faith, in particular, for a party to enter into or continue negotiations when intending not to reach an agreement with the other party.

Article 2.16 (Duty of confidentiality)

Where information is given as confidential by one party in the course of negotiations, the other party is under a duty not to disclose that information or to use it improperly for its own purposes, whether or not a contract is subsequently concluded. Where appropriate, the remedy for breach of that duty may include compensation based on the benefit received by the other party.

Article 2.17 (Merger clauses)

A contract in writing which contains a clause indicating that the writing completely embodies the terms on which the parties have agreed cannot be contradicted or supplemented by evidence of prior statements or agreements. However, such statements or agreements may be used to interpret the writing.

Article 2.18 (Written modification clauses)

A contract in writing which contains a clause requiring any modification or termination by agreement to be in writing may not be otherwise modified or terminated. However, a party may be precluded by its conduct from asserting such a clause to the extent that the other party has acted in reliance on that conduct.

Article 2.19 (Contracting under standard terms)

(1) Where one party or both parties use standard terms in concluding a contract, the general rules on formation apply, subject to Articles 2.20 — 2.22.
(2) Standard terms are provisions which are prepared in advance for general and repeated use by one party and which are actually used without negotiation with the other party.

Article 2.20 (Surprising terms)

(1) No term contained in standard terms which is of such a character that the other party could not reasonably have expected it, is effective unless it has been expressly accepted by that party.

(2) In determining whether a term is of such a character regard is to be had to its content, language and presentation.

Article 2.21 (Conflict between standard terms and non-standard terms)

In case of conflict between a standard term and a term which is not a standard term the latter prevails.

Article 2.22 (Battle of forms)

Where both parties use standard terms and reach agreement except on those terms, a contract is concluded on the basis of the agreed terms and of any standard terms which are common in substance unless one party clearly indicates in advance, or later and without undue delay informs the other party, that it does not intend to be bound by such a contract.

CHAPTER 3 — VALIDITY

Article 3.1 (Matters not covered)

These Principles do not deal with invalidity arising from:
- (a) lack of capacity;
- (b) lack of authority;
- (c) immorality or illegality.

Article 3.2 (Validity of mere agreement)

A contract is concluded, modified or terminated by the mere agreement of the parties, without any further requirement.

Article 3.3 (Initial impossibility)

(1) The mere fact that at the time of the conclusion of the contract the performance of the obligation assumed was impossible does not affect the validity of the contract.
(2) The mere fact that at the time of the conclusion of the contract a party was not entitled to dispose of the assets to which the contract relates does not affect the validity of the contract.

Article 3.4 (Definition of mistake)

Mistake is an erroneous assumption relating to facts or to law existing when the contract was concluded.

Article 3.5 (Relevant mistake)

(1) A party may only avoid the contract for mistake if, when the contract was concluded, the mistake was of such importance that a reasonable person in the same situation as the party in error would only have concluded the contract on materially different terms or would not have concluded it at all if the true state of affairs had been known, and

- (a) the other party made the same mistake, or caused the mistake, or knew or ought to have known of the mistake and it was contrary to reasonable commercial standards of fair dealing to leave the mistaken party in error; or
- (b) the other party had not at the time of avoidance acted in reliance on the contract.

(2) However, a party may not avoid the contract if

- (a) it was grossly negligent in committing the mistake; or
- (b) the mistake relates to a matter in regard to which the risk of mistake was assumed or, having regard to the circumstances, should be borne by the mistaken party.

Article 3.6 (Error in expression or transmission)

An error occurring in the expression or transmission of a declaration is considered to be a mistake of the person from whom the declaration emanated.

Article 3.7 (Remedies for non-performance)

A party is not entitled to avoid the contract on the ground of mistake if the circumstances on which that party relies afford, or could have afforded, a remedy for non-performance.

Article 3.8 (Fraud)

A party may avoid the contract when it has been led to conclude the contract by the other party's fraudulent representation, including language or practices, or fraudulent non-disclosure of circumstances which, according to reasonable commercial standards of fair dealing, the latter party should have disclosed.

Article 3.9 (Threat)

A party may avoid the contract when it has been led to conclude the contract by the other party's unjustified threat which, having regard to the circumstances, is so imminent and serious as to leave the first party no reasonable alternative. In particular, a threat is unjustified if the act or omission with which a party has been threatened is wrongful in itself, or it is wrongful to use it as a means to obtain the conclusion of the contract.

Article 3.10 (Gross disparity)

(1) A party may avoid the contract or an individual term of it if, at the time of the conclusion of the contract, the contract or term unjustifiably gave the other party an excessive advantage. Regard is to be had, among other factors, to

- (a) the fact that the other party has taken unfair advantage of the first party's dependence, economic distress or urgent needs, or of its improvidence, ignorance, inexperience or lack of bargaining skill; and
- (b) the nature and purpose of the contract.

(2) Upon the request of the party entitled to avoidance, a court may adapt the contract or term in order to make it accord with reasonable commercial standards of fair dealing.
(3) A court may also adapt the contract or term upon the request of the party receiving notice of avoidance, provided that that party informs the other party of its request promptly after receiving such notice and before the other party has acted in reliance on it. The provisions of Article 3.13(2) apply accordingly.

Article 3.11 (Third persons)

(1) Where fraud, threat, gross disparity or a party's mistake is imputable to, or is known or ought to be known by, a third person for whose acts the other party is responsible, the contract may be avoided under the same conditions as if the behaviour or knowledge had been that of the party itself.
(2) Where fraud, threat or gross disparity is imputable to a third person for whose acts the other party is not responsible, the contract may be avoided if that party knew or ought to have known of the fraud, threat or disparity, or has not at the time of avoidance acted in reliance on the contract.

Article 3.12 (Confirmation)

If the party entitled to avoid the contract expressly or impliedly confirms the contract after the period of time for giving notice of avoidance has begun to run, avoidance of the contract is excluded.

Article 3.13 (Loss of right to avoid)

(1) If a party is entitled to avoid the contract for mistake but the other party declares itself willing to perform or performs the contract as it was understood by the party entitled to avoidance, the contract is considered to have been concluded as the latter party understood it. The other party must make such a declaration or render such performance promptly after having been informed of the manner in which the party entitled to avoidance had understood the contract and before that party has acted in reliance on a notice of avoidance.
(2) After such a declaration or performance the right to avoidance is lost and any earlier notice of avoidance is ineffective.

Article 3.14 (Notice of avoidance)

The right of a party to avoid the contract is exercised by notice to the other party

Article 3.15 (Time limits)

(1) Notice of avoidance shall be given within a reasonable time, having regard to the circumstances, after the avoiding party knew or could not have been unaware of the relevant facts or became capable of acting freely.
(2) Where an individual term of the contract may be avoided by a party under Article 3.10, the period of time for giving notice of avoidance begins to run when that term is asserted by the other party.

Article 3.16 (Partial avoidance)

Where a ground of avoidance affects only individual terms of the contract, the effect of avoidance is limited to those terms unless, having regard to the circumstances, it is unreasonable to uphold the remaining contract.

Article 3.17 (Retroactive effect of avoidance)

(1) Avoidance takes effect retroactively.
(2) On avoidance either party may claim restitution of whatever it has supplied under the contract or the part of it avoided, provided that it concurrently makes restitution of whatever it has received under the contract or the part of it avoided or, if it cannot make restitution in kind, it makes an allowance for what it has received.

Article 3.18 (Damages)

Irrespective of whether or not the contract has been avoided, the party who knew or ought to have known of the ground for avoidance is liable for damages so as to put the other party in the same position in which it would have been if it had not concluded the contract.

Article 3.19 (Mandatory character of the provisions)

The provisions of this Chapter are mandatory, except insofar as they relate to the binding force of mere agreement, initial impossibility or mistake.

Article 3.20 (Unilateral declarations)

The provisions of this Chapter apply with appropriate adaptations to — any communication of intention addressed by one party to the other.

CHAPTER 4 — INTERPRETATION

Article 4.1 (Intention of the parties)

(1) A contract shall be interpreted according to the common intention of the parties.
(2) If such an intention cannot be established, the contract shall be interpreted according to the meaning that reasonable persons of the same kind as the parties would give to it in the same circumstances.

Article 4.2 (Interpretation of statements and other conduct)

(1) The statements and other conduct of a party shall be interpreted according to that party's intention if the other party knew or could not have been unaware of that intention.
(2) If the preceding paragraph is not applicable, such statements and other conduct shall be interpreted according to the meaning that a reasonable person of the same kind as the other party would give to it in the same circumstances.

Article 4.3 (Relevant circumstances)

In applying Articles 4.1 and 4.2, regard shall be had to all the circumstances, including

(a) preliminary negotiations between the parties;
(b) practices which the parties have established between themselves;
(c) the conduct of the parties subsequent to the conclusion of the contract;
(d) the nature and purpose of the contract;
(e) the meaning commonly given to terms and expressions in the trade concerned;
(f) usages.

Article 4.4 (Reference to contract or statement as a whole)

Terms and expressions shall be interpreted in the light of the whole contract or statement in which they appear.

Article 4.5 (All terms to be given effect)

Contract terms shall be interpreted so as to give effect to all the terms rather than to deprive some of them of effect.

Article 4.6 (Contra proferentem rule)

If contract terms supplied by one party are unclear, an interpretation against that party is preferred.

Article 4.7 (Linguistic discrepancies)

Where a contract is drawn up in two or more language versions which are equally authoritative there is, in case of discrepancy between the versions, a preference for the interpretation according to a version in which the contract was originally drawn up.

Article 4.8 (Supplying an omitted term)

(1) Where the parties to a contract have not agreed with respect to a term which is important for a determination of their rights and duties, a term which is appropriate in the circumstances shall be supplied.
(2) In determining what is an appropriate term regard shall be had, among other factors, to

(a) the intention of the parties;
(b) the nature and purpose of the contract;
(c) good faith and fair dealing;
(d) reasonableness.

CHAPTER 5 — CONTENT

Article 5.1 (Express and implied obligations)

The contractual obligations of the parties may be express or implied.

Article 5.2 (Implied obligations)

Implied obligations stem from

(a) the nature and purpose of the contract;
(b) practices established between the parties and usages;
(c) good faith and fair dealing;
(d) reasonableness.

Article 5.3 (Co-operation between the parties)

Each party shall co-operate with the other party when such co-operation may reasonably be expected for the performance of that party's obligations.

Article 5.4 (Duty to achieve a specific result. Duty of best efforts)

(1) To the extent that an obligation of a party involves a duty to achieve a specific result, that party is bound to achieve that result.
(2) To the extent that an obligation of a party involves a duty of best efforts in the performance of an activity, that party is bound to make such efforts as would be made by a reasonable person of the same kind in the same circumstances.

Article 5.5 (Determination of kind of duty involved)

In determining the extent to which an obligation of a party involves a duty of best efforts in the performance of an activity or a duty to achieve a specific result, regard shall be had, among other factors, to

- (a) the way in which the obligation is expressed in the contract;
- (b) the contractual price and other terms of the contract;
- (c) the degree of risk normally involved in achieving the expected result;
- (d) the ability of the other party to influence the performance of the obligation.

Article 5.6 (Determination of quality of performance)

Where the quality of performance is neither fixed by, nor determinable from, the contract a party is bound to render a performance of a quality that is reasonable and not less than average in the circumstances.

Article 5.7 (Price determination)

(1) Where a contract does not fix or make provision for determining the price, the parties are considered, in the absence of any indication to the contrary, to have made reference to the price generally charged at the time of the conclusion of the contract for such performance in comparable circumstances in the trade concerned or, if no such price is available, to a reasonable price.
(2) Where the price is to be determined by one party and that determination is manifestly unreasonable, a reasonable price shall be substituted notwithstanding any contract term to the contrary.

(3) Where the price is to be fixed by a third person, and that person cannot or will not do so, the price shall be a reasonable price.
(4) Where the price is to be fixed by reference to factors which do not exist or have ceased to exist or to be accessible, the nearest equivalent factor shall be treated as a substitute.

Article 5.8 (Contract for an indefinite period)

A contract for an indefinite period may be ended by either party by giving notice a reasonable time in advance,

CHAPTER 6 — PERFORMANCE

Section 1: Performance in General

Article 6.1.1 (Time of performance)

A party must perform its obligations:

(a) if a time is fixed by or determinable from the contract, at that time;
(b) if a period of time is fixed by or determinable from the contract, at any time within that period unless circumstances indicate that the other party is to choose a time;
(c) in any other case, within a reasonable time after the conclusion of the contract.

Article 6.1.2 (Performance at one time or in installments)

In cases under Article 6. 1. 1 (b) or (c), a party must perform its obligations at one time if that performance can be rendered at one time and the circumstances do not indicate otherwise.

Article 6.1.3 (Partial performance)

(1) The obligee may reject an offer to perform in part at the time performance is due, whether or not such offer is coupled with an assurance as to the balance of the performance, unless the obligee has no legitimate interest in so doing.
(2) Additional expenses caused to the obligee by partial performance are to be borne by the obligor without prejudice to any other remedy.

Article 6.1.4 (Order of performance)

(1) To the extent that the performances of the parties can be rendered simultaneously, the parties are bound to render them simultaneously unless the circumstances indicate otherwise.
(2) To the extent that the performance of only one party requires a period of time, that party is bound to render its performance first, unless the circumstances indicate otherwise.

Article 6.1.5 (Earlier performance)

(1) The obligee may reject an earlier performance unless it has no legitimate interest in so doing.
(2) Acceptance by a party of an earlier performance does not affect the time for the performance of its own obligations if that time has been fixed irrespective of the performance of the other party's obligations.
(3) Additional expenses caused to the obligee by earlier performance are to be borne by the obligor, without prejudice to any other remedy.

Article 6.1.6 (Place of performance)

(1) If the place of performance is neither fixed by, nor determinable from, the contract, a party is to perform:
- (a) a monetary obligation, at the obligee's place of business;
- (b) any other obligation, at its own place of business.

(2) A party must bear any increase in the expenses incidental to performance which is caused by a change in its place of business subsequent to the conclusion of the contract.

Article 6.1.7 (Payment by cheque or other instrument)

(1) Payment may be made in any form used in the ordinary course of business at the place for payment.
(2) However, an obligee who accepts, either by virtue of paragraph (1) or voluntarily, a cheque, any other order to pay or a promise to pay, is presumed to do so only on condition that it will be honoured.

Article 6.1.8 (Payment by funds transfer)

(1) Unless the obligee has indicated a particular account, payment may be made by a transfer to any of the financial institutions in which the obligee has made it known that it has an account.
(2) In case of payment by a transfer the obligation of the obligor is discharged when the transfer to the obligee's financial institution becomes effective.

Article 6.1.9 (Currency of payment)

(1) If a monetary obligation is expressed in a currency other than that of the place for payment, it may be paid by the obligor in the currency of the place for payment unless

(a) that currency is not freely convertible; or
(b) the parties have agreed that payment should be made only in the currency in which the monetary obligation is expressed.

(2) If it is impossible for the obligor to make payment in the currency in which the monetary obligation is expressed, the obligee may require payment in the currency of the place for payment, even in the case referred to in paragraph
(3) Payment in the currency of the place for payment is to be made according to the applicable rate of exchange prevailing there when payment is due.
(4) However, if the obligor has not paid at the time when payment is due, the obligee may require payment according to the applicable rate of exchange prevailing either when payment is due or at the time of actual payment.

Article 6.1.10 (Currency not expressed)

Where a monetary obligation is not expressed in a particular currency, payment must be made in the currency of the place where payment is to be made.

Article 6.1.11 (Costs of performance)

Each party shall bear the costs of performance of its obligations.

Article 6.1.12 (Imputation of payments)

(1) An obligor owing several monetary obligations to the same obligee may specify at the time of payment the debt to which it intends the payment to be

applied. However, the payment discharges first any expenses, then interest due and finally the principal.
(2) If the obligor makes no such specification, the obligee may, within a reasonable time after payment, declare to the obligor the obligation to which it imputes die payment, provided that the obligation is due and undisputed.
(3) In the absence of imputation under paragraphs (1) or (2), payment is imputed to that obligation which satisfies one of the following criteria and in the order indicated:

(a) an obligation which is due or which is the first to fall due;
(b) the obligation for which the obligee has least security;
(c) the obligation which is the most burdensome for the obligor;
(d) the obligation which has arisen first.

If none of the preceding criteria applies, payment is imputed to all the obligations proportionally.

Article 6.1.13 (Imputation of non-monetary obligations)

Article 6.1.12 applies with appropriate adaptations to the imputation of performance of non-monetary obligations.

Article 6.1.14 (Application for public permission)

Where the law of a State requires a public permission affecting the validity of the contract or its performance and neither that law nor the circumstances indicate otherwise

(a) if only one party has its place of business in that State, that party shall take the measures necessary to obtain the permission;
(b) in any other case the party whose performance requires permission shall take the necessary measures.

Article 6.1.15 (Procedure in applying for permission)

(1) The party required to take the measures necessary to obtain the permission shall do so without undue delay and shall bear any expenses incurred.
(2) That party shall whenever appropriate give the other party notice of the grant or refusal of such permission without undue delay.

Article 6.1.16 (Permission neither granted nor refused

(1) If, notwithstanding the fact that the party responsible has taken all measures required, permission is neither granted nor refused within an agreed period or, where no period has been agreed, within a reasonable time from the conclusion of the contract, either party is entitled to terminate the contract.
(2) Where the permission affects some terms only, paragraph (1) does not apply if, having regard to the circumstances, it is reasonable to uphold the remaining contract even if the permission is refused.

Article 6.1.17 (Permission refused)

(1) The refusal of a permission affecting the validity of the contract renders the contract void. If the refusal affects the validity of some terms only, only such terms are void if, having regard to the circumstances, it is reasonable to uphold the remaining contract.
(2) Where the refusal of a permission renders the performance of the contract impossible in whole or in part, the rules on non-performance apply.

Section 2: Hardship

Article 6.2.1 (Contract to be observed)

Where the performance of a contract becomes more onerous for one of the parties, that party is nevertheless bound to perform its obligations subject to the following provisions on hardship.

Article 6.2.2 (Definition of hardship)

There is hardship where the occurrence of events fundamentally alters the equilibrium of the contract either because the cost of a party's performance has increased or because the value of the performance a party receives has diminished, and

- (a) the events occur or become known to the disadvantaged party after the conclusion of the contract;
- (b) the events could not reasonably have been taken into account by the disadvantaged party at the time of the conclusion of the contract;
- (c) the events are beyond the control of the disadvantaged party; and,
- (d) the risk of the events was not assumed by the disadvantaged party.

Article 6.2.3 (Effects of hardship)

(1) In case of hardship the disadvantaged party is entitled to request renegotiations. The request shall be made without undue delay and shall indicate the grounds on which it is based.
(2) the request for renegotiation does not in itself entitle the disadvantaged party to withhold performance.
(3) Upon failure to reach agreement within a reasonable time either party may resort to the court.
(4) If the court finds hardship it may, if reasonable,
 (a) terminate the contract at a date and on terms to be fixed; or
 (b) adapt the contract with a view to restoring its equilibrium.

CHAPTER 7 — NON-PERFORMANCE

Section 1: Non-Performance in General

Article 7.1.1 (Non-performance defined)

Non-performance is failure by a party to perform any of its obligations under the contract, including defective performance or late performance.

Article 7.1.2 (Interference by the other party)

A party may not rely on the non-performance of the other party to the extent that such non-performance was caused by the first party's act or omission or by another event as to which the first party bears the risk.

Article 7.1.3 (Withholding performance)

(1) Where the parties are to perform simultaneously, either party may withhold performance until the other party tenders its performance.
(2) Where the parties are to perform consecutively, the party that is to perform later may withhold its performance until the first party has performed.

Article 7.1.4 (Cure by non-performing party)

(1) The non-performing party may, at its own expense, cure any non-performance, provided that

(a) without undue delay, it gives notice indicating the proposed manner and timing of the cure;
(b) cure is appropriate in the circumstances;
(c) the aggrieved party has no legitimate interest in refusing cure; and
(d) cure is effected promptly.

(2) The right to cure is not precluded by notice of termination.
(3) Upon effective notice of cure, rights of the aggrieved party that are inconsistent with the non-performing party's performance are suspended until the time for cure has expired.
(4) The aggrieved party may withhold performance pending cure.
(5) Notwithstanding cure, the aggrieved party retains the right to claim damages for delay as well as for any harm caused or not prevented by the cure.

Article 7.1.5 (Additional period for performance)

(1) In a case of non-performance the aggrieved party may by notice to the other party allow an additional period of time for performance.
(2) During the additional period the aggrieved party may withhold performance of its own reciprocal obligations and may claim damages but may not resort to any other remedy. If it receives notice from the other party that the latter will not perform within that period, or if upon expiry of that period due performance has not been made, the aggrieved party may resort to any of the remedies that may be available under this Chapter.
(3) Where in a case of delay in performance which is not fundamental the aggrieved party has given notice allowing an additional period of time of reasonable length, it may terminate the contract at the end of that period. If the additional period allowed is not of reasonable length it shall be extended to a reasonable length. The aggrieved party may in its notice provide that if the other party fails to perform within the period allowed by the notice the contract shall automatically terminate.
(4) Paragraph (3) does not apply where the obligation which has not been performed is only a minor part of the contractual obligation of the non-performing party.

Article 7.1.6 (Exemption clauses)

A clause which limits or excludes one party's liability for non-performance or which permits one party to render performance substantially different from what the other party reasonably expected may not be invoked if it would be grossly unfair to do so, having regard to the purpose of the contract.

Article 7.1.7 (Force majeure)

(1) Non-performance by a party is excused if that party proves that the non-performance was due to an impediment beyond its control and that it could not reasonably be expected to have taken the impediment into account at the time of the conclusion of the contract or to have avoided or overcome it or its consequences.
(2) When the impediment is only temporary, the excuse shall have effect for such period as is reasonable having regard to the effect of the impediment on the performance of the contract.
(3) The party who fails to perform must give notice to the oth er party of the impediment and its effect on its ability to perform. If the notice is not received by the other party within a reasonable timc aftei lhe party who fails to perfbrm knew or ought to have known of the impediment, it is liable for damages resulting from such non-receipt.
(4) Nothing in this article prevents a party from exercising a right to terminate the contract or to withhold performance or request interest on money due.

Section 2: Right to Performance

Article 7.2.1 (Performance of monetary obligation)

Where a party who is obliged to pay money does not do so, the other party may require payment.

Article 7.2.2 (Performance of non-monetary obligation)

Where a party who owes an obligation other than one to pay money does not perform, the other party may require performance, unless

(a) performance is impossible in law or in fact;
(b) performance or, where relevant, enforcement is unreasonably burdensome or expensive;
(c) the party entitled to performance may reasonably obtain performance from another source;
(d) performance is of an exclusively personal character; or

(e) the party entitled to performance does not require performance — within a reasonable time after it has, or ought to have, become aware of the nonperformance.

Article 7.2.3 (Repair and replacement of defective performance)

The right to performance includes in appropriate cases the right to require repair, replacement, or other cure of defective performance. The provisions of Articles 7.2.1 and 7.2.2 apply accordingly.

Article 7.2.4 (Judicial penalty)

(1) Where the court orders a party to perform, it may also direct that this party pay a penalty if it does not comply with the order.
(2) 'Me penalty shall be paid to the aggrieved party unless mandatory provisions of the law of the forum provide otherwise. Payment of the penalty to the aggrieved party does not exclude any claim for damages.

Article 7.2.5 (Change of remedy)

(1) An aggrieved party who has required performance of a non-monetary obligation and who has not received performance within a period fixed or otherwise within a reasonable period of time may invoke any other remedy.
(2) Where the decision of a court for performance of a non-monetary obligation cannot be enforced, the aggrieved party may invoke any other remedy.

Section 3: Termination

Article 7.3.1 (Right to terminate the contract)

(1) A party may terminate the contract where the failure of the other party to perform an obligation under the contract amounts to a fundamental nonperformance.
(2) In determining whether a failure to perform an obligation amounts to a fundamental non-performance regard shall be had, in particular, to whether

(a) the non-performance substantially deprives the aggrieved party of what it was entitled to expect under the contract unless the other party did not foresee and could not reasonably have foreseen such result;

(b) strict compliance with the obligation which has not been performed is of essence under the contract;
(c) the non-performance is intentional or reckless;
(d) the non-performance gives the aggrieved party reason to believe that it cannot rely on the other party's future performance;
(e) the non-performing party will suffer disproportionate loss as a result of the preparation or performance if the contract is terminated.

(3) In the case of delay the aggrieved party may also terminate the contract if the other party fails to perform before the time allowed it under Article 7.1.5 has expired.

Article 7.3.2 (Notice of termination)

(1) The right of a party to terminate the contract is exercised by notice to the other party.
(2) If performance has been offered late or otherwise does not conform to the contract the aggrieved party will lose its right to terminate the contract unless it gives notice to the other party within a reasonable time after it has or ought to have become aware of the offer or of the non-conforming performance.

Article 7.3.3 (Anticipatory non-performance)

Where prior to the date for performance by one of the parties it is clear that there will be a fundamental non-performance by that party, the other party may terminate the contract.

Article 7.3.4 (Adequate assurance of due performance)

A party who reasonably believes that there will be a fundamental non-performance by the other party may demand adequate assurance of due performance and may meanwhile withhold its own performance. Where this assurance is not provided within a reasonable time the party demanding it may terminate the contract.

Article 7.3.5 (Effects of termination in general)

(1)Termination of the contract releases both parties from their obligation to 6ffect and to receive future performance.

(2) Termination does not preclude a claim for damages for non-performance.
(3) Termination does not affect any provision in the contract for the settlement of disputes or any other term of the contract which is to operate even after termination.

Article 7.3.6 (Restitution)

(1) On termination of the contract either party may claim restitution of whatever it has supplied, provided that such party concurrently makes restitution of whatever it has received. If restitution in kind is not possible or appropriate allowance should be made in money whenever reasonable.
(2) However, if performance of the contract has extended over a period of time and the contract is divisible, such restitution can only be claimed for the period after termination has taken effect.

Section 4: Damages

Article 7.4.1 (Right to damages)

Any non-performance gives the aggrieved party a right to damages either exclusively or in conjunction with any other remedies except where the non-performance is excused under these Principles.

Article 7.4.2 (Full compensation)

(1) The aggrieved party is entitled to full compensation for harm sustained as a result of the non-performance. Such harm includes both any loss which it suffered and any gain of which it was deprived, taking into account any gain to the aggrieved party resulting from its avoidance of cost or harm.
(2) Such harm may be non-pecuniary and includes, for instance, physical suffering or emotional distress.

Article 7.4.3 (Certainty of harm)

(1) Compensation is due only for harm, including future harm, that is established with a reasonable degree of certainty.

(2) Compensation may be due for the loss of a chance in proportion to the probability of its occurrence.
(3) Where the amount of damages cannot be established with a sufficient degree of certainty, the assessment is at the discretion of the court.

Article 7.4.4 (Foreseeability of harm)

The non-performing party is liable only for harm which it foresaw or could reasonably have foreseen at the time of the conclusion of the contract as being likely to result from its non-performance.

Article 7.4.5 (Proof of harm in case of replacement transaction)

Where the aggrieved party has terminated the contract and has made a replacement transaction within a reasonable time and in a reasonable manner it may recover the difference between the contract price and the price of the replacement transaction is well as damages for any further harm.

Article 7.4.6 (Proof of harm by current price)

(1) Where the aggrieved party has terminated the contract and has not made a replacement transaction but there is a current price for the performance contracted for, it may recover the difference between the contract price and the price current at the time the contract is terminated as well as damages for any further harm.
(2) Current price is the price generally charged for goods delivered or services rendered in comparable circumstances at the place where the contract should have been performed or, if there is no current price at that place, the current price at such other place that appears reasonable to take as a reference.

Article 7.4.7 (Harm due in part to aggrieved party)

Where the harm is due in part to an act or omission of the aggrieved party or to another event as to which that party bears the risk, the amount of damages shall be reduced to the extent that these factors have contributed to the harm, having regard to the conduct of each of the parties.

Article 7.4.8 (Mitigation of harm)

(1) The non-performing party is not liable for harm suffered by the aggrieved party to the extent that the harm could have been reduced by the latter party's taking reasonable steps.
(2) The aggrieved party is entitled to recover any expenses reasonably incurred in attempting to reduce the harm.

Article 7.4.9 (Interest for failure to pay money)

(1) If a party does not pay a sum of money when it falls due the aggrieved party is entitled to interest upon that sum from the time when payment is due to the time of payment whether or not the non-payment is excused.
(2) The rate of interest shall be the average bank short-term lending rate to prime borrowers prevailing for the currency of payment at the place for payment, or where no such rate exists at that place, then the same rate in the State of the currency of payment. In the absence of such a rate at either place the rate of interest shall be the appropriate rate fixed by the law of the State of the currency of payment.
(3) The aggrieved party is entitled to additional damages if the non-payment caused it a greater harm.

Article 7.4.10 (Interest on damages)

Unless otherwise agreed, interest on damages for non-performance of non-monetary obligations accrues as from the time of non-performance.

Article 7.4.11 (Manner of monetary redress)

(1) Damages are to be paid in a lump sum. However, they may be payable in installments where the nature of the harm makes this appropriate.
(2) Damages to be paid in installments, may be indexed.

Article 7.4.12 (Currency in which to assess damages)

Damages are to be assessed either in the currency in which the monetary obligation was expressed or in the currency in which the harm was suffered, whichever is more appropriate.

Article 7.4.13 (Agreed payment for non-performance)

(1) Where the contract provides that a party who does not perform is to pay a specified sum to the aggrieved party for such non-performance, the aggrieved party is entitled to that sum irrespective of its actual harm.
(2) However, notwithstanding any agreement to the contrary the specified sum may be reduced to a reasonable amount where it is grossly excessive in relation to the harm resulting from the non-performance and to the other circumstances.

APPENDIX 5

The Principles of European Contract Law 1998

CHAPTER 1 — GENERAL PROVISIONS

Section 1 — Scope of the Principles

Article 1.101 — Application of the Principles
Article 1.102 — Freedom of contract
Article 1.103 — Mandatory Law
Article 1.104 — Application to questions of consent
Article 1.105 — Usages and Practices
Article 1.106 — Interpretation and Supplementation
Article 1.107 — Application of the Principles by Way of Analogy

Section 2: General Obligations

Article 1.201 — Good Faith and Fair Dealing
Article 1.202 — Duty to Cooperate

Section 3 — Terminology and Other Provisions

Article 1.301 — Meaning of Terms
Article 1.302 — Reasonableness
Article 1.303 — Notice
Article 1.304 — Computation of Time
Article 1.305 — Imputed Knowledge and Intention

CHAPTER 2 – FORMATION
Section 1 — General Provisions

Article 2.101 — Conditions for the Conclusion of a Contract
Article 2.102 — Intention
Article 2.103 — Sufficient Agreement
Article 2.104 — Terms not individually negotiated
Article 2.105 — Merger Clause
Article 2.106 — Written Modification only
Article 2.107 — Promises binding without acceptance

Section 2 — Offer and Acceptance

Article 2.201 — Offer
Article 2.202 — Revocation of an Offer
Article 2.203 — Lapse of an Offer
Article 2.204 — Acceptance
Article 2.205 — Time of Conclusion of the Contract
Article 2.206 — Time Limit for Acceptance
Article 2.207 — Late Acceptance
Article 2.208 — Modified Acceptance
Article 2.209 — Conflicting General Conditions
Article 2.210 — Professional's written confirmation
Article 2.211 — Contracts not Concluded through Offer and Acceptance

Section 3 — Liability for negotiations

Article 2.301 — Negotiations Contrary to Good Faith
Article 2.302 — Breach of Confidentiality.

CHAPTER 3 — AUTHORITY OF AGENTS
Section 1 — General Provisions

Article 3.101 — Scope of the Chapter
Article 3.102 — Categories of Representation

Section 2 — Direct Representation

Article 3.201 — Express, implied and apparent authority
Article 3.202 — Agent acting in exercise of his authority

Section 3 — Indirect Representation

CHAPTER 4 — VALIDITY

CHAPTER 5 — INTERPRETATION

Article 5.101 — General Rules of Interpretation
Article 5.102 — Relevant Circumstances
Article 5.103 — Contra Proferentem Rule
Article 5.104 — Preference to Negotiated Terms
Article 5.105 — Reference to Contract as a Whole
Article 5.106 — Terms to Be Given (Full) Effect
Article 5.107 — Linguistic Discrepancies

CHAPTER 6 — CONTENTS AND EFFECTS

Article 6. 101 — Statements giving rise to contractual obligation
Article 6.102 — Implied obligations
Article 6.103 — Simulation
Article 6.104 — Determination of Price
Article 6.105 — Unilateral Determination by a Party
Article 6.106 — Determination by a Third Person
Article 6.107 — Reference to a Non-Existent Factor
Article 6.108 — Quality of Performance
Article 6.109 — Contract for an Indefinite Period
Article 6.110 — Stipulation in Favour of a Third Party
Article 6.111 — Change of Circumstances

CHAPTER 7 — PERFORMANCE

Article 7.101 — Place of Performance
Article 7.102 — Time of Performance
Article 7.103 — Early Performance
Article 7.104 — Order of performance
Article 7.105 — Alternative performance
Article 7.106 — Performance by a Third Person
Article 7.107 — Form of Payment
Article 7.108 — Currency of Payment
Article 7.109 — Appropriation of Performance
Article 7.110 — Property Not Accepted
Article 7.111 — Money Not Accepted
Article 7.112 — Costs of performance

CHAPTER 8 — NON-PERFORMANCE AND REMEDIES IN GENERAL

CHAPTER 9 — PARTICULAR REMEDIES FOR NON-PERFORMANCE

Section 1 — Right to Performance

Section 2 — Right To Withhold Performance

Section 3 — Termination of the Contract

Section 4 — Price Reduction

Section 5 — Damages and Interest

Article 9.501 — Right to Damages
Article 9.502 — General Measure of Damages
Article 9.503 — Foreseeability
Article 9.504 — Loss Attributable to Aggrieved Party
Article 9.505 — Reduction of loss
Article 9.506 — Substitute Transaction
Article 9.507 — Current Price
Article 9.508 — Delay in Payment of Money
Article 9.509 — Agreed Payment for Non-Performance
Article 9.510 — Currency by Which Damages to be Measured

PRINCIPLES OF EUROPEAN CONTRACT LAW 1998
CHAPTER 1 — GENERAL PROVISIONS
Section 1 — Scope of the Principles

Article 1.101 — Application of the Principles

(1) These Principles are intended to be applied as general rules of contract law in the European Communities.
(2) These Principles will apply when the parties have agreed to incorporate them into their contract or that their contract is to be governed by them.
(3) These Principles may be applied when the parties:

(a) have agreed that their contract is to be governed by "general principles of law", the "lex mercatoria" or the like; or (b) have not chosen any system or rules of law to govern their contract.

(4) These Principles may provide a solution to the issue raised where the system or rules of law applicable do not do so.

Article 1.102 — Freedom of contract

(1) Parties are free to enter into a contract and to determine its contents, subject to the requirements of good faith and fair dealing, and the mandatory rules established by these Principles.
(2)The parties may exclude the application of the Principles or derogate from or vary their effects, except as otherwise provided by these Principles.

Article 1.103 — Mandatory Law

(1) Where the otherwise applicable law allows, the parties may choose to have their contract governed by the Principles, with the effect that national mandatory rules are not applicable.
(2) Effect should nevertheless be given to those mandatory rules of national, supranational and international law which, according to the relevant rules of private international law, are applicable irrespective of the law governing the contract.

Article 1.104 — Application to Questions of Consent

(1) The existence and validity of the agreement of the parties to adopt or incorporate these Principles shall be determined by these Principles.
(2) Nevertheless, a party may rely upon the law of the country in which it has its habitual residence to establish that it did not consent if it appears from the circumstances that it would not be reasonable to determine the effect of its conduct in accordance with these Principles.

Article 1.105 — Usages and Practices

(1) The parties are bound by any usage to which they have agreed and by any practice they have established between themselves.
(2) The parties are bound by a usage which would be considered generally applicable by persons in the same situation as the parties, except where the application of such usage would be unreasonable.

Article 1.106

(1) These principles should be interpreted and developed in accordance with their purposes. In particular, regard should be had to the need to promote good faith and fair dealing, certainty in contractual relationships and uniformity of application.
(2) Issues within the scope of these Principles but not expressly settled by them are so far as possible to be settled in accordance with the ideas underlying the Principles. Failing this, the legal system applicable by virtue of the rules of private international law is to be applied.

Article 1.107 — Application of the Principles by Way of Analogy

These Principles apply with appropriate modifications to agreements to modify or end a contract, to unilateral promises and other statements and conduct indicating intention.

Section 2: General Obligations

Article 1.201 — Good Faith and Fair Dealing

(1) Each party must act in accordance with good faith and fair dealing.
(2) The parties may not exclude or limit this duty.

Article 1.202 — Duty to Co-operate

Each party owes to the other a duty to co-operate in order to give full effect to the contract.

Section 3 — Terminology and Other Provisions

Article 1.301 — Meaning of Terms

In these Principles, except where the context otherwise requires:
(1) 'act' includes omission;
(2) 'court' includes arbitral tribunal;
(3) an 'intentional' act includes an act done recklessly
(4) 'non-performance' denotes any failure to perform an obligation under the contract, whether or not excused, and includes delayed performance, defective performance and failure to co-operate in order to give full effect to the contract.
(5) A matter is 'material' if it is one which a reasonable person in the same situation as one party ought to have known would influence the other party in its decision whether to contract on the proposed terms or to contract at all.
(6) 'Written' statements include communications made by telegram, telex, telefax and electronic mail and other means of communication capable of providing a readable record of the statement on both sides.

Article 1.302 — Reasonableness

Under these Principles reasonableness; is to be judged by what persons acting in good faith and in the same situation as the parties would consider to be reasonable. In particular, in assessing what is reasonable the nature and purpose of the contract, the circumstances of the case, and the usages and practices of the trades or professions involved should be taken into account.

Article 1.303 — Notice

(1) Any notice may be given by any means, whether in writing or otherwise, appropriate to the circumstances.
(2) Subject to paragraphs (4) and (5), any notice becomes effective when it reaches the addressee.
(3) A notice reaches the addressee when it is delivered to it or to its place of business or mailing address, or, if it does not have a place of business or mailing address, to its habitual residence
(4) If one party gives notice to the other because of the other's non-performance or because such non-performance is reasonably anticipated by the first party, and the notice is properly dispatched or given, a delay or inaccuracy in the transmission of the notice or its failure to arrive does not prevent it from having effect. The notice shall have effect from the time at which it would have arrived in normal circumstances.
(5) A notice has no effect if a withdrawal of it reaches the addressee before or at the same time as the notice.
(6) In this Article, 'notice' includes the communication of a promise, statement, offer, acceptance, demand, request or other declaration.

Article 1.304 — Computation of Time

(1) A period of time set by a party in a written document for the addressee to reply or take other action begins to run from the date stated as the date of the document. If no date is shown, the period begins to run from the moment the document reaches the addressee.
(2) Official holidays and official non-working days occurring during the period are included in calculating the period. However, if the last day of the period is an official holiday or official non-working day at the address of the addressee,

or at the place where a prescribed act is to be performed, the period is extended until the first following working day in that place.
(3) Periods of time expressed in days, weeks, months or years shall begin at 00.00 on the next day and shall end at 24.00 on the last day of the period; but any reply that has to reach the party who set the period must arrive, or other act which is to be done must be completed ' by the normal close of business in the relevant place on the last day of the period.

Article 1.305 — Imputed Knowledge and Intention

If any person who with a party's assent was involved in making a contract, or who was entrusted with performance by a party or performed with its assent:

- (a) knew or foresaw a fact, or ought to have known or foreseen it; or
- (b) acted intentionally or with gross negligence, or not in accordance with good faith and fair dealing, this knowledge, foresight or behaviour is imputed to the party itself

CHAPTER 2 — FORMATION
Section 1 — General Provisions

Article 2.101 — Conditions for the Conclusion of a Contract

(1) A contract is concluded if —

- (a) the parties intend to be legally bound, and
- (b) they reach a sufficient agreement without any further requirement.

(2) A contract need not be concluded or evidenced in writing nor is it subject to any other requirement as to form. The contract may be proved by any means, including witnesses.

Article 2.102 — Intention

The intention of a party to be legally bound by contract is to be determined from the party's statements or conduct as they were reasonably understood by the other party.

Article 2.103 — Sufficient Agreement

(1) There is sufficient agreement if the terms:

(a) have been sufficiently defined by the parties so that the contract can be enforced, or
(b) can be determined under these Principles.

(2) However, if one of the parties refuses to conclude a contract unless the parties have agreed on some specific matter, there is no contract unless agreement on that matter has been reached.

Article 2.104 — Terms not individually negotiated

(1) Contract terms which have not been individually negotiated may revoked against a party who did not know of them only if the party invoking them took reasonable steps to bring them to the other party's attention before or when the contract was concluded.
(2) Terms are not brought appropriately to a party's attention by a mere reference to them in a contract document, even if that party signs the document.

Article 2.105 — Merger Clause

(1) If a written contract contains an individually negotiated clause stating that the writing embodies all the terms of the contract (a merger clause), any prior statements, undertakings or agreements which are not embodied in the writing do not form part of the contract.
(2) If the merger clause is not individually negotiated it will only establish a presumption that the parties intended that their prior statements, undertakings or agreements were not to form part of the contract. This rule may not be excluded or restricted.
(3) The parties' prior statements may be used to interpret the contract. This rule may not be excluded or restricted except by an individually negotiated clause.
(4) A party may by its statements or conduct be precluded from asserting a merger clause to the extent that the other party has reasonably relied on them.

Article 2.106 — Written Modification only

(1) A clause in a written contract requiring any modification or ending by agreement to be made in writing establishes only a presumption that an agreement to modify or end the contract is not intended to be legally binding unless it is in writing.

(2) A party may by its statements or conduct be precluded from asserting such a clause to the extent that the other party has reasonably relied on them.

2.107 — Promises binding without acceptance

A promise which is intended to be legally binding without acceptance binding.

Section 2 — Offer and Acceptance

2.201 — Offer

(1) A proposal amounts to an offer if:
- (a) it is intended to result in a contract if the other party accepts it, and
- (b) it contains sufficiently definite terms to form a contract.

(2) An offer may be made to one or more specific persons or to the
(3) A proposal to supply goods or services at stated prices made by a professional supplier in a public advertisement or a catalogue, or by a display of goods, is presumed to be an offer to sell or supply at that price until the stock of goods, or the supplier's capacity to supply the service, is exhausted.

Article 2.202 — Revocation of an Offer

(1) An offer may be revoked if the revocation reaches the offeree before it has dispatched its acceptance or, in cases of acceptance by conduct, before the contract has been concluded under Article 2.205 (2) or (3).
(2) An offer made to the public can be revoked by the same means as were used to make the offer.
(3) However, a revocation of an offer is ineffective if:
- (a) the offer indicates that it is irrevocable; or
- (b) it states a fixed time for its acceptance; or
- (c) it was reasonable for the offeree to rely on the offer as being irrevocable and the offeree has acted in reliance on the offer.

Article 2.203 — Lapse of an Offer

When a rejection of an offer reaches the offeror, the offer lapses.

Article 2.204 — Acceptance

(1) Any form of statement or conduct by the offeree is an acceptance if it indicates assent to the offer.
(2) Silence or inactivity does not in itself amount to acceptance.

Article 2.205 — Time of Conclusion of the Contract

(1) If an acceptance has been dispatched by the offeree the contract is concluded when the acceptance reaches the offeror.
(2) In case of acceptance by conduct, the contract is concluded when notice of the conduct reaches the offeror.
(3) If by virtue of the offer, of practices which the parties have established between themselves, or of a usage, the offeree may accept the offer by performing an act without notice to the offeror, the contract is concluded when the performance of the act begins.

Article 2.206 — Time Limit for Acceptance

(1) In order to be effective, acceptance of an offer must reach the offeror within the time fixed by it.
(2) If no time has been fixed by the offeror acceptance must reach it within a reasonable time.
(3) In the case of an acceptance by an act of performance under art. 2.205 (3), that act must be performed within the time for acceptance fixed by the offeror or, if no such time is fixed, within a reasonable time.

Article 2.207 — Late Acceptance

(1) A late acceptance is nonetheless effective as an acceptance if without delay the offeror informs the offeree that he treats it as such.
(2) If a letter or other writing containing a late acceptance shows that it has been sent in such circumstances that if its transmission had been normal it would have reached the offeror in due time, the late acceptance is effective as an acceptance unless, without delay, the offeror informs the offeree that it considers its offer as having lapsed.

Article 2.208 — Modified Acceptance

(1) A reply by the offeree which states or implies additional or different terms which would materially alter the terms of the offer is a rejection and a new offer.
(2) A reply which gives a definite assent to an offer operates as an acceptance even if it states or implies additional or different terms, provided these do not materially alter the terms of the offer. The additional or different terms then become part of the contract.
(3) However, such a reply will be treated as a rejection of the offer if:
- (a) the offer expressly limits acceptance to the terms of the offer; or
- (b) the offeror objects to the additional or different terms without delay; or
- (c) the offeree makes its acceptance conditional upon the offeror's assent to the additional or different terms, and the assent does not reach the offeree within a reasonable time.

Article 2.209 — Conflicting General Conditions

(1) If the parties have reached agreement except that the offer and acceptance refer to conflicting general conditions of contract, a contract is nonetheless formed. The general conditions form part of the contract to the extent that they are common in substance.
(2) However, no contract is formed if one party:
- (a) Has indicated in advance, explicitly, and not by general conditions, that it does not intend to be bound by a contract on the basis of paragraph (1); or
- (b) without delay, informs the other party that it does not intend to be bound by such contract.

(3) General conditions of contract are terms which have been formulated in advance for an indefinite number of contracts of a certain nature, and which have not been individually negotiated between the parties.

Article 2.2 10 — Professional's Written Confirmation

If professionals have concluded a contract but have not embodied it in a final document, and one without delay sends the other a writing which purports to be a confirmation of the contract but which contains additional or different terms, such terms will become part of the contract unless:

(a) the terms materially alter the terms of the contract, or
(b) the addressee objects to them without delay.

Article 2.211 — Contracts not Concluded through Offer and Acceptance

The rules in this section apply with appropriate adaptations even though the process of conclusion of a contract cannot be analysed into offer and acceptance.

Section 3 — Liability for negotiations

Article 2.301 — Negotiations Contrary to Good Faith

(1) A party is free to negotiate and is not liable for failure to reach an agreement.
(2) However, a party who has negotiated or broken off negotiations contrary to good faith and fair dealing is liable for the losses caused to the other party.
(3) It is contrary to good faith and fair dealing, in particular, for a party to enter into or continue negotiations with no real intention of reaching an agreement with the other party.

Article 2.302 — Breach of Confidentiality

If confidential information is given by one party in the course of negotiations, the other party is under a duty not to disclose that information or use it for its own purposes whether or not a contract is subsequently concluded. The remedy for breach of this duty may include compensation for loss suffered and restitution of the benefit received by the other party.

CHAPTER 3. AUTHORITY OF AGENTS

Section 1 — General Provisions

Article 3.101 — Scope of the Chapter

(1) This chapter governs the authority of an agent or other intermediary to bind its principal in relation to a contract with a third party.

(2) This chapter does not govern an agent's authority bestowed by law or the authority of an agent appointed by a public or judicial authority.
(3) This chapter does not govern the internal relationship between the agent or intermediary and its principal.

Article 3.102 — Categories of Representation

(1) Where an agent acts in the name of a principal, the rules on direct representation apply (Section 2). It is irrelevant whether the principal's identity is revealed at the time the agent acts or is to be revealed later.
(2) Where an intermediary acts on instructions and on behalf of, but not in the name of, a principal, or where the third party neither knows nor has reason to know that the intermediary acts as an agent, the rules on indirect representation apply (Section 3).

Section 2 — Direct Representation

Article 3.201 — Express, implied and apparent authority

(1) The principal's grant of authority to an agent to act in its name may be express or may be implied from the circumstances.
(2) The agent has authority to perform all acts necessary in the circumstances to achieve the purposes for which the authority was granted.
(3) A person is to be treated as having granted authority to an apparent agent if the person's statements or conduct induce the third party reasonably and in good faith to believe that the apparent agent has been granted authority for the act performed by it.

Article 3.202 — Agent acting in exercise of his authority

Where an agent is acting within its authority as defined by article 3.201, its acts bind the principal and the third party directly to each other. The agent itself is not bound to the third party.

Article 3.203 — Unidentified Principal

If an agent enters into a contract in the name of a principal whose identity is to be revealed later, but fails to reveal that identity within a reasonable time after a request by the third party, the agent itself is bound by the contract.

Article 3.204 — Agent acting without or outside his authority

(1) Where a person acting as an agent acts without authority or outside the scope of its authority, its acts are not binding upon the principal and the third party.
(2) Failing ratification by the principal according to article 3.207, the agent is liable to pay the third party such damages as will place the third party in the same position as if the agent had acted with authority. This does not apply if the third party knew or could not have been unaware of the agents lack of authority.

Article 3.205 — Conflict of Interests

(1) If a contract concluded by an agent involves the agent in a conflict of interest of which the third party knew or could not have been unaware, the principal may avoid the contract according to the provisions of articles 4.112 to 4.116.
(2) There is presumed to be a conflict of interest where:
- (a) the agent also acted as agent for the third party; or
- (b) the contract was with itself in its personal capacity.

(3) However, the principal may not avoid the contract:
- (a) if it had consented to, or could not have been unaware of, the agent's so acting; or
- (b) if the agent had disclosed the conflict of interest to it and it had not objected within a reasonable time.

Article 3.206 — Subagency

An agent has implied authority to appoint a subagent to carry out tasks which are not of a personal character and which it is not reasonable to expect the agent to carry out itself. The rules of this Section apply to the subagency; acts of the subagent which are within its and the agent's authority bind the principal and the third party directly to each other.

Article 3.207 — Ratification by Principal

(1) Where a person acting as an agent acts without authority or outside its authority, the principal may ratify the agent's acts.

(2) Upon ratification, the agent's acts are considered as having been authorized, without prejudice to the rights of other persons.

Article 3.208 — Third Party's Right with Respect to Confirmation of Authority

Where the statements or conduct of the principal gave the third party reason to believe that an act performed by the agent was authorised, but the third party is in doubt about the authorisation, it may send a written confirmation to the principal or request ratification from it. If the principal does not object or answer the request without delay, the agent's act is treated as having been authorised.

Article 3.209 — Duration of Authority

(1) An agent's authority continues until the third party knows or ought to know that:

- (a) the agent's authority has been brought to an end by the principal, the agent, or both; or
- (b) the acts for which the authority had been granted have been completed, or the time for which it had been granted has expired; or
- (c) the agent has become insolvent or, where a natural person, has died or become incapacitated; or
- (d) the principal has become insolvent.

(2) The third party is considered to know that the agent's authority has brought to an end under paragraph(l) (a) above if this has been or publicised in the same manner in which the was originally communicated or publicised.
(3) However, the agent remains authorised for a reasonable time to perform those acts which are necessary to protect the interests of the or its successors

Chapter 3 — Indirect Representation

Article 3.301 — Intermediaries not acting in the name of a Principal

(1) Where an intermediary acts:

- (a) on instructions and on behalf, but not in the name, of a principal, or
- (b) on instructions from a principal but the third party does not know and has no reason to know this, the intennediary and the third party are bound to each other.

(2) The principal and the third party are bound to each other only under the conditions set out in Articles 3.302 to 3.304.

Article 3.302 — Intermediary's Insolvency or Fundamental Nonperformance to Principal

If the intermediary becomes insolvent, or if it commits a fundamental non-performance towards the principal, or if prior to the time for performance it is clear that there will be a fundamental non-performance:

(a) on the principal's demand, the intermediary shall communicate the name and address of the third party to the principal; and

(b) the principal may exercise against the third party the rights acquired on the principal's behalf by the intermediary, subject to any defences which the third party may set up against the intermediary.

Article 3.303 — Intermediary's Insolvency or Fundamental Nonperformance to Third Party

If the intermediary becomes insolvent, or if it commits a fundamental non-performance towards the third party, or if prior to the time for performance it is clear that there will be a fundamental nonperformance:

(a) on the third party's demand, the intermediary shall communicate the name and address of the principal to the third party; and

(b) the third party may exercise against the principal the rights which the third party has against the intermediary, subject to any defences which the intermediary may set up against the third party and those which the principal may set up against the intermediary.

Article 3.304 — Requirement of Notice

The rights under Articles 3.302 and 3.303 may be exercised only if notice of intention to exercise them is given to the intermediary and to the third party or principal, respectively. Upon receipt of the notice, the third party or the principal is no longer entitled to render performance to the intermediary.

CHAPTER 4 — VALIDITY

Article 4.101 — Matters not Covered

This chapter does not deal with invalidity arising from illegality, immorality or lack of capacity.

Article 4.102 — Initial Impossibility

A contract is not invalid merely because at the time it was concluded performance of the obligation assumed was impossible, or because a party was not entitled to dispose of the assets to which the contract relates.

Article 4.103 — Mistake as to facts or law

(1) A party may avoid a contract for mistake of fact or law existing when the contract was concluded if:

- (a) (i) the mistake was caused by information given by the other party; or (ii) the other party knew or ought to have known of the mistake and it was contrary to good faith and fair dealing to leave the mistaken party in error; or (iii) the other party made the same mistake, and
- (b) the other party knew or ought to have known that the mistaken party, had it known the truth, would not have entered the contract or would have done so only on fundamentally different terms.

(2) However a party may not avoid the contract if:

- (a) in the circumstances its mistake was inexcusable, or
- (b) the risk of the mistake was assumed, or in the circumstances should be borne, by it.

Article 4.104 — Inaccuracy in Communication

An inaccuracy in the expression or transmission of a statement is to be treated as a mistake of the person who made or sent the statement and Article 4.103 applies.

Article 4.105 — Adaption of Contract

(1) If a party is entitled to avoid the contract for mistake but the other party indicates that it is willing to perform, or actually does perform, the contract as it was understood by the party entitled to avoid it, the contract is to be treated as if it had been concluded as that party understood it. The other party must indicate its willingness to perform, or render such performance, promptly after being informed of the manner in which the party entitled to avoid it understood the contract and before that party acts in reliance on any notice of avoidance.
(2) After such indication or performance the right to avoid is lost and any earlier notice of avoidance is ineffective.
(3) Where both parties have made the same mistake, the court may at the request of either party bring the contract into accordance with what might reasonably have been agreed had the mistake not occurred.

Article 4.107 — Fraud

(1) A party may avoid a contract when it has been led to conclude it by the other party's fraudulent representation, whether by words or conduct, or fraudulent non-disclosure of any information which in accordance with good faith and fair dealing it should have disclosed.
(2) A party's representation or non-disclosure is fraudulent if it was intended to deceive.
(3) In determining whether good faith and fair dealing required that a party disclose particular information, regard should be had to all the circumstances, including:

- (a) whether the party had special expertise;
- (b) the cost to it of acquiring the relevant information;
- (c) whether the other party could reasonably acquire the information for itself; and
- (d) the apparent importance of the information to the other party.

Article 4.108 — Threats

A party may avoid a contract when it has been led to conclude it by the other party's imminent and serious threat of an act:

- (a) which is wrongful in itself, or

(b) which it is wrongful to use as a means to obtain the conclusion of the contract, unless in the circumstances the first party had a reasonable alternative.

Article 4.109 — Excessive benefit or unfair advantage

(1) A party may avoid a contract if, at the time of the conclusion of the contract:

(a) it was dependent on or had a relationship of trust with the other party, was in economic distress or had urgent needs, was improvident, ignorant, inexperienced or lacking in bargaining skill, and

(b) the other party knew or ought to have known of this and, given the circumstances and purpose of the contract, took advantage of the first party's situation in a way which was grossly unfair or took an excessive benefit.

(2) Upon the request of the party entitled to avoidance, a court may if it is appropriate adapt the contract in order to bring it into accordance with what might have been agreed had the requirements of good faith and fair dealing been followed.

(3) A court may similarly adapt the contract upon the request of a party receiving notice of avoidance for excessive benefit or unfair advantage, provided that this party informs the party who gave the notice promptly after receiving it and before that party has acted in reliance on it.

Article 4.110 — Unfair terms which have not been individually negotiated

(1) A party may avoid a term which has not been individually negotiated if, contrary to the requirements of good faith and fair dealing, it causes a significant imbalance in the parties' rights and obligations arising under the contract to the detriment of that party, taking into account the nature of the performance to be rendered under the contract, all the other terms of the contract and the circumstances at the time the contract was concluded.

(2) This Article does not apply to:

(a) a term which defines the main subject matter of the contract, provided the term is in plain and intelligible language; or to

(b) the adequacy in value of one party's obligations compared to the value of the obligations of the other party.

Article 4.111 — Third persons

(1) Where a third person for whose acts a party is responsible, or who with a party's assent is involved in the making of a contract:

- (a) causes a mistake by giving information, or knows of or ought to have known of a mistake,
- (b) gives incorrect information,
- (c) commits fraud,
- (d) makes a threat, or
- (e) takes excessive benefit or unfair advantage, remedies under this Chapter will be available under the same conditions as if the behaviour or knowledge had been that of the party itself.

(2) Where any other third person:

- (a) gives incorrect information,
- (b) commits fraud,
- (c) makes a threat, or
- (d) takes excessive benefit or unfair advantage, remedies under this Chapter will be available if the party knew or ought to have known of the relevant facts, or at the time of avoidance it has not acted in reliance on the contract.

Article 4.112 — Notice of Avoidance

Avoidance must be by notice to the other party.

Article 4.113 — Time limits

(1) Notice of avoidance must be given within a reasonable time, with due regard to the circumstances, after the avoiding party knew or ought to have known of the relevant facts or became capable of acting freely.
(2) However, a party may avoid an individual term under Article 4.110 if it gives notice of avoidance within a reasonable time after the other party has invoked the term.

Article 4.114 — Confirmation

If the party who is entitled to avoid a contract confirms it, expressly or impliedly, after it knows of the ground for avoidance, or becomes capable of acting freely, avoidance of the contract is excluded.

Article 4.115 — Effect of avoidance

On avoidance either party may claim restitution of whatever he has supplied under the contract or the part of it avoided, provided he makes concurrent restitution of whatever he has received under the contract or the part of it avoided. If restitution cannot be made in kind for any reason, a reasonable sum must be paid for what has been received.

Article 4.116 — Partial avoidance

If a ground of avoidance affects only particular terms of a contract, the effect of an avoidance is limited to those terms unless, giving due consideration to all the circumstances of the case, it is unreasonable to uphold the remaining contract.

Article 4.117 — Damages

(1) A party who avoids a contract under this Chapter may recover from the other party damages so as to put the avoiding party as nearly possible into the same position as if it had not concluded the provided that the other party knew or ought to have known the mistake, fraud, threat or taking of excessive benefit or unfair advantage.
(2) If a party has the right to avoid a contract under this Chapter, but does not exercise its right or has lost its right under the provisions of Articles 4.113 or 4.114, it may recover, subject to paragraph (1), damages limited to the loss caused to it by the mistake, fraud, threat or taking of excessive benefit or unfair advantage. The same measure damages shall apply when the party was misled by incorrect information in the sense of Article 4.106.
(3) In other respects, the damages shall be in accordance with the relevant provisions of Chapter 9, Section 5, with appropriate adaptations.

Article 4.118 — Exclusion or restriction of remedies

(1) Remedies for fraud, threats and excessive benefit or unfair advantage-taking, and the right to avoid an unfair term which has not been individually negotiated, cannot be excluded or restricted.
(2) Remedies for mistake and incorrect information may be excluded or restricted unless the exclusion or restriction is contrary to good faith and fair dealing.

Article 4.119 — Remedies for non-performance

A party who is entitled to a remedy under this Chapter in circumstances which afford that party a remedy for non-performance may pursue either remedy.

CHAPTER 5 — INTERPRETATION

Article 5.101 — General Rules of Interpretation

(1) A contract is to be interpreted according to the common intention of the parties even if this differs from the literal meaning of the words.
(2) If it is established that one party intended the contract — to have a particular meaning, and at the time of the conclusion of the contract the other party could not have been unaware of the first party's intention, the contract is to be interpreted in the way intended by the first party.
(3) If an intention cannot be established according to (1) or (2), the contract is to be interpreted according to the meaning that reasonable persons of the same kind as the parties would give to it in the same circumstances.

Article 5.102 — Relevant Circumstances

In interpreting the contract, regard shall be had, in particular, to:

- (a) the circumstances in which it was concluded, including the preliminary negotiations;
- (b) the conduct of the parties, even subsequent to the conclusion of the contract;
- (c) the nature and purpose of the contract;
- (d) the interpretation which has already been given to similar clauses by the parties and the practices they have established between themselves;
- (e) the meaning commonly given to terms and expressions in the branch of activity concerned and the interpretation similar clauses may already have received;
- (f) usages; and
- (g) good faith and fair dealing

Article 5.103 — Contra Proferentem Rule

Where there is doubt about the meaning of a contract term not individually negotiated, an interpretation of the term against the party who supplied it is to be preferred.

Article 5.104 — Preference to Negotiated Terms

Terms which have been individually negotiated take preference over those which are not.

Article 5.105 — Reference to Contract as a Whole

Terms are interpreted in the light of the whole contract in which they appear.

Article 5.106 — Terms to Be Given (Full) Effect

An interpretation which renders the terms of the contract lawful or effective, is to be preferred to one which would not.

Article 5.107 — Linguistic Discrepancies

Where a contract is drawn up in two or more language versions none of which is stated to be authoritative, there is, in case of discrepancy between the versions, a preference for interpretation according to the version in which the contract was originally drawn up.

CHAPTER 6 — CONTENTS AND EFFECTS

Article 6.101 — Statements giving rise to contractual obligation

(1) A statement made by one party before or when the contract is concluded is to be treated as giving rise to a contractual obligation if that is how the other party reasonably understood it in the circumstances, taking into account:

(a) the apparent importance of the statement to the other party;

(b) whether the party was making the statement in the course of business; and

(c) the relative expertise of the parties.

(2) If one of the parties is a professional supplier who gives information about the quality or use of or goods or other property when marketing or advertising them or otherwise before the contract for them is concluded, the statement is M be treated as giving rise to a contractual obligation unless it is shown that the other party knew or could not have been unaware that the statement was incorrect.

(3) Such information and other undertakings given by a person advertising or marketing services, goods or other property for the professional supplier, or by a person in earlier links of the business chain, are to be treated as giving rise to a contractual obligation on the part of the professional supplier unless it did not know and had no reason to know of the information or undertaking.

Article 6.102 — Implied obligations

In addition to the express terms, a contract may contain implied terms which. stem from

(a) the intention of the parties,
(b) the nature and purpose of the contract, and
(c) good faith and fair dealing.

Article 6.103 — Simulation

When the parties have concluded an apparent contract which was not intended to reflect their true agreement, as between the parties the true agreement prevails.

Article 6.104 — Determination of Price

Where the contract does not fix the price or the method of determining it, the parties are to be treated as having agreed on a reasonable price.

Article 6.105 — Unilateral Determination by a Party

Where the price or any other contractual term is to be determined by one party whose determination is grossly unreasonable, then notwithstanding any provision to the contrary, a reasonable price or other term shall be substituted.

Article 6.106 — Determination by a Third Person

(1) Where the price or any other contractual term is to be determined by a third person, and it cannot or will not do so, the parties are presumed to have empowered the court to appoint another person to determine it.
(2) If a price or other term fixed by a third person is grossly unreasonable, a reasonable price or term shall be substituted.

Article 6.107 — Reference to a Non Existent Factor

Where the price or any other contractual term is to be determined by reference to a factor which does not exist or has ceased to exist or to be accessible, the nearest equivalent factor shall be substituted.

Article 6.108 — Quality of Performance

If the contract does not specify the quality, a party must tender performance of at least average quality.

Article 6.109 — Contract for an Indefinite Period

A contract for an indefinite period may be ended by either party by giving notice of reasonable length.

Article 6.110 — Stipulation in Favour of a Third Party

(1) A third party may require performance of a contractual obligation when its right to do so has been expressly agreed upon between the promisor and the promisee, or when such agreement is to be inferred from the purpose of the contract or the circumstances of the case. The third party need not be identified at the time the agreement is concluded.
(2) If the third party renounces the right to performance the right is treated as never having accrued to it.
(3) The promisee may by notice to the promisor deprive the third party of the right to performance unless:

- (a) the third party has received notice from the promisee that the right has been made irrevocable, or

(b) the promisor or the promisee has received notice from the third party that the latter accepts the right.

Article 6.111 — Change of Circumstances

(1) A party is bound to fulfil its obligations even if performance has become more onerous, whether because the cost of performance increased or because the value of the performance it receives has diminished.
(2) If, however, performance of the contract becomes excessively onerous because of a change of circumstances, the parties are bound to enter into negotiations with a view to adapting the contract or terminating it, provided that:

(a) the change of circumstances occurred after the time of conclusion of the contract,
(b) the possibility of a change of circumstances was not one which could reasonably have been taken into account at the time of conclusion of the contract, and
(c) the risk of the change of circumstances is not one which, according to the contract, the party affected should be required to bear.

(3) If the parties fail to reach agreement within a reasonable period, the court may:

(a) terminate the contract at a date and on terms to be determined by the court; or
(b) adapt the contract in order to distribute between the parties in a just and equitable manner the losses and gains resulting from the change of circumstances.

In either case, the court may award damages for the loss suffered through a party refusing to negotiate or breaking off negotiations contrary to good faith and fair dealing.

CHAPTER 7 — PERFORMANCE

Article 7.101 — Place of Performance

(1) If the place of performance of a contractual obligation is not fixed by or determinable from the contract it shall be:

(a) in the case of an obligation to pay money, the creditor's place of business at the time of the conclusion of the contract;

(b) in the case of an obligation other than to pay money, the obligor's place of business at the time of conclusion of the contract.

(2) If a party has more than one place of business, the place of business for the purpose of the preceding paragraph is that which has the closest relationship to the contract, having regard to the circumstances known to or contemplated by the parties at the time of conclusion of the contract.

(3) If a party does not have a place of business its habitual residence is to be treated as its place of business.

Article 7.102 — Time of Performance

A party has to effect its performance:

(1) if a time is fixed by or determinable from the contract, at that time;

(2) if a period of time is fixed by or determinable from the contract, at any time within that period unless the circumstances of the case indicate that the other party is to choose the time;

(3) in any other case, within a reasonable time after the conclusion of the contract.

Article 7.103 — Early Performance

(1) A party may decline a tender of performance made before it is due except where acceptance of the tender would not unreasonably prejudice its interests.

(2) A party's acceptance of early performance does not affect the time fixed for the performance of its own obligation.

Article 7.104 — Order of performance

To the extent that the performances of the parties can be rendered simultaneously, the parties are bound to render them simultaneously, unless the circumstances indicate otherwise.

Article 7.105 — Alternative performance

(1) Where an obligation may be discharged by one of alternative performances, the choice belongs to the party who is to perform, unless the circumstances indicate otherwise.

(2) If the party who is to make the choice fails to do so by the time required by the contract, then:

- (a) if the delay in choosing is fundamental, the right to choose passes to the other party;
- (b) if the delay is not fundamental, the other party may give a notice fixing an additional period of reasonable length in which the party to choose must do so. If the latter fails to do so, the right to choose passes to the other party.

Article 7.106 — Performance by a Third Person

(1) Except where the contract requires personal performance the obligee cannot refuse performance by a third person if:

- (a) the third person acts with the assent of the obligor; or
- (b) the third person has a legitimate interest in performance and the obligor has failed to perform or it is clear that it will not perform at the time performance is due.

(2) Performance by the third person in accordance with paragraph (1) discharges the obligor.

Article 7.107 — Form of Payment

(1) Payment of money due may be made in any form used in the ordinary course of business.

(2) A creditor who, pursuant to the contract or voluntarily, accepts a cheque or other order to pay or a promise to pay is presumed to do so only on condition that it will be honoured. The creditor may not enforce the original obligation to pay unless the order or promise is not honoured.

Article 7.108 — Currency of Payment

(1) The parties may agree that payment shall be made only in a specified currency.

(2) In the absence of such agreement, a sum of money expressed in a currency other than that of the place where payment is due may be paid in the currency of that place according to the rate of exchange prevailing there at the time when payment is due.

(3) If, in a case falling within the preceding paragraph, the debtor has not paid at the time when payment is due, the creditor may require payment in the currency of the place where payment is due according to the rate of exchange prevailing there either at the time when payment is due or at the time of actual payment.

Article 7.109 — Appropriation of Performance

(1) Where a party has to perform several obligations of the same nature and the performance tendered does not suffice to discharge all of the obligations, then subject to paragraph 4 the party may at the time of its performance declare to which obligation the performance is to be appropriated.
(2) If the performing party does not make such a declaration, the other party may within a reasonable time appropriate the performance to such obligation as it chooses. It shall inform the performing party of the choice. However, any such appropriation to an obligation which:

(a) is not yet due, or (b) is illegal, or (c) is disputed, is invalid.

(3) In the absence of an appropriation by either party, and subject to Paragraph 4, the performance is appropriated to that obligation which satisfies one of the following criteria in the sequence indicated:

(a) the obligation which is due or is the first to fall due; (b) the obligation for which the obligee has the least security; (c) the obligation which is the most burdensome for the obligor, (d) the obligation which has arisen first.

If none of the preceding criteria applies, the performance is I proportionately to all obligations.
(4) In the case of a monetary obligation, a payment by the debtor is to be appropriated, first, to expenses, secondly, to interest, and thirdly, to unless the creditor makes a different appropriation.

7.110 — Property Not Accepted

(1) A party who is left in possession of tangible property other than money because of the other party's failure to accept or retake the must take reasonable steps to protect and preserve the property.
(2) The party left in possession may discharge its duty to deliver or return:

(a) by depositing the property on reasonable terms with a third person to be held to the order of the other party, and notifying the other party this; or

(b) by selling the property on reasonable terms after notice to the other party, and paying the net proceeds to that party.

(3)Where, however, the property is liable to rapid deterioration or its preservation is unreasonably expensive, the party must take reasonable steps to dispose of it. It may discharge its duty to deliver return by paying the net proceeds to the other party.

(4) The party left in possession is entitled to be reimbursed or to retain out of the proceeds of sale any expenses reasonably incurred.

Article 7.111 — Money not Accepted

Where a party fails to accept money properly tendered by the other party, that party may after notice to the first party discharge its obligation to pay by depositing the money to the order of the first party in accordance with the law of the place where payment is due.

Article 7.112 — Costs of Performance

Each party shall bear the costs of performance of its obligations.

CHAPTER 8 — NON-PERFORMANCE AND REMEDIES IN GENERAL

Article 8.101 — Remedies Available

(1) Whenever a party does not perform an obligation under the contract and the non-performance is not excused under Article 8.108, the aggrieved party may resort to any of the remedies set out in Chapter 9.

(2) Where a party's non-performance is excused under Article 8.108, the aggrieved party may resort to any of the remedies set out in Chapter 9 except claiming performance and damages.

(3) A party may not resort to any of the remedies set out in Chapter 9 to the extent that its own act caused the other party's nonperformance.

Article 8.102 — Cumulation of Remedies

Remedies which are not incompatible may be cumulated. In particular, a party is not deprived of its right to damages by exercising its right to any other remedy.

Article 8.103 — Fundamental Non-Performance

A non-performance of an obligation is fundamental to the contract if:

(a) strict compliance with the obligation is of the essence of the contract; or

(b) the non-performance substantially deprives the aggrieved party of what it was entitled to expect under the contract, unless the other party did not foresee and could not reasonably have foreseen that result; or

(c) the non-performance is intentional and gives the aggrieved party reason to believe that it cannot rely on the other party's future performance.

Article 8.104 — Cure by Non-Performing Party

A party whose tender of performance is not accepted by the other party because it does not conform to the contract may make a new and conforming tender where the time for performance has not yet arrived or the delay would not be such as to constitute a fundamental nonperformance.

Article 8.105 — Assurance of Performance

(1) A party who reasonably believes that there will be a fundamental non-performance by the other party may demand adequate assurance due performance and meanwhile may withhold performance of its own obligations so long as such reasonable belief continues.
(2) Where this assurance is not provided within a reasonable time, the party demanding it may terminate the contract if it still reasonably that there will be a fundamental non-performance by the other party and gives notice of termination without delay.

Article 8.106 — Notice Fixing Additional Period for Performance

(1) In any case of non-performance the aggrieved party may by notice to the other party allow an additional period of time for performance
(2) During the additional period the aggrieved party may withhold performance of its own reciprocal obligations and may claim damages, but it may not resort to any other remedy. If it receives notice from the other party that the lat-

ter will not perform within that period, or if upon expiry of that period due performance has not been made, the aggrieved party may resort to any of the remedies that may be available under chapter 9.
(3) If in a case of delay in performance which is not fundamental the aggrieved party has given a notice fixing an additional period of time of reasonable length, it may terminate the contract at the end of the period of notice. The aggrieved party may in its notice provide that if the other party does not perform within the period fixed by the notice the contract shall terminate automatically. If the period stated is too short, the aggrieved party may terminate, or, as the case may be, the contract shall terminate automatically, only after a reasonable period from the time of the notice.

Article 8.107 — Performance Entrusted to Another

A party who entrusts performance of the contract to another person remains responsible for performance.

Article 8.108 — Excuse Due to an Impediment

(1) A party's non-performance is excused if it proves that it is due to an impediment beyond its control and that it could not reasonably have been expected to take the impediment into account at the time of the conclusion of the contract, or to have avoided or overcome the impediment or its consequences.
(2) Where the impediment is only temporary the excuse provided by this article has effect for the period during which the impediment exists. However, if the delay amounts to a fundamental nonperformance, the obligee may treat it as such.
(3) The non-performing party must ensure that notice of the impediment and of its effect on its ability to perform is received by the other party within a reasonable time after the non-performing party knew or ought to have known of these circumstances. The other party is entitled to damages for any loss resulting from the non-receipt of such notice.

Article 8.109 — Clause Limiting or Excluding Remedies

Remedies for non-performance may be excluded or restricted unless it would be contrary to ggod faith and fair dealing to invoke the exclusion or restriction.

CHAPTER 9 — PARTICULAR REMEDIES FOR NON-PERFORMANCE

Section 1 — Right to Performance

Article 9.101 — Monetary Obligations

(1) The creditor is entitled to recover money which is due.
(2) Where the creditor has not yet performed its obligation and it is clear that the debtor will be unwilling to receive performance, the creditor may nonetheless proceed with its performance and may recover any sum due under the contract unless:

- (a) it could have made a reasonable substitute transaction without significant effort or expense; or
- (b) performance would be unreasonable in the circumstances.

Article 9.102 — Non-monetary Obligations

(1) The aggrieved party is entitled to specific performance of an obligation other than one to pay money, including the remedying of a defective performance.
(2) Specific performance cannot, however, be obtained where: (a) performance would be unlawful or impossible, or (b) performance would cause the obligor unreasonable effort or expense, or (c) the performance consists in the provision of services or work of a personal character or depends upon a personal relationship, or (d) the aggrieved party may reasonably obtain performance from another source.
(3) The aggrieved party will lose the right to specific performance if it fails to seek it within a reasonable time after it has or ought to have become aware of the non-performance.

Article 9.103 — Damages Not Precluded

The fact that a right to performance is excluded under this Section does not preclude a claim for damages.

Section 2 — Right To Withhold Performance

Article 9.201 — Right to Withhold Performance

(1) A party who is to perform simultaneously with or after the other party may withhold performance until the other has tendered performance or has performed. The first party may withhold the whole of its performance or a part of it as may be reasonable in the circumstances.
(2) A party may similarly withhold performance for as long as it is clear that there will be a non-performance by the other party when the other party's performance becomes due.

Section 3 — Termination Of The Contract

Article 9.301 — Right to Terminate the Contract

(1) A party may terminate the contract if the other party's nonperformance is fundamental.
(2) In the case of delay the aggrieved party may also terminate the contract under Article 8.106 (3).

Article 9.302 — Contract to be Performed in Parts

If the contract is to be performed in separate parts and in relation to a part to which a counter-performance can be apportioned there is a fundamental non-performance, the aggrieved party may exercise its right to terminate under this Section in relation to the part concerned. It may terminate the contract as a whole only if the non-performance is fundamental to the contract as a whole.

Article 9.303 — Notice of Termination

(1) A party's right to terminate the contract is to be exercised by notice to the other party.
(2) The aggrieved party loses its right to terminate the contract unless it gives notice within a reasonable time after it has or ought to have become aware of the non-performance.
(3) (a) When performance has not been tendered by the time it was due, the aggrieved party need not give notice of termination before a tender has been made. If a tender is later made it loses its right to terminate

if it does not give such notice within a reasonable time after it has or ought to have become aware of the tender.

(b) If, however, the aggrieved party knows or has reason to know that the other party still intends to tender within a reasonable time, and the aggrieved party unreasonably fails to notify the other party that it will not accept performance, it loses its right to terminate if the other party in fact tenders within a reasonable time.

(4) If a party is excused under Article 8.108 through an impediment which is total and permanent, the contract is terminated automatically and without notice at the time the impediment arises.

Article 9.304 — Anticipatory Non-Performance

Where prior to the time for performance by a party it is clear that there will be a fundamental non-performance by it the other party may terminate the contract.

Article 9.305 — Effects of Termination in General

(1) Termination of the contract releases both parties from their obligation to effect and to receive future performance but subject to Articles 9.306 to 9.308, does not affect the rights and liabilities that have accrued up to the time of termination.
(2) Termination does not affect any provision of the contract for the settlement of disputes or any other provision which is to operate even after termination.

Article 9.306 — Property Reduced in Value

A party who terminates the contract may reject property previously received from the other party if its value to the first party has been fundamentally reduced as a result of the other party's nonperformance.

Article 9.307 — Recovery of Money Paid

On termination of the contract a party may recover money paid for a performance which it did not receive or which it properly rejected.

Article 9.308 — Recovery of Property

On termination of the contract a party who has supplied property which can be returned and for which it has not received payment or other counter-performance may recover the property.

Article 9.309 — Recovery for Performance that Cannot be Returned

On termination of the contract a party who has rendered a performance which cannot be returned and for which it has not received payment or other counter-performance may recover an amount for the value of the performance to the other party.

Section 4 — Price Reduction

Article 9.401 — Right to Reduce Price

(1) A party who accepts a tender of performance not conforming to the contract may reduce the price. This reduction shall be proportionate to the decrease in the value of the performance at the time this was tendered compared to the value which a conforming tender would have had at that time.
(2) A party who is entitled to reduce the price under the preceding paragraph and who has already paid a sum exceeding the reduced price may recover the excess from the other party.
(3) A party who reduces the price cannot also recover damages for reduction in the value of the performance but remains entitled to damages for any further loss it has suffered so far as these are recoverable under Section 5 of this Chapter.

Section 5 — Damages and Interest

Article 9.501 — Right to Damages

(1) The aggrieved party is entitled to damages for loss caused by the other party's non-performance which is not excused under Article 8.108.
(2) The loss for which damages are recoverable includes:
- (a) non-pecuniary loss ; and
- (b) future loss which is reasonably likely to occur.

Article 9.502 — General Measure of Damages

The general measure of damages is such sum as will put the aggrieved party as nearly as possible into the position in which it would have been if the contract had been duly performed. Such damages cover the loss which the aggrieved party has suffered and the gain of which it has been deprived.

Article 9.503 — Foreseeability

The non-performing party is liable only for loss which it foresaw or could reasonably have foreseen at the time of conclusion of the contract as a likely result of its non-performance, unless the non-performance was intentional or grossly negligent.

Article 9.504 — Loss Attributable to Aggrieved Party

The non-performing party is not liable for loss suffered by AMI aggrieved party to the extent that the aggrieved party contributed to the non-performance or its effects.

Article 9.505 — Reduction of loss

(1) The non-performing party is not liable for loss suffered by the aggrieved party to the extent that the aggrieved party could have reduced the loss by taking reasonable steps.
(2) The aggrieved party is entitled to recover any expenses reasonably incurred in attempting to reduce the loss.

Article 9.506 — Substitute Transaction

Where the aggrieved party has terminated the contract and has made a substitute transaction within a reasonable time and in a reasonable manner, it may recover the difference between the contract price and the price of the substitute transaction as well as damages for any further loss so far as these are recoverable under this Section.

Article 9.507 — Current Price

Where the aggrieved party has the contract and has not made a substitute transaction but there is a current price for the performance contracted for, it may recover the difference between the contract price and the price current at the time the contract is terminated as well as damages for any loss so far as these are recoverable under this Section.

Article 9.508 — Delay in Payment of Money

If payment of a sum of money is delayed, the aggrieved party is entitled to interest on that sum from the time when payment is due to the time of payment at the average commercial bank short-term lending rate to prime borrowers prevailing for the contractual currency of payment at the place where payment is due.

Article 9.509 — Agreed Payment for Non-performance

(1) Where the contract provides that a party who fails to perform is to pay a specified sum to the aggrieved party for such non-performance, the aggrieved party shall be awarded that sum irrespective of its actual loss.
(2) However, despite any agreement to the contrary the specified sum may be reduced to a reasonable amount where it is grossly excessive in relation to the loss resulting from the non-performance and the other circumstances.

Article 9.510 — Currency by which Damages to be Measured

Damages are to be measured by the currency which most appropriately reflects the aggrieved party's loss.

APPENDIX 6

UNCITRAL Model Law on Electronic Commerce

(Edited)
1996 with additional article 5bis as adopted in 1998

UNITED NATIONS
GENERAL ASSEMBLY RESOLUTION 51/162 OF 16 DECEMBER 1996 UNCITRAL MODEL LAW ON ELECTRONIC COMMERCE

Part One. Electronic commerce in general

Chapter I. General Provisions

Article 1. Sphere of application

This Law applies to any kind of information in the form of a data message used in the context of commercial activities.

Article 2. Definitions

For the purposes of this Law:

(a) "Data message" means information generated, sent, received or stored by electronic, optical or similar means including, but not limited to, electronic data interchange (EDI), electronic mail, telegram, telex or telecopy;

(b) "Electronic data interchange (EDI)" means the electronic transfer from computer to computer of information using an agreed standard to structure the information;

(c) "Originator" of a data message means a person by whom, or on whose behalf, the data message purports to have been sent or generated prior to storage, if any, but it does not include a person acting as an intermediary with respect to that data message;
(d) "Addressee" of a data message means a person who is intended by the originator to receive the data message, but does not include a person acting as an intermediary with respect to that data message;
(e) "Intermediary", with respect to a particular data message, means a person who, on behalf of another person, sends, receives or stores that data message or provides other services with respect to that data message;
(f) "Information system" means a system for generating, sending, receiving, storing or otherwise processing data messages.

Article 3. Interpretation

(1) In the interpretation of this Law, regard is to be had to its international origin and to the need to promote uniformity in its application and the observance of good faith.
(2) Questions concerning matters governed by this Law which are not expressly settled in it are to be settled in conformity with the general principles on which this Law is based.

Article 4. Variation by agreement

(1) As between parties involved in generating, sending, receiving, storing or otherwise processing data messages, and except as otherwise provided, the provisions of chapter III may be varied by agreement.
(2) Paragraph (1) does not affect any right that may exist to modify by agreement any rule of law referred to in chapter II.

Chapter II. Application of legal requirements to data messages

Article 5. Legal recognition of data messages

Information shall not be denied legal effect, validity or enforceability solely on the grounds that it is in the form of a data message.

Article 5bis. Incorporation by reference (as adopted by the Commission at its thirty-first session, in June 1998)

Information shall not be denied legal effect, validity or enforceability solely on the grounds that it is not contained in the data message purporting to give rise to such legal effect, but is merely referred to in that data message.

Article 6. Writing

(1) Where the law requires information to be in writing, that requirement information contained therein is accessible so as to be usable for subsequent reference.
(2) Paragraph (1) applies whether the requirement therein is in the form of an obligation or whether the law simply provides consequences for the information not being in writing.

Article 7. Signature

(1) Where the law requires a signature of a person, that requirement is met in relation to a data message if:

(a) a method is used to identify that person and to indicate that person's approval of the information contained in the data message; and

(b) that method is as reliable as was appropriate for the purpose for which the data message was generated or communicated, in the light of all the circumstances, including any relevant agreement.

(2) Paragraph (1) applies whether the requirement therein is in the form of an obligation or whether the law simply provides consequences for the absence of a signature.

Article 8. Original

(1) Where the law requires information to be presented or retained in its original form, that requirement is met by a data message if

(a) there exists a reliable assurance as to the integrity of the information from the time when it was first generated in its final form, as a data message or otherwise; and

(b) where it is required that information be presented, that information is capable of being displayed to the person to whom it is to be presented.

(2) Paragraph (1) applies whether the requirement therein is in the form of an obligation or whether the law simply provides consequences for the information not being presented or retained in its original form.
(3) For the purposes of subparagraph (a) of paragraph (1):

(a) the criteria for assessing integrity shall be whether the information has remained complete and unaltered, apart from the addition of any endorsement and any change which arises in the normal course of communication, storage and display; and

(b) the standard of reliability required shall be assessed in the light of the purpose for which the information was generated and in the light of all the relevant circumstances.

Article 9. Admissibility and evidential weight of data messages

(1) In any legal proceedings, nothing in the application of the rules of evidence shall apply so as to deny the admissibility of a data message in evidence:

(a) on the sole ground that it is a data message; or,

(b) if it is the best evidence that the person adducing it could reasonably be expected to obtain, on the grounds that it is not in its original form.

(2) Information in the form of a data message shall be given due evidential weight. In assessing the evidential weight of a data message, regard shall be had to the reliability of the manner in which the data message was generated, stored or communicated, to the reliability of the manner in which the integrity of the information was maintained, to the manner in which its originator was identified, and to any other relevant factor.

Article 10. Retention of data messages

(1) Where the law requires that certain documents, records or information be retained, that requirement is met by retaining data messages, provided that the following conditions are satisfied:

(a) the information contained therein is accessible so as to be usable for subsequent reference; and

(b) the data message is retained in the format in which it was generated, sent or received, or in a format which can be demonstrated to represent accurately the information generated, sent or received; and

(c) such information, if any, is retained as enables the identification of the origin and destination of a data message and the date and time when it was sent or received.

(2) An obligation to retain documents, records or information in accordance with paragraph (1) does not extend to any information the sole purpose of which is to enable the message to be sent or received.

(3) A person may satisfy the requirement referred to in paragraph (1) by using the services of any other person, provided that the conditions set forth in subparagraphs (a), (b) and (c) of paragraph (1) are met.

Chapter III. Communication of data messages

Article 11. Formation and validity of contracts

(1) In the context of contract formation, unless otherwise agreed by the parties, an offer and the acceptance of an offer may be expressed by means of data messages. Where a data message is used in the formation of a contract, that contract shall not be denied validity or enforceability on the sole ground that a data message was used for that purpose.

Article 12. Recognition by parties of data messages

(1) As between the originator and the addressee of a data message, a declaration of will or other statement shall not be denied legal effect, validity or enforceability solely on the grounds that it is in the form of a data message.

Article 13. Attribution of data messages

(1) A data message is that of the originator if it was sent by the originator itself.
(2) As between the originator and the addressee, a data message is deemed to be that of the originator if it was sent:

(a) by a person who had the authority to act on behalf of the originator in respect of that data message; or

(b) by an information system programmed by, or on behalf of, the originator to operate automatically.

(3) As between the originator and the addressee, an addressee is entitled to regard a data message as being that of the originator, and to act on that assumption, if-

(a) in order to ascertain whether the data message was that of the originator, the addressee properly applied a procedure previously agreed to by the originator for that purpose; or

(b) the data message as received by the addressee resulted from the actions of a person whose relationship with the originator or with any agent of the originator enabled that person to gain access to a method used by the originator to identify data messages as its own.

(4) Paragraph (3) does not apply:

(a) as of the time when the addressee has both received notice from the originator that the data message is not that of the originator, and had reasonable time to act accordingly; or

(b) in a case within paragraph (3)(b), at any time when the addressee knew or should have known, had it exercised reasonable care or used any agreed procedure, that the data message was not that of the originator.

(5) Where a data message is that of the originator or is deemed to be that of the originator, or the addressee is entitled to act on that assumption, then, as between the originator and the addressee, the addressee is entitled to regard the data message as received as being what the originator intended to send, and to act on that assumption. The addressee is not so entitled when it knew or should have known, had it exercised reasonable care or used any agreed procedure, that the transmission resulted in any error in the data message as received.

(6) The addressee is entitled to regard each data message received as a separate data message and to act on that assumption, except to the extent that it duplicates another data message and the addressee knew or should have known, had it exercised reasonable care or used any agreed procedure, that the data message was a duplicate.

Article 14. Acknowledgement of Receipt

(1) Paragraphs (2) to (4) of this article apply where, on or before sending a data message, or by means of that data message, the originator has requested or has agreed with the addressee that receipt of the data message be acknowledged.

(2) Where the originator has not agreed with the addressee that the acknowledgement be given in a particular form or by a particular method, an acknowledgement may be given by:

(a) any communication by the addressee, automated or otherwise, or

(b) any conduct of the addressee,

sufficient to indicate to the originator that the data message has been received.

(3) Where the originator has stated that the data message is conditional on receipt of the acknowledgement, the data message is treated as though it has never been sent, until the acknowledgement is received.

(4) Where the originator has not stated that the data message is conditional on receipt of the acknowledgement, and the acknowledgement has not been received by the originator within the time specified or agreed or, if no time has been specified or agreed, within a reasonable time, the originator:

(a) may give notice to the addressee stating that no acknowledgement has been received and specifying a reasonable time by which the acknowledgement must be received; and

(b) if the acknowledgement is not received within the time specified in subparagraph (a), may, upon notice to the addressee, treat the data message as though it had never been sent, or exercise any other rights it may have.

(5) Where the originator receives the addressee's acknowledgement of receipt, it is presumed that the related data message was received by the addressee. That presumption does not imply that the data message corresponds to the message received.

(6) Where the received acknowledgement states that the related data message met technical requirements, either agreed upon or set forth in applicable standards, it is presumed that those requirements have been met.

(7) Except in so far as it relates to the sending or receipt of the data message, this article is not intended to deal with the legal consequences that may flow either from that data message or from the acknowledgement of its receipt.

Article 15. Time and place of dispatch and receipt of data messages

(1) Unless otherwise agreed between the originator and the addressee, the dispatch of a data message occurs when it enters an information system outside the control of the originator or of the person who sent the data message on behalf of the originator.

(2) Unless otherwise agreed between the originator and the addressee, the time of receipt of a data message is determined as follows:

(a) if the addressee has designated an information system for the purpose of receiving data messages, receipt occurs:

(i) at the time when the data message enters the designated information system; or

(ii) if the data message is sent to an information system of the addressee that is not the designated information system, at the time when the data message is retrieved by the addressee;

(b) if the addressee has not designated an information system, receipt occurs when the data message enters an information system of the addressee.

(3) Paragraph (2) applies notwithstanding that the place where the information system is located may be different from the place where the data message is deemed to be received under paragraph (4).

(4) Unless otherwise agreed between the originator and the addressee, a data message is deemed to be dispatched at the place where the originator has its place of business, and is deemed to be received at the place where the addressee has its place of business. For the purposes of this paragraph:

(a) if the originator or the addressee has more than one place of business, the place of business is that which has the closest relationship to the underlying transaction or, where there is no underlying transaction, the principal place of business;
(b) if the originator or the addressee does not have a place of business, reference is to be made to its habitual residence.

Part Two. Electronic Commerce in Specific Areas

Chapter I. Carriage of Goods

Article 16. Actions related to contracts of carriage of goods

Without derogating from the provisions of part one of this Law, this chapter applies to any action in connection with, or in pursuance of, a contract of carriage of goods, including but not limited to:

(a) (i) furnishing the marks, number, quantity or weight of goods;
(ii) stating or declaring the nature or value of goods;
(iii) issuing a receipt for goods:
(iv) confirming that goods have been loaded;
(b) (i) notifying a person of terms and conditions of the contract;
(ii) giving instructions to a carrier;
(c) (i) claiming delivery of goods;
(ii) authorizing release of goods;
(iii) giving notice of loss of, or damage to, goods;
(d) giving any other notice or statement in connection with the performance of the contract;
(e) undertaking to deliver goods to a named person or a person authorized to claim delivery;
(f) granting, acquiring, renouncing, surrendering, transferring or negotiating rights in goods;
(g) acquiring or transferring rights and obligations under the contract.

Article 17. Transport documents

(1) Subject to paragraph (3), where the law requires that any action referred to in article 16 be carried out in writing or by using a paper document, that requirement is met if the action is carried out by using one or more data messages.

(2) Paragraph (1) applies whether the requirement therein is in the form of an obligation or whether the law simply provides consequences for failing either to carry out the action in writing or to use a paper document.
(3) If a right is to be granted to, or an obligation is to be acquired by, one person and no other person, and if the law requires that, in order to effect this, the right or obligation must be conveyed to that person by the transfer, or use of, a paper document, that requirement is met if the right or obligation is conveyed by using one or more data messages, provided that a reliable method is used to render such data message or messages unique.
(4) For the purposes of paragraph (3), the standard of reliability required shall be assessed in the light of the purpose for which the right or obligation was conveyed and in the light of all the circumstances, including any relevant agreement.
(5) Where one or more data messages are used to effect any action in subparagraphs (f) and (g) of article 16, no paper document used to effect any such action is valid unless the use of data messages has been terminated and replaced by the use of paper documents. A paper document issued in these circumstances shall contain a statement of such termination. The replacement of data messages by paper documents shall not affect the rights or obligations of the parties involved.
(6) If a rule of law is compulsorily applicable to a contract of carriage of goods which is in, or is evidenced by, a paper document, that rule shall not be inapplicable to such a contract of carriage of goods which is evidenced by one or more data messages by reason of the fact that the contract is evidenced by such data message or messages instead of by a paper document.

APPENDIX 7

Incoterms 1990*

EX WORKS (**. . . named place**)

Ex works means that the seller fulfils his obligation to deliver when the has made the goods available at his premises (i.e. works, factory, warehouse, etc.) to the buyer. In particular, he is not responsible for loading the goods on the vehicle provided by the buyer or for clearing the goods for export, unless otherwise agreed. The buyer bears all costs and risks involved in taking the goods from the seller's premises to the desired destination. This term thus represents the minimum obligation for the seller. This should not be used when the buyer cannot carry out directly or indirectly the export formalities. In such circumstances, the FCA term should be used.

FCA Free Carrier (**. . . named place**)

Free Carrier means that the seller fulfils his obligation to deliver when lie has handed over the goods. cleared for export. into the charge of the carrier named by the buyer at the named place or point. If no precise point is indicated by the buyer. the seller may choose within the place or range stipulated where the carrier shall take the goods into his charge. When according to commercial practice, the seller's assistance is required in making the contract with the carrier

---

*1CC No. 460, INCOTERMS 1990, Copyright 10 1990 by ICC Publishing S.A. All rights reserved. Reprinted with the permission of the ICC Publishing Corporation. For a complete explanation of INCOTERMS see, ICC, GUIDE TO INCOTERMS 1990, Pub. No. 461 (1991).

(such is in rail or air transport) the seller may act at the buyer's risk and expense. This term may be used for any mode of transport, including multimodal transport. Carrier means any person who, in a contract of carriage, undertakes to perform or to procure the performance of carriage by rail, road, sea, air, inland waterway or by a combination of such modes. If the buyer instructs the seller to deliver the cargo to a person, e.g. a freight forwarder who is not a carrier, the seller is deemed to have fulfilled his obligation to deliver the goods when they are in the custody of that person. Transport terminal means a railway terminal, a freight station, a container terminal or yard, a multipurpose cargo terminal or any similar receiving point. Container includes any equipment used to unload cargo, e.g. all types of containers and/or flats whether ISO accepted or not, trailers, swap bodies, ro-ro equipment, igloos, and applies to all modes of transport.

FAS Free Alongside Ship (. . . named port of shipment)

Free Alongside Ship means that the seller fulfils his obligation to deliver when the goods have been placed alongside the vessel on the quay or in lighters at the named port of shipment. This means that the buyer has to bear all costs and risks of loss of or damage to the goods from that moment. The FAS term requires the buyer to clear the goods for export. It should not be used when the buyer cannot carry out directly or indirectly the export formalities. This term can only be used for sea or inland waterway transport.

FOB Free on Board (. . . named port of shipment)

Free on Board means that the seller fulfils his obligation to deliver when the goods have passed over the ship's rail at the named port of shipment. This means that the buyer has to bear all costs and risks of loss of or damage to the goods from that point. The FOB term requires the seller to clear the goods for export. This term can only be used for sea or inland waterway transport. When the ship's rail serves no practical purpose, such as in the case of roll-on/roll-off or container traffic, the FCA term is more appropriate to use.

CFR Cost and Freight (. . . named port of destination)

Cost and Freight means that the seller must pay the costs and freight necessary to bring the goods to the named port of destination but the risk of loss of or damage to the goods, as well as any additional costs due to events occurring after the time the goods have been delivered on board the vessel, is transferred from the seller to the buyer when the goods pass the ship's rail in the port of shipment. The CFR term requires the seller to clear the goods for export. This term can only be used for sea and inland waterway transport. When the ship's rail serves no practical purpose, such as in the case of roll-on/roll-off or container traffic, the CPT term is appropriate to use.

CIF Cost, Insurance, and Freight (. . . named port of destination)

Cost, Insurance anti Freight means that the seller has the same obligations as under CFR but with the addition that he has to procure marine insurance against the buyer's risk of loss of or damage to the goods during the carriage. The seller contracts for insurance and pays the insurance premium. The buyer should note that under the CIF term the seller is only required to obtain insurance on minimum coverage. The CIF term requires the seller to clear the goods for export. This term can only be used for sea and inland waterway transport. When the ship's rail serves no practical purposes such as in the case of roll-on/roll-off or container traffic, the CIP term is more appropriate to use.

CPT Carriage Paid To (. . . named place of destination)

Carriage Paid to means that the seller pays the freight for the carriage of the goods to the named destination. The risk of loss of or damage to the goods, as well as any additional costs due to events occurring after the time the goods have been delivered to the carrier, is transferred from the seller to the buyer when the goods have been delivered into the custody of the carrier. Carrier means any person who, in a contract of carriage, undertakes to perform or to procure the performance of carriage, by rail, road, sea, air, inland waterway or by a combination of such modes. If subsequent carriers are used for the carriage to the agreed destination, the risk passes when the goods have been delivered to the first carrier. The CPT term requires the seller to clear the goods for export. This term may be used for any mode of transport including multimodal transport.

CIP Carriage and Insurance Paid To (. . . named place of destination)

Carriage and insurance paid to (. . .) means that the seller has the same obligations as under CPT but with the addition that the seller has to procure cargo insurance against the buyer's risk of loss of or damage to the goods during the carriage. The seller contracts for insurance and pays the insurance premium. The buyer should note that under the CIP term the seller is only required to obtain insurance on minimum coverage. The CIP term requires the seller to clear the goods for export. This term may be used for any mode of transport including multimodal transport.

DAF Delivered at Frontier (. . . named place)

Delivered at frontier means that the seller fulfils his obligation to deliver when the goods have been made available, cleared for export, at the named point and place at the frontier, but before the customs border of the adjoining country. The term frontier may be used for any frontier including that of the country of export. Therefore, it is of vital importance that the frontier in question be defined precisely by always naming the point and place in the term. The term is primarily intended to be used when goods are to be carried by rail or road, but it may be used for any mode of transport.

DES Delivered Ex Ship (. . . named port of destination)

Delivered Ex Ship means that the seller fulfils his obligation to deliver when the goods have been made available to the buyer on board the ship uncleared or import at the named port of destination. The seller has to bear all the costs and risks involved in bringing the goods to the named port of destination. This term can only be used for sea or inland waterway transport.

DEQ Delivered Ex Quay (Duty Paid) (. . . named port of destination)

Delivered Ex Quay (duty paid) means that the seller fulfills his obligation to deliver when he has made the goods available to the buyer on the quay (wharf) at the named port of destination, cleared for importation. The seller has to bear all risks and costs including duties, taxes and other charges of delivering the goods thereto. This term should not be used if the seller is unable directly or indirectly to obtain the import license. If the parties wish the buyer to clear the goods for importation and pay the duty the words ditty unpaid should be used instead of duty paid. If the parties wish to exclude from the seller's obligations some of the costs payable upon importation of the goods (such as value added tax (VAT)), this should be made clear by adding words to this effect: Delivered ex quay. VAT unpaid (... named port of destination). This term can only be used for sea or inland waterway transport.

DDU Delivered Duty Unpaid (. . . named place of destination)

Delivered duty unpaid means that the seller fulfils his obligation to deliver when the goods have been made available at the named place in the country of importation. The seller has to bear the costs and risks involved in bringing the goods thereto (excluding duties, taxes and other official charges payable upon importation as well as the costs and risks of carrying out-customs formalities). The buyer has to pay any additional costs and to bear any risks caused by his failure to clear the goods for import in time. If the parties wish the seller to carry out customs formalities and bear the costs and risks resulting therefrom, this has to be made clear by adding words to this effect. If the parties wish to include in the seller's obligations some of the costs payable upon importation of the goods (such as value added tax (VAT)), this should be made clear by adding words to this effect: Delivered duty unpaid. VAT paid, (.. named place of destination). This term may be used irrespective of the mode of transport.

DDP Delivered Duty Paid (. . . named place of destination)

Delivered duty paid means that the seller fulfils his obligation to deliver when the goods have been made available at the named place in the country of importation. The seller has to bear the risks and costs, including duties, taxes and other charges of delivering the goods thereto, cleared for importation. Whilst the EW term represents the minimum obligation for the seller, DDP represents the maximum obligation. This term should not be used if the seller is unable directly or indirectly to obtain the import license. If the parties wish the buyer to clear the goods for importation and to pay the duty, the term DDU should be used. If the parties wish to exclude from the seller's obligations some of the costs payable upon importation of the goods (such as value added tax (VAT)), this should be made clear by adding words to this effect: Delivered duty paid, VAT unpaid (. . . named place of destination). This term may be used irrespective of the mode of transport.

Differences Between Incoterms 1990 and 2000

The most important differences in substance between the 1990 and 2000 versions concern:

(1) the placing of the export clearance obligation under FAS on the seller (previously on the buyer),
(2) the specification of the seller's obligation to load the goods on the buyer's collecting vehicle and the buyer's obligation to receive the seller's arriving vehicle unloaded under FCA, and
(3) the placing of the import clearance obligation under DEQ on the buyer (previously on the seller).

Also, Incoterms 2000 suggest that instead of removing the notion of "crossing the ship's rail," the so-called FOB-point in FOB, CFR, and CIF, the parties are invited to choose such terms as FCA, CPT, and CIP where delivery of the goods is connected to the handing over of the goods to the carrier. For a complete explanation of Incoterms 2000 see, JAN RAMBERG, ICC GUIDE TO INCOTERMS 2000 (ICC Publication No. 620) (1999)

APPENDIX 8

Commission Regulation (EEC) No. 2349/84 of 23 July 1984 on the Application of Article 85 (3) of the Treaty to Certain Categories of Patent Licensing Agreements as Corrected by QJ 1985, L113134 [OJ 1984, No. L219115] as Amended by Commission Regulation (EEC) No. 151193 of 23 December 1992 [0J 1992, No. L21/8] (Articles 6, 7, 8 & 13 Omitted)

Whereas:

(1) Regulation No 19/65/EEC empowers the Commission to apply Article 85(3) of the Treaty by Regulation to certain categories of agreements and concerted practices falling within the scope of Article 85(1) to which only two undertakings are party and which include restrictions imposed in relation to the acquisition or use of industrial property rights, in particular patents, utility models, designs or trade marks, or to the rights arising out of contracts for assignment of, or the right to use, a method of manufacture or knowledge relating to the use or application of industrial processes.

(2) Patent licensing agreements are agreements whereby one undertaking, the holder of a patent (the licensor), permits another undertaking (the licensee) to exploit the patented invention by one or more of the means of exploitation afforded by patent law, in particular manufacture, use or putting on the market.
(3) In the light of experience acquired so far, it is possible to define a category of patent licensing agreements which are capable of falling within the scope of Article 85(l), but which can normally be regarded as satisfying the conditions laid down in Article 85(3). To the extent that patent licensing* agreements to which undertakings in only one Member State are party and which concern only one or more patents for that Member State are capable of affecting trade between Member States, it is appropriate to include' them in the exempted category.
(4) The present Regulation applies to licences issued in respect of national patents of the Member States, Community patents, or European patents granted for Member States, licences in respect of utility models or 'certified d'utilit' issued in the Member States, and licences in respect of inventions for which a patent application is made within one year. Where such patent licensing agreements contain obligations relating not only to territories within the common market but also obligations relating to non-member countries, the presence of the latter does not prevent the present Regulation from applying to the obligations relating to territories within the common market.
(5) However, where licensing agreements for non-member countries or for territories which extend beyond the frontiers of the Community have effects within the common market which may fall within the scope of Article 85(l), such agreements should be covered by the Regulation to the same extent as would agreements for territories within the common market.
(6) The Regulation should also apply to agreements concerning the assignment and acquisition of the rights referred to in point 4 above where the risk associated with exploitation remains with the assignor, patent licensing agreements in which the licensor is not the patentee but is authorised by the patentee to grant the licence (as in the case of sub-licences) and patent licensing agreements in which the parties' rights or obligations are assumed by connected undertakings.
(7) The Regulation does not apply to agreements concerning sales alone, which are governed by the provisions of Commission Regulation (EEC) No 1983/83 of 22 June 1983 concerning the application of Article 85(3) of the Treaty to categories of exclusive distribution agreements.
(8) Since the experience so far acquired is inadequate, it is not appropriate to within the scope of the Regulation patent pools, licensing agreements entered

into in connection with joint ventures, reciprocal licensing, or licensing agreements in respect of plant breeder's rights. Reciprocal agreements which do not involve any restrictions within the common market should, however, be so included.

(9) On the other hand, it is appropriate to extend the scope of the Regulation to patent licensing agreements which also contain provisions assigning, or granting the rights to use, non-patented technical knowledge, since such mixed agreements. are commonly concluded in order to allow the transfer of a complex technology containing both patented and non-patented elements. Such agreements can only be regarded as full ling the conditions of Article 85(3) for the purposes of this Regulation where the communicated technical knowledge is secret and permits a better exploitation of the licensed patents (know-how). Provisions concerning know-how are covered by the Regulation only in so far as the licensed patents are necessary for achieving the objects of the licensed technology and as long as at least one of the licensed patents remains in force.

(10) It is also appropriate to extend the scope of the Regulation to patent licensing agreements containing ancillary provisions relating to trade marks'. subject to ensuring that the trade-mark licence is not used to extend the effects of the patent licence beyond the life of the patents. For this purpose it is necessary to allow the licensee to identify himself within the 'licensed territory', i.e., the territory covering all or part of the common market where the licensor holds patents which the licensee is authorised to exploit, as the manufacturer of the 'licensed product', i.e., the product which is the subject matter of the licensed patent or which has been obtained directly from the process which is the subject matter of the licensed patent, to avoid his having to enter into a new trade-mark agreement with the licensor when the licensed patents expire in order not to lose the goodwill attaching to the licensed product.

(11) Exclusive licensing agreements, i.e., agreements in which the licensor undertakes not to exploit the 'licensed invention', i.e., the licensed patiented invention and any know-how communicated to the licensee, in the licensed territory himself and not to grant further licences there, are not in themselves incompatible with Article 85(1) where they are concerned with the introduction and protection of a new technology in the licensed territory, by reason of the scale of the research which has been undertaken and of the risk that is involved in manufacturing and marketing a product which is unfamiliar to users in the licensed territory at the time the agreement is made. This may also be the case where the agreements are concerned with the introduction and protection of a new process for manufacturing a product which is already known. In so far as

in other cases agreements of this kind may fall within the scope of Article 85(l), it is useful for the purposes of legal certainty to include them in Article 1, in order that they may also benefit from the exemption. However, the exemption of exclusive licensing agreements and certain export bans imposed on the licensor and his licensees is without prejudice to subsequent developments in the case law of the Court of justice regarding the status of such agreements under Article 85 (1).

(12) The obligations listed in Article 1 generally contribute to improving the production of goods and to promoting technical progress; they make patentees more willing to grant licences and licensees more inclined to undertake the investment required to manufacture, use and put on the market a new product or to use a new process, so that undertakings other than the patentee acquire the possibility of manufacturing their products with the aid of the latest techniques and of developing those techniques further. The result is that the number of production facilities and the quantity and quality of goods produced in the common market are increased. This is true, in particular, of obligations on the licensor and on the licensee not to exploit the licensed invention in, and in particular not to export the licensed product into, the licensed territory in the case of the licensor and the 'territories reserved for the licensor', that is to say, territories within the common market in which the licensor has patent protection and has not granted any licences, in the case of the licensee. This is also true both of the obligation of the licensee not to conduct an active policy of putting the product on the market (i.e., a prohibition of active competition as defined in Article I MOD in the territories of other licensees for a period which may equal the duration of the licence and also the obligation of the licensee not to put the licensed product on the market in the territories of other licensees for a limited period of a few years (i.e., a prohibition not only of active competition but also of 'passive competition' whereby the licensee of a territory simply responds to requests which he has not solicited from users or resellers established in the territories of other licensees - Article 1 (1) (6)). However, such obligations may be permitted under the Regulation only in respect of territories in which the licensed product is protected by 'parallel patents', that is to say, patents covering the same invention, within the meaning of the case law of the Court of Justice, and as long as the patents remain in force.

(13) Consumers will as a rule be allowed a fair share of the benefit resulting from this improvement in the supply of goods on the market. To safeguard this effect, however, it is right to exclude from the application of Article I cases where the parties agree to refuse to meet demand from users or resellers within their respective territories who would resell for export, or to take other steps to

impede parallel imports, or where the licensee is obliged to refuse to meet unsolicited demand from the territory of other licensees (passive sales). The same applies where such action is the result of a concerted practice between the licensor and the licensee.

(14) The obligations referred to above thus do not impose restrictions which are not indispensable to the attainment of the abovementioned objectives.

(15) Competition at the distribution stage is safeguarded by the possibility of parallel imports and passive sales. The exclusivity obligations covered by the Regulation thus do not normally entail the possibility of eliminating competition in respect of a substantial part of the products in question. This is so even in the case of agreements which grant exclusive licences for a territory covering the whole of the common market.

(16) To the extent that in their agreements the parties undertake obligations of the type referred to in Articles 1 and 2 but which are of more limited scope and thus less restrictive of competition than is permitted by those Articles, it is appropriate that these obligations should also benefit under the exemptions provided for in the Regulation.

(17) If in a particular case an agreement covered by this Regulation is found to have effects which are incompatible with the provisions of Article 85(3) of the Treaty, the Commission may withdraw the benefit of the block exemption from the undertakings concerned, in accordance with Article 7 of Regulation No 19/65/EEC.

(18) It is not necessary expressly to exclude from the category defined in the Regulation agreements which do not fulfil the conditions of Article 85(1). Nevertheless it is advisable, in the interests of legal certainty for the undertakings concerned, to list in Article 2 a number of obligations which are not normally restrictive of competition, so that these also may benefit from the exemption in the event that, because of particular economic or legal circumstances, they should exceptionally fall within the scope of Article 85(1). The list of such obligations given in Article 2 is not exhaustive.

(19) The Regulation must also specify what restrictions or provisions may not be included in patent licensing agreements if these are to benefit from the block exemption. The restrictions listed in Article 3 may fall under the prohibition of Article 85(1); in these cases there can be no general presumption that they will lead to the positive effects required by Article 85(3), as would be necessary for the granting of a block exemption.

(20) Such restrictions include those which deny the licensee the right enjoyed by any third party to challenge the validity of the patent or which automatically prolong the agreement by the life of any new patent granted during the life of

the licensed patents which are in existence at the time the agreement is entered into. Nevertheless, the parties are free to extend their contractual relationship by entering into new agreements concerning such new patents, or to agree the payment of royalties for as long as the licensee continues to use know-how communicated by the licensor which has not entered into the public domain, regardless of the duration of the original patents and of any new patents that are licensed.

(21) They also include restrictions on the freedom of one party to compete with the other and in particular to involve himself in techniques other than those licensed, since such restrictions impede technical and economic progress. The prohibition of such restrictions should however be reconciled with the legitimate interest of the licensor in having his patented invention exploited to the full and to this end to require the licensee to use his best endeavours to manufacture and market the licensed product.

(22) Such restrictions include, further, an obligation on the licensee to continue to pay royalties after all the licensed patents ceased to be in force and the communicated know-how has entered into the public domain, since such an obligation would place the licensee at a disadvantage by comparison with his competitors, unless it is established that this obligation results from arrangements for spreading payments in respect of previous use of the licensed invention.

(23) They also include restrictions imposed on the parties regarding prices, customers or marketing of the licensed products or regarding the quantities to be manufactured or sold, especially since restrictions of the latter type may have the same effect as export bans.

(24) Finally, they include ' restrictions to which the licensee submits at the time the agreement is made because he wishes to obtain the licence, but which give the licensor an unjustified competitive advantage, such as an obligation to assign to the licensor any improvements the licensee may make to the invention, or to accept other licences or goods and services that the licensee does not want from the licensor.

(25) It is appropriate to offer to parties to patent licensing agreements containing obligations which do not come within the terms of Articles 1 and 2 and yet do not entail any of the effects restrictive of competition referred to in Article 3 a simplified means of benefiting, upon notification, from the legal certainty provided by the block exemption (Article 4). This procedure should at the same time allow the Commission to ensure effective supervision as well as simplifying the administrative control of agreements.

(26) The Regulation should apply with retroactive effect to patent licensing agreements in existence when the Regulation comes into force where such agreements already fulfil the conditions for application of the Regulation or are modified to do so (Articles 6 to 8). Under Article 4(3) of Regulation No 19/65/EEC, the benefit of these provisions may not be claimed in actions pending at the date of entry into force of this Regulation, nor may it be relied on as grounds for claims for damages against third parties.
(27) Agreements which come within the terms of Articles 1 and 2 and which have neither the object nor the effect of restricting competition in any other way need no longer be notified. Nevertheless, undertakings will still have the right to apply in individual cases for negative clearance under Article 2 of Council Regulation No 17 or for exemption under Article 85 (3),

Has adopted this regulation:

Article 1

(1) Pursuant to Article 85(3) of the Treaty and subject to the provisions of this Regulation, it is hereby declared that Article 85(l) of the Treaty shall not apply to patent licensing agreements, and agreements combining the licensing of patents and the communication of know-how, to which only two undertakings are party and which include one or more of the following obligations:

(a) an obligation on the licensor not to license other undertakings to exploit the licensed invention in the licensed territory, covering all or part of the common market, in so far and as long as one of the licensed patents remains in force;

(b) an obligation on the licensor not to exploit the licensed invention in the licensed territory himself in so far and as long as one of the licensed patents remains in force;

(c) an obligation on the licensee not to exploit the licensed invention in territories within the common market which are reserved for the licensor, in so far and as long as the patented product is protected in those territories by parallel patents;

(d) an obligation on the licensee not to manufacture or use the licensed product, or use the patented process or the communicated know-how, in territories within the common market which are licensed to other licensees, in so far and as long as the licensed product is protected in those territories by parallel patents;

(e) an obligation on the licensee not to pursue an active policy of putting the licensed product on the ‘market in the territories within the common market which are licensed to other licensees, and in particular not to engage in advertising specifically aimed at those territories or to establish any branch or maintain any distribution depot there, in so far and as long as the licensed product is protected in those territories by parallel patents;

(f) an obligation on the licensee not to put the licensed product on the market in the territories licensed to other licensees within the common market for a period not exceeding five years from the date when the product is first put on the market within the common market by the licensor or one of his licensees, in so far as and for as long as the product is protected in these territories by parallel patents;

(g) an obligation on the licensee to use only the licensor’s trade mark or the get-up determined by the licensor to distinguish the licensed product, provided that the licensee is not prevented from identifying himself as the manufacturer of the licensed product.

(2) The exemption of restrictions on putting the licensed product on the market resulting from the obligations referred to in paragraph 1 (2), (3), (5) and (6) shall apply only if the licensee manufactures the licensed product himself or has it manufactured by a connected undertaking or by a subcontractor.

(3) The exemption provided for in paragraph 1 shall also apply where in a particular agreement the parties undertake obligations of the types referred to in that paragraph but with a more limited scope than is permitted by the paragraph.

Article 2

(1) Article 1 shall apply notwithstanding the presence in particular of any of the following obligations, which are generally not restrictive of competition:

(a) an obligation on the licensee to procure goods or services from the licensor or from an undertaking designated by the licensor, in so far as such products or services are necessary for a technically satisfactory exploitation of the licensed invention;

(b) an obligation on the licensee to pay a minimum royalty or to produce a minimum quantity of licensed product or to carry out a minimum number of operations exploiting the licensed invention;

(c) an obligation on the licensee to restrict his exploitation of the licensed invention to one or more technical fields of application covered by the licensed patent;

(d) an obligation on the licensee not to exploit the patent after termination of the agreement in so far as the patent is still in force;

(e) an obligation on the licensee not to grant sub-licences or assign the licence;

(f) an obligation on the licensee to mark the licensed product with an indication of the patentee's name, the licensed patent or the patent licensing agreement;

(g) an obligation on the licensee not to divulge know-how communicated by the licensor; the licensee may be held to this obligation even after the agreement has expired;

(h) obligations:

(i) to inform the licensor of infringements of the patent,

(ii) to take legal action against an infringer,

(iii) to assist the licensor in any legal action against an infringer, provided that these obligations are without prejudice to the licensee's right to challenge the validity of the licensed patent;

(i) an obligation on the licensee to observe specifications concerning the minimum quality of the licensed product, provided that such specifications are necessary for a technically satisfactory exploitation of the licensed invention, and to allow the licensor to carry out related checks;

(j) an obligation on the parties to communicate to one another any experience gained in exploiting the licensed invention and to grant one another a licence. in respect of inventions relating to improvements and new applications, provided that such communication or licence is non-exclusive;

(k) an obligation on the licensor to grant the licensee any more favourable terms that the licensor may grant to another undertaking after the agreement is entered into.

(2) In the event that, because of particular circumstances, the obligations referred to in paragraph I fall within the scope of Article 85(l), they shall also be exempted even if they are not accompanied by any of the obligations exempted by Article 1. The exemption provided for in this paragraph shall also apply where in an agreement the parties undertake obligations of the types referred to in paragraph 1 but with a more limited scope than is permitted by that paragraph.

Article 3

Articles 1 and 2(2) shall not apply where:

(1) the licensee is prohibited from challenging the validity of licensed patents or other industrial or commercial property rights within the common market be-

longing to the licensor or undertakings connected with him, without prejudice to the right of the licensor to terminate the licensing agreement in the event of such a challenge;
(2) the duration of the licensing agreement is automatically prolonged beyond the expiry of the licensed patents existing at the time the agreement was entered into by the inclusion in it of any new patent obtained by the licensor, unless the agreement provides each party with the right to terminate the agreement at least annually after the expiry of the licensed patents existing at the time the agreement was entered into, without prejudice to the right of the licensor to charge royalties for the full period during which the licensee continues to use know-how communicated by the licensor which has not entered into the public domain, even if that period exceeds the life of the patents;
(3) one party is restricted from competing with the other party, with undertakings connected with the other party or with other undertakings within the common market in respect of research and development, manufacture, use or sales, save as provided in Article 1 and without prejudice to an obligation on the licensee to use his best endeavours to exploit the licensed invention;
(4) the licensee is charged royalties on products which are not entirely or partially patented or manufactured by means of a patented process, or for the use of know-how which has entered into the public domain otherwise than by the fault of the licensee or it, undertaking connected with him, without prejudice to arrangements whereby, in order to facilitate payment, the royalty payments for the use of a licensed invention are spread over a period extending beyond the life of the licensed patents or the entry of the know-how into the public domain;
(5) the quantity of licensed products one party may manufacture or sell or the number of operations exploiting the licensed invention he may carry out are subject to limitations;
(6) one party is restricted in the determination of prices, components of prices or discounts for the licensed products;
(7) one party is restricted as to the customers he may serve, in particular by being prohibited from supplying certain classes of user, employing certain forms of distribution or, with the aim of sharing customers, using certain types of packaging for the products, save as provided in Article 1 (1) (7) and Article 2 (1) (3);
(8) the licensee is obliged to assign wholly or in part to the licensor rights in or to patents for improvements or for new applications of the licensed patents;

(9) the licensee is induced at the time the agreement is entered into to accept further which he does not want or to agree to use patents, goods or services which he does not want, unless such patents, products or services are necessary for a technically satisfactory exploitation of the licensed invention;
(10) without prejudice to Article 1(l)(5), the licensee is required, for a period exceeding that permitted under Article 1 (1) (6), not to put the licensed product on the market in territories licensed to other licensees within the common market or does not do so as a result of a concerted practice between the parties;
(11) one or both of the parties are required:

(a) to refuse without any objectively justified reason to meet demand from users or resellers in their respective territories who would market products in other territories within the common market;

(c) to make it difficult for users or resellers to obtain the products from other resellers within the common market, and in particular to exercise industrial or commercial property rights or take measures so. as to prevent users or resellers from obtaining outside, or from putting on the market in, the licensed territory products which have been lawfully put on the market within the common market by the patentee or with his consent; or do so as result of a concerted practice between them.

Article 4

(1) The exemption provided for in Articles 1 and 2 shall also apply to agreements containing obligations restrictive of competition which are not covered by those Articles and do not fall within the scope of Article 3, on condition that the agreements in question are notified to the Commission in accordance with the provisions of Commission Regulation No 27, as last amended by Regulation (EEC) No 1699/75, and that the Commission does not oppose such exemption within a period of six months.
(2) The period of six months shall run from the date on which the notification is received by the Commission. Where, however, the notification is made by registered post, the period shall run from the date shown on the postmark of the place of posting.
(3) Paragraph 1 shall apply only if:

(a) express reference is made to this Article in the notification or in a communication accompanying it; and

(b) the information furnished with the notification is complete and in accordance with the facts.

(4) The benefit of paragraph 1 may be claimed for agreements notified before the entry into force of this Regulation by submitting a communication to the Commission referring expressly to this Article and to the notification. Paragraphs 2 and 3(b) shall apply *mutatis mutandis.*

(5) The Commission may oppose the exemption. it shall oppose exemption if it receives a request to do so from a Member State within three months of the transmission to the Member State of the notification referred to in paragraph 1 or of the communication referred to in paragraph 4. This request must be justified on the basis of considerations relating to the competition rules of the Treaty.

(6) The Commission may withdraw the opposition to the exemption at any time. However, where the opposition was raised at the request of a Member State and this request is maintained, it may be withdrawn only after consultation of the Advisory Committee on Restrictive Practices and Dominant Positions.

(7) If the opposition is withdrawn because the undertakings concerned have shown that the conditions of Article 85 (3) are fulfilled, the exemption shall apply from the date of notification.

(8) If the opposition is withdrawn because the undertakings concerned have amended the agreement so that the conditions of Article 85(3) are fulfilled, the exemption shall apply from the date on which the amendments take effect.

(9) If the Commission opposes exemption and the opposition is not withdrawn, the effects of the notification shall be governed by the provisions of Regulation No 17.

Article 5

(1) This Regulation shall not apply:

(a) to agreements between members of a patent pool which relate to the pooled patents;

(b) to patent licensing agreements between competitors who hold interests in a joint venture or between one of them and the joint venture, if the licensing agreements relate to the activities of the joint venture;

(c) to agreements under which one party grants to the other party a patent licence and that other party, albeit in separate agreements or through connected undertakings, grants to the first party a licence under patents or trade-marks or reciprocal sales rights for unprotected products or communicates to him know-how, where the parties are competitors in relation to the products covered by those agreements;

(d) to licensing agreements in respect of plant breeder's rights.

(2) This Regulation shall nevertheless apply:

(a) to agreements to which paragraph 1(2) applies, under which a parent undertaking grants the joint venture a patent licence, provided that the contract products and the other products of the participating undertakings which are considered by users to be equivalent in view of their characteristics, price and intended use represent:

— in case of a licence limited to production not more than 20%,

— in case of a licence covering production and distribution not more than 10% of the market for all such products in the common market or a substantial part thereof;

(b) to reciprocal licences within the meaning of point 3 of paragraph 1, provided that the parties are not subject to any territorial restriction within the common market with regard to the manufacture, use or putting on the market of the contract products or on the use of the licensed processes.

(3) This Regulation shall continue to apply where the market shares referred to in point (a) of paragraph 2 are exceeded during any period of two consecutive financial years by not more than one-tenth.

Where this latter limit is also exceeded, this Regulation shall continue to apply for a period of six months following the end of the financial year during which it was exceeded.

Article 9

The Commission may withdraw the benefit of this Regulation, pursuant to Article 7 of Regulation No 19/65/EEC, where it finds in a particular case that an agreement by this Regulation nevertheless has certain effects which are incompatible with the conditions laid down in Article 85 (3) of the Treaty, and in particular where:

(1) such effects arise from an arbitration award;

(2) the licensed products or the services provided using a licensed process are not exposed to effective competition in the licensed territory from identical

products or services or products or services considered by users as equivalent in view of their price and intended use;
(3) the licensor does not have the right to terminate the exclusivity granted to the licensee at the latest five years from the date the agreement was entered into and at least annually thereafter if, without legitimate reason, the licensee fails to exploit the patent or to do so adequately;
(4) without prejudice to Article l(l)(6), the licensee refuses, without objectively valid reason, to meet unsolicited demand from users or resellers in the territory of other licensees;
(5) one or both of the parties:

(a) without any objectively justified reason, refuse to meet demand from users or resellers in their respective territories who would market the products in other territories within the common market; or
(b) make it difficult for users or resellers to obtain the products from other resellers within the common market, and in particular where they exercise industrial or commercial property rights or take measures so as to prevent resellers or users from obtaining outside, or from putting on the market in, the licensed territory products which have been lawfully put on the market within the common market by the patentee or with his consent.

Article 10

(1) This Regulation shall apply to:

(a) patent applications;
(b) utility models;
(c) applications for registration of utility models;
(d) 'certificats d'utilité' and 'certificats d'addition' under French law; and
(e) applications for 'certificats d'utilité' and 'certificats d'addition' under French law;
equally as it applies to patents.

(2) This Regulation shall also apply to agreements relating to the exploitation of an invention if an application within the meaning of paragraph 1 is made in respect of the invention for the licensed territory within one year from the date when the agreement was entered into.

Article 11

This Regulation shall also apply to:
(1) patent licensing agreements where the licensor is not the patentee but is authorised by the patentee to grant a licence or a sub-licence;
(2) assignments of a patent or of a right to a patent where the sum payable in consideration of the assignment is dependent upon the turnover attained by the assignee in respect of the patented products, the quantity of such products manufactured or the number of operations carried out employing the patented invention;
(3) patent licensing agreements in which rights or obligations of the licensor or the licensee are assumed by undertakings connected with them.

Article 12

(1) 'Connected undertakings' for the purposes of this Regulation means:

(a) undertakings in which a party to the agreement directly or indirectly:
— owns more than half the capital or business assets, or has the power to exercise more than half the voting rights, or
— has the power to appoint more than half the members of the supervisory board, board of directors or bodies legally representing the undertaking, or
— has the right to manage the affairs of the undertaking;

(b) undertakings which directly or indirectly have in or over a party to the agreement the rights or powers listed in (a);

(c) undertakings in which an undertaking referred to in (b) directly or indirectly has the rights or powers listed in (a).

(2) Undertakings in which the parties to the agreement or undertakings connected with them jointly have directly or indirectly the rights or powers set out in paragraph 1 (a) shall be considered to be connected with each of the parties to the agreement.

APPENDIX 9

Commission Regulation (EEC) No. 4087/88 of 30 November 1988 on the Application of Article 85(3) of the Treaty to Categories of Franchise Agreements [OJ 1988, No. L359/46]

Whereas:

(1) Regulation No. 19/65/EEC empowers the Commission to apply Article 85(3) of the Treaty by Regulation to certain categories of bilateral exclusive agreements falling within the scope of Article 85(l) which either have as their object the exclusive distribution or exclusive purchase of goods, or include restrictions imposed in relation to the assignment or use of industrial property rights.

(2) Franchise agreements consist essentially of licences of industrial or intellectual property rights relating to trade marks or signs and know-how, which can be combined with restrictions relating to supply or purchase of goods.

(3) Several types of franchise can be distinguished according to their object: industrial franchise concerns the manufacturing of goods, distribution franchise concerns the sale of goods, and service franchise concerns the supply of services.

(4) It is possible on the basis of the experience of the Commission to define categories of franchise agreements which fall under Article 85(l) but can normally be regarded as satisfying the conditions laid down in Article 85(3). This is the case for franchise agreements whereby one of the parties supplies goods or provides services to end users. On the other hand, industrial franchise agreements

should not be covered by this Regulation. Such agreements, which usually govern relationships between producers, present different characteristics than the other types of franchise. They consist of manufacturing licences based on patents and/or technical know-how, combined with trade-mark licences. Some of them may benefit from other block exemptions if they fulfil the necessary conditions.

(5) This Regulation covers franchise agreements between two undertakings, the franchisor and the franchisee, for the retailing of goods or the provision of services to end users, or a combination of these activities, such as the processing or adaptation of goods to fit specific needs of their customers. It also covers cases where the relationship between franchisor and franchisees if made through a third undertaking, the master franchisee. It does not cover wholesale franchise agreements because of the lack of experience of the Commission in that field.

(6) Franchise agreements as defined in this Regulation can fall under Article 85(1). They may in particular affect intra-Community trade where they are concluded between undertakings from different Member States or where they form the basis of a network which extends beyond the boundaries of a single Member State.

(7) Franchise agreements as defined in this Regulation normally improve the distribution of goods and/or the provision of services as they give franchisors the possibility of establishing a uniform network with limited investments, which may assist the entry of new competitors on the market, particularly in the case of small and medium-sized undertakings, thus increasing interbrand competition. They also allow independent traders to set up outlets more rapidly and with higher chance of success than if they had to do so without the franchisor's experience and assistance. They have therefore the possibility of competing more efficiently with large distribution undertakings.

(8) As a rule, franchise agreements also allow consumers and other end users a fair share of the resulting benefit, as they combine the advantage of a uniform network with the existence of traders personally interested in the efficient operation of their business. The homogeneity of the network and the constant cooperation between the franchisor and the franchisees ensures a constant quality of the products and services. The favourable effect of franchising on interbrand competition and the fact that consumers are free to deal with any franchisee in the network guarantees that a reasonable part of the resulting benefits will be passed on to the consumers.

(9) This Regulation must define the obligations restrictive of competition which may be included in franchise agreements. This is the case in particular for

the granting of an exclusive territory to the franchisees combined with the prohibition on actively seeking customers outside that territory, which allows them to concentrate their efforts on their allotted territory. The same applies to the granting of an exclusive territory to a master franchisee combined with the obligation not to conclude franchise agreements with third parties outside that territory. Where the franchisees sell or use in the process of providing services, goods manufactured by the franchisor or according to its instructions and or bearing its trade mark, an obligation on the franchisees not to sell, or use in the process of the provision of services, competing goods, makes it possible to establish a coherent network which is identified with the franchised goods. However, this obligation should only be accepted with respect to the goods which form the essential subject-matter of the franchise. It should notably not relate to accessories or spare parts for these goods.

(10) The obligations referred to above thus do not impose restrictions which are not necessary for the attainment of the abovementioned objectives. In particular, the limited territorial protection granted to the franchisees is indispensable to protect their investment.

(11) It is desirable to list in the Regulation a number of obligations that are commonly found in franchise agreements and are normally not restrictive of competition and to provide that if, because of the particular economic or legal circumstances, they fall under Article 85 (1), they are also covered by the exemption. This list, which is not exhaustive, includes in particular clauses which are essential either to preserve the common identity and reputation of the network or to prevent the know-how made available and the assistance given by the franchisor from benefiting competitors.

(12) The Regulation must specify the conditions which must be satisfied for the exemption to apply. To guarantee that competition is not eliminated for a substantial part of the goods which are the subject of the franchise, it is necessary that parallel imports remain possible. Therefore, cross deliveries between franchisees should always be possible. Furthermore, where a franchise network is combined with another distribution system, franchisees should be free to obtain supplies from authorised distributors. To better inform consumers, thereby helping to ensure that they receive a fair share of the resulting benefits, it must be provided that the franchisee shall be obliged to indicate its status as an independent undertaking, by any appropriate means which does not jeopardise the common identity of the franchised network. Furthermore, where the franchisees have to honour guarantees for the franchisor's goods, this obligation should also apply to goods supplied by the franchisor, other franchisees or other agreed dealers.

(13) The Regulation must also specify restrictions which may not be included in franchise agreements if these are to benefit from the exemption granted by the Regulation, by virtue of the fact that such provisions are restrictions falling under Article 85 (1) for which there is no general presumption that they will lead to the positive effects required by Article 85(3). This applies in particular to market sharing between competing manufacturers, to clauses unduly limiting the franchisee's choice of suppliers or customers, and to cases where the franchisee is restricted in determining its prices. However, the franchisor should be free to recommend prices to the franchisees, where it is not prohibited by national laws and to the extent that it does not lead to concerted practices for the effective application of these prices.

(14) Agreements which are not automatically covered by the exemption because they contain provisions that are not expressly exempted by the Regulation and not expressly excluded from exemption may nonetheless generally be presumed to be eligible for application of Article 85 (3). It will be possible for the Commission rapidly to establish whether this is the case for a particular agreement. Such agreements should therefore be deemed to be covered by the exemption provided for in this Regulation where they are notified to the Commission and the Commission does not oppose the application of the exemption within a specified period of time.

(15) If individual agreements exempted by this Regulation nevertheless have effects which are incompatible with Article 85(3), in particular as interpreted by the administrative practice of the Commission and the case law of the Court of justice, the Commission may withdraw the benefit of the block exemption. This applies in particular where competition is significantly restricted because of the structure of the relevant market.

(16) Agreements which are automatically exempted pursuant to this Regulation need not be notified. Undertakings may nevertheless in a particular case request a decision pursuant to Council Regulation No. 17 as last amended by the Act of Accession of Spain and Portugal.

(17) Agreements may benefit from the provisions either of this Regulation or of another Regulation, according to their particular nature and provided that they fulfil the necessary conditions of application. They may not benefit from a combination of the provisions of this Regulation with those of another block exemption Regulation,

Has adopted this regulation:

Article 1

(1) Pursuant to Article 85(3) of the Treaty and subject to the provisions of this Regulation, it is hereby declared that Article 85(l) of the Treaty shall not apply to franchise agreements to which two undertakings are party, which include one or more of the restrictions listed in Article 2.
(2) The exemption provided for in paragraph I shall also apply to master franchise agreements to which two undertakings are party. Where applicable, the provisions of this Regulation concerning the relationship between franchisor and franchisee shall apply *mutatis mutandis* to the relationship between franchisor and master franchisee and between master franchisee and franchisee.
(3) For the purposes of this Regulation:

(a) 'franchise' means a package of industrial or intellectual property rights relating to trade marks, trade names, shop signs, utility models, designs, copyrights, know-how or patents, to be exploited for the resale of goods or the provision of services to end users;

(b) 'franchise agreement' means an agreement whereby one undertaking, the franchisor, grants the other, the franchisee, in exchange for direct or indirect financial consideration, the right to exploit a franchise for the purposes of marketing specified types of goods and/or services; it includes at least obligations relating to:

— the use of a common name or shop sign and a uniform presentation of contract premises and/or means of transport,

— the communication by the franchisor to the franchisee of know-how,

— the continuing provision by the franchisor to the franchisee or commercial or technical assistance during the life of the agreement;

(c) 'master franchise agreement' means an agreement whereby one undertaking, the franchisor, grants the other, the master franchisee, in exchange of direct or indirect financial consideration, the right to exploit a franchise for the purposes of concluding franchise agreements with third parties, the franchisees;

(d) 'franchisor's goods' means goods produced by the franchisor or according to its instructions, and/or bearing the franchisor's name or trade mark;

(e) 'contract premises' means the premises used for the exploitation of the franchise or, when the franchise is exploited outside those premises,

the base from which the franchisee operates the means of transport used for the exploitation of the franchise (contract means of transport);
(f) 'know-how' means a package of non-patented practical information, resulting from experience and testing by the franchisor, which is secret, substantial and identified;
(g) 'secret' means that the know-how, as a body or in the precise configuration and assembly of its components, is not generally known or easily accessible; it is not limited in the narrow sense that each individual component of the know-how should be totally unknown or unobtainable outside the franchior's business;
(h) 'substantial' means that the know-how includes information which is of importance for the sale of goods or the provision of services to end users, and in particular for the presentation of goods for sale, the processing of goods in connection with the provision of services, methods of dealing with customers, and administration and financial management; the know-how must be useful for the franchisee by being capable, at the date of. conclusion of the agreement, of improving the competitive position of the franchisee, in particular by improving the franchisee's performance or helping it to enter a new market;
(i) 'identified' means that the know-how must be described in a sufficiently comprehensive manner so as to make it possible to verify that it fulfils the criteria of secrecy and substantiality; the description of the know-how can either be set out in the franchise agreement or in a separate document or recorded in any other appropriate form.

Article 2

The exemption provided for in Article I shall apply to the following restrictions of competition:

(a) an obligation on the franchisor, in a defined area of the common market, the contract territory, not to:

— grant the right to exploit all or part of the franchise to third parties,

— itself exploit the franchise, or itself market the goods or services which are the subject-matter of the franchise under a similar formula.

— itself supply the franchisor's goods to third parties;

(b) an obligation on the master franchisee not to conclude franchise agreement with third parties outside its contract territory;

(c) an obligation on the franchisee to exploit the franchise only from the contract premises;

(d) an obligation on the franchisee to refrain, outside the contract territory, from seeking customers for the goods or the services which are the subject-matter of the franchise;

(e) an obligation on the franchisee not to manufacture, sell or use in the course A the provision of services, goods competing with the franchisor's goods which are the subject-matter of the franchise; where the subject-matter of the franchise is the sale or use in the course of the provision of services both certain types of goods and spare parts or accessories therefor, that obligation may not be imposed in respect of these spare parts or accessories.

Article 3

(1) Article 1 shall apply notwithstanding the presence of any of the following obligations on the franchisee, in so far as they are necessary to protect the franchisor's industrial or intellectual property rights or to maintain the common identity and reputation of the franchised network:

(a) to sell, or use in the course of the provision of services, exclusively goods matching minimum objective quality specifications laid down by the franchisor;

(b) to sell, or use in the course of the provision of services, goods which are manufactured only by the franchisor or by third parties designed by it, where it is impracticable, owing to the nature of the goods which are the subject-matter of the franchise, to apply objective quality specifications;

(c) not to engage, directly or indirectly, in any similar business in a territory where it would compete with a member of the franchised network, including the franchisor; the franchisee may be held to this obligation after termination of the agreement, for a reasonable period which may not exceed one-year, in the territory where it has exploited the franchise;

(d) not to acquire financial interests in the capital of a competing undertaking, which would give the franchisee the power to influence the economic conduct of such undertaking;

(e) to sell the goods which are the subject-matter of the franchise only to end users, to other franchisees and to resellers within other channels of distribution supplied by the manufacturer of these goods or with its consent;

(f) to use its best endeavours to sell the goods or provide the services that are the subject-matter of the franchise; to offer for sale a minimum range of goods, achieve a minimum turnover, plan its orders in advance, keep minimum stocks and provide customer and warranty services;

(g) to pay to the franchisor a specified proportion of its revenue for advertising and itself carry out advertising for the nature of which it shall obtain the franchisor's approval.

(2) Article 1 shall apply notwithstanding the presence of any of the following obligations on the franchisee:

(a) not to disclose to third parties the know-how provided by the franchisor; the franchisee may be held to this obligation after termination of the agreement;

(b) to communicate to the franchisor any experience gained in exploiting the franchise and to grant it, and other franchisees, a non-exclusive licence for the know-how resulting from the experience;

(c) to inform the franchisor of infringements of licensed industrial or intellectual property rights, to take legal action against infringers or to assist the franchisor in any legal actions against infringers;

(d) not to use know-how licensed by the franchisor for purposes other than the exploitation of the franchise; the franchisee may be held to this obligation after termination of the agreement;

(e) to attend or have its staff attend training courses arranged by the franchisor;

(f) to apply the commercial methods devised by the franchisor, including any subsequent modification thereof, and use the licensed industrial or intellectual property rights;

(g) to comply with the franchisor's standards for the equipment and presentation of the contract premises and/or means of transport;

(h) to allow the franchisor to carry out checks of the contract premises and/or means of transport, including the goods sold and the services provided, and the inventory and accounts of the franchisee;

(i) not without the franchisor's consent to change the location of the contract premises;

(j) not without the franchisor's consent to assign the rights and obligations under the franchise agreement.

(3) In the event that, because of particular circumstances, obligations referred to in paragraph 2 fall within the scope of Article 85(1), they shall also be exempted even if they are not accompanied by any of the obligations exempted by Article 1.

Article 4

The exemption provided for in Article 1 shall apply on condition that:
(a) the franchisee is free to obtain the goods that are the subject-matter of the franchise from other franchisees; where such goods are also distributed through another network of authorised distributors, the franchisee must be free to obtain the goods from the latter;
(b) where the franchisor obliges the franchisee to honour guarantees for the goods, that obligation shall apply in respect of such goods supplied by any member of the franchised network or other distributors which give a similar guarantee, in the common market;
(c) the franchisee is obliged to indicate its status as an independent undertaking; this indication shall however not interfere with the common identity of the franchised resulting in particular from the common name or shop sign and uniform appearance of the contract premises and/or means of transport.

Article 5

The exemption granted by Article 1 shall not apply where:
(a) undertakings producing goods or providing services which are identical or are considered by users as equivalent in view of their characteristics, price and intended use, enter into franchise agreements in respect of such goods or services;
(b) without prejudice to Article 2(e) and Article 3(l)(b), the franchisee is prevented from obtaining supplies of goods of a quality equivalent to those offered by the franchisor;
(c) without prejudice to Article 2 (e), the franchisee is obliged to sell, or use in the process of providing services, goods manufactured by the franchisor or third parties designated by the franchisor and the franchisor refuses, for reasons other than protecting the franchisor's industrial or intellectual property rights, or maintaining the common identity and reputation of the franchised network, to designate as authorised third parties proposed by the franchisee;
(d) the franchisee is prevented from continuing to use the licensed know-how after termination of the agreement where the know-how has become generally known or easily accessible, other than by breach of an obligation by the franchisee;
(e) the franchisee is restricted by the franchisor, directly or indirectly, in the determination of sale prices for the goods or services which are the subject-

matter of the franchise, without prejudice to the possibility for the franchisor of recommending sale prices;
(f) the franchisor prohibits the franchisee from challenging the validity of the industrial or intellectual property rights which form part of the franchise, without prejudice to the possibility for the franchisor of terminating the agreement in such a case;
(g) franchisees are obliged not to supply within the common market the goods or services are the subject-matter of the franchise to end users because of their place of residence.

Article 6

(1) The exemption provided for in Article 1 shall also apply to franchise agreements which fulfill the conditions laid down in Article 4 and include obligations restrictive of competition which are not covered by Articles 2 and 3(3) and do not fall within the scope of Article 5, on condition that the agreements in question are notified to the Commission in accordance with the provisions of Commission Regulation No. 27 and that the Commission does not oppose such exemption within a period of six months.
(2) The period of six months shall run from the date on which the notification is received by the Commission. Where, however, the notification is made by registered post, the period shall run from the date shown on the postmark of the place of posting.
(3) Paragraph 1 shall apply only if:

(a) express reference is made to this Article in the notification or in a communication accompanying it; and

(b) the information furnished with the notification is complete and in accordance with the facts.

(4) The benefit of paragraph 1 can be claimed for agreements notified before the entry into force of this Regulation by submitting a communication to the Commission referring expressly to this Article and to the notification. Paragraphs 2 and 3(b) shall apply *mutatis mutandis.*
(5) The Commission may oppose exemption. It shall oppose exemption if it receives a request to do so from a Member State within three months of the forwarding to the Member State of the notification referred to in paragraph 1 or the communication referred to in paragraph 4. This request must be justified on the basis of considerations relating to the competition rules of the Treaty.

(6) The Commission may withdraw its opposition to the exemption at any time. However, where that opposition was raised at the request of a Member State, it may be withdrawn only after consultation of the advisory Committee on Restrictive Practices and Dominant Positions.
(7) If the opposition is withdrawn because the undertakings concerned have shown that the conditions of Article 85 (3) are fulfilled, the exemption shall apply from the date of the notification.
(8) If the opposition is withdrawn because the undertakings concerned have amended the agreement so that the conditions of Article 85 (3) are fulfilled, the exemption shall apply from the date on which the amendments take effect.
(9) If the Commission opposes exemption and its opposition is not withdrawn, the effects of the notification shall be governed by the provisions of Regulation No. 17.

Article 7

(1) Information acquired pursuant to Article 6 shall be used only for the purposes of this Regulation.
(2) The Commission and the authorities of the Member States, their officials and other servants shall not disclose information acquired by them pursuant to this Regulation of a kind that is covered by the obligation of professional secrecy.
(3) Paragraphs 1 and 2 shall not prevent publication of general information or surveys which do not contain information relating to particular undertakings or associations of undertakings.

Article 8

The Commission may withdraw the benefit of this Regulation, pursuant to Article 7 of Regulation No. 19/65/EEC, where it finds in a particular case that an agreement exempted by this Regulation nevertheless has certain effects which are incompatible with the conditions laid down in Article 85(3) of the EEC Treaty, and in particular where territorial protection is awarded to the franchisee and:

(a) access to the relevant market or competition therein is significantly restricted by the cumulative effect of parallel networks of similar agreements established by competing manufacturers or distributors;

(b) the goods or services which are the subject-matter of the franchise do not face, in a substantial part of the common market, effective competition from goods or services which are identical or considered by users as equivalent in view of their characteristics, price and intended use;
(c) the parties, or one of them, prevent end users, because of their place of residence, from obtaining, directly or through intermediaries, the goods or services which are the subject-matter of the franchise within the common market, or use differences in specifications concerning those goods or services in different Member States, to isolate markets;
(d) franchisees engage in concerted practices relating to the sale prices of the goods or services which are the subject-matter of the franchise;
(e) the franchisor uses its right to check the contract premises and means of transport, or refuses its agreement to requests by the franchisee to move the contract premises or assign its rights and obligations under the franchise agreement, for reasons other than protecting the franchisor's industrial or intellectual property rights, maintaining the common identity and reputation of the franchised network or verifying that the franchisee abides by its obligations under the agreement.

Article 9

This Regulation shall enter into force on 1 February 1989.
It shall remain in force until 31 December 1999.

INDEX

D

F

G

H

J

K

L

M

N

U

Y

Z